Good University Guide 2027

THE TIMES
THE SUNDAY TIMES

Good University Guide 2027

**WHERE TO GO
AND WHAT TO STUDY**

ZOE THOMAS

Published by Times Books
An imprint of HarperCollins Publishers
1 Robroyston Gate,
Glasgow G33 1JN
www.harpercollins.co.uk

HarperCollins Publishers
Macken House, 39/40 Mayor Street Upper,
Dublin 1, D01 C9W8, Ireland

First published in 1993. This edition 2026
© Times Media Ltd 2026

The Times® and The Sunday Times® are registered trademarks of Times Media Ltd

ISBN 978-0-00-878972-5

Main league table and individual subject tables compiled by UoE Consulting Limited. Please see Chapters 1 and 10 for a full explanation of the sources of data used in the ranking tables. The data providers do not necessarily agree with the data aggregations or manipulations appearing in this book and are also not responsible for any inference or conclusions thereby derived.

Text: Zoe Thomas
Data and editorial consultant: Nick Rodrigues
Project editor: Peter Dennis
Design and layout: Davidson Publishing Solutions

All rights reserved. No part of this publication may be reproduced, stored in a retrieval system or transmitted, in any form or by any means electronic, mechanical, photographing, recording or otherwise without the prior written permission of the Publisher and copyright owners.

Without limiting the exclusive rights of any author, contributor or the publisher of this publication, any unauthorised use of this publication to train generative artificial intelligence (AI) technologies is expressly prohibited. HarperCollins also exercise their rights under Article 4(3) of the Digital Single Market Directive 2019/790 and expressly reserve this publication from the text and data mining exception.

The contents of this publication are believed correct at the time of printing. Nevertheless the Publisher can accept no responsibility for errors or omissions, changes in the detail given or for any expense or loss thereby caused.

HarperCollins does not warrant that any website mentioned in this title will be provided uninterrupted, that any website will be error free, that defects will be corrected, or that the website or the server that makes it available are free of viruses or bugs. For full terms and conditions please refer to the site terms provided on the website.

A catalogue record for this book is available from the British Library.

Printed and bound in the UK using 100% Renewable Electricity at CPI Group (UK) Ltd.

10 9 8 7 6 5 4 3 2 1

If you would like to comment on any aspect of this book, please contact us at the above address or online. e-mail: times.books@harpercollins.co.uk

Contents

About the Author 6

Timeline to a University Place 7

How This Book Can Help You 9

Introduction 11

1 The University League Table 18

2 Choosing What and Where to Study 29

3 Assessing Graduate Job Prospects 49

4 The Bottom Line: Tuition Fees and Finance 60

5 Making Your Application 77

6 The Social Inclusion Index 90

7 Finding Somewhere to Live 102

8 Staying Safe and Seeking Help on Campus 115

9 Coming to the UK to Study 123

10 Subject by Subject Guide 132

11 Applying to Oxbridge 271

12 University Profiles 304

Specialist and Private Institutions 439

Index 443

About the Author

Zoe Thomas is a journalist and education writer. She has worked on *The Times and Sunday Times Good University Guide* since 2005 and is a former staff journalist for the Sunday newspaper.

For the past 16 years, she has written extensively for the *Guide*, both its UK and Irish editions, and its sister publication *The Sunday Times Schools Guide, Parent Power*, the annual review of Britain's leading primary and secondary schools. She has a degree in media studies from the University of Sussex.

Acknowledgments

We would like to thank the many individuals who have helped with this edition of *The Times and Sunday Times Good University Guide*, particularly Helen Davies, editor of *The Sunday Times Good University Guide*, and John O'Leary, journalist, education consultant and the former author of this *Guide*. Thanks also go to Nick Rodrigues at The Sunday Times, Peter Dennis, Lauren Murray and Samuel Fitzgerald at HarperCollins Publishers and to Sophie Bradford and Taylor Watson at Greyscale Insights, which has compiled the main university league table and the individual subject tables for this *Guide* on behalf of The Times, The Sunday Times and HarperCollins Publishers. Thanks go to Horseman Bruce Associates (Nicki Horseman) for their assurance on the data analysis. For his work devising our social inclusion ranking, thanks go to Alastair McCall, data journalist and professor of quantitative studies at the University of Buckingham. For their contributions to our Oxbridge profiles thanks go to Claudia Cox (Cambridge) and Phin Hubbard (Oxford). Thank you to the members of *The Times and Sunday Times Good University Guide* Advisory Group for their time and expertise: Christine Couper, director of CouperJones higher education consultants; James Galbraith, senior strategic planner, University of Edinburgh; Josh Gulrajani, director of quality, performance and impact, University of Wolverhampton; Daniel Monnery, pro vice-chancellor external affairs, Northumbria University; Gary Russell, head of strategic planning and performance, Northumbria University; Jackie Njoroge, chief strategy and data officer, University of Salford; Helen Eustace, director of strategic planning, Aberystwyth University; David Totten, head of planning, Queen's University, Belfast; Jenny Walker, head of strategic planning management information, Loughborough University; Patrick Kennedy, higher education consultant; and Richard Puttock, head of business intelligence and data analytics, University of Leeds. Thanks also go to Emily Raven and Kathryn Heywood of Jisc for their technical advice. We also wish to thank all the university staff who assisted in providing information for this edition.

Timeline to a University Place

This book will help you find a university place in September 2027. Though it may seem a long way off, the journey from sixth form to Freshers' Week involves a busy schedule of activities and deadlines that applicants need to tick off in good time. Being prepared for each step as it comes will give you greater flexibility and more options later down the line.

Those applying for degrees in medicine, veterinary medicine and dentistry have an earlier application deadline (October 15, 2026) than the majority of applicants. This is the same date that Cambridge and Oxford universities also require applications to have been submitted. Relevant work experience is required for some degrees including medicine, as are aptitude and pre-assessment tests (detailed further in Chapter 2).

Use the dates below to find the key stages to a university place.

Key dates

February to July 2026
This is the time for chewing things over. What subject are you interested in studying? Where would you like to study it? The chapters of this book will help you whittle down your options with regards to choosing a subject and a university.

March 2026 onwards
Go to university Open Days. They are the best way of getting a feel for a university, its location, and what studying in a particular department or faculty would be like. Applicants need to prebook places and should go to as many Open Days as they can, within reason. Plan carefully and make each one count. Virtual Open Days and events are also offered; they cut down the schlepping on trains and motorways and can fill the gaps where making another trip is not an option. For Open Day dates, consult each university's website – as detailed in Chapter 12.

July 2026
Registration starts for UCAS Apply, the online application system through which you will apply to universities. You will have a maximum of five choices when you complete your form.

September 2026
UCAS will begin to accept completed applications.

October 15, 2026
Deadline for applications to Oxford or Cambridge (you can only apply to one of them), and for applications to any university to study medicine, dentistry or veterinary medicine. Some courses require you to have completed a pre-application assessment test by this date.

January 15, 2027
Deadline for applications for all other universities and subjects (excluding a few art and design courses with a March 2027 deadline). This is the last date you can apply by, but it is better to get your application in beforehand; aim for the end of November 2026.

End of March 2027
Universities should have given you decisions on your applications by now if you submitted them by January 15, 2027.

April 2027 onwards
Apply for student loans to cover tuition fees and living costs.

Early May 2027
By this time, you should have responded to all university decisions. You must select a first choice, and if your first offer is conditional, a second choice, and reject all other offers. Once you have accepted an offer, apply for university accommodation if you are going to need it. Universities have their own housing application deadlines – getting in early will often guarantee a space and may allow you first dibs on your choice of room.

First week of August 2027
Scottish examination results. If your results meet the offer from your first choice (or, failing that, your second choice), your place at university will be confirmed. If not, you can enter Clearing for Scottish universities to find a place on another course.

Second week of August 2027
A-level results announced. If your results meet the offer from your first choice (or, failing that, your second choice), your place at university will be confirmed. If not, you can enter Clearing. If you did better than expected and want to "trade up" you can use the "decline my place" button in your application and enter Clearing.

Mid to late September 2027
Arrive at university for Freshers' Week.

How This Book Can Help You

What and where to study are the fundamental decisions in making a successful university application.

How do I choose a course?
Most degrees last three or sometimes four years, some even longer, so you will need enthusiasm for, and some aptitude in, the subject. Also consider whether studying full-time or part-time will be best for you.
» The first half of Chapter 2 provides advice on choosing a subject area and selecting relevant courses within that subject.
» Chapter 10 provides details for 67 different subject areas. For each there is specific advice and a league table that provides our ranking of universities offering courses.

How will my choice of subject affect my employment prospects?
The course you choose will influence your job prospects after you graduate, so your initial subject decision will have an impact on your life long after you have finished your degree.
» The employment prospects and average starting salaries for the main subject groups are given in Chapter 3.
» The subject tables in Chapter 10 give the employment prospects for each university offering a course.
» Universities are working to increase the employability of their graduates. Examples are given in Chapter 3 and in the profiles in Chapter 12.

How do I choose a university?
While choosing your subject comes first, the place where you study also plays a major role. You will need to decide what type of university you wish to go to: campus, city or smaller town? How well does the university perform in league tables? How far is the university from home? Is it large or small? Is it specialist or general?
» Central to our *Guide* is the main *Times and Sunday Times* league table in Chapter 1. This ranks the universities by assessing their performance not just according to teaching quality and the student experience but also through seven other factors, including research quality, UCAS entry points, and graduate employment prospects.
» The second half of Chapter 2 provides advice on the factors to consider when choosing a university.
» Chapter 12, the largest chapter in the book, contains a page on each university, giving a general overview of the institution as well as data on student numbers, contact details, accommodation provision, and the latest fees available. Note that fees and student support for 2027–28 will not be confirmed until August 2026, and you must check these before applying.
» For those considering Oxford or Cambridge, details of admission processes and profiles of all the undergraduate colleges can be found in Chapter 11.
» Chapter 8 gives advice about student life; focusing on alcohol, drugs, mental health and staying safe on campus.
» Specific advice for international students coming to study in the UK is given in Chapter 9.

How do I apply?

» Chapter 5 outlines the application procedure for university entry. It starts by advising you on how to complete the UCAS application, and then takes you through the process that we hope will lead to your university place for autumn 2027.

Can I afford it?

Note that most figures in Chapter 4 refer to 2025 and there will be changes for 2027, which you will need to check.

» Chapter 4 describes how the system of tuition fees and finance works. It looks at what you are likely to be charged, depending upon where in the UK you plan to study, and how much you can borrow. It also looks at other forms of financial support (including university scholarships and bursaries), and how to plan your budget.
» Chapter 7 provides advice on finding somewhere to live while you are at university. Sample accommodation charges for each university are given in Chapter 10.

How do I find out more?

The Times and Sunday Times Good University Guide website at **thetimes.co.uk/uk-university-rankings** will keep you up to date with developments throughout the year and contains further information and online tables (subscription required).

The UCAS website **ucas.com** offers a wealth of helpful advice and information, as do individual university websites. Statistical information can be found on the Discover Uni website **discoveruni.gov.uk**.

Introduction

Higher education is inextricably linked with the political picture; universities drive economic growth and serve as civic institutions in communities. They pioneer life-changing research and nurture the next generation of leaders. They stimulate social mobility. And they are one of the UK's best exports, boosting Britain's global soft power and welcoming diverse nationalities on campuses up and down the country. For school-leavers flying the nest, they also represent the first tastes of freedom. Even those who are not directly affected by universities' current financial challenges have been gripped by the news that almost half the sector is facing financial deficits in 2025-26. For those with university applicants in the house, conjecture about which individual institutions might be at risk of irretrievable financial abandon, or impacted by job losses and course closures, has joined the usual juggle of A levels, university open days and UCAS applications.

Eager for clarity and a fiscal panacea, the nation waited for the government's post-16 education and skills white paper for higher education. Its contents, published in October 2025, committed to inflationary tuition fee and maintenance loan rises – baked in for the first two years and with the intent to make them automatic in the longer term via legislation when parliamentary time allows. The uplift to tuition fees has been welcomed by the sector. Fees have been kept artificially low for a long period, which has combined with high inflation to shrink the real terms value of teaching income. Vivienne Stern, the chief executive of Universities UK, which represents more than 140 universities, said: "The government has ambitions for our universities to make a stronger contribution to economic growth and individual opportunity, and we share that ambition. It also recognises the financial challenges which are putting pressure on that strength. The decision to raise undergraduate fees in line with inflation in England will help to halt the long-term erosion of universities' financial sustainability, following a decade of fee freezes."

Hot on the heels of the white paper, though, came a blow to cash-strapped universities in the Autumn Budget 2025 – which confirmed an international student levy that will charge universities a £925 per international student for each year of study from August 2028. There is an exemption for the first 220 international students, after this number the levy kicks in. The income it generates will be invested in the reintroduction of grants, which were scrapped under the Conservative government in 2016. Initially worth £1,000 and for "priority" courses only, the Institute of Fiscal Studies estimates the new grants will benefit about 10%

of students. The positive nature of a grant for students has unfortunately come at the cost of extra financial burden to universities. And while there is no extra charge to international students themselves, concerns have been raised that it may be felt through increased fees and reduced investment in support and provision, at a time when the sector is under significant financial pressure and facing growing global competition.

For university applicants and current students, though, affording day-to-day living costs tends to loom largest, and rising tuition fees – which will edge over £10,000 by 2027–28 – add fuel to the "is university worth it?" debate. Maintenance loans are going up at the same rate as tuition fees over the next two years, but it would take an over-inflation boost to level out the real-terms loss of value that soaring inflation has caused. The thorny issue of eligibility also remains: the amount of maintenance loan students get depends on a ladder of household income thresholds, in which middle income families tend to come off worst. Parents' ability to top up their students' coffers is stretched and more students are taking on part-time jobs to fund their studies. Some estimates point that more than two thirds of full-time students have a side job, and all agree that this is the norm for more than half of students.

Research by UCAS showed that the cost of living had increasingly shaped student decisions in the 2025 admissions cycle. Financial support was the second most important consideration for pre-applicants, followed closely by universities' specific cost-of-living support. More than a quarter of students starting university or college in 2025 said they were unsure or unprepared to manage their day-to-day finances. Our *Guide* has always pointed to the financial awards offered by universities in the form of scholarships and bursaries. These have relied on students doing their homework to find out what is available and what they may qualify for – by merit and/or means testing. UCAS has now launched an online tool that gathers provision centrally, pulling together nearly 800 scholarships, bursaries and grants. Find out more about all things student finance in Chapter 4.

University is still a positive, life-changing experience for most who choose it. Government figures in 2025 showed 87.6% of working-age graduates in employment compared to 68% of non-graduates and earning £42,000 average salaries, compared with £30,500 among those without a degree. And while the lofty aspirations of studying solely for the passion of learning have given way to an emphasis on securing a good graduate career, the potential for intellectual inspiration remains among the attractions of university.

After successive increases in applications from 2019 to 2022, demand for university places overall has plateaued – with 758,000 applications for full-time undergraduate places in 2024, up by 500 on 2023 but below the record level from 2022 – although it remains at peak levels among school leavers. A record number of UK 18-year-olds accepted a place in 2024, including record numbers of those from the most disadvantaged backgrounds, out of the second-highest number of applications from UK 18-year-olds (316,850) – in step with the age group's population surge that is working its way up secondary schools.

Fairness of admissions is discussed in greater depth in Chapter 6, The Social Inclusion Index, which features the eighth edition of our dedicated social inclusion league table. Birmingham Newman University has taken the lead in the ranking, which places universities according to nine measures of social inclusion. It reveals how successful (or not) UK universities are at delivering on their social role to attract and retain students with academic potential from all backgrounds. Today's applicants want to know about the composition of the student body they will be joining, and this table helps them in that quest.

In Chapter 8, Staying Safe and Seeking Help on Campus, drinking, drug-taking and personal safety on campuses are front and centre. Aiming to set a realistic tone for parents, it offers helpful advice on how it is possible to give your child their autonomy while also checking in with them.

As the fiscal lens through which deciding what and where to study gets more focused, applicants need to strike a sensible balance between following their dreams and getting into debt unwisely when choosing what and where to study. Investigate the findings of the Graduate Outcomes survey in Chapter 3, which shows what degree-holders are doing 15 months after finishing their degrees. Ideally, in the subjects you want to apply to study, you will see high proportions in high-skilled jobs and/or postgraduate study, and far fewer in jobs deemed low-skilled, or unemployed. We also include salary data within the subject summaries in Chapter 10, though this has never been an ingredient of our rankings.

Most graduates do not regret going to university and carry fond memories of their undergraduate years with them through life – along with career advantages and intellectual enrichment. The right university cannot be pinpointed simply by a league table, but this *Guide* should provide all the information needed to draw up a shortlist for further investigation, which will help you make the right choice in the end.

Evolving higher education

In the 32 years that this book has been published, higher education has experienced numerous changes. Those embarking on degrees from 2025-26 until 2027-28 do so with the knowledge that their tuition fees will rise by inflation each year. After that they will continue to go up each year, although the fine details had yet to be confirmed at the time of writing. Graduates in England used to have 30 years after leaving university to pay off their student debt before the government wrote it off completely, regardless of how much had been repaid. Since 2023-24 however, the deadline for repaying student loans increased to 40 years and the earnings threshold for repayment dropped to £25,000. More graduates than ever will need to repay their student loan in full to the government, plus interest. As universities have sought to weather the financial storm, mergers have taken place – including at leading institutions. City St George's formed in 2024 from City, University of London and St George's – the UK's only medical and health sciences university. An alliance between the universities of Kent and Greenwich, announced in September 2025, has been described as a 'quasi-merger'. There may be more to come.

Covid's intervening years make Brexit feel like a lifetime ago, but it was only on January 31, 2020 that Britain's withdrawal from the European Union completed. The move brought significant change for students from EU countries, Iceland, Liechtenstein, Norway (EEA) and Switzerland, who lost eligibility to UK "home" fees and funding. Instead, since the 2021-22 academic year, they have qualified for the higher rate of "international" tuition rates payable by those from the rest of the world. In 2027, the UK will rejoin the EU's Erasmus foreign exchange programme, which, following Brexit, had been replaced with the Turing Scheme, a national equivalent.

The pattern of applications and enrolments has changed since the original introduction of higher fees in 2012. Students are opting in larger numbers for subjects that they think will lead to well-paid jobs. While there has been a recovery in some arts and social science subjects, the trend towards the sciences and some vocational degrees is unmistakeable. Application numbers within computer science, business-related subjects, medicine, law and engineering were strong in the 2024 cycle. Teaching courses experienced downturns in applications, and the decline in languages at degree level is ongoing. Most students take a degree at least partly to improve their career prospects, so some second-guessing of the employment market is inevitable. But most graduate jobs are not subject-specific, and even the keenest future forecasters are hard-pressed to predict employment hotspots four or five years ahead – which is when today's applicants will be looking for jobs.

The latest Teaching Excellence Framework (TEF) exercise, carried out by the Office for Students (OfS), published its results in December 2023. Ratings of gold, silver, bronze and "requires improvement" were awarded by a TEF panel of independent academic experts and student representatives. As well as their overall ratings, each higher education provider has a rating for the two "aspects" of the TEF: the student experience (encompassing the National Student Survey metrics plus evidence from submissions) and student outcomes (continuation, completion, progression, plus evidence from the submissions). You can find out which ratings were achieved where in Chapter 12 University Profiles. The TEF looks at 107 of the 133 universities profiled in the *Guide*. The other 25 institutions fall outside the survey's area (no Scottish, Welsh or Northern Irish universities were included). Of the 107 surveyed, 34 were given an overall "gold" rating (with 15 of these also achieving gold in the Student Experience and Student Outcome measures); 66 achieved "silver" and 7 were rated "bronze" overall. Only one institution (Goldsmith's) dipped below "bronze" in the student experience category to "requires improvement".

Using this Guide

The merger of *The Times and Sunday Times* university guides 12 years ago began a new chapter in the ranking of higher education institutions in the UK. The two guides had 35 editions between them and, in their new form, provide the most comprehensive and authoritative assessments of undergraduate education at UK universities. Now in its fifth year in our main ranking, Hartpury University is the most recent addition to our league table and ministers are keen for new institutions to shake up the higher education system. Even those with university titles – the first criterion for inclusion in our table – take time to build up the body of data required to make meaningful comparisons.

Some famous names in UK higher education have never been ranked because they do not fit the parameters of a system that is intended mainly to guide full-time undergraduates. The Open University, for example, operates entirely through distance learning, while the London and Manchester Business Schools have no undergraduates. Birkbeck, University of London, which operates a broadly part-time course model, has dropped out of the table, though we still publish a profile of it in Chapter 12.

There are now 67 subject tables, one of them – Cultural Studies – is a new addition that has amalgamated American studies, Celtic studies, East and South Asian studies, and Middle Eastern and African studies – subjects that occupied four separate tables until last year, and which are still referenced separately in Graduate Outcomes and salary comparisons in this year's Subject by Subject chapter. Their small student numbers prompted the merger into a single Cultural Studies table.

A handful of changes to the basic methodology have been introduced, to best reflect the evolving higher education landscape and to ensure the most robust data is used for our calculations. Most recently, restrictions caused by the Data Futures transformation of data collection and reporting in higher education have led to our league table's loss of its student-to-staff ratio metric this year. If such a time comes that the data for this indicator can be robustly relied upon again, we will reinstall it. There is no longer a measure of service and facilities spend – this was removed due to questions over the relevance of such data, and our concerns over the influence of quite small changes year on year on an institution's overall ranking. Meanwhile, for the third year we have included the People & Planet indicator – based on an assessment of universities against 14 ethical and environmental criteria that measure an institution's sustainability. Further detail on the metrics included in our league table follows in Chapter 1. The methodology for the new edition remains stable. The *Guide* has always put a premium on consistency in the way that it uses the statistics published by universities and presents the results. The overriding aim is to inform potential students and their parents and advisers, not to make judgements on the performance of universities. As such, it differs from the government's Teaching Excellence Framework (TEF), which uses some of the same statistics but makes allowance for the prior qualifications of students and uses an expert and student panel to place the results in context.

Guide Award Winners

University of the Year	**Durham**
Runner-up	**Strathclyde**
Shortlisted	**Bath**
	Birmingham
Scottish University of the Year	**Strathclyde**
Welsh University of the Year	**Cardiff**
Specialist University of the Year	**Hartpury**
University of the Year for Graduate Employment	**Imperial College London**
University of the Year for Social Inclusion	**Birmingham Newman**

Our tables use the raw data produced by universities to reflect the undergraduate experience, whatever advantages or disadvantages those institutions might face. We also rank 130 universities, while the TEF uses only three bands, leaving almost half of the institutions in our table on the same middle tier.

Making the right choices

This *Guide* is intended as a starting point to finding the right course, a tool to help navigate the statistical minefield that applicants face as universities present their performance in the best possible light. There is advice on fees and financial questions, as well as all-important employment issues, along with the usual ranking of universities and 67 subject tables.

While some of the leading universities have expanded considerably in recent years, most will remain selective, particularly in popular subjects. Although the offer rate is still promising for now, that does not mean that all students secure the university or course of their dreams. The demand for places is far from uniform, and even within the same university the level of competition will vary between subjects. The entry scores quoted in the subject tables in Chapter 10 offer a reliable guide to the relative levels of selectivity, but the figures are for entrants' actual qualifications. The standard offers made by departments will invariably be lower, and the grades those departments are prepared to accept are often lower still, although they could also be higher if the course is especially over-subscribed.

Making the right choice requires a mixture of realism and ambition. Most sixth-formers and college students have a fair idea of the grades they are capable of attaining, within a certain margin for error. Even with five course choices, there is no point in applying for a degree where the standard offer is so far from your predicted grades that rejection is virtually certain. If your results do turn out to be much better than predicted, there may be an opportunity through Clearing to trade up to an alternative university. Since the relaxation of recruitment restrictions, universities that once took pride in their absence from Clearing have continued to recruit after A-level results day. As a result, the use of insurance choices – the inclusion of at least one university with lower entrance standards than your main targets – has been declining. It is still a dangerous strategy, but there is now more chance of picking up a place at a leading university if you aimed too high with all your first-round choices. Many more UK university applicants who have accepted a place are declining their firm offers to enter Clearing in search of a different course.

The long view

School-leavers who will enter higher education in 2026 were not born when our first league table was published and most will never have heard of polytechnics, even if they attend a university that once carried that title. But it was the award of university status to the 34 polytechnics, over a quarter of a century ago, that was the inspiration for the first edition of *The Times Good University Guide*. The original poly, the Polytechnic of Central London, had become the University of Westminster. Bristol Polytechnic became the University of the West of England, and Leicester Polytechnic morphed into De Montfort University. The new *Guide* charted the lineage of the new universities and offered the first-ever comparison of institutional performance in UK higher education.

The university establishment did not welcome the initiative. The vice-chancellors described the table as "wrong in principle, flawed in execution and constructed upon data which are not uniform, are ill-defined and in places demonstrably false". The league table has changed considerably since then, and its results are taken rather more seriously.

While consistency has been a priority for the *Guide* throughout its 32 years, only four of the original 14 measures have survived. Some of the current components – notably the National Student Survey – did not exist in 1992, while others have been modified or dropped at the behest of the expert group of planning officers from different types of universities that meets annually to review the methodology and make recommendations for the future.

While ranking is hardly popular with academics, the relationship with universities has changed radically, and this *Guide* is quoted on numerous university websites. As Sir David Eastwood, when he was vice-chancellor of the University of Birmingham, said in launching an official report on university league tables that he commissioned as chief executive of the Higher Education Funding Council for England: "We deplore league tables one day and deploy them the next."

Since this book was first published, the number of universities has increased by a third and the full-time student population has rocketed. Individual institutions are almost unrecognisable from their 1993 forms. Nottingham, for example, had fewer than 10,000 students then, compared with more than 35,000 now. Manchester Metropolitan, the largest of the former polys, has experienced similar growth. Yet there are universities now which would have been too small and too specialist to qualify for the title in 1992. The diversity of UK higher education is celebrated as one of its greatest strengths, and the modern universities are neither encouraged nor anxious to compete with the older foundations on some of the measures in our table. Some have made remarkable strides up the rankings, boosted in part by burgeoning research profiles as well as strength in metrics including student satisfaction and graduate prospects. As Thames Valley University in 2001, West London was bottom of our rankings. It is =64th this year, tied with Lincoln – another historic incumbent of the bottom spot (in 1999).

Most universities have had their ups and downs over the years, even Oxford and Cambridge, which tie in fourth place this year. It is the first time in our *Guide*'s 32-year history that neither of these famous and ancient universities has featured in the top three. Both benefit from some of the highest scores for research, entry standards, first and upper-second class degrees, and graduate prospects. But their overall ranks have been constrained by faring less positively in the latest National Student Survey than other universities did. Topping the league table this year for the second year running is the London School of Economics and Political Science (LSE). Its strength in graduate employment is hardwired and there is intellectual stretch in spades for students, who should "expect to encounter ideas you hate, that bite, that go to your identity," LSE's president and vice-chancellor, Larry Kramer, has said. At the same time, the university has succeeded in turning around its rates of student satisfaction spectacularly. Our analysis of students' feedback in successive National Student Surveys ranked LSE 112th for the broad experience as recently as six years ago – now it is =12th. A busy students' union delivers more than 3,000 events, and more than 250 societies and sports clubs keep things lively on top of everything that the capital has to offer. Former No 1 and runner-up for the second consecutive year, St Andrews offers a flexible four-year degree structure which is a big draw, allowing students to take multiple subjects before specialising. This academic breadth is supported by formidable research power and a strong sense of community, as praised by alumnus Prince William. An enduring feature in our league tables top 10, Durham has powered up four places in the past two years, and ranks third this year. In doing so it has outdone Oxbridge – reversing the old joke that Durham is the destination for Oxbridge rejects and earning our University of the Year special award in recognition of its consistent and improving excellence.

1 The University League Table

Students are scholars, learners – and in many ways also consumers – of higher education. The quality of a university matters and applicants are right to be active, engaged and motivated in their search for the best undergraduate course. To evaluate what makes a top university *The Times and Sunday Times University Guide* weighs up university performance measures and combines them in a straightforward way that has armed generations of students with the knowledge and insights to make informed choices.

The table in this chapter focuses on the fundamentals of undergraduate education and makes meaningful comparisons. Every element of the table has been chosen for the light it shines on the experience undergraduates encounter during their degrees, and their future prospects.

When tuition fees were first introduced in 1998, higher education became accountable for the investment it represented to students, their families and to taxpayers more widely. Information and statistics about universities and students came thick and fast as universities and the government adopted a more transparent approach to sharing information. Prior to this sharing of educational facts and figures, the somewhat nebulous notion of "reputation" was what largely counted as the means of judging a university's quality.

The disclosure of data about higher education helps applicants to make informed decisions about what and where to study but navigating this abundance of publicly available information can be a complicated and at times confusing process. This is where our *Guide* can help.

The information contained within our league table gives readers the chance to look under the bonnet of universities' performance. To get the most out of its content, it is worth reading through this introduction to our league table in order to gain an understanding of the measures used. There is no panel of "experts" involved in creating our league table; instead, statistics do the talking. Critics may have reasons to discount any of the measures we use, but the package has struck a chord with readers. Our ranking has built a reputation as the most authoritative arbiter of changing fortunes in higher education.

Over 32 years of publication, our *Guide* has maintained consistency in its evaluations, confident that the measures used are the best currently available for the task. Some changes have been forced upon us though, naturally enough during the course of nearly three decades, and others we have introduced in step with the evolving higher education and broader political landscapes. In building our new league table of eight indicators, the highest weighting is given to scores for student satisfaction with teaching quality and with the wider student experience, graduate prospects and research quality. Following these are entry standards, good honours (firsts and 2:1s) and continuation rates. For the third year, our ranking includes a sustainability metric from People & Planet, which is weighted lower than the other seven.

When universities stopped assessing teaching quality by subject, our table lost its most heavily weighted measure. However, we now have the benefit of the National Student Survey (NSS), which allows us to reflect the student experience. More than two-thirds of final-year undergraduates give their views on the quality of their courses, a remarkable response rate that makes the results impossible to dismiss.

The student satisfaction measure is split in two: "teaching quality" and "student experience" – explained in more detail further down this chapter.

The basic information that applicants need in order to judge universities and their courses does not change, however. A university's entry standards, completion rates, degree classifications and graduate employment rates are all vital pieces of intelligence for anyone deciding where to study. Research grades, while not directly involving undergraduates, bring with them considerable funds and enable a university to attract top academics.

The measures used are kept under review by a steering group of university administrators and statisticians, which meets annually and confers on an ad hoc basis more often than that. The raw data that go into the table in this chapter and the 67 subject tables in Chapter 10 are all in the public domain and are sent to universities for checking before any scores are calculated.

The various official bodies concerned with higher education do not publish league tables, and the Higher Education Statistics Agency (HESA), which supplies most of the figures used in our tables, does not endorse the way in which they are aggregated. But there are now numerous exercises, from the Teaching Excellence Framework to the annual "performance indicators" published by HESA on everything from completion rates to research output at each university, that invite comparisons.

Scrutiny of institutional league table positions is best carried out in conjunction with an examination of the relevant subject table – it is the course, after all, that will dominate your undergraduate years and influence your subsequent career.

How *The Times and Sunday Times* league table works

The table is presented in a format that displays the raw data, wherever possible. In building the university league table, scores for student satisfaction (covering satisfaction with teaching quality and with the wider student experience), research quality and graduate prospects were weighted by 1.5; People & Planet scores were weighted by 0.5; and all other indicators were weighted by 1.

For entry standards, student-staff ratios, first-class and 2:1 degrees and graduate prospects, the score was adjusted for subject mix. For example, it is accepted that engineering and medicine graduates will tend to have better graduate prospects than their peers from English or psychology courses. Comparing results in the main subject groupings helps to iron out differences attributable simply to the range of degrees on offer. This subject-mix adjustment means that it is not possible to replicate the scores in the table from the published indicators because the calculation requires access to the entire dataset.

The indicators were combined using a common statistical technique known as z-scores, to ensure that no indicator has a disproportionate effect on the overall total for each university, and the totals were transformed to a scale with 1,000 for the top score. The z-score technique makes it impossible to compare universities' total scores from one year to the next, although their relative positions in the table are comparable. Individual scores are dependent on the top performer: a university might drop from 60% of the top score to 58% but still have improved, depending on the relative performance of other universities.

Only where data are not available from HESA are figures sourced directly from universities. Where this is not possible, scores are generated according to a university's average performance on other indicators.

The organisations providing the raw data for the tables are not involved in the process of aggregation, so are not responsible for any inferences or conclusions we have made. Every care has been taken to ensure the accuracy of the tables and accompanying information, but no responsibility can be taken for errors or omissions.

The Times and Sunday Times league table uses eight important indicators of university activity, based on the most recent data available at the time of compilation:

- » Teaching quality
- » Student experience
- » Research quality
- » Entry standards
- » Graduate prospects
- » Good honours
- » Continuation rates
- » People & Planet

Teaching quality and student experience

The student satisfaction measure is divided into two components which give final-year undergraduates' views of the quality of their courses. The National Student Survey (NSS) published in 2025, inclusive of overall satisfaction for all UK universities, was the source of the data. The NSS covers seven aspects of a course, which are grouped into themes.

» The teaching quality indicator reflects the average scores of the teaching, learning opportunities, assessment and feedback, and academic support themes. Students answer on a scale from 1 (top) to 4 (bottom), and the score in the table is based on the percentage of positive responses (options 1 and 2).

» The student experience indicator is drawn from the average NSS scores in the organisation and management, learning resources, and student voice themes. Students answer on a scale from 1 (top) to 4 (bottom) and the score in the table is based on the percentage of positive responses (options 1 and 2).

Teaching quality is favoured over student experience and accounts for 67% of the overall score covering student satisfaction, with student experience making up the remaining 33%. The survey is based on the opinion of final-year undergraduates rather than directly assessing teaching quality. Most undergraduates have no experience of other universities, or different courses, to inform their judgements.

Although all the questions relate to courses, rather than other aspects of the student experience, some types of university – notably medium-sized campus universities – tend to do better than others, while those in London, in particular, tend to do worse.

Research quality

This is a measure of the quality of the research undertaken in each university. The information was sourced from the 2021 Research Excellence Framework (REF), a peer-review exercise used to evaluate the quality of research in UK higher education institutions undertaken by the

UK Higher Education funding bodies. The overall quality of research is based on the 2021 REF. The output of the REF gave each institution a profile in the following categories: 4* world-leading; 3* internationally excellent; 2* internationally recognised; 1* nationally recognised and unclassified.

The funding bodies have directed more funds to the very best research by applying weightings. For the current edition of the *Guide*, we used the weightings adopted by UK Research and Innovation (UKRI) and Research England, published in 2020. A 4* output was weighted by a factor of 4, and 3* was weighted by a factor of 1. Outputs of 2* and 1* carry zero weight. The score was weighted to account for the number of staff in each unit of assessment. The score is presented as a percentage of the maximum possible score of 3. To achieve the maximum score, all staff would need to be at 4* world-leading level. There are no scores in this category for Buckingham (as a private university it fell outside of REF 2021).

Entry standards

This is the mean average score, using the UCAS tariff (see page 35), of new students under the age of 21 who took A and AS-Levels, Scottish Highers and Advanced Highers and other equivalent qualifications (e.g. International Baccalaureate). It measures what new students achieved rather than the entry requirements suggested by the universities. The data comes from HESA for 2023-24. The original sources of data for this measure are data returns made by the universities to HESA.

» Using the UCAS tariff, each student's examination results were converted to a numerical score. HESA then calculated an average for all students at the university. The results have then been adjusted to take account of the subject mix at the university.
» A score of 144 represents three As at A-level. Although the vast majority of the top 40 universities in the table have average entry standards of at least 144, it does not mean that everyone achieved such results – let alone that this was the standard offer. Courses will not demand more than three subjects at A-level, and offers are pitched accordingly. You will need to reach the entry requirements set by the university, rather than these scores.

Graduate prospects

This measure is the percentage of full-time, UK-resident graduates working in a high-skilled job and/or undertaking further study 15 months after graduation. The high-skilled employment marker is derived from the new Graduate Outcomes survey, based on 2021-22 graduates and published in 2024. The results have been adjusted for subject mix.

Good honours

This measure is the percentage of graduates achieving a first or upper-second class degree. The results have been adjusted to take account of the subject mix at the university. The data comes from HESA for 2023-24. The original sources of data for this measure are data returns made by the universities to HESA.

» Four-year first degrees, such as MChem, are treated as equivalent to a first or upper-second.
» Scottish Ordinary degrees (awarded after three years of study) are excluded.
» Universities control degree classification, with some oversight from external examiners.

There have been suggestions that, since universities have increased the numbers of good honours degrees they award, this measure may not be as objective as it should be. However, it remains a key measure of a student's success and employability.

Continuation rates
This is the percentage of UK-domiciled full-time undergraduate students still in higher education after one year who either continue at the same provider, or transfer to another UK institution as recorded in the year after entry. The data comes from HESA for 2023-24.

People & Planet
Universities are assessed against 14 ethical and environmental criteria that measure an institution's sustainability. Approximately 45% of marks come from universities' performance on environmental indicators, such as carbon reduction, waste and recycling, water reduction, and use of renewable energy, which are taken from the HESA 2022-23 Estates Management Record covering the period from August 1, 2022 to July 31, 2023. The remaining marks, 55%, are based on analysis of institutional policies on sustainable issues that affect all campus stakeholders, made public by universities online, covering the period from August 1, 2023 to July 31, 2024. These include the food that is served on campus, a university's investments, its curricula, its careers and recruitment activities, workers' rights, and many others.

Rank	Last year's rank		Teaching quality (%)	Student experience (%)	Research quality (%)	Entry standards (UCAS pts)	Graduate prospects (%)	Good honours (%)	Continuation rate (%)	People & planet (%)	Total	Page
1	1	London School of Economics	85.1	85.1	68	185	92.5	90.6	97.6	68.1	1000	381
2	2	St Andrews	89.3	86.9	53.8	208	87.6	90.6	98	38	933	407
3	5	Durham	87	82.2	55.9	178	88.8	90.5	96.8	55.6	906	341
=4	4	Cambridge	85	75.7	69.7	210	90.4	92.1	98.4	37.2	903	328
=4	3	Oxford	85.7	73.4	67	197	90.4	93	97.6	51.5	903	394
6	6	Imperial College London	83.1	82.8	73.9	196	95.9	91.4	96.2	49.1	890	363
7	8	Bath	84.6	85.2	53	171	88.7	88.4	97.2	57.2	861	314
8	9	Warwick	85.6	84.1	60.9	170	86.4	84.8	95.3	47.5	839	428
9	7	University College London	82.3	81	66.8	172	87.5	90.5	96.1	67.2	837	426
10	11	Bristol	82.8	81	66.2	168	83.7	87	97.2	60.8	814	324
11	20	Strathclyde	86.3	84.3	53.1	204	83	82.9	91.7	40.8	803	418
12	10	Loughborough	84.4	85	52.5	153	86.3	84	96.5	52.5	802	383
13	14	Sheffield	87.3	87	59.1	157	82.9	82.8	96.1	46.1	800	410
14	13	Exeter	82.4	81.3	57.5	153	81.9	86.5	96.2	70.9	790	348
15	12	Lancaster	85.5	83.5	57.4	144	82.1	82.1	95.1	53.5	775	369
16	22	Birmingham	83.7	82.1	61.9	151	84.2	83.4	94.6	50.7	765	318
17	19	Southampton	84.1	82.3	60.1	148	84.3	83.4	95.5	47.6	763	414
18	23	Liverpool	85.3	85.6	55.6	141	82	83.1	93.8	58.7	749	377
19	=24	King's College London	81.1	78.5	64.2	164	85.1	84.7	94.5	66.4	748	366
20	=17	York	82.7	79.9	62.8	148	82.7	79.9	96.5	46.3	742	437
21	26	Queen's Belfast	84.1	83	52	154	87.1	77.4	93.8	60.1	740	401
22	16	Glasgow	80.1	75.8	61.2	210	82.3	85.1	93	32.3	735	350
=23	15	Aberdeen	85.7	84	38.7	182	82.2	82.5	92.3	34.7	727	306
=23	36	Dundee	87.2	81.3	51.1	184	83	82	91.6	29.4	727	340
25	=17	Edinburgh	77.7	75.1	61.5	194	81.3	90.8	95.6	37.7	725	345

Rank	Last year's rank		Teaching quality (%)	Student experience (%)	Research quality (%)	Entry standards (UCAS pts)	Graduate prospects (%)	Good honours (%)	Continuation rate (%)	People & planet (%)	Total	Page
26	29	Leeds	81.6	81	57	156	81	85.3	95.1	54.7	720	370
27	=27	Manchester	81.2	79.5	64.4	159	80.8	83.7	95.6	49.3	713	384
=28	32	Cardiff	83	81.8	56.7	146	85.1	77.5	94.7	53.8	712	330
=28	=27	Leicester	85.8	85.7	53.6	126	81	76.4	94.8	54.5	712	374
30	=30	Nottingham	83.2	80.8	56.1	151	83.3	79.2	95.7	44.6	710	391
31	21	Surrey	87.1	84.2	53.3	133	83.7	74.7	92.1	37.2	699	421
32	34	Royal Holloway, London	83.8	83.1	53.6	128	78.7	77.1	93	47.2	687	406
33	=24	Reading	83.4	81.9	51.1	121	80.4	77.8	91.7	74	685	402
34	=30	Newcastle	80.9	79.9	53.6	143	82.4	81.5	93.3	59.3	679	387
35	39	Queen Mary, London	82	79.8	58.7	150	78.6	83.5	92.5	49.9	672	400
36	44	Glasgow Caledonian	84.1	81.5	38.5	166	81.2	83.3	89	58.8	669	351
37	37	Swansea	85.2	83	47.5	123	81	78.1	91.4	64.9	664	423
38	=46	Manchester Metropolitan	87	84.3	42	127	71.6	79.6	89.6	73.6	659	385
39	51	Heriot-Watt	80.7	78.8	48.7	172	82.8	80.6	89	37.7	656	358
40	33	East Anglia	84.1	82	58	128	81	76	92.2	42.2	653	342
41	35	Aston	83.8	82.1	40.9	126	82.6	74.4	93.2	52.8	652	312
42	48	Aberystwyth	89.1	85.1	38.7	115	72.4	73.1	92.3	60.6	635	308
43	=57	Keele	85.4	82.6	42	119	78.6	79.7	92.2	55.9	630	364
44	=46	Essex	86.4	84.2	50	130	72.1	78.8	88	55.4	629	347
45	38	Sussex	84.1	83.2	52.9	130	73	74.1	91.8	48.7	624	422
46	42	Nottingham Trent	86.7	84	41.9	114	71.5	72.9	92.3	66.7	623	392
47	43	Northumbria	83.8	82.4	40.6	128	78.4	78.2	87.4	70.4	622	389
48	49	City St George's	82.9	80.6	51	130	84.9	77.8	89.9	55.5	621	334
49	45	Ulster	86.1	82.4	47.8	125	77.8	81.2	85.8	42.7	620	425
50	61	Robert Gordon	86.8	80.5	20.8	157	81.6	77.6	89.4	51.6	614	403

Rank	Last year's rank		Teaching quality (%)	Student experience (%)	Research quality (%)	Entry standards (UCAS pts)	Graduate prospects (%)	Good honours (%)	Continuation rate (%)	People & planet (%)	Total	Page
51	59	Edinburgh Napier	83.5	80	32.9	155	80	84.2	85.2	51.4	609	346
52	55	Portsmouth	85.8	83	39.1	114	75.1	75.9	92.7	51.3	603	398
53	=40	Arts London	83.6	79	46	141	60.5	79.3	91.9	73.3	600	311
54	62	Chichester	88.5	79.9	20.1	120	74.8	77	90.9	39	597	333
55	63	Stirling	82.2	77.5	43.8	171	75.3	71.9	91.8	30.1	590	417
56	=40	Kent	81.6	77.4	52.9	117	72.1	78.6	91.9	57	589	365
57	68	West of England	84.3	80.6	35.7	122	76.2	75.2	91.5	62.5	586	429
58	70	Plymouth	84.2	79.9	38.6	127	79.7	71.7	91.5	63.5	581	396
59	64	Bangor	84.2	81.4	51.3	123	71.6	71.6	89.3	65.7	577	313
60	60	Hull	87.4	82.5	42.4	109	75.8	71.8	88.4	53.4	574	362
61	=66	Liverpool John Moores	85.8	84.4	32.8	124	73.7	73.6	88.9	56.9	573	379
62	74	Abertay	86.9	82.8	24.6	160	70.9	79.8	85.4	29.8	571	307
63	=84	Edge Hill	86.4	84.5	26.3	119	77.6	72.3	91.2	33.5	564	344
=64	56	Lincoln	84	80.2	38.4	111	72.9	75.2	91.8	52.1	563	375
=64	=57	West London	88.7	86.3	28.7	114	69.4	77.6	85.4	76	563	430
66	=105	Queen Margaret, Edinburgh	85.6	79.8	27.3	165	67	84.1	91.5	29.4	559	399
67	83	Hertfordshire	85.5	83.5	39.2	118	73.1	75.9	89.7	50.5	557	359
68	52	St Mary's, Twickenham	86.3	81.4	29.4	108	79.8	67.9	87.6	34.6	553	408
69	50	Oxford Brookes	85.6	81.7	32.8	112	77.8	65.6	89.3	63.8	552	395
70	75	Plymouth Marjon	89.2	83.1	17.4	121	75.7	76.8	86.8	33.9	551	397
71	=66	Cardiff Metropolitan	84.5	81	32	122	74.4	69.4	87.4	68.7	547	331
72	72	Salford	84.2	78.8	37.8	122	76.6	71.3	88.2	71	541	409
73	=78	Arts Bournemouth	83.9	77.6	23	147	58.3	76.1	93.9	65	532	310
74	86	Lincoln Bishop University	91.2	86.1	11.3	107	76.6	70.5	87.6	33.9	531	375
75	65	SOAS, London	77.9	69.7	51.9	126	75.4	79.4	86	45.1	526	412

Rank	Last year's rank		Teaching quality (%)	Student experience (%)	Research quality (%)	Entry standards (UCAS pts)	Graduate prospects (%)	Good honours (%)	Continuation rate (%)	$People & planet (%)	Total	Page
76	98	Southampton Solent	87	81.5	12.6	112	66	86.3	88	50.9	523	415
77	76	Bath Spa	87.6	82.9	29.3	107	64.8	68.8	89.7	55.7	520	315
78	54	Coventry	86	81.3	33.8	114	74.4	75.6	81	60.8	515	335
=79	82	Bournemouth	80.7	77.7	30.7	108	75.9	73.8	89.7	70.3	514	321
=79	53	Harper Adams	82.6	74.7	19.5	124	74	73.4	91.7	27	514	356
81	109	Canterbury Christ Church	89.5	86.3	26.1	110	75.1	69	81.7	58.3	511	329
82	=94	South Wales	84.9	77.3	27.5	118	71.1	74.8	89.1	63.5	510	413
83	88	Leeds Beckett	85.2	82.7	26.7	115	70.8	71.2	87.7	46.7	507	372
=84	=90	Gloucestershire	84	74.4	21	112	76.4	64.4	90.9	67.9	500	352
=84	104	Teesside	86.5	80.9	28	114	79.2	75.4	84.7	42.2	500	424
86	111	Bradford	81	76.9	29.9	128	77.9	79.5	89.8	52.8	499	322
=87	73	Falmouth	83.3	75.2	48.8	131	58.1	76.5	89.8	43.7	498	349
=87	80	Goldsmiths, London	81.3	72.3	45.5	122	67.1	88.8	84.8	41	498	353
=87	101	Staffordshire	83.6	76.6	30	120	73.7	75.6	88	49.4	498	416
=90	71	Brighton	82.8	77.8	41.4	114	73.3	67.4	88.1	60.5	494	323
=90	112	Leeds Trinity	91.7	88.2	15.1	108	73	59.1	80.5	42.8	494	373
=90	=94	Liverpool Hope	89.9	84.1	22.3	113	65.2	71	86.6	47	494	378
93	96	Lancashire	85.6	80.6	30.4	119	74.3	69.9	85.3	60.4	493	368
94	97	Kingston	84.9	81.8	34.6	117	66.1	71.2	90.4	43.1	491	367
95	=84	Sheffield Hallam	80.7	74.1	36	116	75.5	72.8	89.7	52.5	488	411
96	77	Derby	87.1	81.2	21	110	73.4	67	87.2	49.3	487	339
97	124	Suffolk	92.2	88.7	21.8	109	72	72.4	80.3	34.2	480	419
98	99	Worcester	84.9	80.2	15.3	114	78.6	66.8	85.4	73.4	479	435
99	110	Wales Trinity St David	90.3	85.8	23.8	112	59.6	72.5	88.4	58.2	478	427
100	102	Greenwich	84	80.8	32.9	108	70.6	71.2	87	66.6	477	355

Rank	Last year's rank		Teaching quality (%)	Student experience (%)	Research quality (%)	Entry standards (UCAS pts)	Graduate prospects (%)	Good honours (%)	Continuation rate (%)	People & planet (%)	Total	Page
101	116	Hartpury	88.4	80.8	15.8	120	60	64.8	92.7	n/a	470	357
102	=78	Huddersfield	81.8	76	31.1	118	75	72.5	88.1	51.9	466	361
103	92	Leeds Arts	86.4	81	6	139	59.4	67.1	94.9	42.1	464	371
104	81	Norwich Arts	82.5	76.8	38.8	125	61.9	73.9	90.7	24.6	462	390
105	=105	Sunderland	88.1	82.4	30.5	124	64.7	69.6	85.1	42.2	460	420
106	103	Winchester	83.5	76.5	22	109	69	75	90	44	458	433
107	=90	Birmingham Newman	87.7	84.7	13.3	98	73.9	73.3	85	18.4	456	320
108	113	De Montfort	83.8	80.5	27.4	100	69.3	70.8	85	76.8	451	338
109	89	Chester	82.9	74.9	21.1	119	76.3	76.8	87.4	25.7	448	332
110	121	West of Scotland	87.9	80	19.2	139	73.5	75	77.7	33.7	445	431
111	100	London South Bank	83.6	77.7	28.8	108	75.4	75.2	84.6	37.7	440	382
112	93	York St John	86.4	79.7	19.6	115	69.1	66	87.3	31.9	439	438
113	=107	Birmingham City	84.3	81.2	29	123	70.4	57.4	88.1	57.7	434	319
114	126	East London	87.2	81.7	22.8	114	63.6	80.7	81.4	36.4	433	343
115	120	Westminster	83.3	83	39.7	110	61.2	67.9	86.5	50	425	432
116	117	Middlesex	85.9	80.4	30.4	103	64.7	71.8	81.7	48.9	422	386
117	=107	Brunel London	82.7	79.8	34	114	69.4	61.7	88.2	47.6	413	325
=118	129	Bedfordshire	86.8	81.3	30	101	66.7	61	79	80.7	403	316
=118	125	Northampton	85.5	79.7	13.8	104	69.7	70.1	84.3	45.4	403	388
120	122	Buckinghamshire New	89.2	84.7	17.6	99	69.3	54	81.7	48	394	327
121	123	Wolverhampton	85.7	80.4	21.6	106	73.4	69.9	84.5	10.5	393	434
122	115	Wrexham	84.9	76.1	13.3	109	74.7	72.1	80.6	56.9	391	436
123	130	Anglia Ruskin	83	77.2	30.2	99	69	65.5	85	58.8	382	309
=124	127	London Metropolitan	83.8	80.1	29.2	94	63.4	74.9	81.7	39.2	376	380
=124	118	Roehampton	84.4	81.5	45.9	95	58.1	63.2	89.1	18.2	376	404

Rank	Last year's rank		Teaching quality (%)	Student experience (%)	Research quality (%)	Entry standards (UCAS pts)	Graduate prospects (%)	Good honours (%)	Continuation rate (%)	People & planet (%)	Total	Page
126	119	Greater Manchester	85	78.1	10.6	115	74.8	67.7	82.7	13.9	363	354
127	87	Creative Arts	80.9	71.6	41.2	119	56.8	73	81.3	46.5	357	336
128	114	Buckingham	80.4	65.9	n/a	133	76.4	81.5	83.2	n/a	356	326
129	128	Cumbria	79.2	71.5	13.6	110	74.8	71.4	85.5	27.8	322	337
130	131	Royal Agricultural	72	73.1	24.2	117	68.7	66.9	88.1	23.6	289	405

2 Choosing What and Where to Study

The relative merits of university education are perennial points of discussion, whether in Westminster, the sixth form common room or at a dinner party. Meanwhile, teenagers have been voting with their feet: 279,550 18-year-olds gained a university place in 2024 – a record number of school leavers. By the time they start to engage with the UCAS website, sixth formers will already be accustomed to the choice that runs through education. Those from the UK will have selected GCSEs and A-levels, or Higher and Advanced Higher subjects, from a vast array of options. At this juncture, you need to determine a wise and informed undergraduate choice that is likely to stand the test of time, without losing sight of the ambition and passion that inspires you. This is a milestone that will impact the rest of your life, to one extent or another, on many levels – from the intellectual and professional to the social and personal. Careers, scholarship and friendships are shaped during the undergraduate years. University is the fifth most popular place for couples in the UK to meet, with one in 20 people first encountering their partner there. The place you spend your student years might end up being where you put down roots as a graduate. It's a lot.

And there's a lot of undergraduate courses to choose from – around 32,000 according to the latest count on UCAS for 2026–27 entry. This *Guide* features 133 universities, and there are many colleges that applicants of certain specialisms will also be considering. Students tend to decide on their degree subject before thinking about the institution at which they will study it. Enjoying your subject is a guiding principle for making selections, but employability prospects are also increasingly taken into consideration.

Some subjects and some universities carry more prestige than others. Such judgements are worth bearing in mind, as your future CV will be assessed according to them. This kind of thinking may not sit easily with everyone, but employers treat universities and subjects as yardsticks, not just the results gained on courses. Certain universities, however, may not occupy our upper rankings, but they might have particularly strong departments for individual subjects. Make the most of out of this *Guide*, and cross reference the subject-by-subject information in Chapter 10 with the university profiles and rankings in Chapter 12.

The options are not endless, but they are many. The Graduate Outcomes survey shows what graduates of the subjects you are interested in are doing 15 months after finishing their degrees. Ideally, you will see high proportions in high-skilled jobs and/or postgraduate study, and far fewer in jobs deemed low-skilled, or unemployed. It is a useful tool for new applicants. Be realistic in your choices. The course you apply to should be within your capabilities, although it will also need to keep you interested for three years-plus. A degree should broaden your options later in life, so be sensible about choosing one that can do that for you while keeping an eye on the career horizon. Technological advancements are continually reshaping the world of work, and you want to be abreast of developments. Narrowing your focus at degree stage could limit what is open to you in five to 10 years' time. This *Guide* can inform you of what is possible, and what will make a wise choice.

And naturally, all university thoughts are under the microscope of affordability, with the average graduate debt at £53,000 in 2025 – up 10% in a year – as students increase their borrowing to meet the rising cost of living. Affordability is influencing applicants' decision-making; with rising numbers picking universities close to home so they can save on rent and more than half of students juggling a part-time job with their studies. Finance is in even sharper focus now that annual inclines to tuition fees have been confirmed, following the tighter repayment terms recently introduced under the "Plan 5" student loan. This is covered in more detail in Chapter 4, The Bottom Line. The fiscal precarity of universities themselves adds further perplexity for today's applicants who want to study at university they are confident will weather the financial storm.

Even so, the charms of university remain attractive. It may not be the straightforward golden ticket out of childhood into a carefree young adulthood it once represented, nor the freely accessed financial no-brainer of old, but university continues to provide students with access to myriad new experiences – from their first tastes of freedom and independent living to building their academic and professional foundations for the future. On a fundamental level, many professions require a degree. Looking ahead, as technology replaces routine jobs graduates will be needed for high-tech future economies, some argue. Students still find their vocation at university too. Whether you are in it for the money, the love – or both – university remains beneficial financially, with graduates earning more over their lifetimes than nongraduates.

Getting swept up in the rush of 'what shall I do, where should I apply' hubbub can lead to making a hasty decision that you may regret later. There are growing numbers of students expressing second thoughts about their decisions: in a 2025 survey of more than 10,000 undergraduates 44% said that in hindsight they would have taken a different path – the highest proportion in the five years that the question has been asked in the annual Student Academic Experience Survey by the Higher Education Policy Institute (HEPI) and Advance HE. Another report, *The Benefits of Hindsight: Reconsidering higher education choices*, found that while most undergraduate respondents (65%) were happy with their choice of what and where to study, over a third (35%) said they would have chosen a different course or university (or both) or done something different. It is not surprising that some students have second thoughts after they have enrolled at university; sixth formers are under a lot of pressure to know what they want to do in life and how their degree and chosen university will lead to that – which they are expected to know at age 17. That's why doing the homework now to evaluate what and where to study should make sense in the long run.

Is higher education for you?

Being carried along with the flow is too easy. Maybe all your friends are going to university, or your parents expect it. If you apply for a course in your strongest A-level subject, things should work out OK and your career will look after itself, right? Or perhaps your driving motivation is to leave home in search of the UK's best live music or clubbing scenes, or simply to put a sizeable portion of motorway between you and your parents. Such considerations are natural and will not necessarily lead to disaster. But now is the time to question whether university is the best way of fulfilling your ambitions. There are degree apprenticeships, or training schemes at big firms which could equally help you achieve what you want, minus the need to take out a student loan. If studying for A-levels or equivalent qualifications has felt like torture, now may not be the time for you to go to university. Perhaps a job would be better, and possibly a return to education later in life would suit you more. Love of a subject is an excellent reason for taking a degree; it will help you focus your course search on those that reflect your passion. But if a degree is a means to a career for you, look carefully at employment rates for any courses you consider, and ensure any qualifications you will need are covered by the course.

Narrowing down your options

For now, a scramble for places affects a relatively small proportion of courses that attract intense competition, and there are plenty of places at good universities for candidates with sufficient qualifications. For older applicants returning to education, relevant work experience and demonstrable interest in a subject may be enough to win a place. Too much choice is more of an issue. Start filtering your options by:

» Choosing a subject – or subject area – first, rather than a university. This can reduce the field considerably as not all universities offer all subjects.
» Then factor in personal preferences such as location and type of university – campus or city? – and, by this point, you may already have the beginnings of a manageable list.
» Next up is course content and what life is really like for students.

Today's budding undergraduates are at an advantage in this regard. As well as having access to the informative and accurate contents of university prospectuses and websites, they can connect with current students online and do some digging. Most universities have an "Ask a Student" function, or similar, on their website, which provides them with a link to a student ambassador for a live chat or call back.

Other helpful sources of information are **thestudentroom.com**, the country's largest online student community, and the What I Wish I Knew About University forum on Facebook. Both are peer-to-peer platforms for students and parents to discuss a wide range of university-related questions, share advice and build relationships. Current students on the courses and at the universities you are interested in may be happy to give their appraisals – although, bear in mind, that what they tell you may be biased in some direction or another. Cross-reference anything you have been told with factual sources of information such as ours, or the UCAS website.

The National Student Survey is an objective source of information which is available online, with a range of additional data about the main courses at each institution, at **officeforstudents.org.uk/advice-and-guidance/student-information-and-data**. Visiting the university will give a truer picture yet; better still go to the department where you would be studying.

Setting your priorities

The majority of graduate jobs are not subject-specific; employers value the transferable skills that higher education confers. Rightly or wrongly, however, most employers are influenced by which university you went to, as mentioned above, so the choice of institution remains important. Consider boosting your CV while studying by choosing a university that offers some sort of employment-related scheme. It could be work experience built into your degree, or a particularly active careers service. Nevertheless, it is clear that the prospect of much higher graduate debt is encouraging more students into job-related subjects. This is understandable and, if you are sure of your future career path, possibly also sensible. But much depends on what that career is – and whether you are ready to make such a long-term commitment. Some of the programmes that have attracted public ridicule, such as surf science or golf management, may narrow graduates' options to a worrying extent, but often boast strong employment records.

As you would expect, many vocational courses are tailored to particular professions. If you choose one of these, make sure that the degree is recognised by the relevant professional body (such as the Engineering Council or one of the institutes) or you may not be able to use the skills that you acquire. Most universities are only too keen to make such recognition clear in their prospectus; if no such guarantee is published, contact the university department running the course and seek assurances. In education, for example, by no means do all degrees qualify you to teach.

Even where a course has professional recognition, a further qualification may be required to practise. Both law and medicine, for example, demand additional training to become a fully qualified solicitor, barrister or doctor. Neither degree is an automatic passport to a job: only about half of all law graduates go into the profession. Both law and medicine also offer a postgraduate route into the profession for those who have taken other subjects as a first degree. Law conversion courses, though not cheap, are increasingly popular, and there are a growing number of graduate-entry medical degrees.

One way to ensure that a degree is job-related is to take a "sandwich" course, which involves up to a year in business or industry. Students often end up working for the organisation that provided the placement, while others gain valuable insights into a field of employment – even if only to discount it. The drawback with such courses is that, like the year abroad that is part of most language degrees, the period away from university inevitably disrupts living arrangements and friendship groups. But most of those who take this route find that the career benefits make this a worthwhile sacrifice. Growing numbers of traditional degrees now offer shorter periods of work experience.

Employers' organisations calculate that more than half of all graduate jobs are open to applicants from any subject, and recruiters for the most competitive graduate training schemes often prefer traditional academic subjects to apparently relevant vocational degrees. Newspapers, for example, may prefer a history graduate to one with a media studies degree, while many classics graduates end up in the business world.

A good degree classification and the right work experience are more important than the subject for most non-technical jobs. But it is hard to achieve a good result on a course that you do not enjoy, so scour websites, and email or phone university departments, to ensure that you know what you are letting yourself in for.

What to study?

As well as an interest that is sustainable for three-plus years in the subject you pick, you need to ensure you have the right qualifications to meet its entry requirements. Many economics degrees require mathematics A-level, for example, while most medical schools demand chemistry or biology. The UCAS website is a good starting point; it contains subject profiles and entrance requirements (**ucas.com**), while universities' own sites offer more detailed information. The Russell Group of 24 leading universities' Informed Choices website is another go-to source of information regarding required subjects (**informedchoices.ac.uk**).

Most popular subject areas by applications		**Most popular subject areas by acceptances**	
1 Law	163,325	1 Law	29,830
2 Computer science	128,125	2 Psychology (non-specific)	26,025
3 Psychology (non-specific)	122,965	3 Business studies	22,505
4 Economics	104,065	4 Business and management (non-specific)	21,885
5 Design studies	95,615	5 Computer science	21,080
6 Medicine (non-specific)	88,705	6 Design studies	18,545
7 Sport and exercise sciences	79,040	7 Sport and exercise sciences	16,040
8 Sociology	76,055	8 Language and Area studies	15,785
9 Management studies	73,665	9 Adult nursing	14,795
10 Business studies	70,680	10 Economics	14,485
Source: UCAS End of Cycle report 2024		**Source:** UCAS End of Cycle report 2024	

Making a choice

Your A-levels or Scottish Highers may have been straightforward to choose, but the range of subjects at university is vast. Even subjects you have studied at school may be quite different at degree level – some academic economists prefer their undergraduates not to have taken A-level economics because they approach the subject so differently. Other students are disappointed because they appear to be going over old ground when they continue with a subject that they enjoyed at school. Universities now publish quite detailed syllabuses, and applicants are advised to go through the fine print.

The greater difficulty comes in judging your suitability for the many subjects that are not on the school or college curriculum. Philosophy and psychology sound fascinating (and are), but you may have no idea what degrees in either subject entail – for example, the level of statistics that may be required. Forensic science may look exciting on television – more glamorous than plain chemistry – but it opens fewer doors, as the type of work portrayed in *Silent Witness* is very rare.

Academic or vocational?

There is frequent and often misleading debate about the differences between academic and vocational higher education. It is usually about the relative value of taking a degree, as opposed to a directly work-related qualification. But it also extends to higher education itself, with jibes about so-called "Mickey Mouse" degrees in areas that were not part of the higher education curriculum when most of the critics were students.

Such attitudes ignore the fact that medicine and law are both vocational subjects, as are architecture, engineering and education. They are not seen as any less academic than geography or sociology, but for some reason social work or nursing, let alone media studies and sports science, are often looked down upon. The test of a degree should be whether it is challenging and a good preparation for working life. Both general academic and vocational degrees can do this.

Your school subjects and the UCAS tariff

The official measure by which your results will be judged is the UCAS tariff, which gives a score for each grade of most UK qualifications considered relevant to university entrance, as well as for the International Baccalaureate (IB). The points system is shown on page 35. Two-thirds of

Subject areas covered in this *Guide*

The list below gives each of the 70 subject areas that are covered in detail later in the book (in Chapter 10). For each subject area in that chapter, there is specific advice, a summary of employment prospects and a league table of universities that offered courses in 2020–21, ranked on the basis of an overall score calculated from research quality, entry standards, teaching quality, student experience and graduate employment prospects.

Accounting and Finance
Aeronautical and Manufacturing Engineering
Agriculture and Forestry
American Studies
Anatomy and Physiology
Animal Science
Anthropology
Archaeology and Forensic Science
Architecture
Art and Design
Bioengineering and Biomedical Engineering
Biological Sciences
Building
Business
Celtic Studies
Chemical Engineering
Chemistry
Civil Engineering
Classics
Communication and Media Studies
Computer Science
Creative Writing
Criminology
Dentistry
Drama, Dance and Cinematics
East and South Asian Studies
Economics
Education
Electrical and Electronic Engineering
English
Food Science
French
General Engineering
Geography and Environmental Sciences
Geology
German
History
History of Art
Hospitality, Leisure, Recreation and Tourism
Iberian Languages
Information Systems and Management
Italian
Land and Property Management
Law
Liberal Arts
Linguistics
Materials Technology
Mathematics
Mechanical Engineering
Medicine
Middle Eastern and African Studies
Music
Natural Sciences
Nursing
Pharmacology and Pharmacy
Philosophy
Physics and Astronomy
Physiotherapy
Politics
Psychology
Radiography
Russian
Social Policy
Social Work
Sociology
Sport Science
Subjects Allied to Medicine
Theology and Religious Studies
Town and Country Planning and Landscape
Veterinary Medicine

UCAS tariff scores for main qualifications:

A-levels		AS-levels	
Grade	Points	Grade	Points
A*	56	A	20
A	48	B	16
B	40	C	12
C	32	D	10
D	24	E	6
E	16		

Scottish Advanced Highers		Scottish Highers	
Grade	Points	Grade	Points
A	56	A	33
B	48	B	27
C	40	C	21
D	32	D	15

BTec Level 3			
National Diploma (post-2016)		Extended Certificate	
Grade	Points	Grade	Points
D*	28	D*	56
D	24	D	48
M	16	M	32
P	8	P	16

International Baccalaureate*			
Higher level		Standard level	
H7	56	S7	28
H6	48	S6	24
H5	32	S5	16
H4	24	S4	12
H3	12	S3	6

*The Extended Essay and Theory of Knowledge course are awarded A12, B10, C8, D6, E4
For Foundation Diploma, Extended Diploma and other BTec levels see UCAS website
For other qualifications see: **ucas.com/ucas/ucas-tariff-points**

offers are made in grades, rather than tariff points. This means universities may stipulate the grades they require in specific subjects, and determine which vocational qualifications are relevant to different degrees. In certain universities, some departments, but not others, will use the tariff to set offers. Course profiles on the UCAS website and/or universities' own sites should show whether offers are framed in terms of grades or tariff points. It is important to find out which, especially if you are relying on points from qualifications other than A-levels or Scottish Highers.

Entry qualifications listed in the *Guide* relate not to the offers made by universities, but to the actual grades achieved by successful candidates who are under 21 on entry. This is a useful tool for applicants due to the fact that some courses publish requirements as ABB, for instance, but in reality most entrants achieve AAA. So, in a year of strong year admissions departments may only make offers to applicants with predicted grades that are higher than the minimum requirements. For ease of comparison, a tariff score is included even where universities make their offers in grades.

"Soft" subjects

These are another big factor in what and where you study. The Russell Group scrapped its controversial list of preferred A-levels in 2019, after criticism that it contributed to a devaluation of creative and arts subjects. Previously, however, the group's Informed Choices website had a list of "facilitating subjects" comprising: maths and further maths, English, physics, biology, chemistry, geography, languages (classical and modern) and history, which are required by many degrees and welcomed by Russell Group universities generally.

The website advised sixth-formers to pick the majority of their A-levels from this list and to include at most one "soft" subject. Although these "soft subjects" were not listed specifically, a previous Informed Choices report named media studies, art and design, photography and business studies among the subjects that would normally be given this label. The current Informed Choices website offers more personalised guidance on A-level choices. The facilitating subjects list may be gone, but its legacy is entrenched – which applicants to these universities should be very aware of when selecting their A-levels. It is better to keep more doors open than close any off at sixth form.

For most courses at most universities, there are no such restrictions, as long as your main subjects or qualifications are relevant to the degree you hope to take. Even so, the Russell Group lists are an indication of the subjects that admissions tutors may take more or less seriously, especially if you plan to apply to at least one leading university. Although only the London School of Economics has published a list of "non-preferred" subjects (see below), others may take a less formal approach but still apply similar weightings.

"Traditional academic" and "non-preferred" subjects

The London School of Economics expects applicants to offer at least two of the traditional subjects listed below, while any of the non-preferred subjects listed should only be offered together with two traditional subjects.

Traditional subjects
- Ancient history
- Biology
- Classical civilisation
- Chemistry
- Computing
- Economics
- Electronics
- English (English language, English literature and English language and literature)
- Further mathematics
- Geography
- Government and politics
- History
- Languages: modern foreign, classic and community
- Law
- Mathematics
- Music
- Philosophy
- Physics
- Psychology
- Religious studies
- Sociology

Non-preferred subjects
- Any applied A-level
- Accounting*
- Art and design
- Business studies
- Citizenship studies
- Communication and culture
- Creative writing
- Design and technology
- Drama/theatre studies
- Film studies
- Health and social care
- Home economics
- Information and communication technology
- Leisure studies
- Media studies
- Music technology
- Physical education/sports studies
- Travel and tourism

*The LSE Department of Accounting considers accounting equally with other generally preferred subjects. It will therefore consider accounting alongside one other subject from the non-preferred list. However, the majority of departments continue to regard accounting as a non-preferred subject.

Critical thinking, general studies, global perspectives and research, knowledge and enquiry, project work and thinking skill are normally excluded subjects and will only be considered as a fourth A-level. They will not be accepted as part of a contextual offer.

Source: LSE

Vocational qualifications

The value placed on diplomas and other qualifications by universities can be confusing. The engineering diploma has won near-universal approval from universities (for admission to engineering courses, and possibly some science degrees), but some of the other diplomas are in fields that are not on the curriculum of the most selective universities. Regardless of the points awarded under the tariff, it is essential to contact universities directly to ensure that a diploma or another vocational qualification will be an acceptable qualification for your chosen degree.

Admission tests

The growing numbers of applicants with high grades at A-level have encouraged the introduction of separate admission tests for some of the most oversubscribed courses. There are national tests in medicine and law that are used by some of the leading universities, while Oxford and Cambridge have their own tests in a growing number of subjects. The details are listed on page 38. In all cases, the tests are used as an extra selection tool, not as a replacement for A-level or other general qualifications.

Studying more than one subject

If more than one subject appeals, you could consider Joint Honours – degrees that combine two subjects – or even Combined Honours, which will cover several related subjects. Such courses obviously allow you to extend the scope of your studies, but they should be approached with caution. Even if the number of credits suggests a similar workload to Single Honours, covering more than one subject inevitably involves extra reading and often more essays or project work.

Applicants should also be sure to discuss their even-handed interest in both subjects in the personal statement of their UCAS form. Many students choose a "dual" to add a vocational element to make themselves more employable – business studies with languages or engineering, for example, or media studies with English. Others want to take their studies in a particular direction, perhaps by combining history with politics, or statistics with maths. Some simply want to add a completely unrelated interest to their main subject, such as musical theatre and politics (offered at Liverpool Hope).

At most universities, however, it is not necessary to take a degree in more than one subject in order to broaden your studies. The spread of modular programmes ensures that you can take courses in related subjects without changing the basic structure of your degree. The number and scope of the combinations offered at many of the larger universities is extraordinary. Indeed, it has been criticised by academics who believe that "mix-and-match" degrees can leave a graduate without a rounded view of a subject. But if you are looking for breadth and variety, scrutinise university websites and prospectuses closely as part of the selection process.

What type of course?

Once you have a subject, you must decide on the level and type of course. Most readers of this *Guide* will be looking for full-time degree courses, but higher education is much broader than that. You may have neither the time or the money needed for a full-time commitment of three or four years at this point in life.

Admissions tests

Some of the most competitive courses now have additional entrance tests. The most significant tests are listed below. Note that registration for many of the tests is before 15th October and you will need to register for them as early as possible. All the tests have their own websites. Institutions requiring specific tests vary from year to year and you must check course website details carefully for test requirements. In addition over 50 universities also administer their own tests for certain courses. Details are given at: **ucas.com/undergraduate/applying-university/admissions-tests**

Engineering and Science

Engineering and Science Admissions Test (ESAT): for entry to engineering and science-based subjects at Imperial, Cambridge and University College London. Register from end of July; tests held in October and January.

Law

Law National Admissions Test (LNAT): for entry to law courses at Bristol, Cambridge, Durham, Glasgow, King's College London, London School of Economics, Oxford, SOAS, University College London. Register from August; tests held from September to July.

Mathematics

Mathematics Admissions Test (MAT): for entry to mathematics at Imperial and mathematics and computer science at Oxford. Advised but not compulsory for applicants to mathematics at Warwick. The MAT is also taken into consideration by other universities, including Bath and Durham, for particular courses. Register by mid-September.

The Test of Mathematics for University Admission (TMUA): for entry to some courses in mathematics, computer science or economics at Imperial, Cambridge, London School of Economics, Warwick, Durham and University College London. Register from end of July.

Medical subjects

University Clinical Aptitude Test (UCAT): for entry to medical and dental schools at Aberdeen, Anglia Ruskin, Aston, Bangor, Birmingham, Greater Manchester, Brighton and Sussex Medical School, Bristol, Brunel, Cambridge, Cardiff, Central Lancashire, Chester, City St George's, Dundee, East Anglia, Edge Hill, Edinburgh, Exeter, Glasgow, Hertfordshire, Hull York Medical School, Imperial, Keele, Kent and Medway, King's College London, Lancaster, Leeds, Leicester, Lincoln, Liverpool, Manchester, Newcastle, Nottingham, Oxford, Pears Cumbria School of Medicine, Plymouth, Portsmouth, Queen Mary University of London, Queen's University Belfast, Sheffield, Southampton, St Andrews, Sunderland, Surrey, Swansea, University College London, Warwick and Worcester. Check **ucat.ac.uk/about-ucat** for registration and test dates.

Graduate Medical School Admissions Test (GAMSAT): for graduate entry to medicine at Brunel, Chester, City St George's, Exeter, East Anglia, Pears Cumbria School of Medicine, Keele, Liverpool, Plymouth (and dentistry), St Andrews/Dundee, Sunderland, Surrey, Swansea, Ulster and Worcester. The GAMSAT test is offered in March and September.

Cambridge University

Pre-interview or at-interview assessments take place for most subjects. Full details given on the Cambridge admissions website. See also ESAT, LNAT, TMUA and UCAT above.

Oxford University

Pre-interview tests take place in many subjects and candidates are required to register by early October. Full details given on the Oxford admissions website. Tests are usually held at the candidate's educational institution. See also LNAT and MAT above.

University College London

From 2026 entry, UCL is introducing the TARA (Test of Academic Reasoning for Admissions) for admissions to various mathematics and social science programmes. Register from end of July, tests in September and January.

Part-time courses

Tens of thousands of people each year opt for a part-time course – usually while holding down a job – to continue learning and to improve their career prospects. The numbers studying this way have dropped considerably, but loans are available for students whose courses occupy between a quarter and three-quarters of the time expected on a full-time course.

Repayments are on the same conditions as those for full-time courses, except that you will begin repaying the April four years after the start of your course, or the April after you finish or leave your course, whichever comes first, even if the course has not been completed by then. The downside is that universities have increased their fees in the knowledge that part-time students will be able to take out student loans to cover fees, and employers are now less inclined to fund their employees on such courses.

At Birkbeck, University of London, a compromise has been found with full-time courses taught in the evening. For courses classified as part-time, students pay fees in proportion to the number of credits they take.

Part-time study can be exhausting unless your employer gives you time off, but if you have the stamina for a course that will usually take twice as long as the full-time equivalent, this route should still make a degree more affordable. Part-time students tend to be highly committed to their subject, and many claim that the quality of the social life associated with their course makes up for the quantity of leisure time enjoyed by full-timers.

Distance learning

The pandemic showed that undergraduate teaching and learning is more possible to achieve remotely than many might have thought pre-Covid. If you are confident that you can manage without regular face-to-face contact with teachers and fellow students, distance learning is an option. Courses are delivered mainly or entirely online or through correspondence, although some programmes offer a certain amount of local tuition. The process might sound daunting and impersonal, but students of the Open University (OU), all of whom are educated in this way, are frequently among the most satisfied in the country, according to the results of the annual National Student Survey. Attending lectures or oversized seminars at a conventional university can be less personal than regular contact with your tutor at a distance – factors that mainstream universities have cottoned onto since being forced to pivot to remote teaching and learning in the pandemic.

This mode of study gives students ultimate flexibility to determine when and where they study. Distance learning is becoming increasingly popular for the delivery of professional courses, which are often needed to supplement degrees. The OU takes students of all ages, including school-leavers, not just mature students.

In addition, Massive Open Online Courses (MOOCs) are provided by many of the leading UK and American universities, usually free of charge. As yet, most such courses are the equivalent of a module in a degree course, rather than the entire qualification. Some are assessed formally but none is likely to be seen by employers as the equal of a conventional degree, no matter how prestigious the university offering the course. For those who are uncertain about committing to a degree, or who simply want to learn more about a subject without needing a high-status qualification, they are ideal. MOOCs are also used by sixth-formers to extend their subject knowledge and demonstrate their enthusiasm and capability to admissions tutors. They are certainly worth considering for inclusion in a personal statement and/or to spark discussion at an interview. A number of UK universities offer MOOCs through the Futurelearn platform, run by the Open University (**futurelearn.com**). But the beauty of MOOCs is that they can come from all over the world. Perhaps the best-known providers are Coursera (**coursera.org**), which originated at Stanford University in California, and now involves a large number of American and international universities including Edinburgh, and edX (**edx.org**), which numbers Harvard among its members.

Foundation degrees

Even if you are set on a full-time course, you might not want to commit yourself for three or more years. Two-year vocational Foundation degrees have become a popular route into higher education in recent years. Many other students take longer-established two-year courses, such as Higher National Diplomas or other diplomas tailored to the needs of industry or parts of the health service. Those who do well on such courses usually have the option of converting their qualification into a full degree with further study, although many are satisfied without immediately staying on for the further two or more years that will be required to complete a BA or BSc.

Foundation courses

A growing number of short courses, usually lasting a year, are designed for students who do not have the necessary qualifications to start a degree in their chosen subject. Foundation courses in art and design have been common for many years and are the chosen preparation for a degree at leading departments, even for many students whose A-levels would win them a degree place elsewhere. Access courses perform the same function in a wider range of subjects for students without A-levels, or for those whose grades are either too low or in the wrong subjects to gain admission to a particular course. Entry requirements are modest, but students have to reach the same standard as regular entrants to progress to a degree.

Other short courses

A number of universities are experimenting with two-year degrees, encouraged by the government, squeezing more work into an extended academic year. The so-called "third semester" makes use of the summer vacation for extra teaching, so that mature students, in particular, can reduce the length of their career break. But only at the University of Buckingham, the UK's longest-established private university, is this the dominant pattern for degree courses. Other private institutions are following suit.

Earn while you learn

Degree apprenticeships are a serious alternative to university. They give students the best of both worlds by combining study at degree level with extended work experience at a named industrial or business partner. The government wants more degree apprenticeships and universities are expanding their offerings, which include accountancy, cybersecurity, law, finance, economic and social research, computing, nursing, healthcare sciences, data science, management and some branches of engineering. The average salary while learning is £18,000 but for some it is as high as £26,000. The hours are usually longer than for undergraduates and they have less holiday but degree apprentices graduate debt-free.

The UCAS Career Finder service helps students find jobs and apprenticeships. Applications for an apprenticeship are made directly to employers and, if successful, a student is then linked to a university to study part-time for the associated degree. Weigh up the options on the government's "Find an Apprenticeship" page (**gov.uk/apply-apprenticeship**). Once you register, you can set up email and text alerts to inform you about new apprenticeship roles.

The Sunday Times Top 100 Apprenticeship Employers (**top100apprenticeshipemployers.co.uk**), published in 2025, celebrates the UK's outstanding apprenticeship employers –

recognising the UK's outstanding apprenticeship employers' commitment to creating new apprenticeships, the diversity of their apprentices, and the number of apprentices who successfully complete their apprenticeships.

Such apprenticeships take up to six years to complete and leave the graduate with a Bachelor's or even a Master's degree. Employers including Deloitte, PwC, BMW, Microsoft and the BBC are offering higher-level apprenticeships, although naturally not all are with household names such as these.

Be aware though, that the numbers of degree apprenticeship programmes is relatively small, and the most desirable courses are very competitive to get onto. Plus, the applicant needs to know what they want to do for a job at the point of applying – which not all 17-year-olds do.

Yet more choice

No single guide can allow for personal preferences in choosing a course. You may want one of the many degrees that incorporate a year at a partner university abroad, or to try an exchange via the government's Turing Scheme. Either might prove a valuable experience and add to your employability. Or you might prefer a January or February start to the traditional autumn start – there are plenty of opportunities for this, and not only at post-1992 universities.

In some subjects – particularly engineering and the sciences – the leading degrees may be Masters courses, taking four years rather than three (in England). In Scotland, most degree courses take four years and some at the older universities will confer a Masters qualification.

Those who come with A-levels may apply to go straight into the second year. Relatively few students take this option, but it is easy to imagine more doing so in future at universities that charge students from other parts of the UK the full tuition fees for all years of the course.

Where to study

Several factors might influence your choice of university or college. Obviously, you need to have a reasonable chance of getting in, you may want reassurance about the university's reputation, and its location will probably be important to you as well. On top of that, most applicants have views about the type of institution they are looking for – big or small, old or new, urban or rural, specialist or comprehensive.

Campus universities tend to produce the highest levels of student satisfaction, but big city universities continue to attract sixth-formers in the largest numbers. You may surprise yourself by choosing somewhere that does not conform to your initial criteria but working through your preferences is another way of narrowing down your options.

Entry standards

Unless you are a mature student or have taken a gap year, your passport to your chosen university will probably be a conditional offer based on your predicted grades, previous exam performance, personal statement, and school or college reference. Supply and demand dictate whether you will receive an offer, conditional or otherwise (see Chapter 5). Beyond the national picture, your chances will be affected both by the university and the subject you choose. A few universities (but not many) at the top of the league tables are heavily oversubscribed in every subject; others will have areas in which they excel but may make relatively modest demands for entry to other courses. Even in many of the leading universities, the number of applicants for each place in languages is still not high. Conversely, three As at A-level will not guarantee a place on one of the top English or law degrees, but there are enough universities running courses to ensure that three Cs will give you a chance somewhere.

Universities with highest and lowest offer rates

Highest		Lowest	
University for the Creative Arts	96.7%	University of Oxford	20.3%
Southampton Solent University	95.0%	London School of Economics and Political Science	21.0%
Aberystwyth University	94.4%	University of Cambridge	24.5%
Lincoln Bishop University	93.4%	University of St Andrews	30.0%
University of Sussex	92.7%	Imperial College London	32.8%
SOAS, University of London	92.6%	University College London	35.2%
Northumbria University	91.2%	University of Edinburgh	43.6%
University of South Wales	90.9%	King's College London	44.3%
Nottingham Trent University	90.8%	University of the Arts London	48.4%
University of Kent	90.7%	University of Strathclyde	57.1%

Source: UCAS End of cycle report 2024

University websites and prospectuses and the UCAS website will give you the "standard offer" for each course, but in some cases, this is pitched deliberately low in order to leave admissions staff extra flexibility. The standard A-level offer for medicine, for example, may not demand A*s, but nearly all successful applicants will have one or more.

In Scotland, and increasingly elsewhere in the UK, universities have started to publish two sets of standard offers: their normal range and another with lower grades for applicants from disadvantaged backgrounds.

Contextual offers are a similar practice elsewhere in the UK and are increasingly widespread, using contextualised information about applicants' backgrounds to reduce the entry grades. As already noted, the average entry scores in our tables give the actual points obtained by successful applicants – many of which are far above the offer made by the university, but which give an indication of the pecking order at entry. The subject tables (in Chapter 10) are, naturally, a better guide than the main table (in Chapter 1), where average entry scores are influenced by the range of subjects available at each university.

Best paid graduates
(Median salary 15 months after graduating)

1	Imperial College London	£36,000
2	London School of Economics	£35,000
3	University of Cambridge	£33,750
4	City St George's, University of London	£32,069
=5	UCL (University College London)	£32,000
=5	University of Oxford	£32,000
7	University of Warwick	£31,000
8	King's College London	£30,786
9	University of Bath	£30,600
10	University of Bristol	£30,000

Source: HESA

Most popular universities by main scheme applications 2023

1	University of Manchester	92,500
2	UCL (University College London)	78,330
3	King's College, London	68,510
4	University of Leeds	68,055
5	University of Edinburgh	68,020
6	University of Bristol	63,185
7	Manchester Metropolitan University	59,460
8	University of Birmingham	57,625
9	University of Nottingham	52,165
10	Cardiff University	46,240

Source: UCAS End of Cycle report 2024

Location

The most obvious starting point is the country you study in. Most degrees in Scotland take four years, rather than the UK norm of three, which makes them more expensive for students who come from outside Scotland, especially given the loss of the year's salary you might have been earning after graduation. Chapter 4 goes into the details of the system, but suffice to say that students from Scotland pay no fees, while those from the rest of the UK do.

Nevertheless, Edinburgh and St Andrews remain particularly popular with English students, despite charging them £9,535 (and rising) for the full four years of a degree starting in 2025.

The number of English students going to Scottish universities has increased almost every year since the fees went up, even though there would be no savings, perhaps because the institutions have tried harder to attract them. Fees – or the lack of them – are by no means the only influence on cross-border mobility: the number of Scots going to English universities rose sharply, despite the cost, probably because the number of places is capped in Scotland, but is not any longer in England.

Close to home

Far from crossing national boundaries, however, students also choose to study near home, whether or not they continue to live with their family. This is understandable for Scots, who will save themselves tens of thousands of pounds by studying at their own fees-free universities. But there is also a gradual increase in the numbers choosing to study close to home either to cut living costs or for personal reasons, such as family circumstances, a girlfriend or boyfriend, continuing employment or religion. Some simply want to stick with what they know. A recent survey of sixth-formers by University College London found that one in three students starting university in 2023 may opt to live at home, due to rising costs and family needs affecting the "Covid generation" of school-leavers. Before the pandemic about 20% of first year undergraduates in England lived at home while studying, including mature students. The UCL report found that as many as 34% of 18-year-old school-leavers were considering staying at home if accepted by their first-choice university when exam results were published. The survey found that students from disadvantaged families were more likely to be affected by the financial challenges of studying away from home.

The trend for full-time students who do go away to study, is to choose a university within about two hours' travelling time. The assumption is that this is far enough to discourage parents from springing unannounced visits, but close enough to make the occasional trip home to get the washing done, have a decent meal and see friends. The leading universities recruit from all over the world, but most still have a regional core.

City universities

The most popular universities, in terms of total applications, are nearly all in big cities with other major centres of population within the two-hour travelling window. Students are drawn by the best nightclubs, top sporting events, high-quality shopping, cultural diversity and access to leading galleries, museums and theatres. Especially for those who live in cities already, city universities are a magnet. The big universities also, by definition, offer the widest range of subjects, although that does not mean that they necessarily have the specific course that is right for you. You might not actually go clubbing a lot or hit the shops that much, in spite of the inspiring marketing material that suggests you will, either because you cannot afford to, or because student life is more focused on the university than the city, or even because you are too busy studying.

Campus universities

City universities are the right choice for many young people, but it is worth bearing in mind that the National Student Survey shows that the highest satisfaction levels tend to be at smaller universities, often those with their own self-contained campuses. It seems that students identify more closely with institutions where there is a close-knit community and the social life is based around the students' union rather than the local nightclubs – at least in the first-year when more students tend to live in campus accommodation. There may also be a better prospect of regular contact with tutors and lecturers, who are likely to live on or near the campus.

Few UK universities are in genuinely rural locations, but some – particularly among the more recently promoted – are in relatively small towns. Several longer-established institutions in Scotland and Wales also share this type of setting, where the university dominates the town.

Importance of Open Days

By far the best way to be confident that any university is for you is to visit. The pattern of Open Days varies and many offer virtual as well as physical events. Our profiles in Chapter 12 give each university's website for the latest information. Schools often restrict the number of open days that sixth-formers can attend in term-time, but with dates clustered in the spring and autumn it is usually possible to fit in all those you want to visit. A full calendar of events is available at **opendays.com**.

Bear in mind, if you only attend one or two, that the event has to be badly mismanaged for a university not to seem an exciting place to someone who spends his or her days at school, or even college. Try to get a flavour of several institutions before you make your choice.

How many universities to pick?

When that time comes, of course, you will not be making one choice but five; four if you are applying for medicine, dentistry or veterinary science. (Full details of the application process are given in Chapter 5.) Tens of thousands of students each year eventually go to a university that did not start out as their first choice, either because they did not get the right offer or because they changed their mind along the way. UCAS rules are such that applicants do not list universities in order of preference anyway – indeed, universities are not allowed to know

Top 10 Universities for Quality of Teaching, feedback and support 2023 by % of students satisfied

1	University of Suffolk	92.2
2	Leeds Trinity University	91.7
3	Lincoln Bishop University	91.2
4	University of Wales Trinity Saint David	90.3
5	Liverpool Hope University	89.9
6	Canterbury Christ Church University	89.5
7	University of St Andrews	89.3
8	Buckinghamshire New University	89.2
=8	Plymouth Marjon University	89.2
10	Aberystwyth University	89.1

Source: National Student Survey 2023

Top 10 Universities for Overall Student Experience 2023 by % of students satisfied

1	University of Suffolk	88.7
2	Leeds Trinity University	88.2
3	University of Sheffield	87.0
4	University of St Andrews	86.9
=5	Canterbury Christ Church University	86.3
=5	University of West London	86.3
7	Lincoln Bishop University	86.1
8	University of Wales Trinity Saint David	85.8
9	University of Leicester	85.7
10	University of Liverpool	85.6

Source: National Student Survey 2023

where else you have applied. So do not pin all your hopes on one course; take just as much care choosing the other universities on your list.

The fragmentation of the British university system into groups of institutions is another factor: the Russell Group (**russellgroup.ac.uk**) represents 24 research-intensive universities, nearly all with medical schools; the million+ group (**www.millionplus.ac.uk**) contains many of the former polytechnics and newer universities; the University Alliance (**www.unialliance.ac.uk**) provides a home for 16 universities, both old and new, that identify themselves as professional and technical institutions; while GuildHE (**guildhe.ac.uk**) represents specialist colleges and the newest universities. The Cathedrals Group (**www.cathedralsgroup.ac.uk**) is an affiliation of 15 church-based universities and colleges, some of which are also members of other groups. ResearchPlus is a collective of 10 research-focused universities that formed a strategic partnership in 2025, outside the Russell Group.

Many of today's applicants will barely have heard of a polytechnic, let alone be able to identify which of today's universities had that heritage, but most will know which of two universities in the same city has the higher status. While that should matter far less than the quality of a course, it would be naive to ignore institutional reputation entirely if that is going to carry weight with a future employer. Some big firms restrict their recruitment efforts to a small group of universities (see Chapter 3), and, however shortsighted that might be, it is something to bear in mind if a career in the City or a big law firm is your ambition.

Facilities

The quality of campus facilities is an important factor in choosing a university for most students. Only the course and the university's location tend to have a higher priority. Accommodation is the main selling point for those living away from home, but sports facilities, libraries (24-hour, ideally) and computing equipment also play an important part. Even upgraded campus nightclubs have become part of the facilities race that has followed the introduction of higher fees. Many universities guarantee first-year students accommodation in halls of residence or university-owned flats. It is a good idea to know what happens after that. Are there enough places for second or third-year students who want them, and if not, what is the private market like? Rents for student houses vary quite widely across the country and there have been tensions because of a shortage of student accommodation in places, and sometimes with local residents in some cities. All universities offer specialist accommodation for disabled students – and are better at providing other facilities than most public institutions.

Special-interest clubs and recreational facilities, as well as political activity, tend to be based in the students' union – sometimes known as the guild of students. In some universities, the union is the focal point of social activity, while in others the attractions of the city seem to overshadow the union to the point where facilities are underused. Students' union websites are included with the information found in the university profiles (Chapter 12).

University or college?

This *Guide* is primarily concerned with universities, the destination of choice for the vast majority of higher education students. But there are other options – and not just for those searching for lower fees. A number of specialist higher education colleges offer a similar, or sometimes superior, quality of course in their particular fields. The subject tables in Chapter 10 chart the successes of various colleges in art, agriculture, music and teacher training in particular. Some colleges of higher education are not so different from the newer universities and may acquire that status themselves in future years.

Further education colleges

The second group of colleges offering degrees are further education (FE) colleges. These are often large institutions with a wide range of courses, from A-levels to vocational subjects at different levels, up to degrees in some cases. Although their numbers of higher education students have been falling in recent years, the current fee structure presents FE colleges with an opportunity because they tend not to bear all the costs of a university campus. For that reason, too, they may not offer a broad student experience of the type that universities pride themselves on, but the best colleges respond well to the local labour market and offer small teaching groups and effective personal support.

FE colleges are a local resource and tend to attract mature students who cannot or do not want to travel to university. Many of their higher education students apply nowhere else. But, as competition for university places has increased, they also have become more of an option for school-leavers to continue their studies, as they always have been in Scotland.

Statistical comparisons of FE colleges, with their predominantly local, mature student populations, against universities, where undergraduates make up the main numbers, are not reliable. But it should be noted that the proportion of college graduates unemployed six months after graduation tends to be higher than at universities, and average graduate salaries lower.

Both further and higher education colleges are audited by the Quality Assurance Agency and appear in the National Student Survey, as well as the Teaching Excellence Framework. In all three, their results usually show wide variation. Some demonstrate higher levels of satisfaction among their students than most universities, for example, while others are at the bottom of the scale.

Private universities and colleges

Courses are mainly in business and law, and also in some other specialist fields (see pages 439–42). These were relatively insignificant in terms of size until recently, but the changes to the fee regime may cause numbers at private universities and colleges to grow. By far the longest established – and the only one to meet the criteria for inclusion in our main table – is the University of Buckingham, which is profiled on page 326. The best-known "newcomer" currently is BPP University, which became a full university in 2013 and offers degrees, as well as shorter courses, in both law and business subjects. Like Buckingham, BPP offers two-year degrees with short vacations to maximise teaching time.

Northeastern University London, formerly New College of the Humanities, graduated its first students in 2015, and offers a liberal arts-inspired curriculum. Having started out with fees of nearly £18,000 a year for all undergraduates, the college is now matching the "public sector" at £9,535 a year.

Two other private institutions have been awarded full university status. Regent's University, attractively positioned in London's Regent's Park, caters particularly for the international market with courses in business, arts and social science subjects priced at £23,000–£27,500 a year for 2025–26. However, about half of the students at the not-for-profit university, which offers British and American degrees, are from the UK or other parts of Europe.

The University of Law, as its name suggests, is more specialised. It has been operating as a college in London for more than 100 years and claims to be the world's leading professional law school. It offers law degrees, as well as professional courses, with fees for three-year degrees set at £9,535 per year in 2025–26 for UK students and £11,440 per year for the two-year version. The university has 17 UK campuses, in locations including London (where it has two), Nottingham, Birmingham, Bristol, Manchester and Leeds, as well as at Chester, Exeter,

East Anglia, Reading, Liverpool, Sheffield, Hull, Newcastle, Royal Holloway and Oxford Brookes universities.

Checklist
Choosing a subject and a place to study is a major decision. Make sure you can answer these questions:

Choosing a course
» Will my course enable my career and income goals?
» Do I want to study something I know from school, or something new?
» Are my qualifications right for the course?
» Will I enjoy my studies and stick with them?
» Will there be work experience opportunities?
» Will I cope with the demands made on myself?
» Is there good academic and wellbeing support?

Choosing a university
» Does my dream university offer the right course?
» Do I prefer a campus, city or smaller town setting?
» Should I stay close to home to save money?
» How much will accommodation and study extras cost?
» What do students already there think of the university?
» Does the university have a socially and culturally diverse student population?

There are also growing numbers of specialist colleges offering degrees, especially in the business sector. Walbrook Institute of London (formerly The London Institute of Banking & Finance and before that, ifs School of Finance), also dates back more than 100 years and now has university college status for its courses in finance and banking.

The Dyson Institute of Engineering and Technology, based at Malmesbury, in Wiltshire, welcomed its first 33 undergraduates in 2017 and began awarding its own degrees three years later. Funded entirely by Sir James Dyson, there are no fees, and students work at the nearby Dyson headquarters for 47 weeks a year. The New Model Institute in Technology and Engineering, in Hereford, has received more than £20million in government funding and promises to give students a "head start on becoming a work-ready, world-conscious engineer".

The London Interdisciplinary School was founded in 2017. Based in Whitechapel, east London it had its own degree awarding powers from inception and offers a unique degree in interdisciplinary problems and methods. Black Mountains College was founded in 2019 as a response to the climate emergency and offers an undergraduate degree in sustainable futures: arts, ecology and systems change, in partnership with Cardiff Metropolitan University. It takes time to build a track record, but there should be a market in the areas these new institutions offer.

Sources of information
With more than 130 universities to choose from, the Discover Uni and UCAS websites, as well as guides such as this one, are the obvious places to start your search for the right course.

Discover Uni includes figures for average salaries at course level, as well as student satisfaction ratings and some information on contact hours, although this does not distinguish between lectures and seminars. The site does not make multiple comparisons easy to carry out, but it does contain a wealth of information for those who persevere. Once you have narrowed down the list of candidates, you will want to go through undergraduate prospectuses. All are available online and many universities still print hard copies, should you want a hefty book that includes details of every course to arrive in the post. Beware of generalised claims about the standing of the university, the quality of courses, friendly atmosphere and legendary social life. Stick to the factual information.

While the material that the universities publish about their own qualities is less than objective, much of what you will find on the internet may be completely unreliable, for different reasons. A simple search on the name of a university will turn up spurious comparisons of everything from the standard of lecturing to the attractiveness of the students. These can be seriously misleading and are usually based on anecdotal evidence, at best. Make sure that any information you consider comes from a reputable source and, if it conflicts with your impression, try to cross-check it with this *Guide* and the institution's own material.

Useful websites

The best starting point is the UCAS website (**www.ucas.com**), where there is extensive information on courses, universities and the whole process of applying to university. UCAS has an official presence on Facebook (**facebook.com/ucasonline**) and X (**@UCAS_online**) and now also has a series of video guides (**youtube.com/user/ucasonline**) on the process of applying, UCAS resources and comments from other students.

For statistical information that allows limited comparison between universities (and for full details of the National Student Survey): **discoveruni.gov.uk**

On appropriate A-level subject choice: **informedchoices.ac.uk**

Narrowing down course choices: **coursefindr.co.uk**

For a full calendar of university and college open days: **opendays.com**

Students with disabilities: Disability Rights UK: **disabilityrightsuk.org/guidance-resources**

3 Assessing Graduate Job Prospects

"The only way to do great work is to love what you do," Steve Jobs, the founder of Apple, once said. Such wisdom affirms the approach of many university applicants who follow their heart, applying to study a subject they love at university, whether or not it promises a defined career pathway or a guarantee of high earnings. A more pragmatic approach to subject choice has also emerged in recent years, with current trends in applications depicting a generation conscious of securing solid careers after graduating. The 2024 admissions cycle showed strong student enrolments in courses within business and management, and law. There was also a 6% increase of students accepted onto computing courses, and a 10% uplift to those accepted onto engineering and technology courses, indicating technological and AI advances continuing to drive interest in STEM subjects. Economics and maths degrees had a boom year too, and the number of UK 18-year-olds accepted to 'subjects allied to medicine' was at a record high, totalling 28,495. Meanwhile there were fewer new students starting courses within the humanities and modern languages.

With rising costs of tuition and living, stricter student loans repayments and a tough jobs landscape, applicants are wise to estimate if their investment in undergraduate study will pay off with commensurate career prospects. Predictions about which professions will be resilient to AI add to the mix.

The current jobs market upon graduation is challenging. Martin Birchall, editor of *The Times Top 100 Graduate Employers*, reports that opportunities for university-leavers have now slumped by almost a quarter since 2022, taking graduate recruitment back to a level last recorded in 2012: "The number of graduate jobs on offer from the country's top employers has now fallen three years running, as businesses have struggled with economic uncertainty, tax rises and increasing employment costs. In 2024 alone, graduate vacancies were cut by 14.6% year-on-year – the largest annual fall since 2009 and an even bigger reduction than during the Covid pandemic. The outlook for 2026 remains pessimistic, with employers featured in *The Times Top 100 Graduate Employers* expecting to reduce their graduate recruitment even further in the year ahead."

And despite graduates making a record number of job applications: "an average of 21.7 applications per student (up from 16.4 applications in 2024 and 12.7 applications in 2023)

– fewer final year students were offered a graduate job before leaving university," Birchall notes. Consequently, students' confidence in the graduate job market has dropped dramatically over the past two years, with *The Times Top 100 Graduate Employers* research in 2025 showing 43% of finalists describing the vacancies for new university-leavers as 'limited', up from 37% in 2024, and 25% in 2023. As to what jobs are on their hit list, the most popular destinations were consulting roles, jobs in the media, marketing, finance and law, the research conducted with over 15,000 final year students showed.

When choosing a subject and university, it is useful to be aware that for the majority of graduate jobs (around 70%), graduates from any degree discipline may apply. And whilst many graduate programmes still stipulate that university-leavers should have at least a 2:1 in their degree, the big employers rely on their own battery of tests, online recorded interviews and other assessments during a four or five-stage selection process, to determine whether graduates have developed the right skills, abilities, and experiences to do the roles on offer. "And crucially, they test whether applicants have developed sufficient knowledge and understanding of the jobs they're applying for, and can demonstrate a genuine interest in the roles," says Birchall.

Of course, plenty of university applicants know exactly what they want to study at university, guided by hopes of their dream career. For graduate jobs that require a specific degree – such as engineering, technology, or research and development positions – employers will look closely at the content of the university course an applicant has studied and their academic record, in order to determine they have the technical and other qualifications needed for the roles. If you're considering studying a vocational course as a route into a particular career or sector, check the graduate outcomes from each university offering it.

Figuring out what your values are and the kind of individual you want to be as you grow older is another way of narrowing the field; a sustainable way of life may trump money, for instance. Once you get to university, spend time exploring the different career options you could go onto after graduation, and get as much work experience as you can – be it formal internships, roles within student societies, university sport or part-time jobs, to help develop the skills and aptitude that employers look for.

For those who study for a degree, it still pays to go to university – by a clear margin. Figures published in June 2025 based on the Office for National Statistics' Labour Force Survey showed 87.6% of working age graduates were employed in 2024, compared to 68.0% of nongraduates, and 67.9% of working age graduates were in high-skilled employment in 2024, compared to 23.7% of those who did not go to university. The average salary was £42,000 for graduates, compared with £30,500 for nongraduates, and this gap has remained at about £10,000 since 2007.

According to the Department for Education's latest longitudinal education outcomes data, the average graduate salary a decade after graduation was £34,300. The statistics showed that graduates with economics degrees had the highest salaries ten years after graduating, with an average salary of £68,600. Medicine and dentistry were close behind at £61,000 and mathematical sciences was next at £51,500. Other top-paying degrees included engineering, architecture, computing and the sciences. Taking this longer view of salaries is useful, as industries such as law might pay less in the first year but there is plenty of room for growth – law graduates have an average salary of £23,000 in the first year but £40,500 by year ten, for instance – while nursing and midwifery start well but have lower growth prospects.

Although graduate salaries are perhaps the most obvious way of evaluating whether a degree represents a good bet, they have never been used as a performance measure by *The Times and The Sunday Times Good University Guide* league table rankings. Few would argue that trainee nurses and teachers, for example, should be put off going to university because the professions they are studying towards do not promise megabucks. The social value of some professions may outweigh their financial gains but there is still job security to be found, as well as the rewarding elements of the work. Salaries are also liable to variations including whether a university is located in an area of high or low employment, with high or low wages. We list average salaries for each of the 70 subject groups in this chapter's second table, without including them in our league table calculations.

Graduates are among the highest-skilled workers and play an important role in the economy, they promote innovation and growth. Graduates are also more occupationally and geographically mobile, which helps explain their employment in times of crisis; while unemployment increased during coronavirus, graduates suffered less acutely than those without degrees. As well as specific capabilities related to their subject, graduates have more general transferable skills – such as writing, communication and critical thinking – that contribute to greater career resilience when the world is in extremis. Nick Hillman, the director of the Higher Education Policy Institute, said: "It is still very much worth going to university. You earn more and you pretty much have insurance against unemployment when there's a recession or downturn. Also, it's very difficult to enter most professions nowadays if you don't have a degree. That is just the labour market considerations."

Over a working lifetime the Institute for Fiscal Studies (IFS) calculates that male graduates can expect to be about £130,000 better off than if they had not gone to university, after student loan repayments and extra taxes. For women, this figure is £100,000. Once enrolled, working hard to get a high degree classification also helps, and of course some professions are bigger earners than others. Use our *Guide* to assess graduate prospects by subject area and by university, and to get an idea of the sort of salaries to expect soon after finishing a degree.

Median earnings by degree subject five years after graduation (2017–18 graduates)

Medicine and dentistry	£51,967	General, applied and forensic sciences	£32,300
Economics	£50,400	Law	£32,100
Mathematical sciences	£44,033	Biosciences	£31,488
Engineering	£42,640	Allied health	£31,457
Physics and astronomy	£41,600	Philosophy and religious studies	£30,850
Pharmacology, toxicology and pharmacy	£38,000	Media, journalism and communications	£29,720
Materials and technology	£37,543	Agriculture, food and related studies	£29,400
Medical sciences	£37,050	Sociology, social policy and anthropology	£29,180
Computing	£36,957	History and archaeology	£28,680
Architecture, building and planning	£36,225	Education and teaching	£28,500
Veterinary sciences	£36,150	Sport and exercise sciences	£28,500
Chemistry	£35,400	English studies	£27,683
Politics	£35,400	Psychology	£27,660
Nursing and midwifery	£35,211	Health and social care	£26,500
Languages and area studies	£33,978	Combined and general studies	£25,800
Geography, earth and environmental studies	£33,000	Performing arts	£24,233
Business and management	£32,988	Creative arts and design	£23,880

Source: Department for Education, Graduate Outcomes, November 2025

Graduate prospects in *Good University Guide* rankings

The measure we use to assess graduate prospects takes account of the rates of employment for graduates in the 70 subject areas in our *Guide* and distinguishes between types of work.

The Graduate Outcomes (GO) survey is now in its sixth year, having replaced the Destination of Leavers from Higher Education (DLHE) survey. Both measure the same thing: what graduates do next, but the previous system gathered information six months after graduation, whereas GO conducts its survey 15 months after graduates have finished their degrees.

The longer timeframe better reflects changes in work patterns, with many graduates doing internships, travelling or sampling the jobs market before plumping for a career path. We look at the proportion of graduates in high-skilled jobs and/or postgraduate study. This *Guide* uses a definition of a high-skilled job from the Higher Education Statistics Agency (HESA), which conducts the GO survey.

What graduates are doing 15 months after leaving university by subject studied

Subject	Employed in high-skilled job %	Employed in high-skilled job and studying %	Studying %	Employed in lower-skilled job %	Employed in lower-skilled job and studying %	Unemployed %	Total with positive outcome %
Veterinary Medicine	92	2	1	1	0	2	95
Medicine	81	8	5	0	0	0	94
Nursing	89	4	1	2	0	1	94
Radiography	88	3	2	3	0	2	93
Physiotherapy	87	4	1	2	0	3	91
Dentistry	81	7	1	0	0	3	88
General Engineering	78	3	4	6	0	4	86
Civil Engineering	77	5	4	6	1	4	85
Building	75	8	0	8	0	4	83
Subjects Allied to Medicine	74	4	4	8	1	3	83
Electrical & Electronic Engineering	72	3	6	8	0	5	81
Chemical Engineering	68	4	8	8	0	6	80
Land & Property Management	68	9	2	10	0	4	80
Natural Sciences	50	6	22	7	0	6	78
Mechanical Engineering	68	4	5	10	0	7	77
Materials Technology	53	3	21	10	1	5	77
Bioengineering & biomedical engineering	58	4	15	10	0	5	77
Town & Country Planning & Landscape	66	4	6	12	1	4	77
Architecture	67	5	5	9	0	8	76
Aeronautical & Manufacturing Engineering	65	2	8	13	0	5	76
Physics & Astronomy	52	4	20	10	0	7	75
Pharmacology & Pharmacy	59	7	9	7	1	6	75
Chemistry	51	4	19	11	0	6	74
Mathematics	56	7	11	11	1	7	74
Computer Science	65	4	4	11	1	9	73
Economics	58	9	6	13	1	5	73
Geology	53	3	18	13	0	5	73
Education	64	4	5	17	1	4	72

Subject

Food Science	60	2	9	18	1	3	**71**
Social Work	61	4	4	19	1	4	**70**
Information Systems & Management	62	4	2	17	0	8	**69**
German	56	2	10	18	1	5	**68**
Geography & Environmental Sciences	52	4	11	19	1	5	**67**
Anatomy & Physiology	42	5	19	16	2	5	**66**
Celtic Studies	35	13	17	17	5	0	**65**
Middle Eastern & African Studies	49	5	10	17	1	10	**64**
Liberal Arts	49	5	10	22	1	4	**64**
Theology & Religious Studies	49	5	10	21	2	4	**63**
Italian	46	5	12	22	1	6	**63**
French	50	2	11	21	1	6	**63**
Agriculture & Forestry	53	5	5	32	0	3	**63**
Iberian Languages	49	4	9	22	0	8	**62**
Law	45	6	10	20	2	5	**62**
Biological Sciences	39	3	19	20	1	6	**61**
Politics	46	5	10	22	1	7	**61**
Sport Science	46	5	9	24	1	3	**61**
Anthropology	43	5	12	24	1	6	**60**
Business, Management & Marketing	53	4	3	26	1	7	**60**
Music	49	4	6	26	1	6	**59**
Communication & Media Studies	54	2	3	26	1	8	**59**
Philosophy	42	5	11	22	1	6	**59**
English	43	4	12	23	1	6	**58**
Russian	42	8	9	29	2	3	**58**
Accounting & Finance	44	10	3	26	3	6	**56**
Classics & Ancient History	36	4	15	23	1	6	**55**
History	37	4	14	26	2	5	**55**
Linguistics	38	3	15	28	1	6	**55**
Art & Design	51	2	3	30	1	8	**55**
Archaeology & Forensic Science	40	5	10	27	2	6	**54**
American Studies	38	2	12	31	1	6	**52**
Hospitality, Leisure, Recreation & Tourism	45	2	4	37	1	6	**51**
Social Policy	40	4	7	34	1	6	**51**
Drama, Dance & Cinematics	45	2	3	33	1	8	**51**
East & South Asian Studies	36	3	12	29	2	9	**51**
History of Art, Architecture & Design	41	1	7	32	3	6	**50**
Sociology	36	4	9	32	2	7	**49**
Animal Science	35	3	11	36	2	5	**48**
Psychology	34	5	9	32	2	5	**48**
Criminology	37	4	6	36	2	5	**48**
Creative Writing	36	3	6	30	2	10	**46**

Note: This table is ranked on the proportion of graduates in high-skilled jobs after further study, and those combining low-skilled jobs with further study.
Source: HESA (Higher Education Statistics Agency) 2022–23

What graduates are earning 15 months after graduation by subject studied

Subject	High-skilled work (median) £	Low- and medium-skilled work (median) £
1 Dentistry	42,000	–
2 Medicine	35,000	–
=3 Pharmacology & Pharmacy	33,000	21,050
=3 Veterinary Medicine	33,000	–
5 Economics	31,000	23,750
6 Natural Sciences	30,700	10,500
7 Social Work	30,007	21,419
=8 Aeronautical and Manufacturing Engineering	30,000	23,500
=8 Chemical Engineering	30,000	23,500
=8 Computer Science	30,000	21,000
=8 Electrical and Electronic Engineering	30,000	23,250
=8 General Engineering	30,000	24,500
=8 Materials Technology	30,000	12,000
=8 Mathematics	30,000	21,500
=8 Mechanical Engineering	30,000	24,500
=8 Middle Eastern and African Studies	30,000	–
=8 Physics & Astronomy	30,000	21,250
18 Building	29,000	25,225
19 Civil Engineering	28,800	23,000
=20 Bioengineering and biomedical engineering	28,000	21,000
=20 Philosophy	28,000	21,100
=22 East and South Asian Studies	27,500	20,750
=22 Liberal Arts	27,500	12,000
=22 Politics	27,500	21,676
=25 Anatomy & Physiology	27,000	20,850
=25 Business, Management & Marketing	27,000	22,400
=25 Celtic Studies	27,000	–
=25 Chemistry	27,000	21,500
=25 Classics & Ancient History	27,000	21,000
=25 German	27,000	11,476
=25 Information Systems and Management	27,000	25,000
=25 Town and Country Planning and Landscape	27,000	23,250
33 Iberian Languages	26,900	22,500
34 Anthropology	26,775	20,500
35 Accounting & Finance	26,750	21,500
=36 Agriculture and Forestry	26,500	24,000
=36 Land & Property Management	26,500	21,392
=36 Russian	26,500	12,000
39 Radiography	26,404	–
40 Food Science	26,325	21,000
=41 Biological Sciences	26,000	21,000
=41 Education	26,000	19,000
=41 French	26,000	22,700
=41 Geography & Environmental Sciences	26,000	21,390

=41	Geology	26,000	19,500
=41	History	26,000	20,750
=41	Italian	26,000	12,300
=41	Physiotherapy	26,000	–
=41	Subjects Allied to Medicine	26,000	20,750
50	Nursing	25,675	11,000
=51	Sociology	25,500	21,250
=51	Theology & Religious Studies	25,500	20,350
=53	American Studies	25,000	19,800
=53	English	25,000	20,302
=53	History of Art, Architecture and Design	25,000	22,500
=53	Hospitality, Leisure, Recreation & Tourism	25,000	21,650
=53	Linguistics	25,000	20,500
=53	Music	25,000	20,250
=53	Social Policy	25,000	21,000
=53	Sport Science	25,000	20,750
61	Psychology	24,800	20,200
62	Criminology	24,700	20,750
63	Law	24,500	21,000
=64	Art & Design	24,000	20,500
=64	Creative Writing	24,000	19,500
=64	Drama, Dance and Cinematics	24,000	20,750
67	Archaeology and Forensic Science	23,500	20,000
68	Animal Science	23,400	20,000
=69	Architecture	23,000	21,500
=69	Communication and Media Studies	23,000	20,650

Note: This table is ranked by the median salary of those in highly-skilled employment in each subject area. Where high-skilled salaries are equal, medium-skilled salaries are used as a separator.
Source: HESA (Higher Education Statistics Agency), Graduate Outcomes Survey, published July 2024
Covers graduates in employment and self-employment/freelance work, first degree UK-domiciled students only

---

Future-proof degrees in an AI world
The average Briton changes careers or jobs five to seven times during their lifetime. So, your first job after university doesn't have to be for ever, and experience is transferable. Advances in robotics and artificial intelligence mean some jobs are on the way out, but roles needed to develop new technologies and new solutions are expanding. Automation is changing professions, not wiping them out entirely. The stuff that makes us different from machines, such as emotional intelligence, analytical skills and caring, will be vital in the future jobs market, as will creativity and resilience. A rounded university education with experience both in and out of the classroom or laboratory will help to hone such "soft" skills. As for resilience, Gen Z students have survived a pandemic and they run the gauntlet of social media's distorted realities every day. They may be better at gatekeeping their wellbeing than their parents' generation, but this does not mean they lack resilience.

That said, entry-level jobs have been hit by AI. Data from the recruitment firm Adzuna found that the number of such roles had fallen by 32% since the launch of ChatGPT, the most popular free online AI tool, in November 2022. Lacey Kaelani has been tracking AI threats through the jobs platform that she runs, Metaintro. According to her, the most resilient sectors include software engineering and computer sciences, nursing and healthcare, civil engineering, and psychology or behaviour sciences. She said: "Basic-level software engineering is already being replaced by AI systems but graduates with more advanced degrees and working on their own AI projects are becoming the ones that are best prepared in the labour market ... Meanwhile healthcare can't be automated because it requires physical presence and emotional intelligence and civil engineering requires on-site assessment and in-person work. And as AI handles research and data analysis, psychology and understanding the nuances in human behaviour becomes more valuable."

Graduate employment and underemployment

Competition for graduate jobs, with their salary premium over a working lifetime, remains stiff. The Annual Population Survey carried out by the Office of National Statistics (ONS) estimates that there were over 15 million people with degree or equivalent qualifications working in the UK at the end of 2020 (the most recent data available), and that 43% of the UK working-age population (aged 16–64) had a degree or equivalent.

The high proportion of graduates in the overall population means that they may now take longer than their predecessors to find the right career opening. Employers' ideas of which jobs require a degree, and of the roles for which they prefer graduates change over time. Nurses have not always been required to take a degree, but the job now needs skills that were not part of the profession 30 years ago. The same is true of many occupations. Even in jobs where it may be possible to do the work involved without a degree, having taken one makes it easier to get hired in the first place. The Department of Education estimates that by 2035, 48% of jobs in the UK will require at least an undergraduate degree, up from 36% in 2020.

The graduate labour market

The contents of this *Guide* – particularly in the subject tables – should help to create a nuanced picture. A close examination of individual universities' employment rates in your subject – possibly supplemented by the salary figures on the Discover Uni website – will tell you whether national trends apply to your chosen course (**discoveruni.gov.uk**).

Even without the cost of living crisis, health pandemic and Brexit, for the boom years of graduate employment to return, there will have to be stronger recruitment by small and medium-sized companies, as well as the big battalions. The number of self-employed graduates will increase, in line with universities reporting growing demand for their business start-up and incubator services. If you are considering the graduate entrepreneur route, explore what your chosen university offers, because business hub services vary considerably in scale and sophistication.

Subject choice and career opportunities

For those thinking of embarking on higher education in 2027, the signs are still positive. But in any year, some universities and some subjects produce better returns than others. The tables on the pages that follow give a more detailed picture of the differences between subjects at a national level, while the rankings in Chapters 1 and 10 include figures for each university and subject area.

In the employment table, subjects are ranked according to the proportion employed in jobs categorised by HESA as high-skilled, and include those undertaking further study, whether or not combined with a high-skilled job. Modern universities, in particular, often claim that the whole concept of a graduate job immediately after graduation fails to reflect reality for their alumni. In any case, a degree is about enhancing your whole career, not just your first job out of college.

That said, the tables in this chapter will help you assess whether your course is likely to pay off in career terms, at least to start with. They show both the amount you might expect to earn with a degree in a specific subject, and the odds of being in work. The data was published in 2024 and it reflects the experience 15 months after graduation of those who completed their degrees in 2022, so the picture may have changed by the time you leave university. The pattern of success rates for specific subjects and institutions, however, are unlikely to have changed radically.

It is worth considering that at age 25 the average male graduate earns 5% more per year than the average female graduate, even though women are more likely to get first-class or upper second degrees. By the age of 30 – before most graduates start having children – the gender pay gap in annual earnings has extended to 25%. Without maternity leave to explain such a pay gulf, analysts have suggested it may be down to women choosing degrees that are less likely to translate into as high-paying careers as their male counterparts.

The table of employment statistics from the GO survey reveals some unexpected results. For example, only 59.6% of business, management and marketing graduates are working in high-skilled jobs or doing further study, though this is slightly more than the 56.2% of accounting and finance graduates who achieved similar positive outcomes. The town and country planners, economists and food scientists fare a lot better.

All seven branches of engineering are in the top 20 subjects for starting salaries and for graduate outcomes. The employment table also shows that graduates in some subjects – especially sciences such as physics and astronomy, biological sciences, chemistry and geology – are more likely to undertake further study than in others, such as those in art and design or hospitality.

A range of professions now regard a Masters degree as a basic entry-level qualification. Those going into subjects such as art and design appreciate that these, too, have their own career peculiarities. Periods of freelance or casual work are common at the start of a career and may become an enduring choice. Less surprisingly, doctors, vets and nurses are virtually guaranteed a job, as are dentists (often in the top three) although they have been overtaken by radiographers and physiotherapists in our current edition of the survey.

The second table, on pages 54–55, gives average earnings of those who graduated in 2022–23, recorded 15 months after leaving university. It contains interesting, and in some cases surprising, information about early career pay levels. Few would have placed social work in the top 13 for graduate pay, or guess that law graduates' earnings rank only 61st out of 70 subjects. It is important, of course, to consider the differences between starting salaries and the long-term prospects of different jobs. Over time, the accountants may well end up with bigger rewards, despite being £665 a year worse off than the nurses in our early-career snapshot, as will the lawyers.

In any case, it is important to realise that once you ignore the higher incomes available to medics and other elite professionals, early graduate incomes vary less than you might think from subject to subject.

There is so little between them, in fact, that where high-skilled salaries are equal, medium-skilled salaries are used as a separator. That's why you should consider the lifetime earnings you might derive from these subjects, and your own interests and inclinations, at least as much as this snapshot.

Enhancing your employability

Final year students who had completed work experience – either through a year-long placement as part of their degree or internships during university holidays – were three times more likely to achieve a graduate job offer than students with no work experience at all, according to research by *The Times Top 100 Graduate Employers*.

Graduate employability has become the holy grail of degree education since higher fees were introduced in most of the UK. Virtually every university has an initiative to enhance their graduates' prospects. Many have incorporated specially designed employability modules into degree courses; some are certificating extracurricular activities to improve their graduates' CVs; and many more are stepping up their efforts to provide work experience to complement degrees. Opinion is divided on the value of such schemes.

Some of the biggest employers restrict their recruitment activities to a small number of universities, believing that these institutions attract the brightest minds and that trawling more widely is not cost-effective. The High Fliers survey reported that ten universities targeted by the largest number of leading graduate employers in 2024–25 were Birmingham, Manchester, Nottingham, Warwick, Bristol, Leeds, Bath, Exeter, Imperial College London, and Durham.

Some top law firms and others in the City of London have introduced institution-blind applications, but most graduates do not work in the City, and most students do not go to universities at the top of the league tables. Big employers' links with their favourite recruiting grounds are likely to continue. Widening the pool of universities from which they set out to recruit is costly, and can seem unnecessary if employers are getting the people they think they need. They will expect outstanding candidates who went to other universities to come to them, either on graduation or later in their careers.

University schemes

To hit the ground running as a graduate, students are advised to connect with their university careers service in their first term, where they can access mock assessment centres and practice sessions for the online personality and aptitude tests used by many employers, and get help building their first LinkedIn profile. Increasingly, companies are working with universities to help to shape their curriculums. Today many more degrees than in the past include the chance to study in industry or work abroad – including courses at Russell Group universities. Modules designed to develop the skills needed to succeed in the workplace are embedded within degrees, or students are offered help to find and complete an internship. Make the most of your university's alumni network too.

The value of work experience

The majority of graduate jobs are open to applicants from any discipline. For these general positions, employers tend to be more impressed by a good degree from what they consider a prestigious university than by an apparently relevant qualification. Here numeracy, literacy and communication – the skills needed to function effectively in any organisation – are vitally important.

Specialist jobs, for example in engineering or design, are a different matter however. Employers may be much more knowledgeable about the quality of individual courses, and less influenced by a university's overall position in league tables, when the job relies directly on knowledge and skills acquired as a student. That goes for medicine and architecture as well as computer games design or environmental management. In almost all fields of employment, however, work experience has become increasingly valuable. Research by High Fliers shows that work experience schemes have become an integral part of recruiting new graduates. Students who apply for work experience in their first or second year at university go through similar selection processes to graduates, which works as a kind of pre-vetting for a job after graduation. Many firms now offer paid internships lasting eight to ten weeks to students in their penultimate summer at university (for law it's "vacation schemes" lasting one to three weeks).

If you can make it through the lengthy application process, these internships can be a gateway to securing a prized "return offer", where you are invited back after you graduate to join full-time. Charities and social enterprises such as the 93% Club, Bright Network and Zero Gravity provide support and access to a rapidly developing pipeline into graduate internships and careers at a range of firms including KPMG.

Week-long taster experiences for first-year students are also an option, offered by big graduate employers such as PwC. These are usually held over the Easter break and are sometimes called "spring weeks". Bagging one is competitive: the application process starts in September, as soon as students arrive at university.

Sandwich degrees, which include extended programmes of up to a year at work, have always boosted employment prospects. Graduates frequently end up working where they undertook their placement. And while a sandwich year will make your course take longer, it will not cost a full year's-worth of tuition fees. Many conventional degrees now include shorter placements that should offer some advantages in the labour market.

If you opt for a traditional degree without a work placement, consider arranging your own part-time or temporary employment. The majority of full-time students now take jobs during term time, as well as in vacations, to make ends meet. But such jobs can boost your CV as well as your bank balance. "When you get to that final recruitment round at the assessment centre and they ask, 'Can you tell me where you worked with a team to solve a problem?' you can say, 'I organised a ski trip for 250 students,'" says Martin Birchall, who also edits *The Times High Fliers Research*. "That description brings alive your abilities and achievements."

Plan early for your career

Whatever type of course you choose, it is sensible to start thinking about your future career early in your time at university. Students are wise to dispel the growing tendency to convince themselves that there will be plenty of time to apply for jobs after graduation. In the current employment market all graduates need to offer more than just a degree, whether it be formal work experience, leadership, team work and project management qualities demonstrated through clubs and societies, or commitment to voluntary activities. Get as much experience as you can. Many students finish a degree without knowing what they want to do, but a blank CV will not impress a prospective employer.

Useful websites

Prospects, the UK's official graduate careers website: **prospects.ac.uk**

For career advice, internships and student and graduate jobs: **milkround.com**

For graduate employment (and other) statistics: **discoveruni.gov.uk**

High Fliers research: **highfliers.co.uk**

4 The Bottom Line: Tuition Fees and Finance

The penniless student is an enduring archetype, and most undergraduates will have money on their mind in one way or another. This might be the day-to-day hustle involved in making ends meet on a shoestring, or the overarching financial trade-off of whether the debt they graduate with will be worth the investment. The first tuition fee increase for more than a decade was introduced in the 2025-26 academic year, and it is possible, now, to tot up the tuition costs of a three-year degree for a UK student in England and Wales who started in September 2025. Year one (2025-26): £9,535, plus year two: £9,790 (2026-27), plus year three: £10,050 (2027-28) equals a total of: £29,375. This financial clarity emerged from the post-16 White Paper, published in autumn 2025, in which the government confirmed that the cap on tuition fees will be increased with inflation for the next two academic years. It also announced it will legislate to make the fee increase automatic in future (from 2028-29), conditional on providers achieving a "higher quality threshold" via the Office for Students' quality regime.

No one likes paying more for things, but a sense of certainty is welcome for prospective students making decisions, who prior to the white paper could only estimate how much their fees were going to be in three or four years' time while they were still studying. Unequivocally, rising tuition fees will be embedded in the higher education journey of new undergraduates. That tuition fees have been kept artificially low, at close to their 2010 level for over a decade, has contributed to universities' current financial problems.

The affordability of everyday living is likely to be the most pressing concern for those embarking on a university degree. For most, this is reliant at least in part on access to a sufficient maintenance loan. Students are entitled to borrow an amount each year which reflects their living situation (whether they live at home and whether they study in London) and their household income. At the same time as announcing the tuition fee rises, the government committed to increasing maintenance loans on the same terms, by inflation for the next two years, and with the intent to make it automatic in the longer term via legislation. On current forecasts, the Institute of Fiscal Studies calculates this could mean maximum loan entitlements for those living away from home and studying outside of London will increase from £10,544 in 2025-26 to £10,833 in 2026-27 and £11,132 in 2027-28.

The Labour party has pledged to reintroduce maintenance grants, funded by a levy of £925 per international student from 2028 applied to higher education providers in England. The grants do not have to be repaid by students but will only be available to those studying "priority courses" that support the industrial strategy and the government's missions. The IFS calculated that if the new grants were available to students on priority courses with a household income of less than £25,000, about 10% of students would currently qualify.

In recent years, though, soaring inflation has led to a real-terms loss of value in the maximum amount the poorest students can borrow. Failing to level this out with an above-inflation uplift to maintenance loans means, "the impact of inflation forecast errors has left these cuts baked in for subsequent years," the IFS has noted. Thresholds for eligibility for the maximum amount are another sticking point, with fewer students each year qualifying for the full maintenance loan and students from middle and higher-income households losing out. Parents need to cover the financial shortfall in living costs, the upshot being stretched middle-income families struggling to compensate for the growing gap. Save the Student's National Money Survey 2024 found that maintenance loans fell short of living costs by £502 a month – more than double the shortfall of five years before.

Evoking the mood on campuses, the Russell Group Students' Unions (RGSU), which represents over 750,000 students across 24 universities, made a submission to the government for the 2025 budget stating that "The current maintenance loan system is broken. Support has failed to keep pace with real living costs, leaving students with a significant shortfall." Research by the Higher Education Policy Institute (HEPI) think tank and Loughborough University found that maintenance loans in England now cover just half of students' costs.

The report's researchers estimated that first-year students in halls of residence need £418 per week to cover their living costs – including £158 on rent – more than second- and third-years because of setting-up costs such as buying a laptop and kitchen equipment, and settling-in costs such as freshers' week activities. Overall, students need £21,126 in their first year, the report found, more than twice the maximum annual maintenance loan available to people from low-income households, of £10,544. Across three years this works out at about £61,000 across three years, or up to £77,000 in London. The report found that living costs were slightly lower elsewhere in the UK – £18,244 in Northern Ireland, £19,836 in Scotland and £20,208 in Wales. Students living and studying in Scotland were found to have 59% of their costs covered by the maximum maintenance support and those in Wales have 63% of their costs covered.

Naturally, not all parents can afford to plug the gaps entirely and part-time work is increasingly part of undergraduate life. The HEPI/Loughborough report found that even if students receive the highest levels of maintenance support, they need to work more than 20 hours per week in term-time and holidays on the National Minimum Wage to meet the basic standard of living. The Student Academic Experience Survey 2025, by Advance HE and HEPI, also revealed a dramatic rise in the proportion of full-time undergraduates undertaking paid work working during term time – now at 68%, up from 56% in 2024 and just 42% in 2020.

Such pressures are putting a squeeze on students achieving the "traditional student experience" as students have less disposable income and less time to join clubs and societies. Matt Padley, co-director of the Centre for Research in Social Policy at Loughborough, and one of the authors of the report, said participating in the student experience is especially important in one's first year to make connections and establish friendships. "Finding your feet as a first-year student is difficult enough without having to worry about balancing the costs of 'settling in' against the cost of rent and food."

The vast majority of eligible students take out government-backed student loans for the cost of tuition and make student loan repayments from their earnings. It's important to be aware that although undergraduates – current and new – will be charged increasing sums per year for their university education, these changes do not generate any upfront costs for them. The student loan repayment process remains the same, so the extra fees get added to the overall student loan debt, which only begins to be repaid once students have graduated and are earning over the repayment threshold. Those graduating from a three-year course in 2026, however, will be the first debtors under the Plan 5 repayment system (see page 67 for details). Graduates who started a course between 2012 and 2023 are on the repayment structure known as Plan 2. The move to Plan 5 loans was announced in 2022 and is an attempt to ensure that more graduates pay back more of their loan.

The changes effectively complete the transformation of student 'loans' into a sort of graduate tax, which is paid by those who went to university over their working lifetime in exchange for a degree. The new system is fairer to the taxpayer, ministers say, by reducing the subsidy for university degrees. But as wages stagnate and the job market tightens, fewer graduates are able to repay these loans. Only 44,527 graduates crossed the repayment threshold in 2025, down from around 57,000 in previous years.

So, is it still worth going to university? For new university applicants, the implications of tuition fees, the affordability of studying and loan repayments make this an ever more pressing question. On average workers with a degree are still better off over the course of their working lives – men to the tune of £130,000 and women £100,000, according to the IFS. But the numbers mask stark discrepancies; one in five students would have been better off financially if they had not gone to university, while one in ten students will be about £500,000 better off over their lifetime thanks to their university degree. The IFS found that the subject studied was "hugely important". For example, women were hardly any better off having creative arts and language degrees but law, economics or medicine degrees could earn them at least £250,000 more over a lifetime. Men studying creative arts made less money than those without degrees, but those in medicine or economics were better off to the tune of more than £500,000.

Graduate earnings increase at a faster rate than those of non-graduates. Between the ages of 23 and 31, average earnings grow by 72% for graduates compared to 31% for non-graduates, data analysis by Universities UK revealed in July 2025. Yes, university is increasingly expensive, but the undergraduate experience is far more than a financial pact, and higher earnings later on in life will balance the copy book for most

Tuition fees history

Up until 1998, tuition at UK universities was free. The £1,000 annual fees introduced that year represented a seismic shift in higher education at the time, and in British society more widely. These fees were paid upfront by students at the start of the academic year. In 2006, fees were raised to £3,000 and a new system of variable deferred fees and tuition fees loans was introduced. MPs voted in 2010 to increase tuition fees to £9,000, and this rate kicked in from 2012. The move was met by protest marches, campus occupations and students voting with their feet as evidenced by a downturn in applications to university. Student finance reformed at the same time to include raising the repayment threshold to £21,000 and introducing a variable tiered rate of interest on student loans. Fees up to £9,250 were first introduced in 2017–18 and stayed the same until 2025 when they rose to £9,535. Application and enrolment numbers have regained the ground they lost in the immediate years after 2012, students appearing to have become resigned to the regime.

There are some exceptions to the rates of tuition fees; private providers are not subject to fee caps, and the maximum fee for accelerated degree courses in England is £11,750 in 2026–27 (rising to £12,060 in 2027–28), with commensurate fee loans.

Most students pay the maximum fees, but bursaries and fee waivers bring down the price for students from low-income households, while merit-based scholarships – which are sometimes, but not always linked to household incomes – are similarly valuable to those in receipt of them. This *Guide* quotes the higher headline fees, but even these will vary according to whether you are from the UK or overseas, studying full-time or part-time, and whether you are taking a foundation degree or an honours programme. EU students who enrolled on courses in the UK before Brexit and who are completing their studies still qualify for "home fees". However, any who have joined since Britain left the EU are classed as international students – with higher fees to match. Here we focus on full-time honours degrees for UK undergraduates, and the EU students who escaped the higher international fees: these students make up the biggest group on any UK campus.

An important fact easy to overlook is that some universities guarantee fees will be fixed at the first-year rate for the whole of your course, while others make no such promise. Applicants are advised to check the fees pages of individual universities closely. It is also worth noting that fees cannot exceed 20% of the full-year fee for work placements and up to 15% for a year abroad or Turing year. So, the costs incurred by extending an undergraduate degree to four years by adding a year abroad or in industry are mainly living-related.

Fees and loans

Marginal fluctuations in fee levels and bursary provision between universities tend not to be the basis upon which applicants make their degree choices, however. Numbers from the poorest socio-economic groups are at record levels, although they remain severely under-represented compared with more affluent groups. Most readers of *The Times and Sunday Times Good University Guide* will be choosing full-time undergraduate or foundation degree courses. The fees for 2026 entry are listed alongside each university's profile in Chapter 12 wherever available. Details of English universities' bursaries and scholarships are on the website of the Office for Students (OfS) in the pages on access and participation plans. Universities have their own fees and funding web pages as well, which are good places to source up-to-date information regarding financial help.

Alternative options

Some further education colleges offer substantial savings on the cost of a degree, or offer foundation degrees, but they tend to have very local appeal and their subject range tends to be largely vocational. The private sector offers two-year degrees, such as at the University of Buckingham and BPP University. A two-year course gets you into the workforce faster and reduces spending on living costs. However, this approach also cuts out much chance of holiday earnings and of sandwich courses or placements, where students can often get paid and gain work experience. Tuition fees vary by course at BPP, but the university received a "requires improvement" rating for the student experience in the government's Teaching Excellence Framework 2023, although it fared better for student outcomes with a silver.

Degree apprenticeships

The option of studying for a degree with no fees at all, by taking a degree apprenticeship sponsored by an employer, is growing. Multiverse – the apprenticeship provider run by Euan Blair (son of Tony, the former Labour prime minister) – is the first apprenticeship provider granted a licence to award degrees on the job. Its subject focus is on data, technology, business, and software engineering. Many other degree apprenticeships are in professional areas, such as childcare, nursing, accounting, policing and social work, but there are others in the sciences, business subjects, some social sciences and IT. On the whole, students spend the majority of their time at work with their sponsoring employer – and receiving a wage, rather than having to access loans – with varying periods at university. The degree versus degree apprenticeship debate is fairly even-handed. Financially, degree apprenticeships (called graduate apprenticeships in Scotland) are a no-brainer: you do not pay tuition fees, plus you get paid for a job that is building experience for your future career, rather than a typical part-time role just to boost your current account. Those who last the course of up to five years will be met with immediate employment, and many employers pay those who complete the qualification more than traditional graduates because they will have been with them for longer and be more valuable in the short term.

However, some feel that the apprenticeship route is too new for the long-term prospects to be certain, as is whether the qualification will have the same currency and be as portable as a traditional degree in mid-career. But barriers between vocational and academic education are being broken down, and the numbers enrolling on degree apprenticeships is rising: starts at Level 6 (Bachelors) and 7 (Masters) increased by 20.4% to 60,350 in 2024–25.

Getting the best deal

Student support packages mean applicants can shop around, particularly if their family income is low. But the best deal, even in purely financial terms, is one that leads to a rewarding career. By all means compare the full packages offered by individual universities, but consider too whether marginal differences of a few hundred pounds in headline fees, repaid over 30 or 40 years, matter as much as the quality of the course and the likely advantages it will confer in the employment market. Scottish students can save themselves £29,375 by opting to study in their home country, based on a three-year degree starting in 2025. That is a very different matter to the much smaller saving that is available to students elsewhere in the UK.

Financing your studies

Whatever changes in fees are dictated by government policies, the need for enough money to live on at university and the likelihood that this will involve incurring some debt is unerring. Most students take out both tuition fee and maintenance loans to cover the cost of studying and living. These are technically two types of funding, but the total amount borrowed is known as their Student Loan. Yes, there is going to be a debt and it is likely to be considerable, but student loan debts are not quite like other sorts of commercial borrowing – such as on credit cards or via a mortgage.

As discussed earlier in this chapter, they increasingly work out more like a graduate tax. Each UK country has its own student finance system. The following sections of this chapter relate to the loans and costs incurred by students from England, while the broader content relates to students across the UK. The facts and figures for those from Northern Ireland, Wales and Scotland are detailed separately later in the chapter.

Tuition fee loans

Full-time students can borrow up to the full amount needed to cover tuition fees wherever they study in the UK. This loan is not dependent upon household income. New part-time students can apply for loans of up to £7,145 (the new rate from 2025–26) for tuition fees in an academic year. Students never get their hands on the tuition fee loans cash; the money is paid straight to the university. This way there is no risk of blowing the lot on something other than funding studies, or running late with payments.

Maintenance loans
These are designed to help full-time home students pay for their living expenses – rent, food, travel, bills, going out, clothes, gym fees and so on. Maintenance loans are partly means-tested and the amount that can be borrowed depends on family income, whether the university is in London or elsewhere in the UK, and whether students live at home with their family or independently.

Maximum loan amounts in 2025–26:
» £8,877 for students living at their family home during term time.
» £10,544 for students living away from home, outside London.
» £13,762 for students living away from home, in London.
» £12,076 for students living and studying abroad for at least one term as part of their UK course.

Maintenance loan entitlement, England 2025-26

Household income	Living at home	Living away from home but not in London	Living away from home and studying in London
£25,000 or less	£8,877	£10,544	£13,762
£30,000	£8,132	£9,791	£12,997
£35,000	£7,387	£9,038	£12,231
£40,000	£6,642	£8,285	£11,465
£42,875	£6,214	£7,852	£11,025
£45,000	£5,897	£7,532	£10,700
£50,000	£5,152	£6,779	£9,934
£55,000	£4,407	£6,026	£9,168
£58,349	£3,907	£5,522	£8,655
£60,000	£3,907	£5,273	£8,403
£62,377	£3,907	£4,915	£8,039
£65,000	£3,907	£4,915	£7,637
£70,000	£3,907	£4,915	£6,871
£70,116+	£3,907	£4,915	£6,853

Source: Student Finance England
savethestudent.org/student-finance

In general, students must be under 60 on the first day of the first academic year of their course. However, over-60s can access a lower means-tested loan for living costs, of up to £ 4,461 in 2025–26. Maintenance loans are paid straight into students' bank accounts in three instalments throughout the year. Budgeting to make each loan last until the next instalment is down to students. The final maintenance loan payment is a bit smaller than in the years before, because student life ends in June/July of that year, and with it the entitlement to a student loan.

For most 18-year-old freshers, the sight of their current account being hit with probably its biggest single cash injection ever can bring a rush of blood to the head. More sobering, however, may be the surprise that the interest clock starts ticking on the loan from the day of the initial payment, usually the first day of the first term. It keeps ticking until the April after students finish their course, which is when repayment may or may not begin – depending on the level of earnings. For part-time students earning over the threshold, repayment starts four years after starting to receive the loan, even if they are furthering their studies then rather than working. Repayments are in line with those for tuition fee loans. But critics have said many low and middle-income students could be put off university by having to accrue more debt, and in 2020 the government reintroduced maintenance grants for nurses, as detailed below. More recently in autumn 2025, the government stated its intention to reintroduce maintenance grants for domestic students studying "priority subjects", initially worth £1,000 for students whose household income is below £25,000 a year.

NHS bursaries

Eligible full-time NHS students can apply for a bursary from the NHS, plus a £1,052 grant from the NHS and a reduced maintenance loan from Student Finance England. For those eligible for an NHS bursary, the NHS pays their standard tuition fees directly to their university. Eligible full-time nursing students qualify for a £5,000 a year training grant, paid pro-rata for part-time students. Those who plan on working in a branch of nursing suffering from severe shortages can also access a further £1,000.

Beyond this, another £2,000 is accessible in childcare allowances. Only part of the bursary is means-tested, and some student nurses may be eligible for more bursary funding subject to the means-testing. Student nurses do not have to repay the maintenance grants, as they are not loans. And having the bursary doesn't impact student nurses' access to a full student loan through the Student Loans Company. The NHS Business Services Authority has a Student Services arm which runs the NHS Learning Support Fund, worth investigating by those planning to study health or social work.

Interest rates

Student loan interest rates are based on the Retail Prices Index (RPI), the rate at which prices rise. As this can go up or down, the interest rates can too. The interest rate changes every September, based on the RPI rate of inflation in the year to the previous March. The RPI rate rocketed in recent years, due to high inflation, and was 4.3% in October 2025. As student loans are repaid over a long period, interest rate swings in either direction usually even themselves out. Student loans are fairly flexible; you do not pay if you are not earning enough, and you can overpay whenever you want. If students lose touch with the Student Loans Company, RPI plus 3% is automatically applied to their debt, and penalty charges kick in if anyone tries to avoid paying what they owe.

The disappearing debt

After 40 years in England, or 30 under the old scheme (this varies a little elsewhere in the UK – please see further down this chapter), the debt is written off. Because the repayments seem modest for anyone with a qualifying income, and because of the 40- or 30-year rule, student debt is a lot more forgiving than a mortgage or a credit card, where the bills keep on coming even if you are out of work. The Student Loans Company is probably the only lender in Britain that hands out tens of thousands of pounds without a credit check.

Repaying the student loan

Student loan debt works very differently from other types of borrowing. If you take a personal loan or a mortgage, for example, what you repay is based on how much is borrowed, the interest rate and the loan term. With student loan repayments what you repay is based solely on what you earn. The repayment threshold for the Plan 5 loan for all new students in England is currently £25,000 a year (£2,083 a month or £480 a week) before tax. The first Plan 5 repayments start in the 2026/27 tax year. Once they hit the threshold, university-leavers then pay 9% of anything they earn above this level.

What you'll repay on a Plan 5 student loan

Salary	What you'll repay each year
£24,000	You don't pay
£26,000	£90/year (9% of £1,000)
£35,000	£900/year (9% of £10,000)
£50,000	£2,250/year (9% of £25,000)
£100,000	£6,750/year (9% of £75,000)

Source: moneysavingexpert.com

So, if you earn £30,000 you repay £243.45 a year. A graduate keeps repaying their loan until they have cleared it, or for 40 (or 30 for those on the outgoing loan) years from the April after they graduate. If they have not cleared it by then, the outstanding debt is written off. In other words, the interest added is not the interest paid. That depends on future earnings. Some graduates will not repay any interest, and some will not earn enough to repay all of it. Unlike most debts, which are better to clear as early as possible, students should not start repaying student loans before the April after leaving university, as this can result in overpaying.

The Student Loans Company website has information to guide prospective students through these arrangements and also gives examples of levels of repayment (**www.studentloanrepayment.co.uk**).

Living in one country, studying in another
As each of the countries of the UK develops its own distinctive system of student finance, the effects on students leaving home in one UK nation to go and study in another have become knottier. UK students who cross borders to study pay the tuition fees of their chosen university and are eligible for a fee loan, and maybe a partial grant, to cover them. They are also entitled to apply for the scholarships or bursaries on offer from that institution. Any maintenance loan or grant will still come from the awarding body of their home country. If you are in this position, you must check with the authorities in your home country about the funding you are eligible for. You should also contact your own government about support on offer if you are from the Channel Islands or the Isle of Man.

Applying for support
English students should apply for grants and loans through Student Finance England, Welsh students through Student Finance Wales, Scottish students through the Student Awards Agency for Scotland, and those in Northern Ireland through Student Finance NI or their Education and Library Board. Applications should be made as soon as the offer of a place at university has been received. Don't expect things to happen automatically. For instance, students need to tell the Student Loans Company to pay the tuition fees they owe to the university. Following Britain's departure from the European Union, EU students are charged the same tuition fees as those paid by international students from further afield. International students may be considered for some scholarships and bursaries by individual institutions.

How the fee system works

What follows is a summary of the position for British students in late 2025. Universities in England and Wales have committed to the same rises in tuition fees from 2026. Scottish students studying in Scotland will continue to pay no tuition fees. Northern Ireland had not announced any changes to its fee structure at the time of writing.

While there are substantial differences between the four countries of the UK, there is one important piece of common ground. Upfront payment of fees is not compulsory, and students can take out a fee loan from the Student Loans Company to cover them. This is repayable in instalments after graduation when earnings reach £25,000 for new English students (£28,470 for those on the Plan 2 loan). The most you can borrow to pay fees in 2026–27 is £9,790, rising to £10,050 in 2027–28. There are lower sums for private colleges (up to £6,355) and part-time study, where the cap is £7,145 (from 2025–26) at public institutions and £4,765 at private ones.

There are different levels of fees and support for UK students who are not from England.

New students enrolling at UK universities from all international countries, including those in the EU, pay the same international rate, which is usually much higher than the home rate. EU students already registered on courses before December 31, 2020, qualify for the home rate of fees for the remainder of their course. The latest information on individual universities' fees at the time of going to press is listed alongside their profiles in Chapter 12. With changes, large or small, becoming almost an annual occurrence, it is essential to consult the websites of the relevant government agencies.

Tuition fees by region for courses starting in 2024

Student's home region	Studying in England	Studying in Scotland	Studying in Wales	Studying in Northern Ireland
England	Up to £9,535	Up to £9,535	Up to £9,535	Up to £9,535
Scotland	Up to £9,535	No fee	Up to £9,535	Up to £9,535
Wales	Up to £9,535	Up to £9,535	Up to £9,535	Up to £9,535
Northern Ireland	Up to £9,535	Up to £9,535	Up to £9,535	Up to £4,855
EU and other international*	Variable	Variable	Variable	Variable

*This will not apply to Irish nationals living in the UK and Ireland whose right to study and to access benefits and services is preserved on a reciprocal basis for UK and Irish nationals under the Common Travel Area arrangement.

Source: UCAS ucas.com/money-and-student-life

Fees in England

In England, the maximum tuition fee for full-time undergraduates from the UK will be £9,790 a year in 2026–27 and £7,145 for part-time students. Most courses will demand the maximum rate or close to it. In many public universities, the lowest fees will be for foundation degrees and Higher National Diplomas (HND). Those for foundation degrees have been capped at £5,670 through 2026–27 and 2027–28 at least, to align with the fees for HNDs. These two-year courses remain a cost-effective stepping stone to a full degree, or a qualification in their own right, at many universities and further education colleges. Those universities that offer extended work placements or a year abroad as part of a degree course, will charge much less than the normal fee for this "year out". The maximum cost for a placement year is 20% of the tuition fee, and for a full year abroad, 15%. If you spend only part of the year abroad, you will probably have to pay the whole year's tuition.

Fees and funding in Scotland

At Scottish universities and colleges, students from Scotland pay no fees directly. The universities' vice-chancellors and principals have appealed for charges to be introduced at some level to save their institutions from falling behind their English rivals in financial terms. The Scottish government remains committed to free education, but it is working with the higher education sector to explore the future funding model of Scottish universities. Students whose home is in Scotland and who are studying at a Scottish university apply to the Student Awards Agency for Scotland (SAAS) to have their fees paid for them. Note, too, that three-year degrees are rare in Scotland, so most students can expect to pay four years of living costs.

Students from England, Wales and Northern Ireland studying in Scotland will pay fees at something like the scale that applies in England and will have access to finance at similar levels to those available for study in England.

Many Scottish universities offer a "free" fourth year for non-Scottish students to bring their total fees into line with English universities, but Edinburgh, Glasgow and St Andrews were charging £9,535 in all four years of their degree courses in 2025–26.

Scottish maintenance bursaries and loans 2024–25

Young student (under 25 at start of course)				Independent student (25+)			
Income	Loan	Bursary	Total	Income	Loan	Bursary	Total
Up to £20,999	£9,400	£2,000	£11,400	Up to £20,999	£10,400	£1,000	£11,400
£21,000–£23,999	£9,400	£1,125	£10,525	£21,000–£23,999	£10,400	£0	£10,400
£24,000–£33,999	£9,400	£500	£9,900	£24,000–£33,999	£9,900	£0	£9,900
Over £34,000	£8,400	£0	£8,400	Over £34,000	£8,400	£0	£8,400

Scottish paramedic, nursing and midwifery students studying in Scotland are eligible for bursaries of £10,000 for the first three years and £7,500 for the fourth year of a course, but only if they intend to stay and work in Scotland after qualifying. There is a separate dental bursary scheme.

Source: Students Awards Agency Scotland

Student loans and grants for Scottish students

Scottish students pay no tuition fees at their own universities and can apply for up to £9,535 year as a loan for fees elsewhere in the UK (presumably this will go up in line with the new fees, but Scotland's SAAS agency had not confirmed this at the time of writing). They must reapply for this loan each year.

Unlike the other UK countries, Scotland uses a band system to calculate the combination of bursary and loan, rather than precise household income. So, in 2025–26, students from a family with an income below £20,999 could get a £2,000 Young Students' Bursary (YSB) as well as a loan of £9,400 – making £11,400. For incomes from £21,000 to £23,999, the bursary is £1,125 and the loan remains the same – making £10,525, and for those earning £24,000 to £33,999, the bursary is £500 and the loan is still £9,400, making a total of £9,900. Above £34,000, no bursary is available and the maximum loan falls to £8,400.

These figures are the same regardless of whether students live at home or where they are studying in the UK. Higher loans but more limited bursaries are available for "independent" students – those who are married, mature (25 or over) or without family support. Students must be under 61 to enrol on the first day of their course and to receive a student loan for tuition fees and living costs. Scotland's SAAS agency has the repayment threshold set at £32,745 for those on Plan 4 as of November 2025. Interest is linked to the RPI, as in Northern

Ireland. Repayments continue until the loan is paid off, with any outstanding amount being cancelled after 30 years. As elsewhere in the UK, there are special funds for people with disabilities and other special needs, and for those with children or adult dependants.

Fees and funding in Wales

Welsh universities committed to the same rise in tuition fees as in England for the two years from 2026–27, as they did in 2025 when fees rose to £9,535. For 2025–26, the maximum maintenance award is £10,480 for students living at home, £12,345 for those living away from home and outside London, and £15,415 for those studying in London. The Welsh government has said there will be a 2% rise to maintenance funding for 2026–27. These sums are mainly an outright grant to those from low-income households. So, if total household income is £18,370 or less, £8,100 of the total £12,345 maintenance award is a grant (and therefore does not need to be repaid) and only £4,242 a loan. But if income is over £59,200, then £11,345 is repayable and only £1,000 is a grant. The same logic applies to other levels of support, while part-time students can get a variable loan or grant that depends upon income and the intensity of their course. In addition, students in Wales are also able to apply for Welsh government support for parents of young children, for adult learners, for those with adult dependants and for those with disabilities. This support can cover carer costs as well as equipment and general expenditure.

Tuition fee loans are available to cover the whole of tuition fees in Wales and for Welsh students in Scotland, England or Northern Ireland.

Wales has kept the Plan 2 repayment system, which means that new student borrowers will continue to use the £28,470 repayment threshold and 30-year repayment period. Interest repayments are at RPI.

Student finance in Northern Ireland

The two universities of Northern Ireland are charging local students £4,855 a year for 2025–26. For students from elsewhere in the UK, the fees are £9,535, and they are likely to rise in line with tuition fees in England and Wales, but this was not confirmed at the time of writing. Maintenance loans are of up to £5,250 for students living at home, up to £6,776 for those living away from home outside London, and up to £9,492 for those studying in London. Maintenance grants of up to £3,475 are available to students from households with incomes below £19,203 and these do not have to be repaid. There are partial maintenance grants for students from households with incomes between £19,203 and £41,065. The maximum loan is reduced by the size of any grant received. Loan repayments of 9% of salary start once income reaches £26,065 currently, and interest is calculated on the Retail Price Index or 1% above base rate, whichever is lower. The loan will be cancelled after 25 years, quicker than elsewhere in the UK.

There are also special funds for people with disabilities and other special needs, and for those with children or adult dependants. Students studying in the Republic of Ireland can also borrow up to €3,000 a year to pay their Irish tuition contribution and may be able to get a bursary to study there. Tuition fee loans are available for the full amount of tuition fees, regardless of where you study in the UK.

Affording to live and the cost of living crisis

No one has to pay tuition fees while they are a student, but you still have to find thousands of pounds in living costs to take a full-time degree. Stretching the student budget is an ever-present university challenge, and students have always proved resourceful. The maintenance loan does not provide enough money to cover the real cost of living. University leaders say government forecasts of annual increases to maintenance loans have been inaccurate in each year since 2020–21. Without a mechanism in place to correct for inflation, it means a "significant real-terms cut" has been baked into the system – which the current increases are not sufficient to make up for.

Universities have stepped up financial assistance for students by increasing direct financial aid and non-financial support. Many have opened food banks, which 10% of students surveyed by Save the Student's National Money Survey 2025 said they had used in 2024–25. Over three in five (61%) students skipped meals at least some of the time to save money, the survey also found. Drastic though this sounds, it is unsurprising given the speed with which the cost of food is rising; it began to outpace overall inflation in the summer of 2025, Office for National Statistics data via The Food Foundation found. More than four in ten students (41%) told Save the Student's Money Survey 2025 that they had considered dropping out due to money-related issues. Universities have responded by providing free and low-cost meals, free and subsidised travel, technology loans and money management advisors, as well as enhanced bursaries, grants and rent guarantor schemes for students from under-represented groups, who are at the most risk of dropping out of their studies because of financial challenges.

Typically, the number one source of topping up the coffers is parents, whose financial assistance is explicitly called upon in the government's approach to student funding. Part-time jobs, savings and bursaries and scholarships also contribute to the student purse. The Student Money Survey 2025 found that average undergraduate spending was £1,142 per month (up from £1,104 per month in 2024 and £1,078 per month in 2023), with rent the biggest outlay at an average of £529 per month. More than half (52%) of students received money from their parents – down from 59% in three years, suggesting that parents are also struggling with the rising cost of living.

The amount they are contributing has soared, however, according to the annual NatWest Student Living Index for 2025, which found parent/family monetary support has increased by 57% year-on-year, up from £505.10 per month in 2024 to £794.23 in 2025.

In the tenth year of its publication, the Natwest index also found that 64% of students surveyed had part-time jobs, up from 56% since 2015, while average monthly rent had increased by 52% to £567 and a monthly grocery shop had climbed 43% to £146. The cost of a typical night out was found to have increased from £21.60 to £28.10 in the last five years. Almost a quarter (24%) of students said that they didn't go to nightclubs and one in five (20%) avoided going to the pub. Despite trying to cut back on spending, regrets over spending on non-essentials like eating out (40%) and alcohol (32%) were common, the survey revealed.

Budgeting

Help is at hand to avoid the financial abandon of splurging huge portions of a student loan in the first month. University websites, UCAS at **ucas.com/money-and-student-life/money/budgeting** and **savethestudent.org/save-money** are among the many sources of guidance on preparing a budget. List all likely income (loans, bursaries, part-time work, savings, parental support) and compare this with expected outgoings. It pays to be realistic, rather than too optimistic, about both sides of the equation. "After rent, divide your money by the number of weeks in the term, then subtract 20 per cent for 'oh God, I forgot about …' moments," advises Flora Pringle, educator, teen coach and the author of *Lost in the Leap* on Substack, who also recommends that students learn the art of strategic socialising: "You don't have to attend every social event or buy every round. 'I'm skint this week but happy to come for one drink' is perfectly acceptable."

Aldi, Lidl and other budget supermarkets are godsends when it comes to stretching the budget, even if shopping at one means needing to get a taxi home – share with a housemate and split the cost, there will still be significant savings on the prices at the nearby Tesco Express or Sainsbury's Local. No one is condoning binge drinking, but with "pre-drinks" before a night out popular, great savings can be made by stocking up on the budget versions of drinks and snacks. Shopping online, while not offered by the budget supermarkets, can also be cost effective if you stick to own brand products, as the temptation to pop extra items into the trolley at will is removed and any delivery fee can be shared with housemates. Some parents like to send supermarket deliveries to their student.

Cookery how-tos on YouTube, TikTok, Instagram et al have brought meal prep guidelines to smartphones, bringing culinary skills to the tip of everyone's fingers. Sharing a meal with housemates is great for bonding, while leftovers in Tupperware are a weapon in the fight against blowing the budget on daily café lunches. The same goes for a carry-cup for hot drinks.

More than two-thirds of 18–24-year-olds reported they received no financial education at school, according to a report by the National Association of Student Money Advisors (NASMA). Keeping track of finances is not every student's idea of a good time but it is certain to provide greater freedom for enjoying university life. Most graduates will have to grapple with spreadsheets during their working life, and they make balancing the student budget simpler. Apps can help too, such as Snoop, which lets you connect all your bank accounts and credit cards on one dashboard, so you can keep track of spending. You can set yourself a budget for each spending category and it sends you summaries, showing where you could be overspending to help you cut costs.

Funding timetable

It is vital that you sort out your funding arrangements before you start university. Each funding agency has its own arrangements, and it is very important that you find out the exact details from them. The timings below give general indications of key dates.

March/April
» Online and paper application forms become available from funding agencies.
» You must contact the appropriate funding agency to make an application. This will be the funding agency for the region of the UK that you live in, even if you are planning to study elsewhere in the UK.
» Complete application form as soon as possible. At this stage, select the university offer that will be your first choice.
» Check details of bursaries and scholarships available from your selected universities.

May/June
» Funding agencies will give you details of the financial support they can offer.
» Last date for making an application to ensure funding is ready for you at the start of term (exact date varies significantly between agencies).

August
» Tell your funding agency if the university or course you have been accepted for is different from that originally given them.

September
» Take letter confirming funding to your university for registration.
» After registration, the first part of funds will be released to you.

Make full use of student travel cards and shopping discounts, and shop around for the best calls and data deals on mobile phones. Strength of will around social media advertising should also help with budgeting: Natwest's 2025 survey revealed that 51% of students had been influenced to purchase skincare and makeup products after seeing them on social media, followed by hair care products (39%), and tech accessories (28%).

Study costs

Some courses require much higher course spends than others, and extra financial support may be available for certain – but not all – things. Take out library textbooks or buy them second-hand from students who don't need them anymore to cut back on bills incurred by a long reading list. Lots of reference publications are available for free online too. The average student spent £20 per month on course materials, Save the Student's 2025 survey found.

Overdrafts and credit cards

These are the more expensive forms of debt, and best avoided if at all possible. Many banks offer free overdraft facilities for students but going over the limit without prior arrangement can result in high charges. Credit cards can be useful if managed properly, ideally by setting up a direct debit to pay off the full balance every month, thus avoiding paying any interest. To pay only the minimum charge each month can end up costing a small fortune over a long period.

Those inclined to spend impulsively without keeping track of spending are probably better off without a credit card and should stick with a debit card.

Fraud and scams

Students' financial inexperience, new independence, and digital savviness make them vulnerable to scams and fraud. Scams targeting their bank details are the most common threat – impacting a quarter of those surveyed in the 2025 Natwest Student Living Index. Investment and tax rebate scams were the second-biggest con, with 13% of students reporting they had been targeted by these. Parcel delivery scams, which feature messages that pretend to come from delivery companies, affected 10% of students surveyed. The average loss reported by students who fell victim to scams was £287.60, with 2% losing between £2,000 and £2,999.

Insurance

Most students arrive at university with laptops and other goodies such as games consoles, sports equipment, musical instruments, mobile phones and bikes that are tempting to thieves. It is estimated that around a third of students fall victim to crime at some point during university. A reasonable amount of cover for these items should be found by shopping around, without it costing you an arm and a leg. It may also be possible to add this cover cheaply to parents' domestic contents policy (probably at their expense).

University scholarships and bursaries

Applicants are increasingly shopping around for scholarships and bursaries while applying for university. UCAS will automatically award students any means-tested scholarship based on household income submitted upon application.

There may be fee reductions for groups including local students, which are usually detailed on university websites. There is funding for students with disabilities or family responsibilities; or for those taking subjects such as social work or medicine, with wide public benefit, as well as a range of charities with their own criteria. In some cases, bursaries may make the difference between being able to afford higher education and having to pass up a potentially life-changing opportunity. Some are worth up to £3,000 a year, although most are less generous than this, often because large numbers of students qualify for an award. Some scholarships are even more valuable, and are awarded for sporting and musical prowess, as well as for academic achievement. Most scholarships are not means-tested, but a few are open only to students who are both high performers academically and from low-income families. They can be life-changing: the largest award at the University of East London, for example, is the merit-based vice-chancellor's scholarship of up to £28,605. At the University of Manchester, an annual maintenance bursary of £6,000 as well as fee reimbursement is awarded to two black students of African and Caribbean heritage through the Cowrie Foundation Scholarship, while the University of Hull offers the Chancellor's Scholarship, which provides a full fee waiver to ten undergraduates in any subject.

Some universities have substantial endowments to fund their bursaries and scholarship programmes, such as the prestigious London School of Economics and Political Science, which in recent years has awarded around £4 million annually in scholarships and financial support to its undergraduates. Across the city at the University of West London about half of full-time students qualify for some form of financial assistance, which includes the UWL Aspire Bursary of £100 for student supplies.

The Scholarship Hub, a database of scholarships, suspects UK students could be missing out on funding worth over £150 million a year as organisations offering scholarships often struggle to get enough applications. The database is free, but it requires a subscription to access advice about how to apply and to use enhanced search tools. Most bursaries are means-tested, while scholarships are via open competition. Some universities offer eligible students the choice of accommodation discounts, fee waivers or cash. Most also have hardship funds for those who find themselves in financial difficulties. Many charities for specific industries or professions have a remit to support education, and many have bursaries for anyone studying a related subject. The Directory of Grant-Making Trusts lists bodies that make one-off or regular awards to all kinds of causes, often including deserving students. Only available in hard copy, a library visit to see it for free could be worth the trip.

Take note of the application procedures for scholarships and bursaries. They vary between institutions, and even from course to course within institutions. Specific awards may have specific application deadlines. In some cases, the university will work out for you whether you are entitled to an award by referring to your funding agency's financial assessment. If your personal circumstances change part-way through a course, entitlement to a scholarship or bursary may be reviewed.

Advice on scholarships and bursaries is usually included on a university's website or in its prospectus and many institutions also maintain a helpline. Is the bursary or scholarship automatic or conditional? When will you find out whether your application has been successful? For some awards, this won't be until after exam results.

Students with disabilities

Extra financial help is available to disabled students, whether studying full-time or part-time, through Disabled Students' Allowances, which are paid in addition to the standard student finance package. They are available for help with education-related conditions such as dyslexia, and for other physical and mental disabilities. They do not depend on income and do not have to be repaid. The cash is available for extra travel costs, equipment and to pay helpers. For 2024–25, the maximum amount available for eligible students in England for support – including a nonmedical helper, or specialist equipment – is £27,783 a year.

Further sources of income

There are various types of support available for students in particular circumstances, other than the main loans, grants and bursaries. Support has broadened since the cost of living crisis started to impact students, and the NatWest Student Living Index 2024 shows that income from hardship loans/grants in term time jumped from just £5 a month in 2023 to £290.93 in 2025. Reliance on bank loans also soared from £31 a month in 2023 to £331.92 in 2025.

- » Even without the rising cost of living, undergraduates in financial difficulties can apply for help from their university's student hardship fund. These provide support for anything from day-to-day study and living costs to unexpected or exceptional expenses. The university decides which students need help and how much to award them. These funds often target older or disadvantaged students, and finalists in danger of dropping out. The sums range up to a few thousand pounds, are not repayable and do not count against other income.
- » Students with children can apply for a Childcare Grant. For 2025-26, this was up to £199.62 a week for a first child and up to £342.24 for two or more children. There was also a Parents' Learning Allowance of between £50 and £2,024 a year in 2025-26 for help with course-related costs.
- » Students with a partner, or another adult family member who is financially dependent on them, can apply for an Adult Dependants' Grant of up to £ 3,545 a year for 2025-26.

Part-time work

A part-time term-time job is a fact of life for more than half of students. The challenge is to not let the part-time job get in the way of studying. Student employment agencies, found on many university campuses, match employers with students seeking work, sometimes offering jobs within the university itself. They also ensure both minimum wages and the maximum number of hours worked in term time, typically 15 hours a week. Students sometimes make money from freelance work and student businesses, but most take casual work in shops, restaurants, bars and call centres. Most students get a job during the holidays, including those who don't have one in the term. Three in ten students reported having their own side hustle or business in Save the Student's 2025 survey, most with incomes of under £500 a year but some reporting earnings in the thousands.

Useful websites

The "fees and funding" pages on university websites provide the most up-to-date information on costs of individual courses – especially for rates paid by international students, which vary. Universities also publish details of the financial help available, and how to apply. It is essential to consult the latest information provided by government agencies. The following websites will outline any major developments.

England: **gov.uk/student-finance**

Wales: **studentfinancewales.co.uk**

Scotland: **saas.gov.uk**

Northern Ireland: **studentfinanceni.co.uk**

Office for Students: **officeforstudents.org.uk**

For the basics of fees, loans, grants and other allowances: **gov.uk/student-finance**

UCAS provides helpful advice: **ucas.com/money-and-student-life** as does the student money website: **savethestudent.org**

All UK student loans are administered by the Student Loans Company: **gov.uk/government/organisations/student-loans-company**

HMRC information on the tax position of students: **gov.uk/student-jobs-paying-tax**

For finding out about availability of scholarships: **thescholarshiphub.org.uk** (requires subscription fee). Or go direct to university websites, where their scholarship and bursary provision will be detailed.

5 Making Your Application

Once you have decided what and where to study, it is time to put your research into action. Armed with a list of up to five options, your predicted grades, a carefully written personal statement and favourably informed teacher references, you can submit your university application. The process is deliberately fuss-free; everything happens online and the UCAS hub is an applicant's one-stop-shop for everything from details of around 32,000 courses to open days, key dates and handy to-do lists, along with reminders to keep you on track. It also offers personalised careers information and advice and includes tools such as a personal statement builder and tariff calculator.

So far, so simple. Naturally enough, though, the devil is in the detail and the build-up to submitting an application requires writing, editing and re-writing your personal statement, and keeping referee teachers up to speed on your achievements inside and outside of the classroom so they may write the best possible reference. There is also the matter of bringing your A game to lessons and progress tests, to ensure the highest predicted grades you are capable of. Grades are the most important factor in winning a place at university, but what goes on the application form is more important than many students realise, and it pays to keep your eye on the ball at this stage on the journey to university.

The UK's predicted admissions system is unique among developed countries, and many argue it is hard to navigate and say that applying to university without knowing your results lacks transparency and is hard for students to navigate. Detractors of the system also point to the unfairness of predicted grades, which can be unreliable as well as work against high achievers from disadvantaged backgrounds – whose grades are more likely to be under-predicted, evidence shows. But moving to a post-qualification model (PQA) is not hugely popular with exam boards, whose marking time would be squeezed, or with universities – which may need to delay term start dates and reduce teaching time. In any case, predicted grades are here to stay; despite a long-running debate within the higher education sector, plans to switch to a PQA model were officially shelved in 2022.

Further to the binary discourse over pre- or post-qualification admissions, the chief executive of UCAS, Dr Jo Saxton, believes a dynamic use of Clearing brings a third way into view. This is based on the growing numbers of applicants using UCAS' "decline my place" tool to switch to a different course or applying direct to Clearing. Dr Saxton has said the practice reflect "students exercising the agency that they have in a marketised system", and that if harnessed correctly, it should mean more young people – particularly from disadvantaged backgrounds – securing the right courses for them.

Change has already been instituted within the admissions process, chiefly with the introduction of the new-style personal statement, which was used by the first cohort of students for 2026. Applicants must respond to three structured questions, detailed later in this chapter, which have replaced the 4,000-character essay of old. It is hoped the shift will make the admissions process fairer.

All UK university admissions are handled through UCAS – the service formed in 1992 through the merger of UCCA and PCAS, the former university and polytechnic admissions systems. UCAS makes the process of applying to university as straightforward as possible.

The application process

Almost all applications for full-time higher education courses go through UCAS, including those to the conservatoires, which come with separate guidance and processes on the UCAS website.

Applications for degree apprenticeships are exceptions to the rule, however, and should be made to employers rather than universities. Deadlines differ between employers. You can apply for as many apprenticeships as you want, on top of your university applications. Many recruit through the **gov.uk/apply-apprenticeship** website, which also has links to vacancy information, as does UCAS at **careerfinder.ucas.com**.

Some universities that have not filled all their places on conventional degrees, even during Clearing, will accept direct applications up to and sometimes after the start of the academic year, but UCAS is both the official route and the only way into the most popular courses.

Registering with Apply

Applications kick off by registering with Apply. School and college students will be given a "buzzword" by their tutor or careers adviser – you need this in order to log in to register. It links your application to the school or college so that the application can be sent electronically to your referee (usually one of your teachers) for your reference to be attached. If you are no longer at a school or college, you do not need a buzzword, but you will need details of your referee.

The main screens to be completed in UCAS Apply

» Personal and contact details, and some additional non-educational details for UK applicants.
» Student finance arrangements (UK applicants only), and up to five course choices.
» Details of your education so far, including examination results and those still to be taken.
» Your employment history, listing any paid or voluntary work you have done.
» Your personal statement.
» A reference from one of your teachers.
» View all details to make sure they are correct and reflect your preferences.
» Pay for the application. For 2026–27 it costs £28.50 for up to five courses. This fee is waived for applicants in receipt of free school meals.

Apply is available 24 hours a day, and, when the time comes, information on the progress of your application may arrive at any time. More information is given on the UCAS website. Clicking on "Apply" begins the process for providing your personal details and generating a username and password, as well as reminding you of basic points, such as amending your details in case of a change of address. You can register separate term-time and holiday addresses – a useful option for boarders, who could find offers and, particularly, the confirmation of a place, going to their school when they are miles away at home. Remember to keep a note of your username and password in a safe place.

Throughout the process, you will be in sole control of communications with UCAS and your chosen universities. Only if you nominate a representative and give them your unique nine-digit application number (sent automatically by UCAS when your application is submitted), can a parent or anyone else give or receive information on your behalf, perhaps because you are ill or out of the country.

Video guides on the application process are available on the UCAS website. Once you are registered, you can start to complete the Apply screens. The sections that follow cover the main screens.

Personal details

This information is taken from your initial registration, and you will be asked for additional information, for example, on ethnic origin, to monitor equal opportunities in the application process. UK students will also be asked to complete a student finance section designed to speed up any loan application you might make. Applicants since 2024 entry have been able to select from "man | woman | I use another term | I prefer not to say" when asked for their gender identity.

UCAS also introduced seven new questions in 2023, as part of its commitment to widening participation. They allow students to self-declare important information about their circumstances, so they can be connected to the right support for their needs. The new questions cover:

» Students estranged from their parents
» Students with caring responsibilities
» Students with parenting responsibilities
» Refugees, asylum seekers and those with limited leave to remain in the UK
» Students from UK Armed Forces families
» UK Armed Forces veterans and Service leavers
» A self-declared free school meals question

Choices

In most subjects, you will be able to apply to a maximum of five universities and/or colleges. The exceptions are medicine, dentistry and veterinary science, where the maximum is four, but you can use your fifth choice as a back-up to apply for a different subject.

The other important restriction concerns Oxford or Cambridge, because you can only apply to one or the other; you cannot apply to both universities in the same year, nor can you apply for more than one course there. For both universities you may need to take a written test and submit examples of your work, depending on the course selected. In addition, for Cambridge, many subjects will demand a pre-interview assessment once the university has received your application from UCAS, while the rest will set written tests to be taken at interview.

The deadline for Oxbridge applications – and for all medicine, dentistry and veterinary science courses – is October 15. For all other applications the deadline is January 15 (or March 24 for some specified art and design courses). The other exceptions to this rule are the relatively small but growing number of courses that start in January or February. If you are considering one of these, contact the university concerned for application deadlines.

Most applicants use all five choices. But if you do choose fewer than five courses, you can still add another to your form up to June 30, as long as you have not accepted or declined any offers. Nor do you have to choose five different universities if more than one course at the same institution attracts you – if you are keen on one institution in particular, applying for one course with lower entrance requirements than the other is a good way of hedging your bets.

Universities are not allowed to see where else you have applied, or whether you have chosen the same subject elsewhere. But they will be aware of multiple applications within their own institution. Remember that it is more difficult to write a convincing personal statement if it has to cover two subjects.

For each course you select, you will need to put the UCAS code on the form – and you should check carefully that you have the correct code and understand any special requirements that may be detailed on the UCAS description of the course. It does not matter in what order you enter your choices as all are treated equally. You will also need to indicate whether you are applying for a deferred entry (for example, if you are taking a gap year – see page 88).

Education

This is where you provide details of the schools and colleges you have attended, and the qualifications you have obtained or are preparing for. The UCAS website gives plenty of advice on the ways in which you should enter this information, to ensure that all your relevant qualifications are included with their grades. While UCAS does not need to see qualification certificates, it can double-check results with the examination boards to ensure that no one has exaggerated their results.

In the Employment section that follows, add details of any paid jobs you have had (unpaid or voluntary work should be mentioned in your personal statement).

Personal statement

Applicants for 2027 entry will be the second to submit the new-style personal statement. This has divided the format from one long piece of text into three separate questions, each with a minimum 350-character requirement. The overall 4,000-character limit (including spaces) is the same. The questions are:

Question 1: Why do you want to study this course or subject?

Showcase your motivations for studying the course or courses here, your knowledge of the subject area and interests, and your future plans and why this is a good fit for you.

Question 2: How have your qualifications and studies helped you to prepare for this course or subject?

Under this section, talk about how your studies or training relate to your chosen course, courses or subject area, the relevant skills you have that make you a great candidate, and any relevant educational achievements.

Question 3: What else have you done to prepare outside of education, and why are these experiences useful?

Use this section to highlight work experience, employment or volunteering, as well as personal life experiences or responsibilities. You can also bring in hobbies and extracurricular or outreach activities, achievements outside school or college, and for those no longer in full-time education, this is the place to mention what you've been doing since and how this has equipped you for your chosen course or courses.

By removing the daunting spectre of a personal statement blank page and providing these structured sub-headers, the process is intended to make it easier for applicants to convey their very best talents and experiences. It is hoped that the new format will support the broadest range of applicants to succeed in their applications and remove the advantages that privileged applicants had with regards to coaching and support in writing personal statements.

"The 4,000 total character count remains the same, as does our advice to students," explains Courteney Sheppard, Head of Customer Contact at UCAS. "The personal statement is your opportunity to talk about you and why you want to enrol in a particular course, we encourage students to advocate for themselves, in their own words, and describe the ambitions, skills and experience that will make them suitable for the course."

This is the part of the application where you get to tell the universities why they should pick you. Admissions tutors want to see evidence of your interest, commitment and knowledge of your chosen subject. Avoid using the word "passion" – instead, let it jump off the page. If you enjoy reading, which many people do, say which authors or books inspire you, and why. Again, ensure your account is based on lived experiences, not what you think the UCAS admissions tutor would want you to say. Your UCAS form also has your teacher's reference, and your statement should be in line with their summary of your abilities and interests.

Think hard about why you want to study your chosen subject – especially if it is one you have not taken at school or college – and align your interests and skills with the course. While stopping short of exaggerating or out-and-out lying, this is an opportunity to promote yourself; if that makes you cringe and clam up, ask for help from your parents, friends and teachers. The personal statement is not the place to discuss exam grades – qualifications are covered elsewhere on your UCAS form. Academic staff in charge of admissions look for potential beyond the high grades that increasing numbers of candidates bring. To stand out, do your homework on your chosen degree, show an interest in the subject by listening to podcasts, following lecturers on X, and reading articles. Highlight the experiences you've gained that are related to the syllabus you are applying to – clubs you attend or run, lectures, visits, blogs you have written, work experience and wider reading around the subject.

A part-time job, volunteering and other extracurricular activities can be useful ways of demonstrating that you have the skills and experience for university study. These could involve anything from learning survival skills during the Duke of Edinburgh's Award scheme to taking part in music or sports activities, or helping at a charity. But don't just list your skills – be they communication and leadership or the ability to work in a team and manage time well – try to provide examples of when you have demonstrated them.

Practical work experience or volunteering in medical or caring settings should be included by those applying to study medicine – but don't just list what you've done, reflect on what these experiences taught you about working as a doctor and how you are suited to the training and profession. The same approach goes for other vocational degrees; explain how you see yourself using the qualification. Work experience in any setting requires a similar approach; merely namechecking a prestigious company you have been lucky enough to get a placement at will not impress admissions tutors – tell them what you learnt from the organisation and how it relates to the degree you are applying to study.

Take advice from teachers and, if there is still time before you make your application, look for some subject-related activities that will help round out your statement. Mention the accomplishments that suggest you will turn out to be a productive member of the university and, eventually, a successful graduate. Leading activities outside your school or college are ideal, or other responsibilities you have taken on. Show the admissions tutors that you can take initiative and be self-disciplined, since higher education involves much more independent study than sixth-formers are used to.

Don't be tempted to make sentences complicated – keep them short and don't overuse the thesaurus. Avoid pretentious quotes and clichés, as well as phrases such as "from a young age", "as long as I can remember" and "I have always been interested in". Showing commitment to the full course is important, so admissions officers are convinced you will get good results for its duration. Some applicants' five choices will cover more than one subject, and in this situation try to make more general comments about your academic strengths and enthusiasms and avoid focusing on just one of the courses.

If you are an international (EU and non-EU) student you should also include why you want to study in the UK, detail your English language skills, and any English courses or tests you've taken and why you want to be an international student, rather than study in your own country.

Mature students can talk about any alternative entry requirements you've used – such as an access course – that show skills and knowledge gained through previous experiences. Take advantage of the help offered by your school or college. Your teachers see personal statements every year and will have a feel for ones that have gone down well for former students, despite the new format.

International and EU students
Many universities will continue to accept applications from international students later in the year, until nearer the beginning of the course.

References
Hand-in-hand with your personal statement goes the reference from your school, college or, in the case of mature students, someone who knows you well, but is not a friend or family member. Since 2014, even referees who are not your teachers have been encouraged to predict your grades, although they are allowed to opt out of this process. Whatever the source, the reference has to be independent – you are specifically forbidden to change any part of it if you send off your own application – but that does not mean you should not try to influence what it contains.

Most schools and colleges conduct informal interviews before compiling a reference, but it does no harm to draw up a list of the achievements that you would like to see included, and ensure your referee knows what subject you are applying for. Referees cannot know every detail of a candidate's interests and most welcome an aide-memoire.

The UCAS guidelines skirt around the candidate's right to see their reference, but it does exist. Schools' practices vary, but most now show the applicant the completed reference. Where this is not the case, the candidate can ask UCAS customer service to send a copy of their application as a subject access request, which includes the reference. Better, if you can, to see it before it goes off, in case there are factual inaccuracies that can be corrected.

Timing
Applications are accepted from mid-September onwards, so the autumn half-term is a sensible target date for completing the process. Universities tend to start considering applications as soon as they arrive, so some early applicants will already be holding offers from universities. Other universities will not start making offers until after all applications are in, so offers will be sent out after January 15.

Timetable for applications for university admission in 2027

At the time of writing UCAS had not confirmed the exact dates for the application schedule. Please check the UCAS website for the most recent information.

2026

January onwards	Find out about courses and universities. Check schedule of open days.
February onwards	Attend open days.
May 12	Registration starts for UCAS Apply.
September 1	UCAS starts receiving applications.
October 2	Final day for conservatoire music applications
October 15	Final day for applications to Oxford and Cambridge, and for most courses in medicine, dentistry and veterinary science.

2027

January 13	Final equal consideration date for applications for most other undergraduate courses
January 14–end June	New applications continue to be accepted by UCAS, but only considered by universities if the relevant courses have vacancies.
late February	Start of applications through UCAS Extra.
end March	Universities should have sent decisions on all applications received by January 13.
early May	Final time by which applicants have to decide on their choices if all decisions received by end March (exact date for each applicant will be confirmed by UCAS). **If you do not reply to UCAS, they will decline your offers.** UCAS must have received all decisions from universities if you applied by January 13.
early June	Final time by which applicants have to decide on their choices if all decisions received by early May.
start of July	Any new application received from this time held until Clearing starts. End of applications through UCAS Extra.
July 2	Clearing opens
July 6	International Baccalaureate results published.
early August	Qualifications Scotland (formerly SQA) results published.
August 13	A-level results published.
end August	Last time for you to meet any offer conditions, after which a university might not accept you.
late October	End of period for adding Clearing choices and last point at which a university can accept you through Clearing.

The general deadline for applications through UCAS is January 13, but even those received up to June 30 will be considered if the relevant courses still have vacancies. After that, you will be limited to Clearing, or an application for the following year. If your form arrives with the deadline looming, you may appear less organised than others; your application may therefore be one of a large batch that receives a more cursory first reading. Under UCAS rules, last-minute applicants should not be at a disadvantage, but why take the risk? The best advice is to get your application in early: before Christmas, or earlier if possible.

Next steps

Once your application has been processed by UCAS, you will receive an email confirming that it has been sent to your chosen universities and summarising what will happen next. The email will also confirm your personal ID, which you can use to access the online system that allows you to follow the progress of your application. Check all the details carefully: you have 14 days to contact UCAS to correct any errors.

After that, it is just a matter of waiting for universities to make their decisions, which can take days, weeks or even months. Some obviously see an advantage in being the first to make an offer – it is a memorable moment to be reassured that at least one of your chosen institutions wants you. Others take much longer, perhaps because they have so many good applications to consider, or maybe because they are waiting to see which of their applicants withdraw when Oxford and Cambridge make their offers. Universities are asked to make all their decisions by the end of March, and most have done so long before that.

Interviews

Unless you are applying for a professional training degree in health or education that brings you into direct contact with the public, the chances are you will not have a selection interview. For prospective medics, vets, dentists or teachers, a face-to-face (or video call) assessment of your suitability will be crucial to your chances of success. Likewise in the performing arts, the interview may be as important as your exam grades. Cambridge still interviews around 80% of applicants in all subjects and Oxford interviews about 40% to 45% of applicants (see Chapter 11) while a few of the other top universities also see a significant proportion. But the expansion of higher education has made it impractical to interview everyone, and many admissions experts are sceptical about interviews.

What has become more common, however, is the "sales" interview, where the university is really selling itself to the candidate. There may still be testing questions, but the admissions staff have already made their minds up and are actually trying to persuade you to accept an offer. Indeed, you will probably be given a clear indication at the end of the interview that an offer is on its way. The technique seems to work, perhaps because you have invested time and nervous energy in a sometimes lengthy trip, as well as acquiring a more detailed impression of both the department and the university. The difficulty can come in spotting which type of interview is which. The "genuine" ones require extensive preparation, revisiting your personal statement and reading beyond the exam syllabus. Impressions count for a lot, so dress smartly – even if your interview is being held via video call – and make sure that you are on time. Have a question of your own ready, as well as being prepared to give answers.

While you would not want to appear ignorant at a sales interview, lengthy preparation might be a waste of valuable time during a period of revision. Naturally, you should err on the side of caution, but if your predicted grades are well above the standard offer and the subject is not one that normally requires an interview, it is likely that the invitation is a sales pitch. It is still worth going, unless you have changed your mind about the application.

Offers

When your chosen universities respond to your application, there will be one of three answers:
» Unconditional Offer: This used to be a possibility only if you applied after satisfying the entrance requirements – usually if you were applying as a mature student, while on a gap year, after resitting exams or, in Scotland, after completing Highers. However, some universities competing for bright students now make unconditional offers to those who have predicted high grades – just how high will depend on the university. If you are fortunate (and able) enough to receive one, do not assume that grades are no longer important because they may be taken into consideration when you apply for jobs as a graduate.
» Conditional Offer: The vast majority of students will still receive conditional offers, where each university offers a place subject to you achieving set grades or points on the UCAS tariff.
» Unsuccessful: You do not have the right qualifications or have lost out to stronger competition.

English universities were banned from making "conditional unconditional" offers during the pandemic until September 2021. This type of offer – which only becomes unconditional once an applicant accepts it as their firm choice – once made up 60% of types of offer. Universities UK (UUK), which represents the sector, published its code of fair admissions in 2022, setting out how processes must support "student choice". According to the code, universities should not make conditional unconditional offers, or offers with significantly lower grade requirements based on applicants making their institution a firm choice. Conditional unconditional offer-making has died out since 2023.

Any remaining unconditional offers might tempt a candidate to lower their sights and accept a place that would not have been their first choice otherwise. As long as this is not the case, however, there is no reason to spurn such an offer if it comes, as long as you do not take your foot off the pedal in the run-up to exams. Mark Corver, co-founder of the dataHE consultancy and a former director of analysis and research at UCAS, commented in 2025, "They act to increase the numbers gaining a place and provide early certainty, lowering costs for both applicants and universities. This is becoming more important for students as accommodation costs grow ahead of tuition fees. For lower-tariff universities in particular, being able to offer early certainty to some students is one of the few competitive cards they have left to play."

If you have chosen wisely, you should have more than one offer to choose from, so you will be required to pick your favourite as your firm acceptance. Candidates with conditional offers can also accept a second offer, with lower grades, as an insurance choice. You must then decline any other offers that you have.

You do not have to make an insurance choice – indeed, you may decline all your offers if you have changed your mind about your career path or regret your course decisions. But most people prefer the security of a back-up route into higher education if their grades fall short. Some 24,850 took up their insurance choice in 2024, down from 25,290 in the previous admissions year. You must be sure that your firm acceptance is definitely your first choice because you will be allocated a place automatically if you meet the university's conditions. You cannot change your mind at this stage because UCAS rules will not then allow a switch to your insurance choice.

The only way round those rules, unless your results are better than your highest offer (see Results Day, below), is through direct contact with the universities concerned. Your firm acceptance institution must be prepared to release you so that your new choice can award you a place in Clearing. Neither is under any obligation to do so but, in practice, it is rare for a university to insist that a student joins against their wishes.

UCAS Extra

If things do go wrong and you receive five rejections, it need not be the end of your higher education ambitions. From late February until early July, you have another chance through UCAS Extra, a listing of courses that still have vacancies after the initial round of offers. Extra is sometimes dismissed (wrongly) as a repository of second-rate courses. In fact, even in the boom years for applications, most Russell Group universities still have courses listed in a wide variety of subjects.

You will be notified if you are eligible for Extra and can then select courses marked as available on the UCAS website. You will be able to submit a new personal statement for Extra.

Applications are made, one at a time, through the UCAS Hub. If you do not receive an offer, or you choose to decline one, you can continue applying for other courses. About half of those applying through Extra normally find a place and Extra remains a valuable route for those who need it. Why wait for the uncertainty of Clearing if there are places available on a course that you want?

Results Day

Rule No 1 on results day is to be at home, or at least within easy communication – this is not the day to rely on intermittent wi-fi reception in a far-flung location. The UCAS Hub starts to update from around 8.15am on A-level results day, to inform those who have already won a place on their chosen course. However, it does not show your A-level results, these are obtained from your school or college. If you get the grades stipulated in your conditional offer, the process should work smoothly, and you can begin celebrating. UCAS Hub will let you know as soon as your place is confirmed, and the paperwork will arrive in a day or two. You can phone the university to double check, but it should not be necessary.

If the results are not what you hoped – and particularly if you just miss your grades – you need to be on the phone and taking advice from your school or college. In a year when results are better than expected, some universities will stick to the letter of their offers, perhaps refusing to accept your AAC grades when they had demanded ABB. When places are more liberally available, universities are more likely to forgive a dropped grade to take a candidate who is regarded as promising, rather than go into Clearing to recruit an unknown quantity.

Admissions staff may be persuadable – particularly if there are extenuating personal circumstances. Try to get a teacher to support your case and be persistent. Showing commitment is a good thing.

If your results are lower than predicted, one option is to ask for papers to be re-marked, as growing numbers do each year. The school may ask for a whole batch to be re-marked, and you should ensure that your chosen universities know this. If your grades improve as a result, the university will review its decision, but, if by then it has filled all its places, you may have to wait until next year to start.

If you took Scottish Highers, you will have had your results for more than a week by the time the A-level grades are published. If you missed your grades, there is no need to wait for A-levels before you begin approaching universities. Admissions staff at English universities may not wish to commit themselves before they see results from south of the border, but Scottish universities will be filling places immediately.

Students can use the "Decline My Place" function to enter Clearing, and if they use Clearing Plus, they will be signposted to universities with spaces whose entry requirements match their results. In 2024, 45% of Clearing users contacted only one university, up from 38% in 2019, showing evidence that targeted decision-making is becoming a more prominent feature of Clearing.

Clearing

If results morning did not elicit a "yay, I got in!" moment, put plan B into action and find a university place through Clearing. There will be plenty of options at a good range of universities. Commenting on the process in 2025, the chief executive of UCAS Dr Jo Saxton said perceptions that Clearing was a "bargain basement and for the people who had been unsuccessful" were outdated. "That is definitely not how current applicants perceive it. For current applicants, it's the mechanism by which they change their mind," she said, noting that a fifth of those using Clearing are going back to one of their original five choices. "It's a misrepresentation to suggest that it's a trading-up activity. It is about students trusting their instincts and going back to their curated playlists of favourites, which they've researched and probably visited. They're not blindfolded, throwing a dart at a dart board. It's researched."

In 2024, 38,935 UK 18-year-olds secured a place at university or college through Clearing, slightly fewer than the record number of over 39,000 the year before. Such figures highlight the abundance of options in Clearing, as well as how students are using it as means of re-evaluating their choices. UCAS has found significant growth among those who choose to decline their original place and use Clearing voluntarily to explore and find a new course or university.

Contrary to popular belief, Clearing does not open for the first time on A-level results day, it begins on July 2, (ahead of International Baccalaureate results day on July 6), and runs until October 19. The busiest day, however, will be August 13, when A-level students find out their grades. As long as you are not holding any offers and you have not withdrawn your application, you are eligible automatically. You will be sent a Clearing number via Track to quote to universities.

With recruitment restrictions lifted, universities that used to regard their absence from Clearing as a point of pride are appearing in its vacancy lists, and candidates will see options at the coveted research-led institutions included. Certain courses have more availability than others though, and some subjects, such as medicine and dentistry, rarely show up in Clearing as they are so oversubscribed. Only a handful of universities do not take part these days, including Oxford, Cambridge, Imperial, the London School of Economics, and St Andrews.

The most popular courses may fill up quickly, but many remain open up to and beyond the start of the academic year. And, at least at the start of the process, the range of courses with vacancies is much wider than in Extra. The first step is to trawl through the course vacancy lists on the UCAS website, and elsewhere, before contacting the university offering the course that appeals most (and where you have a realistic chance of a place – do not waste time on courses where the standard offer is far above your grades). Universities have all hands on deck running Clearing hotlines and are adept at dealing with lots of calls in a short period, but even so you can spend a long time trying to get through on the phone while the most desirable places are beginning to disappear.

If you can't get through, send an email setting out your grades and the course that interests you, but keep trying by phone, too. Schools and colleges open on Results Day, and teachers should be willing to help with these calls, especially if you are in a panic. A good way of managing the calls is to let the teacher ring, get through to the university and then pass the phone to the applicant. At the end of calls do a round-up of next steps, as in the melee it is possible to misunderstand or forget things, such as requests for more information or follow-up forms to be filled out.

Wise students will not have waited for Results Day to draw up a list of possible Clearing targets. They will have had their list researched and ready to deploy if the time comes in advance. Research into Clearing options is happening earlier than ever. In 2024, 67% of

Clearing applicants researched potential universities before August, up from 59% last year, reflecting a more deliberate and targeted approach to their choices. Many universities publish lists of courses that are likely to be in Clearing on their websites from the start of August. Reconsider some of the courses you mulled over when making your original application, or others at your chosen universities that had lower entrance requirements. But beware of switching to another subject simply because you have the right grades – you still have to sustain your interest and be capable of succeeding over three or more years. Many of the students who drop out of degrees are those who chose the wrong course in a rush during Clearing. In short, start your search immediately if you find yourself in Clearing, and act decisively, but do not panic. You can make as many approaches as you like, until you are accepted on the course of your choice. Remember that if you changed your personal statement for applications in Extra, this will be the one that goes to any universities that you approach in Clearing, so it may be difficult to return to the subjects in your original application. Most of the available vacancies will appear in Clearing lists, but some of the universities towards the top of the league tables may have a limited number of openings that they choose not to advertise – either for reasons of status or because they do not want the administrative burden of fielding large numbers of calls to fill a handful of places. If there is a course that you find particularly attractive – especially if you have good grades and are applying late – it may be worth making a speculative call. You may be on the spot at just the right moment.

What are the alternatives?

If your results are lower than expected and there is nothing you want in Clearing, there are several things you can do. The first is to re-sit one or more subjects. The modular nature of most courses means that you will have a clear idea of what you need to do to get better grades.

You can go back to school or college or try a "crammer". Although some colleges have a good success rate with retakes, you have to be highly focused and realistic about the likely improvements you can achieve. And some of the most competitive courses, such as medicine, may demand higher grades for a second application.

Other options are to get a job and study part-time, or to take a break from studying and return later in your career. You may have considered an apprenticeship before applying to university; the number and variety are growing all the time, so it may be worth another look. The part-time route can be arduous – many young people find a job enough to handle without the extra burden of academic work. But others find it just the combination they need for a fulfilling life. It all depends on your job, your social life and your commitment to the subject you will study. A number of universities now have a majority of mature students, so you need not be out of place if this is your chosen route.

Taking a gap year

The other popular option is to take a gap year. About 7% of applicants defer their entry until the following year while they travel or do voluntary or paid work, aside from the pandemic years when deferred entries went up. The option is largely the domain of school-leavers, known as "gappers", and a whole industry has grown up around tailor-made activities for them, many in Asia, Africa or Latin America. Some have been criticised for doing more for the organisers than the underprivileged communities that they purport to assist, but there are programmes that are useful and character-building, as well as safe. Most of the overseas programmes are not cheap but raising the money can be part of the experience.

Various organisations can help you find voluntary work. Some examples include vInspired (**vinspired.com**) and Plan my Gap Year (**planmygapyear.co.uk**). Voluntary Service Overseas (**vsointernational.org**) works mainly with older volunteers but has an offshoot, run with five other volunteering organisations, International Citizen Service (**volunteerics.org**), that places 18–25-year-olds around the world.

The alternative is to stay closer to home and make your contribution through organisations like Volunteering Matters (**volunteeringmatters.org.uk**) or to take a job that will make higher education more affordable when the time comes. Work placements can be casual or structured, such as the Year in Industry Scheme (**etrust.org.uk**). Sponsorship is also available, mainly to those wishing to study science, engineering or business. Buyer beware: we cannot vouch for any of these and you need to be clear whether the aim is to make money or to plump up your CV. If it is the second, you may end up spending money, not saving it.

Many admissions staff are happy to facilitate gap years because they think it makes for more mature, rounded students. The longer-term benefits may also be an advantage in the graduate employment market. Both university admissions officers and employers look for evidence that candidates have more about them than academic ability. The experience you gain on a gap year can help you develop many of the attributes they are looking for, such as interpersonal, organisational and teamwork skills, leadership, creativity, experience of new cultures or work environments, and enterprise.

There are subjects – maths in particular – that discourage a break because it takes too long to pick up study skills where you left off. From the student's point of view, you should also bear in mind that a gap year postpones the moment at which you embark on a career. This may be important if your course is a long one, such as medicine or architecture.

If you are considering a gap year, it makes sense to apply for a deferred place, rather than waiting for your results before applying. The application form has a section for deferments. That allows you to sort out your immediate future before you start travelling or working and leaves you the option of changing your mind if circumstances change.

Useful websites
The essential website for making an application is, of course, that of UCAS: **ucas.com/undergraduate/applying-to-university**

For applications to music conservatoires: **ucas.com/conservatoires**

For advice on your personal statement: **ucas.com/undergraduate/applying-university/writing-your-personal-statement/new-personal-statement-2026-entry**

Gap years
For links to volunteering opportunities in the UK: **doit.life**
For links to many gap year organisations: **yearoutgroup.org**

6 The Social Inclusion Index

No longer elitist institutions for the few, universities work hard to widen participation among communities with traditionally low take-up rates in higher education. Such measures go some way to levelling the unequal opportunities experienced by people early in life which make them less likely to benefit from a university education. Social and cultural diversity in higher education nurtures innovation and creativity and creates more choice for students and for graduate employers. Many students will have grown up in communities where there is cultural diversity. Different nationalities, religions and ethnicities in the classroom are no longer something unusual; they are the norm. Cultural diversity in universities is just as important, if not more so. Everyone deserves not only the chance to enter higher education if they have the academic aptitude, but also to feel comfortable doing so regardless of their background. Today's applicants want to know about the composition of the student body they will be joining, and our dedicated social inclusion index – detailed in this chapter – helps steer them in that quest

Universities transform lives and shift the dial on social mobility, as the Sutton Trust educational charity sums up: "Young people from less well-off backgrounds who attend university are more likely to become socially mobile into higher income brackets, and income gaps are lower between graduates from disadvantaged backgrounds and their peers compared to non-graduates." Following this logic, universities may be viewed as engines of social justice through the opportunities they afford for social mobility – a role which has been in sharper focus since the cap on student numbers was abolished in 2015, allowing universities for the first time to recruit as many students as they felt capable of educating.

The fairness of admissions to university has long been high on the political agenda, and the current education secretary Bridget Phillipson has pledged to turn around "baked-in" educational inequalities, to ensure young people from all backgrounds have a chance to "get on in life" after leaving school. The Oxford graduate from Washington in Tyne and Wear said: "Despite growing up in a deeply disadvantaged area, I had the opportunity to go to university – but I was one of the lucky ones. Breaking the link between where a young person grows up and the opportunities they have is central to our mission." UCAS has made a number of changes to encourage more students from low-income families to apply to university, waiving the £28.50 application fee for students in receipt of free school meals, replacing the personal statement with a series of questions, and providing historic entry grades data and offer rates for each course on its web pages – meaning school leavers can potentially make more ambitious choices.

The disadvantages some students experienced when growing up may have impacted their level of knowledge or limited the skills they have accrued and their outlook on what is achievable. But headway is being made on widening access to higher education – as evidenced by admissions figures to UK universities in recent years. Across all UK universities, UCAS data shows a record number of UK 18-year-olds from the most disadvantaged backgrounds securing a place at university or college in 2024. In England, 42,670 students from IMD Quintile 1 accepted a place, 5% more than in 2023. In Scotland, 2,145 Scottish students aged 19 and under from the 20% most disadvantaged postcodes secured a place at university or college in 2024, up 12% on 2023 and more than 50% higher than in 2019 – highlighting sustained effort to widen access to university in Scotland. In Northern Ireland, 1,100 students from the most deprived postcodes accepted a place, up from 1,095 in 2023 (a gain of 0.5%). Only in Wales did the numbers of new students from the most disadvantaged postcodes dip – by 1.7% – to 1,430 in 2024. Dr Jo Saxton CBE, Chief Executive at UCAS said: "I am pleased to see an increased number of UK 18-year-olds accepting places at universities and colleges in 2024. But what I'm even more delighted about, is that we are seeing record numbers of disadvantaged students taking this important next step. Removing barriers – both real and perceived – is an absolute priority for us, and it's encouraging to see those numbers growing."

Analysis by The Spectator of offers made by Oxbridge in the 2024 UCAS application cycle provides a snapshot of progress at these sought-after academic big hitters: of the 80 schools to receive the most offers from Oxbridge, 30 were independent and 50 were state – including grammars, sixth forms, further education colleges and comprehensives or academies. This shows how far these universities have evolved their admissions in recent years: as recently as 2018, a report by the Sutton Trust found that just eight top independent schools had as many Oxbridge acceptances as three-quarters of all schools.

Contributing to widening participation, contextual offers, which undercut published requirements for students who meet widening participation criteria, are now offered by most universities. And with disadvantaged students now 76% more likely to enter higher education compared with 2009, universities' efforts to implement access and participation plans which improve equality of opportunity for students from disadvantaged backgrounds are producing change in the sector.

The distance travelled on increasing diversity among student populations on campuses thus far is commendable, but by no means is it a straightforward upward curve; there was a decline among Quintile 1 entrants in 2023, and in the same year the entry rate gap between the most disadvantaged students (Quintile 1) and the least disadvantaged (Quintile 5) students was its widest since records began in 2005. There also remains work to be done on ensuring students recruited from disadvantaged and minority backgrounds thrive in their studies and succeed after graduation. Dropout rates are higher among disadvantaged students than for those from more privileged backgrounds. A major study of higher education trends over the past 25 years by the Sutton Trust, published in 2023, revealed persistent access gaps for disadvantaged students, particularly at the most selective universities. And with university applications projected to reach one million by 2030, it is feared that progress on widening participation may stall, as contracting offer rates affect disadvantaged students hardest. Time will tell. Whatever the fluctuations, the relevance for would-be students to access detailed information on how diverse and inclusive the institutions they are considering applying to remains constant.

The table

Eight editions on from its introduction, our social inclusion ranking is as pertinent as ever. As well as providing a benchmark by which to measure change going forward, it also shines a light on admissions from some of the under-represented groups on campuses and their subsequent prospects and performance. Today's applicants want to know about the composition of the student body they will be joining, and the tables on pages 98–101 help them in that quest.

We have two social inclusion rankings; one for England and Wales, with Scottish institutions ranked separately on account of a different measure of social deprivation – the Scottish Index of Multiple Deprivation (SIMD) – which better captures the position in the 15 Scottish universities than the POLAR4 (Participation of Local Areas) measure used for England and Wales. SIMD and POLAR4 are not directly comparable: one measures deprivation across several criteria, the other participation in higher education only. The two universities in Northern Ireland, Queen's Belfast and Ulster, are excluded from the ranking owing to differences in the country's school system, which has a high proportion of selective grammar schools, making comparisons with the rest of the UK on social mix invalid via the methodology adopted in this *Guide*.

THE SOCIAL INCLUSION INDEX

We have once again resisted the suggestion to include some or all the measures contained within the social inclusion tables as part of our wider academic ranking. There is good reason for this: a university with a poor record for social inclusion may still have an excellent record for teaching and research. It might be a very good university with an outstanding global and national reputation, but with a socially narrow recruitment profile. By using the two multi-indicator, multi-institution tables that we publish together (alongside the relevant subject table), prospective students can identify which universities are the best fit for them academically and where they might feel most at home socially.

The full list of equally-weighted indicators used in *The Times* and *The Sunday Times* inclusion ranking for England and Wales is:

- » recruitment from non-selective state schools
- » recruitment from all ethnic minorities
- » a measurement of the black awarding gap
- » recruitment of white, working-class males
- » recruitment from deprived areas (using POLAR4)
- » a measurement of the deprived areas dropout gap
- » recruitment of first-generation students
- » recruitment of disabled students
- » recruitment of mature students (those 21 or older on admission)

For Scottish institutions, there is no measure of the deprived areas dropout gap and the deprived areas measure is based on SIMD, rather than POLAR4, as outlined above. With the exception of the admissions data for non-selective state schools, all the other indicators are in the public domain. The uniqueness of this social inclusion ranking is in combining these several strands of data together to build an overall picture of the social mix at each institution, and to measure university performance in two key areas: the gap between the proportion of white students awarded top grades in their degrees and black, Asian and ethnic minority students (known as the black awarding gap), and whether more students from the most deprived areas fail to complete their courses than those recruited from more advantaged districts.

The table is presented in a format that displays the raw data in all instances. No adjustment is made for university location, so a university with a strong, local recruitment pattern in an area of low ethnic minority population is unlikely do well on the measure covering the ethnicity of the intake. This was most notably the case with Wrexham University, which for seven successive years topped our social inclusion ranking overall, but had less than 10% of its intake drawn from ethnic minorities.

However, by combining the indicators using a common statistical technique known as z-scoring, we have ensured no single indicator has a disproportionate effect on the overall total for each university. The totals for each university were transformed to a scale with 1,000 for the top score and the performance of all universities measured relative to that of the university ranked number one.

Just as with our academic ranking, the organisations providing the raw data for the table are not involved in the process of aggregation, and are not responsible for any conclusion or inferences we have made. Every care has been taken to ensure the accuracy of the table and accompanying analysis, but no responsibility can be taken for errors or omissions. The indicators used and what can be learned from them are outlined in turn below.

Non-selective state school admissions

For many years, the Higher Education Statistics Agency (HESA) has published as part of its annual performance indicators, the proportion of students admitted to universities from all state schools. Among the entrants included in this proportion are those attending the 163 state grammars in England and the voluntary grammars in Northern Ireland. However, state school admissions to all universities stripped of the academically-selective grammar school sector are not published elsewhere. Removing the grammar school sector from the equation reveals the proportion of students admitted to each university in 2023-24 (the latest available data) from the largely non-selective state secondary schools (comprehensives and most academies) attended by around 80% of university applicants.

This is the indicator that has seen greatest change over the eight editions of the social inclusion ranking. There are now just three universities where fewer than half the students admitted came from comprehensives and academies: Imperial College London (41.3%, down 2.2 percentage points on the year before's data), Durham (48.6%, up 0.4 of a percentage point) and Cambridge (49.9%, up 0.5 of a percentage point). At the other end of the non-selective state school admissions ranking, Cumbria admitted 100% of its students from this educational background, closely followed by London Metropolitan and Birmingham Newman (both 99%), Wales Trinity St David (98.5%) and East London (98.4%).

Over the eight editions of this ranking, the number of universities where less than half the students are recruited from non-selective state schools has halved, and Oxford has left that cohort completely for the fourth time this year, with 51.6% (53.5% of students drawn from comprehensives and academies in 2021-22). Despite this figure being down 1.9 percentage points compared with last year, it was up 9.1 percentage points over three years, and 12.2 percentage points from our first ranking in 2018 – a sharply accelerating rate of change. Cambridge, which admitted 40.1% of its students from non-selective state schools in our 2018 table, has increased the proportion by a still significant 9.8 percentage points over the intervening period, but now lags behind its principal domestic rival. The rate of change in the school backgrounds of entrants to Oxbridge is vastly outstripping most of its highly-selective rivals – and arguably directly impacting upon them, as the academically capable applicants turned down by Oxbridge find places elsewhere. The much vaunted "brain drain" to American universities – though significant among a clutch of private schools – represents barely a statistical trickle, with most students naturally put off by the much higher costs of studying across the Atlantic.

Despite the recent successes at increasing the numbers of students admitted from the maintained sector at Oxbridge, the reality remains nowhere near proportional parity between state and independent school admissions. Since beating the targets from its previous five-year access plan Cambridge has dropped its state school undergraduate admission targets, but says it will still take applicants' schools into account. Increasingly, the state/private debate is deemed too simplistic. John Blake, the Director of Fair Access and Participation at the Office for Students, said, "we do not require a target on the proportion of pupils from state schools entering a particular university." And anyway, parents of privately educated Oxbridge hopefuls wishing to "game the system" have for a number of years been moving them to top state sixth form colleges and grammar schools for their A-levels.

Our latest data does, though, appear to back up the wider trend towards admitting more students from the non-selective state schools at our most selective universities. Just 15 universities (one fewer than in the previous year's figures and seven fewer than the year before) now take less than 70% of their students from non-selective state schools; 12 of the 15 are members of the highly selective research-led Russell Group. The vast majority of universities (86 in all) admit more than 80% of their students from this demographic.

Ethnic minority admissions

Data gathered from the 2023–24 admissions cycle shows the proportion of entrants to each university drawn from black, Asian, mixed and other ethnic minorities. Eight London universities feature in the top 10, all with at least 70.8% of their students drawn from ethnic minorities, but Bradford is the most ethnically diverse university in England and Wales, recruiting 85.5% of its students from ethnic minorities. Following it are Aston (84.5%), SOAS, University of London (81.2%), Brunel, University of London (80.3%) and City St George's (80.1%). Queen Mary, London is by some distance the most ethnically diverse of the Russell Group student communities and continues to lead the way in the social inclusion ranking overall among the 24-member group.

The least ethnically diverse university is Royal Agricultural, based in Gloucestershire, where 1.5% of the intake was drawn from ethnic minorities, followed by Harper Adams (4%), York St John and Lincoln Bishop (both 7.8%), and Plymouth Marjon (8.1%). Two of the bottom five on this measure are institutions offering largely land-based courses, traditionally attracting low ethnic minority participation. All five universities are in areas of the country with relatively small ethnic minority populations.

Black awarding gap

One of the two university output measures in the social inclusion ranking, the data here is among the most arresting in the survey. We were unable to create a reliable measure of the black awarding gap in eight universities – Aberystwyth, Hartpury, Wrexham, Plymouth Marjon, Lincoln Bishop, York St John, Harper Adams and Royal Agricultural – because there were simply too few black graduates for effective analysis in 2023–24.

Where we could compare the proportions of white and black students gaining first-class or 2:1 degrees, the negative gap in achievement between the groups was at least 20 percentage points in 66 institutions. This is 12 more than in the previous year's data, and six more than the year before. The gap was commendably narrow (less than 10 percentage points) in 10 institutions, six less than in the previous year's figures, and in no universities were black students awarded a higher proportion of top grades than their white counterparts.

The universities with the widest negative percentage point gap for black awarding (showing low proportions of firsts and 2:1s awarded to students from black backgrounds) were Chichester (-47.6%), Leeds Arts (-42.5%), Bath Spa (-37.1%), Canterbury Christ Church (-35.1%), and Birmingham City (-34.9%).

Universities where black students were awarded the most favourable proportions of top-class grades in relation to their white counterparts were Queen Mary, London (-3%), Suffolk (-4.9%), Buckinghamshire New (-6.6%), University College London (-7.4%) and City St George's (-7.5%). One of the top five places here is taken by a Russell Group institution, so often lagging in other areas of the social inclusion ranking, offering evidence that while the numbers ticking a social inclusion box in our highly selective universities might be lower, once admitted, their levels of achievement are hard to tell apart from those drawn from more traditional university-going backgrounds.

White working-class males

There have been countless reports in recent years about the educational underachievement of this group of children. It begins in primary school, accelerates in secondary school, and reaches its logical conclusion with significant underrepresentation at university. As with other measures in our social inclusion ranking, it is not fair to expect universities to correct the systemic failings of the wider education system.

Nevertheless, some universities offer significantly more opportunities to this often-excluded social group. Those doing most are Sheffield Hallam (14.8% of entrants in 2023), Staffordshire and Abertay (both 11.9%), Bath Spa (9.1%), and Aberystwyth (8.9%). At the opposite end of the spectrum, at these institutions white male students with a working-class background make up less than 1 in 100 of students on campus: London School of Economics (0.5%), Bradford (0.8%), and SOAS, University of London (0.9%). White working-class male students are a rare sighting here and at the 63 UK universities where they make up fewer than one in 25 of the student population. This group's access to higher education continues to be one of the more pressing areas in need of action.

Low participation areas (England and Wales only) and deprived areas (Scotland only)

This data is drawn from 2023-24 and looks at the home postcode of all university recruits, putting them into one of five pots, according to the level of participation in higher education. For England and Wales, this indicator records the proportion of students recruited from Quintile 1 (of POLAR4 data) - the 20% of areas that have the lowest participation rates in higher education. In Scotland, this indicator records the proportion of students recruited from the 20% of postcodes with the highest levels of deprivation measured against the Scottish Index of Multiple Deprivation (SIMD20).

Like all indicators, this one has limitations, chief among which is that London overall has high participation rates in higher education relative to the rest of the UK, so very few London-based university entrants fall into Quintile 1 (Q1), meaning that London universities score relatively poorly across the board on this measure, even if they have a socially diverse intake of students. (The strength of performance of many London institutions in other indicators - for example, high recruitment from ethnic minorities and a narrow black awarding gap - confirms this to be the case.)

Teesside (30.9%) and Sunderland (28.5%) record the highest proportions of students recruited from Q1. Both institutions recruit heavily within their immediate surrounds, the northeast being one of the English regions with the lowest participation rates in higher education. Wrexham (27.7%) is ranked third on this measure. Hull (27.4%) and Staffordshire (27.3%) are also in the top five for Q1 recruitment.

At the other end of the scale, London universities account for four of the five institutions with the lowest recruitment from Q1, headed by Brunel, University of London (2.6%) and followed by SOAS, University of London (2.9%), City St George's and Royal Agricultural (both 3%), and Queen Mary, University of London (3.5%).

In Scotland, the highest rates of recruitment of students falling into SIMD20 are to be found at Edinburgh Napier (9.5%) and Heriot-Watt (8.5%), while Highlands and Island (3.9%) and Glasgow (4.4%), have the lowest rates.

Low participation areas dropout gap

This data is drawn from 2023-24 (English universities only) and used in the England and Wales social inclusion ranking only. Drawing upon the same POLAR4 data as above, it measures student outcomes from each of the five social quintiles. The proportion of students dropping out who were recruited from Q1 (the one-fifth of postcodes where university participation is the lowest) is compared with the proportion dropping out who were recruited from Quintiles 2, 3, 4 and 5 (Q2-5). A negative score in this section of the ranking indicates a higher proportion of students is dropping out from Q1 than from areas where more children go to university.

Already under-represented in the student population overall, this measure identifies those universities where Q1 students who do get in are more likely to fail to see their courses through. The universities with the biggest negative percentage point gap for deprived area dropouts - where a bigger proportion of students from the most deprived areas fail to complete their courses than among the rest of the student population - are Roehampton (-7.5%), Westminster and Birmingham Newman (both -6.7%). This is especially concerning for Birmingham Newman, which admits the 11th-highest proportion of students from Q1.

The universities performing most strongly in this aspect of widening participation, where a smaller proportion of students from Q1 drop out compared to the rest of the student population as a whole, are Greater Manchester (+11.9%), Buckinghamshire New (+8.4%), Bedfordshire (+8.3%), Chichester (+7.4%), and St Mary's Twickenham (+7.3%).

First generation students

This measure records the proportion of students recruited from homes where neither parent attended university. This indicator is considered one of the most informative in assessing the overall inclusiveness of university recruitment strategies. Once again, performance varies considerably from the 14 universities where 60% or more of their students identify as first generation - Bradford (73.5%), Birmingham New (72.8%), Wolverhampton (70.7%), Greater Manchester (65.2%), Wales Trinity St David (65.1%), Leeds Trinity (64.8%), Bedfordshire (64.7%), Sunderland (63.1%), Teesside (61.5%), Suffolk (61.3%), East London (61.1%), Huddersfield (61%), Cumbria (60.2%) and Middlesex (60.1%) - to those where fewer than a quarter of students come from homes where parents did not go to university - Cambridge (16%), Oxford (17.6%), St Andrews (18.1%), Edinburgh (18.8%), Bath (21%), Bristol (21.1%), Durham (22.6%) and Imperial College London (24.1%). Of course, as more and more students attend university and, in turn, become parents themselves, the proportions of first-generation students will eventually go down across the board.

Disabled students

This indicator measures the proportion of all students who have declared a disability. It is part of the bigger Office for Students access and participation data and based on the 2023-24 academic year. As with the other indicators, there is a significant difference between the universities at the top – Royal Agricultural, which records 39.4% of students declaring a disability, Falmouth (39%) and Lincoln Bishop (37.3%) – and those at the bottom – Buckinghamshire New (5.4%), Buckingham (6.1%) and Leeds Trinity (8%).

Mature students

Mature students are returners to education and often win places with "life" qualifications, rather than A-levels. This immediately makes the group more diverse than the young entrants, who mostly come straight from school or via a gap year. The age of the student population can have a major impact on the social scene on campus. Older students, particularly those with partners (and quite possibly children) are less likely to be found clubbing or propping up the bar late into the evening. Universities with a very small proportion of mature undergraduates – the LSE (1.3%), Loughborough (1.8%), Bath (2.3%), Oxford (2.4%) and Durham (2.6%) – are likely to have a livelier campus social life than Suffolk (89.2% mature admissions), Canterbury Christ Church (86.8%), Bath Spa (83.3%), Leeds Trinity (80.7%) and Buckinghamshire New (79.9%).

The overall picture

Social inclusion in British universities is evolving and considered a priority in all institutions. However, because of the different starting points for each university, the picture on the ground varies considerably from place to place. Oxford and Cambridge are moving at pace on a number of our measures, but they are not shifting dramatically in our main ranking. This is because our table reflects relative performance and the whole university sector is making strides in improving social diversity on campus. This is a good thing, and the widening use of contextual offers gives this process a chance of continuing despite the challenges presented by the pandemic, which have disproportionately impacted the academic achievement of the disadvantaged.

So, what do this year's social inclusion rankings tell you? It is not possible to appear near the top of them if an institution is only achieving well on one or two of the measures of social inclusion that *The Times* and *The Sunday Times* have chosen. Success in the tables comes from broadly based achievement in recruiting from areas of society least represented in higher education, and then seeing those students progress with their degrees and achieve well.

Appearing near the foot of the tables does not mean social diversity is a non-consideration, simply that the numbers recruited from under-represented groups are vastly lower compared to institutions ranked higher.

A different set of metrics looking at the same subject matter might produce a very different looking table, which is why it is necessary to understand what is being measured here. Based on the measures we have chosen, the top three in the academic rankings – London School of Economics, St Andrews and Durham – appear respectively joint 101st in England and Wales, 13th out of 15 universities in Scotland, and 112th in England and Wales of our social inclusion rankings. Birmingham Newman places 107th in our academic ranking but it is top in England and Wales for social inclusion. Sixteen of the bottom 20 universities for social inclusion in England and Wales (and the bottom three in Scotland) are highly selective Russell Group universities.

Used in conjunction, our academic and social inclusion rankings provide an intriguing insight to likely academic and professional success, the quality of the student experience, and the social, ethnic and educational mix of students likely to be found in the university lecture theatres and the after-hours clubs and bars. But whatever the student recruitment profile of the university you are considering, don't decide where to apply on that basis alone.

If applicants from non-traditional backgrounds don't apply to universities ranked lower for social inclusion, then it only makes it easier for the status quo to prevail.

Social Inclusion Ranking for England and Wales

Ranking	Last year's rank	Institution	State schools (non-grammar) (%)	Ethnic minorities (%)	Black awarding gap (%)	White working-class males (%)	Low participation areas (%)	Low participation areas dropout (%)	First generation students (%)	Disabled (%)	Mature (%)	Total
1	5	Birmingham Newman	99.0	51.5	-27.3	4.0	24.1	-6.7	72.8	25.9	68.4	1000
2	4	Staffordshire	96.2	22.1	-12.9	11.9	27.3	-2.2	59.2	17.7	52.6	984
3	1	Wrexham	97.8	8.7	n/a	7.0	27.7	n/a	59.6	n/a	64.4	943
4 =18		Wales Trinity St David	98.5	10.3	-9.1	5.7	14.0	n/a	65.1	n/a	72.1	892
5	9	Lincoln Bishop	94.6	7.8	n/a	6.8	26.8	3.2	57.7	37.3	35.9	869
6	7	Suffolk	98.3	20.2	-4.9	1.8	27.0	0.9	61.3	9.0	89.2	847
7	13	Sheffield Hallam	96.2	24.8	-27.1	14.8	24.3	2.1	52.9	21.6	17.6	834
=8	12	Creative Arts	93.2	29.0	-13.9	5.5	13.2	-4.3	40.4	21.7	70.6	821
=8 =35		Roehampton	97.6	70.2	-14.5	2.8	4.4	-7.5	59.4	19.1	27.9	821
10	2	Teesside	98.4	17.5	-29.6	8.1	30.9	3.4	61.5	24.2	42.7	817
11	6	Wolverhampton	96.3	62.4	-33.2	3.6	23.0	-2.4	70.7	17.1	41.9	810
12	3	Plymouth Marjon	95.1	8.1	n/a	8.7	17.7	2.4	54.4	29.2	40.5	803
13	8	Sunderland	95.3	18.7	-23.8	7.4	28.5	2.9	63.1	14.7	57.8	795
14 =41		Southampton Solent	95.3	21.2	-16.3	8.3	22.8	1.4	53.1	16.2	41.6	788
15	31	South Wales	84.7	13.4	-17.8	7.5	22.8	n/a	53.0	n/a	42.2	774
16 =73		London Metropolitan	99.0	65.3	-16	3.1	7.8	-1.3	55.7	10.3	68.8	765
17	26	Lancashire	96.0	39.7	-24.5	5.3	12.4	0.2	57.1	27.6	37.0	759
18	14	Leeds Trinity	97.4	40.0	-22.6	2.5	20.9	0.9	64.8	8.0	80.7	755
19 =18		Derby	95.4	34.7	-28.9	7.0	27.2	2.8	52.2	21.2	29.8	741
20	33	Middlesex	97.1	71.1	-25.3	2.1	4.4	-6.4	60.1	16.1	34.4	737
21	17	Chester	95.1	9.9	-14.9	6.5	21.2	0.8	54.6	17.4	28.5	733
22	43	Edge Hill	97.2	10.3	-13.7	5.4	19.3	1.9	55.1	23.1	23.0	729
23 =41		Norwich Arts	94.0	12.1	-9.7	6.0	19.0	1.3	44.0	27.0	13.3	728
24 =38		Liverpool Hope	93.3	16.6	-24.9	8.1	25.0	3.3	51.6	27.1	14.9	727
25	11	Cumbria	100.0	19.4	-22.6	2.8	17.3	-2.2	60.2	12.3	61.2	726
26	16	York St John	95.1	7.8	n/a	7.4	21.0	1.6	47.4	28.9	10.3	725
27	24	Canterbury Christ Church	86.9	28.6	-35.1	5.3	22.6	-2.9	54.1	8.2	86.8	719
28	45	Salford	96.3	42.9	-26.1	4.8	17.8	2.3	53.5	27.2	24.2	718
29	61	Gloucestershire	95.2	13.8	-34.5	7.6	15.9	1.1	48.1	34.0	32.5	707
30	25	De Montfort	95.5	68.0	-18.4	2.5	18.4	2.4	54.7	15.4	26.7	703
31	34	London South Bank	96.9	72.7	-21,5	2.6	5.1	0.4	56.5	19.7	38.1	702
32	37	Coventry	94.1	59.1	-25.5	4.2	15.4	-0.7	55.0	17.4	20.6	699
33	20	Greenwich	94.2	67.3	-27	2.5	7.6	-2.7	59.8	19.9	23.8	693

34 =38	Greater Manchester	97.7	48.3	-25.3	4.3	21.1	11.9	65.2	20.2	63.0	691
=35 15	Bradford	96.2	85.5	-13.9	0.8	10.5	7.2	73.5	16.1	26.5	690
=35 =29	Essex	91.1	41.9	-21	5.6	16.1	0.3	51.0	16.2	28.4	690
37 21	Buckinghamshire New	93.6	40.5	-6.6	6.0	11.5	8.4	52.6	5.4	79.9	682
38 44	Westminster	94.2	76.3	-22.7	2.6	4.5	-6.7	57.2	9.5	12.3	677
39 =22	Anglia Ruskin	94.0	33.9	-26.9	4.1	16.5	0.6	52.2	16.0	52.3	675
40 10	Hull	92.1	19.2	-25.5	2.9	27.4	1.9	54.9	21.8	23.0	667
=41 =22	Huddersfield	95.9	55.5	-24.2	4.0	14.4	1.5	61.0	13.3	20.7	663
=41 50	Northampton	96.4	43.3	-28.7	4.2	17.5	0.3	54.9	17.2	22.6	663
43 55	Goldsmiths, London	92.1	57.1	-17.7	2.2	3.7	0.5	47.7	29.3	21.2	661
=44 51	East London	98.4	65.1	-16.5	1.3	8.6	3.0	61.1	13.8	34.6	659
=44 89	Falmouth	90.9	11.2	-19.2	6.4	12.1	3.2	34.3	39.0	16.9	659
46 52	Portsmouth	91.7	30.1	-25.2	6.1	17.5	1.9	46.7	24.7	13.9	657
47 40	Birmingham City	96.4	69.2	-34.9	2.5	16.8	-1.5	58.7	14.2	18.6	655
48 =62	Northumbria	89.5	14.1	-8.8	6.2	14.6	3.4	48.0	20.0	13.2	647
49 69	West of England	91.4	23.5	-27.5	5.9	16.2	0.9	42.0	26.1	19.7	639
50 81	Bedfordshire	97.6	57.1	-24	2.8	10.2	8.3	64.7	16.9	55.0	637
51 27	Hertfordshire	96.2	60.3	-25.2	2.8	6.7	-2.9	52.2	12.2	26.8	636
52 =35	Bangor	95.9	10.9	-24.9	7.8	16.1	n/a	43.0	n/a	19.8	635
53 47	Winchester	94.1	13.5	28.5	5.4	15.9	1.9	47.5	28.7	19.4	633
=54 49	Liverpool John Moores	91.0	15.2	-21.6	7.6	18.4	3.0	49.7	17.5	14.6	630
=54 64	Manchester Metropolitan	94.1	37.9	-17.5	4.1	15.3	2.1	49.9	17.3	9.8	630
=54 56	Cardiff Metropolitan	93.1	16.3	-23	6.6	17.5	n/a	44.6	n/a	15.5	630
57 =62	Brighton	89.8	27.6	-25.3	5.2	15.2	2.8	44.9	28.6	16.8	629
=58 =29	Lincoln	91.5	12.8	-22.2	6.7	20.3	3.7	51.3	19.1	10.5	620
=58 57	Hartpury	88.6	9.1	n/a	6.3	13.4	-0.7	44.9	22.3	11.3	620
60 71	Worcester	96.6	15.4	-27.4	5.1	16.3	6.0	53.5	24.2	30.8	609
61 53	Keele	85.9	43.7	-20.1	3.9	19.4	4.2	43.5	21.3	11.4	602
62 46	Aberystwyth	90.9	9.2	n/a	8.9	13.4	n/a	39.4	n/a	10.0	601
63 70	Bournemouth	92.7	21.2	-24.8	6.2	12.9	2.5	46.4	22.8	13.0	600
64 =66	Leeds Beckett	91.7	23.1	-24.4	6.2	15.7	3.3	47.5	20.1	10.7	592
65 =73	City St George's	81.5	80.1	-7.5	1.8	3.0	3.3	53.4	13.7	12.8	590
66 68	Kingston	94.2	70.8	-28.6	2.6	6.0	-0.7	51.6	14.0	16.7	587
67 =66	Aston	95.3	84.5	-23.2	1.5	12.4	1.9	53.8	9.0	4.8	586
=68 28	Bath Spa	90.9	13.9	-37.1	9.1	15.0	6.6	41.9	12.4	83.3	577
=68 32	West London	96.5	56.5	-19.2	1.6	7.8	4.3	54.5	10.3	39.0	577
70 60	Leeds Arts	94.0	13.8	-42.5	4.7	17.8	0.5	41.8	34.4	7.5	574
=71 76	Kent	82.4	49.2	-25	4.1	13.2	1.5	44.0	19.8	6.2	561
=71 82	Royal Holloway, London	78.9	48.6	-16	2.6	5.5	-2.0	43.1	19.3	3.7	561
73 58	Brunel, London	91.2	80.3	-21	3.1	2.6	3.6	53.8	12.4	12.8	559
74 75	Queen Mary, London	79.3	77.1	-3	1.9	3.5	4.0	46.8	11.3	8.8	555
75 77	Swansea	92.1	23.2	-18	4.3	12.2	n/a	35.2	n/a	16.8	554
76 85	Oxford Brookes	74.2	24.8	-23.8	2.7	9.2	0.7	34.5	21.9	67.0	553
77 65	Leicester	80.2	68.8	-11.5	2.6	11.6	2.0	38.3	12.1	3.7	552
78 79	East Anglia	85.5	29.2	-15	2.3	13.7	2.3	39.3	20.3	12.8	551
79 84	Nottingham Trent	89.0	37.1	-27.6	4.2	15.7	4.0	42.7	21.6	12.2	549
80 107	University College London	72.6	61.0	-7.4	1.0	5.1	2.0		21.6	3.9	545
81 83	Arts Bournemourh	91.1	17.1	-19.7	2.5	10.0	3.6	42.7	28.6	10.4	543

Social Inclusion Ranking for England and Wales cont.

Ranking	Last year's rank	Institution	State schools (non-grammar) (%)	Ethnic minorities (%)	Black awarding gap (%)	White working-class males (%)	Low participation areas (%)	Low participation area dropout (%)	First generation students (%)	Disabled (%)	Mature (%)	Total
82	54	St Mary's, Twickenham	94.9	33.2	-27.1	4.5	7.0	7.3	51.3	14.6	55.3	539
83	72	Plymouth	85.7	19.8	-26.8	5.9	13.6	3.8	44.3	17.5	22.1	529
84	80	Surrey	81.4	47.1	-21.2	3.1	7.0	-0.8	36.4	17.9	12.1	526
85	103	SOAS, London	82.4	81.2	-12.6	0.9	2.9	6.2	49.4	18.4	7.2	523
86	48	Arts London	88.8	38.0	-15.7	2.7	7.4	4.3	35.9	22.7	12.2	521
87	88	King's College London	75.0	66.1	-18.9	1.6	6.1	-0.5	38.9	16.9	10.9	519
88	114	Buckingham	83.6	59.7	-21.5	1.5	9.4	n/a	n/a	6.1	47.2	512
89	90	Sussex	82.5	29.4	-25.2	1.6	9.9	1.6	36.3	29.2	8.0	499
90	86	Lancaster	77.7	25.6	-21.2	4.3	9.5	0.7	29.6	19.5	3.7	466
=91	93	Manchester	69.7	37.3	-17.6	2.3	9.3	1.7	29.2	23.1	4.6	455
=91	95	Reading	76.7	40.7	-25.7	3.0	8.3	2.6	35.8	22.0	7.4	455
93	87	Sheffield	78.4	22.9	-22.5	3.9	8.9	2.1	28.7	22.6	7.6	452
94	59	Chichester	92.2	10.6	-47.6	5.3	17.0	7.4	44.5	29.0	17.5	451
95	91	York	78.3	16.2	-20.2	4.0	9.5	0.5	28.1	18.6	3.9	445
96	110	Royal Agricultural	63.2	1.5	n/a	3.6	3.0	n/a	36.2	39.4	18.7	442
97	96	Loughborough	66.5	29.6	-15.9	3.6	6.2	1.4	29.4	20.9	1.8	432
98	106	Southampton	69.8	30.3	-22.6	3.2	8.8	1.6	30.1	21.8	5.8	428
99	94	Harper Adams	75.4	4.0	n/a	3.5	7.4	3.6	35.8	28.8	7.7	418
100	97	Birmingham	73.3	42.9	-20.6	2.1	8.9	3.1	33.9	16.3	3.5	412
=101	100	London School of Economics	67.1	61.3	-11	0.5	7.6	5.6	29.5	15.7	1.3	389
=101	92	Warwick	59.9	43.7	-11.7	1.8	6.9	2.5	26.7	15.7	7.1	389
103	99	Nottingham	64.6	35.7	-21.8	1.2	8.5	3.1	28.2	25.1	5.8	387
104	102	Liverpool	74.7	21.9	-24.8	3.6	12.5	6.0	33.3	18.5	5.9	382
105	112	Imperial College London	42.3	65.3	-11	1.7	6.5	-0.3	24.1	10.7	8.1	373
106	98	Cardiff	80.0	21.9	-24.7	3.2	9.6	n/a	29.0	n/a	6.2	370
107	108	Bath	58.0	23.5	-12.5	2.8	4.9	0.3	21.0	17.7	2.3	361
108	111	Oxford	51.6	28.3	-7.6	1.6	6.1	1.9	17.6	21.2	2.4	352
109	105	Leeds	70.0	25.4	-23.1	2.2	9.3	5.6	31.8	18.8	4.6	341
110	101	Bristol	65.5	24.1	-22.2	2.4	6.7	0.3	21.1	16.6	5.2	339
111	104	Newcastle	64.1	16.1	-21.6	2.7	8.8	2.2	29.2	16.0	4.1	337
112	113	Durham	48.8	15.3	-7.5	2.1	9.0	3.5	22.6	20.3	2.6	336
113	115	Cambridge	49.9	34.0	-13.3	1.7	4.8	n/a	16.0	16.5	3.8	316
114	109	Exeter	60.5	16.1	-23.6	2.7	5.4	4.1	25.0	22.4	6.2	299

Social Inclusion Ranking for Scotland

Rank	Last year's rank	Institution	State schools (non-grammar) (%)	Ethnic minorities (%)	Black awarding gap (%)	White working-class males (%)	Deprived areas (%)	First generation students (%)	Disabled (%)	Mature (%)	Total
1	1	West of Scotland	99.1	11.4	-14.4	6.8	6.6	50.8	1.6	55.8	1000
2	2	Abertay	93.3	8.6	n/a	11.9	6.7	47.1	3.5	33.8	995
3	5	Queen Margaret, Edinburgh	95.6	8.5	n/a	4.4	7.9	49.5	7.6	35.1	987
4	10	Robert Gordon	96.0	13.4	-12.8	5.6	6.3	39.0	5.5	38.2	951
5	8	Heriot-Watt	85.7	17.1	-28.6	6.7	8.5	33.9	5.4	11.1	832
6	6	Edinburgh Napier	94.7	11.7	-39.2	4.7	9.5	37.0	5.2	30.2	830
7	9	Dundee	87.7	16.0	-23.1	5.0	6.7	32.6	6.1	27.0	817
8	4	Glasgow Caledonian	96.7	18.2	-33.6	5.9	5.3	45.3	2.2	35.6	787
9	3	Highlands and Islands	97.3	3.6	n/a	6.5	3.9	47.0	3.6	52.5	744
10	7	Strathclyde	88.6	16.3	-21	5.4	5.4	37.1	2.7	13.1	671
11	11	Stirling	90.2	6.4	-46.4	5.5	5.5	38.1	8.8	19.8	631
12	12	Aberdeen	82.1	17.3	-25.7	3.8	5.3	27.5	6.4	12.4	626
13	15	St Andrews	63.9	23.0	-14.7	2.8	6.2	18.1	5.4	9.4	575
14	14	Edinburgh	64.1	16.5	-18.8	2.7	6.1	18.8	5.7	6.3	468
15	13	Glasgow	80.8	15.7	-26.7	3.7	4.4	24.6	2.6	9.4	418

7 Finding Somewhere to Live

Mastering the art of washing up and a flair for vacuuming will go a long way to ensuring domestic bliss with student housemates. Leaving dirty dishes out and not helping with cleaning are the biggest bugbears among undergraduate flatmates, the National Student Accommodation Survey 2025 found. Failing to keep the decibels down, leaving the lights on and letting food rot are also among the no-nos for student sharers, the survey by Save the Student revealed.

For most freshers, university is the first taste of independent living, and a chasm between their academic proficiency and domestic prowess is common enough; learning the ropes of housemate diplomacy is part of the university experience. Student housing runs deeper than who finished the milk, however, and there is more than bricks and mortar to the issue of accommodation for undergraduates. Safe, affordable, and comfortable student digs are inextricably bound to an immersive university experience. Having a suitable roof over their heads influences students' social lives, wellbeing and independence – and ultimately their academic success.

University applicants seeking the broadest study options, unlimited by geographical area, will have living away from home on the cards. Affordability in this context is an educational issue, with steep rents, rising living costs and low maintenance grants prompting increasing numbers of students to live at home, rather than in student accommodation – which represented 30% of those who applied to start their studies in the 2024-25 academic year, according to UCAS. Clearly, the idea of moving away for university can no longer be assumed.

Even so, the majority of students do still "go away" to university, and their September motorway pilgrimages up and down Britain's highways in cars laden with duvets and saucepans are among the indelible rites of passage involved in starting university. To help create a soft landing into undergraduate life most UK universities promise to house all first-year students in halls or in private accommodation partnered with the institution. There are Ts and Cs, of course, notably around confirming the university as first choice and meeting housing application deadlines (detailed with university profiles in Chapter 12).

Nearly two thirds (65%) of first-time university applicants say the availability of accommodation influenced their decision as to where to apply, according to the latest

Least and Most Expensive Places to Rent

Top 15 least expensive locations		Top 15 most expensive locations	
Location	Weighted weekly rent	Location	Weighted weekly rent
Huddersfield	£106	Reading	£164
Preston	£107	Salford	£170
Derby	£108	Bath	£175
Hull	£109	Brighton	£177
Newcastle-under Lyme	£118	Oxford	£178
Sheffield	£123	Exeter	£182
Lincoln	£127	Manchester	£192
Dundee	£128	Durham	£192
Swansea	£130	Guildford	£192
Leicester	£131	Cambridge	£198
Plymouth	£132	Glasgow	£203
Canterbury	£133	Edinburgh	£204
Coventry	£135	York	£206
Norwich	£135	Bristol	£215
Loughborough	£141	London	£296

Source: StuRents, based on 2025-26 academic cycle data. Rents per person per week have been weighted to take into account the price and supply of private purpose-built student accommodation (PBSA) and houses of multiple occupation (HMOs).

Knight Frank Student Accommodation Survey. Housing's influence on decision making for university applicants is not least because of the financial outlay it represents. Paying the rent – always the heftiest financial outlay for students, after tuition fees – is an increasingly big deal, with rents almost 30% higher on average than five years ago. Students – and their families – dig deep to cover accommodation costs. Affordability is compounded by maintenance loans not keeping pace with inflation, and many students only being eligible for slim sums anyway. Rent not only swallows up most of the average maintenance loan; it often outstrips it entirely. Even the maximum maintenance loan is insufficient for 23% of bed spaces in purpose-built student accommodation (PBSA) in England, research by another real estate firm, Cushman and Wakefield, for its 2025 report showed.

Delivered in partnership with UCAS, the Knight Frank survey also revealed student anxiety about the state of the market, with 47% of students expressing worry about a shortage of housing. In an evolving student housing landscape, the accommodation supply is being squeezed from several directions; PBSA, the traditional choice for second and subsequent years of study, private rentals known as "off-street" housing are home to around 44% of students (down from around 50% six years ago). Though the situation varies locally, their supply in general has shortened in recent years as private landlords move out of the student sector for complex reasons including rising borrowing and running costs and increasing overheads.

Changes to legislation – enshrined in the new Renters' Rights Bill which kicks in on 1 May 2026 – that have been designed to improve the rights of renters, may further incline private landlords to step away from renting to students in future. This is due to complexities including its ending of fixed-term tenancy agreements in the student rental market, which relies on an annual cycle from one academic year to the next.

Meanwhile, PBSA developments are increasingly attractive to students for their second and third years. Though typically more expensive than house shares they pose a compelling alternative – kitted out with ensuite rooms, coffee bars, communal study areas, on-site gyms and cinema rooms to recommend them. But having served the sector since the turn of the millennium, the pipeline of PBSA is under pressure too, as developers contend with higher interest rates and increased construction costs. Cushman and Wakefield's report showed that just 88,000 PBSA bed spaces were delivered in the past five years, compared with 158,000 in the previous five years. The new beds were also found to be unevenly distributed across the country, with almost half of them in just three cities – London (3,775), Nottingham (2,593) and Leeds (1,979) – as developers seek the most viable, least risky spots.

Memories remain of the years of "covid bulge" recruitment, when students at universities in cities including Bristol and Glasgow were among those billeted in halls located long distances from their university. Others queued overnight for off-street rentals or signed for houses they had not even viewed. Even without such instances in the most recent recruitment cycles, students are still increasingly starting the search for a second year home almost a year in advance, adding stress to their settling in period as freshers and forcing them to sign up to live with people they may only have known for a few weeks.

Peer reviews of accommodation were also flagged as being important. In total, 74% of applicants said that reviews had an important influence on their decision on where to live, up from 64% in last year's survey. The importance of factors such as access to outdoor space (65%) and a studious atmosphere (54%) confirm that students are also considering lifestyle and academic compatibility when making housing decisions. Branding and reputation were flagged as important by nearly half of applicants, a noticeable increase from previous year's surveys.

New legislation

Students from 2026 onwards will not need to be studying politics degrees to gain first-hand knowledge of new government legislation in action. Labour's version of the Renters' Rights Bill (formerly called "Renters Reform") received Royal Assent in October 2025 and comes into force on 1 May 2027. The biggest overhaul of the rental market in a generation, the bill's headline promises for tenants include abolishing Section 21 "no fault" evictions, banning fixed-term tenancies in favour of periodic ones, and giving tenants the right to exit with two months' notice. The bill also means that landlords will be able to increase rents only once a year, and the rent increase would need to be in line with market rates. The process of securing a rental property in the first place should get easier for tenants. To end bidding wars, all properties will be advertised with an asking rent, which is fixed – it will be illegal for landlords to accept higher offers. They will be banned from asking for or accepting up-front rent payments.

But PBSA remains outside the new rules entirely – keeping fixed terms and allowing providers to ask for more than a month's rent upfront, although PBSA renters will be able to give four weeks' notice if they fail to get their required grades and no longer need their accommodation, if they stop studying and leave the institution, or they withdraw because of illness. The bill has created a new complication for international students with its cap on advance rent payments, as most students from abroad secure a rental by paying six or even 12 months' rent in advance. But under the new rules, international students will need a UK-based guarantor who can vouch for them financially.

For students renting in the off-street market of shared houses, landlords now get Ground 4A – a mandatory possession ground allowing them to evict students between June and September to ensure supply for the next academic year. But ground 4A does not include studio apartments and one- or two-bedroom properties let to students (which account for a third of off-street student housing), and these will be subject to the new regime like other private sector lettings, with no special ground for possession.

Between rising mortgage costs, stricter regulations and now these changes, it is possible that many landlords may decide to leave the market entirely, especially those with one or two properties who can't absorb the added risk. Martin Blakey, the former chief executive of the student housing charity Unipol and a member of the British Property Federation's Student Accommodation Committee, commented: "There will be real and immediate advantages for student renters who will be on assured tenancies, such as the ability to give two months' notice and, perhaps the biggest gain of all for hard-up students, only needing to pay rent four weeks in advance. In the longer term, they will also have minimum standards set under the Decent Homes Standard and will have a right of redress through an ombudsman.

Of course, some may temper these immediate advantages by predicting that the Act will see a reduction in student housing supply resulting in rent rises, an increase in the use of guarantors with rising deposit levels (to counteract the risk of shorter rent payment periods) and that most shared student houses (HMOs) already fall under licencing which should already ensure that the property is safe and being kept in good order. The reality is that no one knows how the Act will affect the market and students specifically."

Living away from home

Most who can afford it see moving away to study as an integral rite of passage. There is no other option for those whose chosen course is at a university further than commuting distance. Others look forward to broadening their experiences in a new, unexplored location. For the fortunate majority, the search for accommodation will be over quickly because the university can offer a place in one of its halls of residence or self-catering flats. But for others, there will be an anxious search for a room in a strange city. Most universities will help with this if they cannot offer accommodation of their own. Save the Student's National Student Accommodation Survey 2025 found that 35% of students were living in properties owned by private landlords, 29% were in university halls, 15% lived with their parents, 14% were in private halls and 3% owned their own property.

The choices you have

» Catered university hall of residence, with individual study bedrooms and a full catering service. Many will have en-suite accommodation.
» Self-catered university halls, flats or houses where you provide your own food.
» Private, purpose-built student accommodation.
» Rented houses or flats, shared with fellow students.
» Living at home.
» Living as a lodger in a private house.

Halls of residence: university-owned and privately-owned

For most parents and carers, their child's university digs will bear little resemblance to the standard of room they might have lived in when studying. Student accommodation has evolved enormously – not only in privately owned blocks, but also in university-owned halls, as ambitious refurbishments modernise campuses up and down the country. First-years are guaranteed a room in halls by most universities, but spaces are usually limited so it pays to meet application deadlines. Applying early might help you get first pick of the different

Term-time accommodation of full-time and sandwich students 2023–24

Other rented accommodation	690,435	30%
Own residence	459,185	20%
Parental/guardian home	429,425	18%
Provider maintained property	353,995	15%
Private-sector halls	208,720	9%
Other	130,315	6%
Not available	65,525	3%

Source: HESA

Top tenancy problems for students

1	Damp	31%
2	Electrical faults	27%
3	Lack of water/heating	27%
4	Leak or flood	21%
5	Rodents/pests	18%
6	Disruptive building work	15%
7	Unnanounced landlord visits	13%
8	Bed bugs	8%
9	Smoke/carbon alarm not working	8%
10	Dangerous living conditions	7%
11	Break-in/burglary	4%
12	Other	2%

Source: National Student Accommodation Survey 2025
Based on over 1,200 responses
www.savethestudent.org

types of room available, too. Any rooms left over are allocated to postgraduates, international students in any year of study and some returning, non-first-year students. Institutions that recruit significant numbers in Clearing have rooms available late in the admissions cycle, but this is not always the case by any means and those gaining their places by Clearing have often been the ones affected by the recent housing shortages. Some universities reserve a small proportion of accommodation for students with families.

While halls are generally the preferred option for freshers, they are also the priciest – not only in private developments but in many cases in university-owned accommodation too, making affordability a sticking point. Some private blocks come with high-spec interiors and swanky extras. Most developments are in big complexes, but there are also niche providers such as Fusion Students, which started as a residential developer before entering into the student market around 12 years ago and now operates in six cities. Its development in Brent Cross, north London, has a gym, a basketball court, boxing studio, cardio studio and zen meditation room. There are monthly events, clubs and chef-catered dinner parties. The list of amenities also includes co-working areas, study spaces, a karaoke room, recording studio, gaming zone, cinema and roof terrace. All bills are included as well as laundry, housekeeping, Fiit (a gym app) membership, concierge, a residents' app and superfast wi-fi. The price of such luxury starts at £292 a week for a single room in a shared three-bedroom apartment and increases to £395 a week for a studio. Student Cribs, which also converts properties to a more luxurious standard than usual digs, now operates in 25 cities.

Unite Students is one of the country's biggest providers. It owns and manages rooms for 70,000 students, working with more than 60 university partners across 22 university towns and cities nationwide. UPP has around 35,000 residential places in complexes built for 15 universities, usually on campus, and where rents are negotiated with the university, often in consultation with the students' union.

Price and location are likely to be more important to students than who owns the property, but when it comes to student accommodation: caveat emptor! Standards can be variable, prices may leave little to live on and private halls are not without negative reviews.

Flat Justice, a not-for-profit tenants' rights group, supported legal actions by 346 dissatisfied students against Unite, following experiences living in halls in Liverpool, London, Coventry and Birmingham. Rats and mice and dust from long-term building work are among the complaints, along with broken radiators, bed bugs, lifts broken for weeks, and students arriving to find an uncleaned flat.

At the top end of the market, private firms usually lead the way, at least in the bigger student cities. Rooms in these complexes are nearly always en-suite and with internet access, and may include other facilities such as your own phone line and satellite TV. Shared kitchens are top-quality and fitted out with the latest equipment. This kind of accommodation naturally comes at a higher price but offers the advantages of flexibility both in living arrangements, inclusive bills and through a range of payment options.

Many new or recently refurbished university-owned halls offer a standard of accommodation that is not far short of the privately built residences. This is partly because rooms in these halls can be offered to conference delegates during vacations. You will probably find them to be in great demand and most students need to get their names down quickly to secure their choice of room. That said, you can often get a guarantee of accommodation if you give a firm acceptance of an offered place by a certain date in the summer. In light of the cost of living crisis, many universities have reported an increased preference for lower-cost accommodation from home and international students. Keen that this does not deter applicants, they are striving to maintain a "rent ladder" in their housing supply, with some lower cost accommodation being available to students who need it.

If you have gained your place through Clearing, this option may not exist, although rooms in private halls might still be on offer at this stage. There have been delays experienced in development completions in recent years and it is wise to ensure, as far as possible, that any new-builds are on time and approved for students to move into.

While a few halls are single-sex most are mixed, and often house over 500 students. In student villages, the numbers are now counted in thousands and are great environments for making friends and becoming part of the social scene.

One possible downside is that big student housing developments can also be noisy places where it can be difficult at times to get down to some work. Surveys of students have revealed that for those who found noise a problem, peace and quiet was a higher priority than access to public transport or good nightlife. Many university libraries, especially new ones, are now open 24 hours a day.

Self-catering

Very few universities offer catered halls of residence and self-catering is the norm. Invest in sturdy crockery and basic utensils – the sort of kit that will survive novice cookery and shared kitchens – and that won't be missed if lost or broken. To avoid reliance on instant noodles and takeaways it is wise to master at least a few culinary basics, and sharing meals with housemates can be a sociable way of settling in.

Catering in university accommodation

Many universities have responded to a general increase in demand from students for a more independent lifestyle by providing more flexible catering facilities. A range of eateries, from fast food outlets to more traditional refectories, can usually be found on campus or in student villages. Students in university accommodation may be offered pay-as-you-eat deals as an alternative to full-board packages.

What to do after the first year?

After your first year of living in university residences you may wish, and will probably be expected, to move out to other accommodation. Of the undergraduates canvassed by the Save the Student National Student Accommodation Survey 2025, 29% said they started looking for their second-year housing in or before November. The main exceptions are the collegiate universities, particularly Oxford and Cambridge, but also others. Students from outside the EU are also often guaranteed university accommodation. At a growing number of universities, where there is a sufficiently large stock of residential accommodation, it is not uncommon for students to move back into halls for their final year. The autumn and winter months are the most common times to view properties for those planning to move.

How much will it cost?

Rents vary so much across the UK that national averages can bear little resemblance to what you end up paying. The 2025 NatWest Student Living Index found a UK average rent for students of £562.67 a month, with the cheapest being £490.64 a month in Milton Keynes, £492.27 in Newcastle and £493.13 per month in Sheffield. Student accommodation website, Students, worked out the ten most expensive UK cities for student rent, listing London at the top (£296 a week), followed by Bristol (£215 per week) and York (£206 a week). Such figures conceal a wide range of actual rents, particularly in London. This was always the case but has become even more obvious with the rapid growth of a luxury market at the same time as many students are willing to accept sub-standard accommodation to keep costs down.

A series of recent reports suggest that the need for good wi-fi has overtaken reasonable rents as students' top priority in choosing accommodation. Savvy accommodation providers are using TikTok channels for reviews and promotion as part of the mix when attracting students. A survey by **mystudenthalls.com** found that a big, bright room, good wi-fi, friendly people, a clean kitchen and a good gym are the top things students say they value in a place to live.

While it is true that going for the cheapest accommodation does not always mean good value if it leaves you cold and unhappy there is a balance to strike. Being able to afford such top-end digs must be a priority. Many students will not receive the full maintenance loan, due to its means-testing against household income. Cash is needed upfront for deposits, and/or a guarantee, probably from your parents, that the rent will be paid. Most universities with a range of accommodation have traditionally found that their most expensive rooms fill up first, and that students appear to have higher expectations than they used to. Although there is a shift towards students applying for the cheaper rooms currently, these are being gradually developed out of the system as universities upgrade their estates.

Another consideration is that both living costs and potential earnings should be factored into calculations when deciding where to live. Taking account of both income and outgoings, the 2025 NatWest student living index shows Lincoln as the most affordable town or city, followed by Bolton and Cardiff.

Living at home

If students live within commuting distance of a good university, the option of dodging hefty rent and household bills is tempting. In 2025, 15% of students lived at home with their parents, according to data collected by Save the Student's annual National Student Accommodation Survey. This may increase, given the rising costs of student housing and of living more broadly, coupled with the willingness of many young people, student or not, to live with their parents well into their twenties.

Stay-at-home students tend to have longer commutes to campus than those in their own digs, the extra journey time a worthwhile compromise. Not only school-leavers live at home; the proportion includes mature students, many of whom live in their own homes rather than with their parents. The trend is four times more common at post-1992 universities than at older universities, reflecting the larger numbers of mature students with family responsibilities at the newer universities and a generally younger and more affluent student population at the older ones.

Before opting to stay at home solely on the basis that it makes financial sense, it is important to consider the relationship with your parents and the availability of quiet space in which to study. You will still be entitled to a maintenance loan, although for 2025–26 it is a maximum of £8,877 in England, rather than £10,544 if you were living away from home outside London, or £13,762 in London. There is no higher rate for anyone living at home in London, which seems unreasonable given the high cost of transport and other essentials in the capital.

The downside is that you may miss out on a lot of the student experience, especially the social scene and the opportunity to make new friends. Research has found that students who live at home are less likely than others to say they are learning a lot at university, and a survey by the Student Engagement Partnership suggests that they find life unexpectedly "tiring, expensive and stressful". But according to a new survey of 1,000 UK students commissioned by Leeds Beckett University, more than half (5%) said staying at home encouraged them to attend more lectures and seminars, perhaps under the watchful eye of parents. If living at home starts to rankle, remember that you can always move on later. Many initially home-based students do so in their second year.

Making your choice

Choosing somewhere cheap is a false economy if it ends up making you feel depressed and isolated. Most students who drop out of university do so in the first few months, when homesickness and loneliness can be felt most acutely. Being warm, rested and well-fed is likely to have a positive effect on your studies. University halls offer a convenient, safe and reliable standard of accommodation, along with a supportive community environment. The sheer number of students – especially first-years – in halls makes this form of accommodation an easy way of meeting people from a wide range of courses and making friends. If meals are included, this extra adds further peace of mind both for students and their parents. But only a tiny proportion of places are catered.

Wherever you choose to live, there are some general points you will need to consider, such as how safe the neighbourhood seems to be, and how long it might take you to travel to and from classes. A survey of travel time between term-time accommodation and university found that most students in London can expect a commute of at least 30 minutes and often over an hour, while students living in Wales are usually much less than 30 minutes away from their university.

Top 10 most annoying housemate problems

1	Leaving dirty dishes out	64%
2	Not helping with cleaning	56%
3	Being excessively loud	46%
4	Leaving lights/appliances on	43%
5	Leaving food to rot	40%
6	Leaving hair in plugholes	28%
7	Not changing loo roll	25%
8	Stealing food	24%
9	Leaving windows open	23%
10	Leaving the toilet seat up	22%

Source: National Student Accommodation Survey 2025
Based on over 1,200 responses
savethestudent.org

In Chapter 12, we provide details of what accommodation each university offers, covering the number of places, the costs, and their policy towards first-year students.

Practical details

Whether starting out in university halls of residence or in a different type of accommodation, you will probably be expected to sign an agreement to cover your rent. Contract lengths vary. They can be for around 40 weeks, which includes the Christmas and Easter holiday periods, or for just the length of the three university terms. These term-time contracts are common when a university uses its rooms for conferences during vacations. Check whether the university has secure storage space for you to leave your belongings. Otherwise, you will have to take everything home or store it between terms.

International students may be offered special arrangements to continue living in halls during the short holidays. Organisations like **hostuk.org** can arrange for international students to stay in a UK family home at holiday times such as Christmas.

Parental purchases

An option for families with the means to do so, is to buy a house or flat and take in student lodgers. This might not be the safe financial bet it once appeared, but it is still tempting for many parents. Estate agents Knight Frank have had a student division since 2007. Those who are considering this route tend to do so from their first year of study to maximise the return on their investment, but be aware that financing is significantly more specialist, and lenders will require 25–30% deposits, apply tougher stress tests and charge higher rates. There is also the management burden to consider. Student lets are much more hands-on than standard buy-to-let: annual tenant turnover, summer voids, cleaning between tenancies, damage beyond normal wear and tear, and chasing rent from multiple students. If you are not local, you will need a letting agent, which typically costs 10–15% of rental income.

Being a lodger or staying in a hostel

A small number of students live as a lodger in a family home, an option most frequently taken up by international students. Students with certain religious affiliations or from a particular country may wish to consider living in a hostel run by a charity catering for a specific group. Most of these are in London. There are also specialist commercial providers such as Mansion Student India, which runs housing for Indian students in the UK (**mansionstudent.co.uk/internationals**).

Renting from the private sector

As discussed earlier in the chapter, the student housing market is under pressure currently, though historically every university city or town has been awash with such accommodation, to the point where so-called "student ghettoes" have emerged. Into this traditional market for rented flats and houses have come the new private-sector complexes and residences, which are experiencing growing demand.

How to start looking for rented property

Start this process as soon as you have accepted a place. Contact your university's accommodation service and ask for its list of approved rented properties. Some have a Student Accommodation Accreditation Scheme, run in collaboration with the local council. To get onto an approved list under such schemes, landlords must show they are adhering to basic standards of safety and security, such as having an up-to-date gas and electric safety certificate.

Security in Student Housing

With multiple students all living under the same roof – each with a laptop, phone and other portable gadgets – student accommodation represents a quick win with big rewards for burglars, so it is worthwhile being security conscious.

» Make sure that your rental property has five-lever mortise locks as well as standard catch locks on the front and back doors. Without these, contents insurance may be invalid. And use them when you go out. Ask if the locks have been changed and, if not, if previous tenants have returned all keys.
» Check that furniture and furnishings provided comply with basic fire resistance standards, that there are working smoke alarms, and that you see up-to-date gas and electricity certificates.
» Be careful about letting anyone in behind you into the house or your halls of residence. People often leave their flat or bedroom doors unlocked. It's best to ask those seeking entry to buzz whomever they're visiting instead.
» Invest in a light-timer for when you're out and don't advertise your departure on social media.
» It might seem slightly over the top, but tuck away your laptop, electronics and any jewellery when you go out. Take valuables home if you're vacating your rooms for any length of time.
» If you prefer your desk at a window, make sure you move costly equipment out of sight when not in use.
» Hide packaging for your laptop, mobile and any other pricey purchases. Just dumping the box next to the bins is tantamount to advertising 'Expensive new gadgets here'.
» Call the taxi from down the street. That way, no one knows which house you've just left empty.
» Not getting contents insurance is a false economy. You may be able to add items to your parents' home insurance.
» Register valuables on the UK National Property Register at **www.immobilise.com**. And use a good bike lock.

Source: **savethestudent.org** and NUS (adapted)

University accommodation officers should also be able to advise you on any hidden charges. For instance, you may be asked to pay a booking or reservation fee, and there are sometimes fees for references or for drawing up a tenancy agreement. The practice of charging a "joining fee", however, has been outlawed.

Speak to older students with first-hand experience. Most universities have a clickable "Chat to a Student" icon on their website. Certain areas of town may be notorious, and you can try to avoid them. What I Wish I Knew About University, a Facebook group featuring over 90,000 members, is increasingly the go-to source of peer-to-peer advice for parents of students.

Making a choice

Once you have made an initial choice of the area you would like to live in and the size of property you are looking for, the next stage is to look at possible places. If you plan to share, it is important that you all have a look at the property. If you will be living by yourself, take a friend with you when you go to view a property, since they can help you avoid any irrational or rushed on-the-spot decisions. Don't let yourself be pushed into signing on the dotted line there and then, despite current market pressures. Take time to visit and consider options, as well as checking out the local facilities, transport and the general environment at various times of the day and on different days of the week.

If you are living in private rented accommodation, it is likely that at least some of your neighbours will not be students. Local people often welcome students, but resentment can build up, particularly in areas of towns and cities that are dominated by student housing. It is important to respect your neighbours' rights, and not to behave antisocially.

Preparing for sharing

It helps to co-habit with people whose outlook on day-to-day living is not too far out of line with your own. There can be a bit of a rush to sign up for second-year houses, which some students do as early as October. While it is good to be ahead of the scrum, you may not yet have met your best friends at this stage. If you have not selected your own group of friends, universities and landlords can help by taking personal preferences and lifestyle into account when grouping tenants together.

Adopt good shared living etiquette from the start to prevent housemate drama further down the line. Organise a cleaning rota for everyone to share the chores, set boundaries around sharing items in communal areas such as bathrooms and kitchens, and be collectively clear about replacing essentials such as loo roll, milk and washing up liquid. Sort out broadband that suits everyone. Be thoughtful about noise levels, especially with regards to music equipment.

The practical details about renting

It is a good idea to ask whether your house is covered by an accreditation scheme or code of standards. Such codes provide a clear outline of what constitutes good practice as well as the responsibilities of both landlords and tenants. Adhering to schemes like the National Code of Standards for Larger Student Developments compiled by the Accreditation Network UK may well become a requirement for larger properties, including those managed by universities. At the very least, make sure that if you are renting from a private landlord, you have their telephone number and home address. Some can be remarkably difficult to contact when repairs are needed or when deposits are due to be returned.

Multiple occupation

If you are renting a private house, it may be subject to the Housing Act 2004 in England and Wales (similar legislation applies in Scotland and Northern Ireland). Licenses are compulsory for all private houses in multiple occupation (HMOs) with three or more storeys and that house five or more unrelated residents. The provisions of the Act also allow local authorities to designate whole areas in which HMOs of all sizes must be licensed. This means that a house must be licensed, well-managed and must meet various health and safety standards, and its owner subject to various financial regulations. There is more on this at **gov.uk** under Private Renting.

Tenancy agreements

Whatever kind of accommodation you go for, you must be sure to have all the paperwork in order and be clear about what you are signing up to. If you are taking up residence in a shared house, flat or bedsit, the first document you will have to grapple with is a tenancy agreement or lease offering an "assured periodic tenancy" – which will replace "assured shorthold tenancies" from 1 May 2027 under the new Renters' Rights Act. Since this is a binding legal document, you should be prepared to go through every clause with a fine-tooth comb. Remember that it is much more difficult to make changes or overcome problems arising from unfair agreements once you are a tenant than before you become one.

For help with understanding some of the clauses, your university accommodation office or students' union is a good place to start. A Citizens Advice Bureau or Law Advice Centre should also be able to offer free advice.

In particular, watch out for clauses that may make you jointly responsible for the actions of others. If you name a parent as a guarantor to cover any costs not paid by you, they may also be liable for charges levied on all tenants for damage that was not your fault. Make sure you keep a copy of all documents and get a receipt (and keep it somewhere safe) for anything you have had to pay for that is the landlord's responsibility.

Contracts with private landlords have tended in the past to be longer than for university accommodation, frequently committing you to paying rent for 52 weeks of the year. Leaving aside the cost, there are probably more advantages than disadvantages to this kind of arrangement. It means you don't have to move out during vacations. You can store your belongings in your room when you go away (but don't leave anything valuable behind if you can help it). You may be able to negotiate a rent discount for periods when you are not staying in the property. The other advantage, particularly important for cash-strapped students, is that you have a base from which to find work and hold down a job during the holidays.

Deposits

On top of the agreed rent, you will need to provide a deposit or bond to cover any breakages or damage. This will probably set you back the equivalent of another month's rent. The deposit should be returned, minus any deductions, at the end of the contract. However, be warned that disputes over the return of deposits are common, with the question of what constitutes reasonable wear and tear often the subject of disagreements between landlord and tenant. About one in six student renters have struggled to get their deposit back, according to successive annual Save the Student surveys.

To protect students from unscrupulous landlords, the 2004 Housing Act introduced a National Tenancy Deposit Scheme under which deposits are held by an independent body. There are details at **citizensadvice.org.uk**. You may also be asked to find guarantors for your rent payments – in practice, usually your parents.

Inventories and other paperwork

Student tenants should get an inventory and schedule of condition of everything in the property. This is another document that should be checked carefully to ensure everything listed is as described. Write on the document anything that is different. The NUS suggests taking photographs of rooms and equipment when first moving in, to provide additional proof. If an inventory is not offered, tenants should make one of their own. You should have someone else witness and sign this, send it to your landlord, and keep your own copy. Keeping in contact with your landlord and developing a good relationship with them will also do you no harm.

You should ask your landlord for a recent gas safety certificate issued by a qualified Gas Safe Register engineer, a fire safety certificate covering the furnishings, and a record of current gas and electricity meter readings.

Being energy efficient has become a high stakes activity since the prices of gas and electricity have spiralled. Freshers who are in halls are likely to be sheltered from the worst of the energy bill rises. But many students in shared houses will be unaware that in most agreements with student letting agents, the energy included is typically subject to a fair use policy – a cap or allowance – that is often based not on units of energy consumed but on sums of money spent. These sums, which may have seemed generous in the past, are being rapidly eclipsed by the rising price of gas and electricity. In the current energy climate, it pays to read the small print regarding fair usage policies to mitigate any shocking bills later down the line.

Students need to take their own readings of meters when they move in. This also applies to water meters if they are expected to pay water rates (although this isn't usually the case). Putting lids on pans, not overfilling the kettle, layering up warm clothes instead of turning up the radiators and switching off the lights will save money and cut down on carbon emissions. The NUS issues its own advice on how to keep down energy bills, at **studentswitchoff.org**.

Students are not liable for council tax if they are sharing a house only with other full-time students. However, they may be liable to pay a proportion of the council tax bill if they are sharing with anyone who is not a full-time student. In this instance, the student may need to get a council tax exemption certificate from their university as evidence that they are not liable for it.

Safety and security

Once you have arrived and settled in, freshers should remember to take care of their own safety and the security of their possessions. They are particularly vulnerable when they are still getting used to new-found independence. This may help explain why so many students are burgled or robbed in the first six weeks of the academic year. Valuable portable items such as mobile phones, tablets and laptops should be taken care of – not left on display – and covered by insurance. Students' unions, universities and the police can provide plenty of practical guidance upon arrival at university.

Useful websites

For advice on a range of housing issues: **readytorent.nus.org.uk** and **nus.org.uk/student-housing-hub**

The Shelter website has separate sections covering different housing regulations in England, Wales, Scotland and Northern Ireland: **shelter.org.uk**

As examples of providers of private hall accommodation: **upp-ltd.com**, **unitestudents.com**, **imperialhomesolutions.co.uk** and **student-cribs.com**

A number of sites will help you find accommodation and/or potential housemates, including: **accommodationforstudents.com**, **uniplaces.com**, **sturents.com**, **studentpad.co.uk**, **studentcrowd.com** and **student.spareroom.co.uk**

Accreditation Network UK is at: **anuk.org.uk**

hostuk.org helps international students meet British people and families in their homes

8 Staying Safe and Seeking Help on Campus

Fresh out of school and heady with freedom, new undergraduates have independence at their fingertips. And there's a lot to navigate, from sex, drugs and alcohol to learning the washing machine symbols and mastering the art of bolognese on a budget. As the dust settles after the university drop-off rite of passage – complete with customary halls room kit-out with strings of fairy lights and scatter cushions – the reality of all that independence hits home. Parents and carers may dimly recollect an awkward hug goodbye and a "see you at Christmas" when we first left home, but rearing children is light years away now – with digital stalking and endless chatter on school WhatsApp groups all part of the picture. Letting go for parents may be as hard to do as giving up the Life360 subscription or resisting the urge to monitor their every move on FindMyiPhone. Naturally, not all parents worry about how they can safely send homemade pies in the post to their new students – as some do – and not everyone packs off their fresher with "open when" envelopes ("...when you're sick" (paracetamol, vitamin C); "...when you need a coffee" (Starbucks voucher)). But most will be concerned about their basic safety and happiness.

Starting university is a time of huge change for students. Many find it hard to settle in – whether that is struggling to find like-minded types to make friends with, feeling anxious about degree-level learning, or having a confidence wobble upon encountering peers who are at least as clever and hardworking as they are. Financial worries have always been part of the student scene, but with maintenance loans barely covering the rent and huge increases to other living costs, some students risk being priced out of socialising. Such concerns seem paradoxical, given that traditional worries are about students going out too much. The rise of "cancel culture" on campuses is an added complication, with peer-on-peer policing about deemed misdemeanours – ranging from inappropriate sexual behaviour or the misuse of pronouns to "offensive" political views – at times causing students to be shunned by each other. And for some students, the pressure of not wanting to let anyone down – including their parents who are often making personal sacrifices to contribute to their bills – weighs heavy.

Despite both the traditional and the contemporary concerns, parents are advised to switch off the helicopter rotors and give their child independence, while also checking in with them around the major issues: drinking, taking drugs, sex and staying safe – physically and mentally – on campus.

The extent to which universities are "in loco parentis" is an issue of discussion within the higher education sector. The age of majority was lowered to 18 from 21 in 1970, meaning that universities could do away with rules around hall of residence curfews, restrictions on guests and dress codes. Constraints like that would seem ridiculous now. Universities are also too big to keep tabs on all students all the time. But universities do provide support and guidance to students on issues of alcohol, drugs, sexual consent and respect, and all have services to support student wellbeing and mental health. Courses on these issues are occasionally mandatory, but in most cases, they need to be sought by students themselves via student services at the university and/or its students' union.

From the first round to last orders

Historically, university life has been inextricably linked to drinking alcohol, with big nights out a cornerstone of the student experience. Stereotypes of student binge drinking abound – fuelled by university social scenes which revolve around campus or college bars and Freshers' Week itineraries packed with club nights and boozy social mixer events. This extends to accommodation, with pre-drinks a cheap alternative to paying bar prices, and students often aiming to get sozzled enough before they go out to ensure they spend little once they do. The long-term health conditions caused by regular over-consumption of alcohol are unlikely to be at the forefront of the minds of freshly independent 18-year-olds as they knock back another shot, but those drinking to excess can find themselves missing deadlines, involved in antisocial behaviour or letting their guard down around personal safety.

Social norms around drinking are changing, however, and a drinking culture prevails for those who want it, but students no longer have to drink to make friends. There is increased awareness of the mental and physical toll of getting drunk. The rising cost of living – including alcohol – is also reshaping the student experience. A cost of living analysis compiled by NatWest bank found that half the students questioned were going on fewer nights out to save money, while a fifth avoided the pub altogether and almost a quarter had never set foot in a nightclub. Research by the charity Drinkaware found that one in five young adults aged 18 to 24 are teetotal and under-25s are less likely to drink alcohol than any other generation. The proportion of under-25s who say they are non-drinkers or have not had alcohol in the past year rose from 19% in 2011 to 38% in 2021 – and that grew to 42% among young women. The trend has led to the rise of alcohol-free accommodation at universities – including at Liverpool, Southampton, Keele, St Andrews, Bath, Surrey, Birmingham, Bristol, and Swansea. Manchester offers "lifestyle-moderated" halls, which are more reserved with respect to parties, alcohol and noise. Sober societies are also common throughout UK universities.

So far so sensible. But although abstaining from alcohol is on the rise among young people, the Drinkaware report, published in 2023 and based on a survey of 10,000 adults, also found that members of Gen Z were more likely to drink in harmful quantities. Three quarters of young adults said they binged – defined as having at least four pints or glasses of wine in a single drinking session, but only two thirds of over-25s did. Plus, the survey found that young adults were twice as likely to experience memory loss due to drinking and were also more likely to have anxiety and depression. Karen Tyrell, Drinkaware's chief executive, believes: "We need to normalise conversations around alcohol, making it easier for people to speak up and get help."

For anyone wanting to encourage moderation to their student offspring, preaching sobriety tends not to be the most effective approach. The team behind the NUS Alcohol Impact survey advise fostering an open chat about alcohol over-consumption. A good way to get the conversation going is by explaining how to take care of someone else who has drunk to excess.

A harm reduction approach is even more important when hall parties take over. Pack an alcohol measure with your student's kitchen equipment (some universities give them out to encourage drinking responsibly). If having one does not result in your child fastidiously keeping a drinks diary, it could at least slow down the sloshing of another huge glug.

Finally, trust them to make good decisions. The Students, Alcohol and Drugs 2024-25 survey by SOS-UK found that most students (83%) agree that drinking too much too quickly can cut short a great night out with friends. Three quarters (75%) agree that they don't have to get drunk to have a good night out, and that they don't like socialising with people who get very drunk and ruin the night for others. The survey was completed as part of the SOS-UK Drug and Alcohol Impact programme, which embeds responsible drinking on campuses and refocuses conversations on drugs.

Chasing the high

There are lots of assumptions about students' inclinations for taking drugs, but "essentially there's very little written about student drug use", says Professor Nic Beech, vice-chancellor at the University of Salford and chair of the Universities UK (UUK) student drug use taskforce, which convened in 2022 to help universities understand and address student drug use and published its report in 2024. Summarising, Professor Beech said: "As educators, our priority is to see students succeed and we know that drug use can work against this, impacting students' health, wellbeing, education, and future careers. Around one in eight of those we surveyed said they had used drugs in the past twelve months, and almost half of those wanted to reduce their use – but the evidence also shows fear can be a big deterrent in students seeking help to change their drug behaviour. Universities need to take a proactive role in showing students the risks of using drugs, but also in providing support to both users and non-users."

The Students, Alcohol and Drugs 2024-25 report found that 79% of respondents did not currently use drugs, over a quarter had used drugs whilst at university (27%), and 2% used drugs daily or almost daily. Of those that did use – or had used – drugs, the majority (64%) did so for recreation, with nearly a quarter (24%) to enhance their social interactions. Only 1% reported that they used drugs to cope with bullying or harassment or to perform better athletically. Cannabis was found to be the most frequently reported drug among students, with over two thirds (69%) saying they used cannabis (11% of students reported using it daily or almost daily). This was followed by powder cocaine (26%), ketamine (23%), ecstasy/MDMA (22%), magic mushrooms (21%), poppers (20%) and LSD (10%).

UUK's taskforce findings reported that of students who had taken drugs, more than half said they did so to have fun. A third reported relaxation, and another third bonding with friends as motivations. "Study drugs" such as Ritalin and Modafinil may also be used by students, purportedly taken to improve concentration and keep them writing essays into the early hours.

Just say no?

A solely punitive approach to drug use isolates students rather than aiding them. "The trouble is that as soon as people feel isolated their wellbeing goes down, they are hesitant to socialise and that puts them more into the position where drugs and alcohol are likely to be the sort of thing that they go to," notes Professor Beech.

The UUK student drug use taskforce encompassed a survey of nearly 4,000 students. It found that 18% said they had used drugs in the past and, within this group, two-thirds had used drugs in the past twelve months – equating to around one in eight (12%) of those surveyed. This is notably lower than a rate of use identified by the Office for National Statistics, that 17.6% of 16-24-year-olds in England and Wales reported drug use in the year to

March 2023. Meanwhile, in Scotland, the Scottish Crime and Justice Survey covering the years 2018–2020 found that 23.5% of individuals aged 16–24 reported using drugs in the year prior to being surveyed. One of the more commonly reported reasons for taking drugs was to deal with anxiety and mental health issues.

The taskforce's findings recommend moves away from a "zero-tolerance" approach to one focused on "harm reduction" with support and education prioritised over disciplining students who are using drugs. "As well as tackling supply and reducing demand, if we want to help students succeed in education, we need to make it easier for them to access help where they need it, to be effectively informed and to retain the hope of success, which is a foundational motivation for learning," said Professor Beech.

Similarly, the Drug and Alcohol Impact scheme (organised by SOS-UK) aims to move the conversation on drugs towards reducing harm, and building healthier, safer, more productive student communities. Students for Sensible Drug Policy (SSDP) is an international grassroots organisation, advocating a change in drug policy on campuses, an "end to the war on drugs" and acknowledgement of the many reasons behind drug use, including mental health management and peer pressure. The goal is to empower students to make informed decisions, stating that pastoral and medical needs will always be prioritised over disciplinary proceedings.

This is not to say that drugs will soon be permissible on campuses. Many universities take a firmer line than the law, penalising students for technically legal drug use. Accommodation contracts often have an outright ban on drugs, threatening eviction.

What can parents do?

Open dialogue equips your child with harm reduction knowledge. By discussing the effects of certain drugs, and what to do if someone has a bad reaction or overdoses, students will garner information that could end up saving a life. To facilitate such a potentially thorny chat, the NUS Alcohol and Drugs Impact scheme recommends taking a bystander approach. By saying "your friends may take drugs, these are the risks they are undertaking" you make sure that they get the information for themselves while not directly tackling them on it. This may help young people to understand the risks in a non-judgmental, safe space.

University drug policies vary, so read the fine print. Websites such as **talktofrank.com** provide information on the effects that different substances can have and advice on how to talk to young people about drugs.

Consent

Sexual assault and violence on UK campuses is a very real problem, as highlighted by the website **everyonesinvited.uk**. First launched in 2020, it reports survivors' testimonies of sexual abuse – including in 93 institutions profiled in the *Good University Guide*. Through freedom of information requests, Eva Tutchell and John Edmonds, authors of *Unsafe Spaces: Ending Sexual Abuse in Universities*, estimate there are between 50,000 and 100,000 sexual assaults at British universities every year. "The first thing that amazed us was that universities, research-based organisations, have made no real attempt to collect authoritative information about sexual assaults on campuses," Edmonds says. "If you haven't got the evidence, the specialist knowledge, how do you put together a programme that is likely to work? They rely on reports made by students and by junior staff, but everybody knows that these sexual assaults are massively underreported." The NUS thinks that universities need to look at their reporting systems. Are any universities getting it right? Edmonds and Tutchell conclude that there are a few who "haven't always got it right, but are taking it seriously".

Sex and relationships among students

Findings of a poll of students' personal lives by the Higher Education Policy Institute (HEPI) for its report Sex and Relationships Among Students, published in 2021, revealed that more than half of students think it should be compulsory to pass a sexual consent assessment before entering higher education. Most students (59%) reported that they were "very confident" about "what constitutes sexual consent" but only half as many (30%) said they were "very confident" about how to navigate sexual consent after alcohol has been consumed. Two-thirds of students said they knew how to challenge inappropriate sexual behaviour (with 23% saying they feel "very confident" in doing so and 43% "fairly confident").

The Emily Test charity campaigns for better protection for students. Its chief executive is Fiona Drouet, whose daughter, Emily, was a law undergraduate at Aberdeen University when she was subjected to a campaign of gender-based violence by her boyfriend, a fellow student, which ended tragically in her taking her own life.

Reframing the birds and the bees

Understanding the intricacies of consent is the key to helping your child protect themselves and others, and the advice from Mandy Saligari, a therapist who specialises in treating teenagers and young adults "So, start off by saying, 'I know you are going to roll your eyes, but I need you to listen because this is important'. Do not get put off by your child saying, 'Oh, no!' – you have the right to fulfil your parental duty.

"Teenagers need to understand that there is no 'point of no return'. At any stage, either party can stop and say, 'I do not want to do this'. You are not a prick-tease if you go three-quarters of the way and then say you don't want to continue. And if you are a boy and you hear 'No', stop straight away. Tell your teenager they should not be afraid to assert their sexual boundaries."

The uncomfortable truth is that most people who experience sexual violence, experience it from someone close or known to them, or perhaps someone who doesn't actually understand what consent is. In retrospect, following Emily's suicide, Drouet thinks that she was a naive parent. She'd tell her daughter to mind her drink wasn't spiked and not be out alone, but never discussed coercion or abuse. "I never said: 'this is what you should do if you find yourself in a relationship where you feel you're not free to do the things that you want to do, you're being put down all the time, you're being blackmailed or asked to do things sexually that you're not comfortable with," she said.

Another thing to do as a parent is to make sure your child feels able to talk to you without judgment or blame. According to Edmonds, until you start talking to victims, you don't realise "how little you know – the hurt, the secrecy, the guilt, the whole gamut is just awful." Sex education in schools increasingly covers consent, but this needs bolstering from parents to equip your child with practical information about support services on offer. Universities are, though, increasingly providing a reporting function for anyone subjected to any kinds of abuse on campus. Make sure your child knows how to access contraceptive services and sign up to a GP as soon as possible.

Happy ever after

Finally, remind yourself that romance isn't dead: university is the fifth most popular place for couples in the UK to meet, with one in 20 people meeting their partner there, according YouGov polling in 2025. And with university relationships less likely to end in divorce – as tracked by research from the Marriage Foundation charity – what starts on campus could last for a lifetime.

Cancel culture

We are used to public speakers being no-platformed on campuses from time to time but so-called "cancel culture" is adding another dimension to inter-student relations. Naming and blaming each other for misdemeanours, students act as judge, jury and executioner in their exclusion of others from social circles. Twenty-year-old University of Oxford student Alexander Rogers killed himself within a week of being shamed by university friends in 2024. His death followed a post-pub tryst, which the woman involved told friends had left her feeling "uncomfortable", though no formal complaint was lodged, while others explained he had "messed up" and they needed space from him. Shortly afterwards, the third-year material sciences student left a goodbye note describing an "unintentional but unforgivable" act.

The coroner, Nicolas Graham, thought the punishment of ostracisation played an influential role in his suicide. He cited an independent review commissioned by Rogers' college, Corpus Christi, describing an "established and normalised" culture in which "students could rush to judgment without knowledge of all the facts, could shun those accused, and a 'pile-on' might occur where a group would form a negative view about another individual". According to the report, "This culture was not limited to Oxford University. It is an issue for the higher education sector as a whole." The coroner urged ministers to take cancel culture – "the exclusion of students from social circles based on allegations of misconduct, often without due process or a fair hearing" – seriously.

Troubled minds

The proportion of students who disclosed a mental health condition to their university increased rapidly from under 1% in 2010–11 to 5.8% in 2022–23. Surveys of students where responses are confidential have found much higher rates of poor mental health than disclosed to universities. In a 2022 survey by the mental health charity Student Minds, 57% self-reported a mental health issue and 27% said they had a diagnosed mental health condition. A survey of 4,500 university students, carried out by the National Union of Students in 2022, found that nine in in ten said their mental health was impacted by the cost of living, and a quarter of students said financial worries were having a major impact on their mental health, as increasing numbers cut down on essentials. The consequences of mental health issues for students range from poor academic performance and dropping out of university to self-harm and suicide.

It's a lot to contend with when you are trying to find your way in life, with the added pressure to perform, to succeed and to not let your family down.

Anxiety, depression and suicidal feelings are the three most common mental health problems among students, according to Mind, the mental health charity. The onset of mental health conditions often overlaps with the age when most students go to university. "The start of a new academic year is a key pressure point. Students may be worried about their academic capability, establishing new friendships, or making ends meet financially," notes Jenny Smith, policy manager at Student Minds.

Tackling the load

There has been a lot of positive work to address mental health in universities and colleges – but they are autonomous institutions and therefore provision varies. Most commonly, students can access wellbeing services for low-intensity support, counselling services for those with moderate mental distress, and disability services for students who receive disabled students' allowances and have a diagnosed mental health condition.

All universities profiled in our *Guide* offer mental health services to students, and although provision and funding levels differ by institution, most have sharpened their focus on how best to support students. Many have a platform that allows students to self-refer for mental health help, so they do not have to go via the GP or any other channels. Therapies might be one-off counselling, or a course of sessions, or students might be referred to wellbeing self-help groups. Access to the Togetherall online mental health service is freely available to students throughout the country. Therapy pets have begun visiting campuses to lift people's spirits and some student welfare services prescribe physical exercise to improve students' overall wellbeing. Talks on managing procrastination or perfectionism are given by the welfare services at lots of universities and there are workshops available to help with study skills. Access to university-run mental health services is different to the NHS (though universities will refer students to the NHS if necessary) and many promise same-day triage appointments to anyone in need. However, a 2023 survey of 4,000 UK students by the Tab student news site and Campaign Against Living Miserably (CALM), a suicide prevention charity, found just 12% of respondents thought their university handled the issue of mental health well.

The diagnosis of neurodivergent conditions in students is another field that universities are increasingly on the ball about. At Newcastle University, a Neurodevelopmental Assessment Service (NDAS) assesses and diagnoses attention deficit hyperactivity disorder (ADHD) and autism on campus. More than 200 students approached it for an assessment in 2023. Dr Fiona Gullon-Scott, a clinical psychologist who launched the service in 2022 describes how students make it as far as university without a formal diagnosis, because they are bright and have been well scaffolded at home and school, "but at university, where there's very little structure and they're managing the minefield of new social situations as well as independent learning, they've found themselves unravelling." An ADHD diagnosis can result in extra time in exams, funding for specialist mentoring and reasonable adjustments to work deadlines, as well as medication in some cases.

How can parents help?

The role of a parent or guardian has never been more important. Family and friends are often the first to know when students are unwell. If your prospective student is worried about the future, tell them that they are not alone. Suggest that, while there are many things that are out of our control, they can always reach out to you with their concerns and to other people at university. Research what support is available to your child and spend time brainstorming helpful strategies together. For those consumed by money worries, practical help with creating a budget can help with their burden.

Student Minds has launched Student Space, offering free wellbeing resources and support via phone, text, webchat or email to all university students in England and Wales. For parents and carers worried about their child's mental health, the Parents' Helpline at Young Minds offers free, confidential advice. For other resources and information visit the Student Minds parents' FAQ page at **studentminds.org.uk/supportforparents.html**.

Digital personas

Even post-pandemic, this generation of students is experiencing the most online-based higher education experience to date. In the past decade, universities have increasingly seen coursework set, essays handed in and gradings taking place digitally. Lectures are recorded and uploaded onto student interfaces.

Along with online learning, students should be aware of the impact their online persona has. Posting on social media and messaging online is not private, and many students have been exposed in supposedly confidential group chats, or by statuses on a private profile. Once posted online – be it a compromising photo, crass opinion or cruel "banter" – then it is there to stay. Digital footprints are permanent.

Students at Durham rightly fell foul of this in September 2020, when a group chat containing multiple misogynistic, racist and discriminatory views was leaked. One student had his offer withdrawn. In a similar online exposure, 11 students at Warwick were suspended for making rape jokes, racist statements and antisemitic slurs in an online conversation.

Remind your child that things they post today may be seen not only by their university but by future employers. Caution them not to post anything they wouldn't be comfortable having read back to them in an interview, or in front of a lecture hall of peers.

Universities have social media guidelines for students and your child will be seen as a representative of the university, whether posting on a private page or not. Clue them up on this before they go and remind them that nothing is truly private.

Keeping an eye online

Your child is unlikely to accept you as a friend on social media sites or share everything with you. If you give them space, they are more likely to willingly talk to you when they want to. Encourage privacy settings so their posts can't be shared beyond the intended audience.

If you're concerned that they might be feeling isolated, stay in touch. The key is open dialogue and reserving your own judgment. Developing this relationship before your child goes to university will reap dividends as they navigate their time away.

Useful websites

For alcohol information: **alcoholimpact.nus.org.uk** and **www.drinkaware.co.uk**

For information about drugs: **talktofrank.com** and **ssdp.org**

For information around consent: **nusconnect.org.uk** and **revoltsexualassault.com**

For information about mental health services the first point of reference should be a university's student support services.

For more general information: **www.studentminds.org.uk**, **www.youngminds.org.uk** and **sobergirlsociety.com**

9 Coming to the UK to Study

"The UK is a wonderful and safe place to come and study. Our country is home to some of the best universities in the world," said Bridget Phillipson in a 2025 video highlighting the benefits of a UK university education and promoting the country's post-study work opportunities for international students. "An education from a British university has been the springboard to success for so many global trailblazers, from politics to business, from the arts to the sciences," the secretary of state for education noted, "In fact, dozens of current and recent world leaders studied here in the UK. And our universities have driven some of the most exciting and valuable research anywhere in the world." The message from the government to eligible students considering coming to UK universities is intended to be loud and clear: Britain's campuses want you.

Phillipson's reassurances follow government measures to tighten student visas, which came into force in January 2024, preventing international students on undergraduate degrees or taught postgraduate courses from bringing family members on a student visa, as the government looks for ways to get net migration numbers down. Even so, the Graduate Route visa – introduced in 2021 and allowing students to live and work in the UK for two years after graduation, or three years for PhD graduates – was reaffirmed soon after Labour came into power in 2024, to add to the appeal of the UK as a study destination.

As the government seeks to juggle the wider political agenda, the education secretary's stance reinforces an established pride in the strength of UK universities, which are widely considered one of the country's most important and successful exports: the UK is the second most popular global destination for international students after the US. Often hubs for students from over 100 countries, UK universities are renowned for offering high-quality teaching and research. Added to their academic gravitas, life on campuses up and down the country is welcoming and diverse.

The share of international students in the UK has steadily increased since the 1990s. According to UNESCO data there were more than 707,000 international students studying in UK higher education in 2023, which findings by the Migration Observatory at the University of Oxford support – these show that in the 2023–24 academic year, around 730,000 international students were studying in UK higher education institutions, representing a quarter of all those studying in UK universities. That was 4% less than in the year before, when the number of international students in British universities reached a record high, and reflects the government measures to tighten student visas, which came into force in January 2024.

Brexit triggered the withdrawal of home fee status for EU undergraduates, meaning that students from the EU have had to pay significantly higher international fees since 2021. Consequently, the end of free movement has more than halved the footfall of European undergraduates on British campuses: in 2024, there were around 22,000 EU applications to undergraduate courses in the UK, 58% fewer than in 2020. But the recent growth – and slight subsequent decline – in the total number of international students was mostly driven by those coming from non-EU countries, whose number more than doubled between 2018-19 and 2022-23.

India overtook China to be the largest single source of international students in 2023-24. Taken together, India and China sent over 40% of all international students to the UK (22.7% and 20.5% respectively), equating to 316,000 students. Students from Nigeria represented the third-biggest group, followed by those from Pakistan. The figures include postgraduates (the fastest-growing group) as well as undergraduates (who are the focus of our *Guide*). Within the European Union, Ireland sends more students to UK providers than any other EU country. It is hoped that online learning may help re-engage students from the EU. There is also the GREAT Scholarships system for postgraduate students from 18 countries around the world, including three in the EU. Some UK universities also offer their own scholarships and bursaries to support EU students.

The range of tuition fees charged by each university for international students (which includes students from EU countries) is listed with its dedicated university profile in Chapter 12 of our *Guide*. Most fall broadly between around £11,000 and £25,000, with classroom-based subjects such as the humanities at the cheaper end. Subjects such as the engineering disciplines can cost over £35,000 while medical degrees can reach over £57,000.

International students enrich the UK higher education system, both culturally and financially, contributing to the national economy – creating net economic benefits of £37.4 billion, according to estimates by economic consultancy London Economics. There are intangible benefits too. International students give institutions access to a wider pool of talent. As graduates, they either contribute to wealth creation here or return home with an attachment to Britain that can develop into trade, investment or political capital on the world stage later down the track. According to the 2025 Soft-Power Index analysis by HEPI/Kaplan, 59 world leaders (defined as monarchs, presidents and prime ministers) studied in the UK; only the United States takes credit for more.

Why study in the UK?
There is much to recommend a degree in Britain. It is home to four of the world's top ten institutions and 17 in the top 100, as recognised by the QS 2026 World University Rankings, while Times Higher Education's World University Rankings 2026 have Oxford in first place globally and include 26 British universities in the top 200. Students throughout UK universities benefit from being immersed in the English language, and global surveys have shown that British universities are seen to offer high quality in a relatively safe and diverse environment. London was the QS Best Student City for six years running and ranks third in the 2026 league table, where it remains top in Europe. Degree courses here, both undergraduate and postgraduate, are shorter than the average length worldwide, which helps balance our relatively high living costs. The fall in the value of the pound recently has added to the country's appeal.

As well as the strong reputation of UK degrees and the opportunity to be taught in and soak up the English language, research shows that most international graduates are well-rewarded by studying in the UK. A report by Universities UK, published in 2024, found that "international graduates clearly value their UK study experience, recognising that the high quality learning experience opens doors for positive career outcomes and progression. Most international students find a job soon after graduating and are satisfied with their role and benefits."

The report detailed the perspectives and experiences of over 10,000 international graduates from 196 countries and territories. Results showed that 59% of respondents chose to study in the UK because of the perceived quality of the study experience, and the majority reported that the reality lived up to the expectation. Nearly three-quarters (73%) of those surveyed felt that the Graduate Route visa met their expectations, reporting higher job satisfaction compared to those on other visa types, and 71% felt a lasting connection with the UK, while 57% said they were more likely to engage in business with the UK due to their educational experiences.

The top countries for sending international students to the UK

EU countries (top 20)		% of international students	Non-EU countries (top 20)		% of international students
Ireland	9,690	1.3	India	166,310	22.7
France	8,680	1.2	China	149,885	20.5
Italy	7,160	1.0	Nigeria	57,505	7.9
Spain	7,110	1.0	Pakistan	45,720	6.2
Germany	7,105	1.0	United States	23,250	3.2
Greece	4,155	0.6	Hong Kong (Special Administrative Region of China)	17,250	2.4
Romania	4,130	0.6			
Cyprus (European Union)	3,715	0.5	Malaysia	12,760	1.7
Poland	3,665	0.5	Nepal	12,715	1.7
Portugal	2,895	0.4	Bangladesh	12,285	1.7
Netherlands	2,240	0.3	Saudi Arabia	9,680	1.3
Belgium	1,830	0.2	United Arab Emirates	8,535	1.2
Bulgaria	1,555	0.2	Canada	7,840	1.1
Sweden	1,490	0.2	Sri Lanka	7,250	1.0
Czech Republic	1,240	0.2	Kuwait	6,640	0.9
Hungary	1,085	0.1	Turkey	6,555	0.9
Austria	1,065	0.1	Singapore	6,500	0.9
Lithuania	935	0.1	Thailand	6,180	0.8
Gibraltar	915	0.1	Ghana	5,760	0.8
Slovakia	820	0.1	Korea (South)	5,270	0.7
			Indonesia	4,660	0.6
Total (all non-UK EU)	**71,480**		**Total (all non-EU)**	**572,550**	

Note: First degree non-UK students

Students who take the plunge to travel abroad to study are likely to be bright and highly motivated, so some positivity in such students' outcomes is to be expected. And, unless they have government scholarships, most international students have to be from relatively wealthy backgrounds to afford the fees and other expenses involved.

International student satisfaction

In the latest survey by Etio (formerly i-graduate), the student polling organisation, 90% of international students declared themselves satisfied with their experience of UK universities, 80% said they would recommend their institution and 86% said their programme was good value for money (each metric in line or slightly above the global benchmarks). Career and employability aspects featured strongly in their feedback. Satisfaction with all aspects of careers support – such as advice and guidance on careers, training, opportunities for placements and networking with alumni – all scored higher than the global benchmarks. Library services, feeling safe and secure on campus, and the ability to submit work remotely were also high-scoring areas for UK universities among the international students surveyed.

The number of students taking UK degrees through a local institution, distance learning or a full branch campus of a UK university was already growing even before covid's acceleration of blended online learning. Around 30 UK universities have a physical presence overseas and the success of these international hubs has led to the formation of a UK University Overseas Campuses Network, representing institutions providing a British education to more than 60,000 students. Most branch campuses are in Asia or the Middle East. Coventry – among the most popular UK universities with international students – has a campus in Poland.

Where to study in the UK

Most of the UK's universities and other higher education institutions are in England. Of the 133 universities profiled in this *Guide*, 109 are in England, 15 in Scotland, seven in Wales and two in Northern Ireland. Fee limits in higher education for UK and EU students are determined separately in each administrative area. All undergraduates from outside the UK are now charged the international rate of fees. Within the UK, the cost of living varies by geographical area. London is home to University College London, the most popular university with international students for ten years running, even though it is in the most expensive city. Incoming students should find out as much as they can about what living in Britain is like. Further advice and information is available through the British Council at its offices worldwide, at more than 40 university exhibitions that it holds around the world every year, or at its Education UK website: **study-uk.britishcouncil.org**. Also useful is the information provided by the UK Council for International Student Affairs (UKCISA) at **ukcisa.org.uk**.

Universities in all parts of the UK invest heavily in the best academic staff, buildings and equipment, and take part in rigorous quality assurance monitoring. The Office for Students is the chief regulatory body for higher education in England, overseeing organisations such as the Quality Assurance Agency for Higher Education (QAA), which remains the arbiter of standards. Professional bodies also play an important role in relevant subjects.

Although many people from outside the UK associate British universities with Oxford and Cambridge, the reality at most higher education institutions is quite different. Some universities do still maintain ancient traditions, but most are modern institutions that place at least as much emphasis on teaching as on research and offer many vocational programmes,

The universities most favoured by EU and non-EU students

Institution (top 20)	EU students	Institution (top 20)	Non-EU students
University College London	1,840	University College London	10,730
Ulster University	1,550	Manchester	8,890
Edinburgh	1,545	King's College London	6,785
King's College London	1,520	Coventry	6,710
Warwick	1,065	Edinburgh	6,610
Bath	1,015	University of the Arts, London	6,600
Queen's University Belfast	995	Leeds	5,040
Manchester	950	Bristol	4,785
Imperial College London	930	Liverpool	4,455
Queen Mary University of London	910	Imperial College London	4,350
University of the Arts, London	900	Birmingham	4,345
Glasgow	830	West of England	4,040
Westminster	720	Warwick	3,910
Exeter	645	Sheffield	3,885
Bristol	630	Durham	3,790
City, University of London	630	De Montfort University	3,500
Greenwich	595	Hertfordshire	3,430
Southampton	595	Glasgow	3,310
Aberdeen	585	Westminster	3,225
West London	585	Exeter	3,130

Note: First degree non-UK students

often with close links to business, industry and the professions. The table above shows the universities that are most popular with international students at undergraduate level. Although some are among the most famous names in higher education, others achieved university status only in the past 30 years.

What subjects to study?

Strongly vocational courses are favoured by international students. Many of these in professional areas such as architecture, dentistry or medicine take one or two years longer to complete than most other degree courses. Traditional first degrees are mostly awarded at Bachelor level (BA, BEng, BSc, etc.) and last three to four years. There are also some "enhanced" first degrees (MEng, MChem, etc) that take four years to complete. The relatively new Foundation degree programmes are almost all vocational and take two years to complete as a full-time course, with an option to study for a further year to gain a full degree. The table below shows the most popular subjects studied by international students. You need to consider the details of the degree you wish to study and ensure that you have looked at the ranking of that university in our main league table in Chapter 1 and in the subject tables in Chapter 10.

The most popular subjects for international students

Subject of study	EU students	Non-EU students	Total students	% of all international students
Business and management	9,500	64,830	349,835	27
Design, and creative and performing arts	4,760	17,210	147,020	8
Social sciences	4,665	19,220	193,360	9
Subjects allied to medicine	4,055	15,680	231,390	7
Engineering and technology	4,045	24,450	121,060	10
Computing	2,815	21,605	121,365	9
Law	2,375	11,920	96,125	5
Biological and sport sciences	2,370	6,740	90,385	3
Psychology	2,120	6,325	100,070	3
Language and area studies	1,625	3,280	57,675	2
Physical sciences	1,495	5,295	48,860	2
Medicine and dentistry	1,400	6,470	61,520	3
Historical, philosophical and religious studies	1,335	3,930	57,750	2
Architecture, building and planning	1,000	4,790	42,490	2
Mathematical sciences	990	6,750	33,285	3
Media, journalism and communications	890	5,035	32,215	2
Combined and general studies	515	980	18,295	1
Geography, earth and environmental studies (natural sciences)	415	1,880	24,465	1
Veterinary sciences	300	1,770	10,065	1
Education and teaching	275	2,080	43,325	1
Agriculture, food and related studies	255	900	9,800	0
Geography, earth and environmental studies (social sciences)	115	490	8,430	0
Total	**47,325**	**231,625**	**1,898,790**	

Note: First degree non-UK students

English language proficiency

The universities maintain high standards partly by setting demanding entry requirements, including proficiency in English. For international students, this usually includes a score of at least 5.5 in the International English Language Testing System (IELTS). Under visa regulations introduced in 2011, universities are able to vouch for a student's ability in English. This proficiency will need to be equivalent to an "upper intermediate" level (level B2) of the CEFR (Common European Framework of Reference for Languages) for studying at an undergraduate level (roughly equivalent to an overall score of 5.5 in IELTS).

There are many private and publicly funded colleges throughout the UK that run courses designed to bring the English language skills of prospective higher education students up to the required standard. However, not all of these are government approved. Some private organisations such as INTO (**intostudy.com**) have joined with universities to create centres running programmes preparing international students for degree-level study. The British Council also runs English language courses.

Tougher student visa regulations were introduced in 2012 and have since been refined. Although under the current system, universities' international students should not be denied entry to the UK, as long as they are proficient in English and are found to have followed other immigration rules, some lower-level preparatory courses taken by international students have been affected. It is, therefore, doubly important to consult the official UK government list of approved institutions (web address given at the end of this chapter) before applying.

How to apply

The information below is best read in conjunction with that provided in Chapter 5, which deals with the application process in detail. Some international students apply directly to a UK university for a place on a course, and others make their applications via an agent in their home country. But most applying for a full-time, first-degree course do so through the Universities and Colleges Admissions Service (UCAS). If you take this route, you will need to fill in an online UCAS application form at home, at school or perhaps at your nearest British Council office. There is plenty of advice on the UCAS website about the process. Whichever way you apply, the deadlines for getting your application in are the same.

Applications for most courses starting in September 2027 must be received at UCAS by 14 January, 6pm UK time, 2027 for equal consideration. Applications can be sent after this, but providers cannot guarantee they will be given equal consideration. Note that some art and design courses have a later deadline of 24 March. Applications for Oxford and Cambridge and for all courses in medicine, dentistry and veterinary science have to be received at UCAS by 15 October each year.

Entry and employment regulations

As discussed above, visa regulations have been the subject of continuing controversy in the UK. Recent governments have been criticised for increasing visa fees, doubling the cost of visa extensions, and ending the right to appeal against refusal of a visa. The current points system for entry – formerly known as Tier 4 which came into effect in 2009 – was replaced with the Student visa in 2020. Under this scheme, prospective students can check whether they are eligible for entry against published criteria, and so assess their points score. Universities are also required to provide a Confirmation of Acceptance for Studies (CAS) to their international student entrants, who must have secured an unconditional offer, and the institution must appear as a "Student sponsor" on the Home Office's Register of Sponsors. Prospective students must demonstrate that, as well as the necessary qualifications, they have English language proficiency and enough money for the first year of their specified course. This includes the full fees for the first year and, currently, living costs of £1,529 a month, up to a maximum of nine months, if studying in London (£1,171 a month in the rest of the UK). Under the current visa requirements, details of financial support are checked in more detail than before.

All students wishing to enter the UK to study are required to obtain entry clearance before arrival. The only exceptions are British nationals living overseas, British Overseas Territories citizens, British protected persons, British subjects, and non-visa national short-term students who may enter under a new Student Visitor route. All overseas students must now obtain a student visa, including those from EU countries, Iceland, Liechtenstein, Norway and Switzerland. Fees are currently £524 for applicants outside the country, plus an annual healthcare surcharge of £776 per year.

As part of the application process, biometric data will be requested and this will be used to issue you with a Biometric Residence Permit (BRP). You will need a BRP to open a UK bank account, rent accommodation or establish your eligibility for benefits and services or to work part-time, for example. The details of the regulations are continually reviewed by the Home Office. You can find more at **gov.uk/student-visa**.

Irish nationals have the right to live and work in the UK, under the UK-Ireland Common Travel Area arrangements. Irish students will not need to apply for a student visa or the graduate immigration route.

Bringing your family

Since 2010, international students on courses of six months or less have been forbidden to bring a partner or children into the UK. The latest reforms extend this prohibition much wider, to include all international students – other than those on postgraduate research courses. The family members these students are allowed to bring are their husband or wife, civil partner (a same-sex relationship that has been formally registered in the UK or your home country) or long-term partner and dependent children. It is important to check the latest information at **ukcisa.org.uk**.

Support from British universities

Support for international students is more comprehensive than in many countries and begins long before you arrive in the UK. Many universities have advisers in other countries. Some will put you in touch with current students or graduates who can give you a first-hand account of what life is like at a particular university. Pre-departure receptions for students and their families, as well as meet-and-greet arrangements for newly arrived students, are common. You can also expect an orientation and induction programme in your first week, and many universities now have "buddying" systems where current students are assigned to help new arrivals. Each university also has a students' union that organises social, cultural and sporting events and clubs. Both the university and the students' union are likely to have full-time staff whose job it is to look after the welfare of students from overseas.

International students with pre-settled/settled status under the EU Settlement Scheme and studying in the UK for six months or more have free access to the National Health Service (NHS). They also benefit from subsidised dental and optical care under NHS rules. Non-EU students have to pay a healthcare surcharge to benefit from this.

Those international students coming into the UK on a student visa or any other visa that included paying the Immigration Health Surcharge as part of their visa application are then also entitled to free access to the NHS and can register with a GP as a permanent patient.

At university, you will naturally encounter people from a wide range of cultures and walks of life. Getting involved in student societies, sport, voluntary work, and any of the social activities on offer will help you gain first-hand experience of British culture, and, if you need it, will help improve your command of the English language.

Useful websites
The British Council, with its dedicated Study UK site designed for those wishing to find out more about studying in the UK: **study-uk.britishcouncil.org**

The UK Council for International Student Affairs (UKCISA) provides a wide range of information on all aspects of studying in the UK: **ukcisa.org.uk**

UCAS, for full details of undergraduate courses available and an explanation of the application process: **ucas.com/international/international-students**

For the latest information on entry and visa requirements: **gov.uk/student-visa**
Register of student sponsors for educational establishments: **gov.uk/government/publications/register-of-licensed-sponsors-students**

For a general guide to Britain, available in many languages: **visitbritain.com**

10 Subject by Subject Guide

Not all undergraduate degrees from all universities are the same, even if they carry the same title. The topics, content and structure of courses vary widely, and each institution has distinctive approaches to teaching and assessment methods, contact hours and feedback. The relative effectiveness of such idiosyncrasies is reflected in students' reviews of their courses in the annual National Student Survey. Meanwhile, some academic departments are staffed by scholars conducting world-leading research in their field, and some courses establish links with industry partners that pave the way for covetable student work placements and graduate jobs. Students may also be interested in the academic calibre of their peers – as measured by the yardstick of the entry grades they achieved – to help estimate if a course is the right fit for them.

Such factors contribute to the quality of a degree – which applicants evaluating what and where to study should consider with at least as much weight as the prestige of a university. The quality of a course is particularly important in the immediate term while studying, because the extent to which a degree meets your expectations and ambitions will determine what you get out of it, and ultimately how well you do.

The 67 tables in this chapter drill down into the experience students are likely to have on their chosen course and the career prospects they might expect after graduating. The statistics harnessed to create our subject rankings create tables that help applicants weigh up the relative strengths of a certain subject at various institutions. Perhaps surprisingly, the best course in the subject you want to study might not be at the university with the highest league table position or the oldest foundation. Some fairly modest universities are specialists in niche areas – as evidenced by their research outputs, graduate career successes and feedback from current students. Or, it could turn out that the best course happens to be offered at a top-end, ancient university that you had not considered before. Or maybe the subject you loved at A-level is taught quite differently at degree level and would turn out an uninspiring choice for a three-year undergraduate commitment.

Employment prospects are another factor; they might be poor in the subject you love – but digging down into the outcomes of previous graduates at individual institutions may elicit those that buck the trend and bring the best of both worlds within sight.

This chapter offers pointers to the leading universities in a wide range of subjects. Many, such as history and mathematics, have their own table. Others are grouped together in broader categories, such as "subjects allied to medicine". If you see a dash (–) this denotes a score is not available because the number of students is too small for the outcome to be statistically reliable. Please also be aware that it is possible not all institutions listed in a particular area will be running courses in 2026–27, as university curriculums vary frequently.

The subject tables include scores from the National Student Survey (NSS). These distil the views of final-year undergraduates on various aspects of their course, with the results presented in two columns. "Teaching Quality" reflects the average scores in the sections of the survey focusing on teaching, assessment and feedback, learning opportunities and academic support. "Student Experience" is derived from the average of the NSS sections covering organisation and management, learning resources, and student voice. The three other measures used in our tables are research quality, students' entry qualifications and graduate employment outcomes. The Education table uses a fifth indicator, Ofsted grades, a measure of the quality of teaching based on Ofsted inspections of teacher training courses. None of the measures are weighted. A full explanation of the measures is given below.

Cambridge is again the most successful university among our subject rankings. It tops 15 of the 67 tables (including the joint lead with Edinburgh in Education); St Andrews heads 10 (including the joint lead with Oxford in English); Oxford and Glasgow lead in five each; the LSE and Imperial each come top in four subject tables; Strathclyde and Warwick top three tables each; and Durham and Strathclyde are each first in two tables. Fifteen other universities top one table each.

New this year, our Cultural Studies table incorporates courses within American studies, Celtic studies, East and South Asian studies, and Middle Eastern and African studies. Formerly occupying four separate tables, these subject areas continue to be referenced separately in Graduate Outcomes and salary comparisons in this year's *Good University Guide*. But their small student numbers have prompted their amalgamation into a single main Cultural Studies table.

Teaching Quality and Student Experience

The student satisfaction measure is divided into two components, that give students' views of the quality of their courses. Following consultation with our steering group, *The Times and Sunday Times Good University Guide 2027* used the NSS 2025.

i) Teaching quality: The teaching quality measure reflects the average scores of the teaching, learning opportunities, assessment and feedback, and academic support themes. Students answer on a scale from 1 (top) to 4 (bottom), and the score in the table is based on the percentage of positive responses (options 1 and 2).

ii) Student experience: The student experience measure is drawn from the average NSS scores in the organisation and management, learning resources, and student voice themes. Students answer on a scale from 1 (top) to 4 (bottom) and the score in the table is based on the percentage of positive responses (options 1 and 2).

Teaching quality is favoured over student experience and accounts for 67% of the overall score for student satisfaction, with student experience making up the remaining 33%.

Research quality

This information is sourced from the 2021 Research Excellence Framework (REF), a peer review exercise used to evaluate the quality of research of UK higher education institutions, undertaken by the Higher Education Funding Bodies. The output of the REF gave each institution a profile in the following categories: 4* world-leading; 3* internationally excellent; 2* internationally recognised; 1* nationally recognised; and unclassified. The funding bodies have directed more funds to the very best research by applying weightings. For the 2026 edition of our *Guide*, we used the weightings adopted by UK Research and Innovation (UKRI) and Research England, published in 2020. A 4* output was weighted by a factor of 4, and 3* was weighted by a factor of 1. Outputs of 2* and 1* carry zero weight. The score was weighted to account for the number of staff in each unit of assessment. The score is presented as a percentage of the maximum possible score of 3. To achieve the maximum score, all staff would need to be at 4* world-leading level. There are no scores in this category for Buckingham (as a private university it fell outside of the REF 2021).

Entry standards
These are the average mean tariff point scores on entry for first-year, first-degree students under 21 years of age based on A- and AS-levels, and Highers and Advanced Highers, and other

---

The subjects listed below are covered in the tables in this chapter:

- Accounting and Finance
- Aeronautical and Manufacturing Engineering
- Agriculture and Forestry
- Anatomy and Physiology
- Animal Science
- Anthropology
- Archaeology and Forensic Science
- Architecture
- Art and Design
- Bioengineering and Biomedical Engineering
- Biological Sciences
- Building
- Business, Management and Marketing
- Chemical Engineering
- Chemistry
- Civil Engineering
- Classics and Ancient History
- Communication and Media Studies
- Computer Science
- Creative Writing
- Criminology
- Cultural Studies (incorprating American, Celtic, East & South Asian, and Middle Eastern & African Studies courses)
- Dentistry
- Drama, Dance, Cinematics and Photography
- Economics
- Education
- Electrical and Electronic Engineering
- English
- Food Science
- French
- General Engineering
- Geography and Environmental Sciences
- Geology
- German
- History
- History of Art, Architecture and Design
- Hospitality, Leisure, Recreation and Tourism
- Iberian Languages
- Information Systems and Management
- Italian
- Land and Property Management
- Law
- Liberal Arts
- Linguistics
- Materials Technology
- Mathematics
- Mechanical Engineering
- Medicine
- Music
- Natural Sciences
- Nursing
- Pharmacology and Pharmacy
- Philosophy
- Physics and Astronomy
- Physiotherapy
- Politics
- Psychology
- Radiography
- Russian and East European Languages
- Social Policy
- Social Work
- Sociology
- Sports Science
- Subjects Allied to Medicine
- Theology and Religious Studies
- Town and Country Planning and Landscape
- Veterinary Medicine

equivalent qualifications (for example, the international baccalaureate). Data is from 2023–24. Tariff points refer to the score assigned by UCAS to grades from A-levels and equivalent qualifications that are used by universities to determine if their entry requirements have been met. Entrants with zero tariffs were excluded from the calculation. International A-level outcomes are not included in the HESA-sourced tariff point calculations. Each student's examination grades were converted to a numerical score using the UCAS tariff. The points used in the tariff appear on page 35.

Graduate prospects

This is the percentage of graduates in high-skilled jobs or undertaking graduate-level study 15 months after graduation, recorded in the Graduate Outcomes survey published in 2024 and based on 2021–22 graduates. A low score on this measure does not necessarily indicate unemployment – some graduates may have taken jobs that are not categorised as professional work. The averages for each subject are given at the foot of each subject table in this chapter and in two tables in Chapter 3, see pages 52–5. Note that in the tables that follow, when a figure is followed by a *, it refers to data from a previous year.

Average graduate salaries are published at the foot of the tables but these are not a component of the rankings' methodology.

Accounting and Finance

Often taken together, accounting and finance share a focus on matters monetary, business and management. Maths A-level is useful but not an essential requirement, except by a few leading universities. Business, economics and statistics are among the other A-levels that universities look for. For the fourth year running, the London School of Economics takes first place in our Accounting and Finance table. It outdoes all 99 other universities for the quality of its research and claims the best graduate prospects. Warwick is runner-up for the third year in a row, its overall position boosted by the second-best rates of student satisfaction with the broad experience. Entry standards vary considerably by institution, from 27 universities averaging over 144 UCAS points (equal to three As at A-level), topped by Glasgow with 226 UCAS points down to London Met which averaged just 74 UCAS points among its accounting and finance entrants. Aberystwyth (42nd overall) comes top for students' evaluation of teaching quality and the broad experience, while Dundee (13th overall) and Edge Hill (48th) place in the top four for both.

Following the LSE for graduate prospects is Bristol, with 92.7% of graduates in high-skilled jobs or further study 15 months after degrees, then Queen's, Belfast – which has been in the top three for the metric in this table for the past four years. More than 90% of graduates from Exeter, Bath, Sheffield and Warwick had also achieved these career outcomes when surveyed. But, perhaps surprisingly, accounting and finance overall do not set our graduate prospects measure alight, ranking 54th out of 70 subject areas.

An evolution is underway in the professional landscape, as Alnoor Bhimani, professor of management accounting, London School of Economics explains: "The field is seeing the biggest business transformation ever witnessed, with newly emerging accountability systems, novel asset classes and financial innovations, and disruptive AI-based digital technologies changing the form and way financial information is used. " Demand for the subjects is rising; finance degrees attracted nearly 51,600 applications for 2024 entry and accounting received around 57,200 (up 8% and 9% respectively year-on-year).

Accounting and Finance	Teaching quality %	Student experience %	Research quality %	Entry standards (UCAS points)	Graduate prospects %	Overall score
1 London School of Economics	87.3	90.6	69	190	96.9	100
2 Warwick	90.9	94.4	65.2	181	90	99.5
3 Bath	92	90.3	65.2	160	90.7	98
4 Strathclyde	86	85.8	52.5	210	83.6	96.6
5 Glasgow	78.9	83.8	57.2	226	84.7	96.1
6 City St George's	89.5	90.6	67.2	146	85.3	95.9
7 Leeds	88	89.7	62.3	158	84.9	95.6
8 Liverpool	92.7	93.7	58	147	79.5	95.3
9 Sheffield	89.1	91.1	48.8	154	90.3	95.1
10 Durham	90.1	89.9	55.8	140	89.8	95
=11 Edinburgh	80.6	84	59	187	85.5	94.4
=11 King's College London	88.2	88.6	63	144	-	94.4
13 Dundee	95.6	94	28.5	174	77.8	94.3
14 University College London	82.3	85.8	62.3	167	-	93.6
=15 Birmingham	84	88.2	55.2	149	87.5	93.4
=15 Queen's, Belfast	85.3	86.8	40.5	162	92.2	93.4

17	Manchester	80.8	83.7	66.2	157	85	93.3
18	Lancaster	85.2	86.6	59.2	137	86.2	93
19	Exeter	82.5	80.5	63.5	139	91.2	92.9
20	Loughborough	84.7	90.3	49.2	143	87.7	92.8
21	Newcastle	85.8	86	40.5	146	87.9	91.8
22	Southampton	87.1	88.9	52	134	78.8	91.7
23	Bristol	79.4	82.6	46	153	92.7	91.5
24	Ulster	90.2	86.2	45.8	122	82.9	91.4
25	Surrey	87.2	88.7	54.8	127	76.2	91.2
26	Cardiff	82.3	85.3	56	151	75.9	91.1
27	Stirling	82.5	79	38.2	173	84.3	91
=28	Aberdeen	85.4	87.3	32.2	158	79	90.4
=28	Nottingham	80	80.8	46.8	149	86.9	90.4
30	Reading	84.5	86.5	46.2	124	84.3	90.2
31	Swansea	91.7	91.8	38.8	117	74.5	90.1
32	Heriot-Watt	78.7	83.7	38.2	170	80.9	89.9
33	Aston	85.1	86.4	43.5	125	79.2	89.4
34	Sussex	86	85.1	50.7	123	72.9	89.3
35	Leicester	87.6	86.8	45.8	116	75.1	89.2
36	Portsmouth	92.8	94	37.8	104	69	88.9
37	Queen Mary, London	83.1	82.6	53.2	137	68.8	88.7
=38	East Anglia	82.5	80.3	57.8	117	76.1	88.6
=38	Royal Holloway	87.1	88.1	43	122	70.5	88.6
40	Edinburgh Napier	84.9	90.3	20	155	74.1	88.4
41	Robert Gordon	88.9	84.8	19	182	60.3	88.3
42	Aberystwyth	96.2	94.9	22.8	96	-	88.2
43	Liverpool John Moores	92.1	91.2	21	114	72.4	87.7
=44	Glasgow Caledonian	83.3	83.3	25.8	173	65.2	87.6
=44	Manchester Metropolitan	90	89.3	42.8	115	60.3	87.6
46	Nottingham Trent	89.6	87.1	34.2	106	71.8	87.4
47	Lancashire	91.7	89.1	28.2	118	64.3	87.1
48	Edge Hill	94	94.2	21	118	60	86.9
49	Kent	83	80.5	37.2	117	77.9	86.8
=50	Gloucestershire	90.9	87.7	8.8	112	80.6	86.7
=50	Plymouth	89.2	93.9	28.7	108	65.4	86.7
=52	Keele	87.2	88.3	24.8	101	74.1	85.9
=52	Oxford Brookes	84.8	86.5	26	108	75.8	85.9
54	Chester	87.5	87.1	25.2	104	72.3	85.8
55	Wolverhampton	91.4	92.8	20.2	98	64.9	85.5
56	Essex	82.8	84.5	39.8	113	65.1	85.4
57	Northumbria	79	82.4	28.2	122	77.3	85.2
58	SOAS, London	83.9	76.4	44.2	109	-	85.1
59	Hull	85.3	91.1	29.5	97	67.4	85
60	Hertfordshire	87.2	89	29	108	59.8	84.8
=61	West of England	86	84.1	27.3	110	66.5	84.7
=61	York	71.9	74.3	50.5	147	-	84.7
63	Greenwich	87.9	87.6	33.2	99	58.5	84.5
64	Westminster	82.9	86.3	37.5	114	57.4	84.3

Accounting and Finance cont.

	Teaching quality %	Student experience %	Research quality %	Entry standards (UCAS points)	Graduate prospects %	Overall score
=65 Bangor	84.5	78.7	32.2	116	61.4	83.9
=65 Roehampton	87.3	81.5	32.8	90	-	83.9
=65 South Wales	87.8	86.2	9	113	67.8	83.9
=65 Winchester	88.8	85	22.2	98	64.2	83.9
69 Staffordshire	82.3	80.7	38.8	-	60	83.7
=70 Brunel	85	81.2	30.2	105	61.2	83.4
=70 Coventry	85	84.4	33.2	97	59.7	83.4
=70 Salford	87.7	88.6	24.8	111	51.8	83.4
=73 Bedfordshire	90.7	90.9	22	97	52.2	83.3
=73 Lincoln	85.7	78.2	25	105	65.8	83.3
75 Derby	87.9	89.1	18	96	60.4	83.1
76 East London	91.6	90.1	11	94	58	82.9
77 Middlesex	83.8	82.6	46.2	94	50.9	82.8
78 West of Scotland	88.1	85.8	10.5	123	53.2	82.5
79 Teesside	92.4	84	-	96	63.7	82.1
=80 Sheffield Hallam	76.9	76.4	23.5	109	73.5	82
=80 Sunderland	92.3	89.7	-	106	53.8	82
82 Brighton	79.6	77.2	28.5	95	68.9	81.8
=83 Bournemouth	77.7	77.8	23	97	73.3	81.6
=83 Leeds Beckett	85.1	82.4	8.2	105	64.4	81.6
=85 Bradford	77.7	81.6	38.2	112	52.1	81.5
=85 Kingston	83.8	82.7	24	101	55.6	81.5
=85 Northampton	92.6	93.3	1.2	87	53.8	81.5
88 Worcester	88.8	77	12.5	98	-	81.4
89 York St John	79.5	69.4	9.8	106	81.2	81.2
90 London South Bank	84.1	85.3	21.5	104	49.9	81
91 Huddersfield	78.8	76.5	23.2	110	62.2	80.9
92 Greater Manchester	86.4	81.5	0	-	66	80.7
93 De Montfort	84.5	83.3	19	89	56.9	80.6
94 West London	87.1	88.6	-	104	52.3	80.2
95 Anglia Ruskin	83.1	81.6	45.8	76	42.7	80.1
96 Canterbury Christ Church	82.7	75.1	13.2	96	62.2	79.8
97 Birmingham City	82.7	83.6	11.2	115	47.8	79.6
98 Cardiff Metropolitan	80.7	83.9	14	99	54.5	79.4
99 Abertay	76.9	82.1	-	106	62.1	78.2
100 London Metropolitan	70.7	79	22	74	55.8	75.7

Employed in high-skilled job	43%	Employed in lower-skilled job		26%
Employed in high-skilled job and studying	10%	Employed in lower-skilled job and studying		3%
Studying	3%	Unemployed		6%
High-skilled work (median) salary	£26,750	Low/medium skilled salary		£20,000

Aeronautical and Manufacturing Engineering

The courses under this category focus predominantly on aeronautical or manufacturing engineering (often called production engineering) but the table also contains some courses with the mechanical title. Most courses require maths and physics, other desirable subjects include further maths, chemistry, computer science, and design technology. An awareness of AI methods is also increasingly useful, notes Professor Ian Craddock, head of the School of Civil, Aerospace and Design Engineering, University of Bristol, who says: "Our graduates will develop new ways of generating power from wind and waves; reduce the carbon emissions of our air travel through the introduction of electric and hydrogen-powered aircraft; help protect vulnerable communities worldwide from rising sea levels; and deploy AI to improve recycling of precious raw materials."

Imperial tops the table for the fifth year running, its position boosted by having the top research rating in the subjects as well as the second-best graduate prospects. Southampton moves up two places to rank third place this year, while Cambridge is steady in the runner-up spot. Fifth-place Sheffield is in the top four for both measures of student satisfaction: teaching quality and the broad experience, metrics topped by West of Scotland – in 17th place overall and the highest-ranked post-1992 university.

Entry standards can be stiff: led by Cambridge with 222 UCAS points averaged by entrants, a third of the universities in our table average over 144 UCAS points, although there are still some places to be found with more modest grades – such as at Nottingham Trent, which ranks 21st overall and averages 104 UCAS points.

Subjects categorised by UCAS as aeronautical and aerospace engineering have attracted rising demand, which neared 27,000 in 2024, when over 20,400 students gained offers. Production and manufacturing engineering drew over 11,000 applications in the same admissions cycle, and just around 9,500 received offers.

With average starting salaries of £30,000 the subjects rank =5th and they place 20th in our graduate prospects measure, based on almost two-thirds of graduates being in high-skilled jobs when surveyed 15 months after their degree and around one in ten engaged in further study.

Aeronautical and Manufacturing Engineering	Teaching quality %	Student experience %	Research quality %	Entry standards (UCAS points)	Graduate prospects %	Overall score
1 Imperial College	85.8	85.6	81	213	98.1	100
2 Cambridge	81.3	82.1	77.2	222	97	98.5
3 Southampton	88	86.7	70	168	94.3	95.3
4 Bristol	80.7	78.7	68	200	94.6	94.8
=5 Sheffield	88.5	89.2	66.8	169	86.2	93.6
=5 University College London	80.8	79.4	70	184	-	93.6
7 Nottingham	87	84.1	59	154	91.5	91.8
8 Heriot-Watt	77.5	78.3	55.5	196	-	91
9 Bath	77.9	75.4	49.5	190	94.4	90.7
10 Glasgow	71.4	65.8	61.5	210	91.4	90.5
11 Manchester	74.4	67.6	63	185	89.7	89.4
12 Loughborough	84.9	83.6	46.5	154	89.2	89.1
13 Queen's, Belfast	81.8	80.3	51	159	86.2	88.4
=14 Leeds	81.1	81.9	64.8	168	72.6	87.9
=14 Liverpool	80.1	78.7	57	144	87.9	87.9

Aeronautical and Manufacturing Engineering cont.

	Teaching quality %	Student experience %	Research quality %	Entry standards (UCAS points)	Graduate prospects %	Overall score
16 Surrey	81.1	78.4	55.2	137	88.2	87.4
17 West of Scotland	98.6	90.3	16.5	133	-	86.8
18 Sussex	86.7	84.5	29.5	141	84.6	85.6
=19 Swansea	85	80.6	48.8	129	79.7	85.4
=19 Ulster	82.5	76.1	49.8	125	85.4	85.4
21 Nottingham Trent	83.6	81	59	104	-	85.2
22 Strathclyde	64.8	65.4	52.8	-	100	84.7
23 Queen Mary, London	75	70.5	66	146	76.1	84.6
24 Leicester	80.3	74.7	39.8	125	85.5	83.5
25 Portsmouth	92.3	88.9	21	120	77.2	83.3
26 Aston	84.8	70.7	35.2	120	84.6	83
27 Brighton	86.1	80.9	36.5	106	80.2	82.6
28 Sheffield Hallam	82.3	74.3	30	117	85.1	82
29 De Montfort	88.5	85.5	21.8	95	-	80.2
30 Teesside	84	85.7	18.8	106	77.8	79.8
31 Coventry	78.5	67.6	23.5	116	84.3	79.3
32 East London	81	77.4	21.2	121	-	79.1
33 Hertfordshire	78.9	79.2	33	113	70.9	78.8
=34 Brunel	69.6	70.7	33	125	80	78.5
=34 City St George's	78.7	77.9	32.5	116	69.2	78.5
36 Salford	73.3	66.4	33.2	116	79.7	78.3
37 South Wales	86.3	78.5	26.8	110	63.8	78.1
38 West of England	68.5	61.9	30.8	123	84.2	77.8
39 Birmingham City	78.6	79.2	17.5	119	70.3	77.1
40 Sunderland	82.8	75.6	29.2	-	60.9	76.9
41 Greater Manchester	77.5	66.6	22	122	-	76.7
42 Lancashire	75.6	68.7	23	116	73.5	76.5
43 Kingston	81.5	78.1	17.2	110	67	76.3
44 Staffordshire	74.7	77	25.5	104	55.7	72.8
45 Huddersfield	62.9	59.8	32.5	116	-	72.4
46 Wolverhampton	71.1	58.7	18.2	91	70.6	71.4
47 Derby	76.4	62.2	14	116	49.2	69.8

Employed in high-skilled job	65%	Employed in lower-skilled job		13%
Employed in high-skilled job and studying	2%	Employed in lower-skilled job and studying		0%
Studying	8%	Unemployed		5%
High-skilled work (median) salary	£30,000	Low/medium skilled salary		£22,000

Agriculture and Forestry

Agriculture and its related disciplines involve developing solutions for sustainably feeding the growing population while protecting the environment. "The scientific evidence is unequivocal: we have exceeded our planetary boundaries in terms of climate change, biodiversity loss and natural nutrient cycles," comments Professor Michael Lee, deputy vice-chancellor, Harper Adams University.

Bangor takes the lead in our new Agriculture and Forestry table, up from third place last year, its position buoyed by strong performance across the table including the second-highest entry standards and research quality that is outdone only by Queen's, Belfast – runner-up this year after four years at No 1. The most satisfied students are at Nottingham Trent, which leads on both measures derived from the National Student Survey: teaching quality and wider undergraduate experience. Nottingham, which topped the table five years ago, settles for fourth place this year, while Newcastle moves up a place to third. Ranking eight, Harper Adams (which comes top for graduate outcomes) is ahead of the other two specialist institutions in the table, Hartpury and Royal Agricultural.

Perhaps showing early signs of the "Jeremy Clarkson effect" reported by the Royal Agricultural University, which in September 2025 noted increased applications to its rural land management degree. Demand for places to study agriculture degrees more broadly across all universities edged up a little in 2024 – to over 6,800 and most (around 5,800) received an offer and close to 2,000 new students enrolled. Forestry and arboriculture attract much smaller numbers, with just 240 applicants and 85 new undergraduates in 2024.

The two subjects place 41st out of the 70 subjects in our graduate prospects ranking, based on more than six in ten graduates working in high-skilled jobs and/or furthering their studies 15 months after degrees. Average early career salaries of £26,000 compare more favourably still – ranking agriculture and forestry =28th.

Agriculture and Forestry	Teaching quality %	Student experience %	Research quality %	Entry standards (UCAS points)	Graduate prospects %	Overall score
1 Bangor	81.2	76	67.5	144	-	100
2 Queen's, Belfast	69.9	72.8	69.2	146	70.2	98.1
3 Newcastle	81.8	79.2	42.8	140	70	96.7
4 Nottingham	86.8	85.2	52	138	62.5	96.5
5 Reading	90.5	86.8	42.5	122	-	95.5
6 Aberystwyth	79.2	82.1	48.8	126	-	94.2
7 Nottingham Trent	92.5	89.4	30.8	118	-	93.8
8 Harper Adams	82.2	76.1	19.5	122	75.1	92.9
9 Hartpury	91.6	86.2	-	106	64.3	87.3
10 Royal Agricultural	71.1	73.8	24.2	119	59.6	85.7

Employed in high-skilled job	53%	Employed in lower-skilled job	32%
Employed in high-skilled job and studying	5%	Employed in lower-skilled job and studying	0%
Studying	5%	Unemployed	3%
High-skilled work (median) salary	£26,500	Low/medium skilled salary	£24,500

Anatomy and Physiology

In a table dominated by the older institutions, Edinburgh occupies the top spot for the second year in a row, its rank driven by strong performances across all metrics without coming first in any individually. Aberdeen, the winner for the two years prior to Edinburgh's ascent and now in sixth place, leads graduate prospects and Dundee is in front for research and for student satisfaction with teaching quality. Bangor does best for students' evaluation of the broad experience, followed by Nottingham and then Leicester, while Queen's, Belfast takes second place overall. Oxford and Cambridge tied at No 1 in this table only four years ago, but neither university have sufficient data for the subjects to be included in our current edition.

Very few courses in this table actually have the title of anatomy or physiology – far more common are degrees titled biomedical science. The subject involves studying the structure and function of the human body, covering molecular and cellular mechanisms. A two-science minimum at A-level usually means biology and chemistry, although physics is also an option. The leading universities look for maths too. It is a good idea to attend university open days and look at websites to find a particular course of interest, as their content may differ across institutions.

Courses within biomedical science, anatomy and physiology attracted over 58,000 applications and around 11,000 new student admissions in 2024. In terms of jobs, "Anatomy and physiology provides good grounding for careers in relevant research, clinical scientist roles or scientific or medical information, marketing or sales," says Dr Katherine Brooke-Wavell, senior lecturer in human biology, Loughborough University. Anatomy and physiology rank 34th out of 70 subject areas in our graduate employment index, while average starting salaries of £25,900 put the subjects 36th.

Anatomy and Physiology	Teaching quality %	Student experience %	Research quality %	Entry standards (UCAS points)	Graduate prospects %	Overall score
1 Edinburgh	76.5	74.4	69.2	206	89.4	100
2 Queen's, Belfast	91.9	83	69.2	160	-	99.4
3 Dundee	94.5	90.1	78	170	73.9	98.4
4 University College London	81.6	82.6	64	186	-	98.2
5 Manchester	80.9	83.7	69.5	165	-	97.4
6 Aberdeen	87.3	89.7	33.2	207	90	96.7
7 Loughborough	81.8	87.2	66.8	159	83.1	95.8
8 Bangor	92.8	95.2	59.8	132	-	95.6
9 Swansea	76.3	74.5	66.8	115	97.8	95.2
10 Bristol	86.5	87.9	57.4	156	83.5	94.8
11 Glasgow	85.4	80.9	55.8	205	74.9	94.7
=12 Liverpool	84.8	87.9	46.8	151	88.2	93.7
=12 Newcastle	78.3	78	58.8	168	-	93.7
14 Nottingham	90.4	92.3	54	143	79.2	92.8
15 Leicester	87.7	92.2	53.5	127	-	91.9
=16 Manchester Metropolitan	81.6	79.9	51.2	126	86.4	90.8
=16 Portsmouth	87	84.5	57.5	116	-	90.8
18 City St George's	93.8	73.3	48.8	122	-	89.7
19 Essex	91.5	90.4	42.5	115	82.2	89.5
20 Leeds	77.4	75.8	52	149	76	88.1
21 West of England	79.9	78.9	42.8	117	74.2	84
22 Westminster	86.4	84.7	36.8	94	-	83.2
23 Huddersfield	85.9	77	22.5	133	-	82.6
24 Ulster	52.1	43.2	53.5	117	73.5	77.8

Employed in high-skilled job	42%	Employed in lower-skilled job		16%
Employed in high-skilled job and studying	5%	Employed in lower-skilled job and studying		2%
Studying	19%	Unemployed		5%
High-skilled work (median) salary	£27,000	Low-/medium-skilled salary		£20,000

Animal Science

Led by Glasgow at No 1 the top three of our table has been the same for three years running, except that this year UCL joins Manchester to tie in third place. Glasgow's rank is boosted by the highest entry standards by some distance, with new entrants averaging 216 UCAS points. Manchester, in joint third place overall, is top for research. Lincoln, the table's highest-ranked modern university, moves into the top 10 (eighth), its performance enhanced by coming top for student satisfaction with the wider experience and third for teaching quality, a metric topped by Derby with Nottingham Trent runner-up, while the Royal Agricultural College is bottom.

The best graduate outcomes – with 88.9% of graduates in high-skilled jobs or further study 15 months on from their degrees, were found at the Royal Veterinary College. Conversely, at Plymouth only 29.4% of graduates had achieved these outcomes. Harper Adams, in 19th place overall, leads the four specialist institutions, followed by Hartpury (20th).

This is the 11th edition of our Animal Science table, which was first launched to reflect the growing interest in the subject area and is extracted from the agriculture category – with courses ranging from veterinary nursing and equine science to animal behaviour. Students learn about animal physiology, behaviour and welfare, which Dr Beth Nicholls, principal research fellow in ecology and evolution at the School of Life Sciences, University of Sussex explains is "critical for sustainable farming, wildlife preservation and understanding zoonotic diseases. They play a vital role in improving livestock productivity, developing humane animal management practices and ensuring food security." Transferable skills include data analysis, report writing, and delivering effective presentations. High roller starting salaries are not what draws animal science students, however. The subject ties with creative writing at the bottom of our salaries ranking, with annual average wages of £22,000 for graduates. Early career prospects more broadly also fare poorly, relative to other subjects, ranking 67th out of 70 – with just under half of graduates employed in high-skilled jobs or postgraduate study 15 months on from their degrees. Demand has cooled in the past two years, and in 2024 animal science attracted just over 8,000 applications and around 1,900 students were accepted onto courses.

Animal Science	Teaching quality %	Student experience %	Research quality %	Entry standards (UCAS points)	Graduate prospects %	Overall score
1 Glasgow	87.2	82.1	64.8	216	73.5	100
2 Bristol	84.9	80.3	60.2	152	82.7	95
=3 Manchester	81.9	80.4	69.5	174	64.9	94.2
=3 University College London	73.8	74.1	64	205	-	94.2
5 Liverpool	82.5	82.1	68.2	150	73.5	93.9
6 Queen's, Belfast	83	74.2	69.2	160	69.2	93.3
7 Nottingham	80.3	85.7	52	145	82.3	93
8 Lincoln	92	89.8	42.5	120	65.7	90.8
9 Aberystwyth	88.8	87.8	48.8	121	66.3	90.7
10 Royal Holloway	87.3	84.6	43.5	130	-	89.6
11 Newcastle	77.8	80.3	58.8	124	71.9	89.1
12 Bangor	78.7	78.7	67.5	127	53.6	87.5
13 Sussex	78.8	68.5	49.8	135	69	87.3
14 Oxford Brookes	85.9	77.7	39.5	111	59.3	85.6
15 Plymouth	87	86.1	58.2	122	29.4	85.3
16 Liverpool John Moores	85.1	83.6	28.7	124	50	84.5

Animal Science cont.

	Teaching quality %	Student experience %	Research quality %	Entry standards (UCAS points)	Graduate prospects %	Overall score
17 Anglia Ruskin	88.4	77.8	17.8	119	54.2	83.7
18 Derby	93.1	87.6	-	111	54.8	83.6
19 Harper Adams	83.7	75.2	-	123	73.2	83.4
20 Hartpury	87.2	78.3	15.8	121	53.1	83.2
21 Royal Veterinary College	75.9	68.6	-	122	88.9	83
22 Nottingham Trent	92.1	87.6	-	122	42.9	82.3
23 Chester	78.5	76.6	6.2	118	64.5	81.2
24 Cumbria	90.2	75.3	-	101	54.4	80.4
25 Royal Agricultural	72.7	73.3	-	123	46.1	76
26 Cumbria	77.2	59.2	—	116	54.4	75.7
27 Royal Agricultural University	61.6	58.2	—	118	46.1	71

Employed in high-skilled job	35%	Employed in lower-skilled job	36%
Employed in high-skilled job and studying	3%	Employed in lower-skilled job and studying	2%
Studying	10%	Unemployed	5%
High-skilled work (median) salary	£23,400	Low-/medium-skilled salary	£20,000

Anthropology

Anthropologists investigate wide-ranging fields such as religion, gender, geopolitics, climate change, robotics and AI, human rights, social media, and capitalism. "By developing critical and flexible thinking, anthropology students explore stimulating subjects they did not know about, or specialise in topics they are already passionate about, leading to excellent opportunities of employment," says Dr Diana Ibañez-Tirado, senior lecturer in social anthropology, University of Sussex. When last surveyed 15 months after finishing their degrees, around six in ten graduates were working in high-skilled jobs, furthering their studies, or doing both – ranking anthropology 47th in the employment table of 70 subject areas. For average starting salaries, annual earnings of £25,200 place it 44th.

St Andrews retains the top spot in our new Anthropology table for the second year in a row, boosted by the best rates of student satisfaction with teaching quality and second-best scores for students' evaluations of the wider experience – in which Oxford Brookes (19th overall) comes top. Former No 1 in the table, London School of Economics (LSE), is runner-up this year – though still comes out top for research. Oxford has slipped 10 places to rank 11th, while third-place Durham is top for graduate prospects. East Anglia, in fourth place overall, is only marginally behind LSE for its research quality in anthropology, based on outcomes of the Research Excellence Framework 2021. The study of humans and human society, from the physical evolution of the human body and brain, to the political, cultural and linguistic practices of modern societies, anthropology has tended to be the preserve of old universities. Plymouth, in 18th place, is the top-ranked post-1992 university.

Led by Cambridge, where anthropology students averaged the highest entry standards of 192 UCAS points, over half of the table (12 universities) averaged over 144 UCAS points (equivalent to AAA at A-level). The subject attracts small numbers of students: four years of declining enrolments brought the number of new anthropology undergraduates to 1,025 in 2024.

Anthropology

	Teaching quality %	Student experience %	Research quality %	Entry standards (UCAS points)	Graduate prospects %	Overall score
1 St Andrews	92.2	90.5	49.2	189	-	100
2 London School of Economics	89.1	85.7	73.2	172	68.8	98.7
3 Durham	89.1	81.7	54.8	166	87.8	98.6
4 East Anglia	88.1	84.1	70.8	129	78.5	96.6
5 University College London	85	78.5	52.2	154	87.5	95.7
6 Birmingham	84.9	84	67	136	-	95.4
=7 Cambridge	83.6	69.1	40.8	192	86.9	95.3
=7 Manchester	87.5	85.9	61.3	154	71.7	95.3
9 Exeter	85.2	88.3	46.8	148	84.3	94.5
10 SOAS, London	89.1	75.3	61.8	125	-	93.5
11 Oxford	82.7	56.5	54.2	183	-	93.3
12 Aberdeen	87.7	80	42.2	163	-	92.8
13 Bristol	80.8	81.4	58.8	150	73.1	92.5
14 Sussex	85	85.9	53.8	137	69.3	91.4
15 Edinburgh	69.4	68.8	51.7	190	76.8	91.1
16 Brunel	91.8	88.4	34.8	-	70.6	90.6
17 Queen's, Belfast	85.9	81.6	41.5	143	-	90
18 Plymouth	84.4	81.2	47.1	120	-	88.4
19 Oxford Brookes	91.3	93.2	34.8	111	68.8	88.1
20 Bournemouth	90.2	85.6	50.5	102	61.1	87.6
21 Goldsmiths, London	86.2	68.8	51.5	128	56.2	86.3
22 Liverpool John Moores	86.2	81.2	28.7	120	-	84.5
23 King's College London	76	79.1	-	171	83.3	84.2

Employed in high-skilled job	43%	Employed in lower-skilled job	24%
Employed in high-skilled job and studying	5%	Employed in lower-skilled job and studying	1%
Studying	12%	Unemployed	6%
High-skilled work (median) salary	£26,775	Low-/medium-skilled salary	£19,000

Archaeology and Forensic Science

While most archaeology courses have no subject requirements, the leading universities will usually want a science. Geography and history are also relevant A-levels. Single honours archaeology degrees attracted 975 new students in 2024, while 2,370 students were accepted onto courses classified by UCAS as forensic and archaeological sciences. "Archaeology and heritage isn't just about the past; this is an exciting, evolving field in which skills traditionally used to uncover historical secrets are increasingly being applied to help us better understand our present and future," says Karina Croucher, professor in the School of Archaeological and Forensic Science at the University of Bradford, who adds: "Archaeology and forensic sciences involves geophysics, drones, analytical chemistry, CT scanning, the use of augmented and virtual reality to present and analyse data, and an array of scientific and humanities research approaches, leading to multiple career pathways, from teaching and museums to specialist roles in crime scene investigation and more."

Tenure at the top of our Archaeology and Forensic Science table has shifted to Aberdeen this year, its position buoyed by the top rates of student satisfaction with teaching quality and third highest entry standards (outdone by Glasgow and Edinburgh). University College London, in third place overall, has the best graduate prospects. Last year's No 1 – Oxford – has dropped to =15th. Reading ranks seventh overall but it is top for research quality, based on outcomes of the most recent Research Excellence Framework in 2021. For student satisfaction with the broad experience, Lancashire is unbeaten and comes third for teaching quality

In our graduate employment table of 70 subject areas, archaeology and forensic sciences rank 59th, based on over 54% of graduates working in high-skilled jobs and/or furthering their studies 15 months on from their degrees. More than a quarter (27%) were employed in jobs deemed "low-skilled", however. Starting salaries of £22,585 put the subjects fourth from bottom in the pay index of 70 subject areas.

Archaeology and Forensic Science	Teaching quality %	Student experience %	Research quality %	Entry standards (UCAS points)	Graduate prospects %	Overall score
1 Aberdeen	96.8	90.2	44.2	189	-	100
2 Durham	89.9	78.9	70.2	168	82.5	99.4
3 University College London	88.9	80.6	55.8	142	95.7	98.5
=4 Cambridge	88	70.2	71	180	-	98.3
=4 Glasgow Caledonian	94.4	91	61	160	75.8	98.3
6 Edinburgh	81.4	79	59.1	195	-	96.5
=7 Dundee	84.3	87.7	50.2	184	-	95.9
=7 Reading	92	87.7	76.5	114	-	95.9
9 Southampton	91.6	89	69.8	131	73.7	95.8
10 Exeter	90.3	90.7	58.8	138	77.5	95.6
11 Leicester	93.7	88	70	113	-	95.3
12 Glasgow	91	84.3	54.2	196	56.5	94.1
13 Newcastle	94.7	86.9	47.8	126	74.1	93.2
14 Robert Gordon	96.8	90.2	-	184	77.4	92.9
=15 Keele	90.7	86.1	48	128	76.6	92.8
=15 Oxford	84.9	55.1	61.8	172	-	92.8
17 Cardiff	86.8	83.1	58	133	72.7	92.3
18 Queen's, Belfast	88.4	85.3	51.2	135	-	92.1
19 Lincoln	92	90.8	27.8	112	81.8	90.9
20 York	80.8	74.5	63	132	73.6	90.8
21 Nottingham	87.9	78.2	51.5	125	-	90
22 Birmingham	80.4	76.7	54.2	144	-	89.7
23 West of Scotland	90.4	80.5	28.7	147	-	89.4
24 Lancashire	95.1	94.9	32.8	110	66.4	88.9
25 Northumbria	78.9	76.8	53.5	129	71.6	88.5
26 Liverpool	82	76.1	43.5	131	72.8	88.4
27 Bradford	89.2	85.6	38.2	118	-	88.3
28 Kingston	90.2	86.5	38.5	112	67.7	88.1
29 Nottingham Trent	91.8	84.3	-	132	78.9	87.4
30 Bournemouth	83.4	80.3	50.5	102	67.3	86.5
31 Hull	89.2	83.2	55.5	94	56.6	85.7

32	Liverpool John Moores	78.3	80.3	28.7	130	72.2	85.6
33	Kent	88.9	87.5	-	126	74.6	85.4
34	Wales Trinity St David	91.2	73.5	31	109	-	85.2
35	Staffordshire	86.9	76.2	31	104	67.7	84.7
36	Portsmouth	82.8	82.1	33	116	-	84.4
37	De Montfort	90.2	90.6	-	105	72.4	83.9
38	Winchester	91.6	73.8	16	98	64.6	82.5
39	Teesside	87.4	81.1	18.8	109	60.7	82.4
40	Derby	86.5	87.3	-	102	72.1	82.3
41	Canterbury Christ Church	83.4	76	17.8	106	68.1	82.2
42	West of England	87.1	84.1	-	126	63.9	82.1
43	Chester	87.2	78.8	22.5	107	57.9	81.8
44	Coventry	91.6	84.9	-	107	61.6	81.4
45	Anglia Ruskin	80.4	67.4	33.8	90	60.4	79.7
46	West London	74.5	71.1	-	117	73.7	79.3
47	Greenwich	87.5	75.3	-	110	54.5	78
48	South Wales	73	63.8	-	125	69.6	77.9
49	Wolverhampton	75.9	77.3	-	108	47.8	73.4

Employed in high-skilled job	40%	Employed in lower-skilled job	27%
Employed in high-skilled job and studying	4%	Employed in lower-skilled job and studying	2%
Studying	10%	Unemployed	6%
High-skilled work (median) salary	£23,500	Low-/medium-skilled salary	£19,000

Architecture

"This is a deeply interdisciplinary subject, combining humanities, arts, social sciences and technology," says Professor Flora Samuel, head of the Department of Architecture, University of Cambridge, "Whether or not you decide to be an architect – it is a tough and often poorly paid profession – a degree in architecture will set you up with a range of transferable skills, allowing you to pivot into a variety of jobs." Demand for architecture degrees increased in 2024, when the subject attracted over 35,300 applications and 6,035 undergraduates were accepted onto courses (up from 5,660 the year before). Early career trajectories are positive; two-thirds of graduates were in professional jobs 15 months after their degrees according to the latest data, which combined with around 10% in postgraduate study and/or a professional-grade job ranks the subject 19th out of 70 areas. Early career salaries compare less favourably however, with average annual earnings of £23,000 putting the subject in the bottom ten.

Loughborough tops the Architecture table for the third year running, its position boosted by the top graduate prospects – with 100% of graduates securing high-skilled jobs or furthering their studies 15 months on from their degrees. Loughborough also has the second-best research quality rating and top 15 rates of student satisfaction with both teaching quality and the wider experience. Runner-up Leeds is unbeaten for both measures of student satisfaction: teaching quality and the wider experience, in which East London (40th overall) is in second place. At the other end of the scale, architecture students at Lincoln reported the lowest rates of satisfaction with teaching quality, and those at Arts Bournemouth were least content with the broad experience. Sheffield is down one place to rank third in the main table this year. The highest entry standards are at Strathclyde (198 UCAS points) and range down to 94 UCAS tariff points averaged by entrants to East London. Cambridge leads the field in research.

There are usually no essential subjects required to study architecture, although the leading universities will look for a mixture of art and science, and a portfolio is essential. It takes most architects seven years to fully qualify, of which a degree is the first step. Such a timeframe asks a lot of students' dedication to the profession and of their financial wherewithal to support themselves. Course materials add to costs. Study time is spent drawing, making and researching through design.

Architecture	Teaching quality %	Student experience %	Research quality %	Entry standards (UCAS points)	Graduate prospects %	Overall score
1 Loughborough	94.1	85.8	72	177	100	100
2 Leeds	98.3	98.1	64.8	168	-	99.3
3 Sheffield	91.8	90.9	71.8	177	89.4	96.7
4 Edinburgh	84	82.3	59	188	92.2	94.4
5 Cardiff	85.3	86.1	67.5	163	92.1	94.2
6 Queen's, Belfast	95.1	91.4	36.5	160	96.3	93.6
7 Cambridge	77.3	69.2	74.8	187	88	92.6
8 Nottingham	86.6	71.3	59	169	91.5	92.5
9 Bath	84	79.2	49.5	181	92.1	92.4
10 Manchester School of Architecture	89.3	86.6	53.2	164	88.5	92.2
11 Liverpool	90.9	89.1	55.2	142	88.6	91.5
12 Strathclyde	86	75.4	50.2	198	81.7	90.8
13 University College London	88.5	73.2	61	167	82.8	90.6
14 Dundee	94.9	82.4	-	181	97	89.9
15 Oxford Brookes	88.3	86.1	33.2	150	91.3	89.2
16 Newcastle	84.9	78.8	56	144	85.5	88.7
17 Lancaster	80.1	62.4	59.5	158	-	88.4
18 Ulster	89.4	89.3	54.2	127	81.1	87.7
19 West of England	91.5	87.3	40.8	146	80.9	87.6
20 Liverpool John Moores	89.4	83	38.2	119	89.8	87.1
21 Arts London	75	71.4	46	152	91.2	86.9
22 Birmingham City	90.8	88.3	31.2	129	85.7	86.4
23 Sheffield Hallam	85.3	70.2	43.2	116	91.2	86.1
24 Coventry	80.9	76.3	54.2	115	88	86
25 Reading	81.8	67.9	53.5	133	-	85.9
26 Edinburgh Napier	80	78.3	38	160	83.1	85.7
=27 Brighton	81.6	75	53	112	87.1	85.4
=27 Kent	79.7	73.6	61	119	83.7	85.4
=29 Robert Gordon	85.7	70.8	14	162	89.5	85.3
=29 Westminster	89.8	87.1	38.2	128	80.2	85.3
31 Leeds Beckett	83.8	79.9	24.5	120	92.5	84.7
32 Kingston	82.4	76.1	63	132	73.6	84.5
=33 Creative Arts	87.8	81.7	41.2	118	81.1	84.4
=33 Salford	84.1	75.5	43.5	106	87.5	84.4
35 Wolverhampton	95.1	89.6	20	112	-	84.2
36 Nottingham Trent	85.9	77.9	38	115	84.5	84.1
37 Plymouth	76.7	66	49	116	87.3	83.5

=38	Greenwich	83.7	76.9	30	112	87.1	83
=38	Northumbria	84.4	79.3	25	135	82.5	83
40	East London	95.9	92.6	25	94	78.8	82.5
41	London South Bank	84.4	70.7	35	104	85.7	82.3
42	De Montfort	77.5	78.5	40.5	107	80	80.7
43	Portsmouth	80.1	76.5	41.8	109	75	79.9
44	Huddersfield	84.4	71.3	36.5	115	71.8	79.3
45	Gloucestershire	80.6	60.5	24	121	-	78.5
46	Lincoln	68.7	65.6	12.2	106	94.1	78.2
47	Anglia Ruskin	80.9	73.6	23.8	95	-	77.3
48	Hertfordshire	74.1	64.2	24.2	106	-	75.6
49	London Metropolitan	89.1	74.9	-	116	68.3	74.9
50	Arts Bournemouth	71.8	58.2	23	126	70.4	74.2

Employed in high-skilled job	67%	Employed in lower-skilled job	9%
Employed in high-skilled job and studying	5%	Employed in lower-skilled job and studying	0%
Studying	5%	Unemployed	8%
High-skilled work (median) salary	£23,000	Low-/medium-skilled salary	£20,000

Art and Design

Most art and design courses are at the post-1992 universities and/or the specialist arts institutions, but the older universities dominate the top 10 of our table due largely to their higher entry standards – although most artists would argue that entry grades are less significant than in other subjects. Selection rests primarily on the quality of candidates' portfolios and many undergraduates enter via a one-year Art Foundation course. Even the research-led Russell Group of universities do not require any essential A-levels, although they do advise that art and design subjects are preferred.

Oxford remains at the top of the Art and Design table for the fifth year running, its ranking boosted by results of the latest Research Excellence Framework 2021, which put it comfortably in front of all other universities in the table. Behind Oxford on research quality is Westminster, which sits 30th overall. Oxford also attracts by far the highest entry standards, with entrants averaging 228 UCAS points. Glasgow also averaged over 200 UCAS points and Newcastle (which topped the table five years ago) is only just behind with 199 UCAS points. At the other end of the scale only three universities (London South Bank, Winchester and Buckinghamshire New) have entry standards below 100 tariff points, on average.

In seventh place, Kingston is the highest-ranked modern university while Arts London, at 27th, places the highest of the six specialist institutions, ahead of Falmouth (=36th). Bangor leads for both measures of student satisfaction: teaching quality and students' wider experience. Otherwise, our National Student Survey (NSS) analysis found modern universities to have the edge over their older peers for satisfaction rates, with Liverpool Hope second for both, Glasgow Caledonian third for the broad student experience and Suffolk third for teaching quality.

Art and design are among the biggest recruiters in higher education, with more than 124,000 applications in 2024 and over 14,000 new students starting courses. Design studies is much the largest area while fine art – though it accounts for a far smaller proportion of students – still attracted 4,335 new starters in 2024. The subjects usually feature in the lower-reaches of employment tables, though there are 12 subject areas below them in our latest ranking of 70. For salaries the subjects are =62nd, based on average early career incomes of

£23,000. The trend for graduates to not necessarily proceed straight into high-skilled jobs tends not to be a surprise to artists and designers, who accept they may have a period in low-paid self-employment early in their career. Based on our analysis of the Graduate Outcomes survey, Winchester (80th overall) is top, followed by Loughborough (fourth) and University College London – which each had 80.8% of graduates already in professional jobs or further study 15 months after their degrees.

Art and Design

	Teaching quality %	Student experience %	Research quality %	Entry standards (UCAS points)	Graduate prospects %	Overall score
1 Oxford	80	77	88.8	228	-	100
2 University College London	92.5	87.8	64.7	198	80.8	98.8
3 Goldsmiths, London	91.8	87.7	57.5	171	72.9	93.1
4 Loughborough	84.7	80.5	51.7	172	81.2	92.9
5 Leeds	83.1	80.9	54.8	163	76	90.7
6 Dundee	86	76.8	57.2	193	66	90.5
7 Kingston	87.3	82.6	63	158	69.2	90.2
8 Newcastle	80.1	75.2	61	199	62.7	89
9 Manchester	87.3	86.7	63	136	68.4	88.6
=10 Manchester Metropolitan	85.6	82.6	51.7	145	72.7	88.5
=10 Sunderland	89.6	82.9	49.8	122	76.2	88.5
=12 Lancaster	81.7	77.2	59.5	159	-	88.4
=12 Reading	84.9	84	51.8	125	77.3	88.4
14 Edinburgh Napier	89.2	74.4	23.5	179	73	88
=15 Northumbria	87	80.2	45.8	141	73.7	87.9
=15 Nottingham Trent	88.1	85.2	53	126	72.5	87.9
17 Southampton	88.9	83.9	56.5	130	67.8	87.2
18 Glasgow Caledonian	91.9	92.1	13.8	172	68.3	86.8
19 Sheffield Hallam	87.9	81.4	57	125	67.9	86.5
20 Bangor	98.6	95.3	40.2	110	66.7	86.4
=21 Cardiff Metropolitan	84.8	77.1	56.2	124	70.8	86.2
=21 Edinburgh	84.9	81.5	54	160	61.5	86.2
23 Ulster	88.4	79.9	54.5	124	67.9	86.1
=24 Glasgow	59.2	56.6	68.8	202	-	85.6
=24 Robert Gordon	94.1	85.3	13.8	150	70.1	85.6
26 Coventry	82.8	75	54.2	119	72.7	85.5
27 Arts London	84.7	79.6	46	146	65.5	85.2
28 Bournemouth	84.3	84.2	38.5	100	78.7	85.1
29 Staffordshire	86.8	77.6	53.5	125	65.8	84.9
30 Westminster	85.5	83.1	75.5	131	55	84.8
=31 Canterbury Christ Church	95.1	91.8	38	104	-	84.6
=31 Worcester	89.3	82.7	19.2	125	75.2	84.6
33 Portsmouth	85.9	80.3	41.8	114	71.8	84.5
34 Teesside	89.3	82.4	49.2	123	63.2	84.3
35 Greenwich	84.2	79.9	30	114	76.9	84.2
=36 Falmouth	84.8	74.2	48.8	146	62	84
=36 Oxford Brookes	92.5	82.6	25.5	140	64.7	84

38	Liverpool John Moores		85.9	81.8	38.2	151	61	83.7
39	West of England		85.9	78.5	36	145	63.9	83.6
40	Lancashire		90.4	89	35.2	123	63.3	83.5
41	Abertay		81.6	74.9	-	173	73.3	83.1
42	De Montfort		86.9	80.3	32	121	68.3	82.9
43	Middlesex		88.9	80.6	41.2	110	64.8	82.6
=44	Aberystwyth		82.8	74.4	41	136	63.9	82.5
=44	Norwich Arts		85.6	80	38.8	126	63.8	82.5
46	Wolverhampton		89.3	83.4	35.2	134	59.5	82.4
47	Lincoln		85.8	78.2	43.8	118	63.8	82.3
=48	Birmingham City		89.1	84.6	31.2	130	60.9	82.1
=48	Brighton		79.2	72.2	53	131	62.6	82.1
=48	London Metropolitan		92.3	86.5	42.2	108	59.5	82.1
51	Gloucestershire		81.6	71.2	45	115	67.4	81.8
52	Huddersfield		81.7	73.7	30.8	128	68.3	81.7
53	South Wales		88.9	79.7	35.8	123	60.8	81.6
54	Leeds Beckett		86.1	79.8	29.2	114	67.3	81.5
55	Arts Bournemouth		87.4	82.8	23	150	57.7	81.1
56	Plymouth		77.6	68.8	26.5	125	70.4	80.2
57	Heriot-Watt		76.3	61.8	34.2	157	61.2	80
58	Buckinghamshire New		90	87.8	41.2	85	60.1	79.9
59	Chester		81.7	76.8	26.2	133	61.1	79.5
60	Liverpool Hope		95.8	93.3	12.5	124	53.2	79.1
61	York St John		76.9	64.3	5.8	126	75.6	78.9
=62	Greater Manchester		89.9	83.7	17.8	111	59.8	78.8
=62	Leeds Arts		87	82.3	6.2	142	59.1	78.8
64	Salford		86.7	80.2	-	131	64.9	78.7
65	Wales Trinity St David		86	76.2	20.8	127	56.9	78
=66	Creative Arts		78.8	69.4	41.2	125	56	77.9
=66	Suffolk		95.5	81.4	-	102	63.3	77.9
=68	Anglia Ruskin		85	73.9	31.2	112	57.3	77.8
=68	Bath Spa		83	72.4	18.5	120	62.3	77.8
70	Derby		84.2	66.3	19.5	107	64.8	77.5
71	London South Bank		85.7	77.5	-	98	70.6	77.4
72	Northampton		88.1	81.5	12.2	100	61.7	77.2
73	Cumbria		75.9	64	23.2	116	65.8	76.9
74	Hertfordshire		86	78.9	24.2	115	51.6	76
75	East London		83.5	78.5	14.8	108	55.2	74.8
76	Wrexham		83.4	65.3	3.2	122	56.9	73.9
77	Kent		85.6	74.7	-	111	55.9	73.6
78	Southampton Solent		83.1	72.2	-	109	57.6	73.3
79	West London		75.1	64.6	-	103	65.8	72.9
80	Winchester		59	47.1	-	95	81.5	72.2
81	Bedfordshire		66.1	49.5	-	110	68	71

Employed in high-skilled job	50%	Employed in lower-skilled job	30%
Employed in high-skilled job and studying	2%	Employed in lower-skilled job and studying	1%
Studying	3%	Unemployed	8%
High-skilled work (median) salary	£24,000	Low-/medium-skilled salary	£20,000

Bioengineering and Biomedical Engineering

Ageing populations, the demand for new treatments for chronic conditions and the need to respond rapidly to evolving disease challenges have brought about growth in biomedical engineering and bioengineering among universities worldwide over the past two decades. The discipline collectively involves a range of engineering and scientific skills, including some of the newest areas of science in genomics imaging and computing to meet those challenges. "It's about developing and using technology to enhance human health and improve quality of life. We apply maths and physics in context, bringing everything together in a practical way. We measure human signals to better understand the body, focusing on preventing and curing diseases, healthy ageing, and enhancing human potential," says Dr Markus Pakleppa, senior lecturer in biomedical engineering, School of Science and Engineering, University of Dundee – which retains the lead in our Bioengineering and Biomedical Engineering table, now in its fifth year of publication and extending to 25 universities, 11 more than two years ago.

Dundee's win is based on strong performance across the table's metrics, without coming top in any individually. The highest entry standards are at Cambridge (runner-up overall), while fourth place Imperial achieved the best results in the subjects in the latest Research Excellence Framework 2021. In 16th place overall, Nottingham Trent is the highest-ranked post-1992 university.

For student satisfaction with both teaching quality and the wider experience Sheffield (third overall) does best, followed by Hull and Essex respectively. At the opposite end of the scale, students at City St George's and Ulster expressed much lower rates of satisfaction in our latest National Student Survey analysis, and the universities share the bottom two spots for teaching quality and the wider experience.

Demand for the degrees increased for the fourth year running in 2024, nearing 9,000 applications, of which 1,500 new undergraduates were accepted onto courses. Graduate bioengineers may go on to develop prosthetics and biomedical implants, 3D medical imaging or image-guided and robot-assisted surgery – among a range of career pathways. Some biomedical graduates apply for places on the Graduate Entry into Medicine programmes. There are insufficient employment data so far for 11 out of the 25 universities in our table, of which Imperial stands out for achieving the highest rate (98.1%) of graduates in high-skilled work or further study 15 months on from their degrees, closely followed by Cambridge (97.2%) and Reading (96%). In our graduate prospects ranking of 70 subject areas, bioengineering and biomedical engineering sit 17th. Full-time further study accounts for a sizeable proportion (15.4%) of the 77.3% of graduates who were in high-skilled jobs and/or studying 15 months on from their degrees. The subjects rank 20th for starting salaries.

Bioengineering and Biomedical Engineering	Teaching quality %	Student experience %	Research quality %	Entry standards (UCAS points)	Graduate prospects %	Overall score
1 Dundee	87.3	85.6	78	216	-	100
2 Cambridge	80.4	80.8	73.5	222	97.2	96.5
3 Sheffield	94.5	90	66.8	162	92	95.9
4 Imperial College	79.3	77.5	81	185	98.1	95.2
5 Oxford	80.4	74.8	69.5	213	94	94.2
6 Southampton	86.4	84.8	70	161	-	94
7 Leeds	82	82.3	64.8	190	-	93.2
8 Strathclyde	89.3	83	52.8	211	84.3	93

9 Loughborough	83.3	83.7	66.8	150	92.5	91.9
10 University College London	77.1	75	64	171	-	89
11 King's College London	86	85.3	50	152	83.8	88.8
12 Essex	89.6	89.4	42.5	140	-	88.7
13 Surrey	83.3	81.8	55.2	126	-	87.1
14 Reading	80.6	79.4	54	104	96	86.9
15 Queen Mary, London	76.3	72.8	50.5	162	88.9	86.5
16 Nottingham Trent	82.3	80.5	59	104	80.8	85.7
17 Hull	91	87	36.2	108	-	85.2
18 Cardiff	75.2	74.8	54	139	-	84.1
19 Swansea	81.4	76.4	48.8	114	-	83.5
20 Ulster	72.6	68.1	49.8	131	89.1	83.3
21 Salford	84.7	83.3	37	121	74.8	83.1
22 Aston	78.6	73.9	46	124	-	82.3
23 City St George's	71.2	70.6	32.5	118	-	76.2
24 Birmingham City	82.6	85.5	-	104	65.2	74.7
25 Bradford	79.3	76.7	-	122	57.1	72.5

Employed in high-skilled job	58%	Employed in lower-skilled job		10%
Employed in high-skilled job and studying	4%	Employed in lower-skilled job and studying		0%
Studying	15%	Unemployed		5%
High-skilled work (median) salary	£28,000	Low-/medium-skilled salary		£22,000

Biological Sciences

Of the specialisms within the Biological Sciences grouping, biology is the most popular – with over 24,000 applications and nearly 4,000 new students in 2024. It is closely followed by molecular biology, biophysics and biochemistry, which had over 3,700 enrolments in the same admissions round, while zoology attracted more than 1,800 new students.

There has been growing interest in the study of ecology and environmental biology, which attracted over 11,000 applications for 2024 entry and 2,115 new student enrolments. Many of the leading universities will demand two sciences at A-level, or the equivalent – usually biology and chemistry – for any of the biological sciences.

For the 21st year, Cambridge tops the Biological Sciences table, its tenure strengthened once more by fiercely high entry standards – with new undergraduates averaging 224 UCAS tariff points. Cambridge also boasts the best graduate prospects and second-highest research quality rating. But based on the outcomes of the Research Excellence Framework 2021, it is Dundee that tops all 89 universities in our table for its strength in biological sciences research, while tying with Durham overall in ninth place. Performing strongly across all measures, St Andrews moves up a place to rank second, while former runner-up Oxford drops to fifth position.

The upper reaches of our table are dominated by universities with old foundations across the UK. In 22nd place, Glasgow Caledonian is the top-ranked modern university, while Ulster in Northern Ireland (41st overall) claims rates of employment second only to Cambridge – with 91.3% of its biological sciences graduates in high-skilled jobs and/or further study 15 months on from their degrees. The post-1992 universities do best on rates of student satisfaction, derived from the National Student Survey: Anglia Ruskin is top for teaching quality, followed by West of Scotland, while Edinburgh Napier is unbeaten for students' evaluation of the wider experience, followed by Gloucestershire.

Nearly one in five (19.1%) of biological sciences graduates were engaged in further study 15 months after the undergraduate degrees, according to our Graduate Outcomes survey analysis, while 39.1% were in high-skilled jobs and 4% were combining work with studying – placing the biological sciences in the lower half (44th) of our 70-subject employment index. For starting salaries, they place =46th.

Biological Sciences	Teaching quality %	Student experience %	Research quality %	Entry standards (UCAS points)	Graduate prospects %	Overall score
1 Cambridge	85.5	82.1	73.5	224	94.3	100
2 St Andrews	89	89.1	49.5	196	88.7	96.3
3 Strathclyde	87.2	84.3	65.8	216	78.8	96.2
4 Glasgow	89.5	84.6	55.8	210	82.2	96.1
5 Oxford	83.7	75.2	69.5	198	89.4	95.9
6 Bristol	89.3	90.2	67.2	163	83.2	95.4
7 Edinburgh	81.3	78.1	69.2	200	86.2	95
8 Sheffield	86.3	88.3	70.2	164	82.9	94.8
=9 Dundee	81.6	78.4	78	189	82.4	94.7
=9 Durham	90.4	84.9	44	178	89.6	94.7
=9 Loughborough	90.4	89.2	66.8	143	84.9	94.7
12 Queen's, Belfast	84.1	86.8	69.2	153	87.4	94.2
13 Bath	85.1	83.5	49.2	165	89.8	93.1
14 Imperial College	78.5	75.2	63.2	181	89.9	93
=15 Manchester	81.3	81.5	69.5	169	82.8	92.9
=15 Surrey	91.5	92.1	58	123	83.3	92.9
17 York	83.1	81.5	66	151	86.8	92.8
18 University College London	78.1	80.7	64	184	84.6	92.7
19 Lancaster	91.2	88.4	59.1	150	75.6	92.5
20 Liverpool	83.8	85.1	68.2	142	80.9	91.9
21 Cardiff	84.2	82.5	53.5	151	86.6	91.8
22 Glasgow Caledonian	95.5	89.5	61	145	65.4	91.5
23 Aston	91.5	87	46	113	87.1	91.2
24 King's College London	82.1	82	50	164	84.3	91
25 Abertay	94.7	87.8	-	176	88.2	90.8
26 Leicester	86.6	90	53.5	123	81.6	90.6
=27 Essex	92.5	87.8	42.5	117	82.2	90.4
=27 Stirling	87.8	84.1	45.8	170	73.7	90.4
29 Aberdeen	86	86.6	33.2	182	76.7	90.2
30 Leeds	80.9	80.9	52	148	85.1	90.1
31 Queen Mary, London	83.9	81	50.5	143	82.6	89.9
32 East Anglia	84.6	86.6	56	123	80.1	89.7
33 Warwick	81.6	81.5	46.5	155	82.4	89.6
=34 Exeter	81	79.4	60.5	156	75.3	89.4
=34 Royal Holloway	86.9	87.4	43.5	124	82.4	89.4
=34 Southampton	78.8	81	53.5	145	84	89.4
37 Swansea	86.8	86.7	64.2	123	70.3	89.2
38 Nottingham	81.8	79.7	50.2	147	80.5	89

39	City St George's	82.9	79.4	48.8	125	85.7	88.9
40	Birmingham	79.7	74	57	149	81.1	88.8
41	Ulster	82.5	74.8	53.5	102	91.3	88.7
=42	Liverpool John Moores	89.3	91	28.7	113	83.8	88.5
=42	Portsmouth	87.8	84.6	41.2	113	82.2	88.5
44	Gloucestershire	93	94	25.8	101	82.4	88.4
45	Keele	86.4	87.8	39.2	120	80.5	88.3
46	Bangor	79.3	78.7	67.5	123	-	88
=47	Heriot-Watt	80.1	78.9	32.8	174	77.5	87.5
=47	Plymouth	85.1	83.3	42.9	133	75	87.5
=47	Staffordshire	88.7	80	30.8	-	80	87.5
=47	Sussex	82.5	88.7	49.8	132	72.3	87.5
=51	Northumbria	79.4	81	53.5	121	80.1	87.3
=51	Reading	85.4	82	54	117	72.6	87.3
53	Coventry	88.8	77.6	47.2	105	77.7	87.2
54	West of Scotland	97.9	94	30.8	141	55.7	87
55	Newcastle	76.6	77.2	58.8	136	75.3	86.7
56	Hertfordshire	85.1	82.1	48	94	78.8	86.5
=57	Aberystwyth	86.4	84.6	48.8	111	70.4	86.4
=57	Brighton	87.9	87.6	50.5	103	68.3	86.4
=57	Edinburgh Napier	96.7	95.6	-	146	68.5	86.4
=57	West of England	89.3	86.5	42.8	116	67.3	86.4
61	Manchester Metropolitan	84.7	82.8	44.8	119	71.9	86.1
62	Nottingham Trent	90.8	87.7	43.5	113	63.8	86
=63	Hull	88.7	81.8	42	103	69.4	85.3
=63	Kingston	90.5	85	38.5	100	68.6	85.3
65	Kent	82.8	75.7	50	107	73.9	85.2
66	Oxford Brookes	84.6	80.1	39.5	99	77	85.1
67	Edge Hill	87.6	85.2	13.8	113	79	84.8
68	Huddersfield	82.4	85.2	24	120	76.8	84.6
69	Anglia Ruskin	98.4	92.1	33.8	87	56.5	84.3
70	Roehampton	85.2	84.7	37.5	92	-	84.1
=71	Salford	84.9	82.7	37	116	66.3	83.9
=71	Sheffield Hallam	89.3	79.5	16.8	105	76.2	83.9
73	Worcester	87.6	85.4	7.8	113	75.8	83.5
74	Derby	85.2	91.2	-	103	80.5	83
75	Bournemouth	83.9	82.6	29.2	103	69.7	82.8
76	Bath Spa	89.5	89.7	-	106	72.5	82.5
77	Lincoln	87.3	80.1	-	108	76.2	81.8
78	Robert Gordon	82	75.2	-	128	78.9	81.6
79	Royal Veterinary College	79	72.6	-	131	79.1	80.7
80	Greenwich	79.8	77.4	-	100	82.3	80.4
81	Canterbury Christ Church	83.4	82	9.5	94	70.8	80.2
82	Westminster	78.6	78.1	36.8	106	58.9	79.7
83	South Wales	87.1	77.3	16.2	128	51	79.2
84	Brunel	80.6	78.3	-	115	70.8	79.1
85	Northampton	85	84.3	14	83	62.5	78.9
86	Bradford	78.4	73.5	-	112	70.2	77.8

Biological Sciences cont.

	Teaching quality %	Student experience %	Research quality %	Entry standards (UCAS points)	Graduate prospects %	Overall score
87 Wolverhampton	85.8	76.7	-	120	56.7	77.7
88 Chester	72.6	65.8	6.2	106	72.6	76.3
89 Cumbria	84.7	69.8	-	99	59.2	75.9

Employed in high-skilled job	39%	Employed in lower-skilled job	19%
Employed in high-skilled job and studying	3%	Employed in lower-skilled job and studying	1%
Studying	19%	Unemployed	6%
High-skilled work (median) salary	£26,000	Low-/medium-skilled salary	£21,000

Building

Heriot-Watt returns to the top spot of the Building table this year, having placed third in our previous edition, its overall rank boosted by the highest entry standards of 163 UCAS points, which entrants to third place University College London also achieved. Last year's No 1 in the table, Loughborough leads for research, based on outcomes of the Research Excellence Framework 2021. Nottingham and Ulster are steady in second and fourth place respectively for the third consecutive year.

Students at De Montfort in Leicester were the most satisfied with their teaching quality, our National Student Survey analysis shows, followed by those at Robert Gordon and Derby. For the wider experience, Huddersfield claims the highest rates of student satisfaction, with Derby and Kingston following it.

"Given the way buildings impact our lives every day, choosing to study a subject within 'building' will mean a career that has the potential to profoundly change our society for the better. You'll master the art and science of constructing buildings that make people happy and healthy, and, importantly, are inclusive and sustainable," says Dr Chaitali Basu, associate director of digital construction, University of the West of England.

Building courses include surveying, construction, building services engineering and construction management. They have attracted growing numbers of admissions and 2024 proved a bumper year for building undergraduate enrolments – with nearly 6,800 new starters accepted onto degrees. Applicants may be drawn by the firm foundations offered by the subject's career prospects: building ranks ninth in our employment table, based on more than four in five graduates being employed in high-skilled jobs and/or furthering their studies within fifteen months of finishing their degrees. Rates of pay are also encouraging too, the £28,500 average annual incomes earned by building graduates tying the subject with civil engineering at =17th place in our salaries index. Degree apprenticeships, although not included in our table, offer an increasingly popular route into the construction industry.

Building	Teaching quality %	Student experience %	Research quality %	Entry standards (UCAS points)	Graduate prospects %	Overall score
1 Heriot-Watt	84.4	83.5	59	163	89.6	100
2 Loughborough	77.3	80.1	72	135	98.8	99.6
3 University College London	86.6	77.1	61	163	79.2	97.3

Rank	University						
4	Reading	87.2	86	53.5	109	95.7	96.9
5	Nottingham	85.2	79.7	59	134	87.5	96.6
6	Plymouth	88.2	78.3	49	118	92	95.6
7	Salford	84.4	85.4	43.5	113	90.7	94
8	West of England	82.7	83.7	40.8	115	92.9	93.8
=9	Huddersfield	88.7	90.3	36.5	108	-	93.6
=9	Ulster	79.4	76.8	54.2	126	87.4	93.6
11	Robert Gordon	90.4	84.7	14	-	95.5	93.5
=12	Oxford Brookes	84	80.6	33.2	119	91.3	92.8
=12	Sheffield Hallam	81.6	77.2	43.2	117	90.8	92.8
14	Nottingham Trent	84.2	83.8	38	108	90.7	92.6
15	Portsmouth	87.7	83.5	21	108	93	91.8
=16	De Montfort	91.7	86.6	40.5	83	-	91.6
=16	Edinburgh Napier	72.3	78.1	38	147	85.7	91.6
=16	Glasgow Caledonian	76.7	72.1	30.2	149	87.5	91.6
=19	Aston	83.7	82.8	35.2	120	83.3	91.2
=19	Liverpool John Moores	81.6	81.4	28.7	115	90.6	91.2
=21	Coventry	80.1	76.4	23.5	109	95.8	90.5
=21	Northumbria	79.2	81.4	25	127	88	90.5
23	Brighton	85	80.3	36.5	102	82.5	89.5
24	Greenwich	83.8	83.6	30	104	83.3	89.1
25	Westminster	82	75.8	38.2	111	74.2	87.2
26	Kingston	89.5	86.7	17.2	100	76.9	87
=27	Anglia Ruskin	82.4	76.6	23.8	98	82.6	86.5
=27	Leeds Beckett	74.5	75.9	24.5	105	86.5	86.5
29	Birmingham City	82.9	79.3	34.8	112	70.1	86.3
30	London South Bank	68.1	59.7	35	118	83.3	85
31	Derby	89.8	88.9	-	79	83.3	84.9
32	Lancashire	79.5	76.6	-	117	79.4	83.8
33	Wolverhampton	79.4	73.5	20	92	-	83.7

Employed in high-skilled job	75%	Employed in lower-skilled job	8%
Employed in high-skilled job and studying	8%	Employed in lower-skilled job and studying	0%
Studying	0%	Unemployed	4%
High-skilled work (median) salary	£29,000	Low-/medium-skilled salary	£24,450

Business, Management and Marketing

The wide choice of institutions offering courses within our Business, Management and Marketing table reflects the popularity of the various branches of the subjects and ranks 119 universities this year. Growing demand in these fields has been well documented, as university applicants veer towards subjects they think will offer encouraging graduate job prospects. Despite a year-on-year dip in the number of applications and enrolments to the subjects in 2024 their popularity continued to far outstrip levels of demand five years ago, with business and management degrees attracting 60,980 applications (down from 64,485 the year before) and nearly 22,000 new students, and business studies degrees receiving 70,680 applications and 22,505 enrolments. Management studies degrees attracted 73,665 applications and 11,295 new starters in 2024, while marketing courses welcomed 8,010 new students from 40,765 applications – demand well above the years prior to 2020. The huge number of options means there should also be plenty of opportunities to secure a place through Clearing. Some of the most famous business schools are absent from this table because they only offer postgraduate qualifications such as MBAs, whereas our Guide details undergraduate provision.

Oxford has returned to the top of our Business, Management and Marketing table this year, buoyed by the best graduate prospects (almost all graduates (99.6%) were employed in high-skilled jobs or continuing their studies within 15 months) and average entry standards (214 UCAS points) which are second only to those at St Andrews (216 points), in =6th place overall and formerly a repeat leader of the table. The London School of Economics, in fourth place overall, achieved the best results in the REF 2021 and therefore tops our research quality rating, in which it is followed by City St George's (14th), Oxford and Manchester (=10th).

In our analysis of the latest National Student Survey the universities that nailed the highest scores for satisfaction with teaching quality rank in the middle to lower reaches of the table overall. Aberystwyth (in 31st place overall) came top for this measure, followed by Staffordshire (=44th) and West London (=91st). West London (=88th) and Suffolk (=111th) take first and second place in our measure for student satisfaction with the wider experience, where they are followed by Warwick.

But graduate prospects are the most closely correlated aspect of the business ranking to the complete result. Seven of the top 10 for this measure rank in the top 10 for business, management and marketing overall. Our analysis of graduate employment in high-skilled jobs or postgraduate study 15 months on from degrees showed that following Oxford are LSE (96.4%), Bath (92.1%) and Durham (91.8%). By contrast, Suffolk is at the foot of our employment ranking with 48.5% of graduates in high-skilled work or study after 15 months.

"There are more than 5.5 million private-sector businesses in the UK, which offer four out of five jobs, so it's no wonder that business and management graduates are in demand. A degree in these subjects provides knowledge and skills that are specific to core careers in important industries, such as banking, finance, consumer goods, accounting and consulting. It also prepares students to succeed in a range of managerial and support roles in any organisation, including in the public and non-profit sectors. And it can provide the perfect launching pad for young entrepreneurs to start their own business," says Juan López-Cotarelo, associate professor in the Organisation and Human Resource Management group, University of Warwick. As a subject area overall however, business, management and marketing manage only 48th place in our 70-subject table, but they compare more favourably in our earnings index (=28th).

Business, Management and Marketing	Teaching quality %	Student experience %	Research quality %	Entry standards (UCAS points)	Graduate prospects %	Overall score
1 Oxford	86.4	80.5	66.2	214	98.2	100
2 Warwick	90	91.9	65.2	188	89.5	99.2
3 King's College London	85.4	87.4	63	191	90.9	97.7
4 London School of Economics	84.1	84.3	69	173	96.4	97.4
5 University College London	87.8	88.1	62.3	169	91.3	97
=6 Bath	85.1	84.7	65.2	161	92.1	95.8
=6 St Andrews	83.7	82.7	48.2	216	85.8	95.8
8 Strathclyde	85	83.4	52.5	205	84.2	95.7
9 Edinburgh	77.6	80.1	59	188	88.4	93.8

=10	Leeds	83.1	85.9	62.3	155	84.1	93.5
=10	Manchester	82.1	82.9	66.2	159	84.1	93.5
=12	Durham	83.1	85.4	55.8	143	91.8	93.3
=12	Liverpool	86.1	87.5	58	140	85.5	93.3
14	City St George's	81.5	80.3	67.2	172	78.7	93
15	Exeter	82.7	82.7	63.5	143	87.7	92.9
16	Loughborough	82.2	85.2	49.2	147	90.3	92.3
=17	Bristol	80.8	82.4	46	160	88.9	91.8
=17	Lancaster	83.7	83.5	59.2	135	84.1	91.8
19	Aberdeen	83.5	84.8	32.2	177	84.4	91.7
20	Dundee	90	87.6	28.5	177	74.6	91.6
21	Birmingham	80.1	82.1	55.2	144	88.2	91.5
=22	Cardiff	80.5	83.9	56	147	82.5	91.1
=22	Glasgow	70.7	75.3	57.2	206	80.6	91.1
24	Sheffield	83.2	88.7	48.8	138	81.7	91
25	Queen's, Belfast	81.6	82.5	40.5	148	86.6	90.4
26	Surrey	84.9	84.3	54.8	131	77.3	90.3
27	Nottingham	80	84.9	46.8	149	81.7	90.2
28	Southampton	82.5	82.1	52	131	82.5	90.1
=29	Stirling	80	83.5	38.2	174	75.1	89.6
=29	York	79.7	83.5	50.5	136	81.9	89.6
31	Aberystwyth	94	91.7	22.8	124	74.7	89.3
32	Sussex	82.8	83.5	50.7	125	78.3	89.1
33	Reading	79.7	81.4	46.2	125	84.5	88.6
34	Queen Margaret, Edinburgh	91.6	86.8	7.5	163	72.4	88.5
35	Manchester Metropolitan	87.3	85	42.8	123	71.9	88.4
36	Heriot-Watt	76.4	77.7	38.2	168	79.2	88.2
37	Glasgow Caledonian	82.6	82.2	25.8	170	73	88.1
=38	Aston	80.1	78.4	43.5	126	83.8	88
=38	Ulster	83.3	81.4	45.8	119	78.3	88
40	Royal Holloway	82.4	85.3	43	123	75.6	87.9
=41	Canterbury Christ Church	91.9	89.9	38	100	68.3	87.7
=41	East Anglia	79	80.7	57.8	119	75.5	87.7
43	Newcastle	75.7	79.5	40.5	141	83.4	87.6
=44	Nottingham Trent	87	86.9	34.2	110	75.2	87.4
=44	Robert Gordon	90.4	89.2	19	143	65.9	87.4
=44	Staffordshire	94	90.6	38.8	104	60.9	87.4
=47	Hull	88.2	89.9	29.5	98	77.2	87.2
=47	Queen Mary, London	80.1	80.9	53.2	152	61.2	87.2
=47	Swansea	82.4	81.9	38.8	121	77.4	87.2
50	Leicester	80.5	82.5	45.8	121	75.4	87.1
51	Lancashire	89.3	86.6	28.2	123	68.8	87
52	Edge Hill	88.8	91.6	21	112	73.2	86.9
=53	Bangor	89.7	80	32.2	114	-	86.8
=53	Northumbria	82.3	83.7	28.2	124	79.3	86.8
=53	Plymouth	86.6	84.9	28.7	111	76.4	86.8
=53	Portsmouth	84.6	82.9	37.8	114	74.6	86.8
57	Oxford Brookes	85	85.4	26	110	79.9	86.6

Business, Management and Marketing cont.

	Teaching quality %	Student experience %	Research quality %	Entry standards (UCAS points)	Graduate prospects %	Overall score
58 Kent	82.3	78.4	37.2	123	75.9	86.4
59 Liverpool John Moores	86.5	87	21	119	72.5	86
60 West of England	85.3	85.9	27.3	112	72.9	85.9
=61 Buckingham	92	84.3	-	97	86.6	85.8
=61 Teesside	85.3	78.9	49.2	97	69.7	85.8
=63 Arts London	80.8	79.9	46	130	64.6	85.7
=63 Hertfordshire	88.9	87.8	29	112	63.9	85.7
=65 Edinburgh Napier	80	81.8	20	142	76.1	85.6
=65 Keele	82.4	85.7	24.8	108	78.9	85.6
67 Chichester	89.9	84.5	1.2	108	83.3	85.5
68 Derby	88.6	85.4	18	105	74.2	85.4
69 Brunel	85.5	86.7	30.2	118	63.5	85.2
70 Lincoln	84.5	83	25	101	77.4	85.1
71 Falmouth	81.8	76.3	48.8	122	62.9	85
=72 Bath Spa	88.2	86.3	23.8	97	68.7	84.7
=72 Chester	84.6	75.5	25.2	115	75.4	84.7
=74 Anglia Ruskin	86.5	85	45.8	92	59.9	84.6
=74 Bradford	84.3	83.6	38.2	112	61.6	84.6
=74 Coventry	87.9	86.2	33.2	105	59.8	84.6
77 Birmingham City	88.9	88.5	11.2	117	64.8	84.4
78 South Wales	91.7	87.4	9	113	64.1	84.3
=79 Essex	82.2	84.3	39.8	117	58.5	84.1
=79 Middlesex	83.6	83.2	46.2	100	59.2	84.1
=81 De Montfort	88.8	87.8	19	88	66.5	83.6
=81 York St John	84.1	78.3	9.8	110	78.7	83.6
=83 Brighton	80.1	80.5	28.5	106	72.1	83.5
=83 Wolverhampton	87.6	84	20.2	100	65.2	83.5
85 Gloucestershire	86.2	80.3	8.8	102	76.6	83.4
86 Westminster	82.7	83.9	37.5	110	56.4	83.2
87 Leeds Trinity	92.4	89.9	-	99	64.7	83.1
=88 Greenwich	85.2	84.7	33.2	105	55.2	83
=88 London South Bank	83.1	82.3	21.5	107	67.2	83
=88 Southampton Solent	87.8	84.1	-	108	71.9	83
=88 West London	92.9	92.1	-	115	55.5	83
=92 Bournemouth	76.8	78	23	102	79.5	82.8
=92 Leeds Beckett	82.6	82.3	8.2	109	74.6	82.8
94 Salford	81	82	24.8	113	62.5	82.4
95 Huddersfield	82	81.4	23.2	118	60.4	82.3
96 Worcester	78.5	76.7	12.5	108	79.2	82.2
97 Abertay	79.4	79.7	-	155	64.4	82
98 SOAS, London	75.3	72.3	44.2	108	-	81.9
99 Buckinghamshire New	93.7	91.8	-	88	56.4	81.6
=100 Kingston	81.6	79	24	104	62.6	81.5
=100 Roehampton	84.5	83.8	32.8	91	53.5	81.5

Rank	University						
=102	Cardiff Metropolitan	76.7	73	14	115	76.6	81.4
=102	Greater Manchester	89.1	85.2	-	113	57.7	81.4
104	East London	88.8	82.2	11	112	53.1	81.3
105	Wales Trinity St David	92.2	90.5	-	99	52.7	81.2
106	Sheffield Hallam	76.5	73.3	23.5	110	70.5	81.1
=107	Cumbria	86.8	83.4	7.8	96	61.5	81
=107	Goldsmiths, London	76.9	72.3	29.7	116	63.5	81
=109	Liverpool Hope	86.1	82.2	-	107	63.7	80.9
=109	West of Scotland	80	73.6	10.5	122	67.4	80.9
=111	London Metropolitan	83.2	79.3	22	86	63.3	80.7
=111	Northampton	85.9	85.5	13.2	89	58.2	80.7
=111	Suffolk	94	91.9	-	93	48.5	80.7
=111	Sunderland	90.1	87.9	-	105	52.8	80.7
115	Winchester	76.5	73.4	22.2	96	73.1	80.6
116	Creative Arts	72.3	71	41.2	98	67.9	80.5
117	St Mary's, Twickenham	80.1	75.5	-	97	73.8	79.6
118	Bedfordshire	81.5	79.9	22	92	52.9	79.1
119	Royal Agricultural University	72.6	72.3	-	112	70.2	77.7

Employed in high-skilled job	53%	Employed in lower-skilled job		26%
Employed in high-skilled job and studying	4%	Employed in lower-skilled job and studying		1%
Studying	3%	Unemployed		7%
High-skilled work (median) salary	£27,000	Low-/medium-skilled salary		£21,800

Chemical Engineering

Cambridge has extended its lead in our Chemical Engineering table, having toppled Oxford from No 1 two years ago by the narrowest of margins (0.1%) and furthering its lead last year it is now ahead of this year's runner-up Oxford by 4.3%. Helping Cambridge to the top of the table are the highest entry standards in the subject by far, with entrants averaging an eye-watering 235 UCAS tariff points. It also leads for graduate prospects; almost all Cambridge graduates in the subject were employed in high-skilled jobs or furthering their studies when surveyed 15 months on from their degrees. Even at the opposite end of the scale at Queen Mary, more than three-quarters of graduates had achieved the most desired outcomes. Imperial is third overall but unbeaten for research quality, based on its results in the latest Research Excellence Framework in 2021. Chemical engineering students throughout the table tend to arrive with good grades; over half of the universities have entry standards that equate to AAA or above at A-level (144 UCAS points). But less highly qualified applicants should not be put off as there are plenty of institutions with more accessible entry standards too, such as Surrey, ranked 22nd overall and averaging 126 UCAS points. Applicants will need maths, which is essential for chemical engineering degrees, and while chemistry or physics are required the leading universities will usually expect both. Most courses offer industry placements in the final year and lead to Chartered Engineer status. Applications and enrolments increased in 2024's admissions cycle, and nearly 2,700 students were accepted onto courses.

The highest levels of student satisfaction with teaching quality were found at Teesside, based on our latest National Student Survey analysis, followed by Bradford. For student evaluation of the broad experience, Teesside is top again, followed by Newcastle (=10th overall) and then Portsmouth (31st).

Creating useful products from raw materials, chemical engineering combines natural sciences with life sciences, maths and economics. Chemical engineering graduates are in demand; four in five were employed in high-skilled jobs and/or postgraduate study when surveyed 15 months on from their degrees – only 11 subjects do better in our employment ranking. Average early career salaries of £30,000 compare even more favourably, ranking =5th out of 70 subject areas.

Chemical Engineering	Teaching quality %	Student experience %	Research quality %	Entry standards (UCAS points)	Graduate prospects %	Overall score
1 Cambridge	87.6	81.1	77.2	235	97.1	100
2 Oxford	80.4	74.8	77.5	213	94	95.7
3 Imperial College	87.3	88.4	81	202	86.8	95.5
4 Edinburgh	84.4	85.8	55.5	176	93.8	93.3
=5 Bath	87.1	88.2	49.5	167	93.8	92.9
=5 Southampton	86.4	84.8	70	154	-	92.9
7 Strathclyde	85.6	82.9	52.8	206	88.8	92.8
8 Birmingham	83	84.1	63.7	161	91.6	92.1
9 Nottingham	84.4	83.8	59	158	92	91.9
=10 Heriot-Watt	87.7	80.4	55.5	180	86.1	91.1
=10 Newcastle	90.8	92.3	58.5	130	88.3	91.1
12 University College London	76.5	78.2	70	164	91.4	90.9
13 Loughborough	85.5	82.4	46.5	146	92.7	90.4
14 Leeds	73.9	73.1	64.8	161	93.6	90.1
=15 Queen's, Belfast	81.4	75.4	51	162	91.4	89.9
=15 Sheffield	81	82.9	66.8	169	84.9	89.9
17 Ulster	89.3	88.7	49.8	126	-	89.4
18 Manchester	81.7	82.1	63	167	84.2	89.3
19 Swansea	92.1	89.4	48.8	111	85.7	88.3
20 Aberdeen	84	85.1	35.8	177	85.4	88.2
21 Teesside	98.4	97.2	18.8	90	85.7	86.2
22 Surrey	82.2	85.4	55.2	126	82.2	86.1
23 Aston	86.2	77.3	35.2	113	88.3	85.8
24 Bradford	92.2	89.4	27	130	80.4	85.3
=25 Hull	88.9	81.8	36.2	88	85.1	84.5
=25 Queen Mary, London	76.3	74	66	147	77.8	84.5
27 Lancaster	83.1	80.2	44.8	144	78.4	84.4
28 Chester	80.8	76.8	15.8	119	91.3	84
29 Greenwich	85.1	82.5	31.5	104	-	83.7
30 Brunel	79	73.9	33	120	-	82.4
31 Portsmouth	79	90.5	21	116	-	82.1
32 Sheffield Hallam	78.2	71.7	30	-	80.8	80.3
33 London South Bank	80.9	76.5	27.3	97	79.4	79.9
34 Derby	70.8	46.9	14	126	-	75.2

Employed in high-skilled job	68%	Employed in lower-skilled job	8%
Employed in high-skilled job and studying	4%	Employed in lower-skilled job and studying	0%
Studying	8%	Unemployed	6%
High-skilled work (median) salary	£30,000	Low-/medium-skilled salary	£23,000

Chemistry

Up one place to rank No 1 in this year's table St Andrews' overall position is buoyed by a perfect record on career prospects among its chemistry graduates – with 100% employed in high-skilled jobs or furthering their studies 15 months after their degrees. Cambridge is down a place in this year's runner-up spot, but still attracts the highest entry standards of 224 UCAS points. Entry standards are generally high to study chemistry, and 22 universities average over 144 UCAS tariff points (equivalent to AAA at A-level). Bristol, in 12th place overall, pips Cambridge to first place for research, based on the results of the latest Research Excellence Framework 2021. In a table traditionally dominated by the older universities at its upper end, Plymouth is the top-ranked modern institution in =21st place, taking over from Northumbria which was formerly chemistry's top-ranked post-1992 university but has fallen from tenth place only two years ago to =38th this year. In our new National Student Survey analysis, Keele (26th overall) is top for student satisfaction with teaching quality, followed by Nottingham Trent (=29th) and Leicester (=16th). For students' evaluation of the wider experience, Keele leads again, with Leicester and Bath (8th) second and third respectively. In contrast, chemistry students at Reading (48th in the table) reported the lowest rates of satisfaction with the broad student experience and teaching quality.

Chemistry A-level, or equivalent qualification, is almost always a prerequisite and the leading universities will also look for maths and/or at least one other science – it is worth checking which second science individual institutions ask for, as these may differ. Courses include laboratory and experimentation work, alongside independent and group research projects and industry experience or placements.

Nearly a fifth of chemistry graduates (18.7%) had progressed to postgraduate study when surveyed 15 months after their degrees, the Graduate Outcomes survey shows, while more than half were working full-time in high-skilled jobs and 4.4% were combining study and jobs – which combine to rank chemistry 23rd out of 70 subject areas for graduate prospects. The subject places in the top 25 for early career earnings too. Applications exceeded 31,500 for 2024 entry, their highest to date, and over 5,300 new chemistry students were accepted onto courses – reflecting an uplift in new starters as well. Options for aspiring undergraduates are broad: with 122 universities and colleges offering courses in 2026–27.

Chemistry	Teaching quality %	Student experience %	Research quality %	Entry standards (UCAS points)	Graduate prospects %	Overall score
1 St Andrews	89	85.3	66.8	215	100	100
2 Cambridge	85.5	82.1	80	224	94.3	99.4
3 Strathclyde	93.1	90.1	56.8	205	85	95.8
4 York	88.7	85.8	71	154	91.4	94.9
5 Oxford	79.6	69.7	74	199	94.4	94.8
=6 Edinburgh	78.9	78.8	66.8	200	94.3	94.7
=6 Imperial College	84.6	86.4	75.5	188	85.4	94.7
8 Bath	87.9	92.1	64.5	162	89.8	94.5
9 Durham	88	85	55	180	91.4	94.2
10 Liverpool	83.8	86.7	72.8	142	93.7	93.9
11 Queen's, Belfast	90.8	78	48.8	156	97.4	93.8
12 Bristol	81.9	79.1	80.5	172	86.1	93.3

Chemistry cont.

	Teaching quality %	Student experience %	Research quality %	Entry standards (UCAS points)	Graduate prospects %	Overall score
=13 King's College London	82.8	77	74.2	156	91	93
=13 University College London	83.6	83.3	76	172	83.7	93
15 Warwick	85	82.3	63.2	153	90.2	92.4
=16 Leicester	94.6	92.2	51.2	125	89	92.3
=16 Sheffield	88.1	86.1	62.7	148	87	92.3
18 Birmingham	88.8	86.7	53.5	152	87.2	91.7
19 Cardiff	87.5	80.8	57.8	136	91.3	91.5
20 Manchester	82.7	81.5	72.2	159	83.2	91.3
=21 Plymouth	93.5	91.1	40.8	120	91.2	91
=21 Southampton	86	86.1	61.8	149	84.4	91
23 Heriot-Watt	93.7	87.4	32.8	186	80.7	90.7
24 East Anglia	85.4	82.6	54	124	93.2	90.6
25 Glasgow	80.4	66.6	55.5	202	85.7	90.5
26 Keele	96.1	95.1	48	116	82.2	90.3
27 Nottingham	85.6	82.8	58.2	142	85	90
28 Newcastle	84.8	80.6	62.7	137	84.2	89.6
=29 Leeds	84.1	77.6	50.2	152	85.3	88.9
=29 Nottingham Trent	95	90	59	101	78.1	88.9
=31 Lancaster	93	90.1	30.2	142	82.1	88.4
=31 Swansea	93.8	89.4	43	117	81.2	88.4
33 Surrey	89.5	83.5	55.2	120	80.8	88.3
34 Queen Mary, London	82.7	78.6	62.5	140	78.7	87.7
=35 Loughborough	83.1	81.9	34.8	141	87.9	87.3
=35 Sussex	84.5	78.8	43.5	130	86	87.3
37 Aberdeen	88.8	78.6	39.5	146	80	87.1
=38 Manchester Metropolitan	84.7	80.2	45.5	128	82.4	86.7
=38 Northumbria	82.6	81.6	53.5	118	-	86.7
40 Aston	89.7	87.3	35.2	108	-	86.1
41 Kent	83.5	79.1	40.2	101	79.7	83.4
42 Huddersfield	91.5	81.9	18.5	101	80.2	83.3
=43 Bradford	84.3	82.8	25	117	-	82.9
=43 Sheffield Hallam	86.4	77.2	-	110	91.5	82.9
45 Lincoln	76.2	66.6	42.2	102	80.9	81.1
46 Salford	85.4	78.6	37	112	64.7	80.1
47 Greenwich	80.5	70.7	32.8	91	-	79.5
48 Reading	76.2	60.6	36	106	78	79.4
49 Kingston	78.5	77.8	38.5	104	68.6	79.1
50 Lancashire	77.9	65.9	-	126	80	77.7
51 Chester	76.9	75.3	14	103	-	76.9
52 De Montfort	79.4	84.6	-	92	68.8	74.8

Employed in high-skilled job	51%	Employed in lower-skilled job	11%
Employed in high-skilled job and studying	4%	Employed in lower-skilled job and studying	0%
Studying	19%	Unemployed	6%
High-skilled work (median) salary	£27,000	Low-/medium-skilled salary	£20,000

Civil Engineering

As the future brains behind the design, construction and maintenance of roads, bridges, pipelines, processing plants, buildings and harbours, civil engineering students learn how to apply physics, maths and mechanics to structural design. Professor Carlo Prato, head of the School of Civil Engineering, University of Leeds, notes that civil engineers are also "integral to the provision of everything from clean air and water to renewable energy and carbon reduction," and says that "civil engineering can lead to a diverse range of careers as well as provide the knowledge and practical skills to tackle some of the planet's most complex problems." As well as A-levels and Scottish Highers, BTEC qualifications are a popular means of entry into a civil engineering undergraduate degree, but applicants should check with individual universities for their preferred entry requirements. Some degrees in the subject are four-year courses leading to an MEng; others are sandwich courses that include a work placement.

Leading a shake-up of the top 10 of our Civil Engineering table, Imperial is up one place to take the top spot, swapping places with last year's No 1 and this year's runner-up Cambridge, which led our table for 16 years until four years ago. Imperial has a peerless research quality rating, based on the results of the Research Excellence Framework 2021, and along with Edinburgh (11th overall) and Surrey (18th) it achieves a perfect 100% of civil engineering graduates in high-skilled jobs or postgraduate study 15 months on from their degrees. Southampton has risen five places to rank third while Bath has dropped eight to place =12th. The highest rates of student satisfaction with teaching (as derived from our latest National Student Survey analysis) are found at Dundee (=5th overall), Ulster (=16th) and Southampton, while students' evaluations of the broader experience put Dundee in front again, followed by West of Scotland (25th overall) and Birmingham City (31st). Civil engineering students at Anglia Ruskin place the university bottom for satisfaction the wider experience, a position London South Bank holds for teaching quality.

A regular among the top 10 subjects for graduate prospects, civil engineering ranks eighth this year. When surveyed 15 months on from their degrees, more than 85% of graduates were working in high-skilled jobs and/or furthering their studies. Promising average starting salaries of £28,500 put civil engineering =17th out of 70 subject areas for earnings. But a second consecutive decrease in demand brought applications under 22,000 in 2024, although the number of new students accepted onto courses increased a little to 4,035.

Civil Engineering	Teaching quality %	Student experience %	Research quality %	Entry standards (UCAS points)	Graduate prospects %	Overall score
1 Imperial College	83.3	84.9	81	188	100	100
2 Cambridge	80.4	80.8	77.2	222	97.2	99.8
3 Southampton	92.7	90.3	70	166	91.2	98
4 Oxford	80.4	74.8	77.5	213	94	97.8
=5 Bristol	89.4	85.6	68	176	91.2	97.2
=5 Dundee	96.4	95.8	50.2	162	91.2	97.2
7 Strathclyde	85.7	83.1	52.8	199	95.9	97.1
8 Sheffield	88.7	89.5	66.8	162	92.2	96.7
9 Glasgow	79.5	78.8	61.5	214	93.2	96.3
10 Leeds	89	89.3	64.8	156	91	95.8
11 Edinburgh	81	77.7	55.5	181	100	95.7
12 Bath	86	84.2	49.5	165	98	95.4

Civil Engineering cont.

	Teaching quality %	Student experience %	Research quality %	Entry standards (UCAS points)	Graduate prospects %	Overall score
13 Nottingham	89.4	90.8	59	150	89.7	94.8
14 Loughborough	84.8	83.2	72	137	93.5	94.5
15 Heriot-Watt	81.4	74.8	55.5	185	94.2	94.2
=16 Liverpool	88.2	86.8	57	138	93.1	94.1
=16 Ulster	92.8	90.2	49.8	125	93.6	94.1
18 Surrey	84.7	83.6	55.2	121	100	93.5
=19 Aberdeen	87.9	84.6	35.8	152	95.7	93.1
=19 University College London	79.2	78	70	158	91.3	93.1
21 Birmingham	77.4	72.9	63.7	149	98.2	92.8
22 Manchester	78	74.8	63	149	96.9	92.7
23 Queen's, Belfast	78.8	76.7	51	151	98.7	92.5
24 Newcastle	79.9	81.8	58.5	126	93.5	91.2
25 West of Scotland	89.5	95.3	16.5	-	91.3	90.9
=26 Edinburgh Napier	84.2	78	22.8	172	93.1	90.8
=26 Hertfordshire	89.3	82	33	137	-	90.8
28 Cardiff	78.3	80.4	54	139	92.6	90.7
=29 Exeter	81.2	75.1	47	151	91.4	90.6
=29 Plymouth	90	87.1	32.5	119	92	90.6
31 Birmingham City	91.9	91.6	17.5	123	91.2	90
32 Greenwich	91.2	89.2	31.5	100	91.9	89.9
33 Swansea	82.9	79	48.8	117	92.5	89.8
34 Nottingham Trent	83.4	81.8	38	106	90.6	88
35 West of England	77.1	80.5	30.8	134	93	87.9
36 Glasgow Caledonian	82.8	84.7	12.8	161	86.2	87.7
37 Teesside	84.8	84.6	18.8	-	88.5	87.2
38 Reading	74.1	78.5	53.5	122	-	87.1
39 City St George's	79.6	78.7	32.5	109	92.9	87
40 Bradford	89.3	84.6	27	110	83.3	86.8
41 Aston	79.6	78.5	35.2	126	-	86.7
42 Northumbria	76.4	77.2	43	122	87.5	86.5
=43 Coventry	87	76.8	23.5	106	88.9	86.4
=43 Liverpool John Moores	76.6	71.8	45.5	110	90.6	86.4
=45 Brunel	90.6	88.3	33	107	76.6	86.2
=45 Portsmouth	83.8	82.5	21	120	86.6	86.2
47 Brighton	77.4	76.6	36.5	122	-	85.5
48 Salford	84.3	75.9	33.2	110	83.3	85.4
49 Sheffield Hallam	78.2	71.7	30	127	-	84.7
50 Kingston	89.3	89.7	17.2	108	74.1	83.8
51 West London	80.8	81.2	13.8	117	83.8	83.7
52 Derby	81.3	84.5	14	95	-	82.7
53 Wolverhampton	76.4	73.1	18.2	96	-	80.3
54 Leeds Beckett	79.7	77.5	24.5	100	72.5	80.2
55 East London	83	81.5	21.2	114	64	79.7
56 London South Bank	72.8	68.7	27.3	116	73.8	79.3
57 Anglia Ruskin	73.8	66.5	23.8	91	-	78.8

Employed in high-skilled job	77%
Employed in high-skilled job and studying	5%
Studying	4%
High-skilled work (median) salary	£28,800
Employed in lower-skilled job	6%
Employed in lower-skilled job and studying	1%
Unemployed	4%
Low-/medium-skilled salary	£21,000

Classics and Ancient History

Classics takes in the broad literature, history and culture of Ancient Greek and Roman societies spanning 1,500 years, and can include architecture, religion and philosophy. Some courses will want Latin or Greek A-level, while others will allow students to learn the languages from scratch once they have enrolled. Several universities teach the subjects as part of modular courses, but not on their own. "Employers will love you; my former students run museums, civil service departments, schools, pop groups, theatres, banks, advertising agencies, and travel, data analysis and broadcasting companies. One is now an MP," says Professor Edith Hall, Department of Classics and Ancient History, University of Durham.

Leicester has staged a huge 22-place ascent of our new Classics and Ancient History table to take the No 1 spot, ousting last year's top university St Andrews into joint second place with Durham. Spurring Leicester's lead is superb feedback from its classics and ancient history students in the latest National Student Survey (NSS), which has placed Leicester top for both measures of student satisfaction: teaching quality and the broad experience. Conversely, University College London (in 22nd place overall) comes bottom for each of these NSS-led metrics. St Andrews is top for graduate prospects – with 96.5% of graduates engaged in high-skilled jobs and/or further study within 15 months of their degree, and boasts peerless rates of student satisfaction with teaching quality and the wider experience, while Cambridge (which enjoyed a 16-year reign at the top of the table until four years ago) has the highest entry standards of 206 UCAS points. For research quality in the subjects, Warwick ranks No 1, based on results of the latest Research Excellence Framework 2021, where it is closely followed by King's College London and Manchester, which tie in our analysis. Conversely, Manchester finishes bottom for each of these student-led measures. Independent schools dominate provision of Latin and Greek at A-level and at half of the universities in our table entrants averaged over 144 UCAS points, equal to three As at A-level.

Classics and ancient history rank =55th in our employment table of 70 subject areas, based on over a third of graduates working in high-skilled jobs 15 months after their degrees, 14.9% furthering their studies and around 5% combining work and study. Although not an ingredient of our subject ranking overall, in our pay index the subjects fare a little more strongly, placing =46th. After three years of rising numbers, classics attracted a cooler 7,715 applications in 2024 (down from nearly 8,200 the year before), while the number of students enrolling was the same for the second year running, with 1,395 new classics students accepted onto degrees.

Classics and Ancient History	Teaching quality %	Student experience %	Research quality %	Entry standards (UCAS points)	Graduate prospects %	Overall score
1 Leicester	96.9	96.3	70	119	-	100
=2 Durham	89.5	84.8	57.8	179	86.8	99
=2 St Andrews	91.3	88.8	42.5	184	96.5	99
4 Oxford	85.1	67.9	60	193	91.3	98.9
5 Manchester	94.2	86	65.5	144	82.3	98.6
6 Warwick	91.4	77.4	65.8	158	77.8	97.2
7 Cambridge	86.4	68.2	48.8	206	84.2	96.1

Classics and Ancient History cont.

	Teaching quality %	Student experience %	Research quality %	Entry standards (UCAS points)	Graduate prospects %	Overall score
8 King's College London	84.2	76.7	65.5	156	77.2	95
9 Glasgow	79.5	76.1	62.5	169	-	94.3
10 Exeter	85.3	80.5	61.5	146	76.4	93.9
11 Royal Holloway	91	81.2	53.5	121	84.7	93.7
=12 Leeds	86	83.8	52	141	77.9	92.1
=12 Nottingham	88.3	84.7	51.5	130	78.6	92.1
14 Liverpool	87.9	86.3	43.5	126	81.4	90.7
15 Bristol	83.4	79.1	52.8	152	71.3	90.5
16 Birmingham	88.3	80.1	54.2	137	66.7	90.1
17 Kent	89.3	72.5	58.8	104	73.8	90
18 Edinburgh	76.4	72.4	51.5	177	69.3	89.2
19 Swansea	93	86.4	45.2	112	65.1	87.8
20 Newcastle	85.9	78.4	42	134	71.6	87.5
21 Reading	92.1	87.5	43.2	112	66.3	87.4
22 University College London	76	65.2	44.2	159	73.9	86.7
23 Cardiff	88.7	85.3	42.2	118	63	85.9

Employed in high-skilled job	36%	Employed in lower-skilled job	23%
Employed in high-skilled job and studying	4%	Employed in lower-skilled job and studying	1%
Studying	15%	Unemployed	5%
High-skilled work (median) salary	£27,000	Low-/medium-skilled salary	£20,000

Communication and Media Studies

This subject table covers a wide range of courses; some focus on the history and theory of media and culture in society, while others range from practical production for TV, film and radio to script-writing or journalism. "The media is vital to the conduct and framing of national and global politics. As citizens and consumers we navigate an ever more complex, high-choice communication environment. The creative and cultural industries are of immense economic value, but it's not just about the money. There is so much in popular culture that deserves to be valued and analysed. Media and communication programmes offer an exciting interdisciplinary field of study that puts you at the heart of these critical debates," says Professor David Deacon, head of the Department of Communication and Media, Loughborough University. After years of rising applications to the subjects, demand for them cooled for the second consecutive year in 2024's admissions cycle, when just over 62,200 applied and 11,605 new students were accepted onto courses.

Strathclyde returns to the top of our Communication and Media Studies table this year, boosted by the highest entry standards of 204 UCAS points, swapping places with last year's No 1 Loughborough, which settles for second. For research, =6th-place Cardiff achieves the top score in our analysis of the Research Excellence Framework 2021, followed by Goldsmiths, Loughborough and Southampton. In our latest National Student Survey analysis, Staffordshire (18th overall) is top for teaching quality, followed by Lancaster (16th) and Wolverhampton (=49th), and for the student experience Lancaster is in front, followed by Loughborough and Sheffield – which ranks third overall for the second year running. Huddersfield, London Met and Goldsmiths occupy the bottom three ranks for both measures of student satisfaction.

Entry grades span a broad spectrum, from 204 UCAS points at Strathclyde down to 85 points at Anglia Ruskin – one of nine universities to average below 100 points in the UCAS tariff.

Low starting salaries tend to be the norm in media industries, and average annual pay of £23,000 for those with communication and media studies degrees ranks the subjects in the bottom ten of our pay index. They compare better in our graduate prospects table, placing 50th out of 70 subject areas this year. Most communication and media studies students will be wise to the dearth of "professional"-grade roles upon graduation, but career prospects vary considerably by university. At least four in five of those who studied at 11 universities had achieved the desired career outcomes 15 months after graduating, led by Gloucestershire (=27th overall), City St George's (=8th), Newcastle (=8th) and Leeds (4th). At the opposite end of the scale, less than half of those with degrees in the subjects from Northampton (79th overall) and London Metropolitan (80th) had achieved the same outcomes within the same timeframe.

Communication and Media Studies	Teaching quality %	Student experience %	Research quality %	Entry standards (UCAS points)	Graduate prospects %	Overall score
1 Strathclyde	84.1	83.1	58.8	204	80	100
2 Loughborough	89.3	90.2	71.8	138	84.6	98.6
3 Sheffield	90.4	90	59.5	142	84.8	97.8
4 Leeds	86.1	84.3	50.2	152	85.5	96.1
5 Warwick	83.7	78.3	68.8	155	79.3	96
=6 Cardiff	80.3	77.9	77	141	84.5	95.8
=6 University College London	86.1	88.8	56.8	150	-	95.8
=8 City St George's	87.7	87.3	42.8	132	88.5	94.8
=8 Newcastle	81.5	82.7	60.8	136	86.8	94.8
10 Glasgow Caledonian	87.6	79	38.5	168	78.7	94.6
11 Queen Mary, London	87.8	73	76.4	140	69.4	94
12 Leicester	84.9	82.1	68.6	124	78.6	93.8
=13 Edinburgh Napier	88.2	82.7	38.8	154	77.1	93.7
=13 Liverpool	85.3	85.7	55.2	131	80.1	93.7
15 King's College London	82.1	83.7	64.5	148	71.6	93.5
16 Lancashire	95.5	91.6	31.8	119	79.7	93.2
17 Stirling	86.1	79.7	44.5	172	67	93.1
18 Staffordshire	98.2	86.5	31.5	114	77.9	92.5
19 Exeter	81.2	78.8	55.9	142	76.6	92.4
=20 Lancaster	89.1	73.5	60.2	130	72.7	92.3
=20 Robert Gordon	90.6	85.6	26	147	76	92.3
22 Salford	88.4	82.4	49.8	123	75.3	91.8
23 Nottingham	84.7	84.9	54.8	131	69.8	91.4
24 Northumbria	87.3	84.2	45.8	126	72.2	90.9
=25 Arts London	88	85.8	46	130	67.2	90.7
=25 Southampton	83.1	81.6	69.2	137	59.1	90.7
=27 Essex	81.4	75.4	49.8	128	78.9	90.4
=27 Gloucestershire	89.2	75.3	23.8	107	92.7	90.4
=29 Manchester Metropolitan	86	78.6	51.7	120	72.3	90.1
=29 Swansea	88.8	88.6	31.5	127	71.4	90.1
31 Nottingham Trent	87.8	79.7	42.5	110	78.3	90

Communication and Media Studies cont.

	Teaching quality %	Student experience %	Research quality %	Entry standards (UCAS points)	Graduate prospects %	Overall score
=32 Royal Holloway	81.6	77	63.7	126	67.9	89.9
=32 Sussex	83.7	82	61.8	124	64.6	89.9
=34 Sunderland	93.5	87.5	25.5	120	70.3	89.7
=34 West London	94.8	80.7	45.5	98	-	89.7
36 Canterbury Christ Church	91.9	85.3	38	96	75.9	89.5
37 West of England	85.6	79.4	48.2	117	70.6	89.2
=38 Birmingham City	89.2	83.4	40.8	122	65.1	89.1
=38 East Anglia	82.9	79.7	50.2	118	71.8	89.1
=40 Coventry	85.8	82.7	54.2	107	68.1	88.9
=40 Queen Margaret, Edinburgh	84.8	75	33	157	63.5	88.9
42 Teesside	92.9	77.2	49.2	94	69.2	88.6
43 Derby	91.5	84.8	24	109	74.1	88.5
44 Anglia Ruskin	89.1	86.6	53.8	85	-	88.4
45 Westminster	89.5	87	50	103	62.2	88.3
46 Bournemouth	80.1	75.8	47.2	109	79	88.2
=47 Goldsmiths, London	76.4	68.3	72.8	120	67.5	88
=47 Ulster	84.9	73.9	35	124	73.1	88
=49 Kingston	83.7	73.9	45	118	69.3	87.6
=49 Wolverhampton	95.3	84.9	31.5	91	-	87.6
51 Leeds Trinity	91.8	84.2	-	113	80.4	87.4
=52 Hertfordshire	79.2	76.8	24.2	121	82.7	87.3
=52 Leeds Beckett	86.3	82	26.5	115	71.9	87.3
=54 Bath Spa	88.4	81.2	42	118	59	87.2
=54 Keele	89	79.3	54.8	110	55.6	87.2
=54 Oxford Brookes	85.5	81.9	21.5	126	70.6	87.2
=54 Sheffield Hallam	83.2	73.8	46	116	68.6	87.2
=58 Falmouth	85	78.1	48.8	124	57.4	87
=58 Liverpool John Moores	87.1	81.9	22.2	124	68	87
60 Edge Hill	84.2	80.1	39.8	114	66.9	86.9
61 Portsmouth	85.7	79.7	30.2	113	68.9	86.5
62 Bangor	84.5	80.5	33.2	144	53.3	86.3
63 Brighton	82.5	75.9	44.2	110	66.5	86.1
64 Winchester	86.4	79.9	29.2	108	67.5	85.9
65 East London	82.6	71.3	34.2	114	70.7	85.7
66 Southampton Solent	90.7	87.7	9.5	112	65.4	85.6
67 Hull	91.4	84.1	35	101	54.4	85
68 South Wales	80.8	74.5	35.8	122	62.6	84.9
69 Roehampton	82.7	79.3	53	94	59.6	84.8
70 Lincoln	81.7	78.1	33.5	109	65.3	84.6
71 Worcester	89.8	81.5	5.8	105	69.9	84.5
72 Chester	86.9	79.8	21	113	60.9	84.2
73 Brunel	88	85.3	-	106	71.6	84.1
74 De Montfort	85.5	84	24	99	61.2	83.5
75 Liverpool Hope	86.9	76.6	-	116	69.4	83.4

76 West of Scotland	89.9	72.7	19.2	-	61	83.3
77 York St John	88.7	80.6	-	111	64.3	82.9
78 Huddersfield	71.1	60	49.8	112	64.3	81.7
79 Northampton	88.9	82	-	98	48.7	78.9
80 London Metropolitan	73.7	67	-	99	49.2	73.4

Employed in high-skilled job	53%	Employed in lower-skilled job	26%
Employed in high-skilled job and studying	2%	Employed in lower-skilled job and studying	1%
Studying	3%	Unemployed	8%
High-skilled work (median) salary	£23,000	Low-/medium-skilled salary	£19,300

Computer Science

Leading our new Computer Science table is Imperial, boosted by its students in the subject averaging 220 UCAS points – the highest entry standards – as well as securing the best results in computer science in our analysis of the Research Excellence Framework 2021, followed by last year's No 1 in the table, Oxford. There are seven universities where entry standards tip over 200 UCAS points and 34 average over 144 points (equal to three As at A-level), but with such a popular degree there are also places to be found with more accessible requirements. Our analysis of the latest National Student Survey shows students at East London (in =79th place overall) to have the highest rates of satisfaction with teaching quality and the broad experience, while Birmingham (fourth overall) also places in the top three for both. Computer science is the fastest-growing subject area in the UK, and the interest in computing degrees comes amid the rise in the popularity of AI and gaming. As a UCAS subject group, computing received 204,700 applications in 2023, a 5% increase year-on-year and around 38% more than six years before in 2019, while the numbers of students accepted onto courses reached over 38,000 in 2024 (up 24% compared with six years earlier). Courses encompass a number of areas, taking in everything from computer science (the largest area) and software engineering to AI (a sector in which applications and enrolments have more than doubled in the past six years), video games design and animation.

Job security in an evolving industrial landscape is part of the appeal. Thirty universities report at least 90% of their computer science graduates as being in high-skilled jobs or postgraduate study within 15 months. Oxford achieves a perfect 100%. Job prospects for computer science graduates are pretty good throughout the table, with only 17 of the 114 universities registering rates of high-skilled work/postgraduate study beneath 70%. As a whole, computer sciences ranks 25th out of our employment ranking's 70 subject areas. Although earnings are not an ingredient of our main subject rankings, applicants are often drawn to degrees within computer science on the basis of healthy graduate pay cheques; starting salaries of £29,860 rank the subject 14th out of 70 in our pay index.

Tom Curtin, industrial liaison officer, Department of Computing, Imperial College London notes: "Computer scientists have provided the digital systems at the heart of everything we do, driven the technology sector providing the basis for almost every trillion-dollar company to emerge over the past decade and, in the near future, will be at the helm of the next industrial revolution, driven by AI." Applicants are advised to ensure their maths skills are up to scratch, keep abreast of technology and data science news, and experiment with new computing technologies. Computing as a whole remains a male-dominated field: in 2024 only 21% of all applications were made by females and 20% of those accepted onto computing courses were female students.

Computer Science

	Teaching quality %	Student experience %	Research quality %	Entry standards (UCAS points)	Graduate prospects %	Overall score
1 Imperial College	86.9	84.9	94.8	220	97	100
2 Oxford	89.7	81.4	85.8	211	100	99.4
3 Cambridge	87.8	80.5	78.2	216	94.8	97.3
4 Birmingham	92.4	92.4	82.8	167	97.2	97.2
5 St Andrews	88.4	90	41.2	218	99.1	95.6
6 University College London	77.9	80.2	82.2	199	95.2	94.2
7 Warwick	78.8	81	81.8	198	93	94
8 Bristol	84.6	83.3	76	176	94.7	93.8
9 Glasgow	79.8	80.8	71.8	209	91.4	93.5
10 Durham	82.3	81.9	59	199	96.6	93.4
11 Manchester	78.1	78.3	71.2	189	97.5	92.8
12 Edinburgh	71.5	70.1	81.2	212	92	91.9
13 Sheffield	81.5	84.5	69.8	168	92.5	91.5
14 Bath	81.7	85	52.2	187	93.1	91.2
15 Dundee	87.9	81.1	53.5	184	86.8	90.9
16 Southampton	74.7	76.2	70.8	174	92.4	89.6
17 Queen Mary, London	81.7	80.7	74.2	155	84.9	89.2
18 Leeds	76.3	75.9	72	161	92.1	89.1
19 King's College London	71	72.2	68	176	96	88.9
=20 Lancaster	79.1	79.8	64.8	151	92.4	88.7
=20 Loughborough	84.2	86.5	46.5	156	90.3	88.7
=20 Strathclyde	78.8	74.4	46.2	202	87.6	88.7
23 Liverpool	79.7	82.6	61	137	94.2	88.2
24 York	73.9	73.8	72.5	153	93.5	88.1
25 Surrey	82	85.5	50.5	139	92.4	87.7
26 Royal Holloway	80.2	78.6	65	127	91.8	87.2
27 Exeter	79.1	81.8	45.5	148	93.8	87.1
28 Sussex	81.6	82.7	59.2	131	88.6	86.9
29 Nottingham	73	73.3	63.5	161	89.7	86.6
30 Swansea	83.9	83.6	46.5	128	90.7	86.5
31 Cardiff	73.8	74.9	57.8	152	91.7	86.2
32 Newcastle	73.6	76.2	60.5	137	91.9	85.6
33 Leicester	82.4	83.1	41.8	131	89.4	85.5
34 Queen's, Belfast	71.5	75.4	51	148	92.3	84.9
=35 Essex	80.1	80.5	53.5	126	85.7	84.8
=35 Heriot-Watt	71.3	70.9	39.5	179	90	84.8
37 Edinburgh Napier	78.8	76.2	47.2	155	82.6	84.7
38 Manchester Metropolitan	85.3	82.8	29.2	138	83.6	84.1
39 East Anglia	80.2	79.9	41.8	120	88.7	83.7
40 Aberystwyth	86.1	79.5	43.8	110	84	83.6
41 Ulster	82.1	80.4	38	118	87.2	83.4
42 Aston	80.4	78.1	29.2	131	89.5	83.2
43 Aberdeen	73.1	74.2	44	161	-	83.1
=44 Glasgow Caledonian	83.6	81.5	13.8	159	81.2	82.9

=44 Northumbria	83.4	79.3	25.8	126	87.6	82.9
=44 Portsmouth	86.1	84.4	32.8	119	80.7	82.9
47 Brunel	85	81.2	37.5	121	78.7	82.5
48 Reading	77.5	79.1	39.8	120	87	82.4
49 Worcester	89.1	89.9	12.5	107	86	82.3
50 Abertay	85	80	-	162	82.8	82.2
51 Kent	74.8	74	57.2	123	81.1	82
52 City St George's	69.9	73.1	47.5	136	86.7	81.8
=53 Bangor	81.8	78.7	40.2	124	77.1	81.6
=53 Lincoln	77.4	81.1	44	106	84.5	81.6
55 Robert Gordon	83.3	75.4	16	157	77.5	81.5
=56 Coventry	87.4	84.8	23.5	106	80.5	81.3
=56 Plymouth	78.2	74.7	32	124	85.4	81.3
=58 Hull	82.8	83.1	31.2	108	81.8	81.2
=58 Sunderland	90.3	89.6	14.5	102	80	81.2
=58 West of England	78.8	77.5	32.2	121	83.8	81.2
=61 Brighton	81.1	81.7	32.5	109	80.9	80.7
=61 Chester	82.6	78	13.2	128	83.9	80.7
=63 Birmingham City	85	84	23.2	120	75.6	80.6
=63 Stirling	76	64.6	24	161	81.1	80.6
65 Arts London	82.3	77.8	46	126	68.3	80.5
66 Teesside	92.2	88.3	18.8	125	65.3	80.4
=67 South Wales	86.8	80.3	18.8	126	74.3	80.3
=67 West of Scotland	90.3	80.8	18	130	69.1	80.3
69 Liverpool John Moores	84.2	82.1	26	121	74.1	80.2
70 Nottingham Trent	82.7	77.5	26	114	79	80
71 Huddersfield	77.8	75.2	26.5	117	83.8	79.9
72 Staffordshire	81.8	71.9	25.5	122	79.7	79.8
=73 Greater Manchester	92.8	88.8	-	114	73.8	79.7
=73 Hertfordshire	77.3	79.5	41.2	124	72.3	79.7
=73 Wolverhampton	84.6	84.3	12.5	95	85.3	79.7
=76 Bournemouth	80.1	76.7	22.2	112	82.7	79.5
=76 Oxford Brookes	81.7	78.8	24.2	105	80.8	79.5
78 Keele	79.3	81.5	20.8	112	81.8	79.4
=79 East London	96	96.7	28.7	103	52.7	78.9
=79 Edge Hill	78.1	80.4	20	119	79.4	78.9
81 Sheffield Hallam	80.9	77.3	17	120	78.1	78.8
82 Leeds Beckett	82.2	79.2	18.2	117	74.7	78.5
=83 Bedfordshire	86	85	15.2	95	74.2	78
=83 Kingston	82	84	23.5	108	70.8	78
85 Falmouth	75.5	61.5	48.8	130	67.4	77.6
86 De Montfort	79.2	79.3	25	96	77.2	77.5
=87 Bath Spa	84.1	74.2	-	100	84	77.4
=87 Westminster	81.1	83.8	24	107	69	77.4
=89 Bradford	76.9	73.2	20.5	120	75	77.1
=89 Goldsmiths, London	76.9	70.9	28.5	104	77.2	77.1
91 Salford	75.3	73.5	28.2	122	71.4	76.9
92 Liverpool Hope	84.3	71.7	19.5	109	69.6	76.8

Computer Science cont.

	Teaching quality %	Student experience %	Research quality %	Entry standards (UCAS points)	Graduate prospects %	Overall score
93 London South Bank	81.1	81.9	-	107	78	76.6
94 Greenwich	77.5	75.8	28	110	69.6	76.5
95 York St John	73	67.1	-	107	93.2	76.4
96 Anglia Ruskin	84	82.8	10	88	74.3	76.3
97 Roehampton	81	78.7	53	86	58.5	76.2
98 Buckinghamshire New	82.3	68.3	-	102	81.6	76
99 Derby	74.5	72	15.8	110	77.8	75.9
=100 Wales Trinity St David	82.2	78.4	-	128	68	75.8
=100 West London	81.9	84.2	20	105	63	75.8
102 Gloucestershire	78.3	67.5	6.2	109	79.3	75.6
103 Northampton	78.5	74.8	8.5	97	77.3	75.3
104 Southampton Solent	81.6	74.8	-	111	71.7	75
105 Cardiff Metropolitan	77.9	77.6	-	116	72.9	74.9
106 Middlesex	81.8	74.3	20.2	103	63.9	74.8
107 Lancashire	73.5	67.2	17.8	114	72	74.3
108 Canterbury Christ Church	75.2	71.6	16.8	110	66.4	73.6
109 Norwich University of the Arts	75.3	70.5	-	130	61.2	72.1
110 London Metropolitan	75.1	73.2	13.2	80	68.8	71.8
111 Suffolk	71.6	59.1	-	103	72	70.6
112 Winchester	58.3	53.6	-	107	87.8	70.4
113 Creative Arts	82.8	73.2	-	113	41.3	68.7
114 Wrexham	65.8	65.7	1.5	80	64.3	66.7

Employed in high-skilled job	65%	Employed in lower-skilled job	11%
Employed in high-skilled job and studying	4%	Employed in lower-skilled job and studying	1%
Studying	4%	Unemployed	9%
High-skilled work (median) salary	£30,000	Low-/medium-skilled salary	£20,000

Creative Writing

Taking the lead in our new Creative Writing table, Strathclyde attracts the highest entry standards among its creative writing students and places in the top ten for teaching quality. In third place this year Newcastle topped last year's table and has the top research in the field, based on results of the Research Excellence Framework 2021, followed by Leeds (17th overall), and runner-up Nottingham. Another former creative writing No 1, Warwick, takes fourth place this year. Creative writing students tend to enjoy their studies, as represented in our latest National Student Survey analysis, which shows high rates of satisfaction with teaching quality throughout the table. These are topped by Hull, which places =13th overall. Nottingham does best for students' evaluation of the broader experience.

Applicants to creative writing courses may not be motivated by immediate professional full-time employment upon graduation, which is perhaps why only 20 of the 49 universities tabled post a graduate prospects score. Of these, West of England does best based on 77.2% of its graduates being employed in high-skilled work and/or further study within 15 months – a proportion which falls to 44.8% at Chichester. As a whole, creative writing sits at the foot of our employment ranking of 70 subject areas this year. More than four in ten graduates were in high-skilled work and/or further study when surveyed 15 months after their degrees, but three in ten were in jobs deemed "low-skilled" and around one in ten were unemployed – the highest unemployment rate of any subject group. Creative writing is also bottom of the salaries table, jointly with animal science.

After two years of rising demand for creative writing courses, applications for 2024 entry dipped by around 10%, when just under 7,400 applied for degrees. New student enrolments also decreased to 1,640 undergraduates accepted onto creative writing programmes, the lowest number in six years. There remain 109 universities and colleges offering the subject in 2026–27, four fewer than the year before.

Creative Writing	Teaching quality %	Student experience %	Research quality %	Entry standards (UCAS points)	Graduate prospects %	Overall score
1 Strathclyde	94	84.4	58.8	198	-	100
2 Nottingham	94.6	95.2	70.5	152	-	98
3 Newcastle	89.8	82.7	83.8	142	-	95.7
=4 Dundee	93.8	88.3	40.8	173	-	94.6
=4 Warwick	86.1	81	64.8	172	-	94.6
6 University College London	90.2	87.7	61.5	150	-	93.9
=7 Birmingham	84.9	83	68.8	144	74.6	92.8
=7 Exeter	84.4	82	59.5	168	-	92.8
9 Keele	95.5	88	54.8	126	-	92
=10 East Anglia	83.6	79.9	67	140	75.5	91.8
=10 Royal Holloway	88.2	85.9	60.5	142	-	91.8
12 Bangor	95.7	93	44.2	-	67.4	91.6
=13 Hull	97.6	92.8	55.5	107	-	91.2
=13 Lancaster	90.6	86.1	48	146	-	91.2
15 Birmingham City	91.5	90.3	65.5	114	-	91.1
16 Sussex	87.5	83.8	67	128	-	90.8
17 Leeds	79.2	71.9	73.2	156	-	90.5
=18 Coventry	94.2	91	54.2	112	-	90.1
=18 Manchester Metropolitan	89.5	78.6	61.8	122	70.1	90.1
20 Brunel	95.4	93.2	42.8	112	67.4	89.2
21 West of England	92.3	90.1	32.2	115	77.2	89.1
22 Plymouth	90.3	73.1	60.5	118	-	88.3
23 Kent	86	77.1	64.5	121	-	88.2
24 York St John	96.6	88.1	22.8	107	72.7	87.4
25 Lincoln	94.8	86.2	36	107	-	86.4
26 Reading	85.1	75.8	51	126	-	86.1
=27 Kingston	86.1	68	47	132	-	85.7
=27 Westminster	87.4	87.3	55.5	97	-	85.7
29 Nottingham Trent	88.9	79.9	39.2	121	-	85.6
30 Brighton	84.2	77.3	44.2	101	74.5	85.5
=31 Edge Hill	93.1	79.7	32.8	118	60.8	85.4
=31 Gloucestershire	92.5	89.8	32.8	114	59.2	85.4
=31 Liverpool John Moores	80.6	74	58	123	63.2	85.4

Creative Writing cont.

	Teaching quality %	Student experience %	Research quality %	Entry standards (UCAS points)	Graduate prospects %	Overall score
34 Sheffield Hallam	86.9	70.4	50.7	118	-	85.2
35 Aberystwyth	89.7	84.8	25.5	113	66.2	84.7
36 Chichester	94.2	88.7	37.2	124	44.8	84.2
=37 Bath Spa	88.1	82	51.7	112	50.9	83.8
=37 Salford	86.4	72.7	26.5	125	65.3	83.8
39 Liverpool Hope	85.5	84.4	36	116	-	83.7
40 Portsmouth	86.6	81.7	30.8	107	65.7	83.6
41 Anglia Ruskin	87.8	83	46	92	-	83.2
=42 Falmouth	80.4	73.6	48.8	119	-	83
=42 Leeds Beckett	91.5	79.4	30.8	103	-	83
44 Arts Bournemouth	86.9	85.2	23	120	-	82.7
45 Greenwich	86.7	80.7	26.5	109	-	81.5
46 Worcester	89	83.4	19.2	107	-	81.2
47 Winchester	86.8	76.6	16.2	112	56.1	80
48 De Montfort	83.5	60.4	54.5	92	51.7	79.6
49 Chester	78.2	68.8	25	122	-	78.3

Employed in high-skilled job	36%	Employed in lower-skilled job	30%
Employed in high-skilled job and studying	3%	Employed in lower-skilled job and studying	2%
Studying	6%	Unemployed	10%
High-skilled work (median) salary	£24,000	Low-/medium-skilled salary	£19,000

Criminology

Sheffield has ousted Loughborough at the top of our Criminology table, boosted by the best score for graduate job prospects – based on 82.8% of its criminology graduates being in high-skilled work and/or further study within 15 months, and entry standards that rank in the top five. Runner-up Loughborough continues to perform strongly across all metrics, and its criminology students gave the the most positive feedback on their broad experience in the latest National Student Survey (NSS), followed by those at Manchester Met (25th overall) and tenth-place Lancaster. For students' evaluation of teaching quality Suffolk comes out top, and ranks =38th overall. Kent is in the lead for research in our analysis of the latest Research Excellence Framework 2021, where it is followed by Southampton (fourth in the main table) and City St George's (18th).

"What is crime? Why does it occur? And what are the best ways to address it?" asks Dr Donna Marie Brown, associate professor in criminology, Durham University. Covering topics including policing, prisons and youth justice, criminology students learn about criminological theory, the roles of criminal justice agencies and the impact of crimes on victims and communities. Now in its tenth year and stretching to 88 universities, our Criminology table reflects this growing undergraduate field, offered by 156 universities and colleges across 1,260 courses for 2026-27, either by itself, as part of a joint honours degree, or within a broader social science degree. Sociology and psychology are welcomed by some university departments, but there are no specific entry requirements for criminology degrees, apart possibly from GCSE maths, since the course is likely to involve the use of statistics.

Career opportunities further down the line include the police force, prison service, Home Office, charities or law practice. But overall, criminology comes second from bottom of our employment index, where it is held back by the almost equal proportion of graduates that start out in low-skilled jobs (36.2%) as in high-skilled employment (37.2%). Average early career salaries of £23,000 compare more favourably with other subject areas, and criminology ranks =62nd out of 70.

Criminology

	Teaching quality %	Student experience %	Research quality %	Entry standards (UCAS points)	Graduate prospects %	Overall score
1 Sheffield	86.7	86.6	55	149	82.8	100
2 Loughborough	85.8	90.1	55.8	138	82.5	99.1
3 Bath	86	82.9	59.5	147	-	96.9
4 Southampton	85.3	84.1	66.8	137	71.1	96.8
5 Durham	85.1	79.2	53	158	70.7	96.6
6 University College London	84.2	83.4	61.5	144	-	96.3
7 Queen's, Belfast	87.5	84	56.5	140	69.8	96.2
8 York	85.1	83.6	58	136	72.2	95.8
9 Stirling	80.6	81.8	47.5	180	64.6	95.7
10 Lancaster	89.6	88.5	48	132	69.7	95.5
11 Exeter	83	83	46.8	152	70.8	95.2
12 Essex	86.9	82.1	62.5	147	59.3	94.8
=13 Cardiff	81.9	83.7	54	144	69	94.5
=13 Nottingham	86.6	86.1	54	137	65.3	94.5
15 Leicester	85.1	86	52.2	123	67.3	93.1
16 Swansea	87.4	87.3	27.8	130	72.2	92.8
17 Birmingham	81.2	84.3	61	134	61.5	92.6
18 City St George's	81.3	82.5	64	117	64.2	91.7
19 Plymouth	83.4	80.4	50.5	115	69.7	91.6
20 Liverpool	81.3	83.5	55	131	61.3	91.4
21 West London	89.1	87.3	39	105	65.4	90.6
=22 Lancashire	84.7	76.6	51.5	115	64.6	90.5
=22 Royal Holloway	80.3	80.5	38	124	70.9	90.5
24 Wrexham	92.3	84.4	20.5	115	66.7	90.3
25 Manchester Metropolitan	88.2	88.9	32.8	117	61.5	90
26 Sussex	84.8	79.9	41	120	63.8	89.9
27 Huddersfield	84.6	81.8	43.5	108	65.3	89.6
28 Surrey	91.3	87.2	-	128	67.7	89.5
29 Portsmouth	84.4	84.5	33	113	65.9	89.2
30 Manchester	79.6	78.3	40.8	148	55.8	89.1
31 West of England	82.1	79	35.2	110	69.7	88.9
32 Birmingham City	87.9	85.7	25.8	120	58.6	88.4
33 Bedfordshire	90.4	84.7	50.2	76	-	88.3
34 Liverpool John Moores	87.8	87.6	15.8	119	62.1	88.1
35 Ulster	86.7	81	53.8	115	47.7	87.8
=36 Kent	77.2	73.5	72.2	106	56.1	87.7
=36 Liverpool Hope	91.4	85.7	21.2	112	57	87.7

Criminology cont.

	Teaching quality %	Student experience %	Research quality %	Entry standards (UCAS points)	Graduate prospects %	Overall score
=38 Suffolk	95.6	87	21.8	87	-	87.5
=38 Westminster	85.8	84.3	31.5	99	63.4	87.5
=40 Keele	86.5	82.3	33.2	99	62	87.4
=40 Lincoln	77.8	79.8	51	104	62.9	87.4
42 South Wales	82.6	74.7	33.5	111	64.2	87.2
=43 Bangor	82.3	74.5	33.2	121	-	87.1
=43 Hull	81.2	80.6	53.8	98	57.9	87.1
45 Nottingham Trent	86.6	83.6	29.5	106	58.7	87
46 Aberystwyth	84.4	81.6	34.2	100	61.9	86.9
=47 Abertay	85.6	79.8	-	146	58.5	86.7
=47 Edge Hill	87.9	87.9	17.5	114	56.6	86.7
=49 Middlesex	84.3	80.4	27.8	96	66.1	86.6
=49 Worcester	88.7	83.2	12.8	104	64.3	86.6
51 Bournemouth	82.3	79.4	10.2	105	73.4	86.5
=52 London Metropolitan	91.5	87.7	-	104	63.5	86.2
=52 Sheffield Hallam	85.4	79	26.2	110	58.7	86.2
=54 Greenwich	82.5	81.5	37	102	58.6	86.1
=54 Northumbria	71.8	67.9	42	130	63.1	86.1
56 Sunderland	85.5	75.8	39.5	102	56	86
57 Salford	81.2	80.9	44.5	114	51	85.9
58 Edinburgh Napier	80.8	77.7	35.2	150	42.2	85.8
=59 Birmingham Newman	82.1	75	13.8	89	76.8	85.6
=59 Derby	86.1	81.4	25.5	106	56.7	85.6
=61 Brighton	84	80.1	34	95	55.4	84.6
=61 Chichester	90.5	87.1	3	102	-	84.6
=63 Teesside	88.5	80.2	18.2	104	52.7	84.3
=63 York St John	90.9	83.3	-	106	56.6	84.3
65 Roehampton	80.2	77.7	40.2	93	56.9	84.2
66 Canterbury Christ Church	89.8	86	-	104	56.6	84
=67 Kingston	83.2	84.1	27	107	50.2	83.9
=67 Staffordshire	80.5	65.8	18.2	105	66.4	83.9
69 Coventry	85.2	77.6	-	103	64.4	83.6
=70 De Montfort	81.7	78.4	43.2	88	52.5	83.5
=70 Leeds Beckett	81.4	83.2	17.8	106	56	83.5
=70 Leeds Trinity	89.3	82.1	-	106	56.2	83.5
=70 Winchester	81.9	77.8	16.5	99	61.3	83.5
74 Southampton Solent	86.6	80.5	9.5	98	57.2	83.2
75 East London	81.2	75.8	40	86	53.2	82.7
=76 Chester	87.9	88.4	12.8	119	38.5	82.4
=76 Oxford Brookes	85.3	83.4	28.2	102	42.9	82.4
78 Wolverhampton	85.9	79	12.2	94	-	82.3
79 St Mary's, Twickenham	85.8	84.2	10.5	89	-	82
80 Hertfordshire	77.9	72	-	106	66.2	81.8
81 London South Bank	79.4	79.7	27.8	92	52.8	81.7

82 Bradford		81.8	78.9	-	108	51.4	80.3
83 Bath Spa		83.1	82.6	-	80	58.9	80
=84 Anglia Ruskin		76.1	60.9	35.5	95	51.4	79.7
=84 Gloucestershire		80.1	69.2	-	96	60.3	79.7
86 Northampton		79.1	78.8	4.2	84	39.6	74.9
87 Buckinghamshire New		71.4	65.1	12.5	78	-	73.2
88 Cumbria		63.8	45.3	8.2	85	-	68.1

Employed in high-skilled job	37%	Employed in lower-skilled job	36%
Employed in high-skilled job and studying	4%	Employed in lower-skilled job and studying	2%
Studying	6%	Unemployed	5%
High-skilled work (median) salary	£24,700	Low-/medium-skilled salary	£20,500

Cultural Studies

New this year, our Cultural Studies table incorporates courses within American studies, Celtic studies, East and South Asian studies, and Middle Eastern and African studies. Formerly occupying four separate tables, these subject areas continue to be referenced separately in Graduate Outcomes and salary comparisons in this year's *Good University Guide* (see pages 51–55). But the small – and diminishing – numbers of students they attract have prompted their amalgamation into a single main Cultural Studies table. At No 1 in our inaugural ranking is University College London (the leading university for American studies in our last edition), its position buoyed by the top research rating, based on results of the latest Research Excellence Framework 2021. Runner-up the London School of Economics has the second-highest entry standards – 196 UCAS points – jointly with Oxford (sixth place overall).

American studies degrees combine disciplines including history, politics and literature, concentrating on the United States as well as Latin America and the Caribbean. Students often have the chance to spend a year at a university across the pond as part of a four-year course. The subject helps students understand challenges such as inequality, climate crisis, international security and migration. Universities look for English language, English literature and history A-levels, while politics is also considered useful. Graduates of American studies are set up for a range of careers, working at home and abroad, in business, government, the civil service, NGOs and charities or education. But American studies ranks only 60th out of 70 subject areas for graduate prospects 15 months after degrees, while average starting salaries of £24,000 place it =54th.

For Celtic studies, the content of courses caters largely to each university's host Celtic nation. Universities in Wales focus predominantly on degrees in Welsh history, culture and language, and those in Scotland and Ireland cover similar themes but with the focus on Gaelic, Scottish or Irish studies. The subject encompasses topics including history, mythology and folklore, modern literature, linguistics, and contemporary struggles for the revitalisation of languages such as Welsh, Scottish Gaelic and Irish. Most students become fluent in at least one of the languages. Career prospects for those with a Celtic studies degree have tended to be positive. The subject ranks 35th in our employment ranking of 70 subject areas and places =23rd in our salaries index, based on average annual earnings of £26,500.

East and South Asian Studies degrees encompass Chinese studies, Japanese studies and South Asian studies. The subjects are offered by only a small number of universities in the UK, among them SOAS in London (in 23rd place of our table overall), which also offers a range of languages including Burmese, Indonesian, Thai, Tibetan and Vietnamese.

"Students learn about the events that have shaped the so-called 'subcontinent' over three millennia and resonated well beyond its boundaries, such as the composition of the Vedas to the rise of Hinduism and Buddhism; the early development of intellectual traditions in fields such as philosophy, linguistics and mathematics; the spread of Islam and the rise of the Persianate culture; the 'encounter' with the Europeans and the experience of colonialism; and the fight for independence up to the emergence of India as an economic and political powerhouse on the global scene," explains Dr Vincenzo Vergiani, professor of Sanskrit, Faculty of Middle Eastern Studies, University of Cambridge. Most undergraduates learn their chosen language from scratch, although universities expect to see evidence of potential in other modern language qualifications. East and South Asian studies rank 64th in our graduate employment list of 70 subject areas, while starting salaries of £25,000 compare more favourably, =46th place of our pay index.

Students of Middle Eastern studies may become versed in the key languages of Arabic, Hebrew, Persian and Turkish. As a grouping, the subjects place 36th in our graduate prospects index and those with a degree in Middle Eastern and African studies earn £28,000 graduate salaries, on average, ranking the subject in the top 20 of our pay list.

Cultural Studies

	Teaching quality %	Student experience %	Research quality %	Entry standards (UCAS points)	Graduate prospects %	Overall score
1 University College London	87.5	81	140.8	153		100
2 London School of Economics	91.1	86.1	59.5	196		94.3
3 Cardiff	94.4	90.4	55.5	150		93.1
4 Aberystwyth	97.5	98.9	41.2	166		91.9
5 Bangor	97.1	90.3	42	176		91.2
6 Oxford	80	58.5	62.3	196		90.6
7 Cambridge	87.7	71	45.2	190		89.2
8 East Anglia	85.8	85.2	63	-		88.5
9 Sussex	89.6	80.6	65.1	130		88.4
10 Queen's, Belfast	93.3	87.4	37	153		87.4
11 Nottingham	86.8	88.3	62.6	131		87
=12 Exeter	84.2	82.2	65.8	138		86.8
=12 Newcastle	89.4	86.8	61.8	126		86.8
14 Manchester	83.8	81.5	62.6	145		86.4
15 Durham	78.8	64.3	44.8	179		86.3
16 Ulster	94.8	91.3	37	133		86.1
17 Birmingham	83.3	83.7	68.8	-		85.7
18 Swansea	92.9	90.3	45.2	106		85.5
19 Edinburgh	71.8	67.5	48.2	179		84.9
20 Liverpool	83.2	83.9	65.5	123		84.7
21 Glasgow	88.2	82.1	40.8	206		84.6
22 Sheffield	88.8	83.3	48.8	153		84.2
23 SOAS, London	78.6	66.4	60	125		83.8
24 Leeds	78.2	74.5	52	151		83.4
25 Oxford Brookes	88.4	87.5	36	111		81.3
26 Westminster	86.2	85	24.5	111		78.5
27 Lancashire	78.6	68	31.8	114		74.1

American studies

Employed in high-skilled job	38%	Employed in lower-skilled job	31%
Employed in high-skilled job and studying	1%	Employed in lower-skilled job and studying	0%
Studying	12%	Unemployed	6%
High-skilled work (median) salary	£25,000	Low/medium skilled salary	£20,000

Celtic studies

Employed in high-skilled job	35%	Employed in lower-skilled job	17%
Employed in high-skilled job and studying	13%	Employed in lower-skilled job and studying	5%
Studying	17%	Unemployed	0%
High-skilled work (median) salary	£27,000	Low-/medium-skilled salary	N/A

East and South Asian studies

Employed in high-skilled job	36%	Employed in lower-skilled job	29%
Employed in high-skilled job and studying	3%	Employed in lower-skilled job and studying	2%
Studying	12%	Unemployed	9%
High-skilled work (median) salary	£27,500	Low-/medium-skilled salary	£20,000

Middle Eastern and African studies

Employed in high-skilled job	49%	Employed in lower-skilled job	17%
Employed in high-skilled job and studying	5%	Employed in lower-skilled job and studying	1%
Studying	10%	Unemployed	10%
High-skilled work (median) salary	£30,000	Low-/medium-skilled salary	N/A

Dentistry

Returning to the top of the Dentistry table is Glasgow, which topped it for a seven-year run until Queen's, Belfast took the helm for the past two years. But with just 15 undergraduate dental schools across the country, this is one of the smaller and more stable subject rankings and this year's table differs very little from our previous edition, albeit with some reshuffling, such as Dundee gaining two places to rank second and Bristol edging one place down to fourth. The dental school at Glasgow was established in 1879. It has the highest average entry grades in the UK (236 UCAS points), sits fourth for research and seventh for student satisfaction with the broad experience, as well as fifth for teaching quality – both measures derived from our National Student Survey analysis. Dundee and Liverpool each achieve perfect 100% rates of graduate employment in high-skilled jobs and/or further study 15 months after degrees. King's College London is top for research but bottom for both measures of student satisfaction, teaching quality and the wider experience. The table is dominated by older universities, with only Plymouth and Lancashire representing the modern university sector.

The increasing demand for dentistry degrees continued to climb in 2024 when applications rose to nearly 26,700 – a 15% increase year-on-year and reflecting a huge longer-term surge of around 81% across the past six years. The number of dental school places available is capped by the government, as with medicine, creating a notoriously competitive recruitment landscape: 1,485 dentistry students began courses in 2024. Career prospects are reliably positive. Dentistry remains the No 1 most lucrative option for graduates, with a median starting salary of £42,000. Although graduate outcomes are not as consistently high as for medicine, most graduates (88.4%) from five-year dentistry courses are in a high-skilled job as a dentist or enrolled on postgraduate study within 15 months – which ranks dentistry sixth in our employment index.

Dentistry

	Teaching quality %	Student experience %	Research quality %	Entry standards (UCAS points)	Graduate prospects %	Overall score
1 Glasgow	92.8	80.5	63.5	236	97.4	100
2 Dundee	92.2	88.9	60.8	225	100	98.2
3 Queen's, Belfast	98.4	98.6	66.2	179	93.4	95
4 Bristol	94.9	94.3	70.9	174	95.5	94.8
5 Newcastle	92.3	89.3	65.8	171	97.3	91.8
6 Liverpool	96.4	93.2	63.2	166	100	91.3
7 Sheffield	89	73.6	63.7	164	94.8	88.2
8 Cardiff	87.1	72.6	58.8	173	96.2	87.6
9 Leeds	85	79.2	65	154	95.2	86.8
10 Manchester	71.4	61.3	71.2	167	96.8	86.7
11 Birmingham	88.1	76.3	55	161	95.7	85.1
12 King's College London	51.6	44.9	76.2	162	94.2	82.6
13 Plymouth	93.1	89	39.5	160	95.6	81.8
14 Queen Mary, London	70.6	60.9	54.8	170	96.8	81.6
15 Lancashire	83.6	66.9	35.5	-	97.7	74.6

Employed in high-skilled job	81%	Employed in lower-skilled job	0%
Employed in high-skilled job and studying	7%	Employed in lower-skilled job and studying	0%
Studying	1%	Unemployed	3%
High-skilled work (median) salary	£42,000	Low-/medium-skilled salary	N/A

Drama, Dance, Cinematics and Photography

A shake-up of the table has brought Warwick to the top this year, its overall rank boosted by strong performances across all metrics, without leading in any individually. Entrants to Warwick averaged 168 UCAS points, the highest entry standards south of the border, while Glasgow tops the table with 191 UCAS points. Third-place Manchester is in front for research quality, based on results of the Research Excellence Framework 2021, where it is closely followed by the Central School of Speech and Drama, Royal Holloway (21st overall) and Queen Mary, London – which has gained one place rank as runner-up. In =34th place overall, Central ranks fourth among the six specialist institutions, behind Guildhall (8th), Royal Conservatoire of Scotland (22nd) and Trinity Laban (23rd), and ahead of Rose Bruford (=41st), and LAMDA (92nd).

Students at Bedfordshire expressed the highest rates of satisfaction with teaching quality and the wider experience in our latest National Student Survey (NSS) analysis. Conversely, those at Brighton (in 98th place overall) gave the least positive reviews of teaching quality, while St Mary's Twickenham is bottom for student satisfaction with the wider experience for the second year running.

Two universities: Surrey (10th in the table) and East Anglia (40th) registered over 80% of their graduates employed in high-skilled jobs and/or furthering their studies within 15 months of their degrees. Around half that proportion (41.8%) had achieved the same outcomes among graduates of Brighton – one of five universities with less than half of its graduates achieving these outcomes 15 months on, along with West of Scotland, Bedfordshire, Hertfordshire, and Liverpool Hope. The subjects as a whole rank 63rd out of the 70 in our employment ranking.

Although 20 institutions averaged over 144 UCAS among their entrants (equivalent to AAA), performance or portfolio are often more important criteria for entry and there are plenty of courses with accessible entry standards. Dr David Butler, senior lecturer in drama and film studies, University of Manchester advises applicants to: "Keep a diary of the productions you watch or listen to, jotting down moments and uses of set design, colour, sound, music, dialogue and gesture, etc. that stood out for you, to heighten your powers of perception."

Courses are broad-based within our Drama, Dance, Cinematics and Photography table, covering the four disciplines (although UCAS pairs photography with cinematics under the same grouping), and ranging from acting, theatre studies and performing arts to professional and commercial dance, film studies and photography. Joint honours courses, such as drama studies and English, are also incorporated.

Drama, Dance, Cinematics and Photography	Teaching quality %	Student experience %	Research quality %	Entry standards (UCAS points)	Graduate prospects %	Overall score
1 Warwick	91.4	86	68.8	168	70.4	100
2 Queen Mary, London	92.3	84.7	76.4	138	77	99.5
3 Manchester	85.1	80.4	80.5	160	73.3	99.2
4 City St George's	94.6	81.5	66.5	153	-	98.9
5 Glasgow	81.8	77.9	60.5	191	68.5	98.1
6 Exeter	84.6	80.8	62.3	159	77.1	98
7 Durham	94	92.8	59.5	140	-	97.1
8 Guildhall School of Music and Drama	88.1	72.2	61.3	154	74.6	96.8
9 Aberdeen	90.2	83.7	32.5	178	-	96.4
10 Surrey	84	68.8	43.8	156	83	96
11 Essex	92	82.8	34.2	164	70.1	95.7
12 Birmingham	89.2	81.8	50.2	149	70.2	94.9
=13 Bristol	83.1	82.5	64.2	156	65.4	94.5
=13 Lancaster	87.3	78.9	59.5	158	63.8	94.5
15 York	78.2	64.2	58.2	156	74.4	93.4
=16 Edinburgh	78.1	69.7	59.2	180	56.9	91.9
=16 Manchester Metropolitan	83.1	75.6	61.8	140	65.7	91.9
18 West of England	87.6	80.5	48.2	144	62.6	91.6
=19 Coventry	89.1	83	55.5	115	68.5	91.3
=19 Leeds	83.5	73	56.8	150	61.8	91.3
21 Royal Holloway	79.1	71.3	78.5	134	64.2	91.2
22 Royal Conservatoire of Scotland	88.1	77.5	35.2	160	59.3	90.9
23 Trinity Laban	84	73	38	129	75.6	90.7
=24 Aberystwyth	91.3	83.6	44.5	119	65.9	90.4
=24 Northumbria	88.3	84.1	45.8	129	63.7	90.4
26 Edinburgh Napier	81.3	68.5	8.5	182	68.1	90.3
=27 Kent	87.2	81.4	74.8	124	55.1	90.2
=27 Nottingham Trent	90.7	81.2	53	125	60	90.2
=29 Birmingham City	88.5	75.2	46.5	130	63.1	89.8
=29 Newcastle	79.1	71.6	59.2	142	-	89.8
31 Westminster	79	75.1	75.5	133	58.9	89.7
32 Sunderland	89.4	82.9	49.8	128	57.3	89.2
33 Queen's, Belfast	83.5	75	46.8	142	59.5	88.9

Drama, Dance, Cinematics and Photography cont.	Teaching quality %	Student experience %	Research quality %	Entry standards (UCAS points)	Graduate prospects %	Overall score
=34 Central School of Speech and Drama	77.4	64.3	79.8	108	68.3	88.5
=34 Goldsmiths, London	76.8	57.8	46.8	126	76.8	88.5
36 Queen Margaret, Edinburgh	91.1	78.5	-	166	57.6	88.1
37 Salford	87.4	78.3	30.2	135	61.3	88
=38 Canterbury Christ Church	90.7	87.7	38.5	115	59.4	87.8
=38 Plymouth	88.7	78.4	49.8	114	60	87.8
40 East Anglia	82.5	69.8	-	129	81.8	87.6
=41 Kingston	81	73	45	130	63.2	87.5
=41 Rose Bruford	90.2	72.4	19	138	61.9	87.5
=43 Lancashire	91.2	86.1	19	119	63.3	87.2
=43 Portsmouth	87.5	81.8	30.2	120	63.2	87.2
=45 Chichester	90.4	80.1	13.2	126	64.9	87.1
=45 Ulster	84.2	81.1	49	115	60.4	87.1
=45 Wolverhampton	95.5	90	6.8	117	63.4	87.1
48 Falmouth	82.6	77.1	48.8	131	56.4	87
=49 De Montfort	81.9	70.3	45	112	68.1	86.8
=49 Lincoln	89.8	82.9	37.2	117	57.7	86.8
51 Liverpool John Moores	91	83.3	22.2	128	57.6	86.7
52 Reading	78.1	71.9	59	130	57	86.5
=53 Hull	84.6	79.1	35	110	66.2	86.4
=53 Roehampton	81.5	57.5	68.8	100	66.7	86.4
=53 Staffordshire	90.3	83.6	31.5	119	56.9	86.4
=56 Greenwich	89.1	82.4	-	130	65.5	86
=56 Leeds Trinity	93.1	84.4	11.2	122	-	86
=58 Greater Manchester	90.2	82.9	-	126	65.1	85.8
=58 Leeds Arts	85.9	79	2.8	137	64.7	85.8
=60 Arts London	79.1	72.9	46	138	54.8	85.7
=60 Edge Hill	88.2	82.3	-	123	67.8	85.7
=62 Gloucestershire	84.2	70.2	45	116	59.4	85.5
=62 Sussex	80.5	68.1	48	136	54.1	85.5
64 Northampton	87.7	73.5	30.2	116	60.7	85.4
65 Arts Bournemouth	80.7	72.9	23	148	56.6	85.1
66 West London	80.6	61.8	32.2	124	65.3	85
=67 Bath Spa	87.9	78.1	26	118	57.7	84.8
=67 Buckinghamshire New	89.5	81.2	-	111	68.9	84.8
=67 Hertfordshire	84.4	81	42.5	131	48.1	84.8
70 Middlesex	88.2	76.6	26	120	54.4	84
71 Worcester	86.8	86.7	5.8	117	60.5	83.7
=72 Liverpool Hope	93.3	80.9	17.5	120	49.3	83.4
=72 Winchester	82.9	67.1	32.5	119	57.6	83.4
74 Anglia Ruskin	75.6	66.6	61.8	106	57.7	83.3
=75 Bournemouth	78.9	72.4	38.5	122	55.3	83.2
=75 East London	82.1	70.4	13	136	57.5	83.2
77 South Wales	81.6	69.8	35.8	118	56.3	83.1

Rank	University						
78	London Metropolitan	92.6	91.9	-	117	51.9	82.6
=79	Creative Arts	76.6	71.2	41.2	119	55.4	82.5
=79	West of Scotland	89.2	83	19.2	134	42.9	82.5
81	York St John	81.3	70.5	33.2	120	52.8	82.2
=82	Plymouth Marjon	74.8	63.1	-	125	71.7	81.9
=82	Sheffield Hallam	88.7	77.2	-	120	56.5	81.9
=82	Southampton Solent	86	80.2	-	116	59.6	81.9
85	Wales Trinity St David	89.3	79.8	-	129	50.5	81.7
=86	Chester	79.3	69.9	21	117	59.3	81.6
=86	Derby	83.7	78.8	-	114	61.8	81.6
88	Norwich Arts	81.8	75.5	-	124	60.1	81.5
89	Huddersfield	83.3	66.8	20	117	55.4	81.2
90	Leeds Beckett	76.6	62.2	15.8	130	58.6	80.9
91	Brunel	77.5	68.5	38	113	53.2	80.8
92	LAMDA	88.3	73	-	93	64.5	80.6
93	London South Bank	87.1	74.2	-	115	55	80.3
94	Bedfordshire	97.2	95.1	-	96	45.1	79.8
95	Oxford Brookes	72.2	63.4	21.5	128	-	78.9
96	Cumbria	76.9	71	-	121	57.4	78.8
97	St Mary's, Twickenham	77	53.7	-	114	57.1	76.4
98	Brighton	68.7	58.9	44.2	118	41.8	75.9

Employed in high-skilled job	45%	Employed in lower-skilled job	33%
Employed in high-skilled job and studying	2%	Employed in lower-skilled job and studying	1%
Studying	3%	Unemployed	8%
High-skilled work (median) salary	£24,000	Low-/medium-skilled salary	£20,000

Economics

Applications to study economics soared past 104,000 in 2023 (up 3% year on year and reflecting a 22% uplift in demand across the past six years) and new student enrolments increased too, by around 4%, with nearly 14,500 undergraduates accepted onto economics courses. Maths A-level (or equivalent qualification) is usually required by the leading universities, while philosophy, sociology, government and politics, further maths and economics may be useful. Applicants are advised to become comfortable with mathematics because it's used extensively in economics. Dr Michael Gmeiner and Professor Dimitra Petropoulou, Department of Economics, London School of Economics and Political Science (LSE) say: "An economics degree is rigorous and highly applicable to the real world, equipping students with the skills to analyse the important issues of our time. From big concepts such as inflation, unemployment, climate change, poverty and wealth inequality to individual-level decision-making behaviour, economists use theory and data analysis to understand how people behave and interact, and design policies to foster positive change. Critical thinking, data analysis and coding skills make graduates desirable across a range of sectors. Opportunities include roles in government, consulting, tech companies and finance."

Economics graduates are among the best paid, commanding median salaries of £30,000 – only four of the 70 subjects in our earnings index place higher. Economics sits 26th in our employment ranking (down five places), with the latest data showing just under three-quarters of graduates in high-skilled jobs and/or postgraduate study within 15 months of degrees.

Warwick ranks No 1 in our Economics table for the fourth consecutive year. Its convincing performance is driven by strength in all five areas measured in our ranking – including top-15 finishes for both measures of student satisfaction and the second-best score for research quality and the second highest entry standards – without being unbeaten on any individually. In runner-up position overall, the London School of Economics (LSE) topped our Economics table four years ago and claims the best graduate prospects jointly with Cambridge and King's College London. The LSE also leads for research in the field, based on results of the Research Excellence Framework 2021, but sits second to Warwick due largely to being outdone on rates of student satisfaction, for which LSE ranks in the top 30 for teaching quality and the wider experience, measures derived from the National Student Survey.

Cambridge is steady in third place overall, jointly with Oxford this year. Ranking fifth in the table, St Andrews leads on entry standards with 217 UCAS points averaged by its new entrants. Economics students at Hertfordshire (in 39th place overall) are by a clear margin the most satisfied with their teaching quality and the wider experience for the third year running. Those at Huddersfield, Brighton and London South Bank registered in the top three across these metrics. Conversely, economics undergraduates at York (44th place) and Newcastle (=48th) expressed the lowest rates of contentment with teaching quality, positions held by Chester (61st) and SOAS, London (68th) for the wider experience.

Economics	Teaching quality %	Student experience %	Research quality %	Entry standards (UCAS points)	Graduate prospects %	Overall score
1 Warwick	89.1	88.4	76.5	192	93.3	100
2 London School of Economics	85	86.4	80.8	193	96.2	99.8
=3 Cambridge	81.2	75	68.2	213	96.2	97.1
=3 Oxford	86.3	75.6	62	205	94.8	97.1
5 St Andrews	89.3	88.2	31.2	217	91	95.9
=6 Durham	86.5	86.5	55.8	173	92.9	95.7
=6 University College London	77.4	83.4	72.5	181	94.8	95.7
8 Leeds	81.8	89.5	62.3	166	91.2	95
=9 Nottingham	79.6	84.4	64.5	172	91.1	94.3
=9 Strathclyde	84.4	83.1	52.5	193	86.6	94.3
11 Glasgow	76.5	77.9	57.2	215	87.8	93.6
12 Heriot-Watt	89.1	86.1	38.2	172	86.4	93.2
13 Birmingham	82.9	84.5	55.2	151	91.2	93.1
14 Sheffield	86.6	89.4	48.8	153	85.9	93
15 Liverpool	85.8	88.8	58	141	84.4	92.9
=16 Bristol	77.2	79.7	60.2	174	90.4	92.6
=16 Lancaster	84.2	84	59.2	136	88.7	92.6
18 Exeter	82.2	85.3	44.8	164	91.4	92.5
19 Edinburgh	75.6	76.7	50.2	196	92.8	92.3
20 Aston	90.1	89.7	43.5	119	89	92.2
21 Loughborough	83.8	85.7	49.2	157	85.7	92.1
22 Bath	82	87.5	25.2	178	94.4	91.8
23 Queen Mary, London	78.5	81.4	60.5	155	87.4	91.7
=24 Cardiff	79.2	80.5	56	146	90.7	91.3
=24 Manchester	79.7	81.6	54.5	154	87.6	91.3

Rank	University						
=24	Surrey	86.2	89.1	54.2	126	81.8	91.3
=27	East Anglia	84.6	86.3	46.2	127	87.8	90.8
=27	Stirling	87.5	84.1	38.2	152	82.4	90.8
29	Queen's, Belfast	79.5	82.4	40.5	152	93	90.7
30	Brighton	96.3	95.6	28.5	93	-	90.5
31	Ulster	86.9	86.9	45.8	117	81.3	89.7
=32	Southampton	80.2	83.1	42	141	87.4	89.5
=32	Sussex	84.1	83.5	52	126	79.6	89.5
34	Leicester	82.3	85.3	45.8	117	86.3	89.3
35	King's College London	82.2	83.3	-	185	96.2	89.2
36	Royal Holloway	82	84.9	53.8	118	78.9	88.7
37	Essex	85.2	85.4	59.5	108	71.2	88.4
38	Hull	87	83	29.5	108	88.6	88.3
=39	Aberdeen	86	87	32.2	160	70	88.2
=39	Hertfordshire	96.5	97.9	29	112	63.7	88.2
41	Swansea	90.7	88.4	38.8	106	73.6	88.1
42	Coventry	91.1	89.9	33.2	101	75.9	88
43	Nottingham Trent	89.1	88.6	34.2	108	75.9	87.8
44	York	71.1	73.4	48.8	145	90.2	87.5
45	Plymouth	87.3	81.7	28.7	117	80	87.1
=46	Manchester Metropolitan	81.6	85.8	42.8	115	76.1	86.9
=46	Portsmouth	87.6	89	37.8	110	70.2	86.9
=48	Newcastle	72.2	77.8	40.5	146	86.8	86.8
=48	Reading	80	76	46.2	113	82.9	86.8
50	Oxford Brookes	81.5	85.4	26	110	81.8	85.7
51	Greenwich	88.2	89.2	33.2	98	67.2	85.4
52	Keele	80.2	81.2	24.8	99	88.3	85.3
53	Dundee	77.8	76.5	-	171	88.9	85.2
54	Kent	81	80.1	29.5	110	80.8	85.1
55	London South Bank	92.9	88	-	99	75.9	84.4
=56	City St George's	77.6	81.2	32.5	116	73.5	83.7
=56	West of England	83.8	77.5	27.3	110	72	83.7
58	Bournemouth	81.7	80.7	23	99	77.5	83.5
59	Huddersfield	85.1	90.8	23.2	102	64.2	83.4
60	Lincoln	79.2	86.1	-	102	86.2	82.6
61	Chester	87.3	70.8	12.8	112	-	82.4
62	Aberystwyth	81.3	73.4	22.8	112	-	82.3
=63	Leeds Beckett	76.5	81.4	8.2	109	80	81.5
=63	Sheffield Hallam	83.2	80.7	-	104	77.6	81.5
=65	Kingston	82.2	79.2	24	98	66	81.4
=65	Westminster	83.2	81.7	37.5	99	54.5	81.4
67	De Montfort	84.3	85.3	-	79	76.7	80.9
68	SOAS, London	77.7	72.5	-	126	78.6	80.5
69	Brunel	82.9	79.1	16	105	62.1	80.3
=70	Goldsmiths, London	84.8	76.3	-	95	68.4	79.3
=70	Middlesex	88.5	89.3	-	84	57.6	79.3
72	Northampton	85.6	82.3	1.2	73	-	79.2
73	Birmingham City	80.4	79.3	11.2	112	54.9	78.3

Employed in high-skilled job	58%	Employed in lower-skilled job	13%
Employed in high-skilled job and studying	9%	Employed in lower-skilled job and studying	1%
Studying	6%	Unemployed	5%
High-skilled work (median) salary	£31,000	Low-/medium-skilled salary	£22,500

Education

Tying in first place of our new Education table, Cambridge and Edinburgh have risen one and two places respectively, their leading overall rank supported by strong performances across the metrics in the ranking, without topping any individually. Last year's No 1, Durham, is down five places to sit sixth overall, but still claims the top research rating in the field – based on results of the latest Research Excellence Framework in 2021. Our table focuses exclusively on undergraduate provision, which explains the absence of some of the best-known education departments, which only offer postgraduate courses. Degrees at Cambridge, for instance, combine the academic study of education with other subjects but do not offer Qualified Teacher Status. The top four for entry standards are exclusively Scottish universities, which benefit from the favourable tariff conversion for Scottish secondary qualifications. For student satisfaction with teaching quality, West London (ranked 80th in the table), Sussex (13th) and Hertfordshire occupy the top three spots. For student satisfaction with the broader experience West London is top again, followed by Hertfordshire and Manchester Met (=33rd overall). At the foot of both rankings is Stirling (placed 31st in the main table), our latest National Student Survey analysis shows.

Our Education table includes inspection data by Ofsted for universities in England, adding an extra column which distinguishes it from the other subject rankings in our Guide. Fifteen universities achieve the top score (four) from Ofsted. These are, in descending order: Cambridge, Manchester, Bristol, Durham, Nottingham, Brighton, Warwick, Winchester, Edge Hill, St Mary's, Twickenham, Southampton, University College London, Chichester, Chester, and Worcester. Only Chester at 37th and Worcester at 47th – both with Ofsted's highest rating – rank outside our top 30.

"Informed by cutting-edge research, policy and practice and supported by the latest learning technologies, you will be empowered to implement change and transform people's lives for the better. What can we do to improve how they learn? How can we overcome the many educational barriers young people face? How can we use educational, sociological and psychological research to make a positive impact on their lives?" say Dr Trevor Grimshaw, Dr Ioannis Costas Batlle and Dr Sam Carr, Department of Education, University of Bath, who advise applicants to "Find the recommended reading lists and start training yourself to analyse the literature critically, noting down your key questions as you read."

Applications to teacher training BEd degrees – the most common route into primary teaching – declined for the third year running in 2024 when 39,440 applied – a 10% decrease compared with 2023 and 29% lower than 2021's boom year for applications to teacher training. But the number of students who gained places was more stable, only dipping by 1%, and 8,840 undergraduates were accepted onto courses in 2024. Academic studies in education degrees are also encompassed in our ranking and demand for the subject has also waned in recent years; it attracted 26,540 applications in 2024, while 6,160 new undergraduates began courses – the fewest in six years after consecutive decreases.

Secondary school teachers are more likely to take the Postgraduate Certificate in Education, or to train through the Teach First or Schools Direct programmes, which are not included in our table's statistics.

Education sits 28th in our employment ranking of 70 subject areas. The demands for new primary and secondary teachers vary across the country, creating differing graduate outcomes scores at universities. St Mary's, Twickenham tops the table's graduate prospects index this year, with 93.4% of graduates in high-skilled work and/or postgraduate study 15 months after their degrees. Though not an ingredient of our ranking, teachers' pay is of interest to many. Median graduate salaries of £25,714 for those in high-skilled jobs places education just outside the upper half of subject areas, at =38th.

Education

	Teaching quality %	Student experience %	Research quality %	Ofsted rating	Entry standards (UCAS points)	Graduate prospects %	Overall score
=1 Cambridge	89.6	79.9	67.8	4	182	88	100
=1 Edinburgh	88.6	88.6	51	-	196	88.8	100
3 Glasgow	86.3	77.3	64.5	-	187	83.6	97.4
4 Manchester	90	91.3	67.5	4	133	-	97.3
5 Bristol	87.2	89.1	67.5	4	140	85.7	96.7
6 Durham	83.5	73.9	73.2	4	139	92.5	96.5
7 Strathclyde	91.7	88.4	20.8	-	202	80.7	96.3
8 Dundee	90.1	88.1	35.2	-	166	87	95.8
9 Aberdeen	91.9	89.4	23	-	170	85.9	95.4
10 Cardiff	89.7	90.3	72	-	138	80.4	95.3
11 Bath	88.3	88.6	47.8	-	147	86.8	94.9
12 Nottingham	83.8	84.5	61.5	4	139	-	94.8
13 Sussex	94.1	86.2	64.8	3.4	112	87.8	94.6
14 Birmingham	85.4	89.6	70.5	3.5	142	81.1	94.1
=15 Brighton	92	88.2	37.5	4	122	84.9	94
=15 Warwick	91.1	90.6	55.8	4	132	75.3	94
17 Winchester	90.4	88.2	28	4	121	89.6	93.9
18 West of Scotland	93.2	86.8	17.5	-	182	77.7	93.8
19 Edge Hill	89.8	88.7	30.8	4	122	82.4	92.5
=20 Leeds	84.8	89.2	44.2	-	139	84.8	92.4
=20 St Mary's, Twickenham	92.6	90.8	-	4	109	93.4	92.4
22 Southampton	85.5	87.3	41	4	124	-	92.3
23 University College London	85.1	85.6	68.8	4	148	65.4	92.2
24 Northumbria	90.5	79.6	42	3	131	89.9	91.7
25 Roehampton	91.2	84.8	53.5	3.5	116	79.6	91.6
26 Chichester	90.7	88.1	5.2	4	124	85	91.4
27 Bangor	88.6	77.9	42	-	137	82.1	91.2
28 Sheffield Hallam	87.1	80.7	39.2	3.7	126	81.7	90.9
29 East Anglia	85.9	88.6	41.2	3	128	87.7	90.6
30 Sheffield	88.8	87.5	62	3	137	74.1	90.5
31 Stirling	71	57.3	53.2	-	185	85.7	90.4
32 Derby	88.1	83.4	29.2	3.5	120	84.5	90.2
=33 Manchester Metropolitan	92.1	91.5	42.8	3	126	77.7	90.1
=33 Plymouth Marjon	93.6	88.1	14	3.3	121	84.2	90.1
35 West of England	90.3	85.6	48.5	3	117	81.3	89.8
36 York	82.9	76.7	70.8	3.3	142	69.7	89.5

Education cont.

	Teaching quality %	Student experience %	Research quality %	Ofsted rating	Entry standards (UCAS points)	Graduate prospects %	Overall score
=37 Chester	83.8	74.8	16.2	4	125	82.7	89.2
=37 Newcastle	89.3	83	36.8	3.2	125	-	89.2
=37 Nottingham Trent	91.2	87.4	29.5	3	119	83.1	89.2
40 Reading	83.1	80.1	41.8	3	125	87	89
41 Northampton	90.6	90.1	28.2	3	113	83.5	88.9
=42 Cardiff Metropolitan	91.9	90.6	17.5	-	123	77.9	88.8
=42 Swansea	89.2	85.7	46.5	-	124	71.9	88.8
44 Keele	86.8	86.1	33.2	-	116	81.1	88.7
45 York St John	88	82.5	24.5	3.2	131	80.9	88.6
46 Bedfordshire	92.8	85.9	21	3.1	107	83.7	88.5
47 Worcester	87.7	80.6	10.8	4	113	78.7	88.4
48 Anglia Ruskin	90.7	86.2	16.2	-	103	84.8	88
49 Hertfordshire	94	93.3	9.5	3	122	78.3	87.9
50 Kingston	87	83	28.5	3	125	80.2	87.6
=51 Liverpool Hope	93.8	84.6	23.8	3	117	76.3	87.5
=51 Liverpool John Moores	88.5	88.9	21.8	3	134	75.5	87.5
53 Gloucestershire	91.4	87.9	16.2	3	116	79.6	87.4
=54 Leeds Trinity	89.5	83.2	8	3	121	83.4	87.1
=54 South Wales	94	87.8	-	-	112	77.6	87.1
=54 Wolverhampton	93.9	90.3	10.5	3	93	84.5	87.1
57 Lincoln Bishop	90.9	86.3	10.2	3	114	81.2	86.8
=58 Bath Spa	78.9	72.9	31.5	3.7	106	82.2	86.6
=58 Coventry	87.2	83.5	54.2	3	102	73.1	86.6
60 Greater Manchester	87.3	84.9	7.8	3	99	86.7	85.9
=61 Birmingham City	86.3	81.7	11.8	3	128	76.6	85.5
=61 Brunel	88.8	84.7	20.8	3	111	75	85.5
=61 Leeds Beckett	89.5	82.1	17.2	3	114	75.5	85.5
=64 Greenwich	86.3	82.2	17	3	111	79.2	85.4
=64 Huddersfield	88.7	78.5	31.2	3.1	117	69.5	85.4
=64 Teesside	91.6	86.6	18.2	3	108	72.8	85.4
67 Staffordshire	84.9	79	18.2	3	125	76	85.2
68 East London	88	82.9	11.2	3	110	78.4	85.1
69 Oxford Brookes	83.3	68.2	36	2.3	127	84.5	85
70 Plymouth	79.4	77.3	39.2	3	122	75	84.9
71 Canterbury Christ Church	82.6	76.9	29.5	3	110	78.3	84.8
72 Birmingham Newman	85.4	83.4	4.8	3	116	79.2	84.6
73 Sunderland	83.5	76.8	9.2	3	126	78.1	84.5
74 Lincoln	86.1	82.1	28.5	-	107	71.3	84.2
=75 Cumbria	83.7	71.3	8.5	3	120	79.3	83.9
=75 Middlesex	85.3	84.9	15.5	3	107	74.3	83.9
77 Portsmouth	75.3	71.5	51.7	3.5	121	62.7	83.4
=78 Aberystwyth	84.7	75.4	-	-	124	73.3	82.8
=78 Lancashire	87.4	84.8	-	-	119	68.8	82.8
80 West London	97	95.8	-	-	124	52.5	82.7

=81 De Montfort	87.4	90.2	-	-	98	72.5	82.6
=81 Hull	83.9	77.8	31.5	2.2	116	76.5	82.6
83 London South Bank	81.3	71.5	-	3	103	79.6	81.6
84 London Metropolitan	82.5	77.2	6.5	3	102	73.9	81.5
85 Wales Trinity St David	89.8	78.3	11.8	-	86	69.7	81.1
86 Goldsmiths, London	78	67.6	29.5	3	111	60.9	79.3

Employed in high-skilled job	64%	Employed in lower-skilled job	17%
Employed in high-skilled job and studying	4%	Employed in lower-skilled job and studying	1%
Studying	5%	Unemployed	4%
High-skilled work (median) salary	£26,000	Low-/medium-skilled salary	£19,000

Electrical and Electronic Engineering

High entry standards to electrical and electronic engineering degrees are the norm at the leading institutions; at Cambridge – the table's overall frontrunner – entrants averaged an extraordinary 222 UCAS tariff points. It is one of six universities where entry tariffs tip over 200 UCAS points, while 21 universities recorded over 144 points (equivalent to AAA at A-level) according to the latest data. Imperial, tied with Oxford in joint third place overall, has the edge for research quality – based on results of the Research Excellence Framework 2021. Oxford sits second for research. The QS world rankings 2025 put Cambridge and Oxford in the top 10 for the subject, and Imperial 12th. For student satisfaction, Royal Holloway (in =18th place overall) comes top for students' evaluation of teaching quality and the broad experience, but otherwise the upper reaches are dominated by the table's modern universities – including Edinburgh Napier (=25th) and Northumbria (33rd) for the broad experience, and Greenwich (35th) and London South Bank (54th) for teaching quality.

The best graduate prospects are found at Cambridge, where nearly all (97.2%) graduates were working in high-skilled jobs and/or enrolled in postgraduate study within 15 months. It is one of 20 universities to register at least 90% for this measure. The subject as a whole ranks =5th in our salaries index pay and compares almost as favourably in our employment table, where it ranks 11th.

"Electrical and electronic engineering is pivotal to modern innovation, driving advancements in renewable energy, telecommunications and electric vehicles. Students gain cutting-edge knowledge and hands-on experience in these fields, as well as problem-solving skills and a strong foundation in maths and physics, preparing them to tackle global challenges," say Dr Mohamed K Darwish, course director for MSC in advanced electronic and electrical engineering, and Dr Konstantinos Banitsas, lecturer and researcher, Department of Electronic and Computer Engineering, Brunel University.

Maths is a required subject, along with a second science such as physics, electronics or chemistry. Electrical and electronic engineering attracts the second-highest number of applications and enrolments among the engineering disciplines (behind mechanical engineering). Rising demand for the subject continued in 2024, when applications and enrolments to electrical and electronic engineering reached 23,090 and 5,325 respectively – record levels for both.

Electrical and Electronic Engineering

	Teaching quality %	Student experience %	Research quality %	Entry standards (UCAS points)	Graduate prospects %	Overall score
1 Cambridge	80.4	80.8	77.2	222	97.2	100
2 University College London	87.8	86.3	70	176	-	98.4
=3 Imperial College	78.6	76.4	81	207	95	98.1
=3 Oxford	80.4	74.8	77.5	213	94	98.1
5 Southampton	86	84	70	176	95.5	97.3
6 Strathclyde	84.9	80.6	52.8	207	90.9	95.8
7 Sheffield	85.7	84.3	66.8	158	94.1	95.4
8 Queen Mary, London	89.6	87.8	66	137	93.8	95.2
9 Leeds	82	81.4	64.8	160	96.8	94.7
10 Glasgow	74	64.5	61.5	217	96.1	94.3
11 Edinburgh	74.9	77.1	55.5	215	-	94.1
12 Manchester	83.3	83.4	63	155	92.5	93.7
13 Heriot-Watt	83.9	79.9	55.5	160	93.2	93.2
14 Liverpool	86	84.7	57	130	95.9	92.9
15 King's College London	81.7	84.4	62	150	-	92.5
16 Nottingham	82.3	81.7	59	141	94.3	92.2
17 Loughborough	84.8	79.9	46.5	152	93.1	91.7
=18 Queen's, Belfast	78.8	82	51	163	92.7	91.6
=18 Royal Holloway	96.6	93.3	33	120	-	91.6
20 Bristol	78.9	75.6	72.8	153	86.5	91.5
21 Cardiff	84.3	83.9	54	136	90.9	91.3
22 Exeter	83.8	79	47	140	92.7	90.6
23 Aberdeen	81.6	80.5	35.8	157	93.3	90.1
24 Robert Gordon	85.6	73.8	20.5	173	93.8	89.9
=25 Edinburgh Napier	90.8	92.6	22.8	-	85.7	89.6
=25 Newcastle	84.8	84.5	58.5	120	84.7	89.6
27 Bath	74.6	73.2	49.5	167	89.2	89
=28 Hull	90.4	88.5	36.2	116	-	88.9
=28 Surrey	82.2	80	55.2	121	88.1	88.9
30 Salford	90.4	86.2	33.2	120	86.2	88.6
31 Plymouth	86	79.8	32.5	123	93.2	88.5
32 Lancaster	82.6	81	44.8	134	-	88.2
33 Northumbria	88.6	91.8	43	124	76.5	88
34 Birmingham	80.6	77.6	63.7	138	76.2	87.8
35 Greenwich	91.2	87.5	31.5	108	-	87.6
=36 Essex	76.2	80.1	53.5	144	81.4	87.3
=36 Lancashire	86.1	90.3	23	135	-	87.3
=36 Manchester Metropolitan	82.4	77.1	45.5	120	87.5	87.3
39 York	81.9	69.4	49.8	128	85.1	87
40 Glasgow Caledonian	88.2	86.8	12.8	165	77	86.8
41 Swansea	77.2	79	48.8	112	89.7	86.5
42 Ulster	82.2	78.2	49.8	110	-	86.3
43 Liverpool John Moores	81.8	83.8	45.5	128	76.7	86
44 City St George's	81.8	83	32.5	130	-	85.9
45 Coventry	83	76.3	23.5	139	81.2	84.8

46 West London		88.2	86.3	13.8	119	-	84.6
47 Hertfordshire		82	75.4	33	122	-	84.4
48 Brighton		82.5	76.9	36.5	110	-	84.2
49 West of England		82.4	81	30.8	107	-	83.5
50 Teesside		86.4	84.7	18.8	111	77.8	83.3
51 Lincoln		82.4	71.6	24	129	-	83.2
52 Portsmouth		84	82.6	21	107	80.8	83.1
53 Birmingham City		85.5	80.3	17.5	130	74.4	83
54 London South Bank		91.2	89.9	27.3	109	58.7	81.7
55 Kent		72.5	71.2	41.5	112	79.5	81.5
56 Derby		86.1	76.3	14	123	72.1	81.4
57 Brunel		75.7	74	33	115	77.3	81.3
58 Sheffield Hallam		77.1	69	30	117	76.4	80.7
59 Staffordshire		80.1	71.3	25.5	104	-	80.4
60 Westminster		86.5	82.5	24	106	63.9	80.3
61 Nottingham Trent		74	79.9	59	108	58.3	79.9
62 Aston		72.2	53.2	35.2	126	-	78.8
63 Northampton		82	76.5	8.5	82	-	77
64 De Montfort		73.7	65.4	21.8	96	-	76
65 Chichester		73.3	63.5	12.5	101	-	74.7
66 South Wales		64	61	26.8	-	71.4	72.7

Employed in high-skilled job	72%	Employed in lower-skilled job	8%
Employed in high-skilled job and studying	3%	Employed in lower-skilled job and studying	0%
Studying	6%	Unemployed	5%
High-skilled work (median) salary	£30,000	Low-/medium-skilled salary	£21,000

English

In a tie at the top of our new table Oxford has returned to the No 1 spot it slipped from last year and joined St Andrews – which leads the table for the second consecutive year. Averaging 202 UCAS points among its English degree entrants, St Andrews has the highest entry standards. Cambridge and University College London are steady in third and fourth place respectively. Newcastle sits 14th overall but is peerless for its research in the subject, while Edinburgh (=24th) achieves the second-best research quality score. At more than a quarter (23) of the universities listed, students arrived with upwards of 144 UCAS points (equivalent to three As at A-level) but there are also six universities registering 100 points or less. Teesside, in =39th place overall, has the lowest entry standards (92 UCAS points) but comes top for student satisfaction with teaching quality. Lincoln Bishop (62nd in the table) does best for students' evaluation of the broad experience.

English literature is usually required for entry. Some English degrees offer an equal balance of literature and language, while others specialise in one or the other – a distinction usually clear in the course title. English is also frequently paired with other subjects in joint honours degrees. "An English degree offers a unique opportunity for you to engage with the rich global heritage of creativity in the English language and to enhance your own linguistic, critical and creative abilities. The skills and knowledge you will acquire are so fundamental, they will prepare you not just for any career but for any future you care to make for yourself," says Professor Peter D McDonald, tutor in English, St Hugh's College, University of Oxford.

English has not been immune to the declining popularity of humanities subjects, but despite some universities making the controversial decision to drop their degrees in English literature (amid pressure from government to ensure graduates go straight into well-paid jobs) demand for degrees in English studies, English language and English literature registered only a small year-on-year dip in 2024 to 44,785 applications and 8,205 new student enrolments. The longer-term view shows a 17% drop in admissions in the last six years, however. Our analysis of the latest Graduate Outcomes survey shows almost six in ten English graduates (58.3%) employed in high-skilled jobs and/or postgraduate study 15 months on, ranking the subject =52nd out of 70. These outcomes vary considerably by university, ranging from 91.5% in high-skilled jobs/postgraduate study at Aston to 60.8% at Hertfordshire. Average graduate salaries of £24,500 put English 53rd. There remain plenty of universities to study English at. The UCAS website showed 905 courses in English literature at 108 universities and colleges for 2026–7. For English degrees more broadly, there were 1,580 courses offered by 132 providers.

English	Teaching quality %	Student experience %	Research quality %	Entry standards (UCAS points)	Graduate prospects %	Overall score
=1 Oxford	90.7	78	69.8	187	83.3	100
=1 St Andrews	87.1	84.1	61.8	202	84.3	100
3 Cambridge	84.4	70.9	65	201	88.3	99.5
4 University College London	90.4	86.4	61.5	178	83.2	99
5 Leicester	96.1	93.4	67.8	115	86.9	98.6
6 Aberdeen	94.8	92.4	53.8	167	80.2	98.2
7 York	88.9	86.8	70.2	155	81.9	97.9
8 Strathclyde	88.5	86.3	58.8	195	76.5	97.5
9 Durham	86.2	73.2	55.5	188	85.6	97.4
10 Nottingham	88.8	86.9	70.5	148	81.4	97.3
11 Warwick	87	79.1	64.8	158	84.6	97
12 Southampton	86.6	88.3	69.2	142	82.4	96.6
13 Birmingham City	94	94.2	65.5	112	82.6	96.5
14 Newcastle	86.8	82.8	83.8	137	78	96.4
15 Birmingham	88.6	85.5	68.8	147	77.1	95.7
16 King's College London	83.5	80.1	70.8	161	78.9	95.6
17 Exeter	84.1	83.7	59.5	159	82.5	95.5
18 Glasgow	84.9	78.8	61.8	193	73.2	95.3
=19 Leeds	81.7	79.9	73.2	152	79.4	95
=19 Royal Holloway	87.4	84.5	60.5	135	82.9	95
=19 Surrey	89	81.7	63	126	83.4	95
22 Edinburgh Napier	93.2	90.7	48.2	156	75.5	94.9
23 Liverpool	87.1	87.5	65.5	132	80	94.8
=24 Cardiff	87.9	85.1	67.2	133	77	94.3
=24 Edinburgh	76.5	70.7	74.5	174	79.1	94.3
26 Sheffield	88.4	89.1	62.3	150	73.2	94.2
27 Canterbury Christ Church	96.8	87.1	53.2	-	72.3	94
28 Liverpool John Moores	93.9	90.7	58	113	77.3	93.9
29 Lancaster	93.3	87.8	48	136	75.9	93.4
30 Manchester Metropolitan	89.9	85.6	61.8	117	78.1	93.3

Rank	University					
31	Loughborough	91	83.7	54.5	138	75.1	93.2
32	Sussex	87.2	84.2	67	127	74.6	93
33	Keele	95.6	91.1	54.8	110	74.4	92.9
34	Manchester	81.1	76.2	66.5	157	75	92.8
=35	Aston	86.3	84.1	38	112	91.5	92.7
=35	Queen's, Belfast	87.5	83.1	47.5	144	78.5	92.7
37	East Anglia	86.2	82.7	67	132	73.1	92.5
38	Queen Mary, London	89.2	84.7	59.5	136	71.4	92.3
=39	Bath Spa	87.5	80.6	51.7	115	82.8	92.2
=39	Teesside	98.7	90.7	49.2	92	-	92.2
41	Northumbria	92.1	85.4	54	122	74.1	92.1
42	Reading	87.4	80.1	51	119	81.4	92
=43	Bristol	78.8	75.4	54.5	164	77.7	91.8
=43	Swansea	92.2	87.5	60	130	67.3	91.8
45	Oxford Brookes	93.3	78.4	72.8	116	66.5	91.7
46	Huddersfield	88.6	74.5	60	106	80	91.6
=47	Brunel	94.1	95	42.8	115	73.3	91.5
=47	Dundee	86.7	82.9	40.8	166	72.6	91.5
49	Sunderland	-	-	40.5	96	87.5	91.4
50	Kingston	92.4	79.1	47	126	-	91.3
51	Sheffield Hallam	92.7	89.3	50.7	104	74.2	91.1
52	Coventry	93.5	92.2	54.2	95	71.8	90.7
=53	Northampton	98.5	95.2	30.2	104	-	90.6
=53	Stirling	84.7	81.6	47.5	170	67.4	90.6
55	Westminster	88.9	87	55.5	103	72.7	90
56	Kent	86.2	80.6	64.5	111	70.7	89.9
57	Chichester	94.2	88.8	37.2	108	-	89.8
=58	Falmouth	82.3	82.9	48.8	137	-	89.7
=58	Plymouth	90.4	76.3	60.5	117	68.1	89.7
60	Hull	89	83.7	55.5	106	71.6	89.6
61	De Montfort	86.2	83.5	54.5	97	76.3	89.5
62	Lincoln Bishop	98.5	99.2	19	103	-	89.1
=63	Goldsmiths, London	81.8	65.7	46	122	80.1	88.5
=63	Hertfordshire	97.6	92.6	42.5	113	60.8	88.5
65	Birmingham Newman	93.1	88	43.8	84	-	88.3
66	Essex	82.5	77.1	49.8	123	-	88
67	Salford	90.1	83.9	26.5	110	75.7	87.8
68	Nottingham Trent	92.3	83.6	39.2	109	68	87.7
69	City St George's	86	86.4	43.8	101	-	87.4
70	Roehampton	88.7	84.3	50.5	118	62.5	87.3
71	York St John	94.4	90.7	22.8	108	69.7	87.2
=72	Greenwich	92.3	86.9	26.5	104	71.3	87
=72	Liverpool Hope	90.9	85.6	36	108	67.6	87
74	Lancashire	89.7	87.1	33.8	103	70.1	86.9
=75	Edge Hill	80.2	74.2	32.8	109	81.6	86.8
=75	Wolverhampton	88.1	81.2	44	98	70	86.8
77	Ulster	86.6	79.4	41	105	71	86.7
78	Gloucestershire	93.1	89.7	32.8	105	65.2	86.6

English cont.

	Teaching quality %	Student experience %	Research quality %	Entry standards (UCAS points)	Graduate prospects %	Overall score
79 Lincoln	88.8	81.3	36	111	68.8	86.5
80 Bangor	89.8	82.1	44.2	112	63	86.4
81 Portsmouth	89.1	87.9	30.8	110	66.7	85.9
82 Aberystwyth	86.9	83.1	25.5	116	70.2	85.7
83 Leeds Beckett	92.8	80.4	30.8	107	62.8	84.9
84 Brighton	74.8	70.7	44.2	108	74.7	84.5
85 Chester	88.5	67.9	25	122	67.6	84.4
86 Worcester	89.8	80	19.2	104	-	84
87 Bournemouth	-	-	22.5	113	70.8	83.9
88 West of England	82.7	80.6	32.2	111	66.1	83.8
89 Anglia Ruskin	72.9	62.1	46	121	71.2	83.5
90 Winchester	92.4	71.2	16.2	115	61.9	82.5

Employed in high-skilled job	43%	Employed in lower-skilled job	23%
Employed in high-skilled job and studying	4%	Employed in lower-skilled job and studying	1%
Studying	12%	Unemployed	6%
High-skilled work (median) salary	£25,000	Low-/medium-skilled salary	£19,500

Food Science

Degrees under this grouping encompass a broad range of courses, from nutrition and dietetics – which offer opportunities to study alongside doctors, nurses and other health professionals in hospitals – to food manufacturing and professional cookery. There is even a BSc in Baking Science and Technology, offered by London South Bank at its National Bakery School. "Never has there been a more critical time for our global society to comprehend the importance of what we feed our bodies and how nutrients affect our short and long-term health. Understanding our human metabolic demands for nutrients and improving health through optimal, safe and appropriate food is exactly what is studied in the subject areas of nutrition science and food science," says Professor Susan Lanham-New, head of the Department of Nutritional Sciences, University of Surrey. Applicants are advised to ensure that courses are approved by the accrediting bodies – for nutrition science degrees it is the Association for Nutrition and for food science degrees it's the Institute of Food Science and Technology. Food science courses usually feature in the top 30 of our employment and salaries rankings, as they do this year in 29th and =28th place respectively.

Glasgow takes the lead in our new Food Science table's tightly packed top three, ousting Queen's Belfast into second place jointly with Surrey – which maintains its long-held top three record in the ranking. Glasgow's lead is secured by the highest entry standards by far (224 UCAS points), but it fares less strongly for student satisfaction. Queen's Belfast is in front for research quality, based on its results in food science areas in the Research Excellence Framework 2021. In our National Student Survey analysis Abertay (sixth place in the main table) achieved the best feedback from students for teaching quality and Surrey leads for their evaluation of the broad experience where it is followed by Liverpool John Moores (in 14th place overall). At the other end of scale, students at Coventry reported the lowest rates of satisfaction with teaching quality and those at Harper Adams gave the poorest reviews for the wider experience.

Food Science

	Teaching quality %	Student experience %	Research quality %	Entry standards (UCAS points)	Graduate prospects %	Overall score
1 Glasgow	76.1	68.6	64.8	224	-	100
=2 Queen's, Belfast	89.4	84.7	69.2	147	92.6	98.2
=2 Surrey	94.2	97.3	58	133	95.1	98.2
4 Glasgow Caledonian	83.6	68.9	61	184	90	97.2
5 Plymouth	90.9	88.3	58.2	148	87.8	96.5
6 Abertay	96.1	93.9	28.2	170	76.9	94.2
7 Hertfordshire	91.3	86.6	42.5	119	100	94.1
8 Ulster	90	86.1	53.5	134	87.3	94
9 Reading	90.6	89.3	42.5	125	90.9	92.8
10 Nottingham	82.4	73.3	52	149	88.6	92.3
11 Newcastle	86.3	78.5	65.8	149	68.6	91.8
12 Leeds	80.4	81.3	45.5	150	87	91.3
13 Manchester Metropolitan	90.4	91.3	36	136	76.5	90.2
14 Liverpool John Moores	92.8	95.5	26.5	124	-	89.6
15 Chester	83.5	68.1	31	133	95	89.2
16 Nottingham Trent	93.3	92.9	30.8	115	-	89.1
17 Robert Gordon	92.9	92.9	-	151	83.3	88.8
18 Liverpool Hope	91.8	87.3	15	136	-	87.7
=19 Bournemouth	86.4	87.3	29.2	127	79.4	87.6
=19 Cardiff Metropolitan	91.4	83.2	-	155	81.2	87.6
21 Westminster	88.4	90.3	36.8	120	73.5	87.5
22 Oxford Brookes	81.9	71.5	39.5	126	-	85.6
23 Harper Adams	83.2	67.3	19.5	116	92.7	85.4
24 Coventry	74.6	68.4	24.8	144	82.4	84.3
=25 Leeds Beckett	86.6	88.4	-	120	85.1	84.2
=25 Queen Margaret, Edinburgh	89.3	88.8	-	145	70	84.2
27 King's College London	87.6	72.1	-	141	78.3	83.8
28 Edge Hill	92	92.1	-	128	62.5	82.2
=29 London Metropolitan	81.1	75.8	-	121	84.8	81.7
=29 Sheffield Hallam	83.7	80.8	-	116	82	81.7
31 St Mary's, Twickenham	85.3	77.4	-	116	73.5	80.3
32 London South Bank	89.2	67.6	-	100	50	74.4

Employed in high-skilled job	60%	Employed in lower-skilled job		18%
Employed in high-skilled job and studying	2%	Employed in lower-skilled job and studying		1%
Studying	8%	Unemployed		3%
High-skilled work (median) salary	£26,325	Low-/medium-skilled salary		£21,000

French

Topping the French table for the second year in a row, St Andrews attracts high entry standards in the subject – with its students of French averaging 210 UCAS points (only Glasgow has higher) – and boasts excellent rates of satisfaction: in our National Student Survey analysis it comes third for teaching quality and second for the broad experience.

"Students will be challenged to engage with various aspects of Francophone cultures and history, such as world-changing revolutionary ideas, genre-bending literature and groundbreaking cinema. By developing linguistic proficiency and critical-thinking skills in tandem, this unique combination of analytic, transcultural and communicative competencies ensures that French students are highly sought-after graduates," notes Dr Angela O'Flaherty, lecturer in French, Department of Language and Linguistic Science, University of York – which ranks fourth overall in our table and No 1 for research quality in the subject.

Throughout our French ranking, degrees attract high entry standards: 22 out of the 27 universities tabled average upwards of 144 UCAS points (equivalent to AAA at A-level). Unusually, there are no universities with post-1992 foundations – reflecting the long decline in the popularity of studying modern languages. Applications and enrolments continued their downward trend in 2024, when 4,125 applied and 750 undergraduates were accepted onto courses. But those with French in their sights still have options; the UCAS website showed 858 courses in French offered by 65 colleges and universities in 2026–27, many offered as part of dual honours courses in conjunction with a wide variety of other subjects. Applicants are advised to listen, watch or read about their interests (culture, sport, history, music etc) in French.

Compared with other subject areas, French sits 40th in our employment index of 70 and 45th for graduate salaries.

French

	Teaching quality %	Student experience %	Research quality %	Entry standards (UCAS points)	Graduate prospects %	Overall score
1 St Andrews	93.3	90.7	51.5	210	-	100
2 Cambridge	92.5	70.6	61	198	91.5	99.7
3 Lancaster	93	86.6	68.5	149	-	97.5
4 York	87.4	84.7	74.8	147	-	96.6
5 Bristol	88.5	81.4	64	163	81.3	95.2
6 Warwick	91.7	89.6	46.2	153	85.5	94.2
7 Surrey	93.9	96	63	109	-	94
8 Liverpool	91.8	90.2	59	132	-	93.9
9 Oxford	86.5	65.9	51.2	188	83.8	93.6
10 Durham	87.2	77.1	46	173	85.6	93.3
11 Queen's, Belfast	93.7	90	37	158	83.4	93.1
12 Manchester	84.2	81.1	59.5	151	82.1	92.8
=13 Newcastle	85.2	83.4	61.8	134	83.6	92.7
=13 Royal Holloway	90.2	86.3	60	127	-	92.7
15 University College London	83.3	80.1	56	167	-	92.5
16 Birmingham	87.5	83.2	54.8	150	79.8	92.4
17 Bath	89	88.8	31.8	156	89.1	92.2
=18 Nottingham	81.4	87.4	62	144	-	91.9
=18 Southampton	91.9	83.4	47.8	145	-	91.9
=18 Stirling	82.9	78.4	47.5	184	-	91.9
21 Exeter	84.3	80.6	50	151	82.9	91.4
22 King's College London	82.4	76.4	51.2	160	81.1	91
=23 Cardiff	89	87.6	55.5	131	72.7	90.2
=23 Leeds	84.5	79	52	158	74.9	90.2
25 Edinburgh	77.4	74.6	45.8	184	73.2	88.4

26 Glasgow		83.6	80.2	25.5	214	66.8	87.7
27 Queen Mary, London		79.8	76.5	51.1	144	66.7	85.7

Employed in high-skilled job	50%	Employed in lower-skilled job	21%
Employed in high-skilled job and studying	2%	Employed in lower-skilled job and studying	1%
Studying	11%	Unemployed	6%
High-skilled work (median) salary	£26,000	Low-/medium-skilled salary	£23,000

General Engineering

Bristol is up two places to take the lead in our General Engineering table, ousting Imperial – which is down four places to rank fifth this year. Bristol's win is secured by much improved rates of satisfaction among its general engineering students: in our new National Student Survey (NSS) analysis their evaluations put Bristol in the top four for teaching quality and the broad experience. Bristol led this table for a three-year stretch before Cambridge (runner-up this year) took the helm, followed by Imperial and it tops the graduate prospects ranking – with a perfect 100% of general engineering students employed in high-skilled jobs and/or further study within 15 months. Imperial remains unbeaten for research quality, while Sheffield (in third place overall) is hitting all the right notes with its general engineering students, whose NSS feedback ranks it top for teaching quality and the broad experience, where it is followed by Strathclyde (eighth in the table) for both. General engineering students entering Cambridge averaged 222 UCAS points, putting the university at the front for entry standards – which are higher than 144 points (equivalent to AAA) at 14 universities. But the subject can also be accessed with more modest grades, such as the 112 UCAS points averaged by general engineering students at Swansea, which places 17th overall.

Students opting for the general strand of engineering gain the flexibility that the breadth of the subject allows in their future careers, while degrees also provide opportunities to specialise in a specific area of interest. "This approach equips graduates with versatile problem-solving skills and a holistic understanding of engineering, making them highly adaptable and sought-after. By engaging with cutting-edge research and innovative projects, students gain hands-on experience and a competitive edge in the job market," says Dr Andy Nichols, general engineering course director, University of Sheffield.

General engineering makes a convincing choice for careers prospects. It ranks seventh in our employment index and =5th for starting salaries. Having followed an upward curve for a decade or so applications have levelled out and in 2023 the subject attracted 21,255 applications and just under 4,000 new undergraduates were accepted onto courses.

General Engineering	Teaching quality %	Student experience %	Research quality %	Entry standards (UCAS points)	Graduate prospects %	Overall score
1 Bristol	89.8	85.2	68	174	100	100
2 Cambridge	80.4	80.8	77.2	222	97.2	99.9
3 Sheffield	95.1	88.9	66.8	190	89.7	98.9
4 Oxford	80.4	74.8	77.5	213	94	97.8
5 Imperial College	78.3	80.7	81	186	95.9	97.4
6 University College London	86.4	73.4	70	179	-	96.6
7 Durham	85.6	72	52.8	204	95.4	96.4

General Engineering cont.

	Teaching quality %	Student experience %	Research quality %	Entry standards (UCAS points)	Graduate prospects %	Overall score
8 Strathclyde	90.1	87.4	52.8	186	88.9	96
=9 King's College London	85.5	83	62	158	-	95.2
=9 Queen Mary, London	85.8	85.8	66	144	-	95.2
11 Heriot-Watt	83	78.9	55.5	172	-	94.2
12 Liverpool	86	83.1	57	131	-	93
13 Loughborough	81.8	70.4	46.5	162	90.9	91.3
14 Cardiff	81.6	77.4	54	140	-	91.2
=15 Lancaster	82.6	81	44.8	142	-	91
=15 Warwick	77.6	79.2	56.2	155	88.5	91
17 Swansea	84.5	81.7	48.8	112	-	90.1
18 Ulster	80.5	74.1	49.8	122	89.4	89.1
19 Liverpool John Moores	85.9	84.3	45.5	115	83.3	88.6
20 Exeter	68.9	71.8	47	155	91.3	88.3
21 West of Scotland	87.1	84.5	16.5	-	85.3	87.9
22 Brunel	82.7	70.7	33	119	90	87.8
23 York	79.6	70.1	49.8	118	-	87.6
=24 Lincoln	82.4	71.6	24	118	-	85.6
=24 Robert Gordon	81.6	73.7	20.5	124	-	85.6
26 Lancashire	79.2	74.2	23	122	-	85.1
27 London South Bank	74.6	66.1	27.3	131	-	83.8
28 Coventry	76	69	23.5	124	81.4	82.8
29 Bournemouth	82.3	78.3	14	103	79.8	82.7
30 Northampton	82	76.5	8.5	81	-	81.7
31 Wrexham	74.2	68.5	16.2	91	-	80
32 Glasgow Caledonian	68.6	69.6	12.8	-	82	78.6

Employed in high-skilled job	78%	Employed in lower-skilled job	6%
Employed in high-skilled job and studying	3%	Employed in lower-skilled job and studying	0%
Studying	4%	Unemployed	4%
High-skilled work (median) salary	£30,000	Low-/medium-skilled salary	£23,000

Geography and Environmental Science

Our table incorporates the different strands of geography – physical and human. The former focuses on physical processes and natural environments, the latter concerns human societies and the links between people and the planet. Environmental science studies the earth's physical, chemical and biological processes and looks at what impacts the planet in terms of social, political and cultural developments. "Are you fascinated with finding out how nature works – and how people interact with it?" asks Dr Hannah Cloke, professor of hydrology, University of Reading, "Geography and environmental science help to find patterns and make sense of the mess. Most of the biggest issues the world faces, like climate change, biodiversity loss or war, need both human and physical solutions, which is why geographers see the world in this way."

Durham is No 1 in the table for the second consecutive year, buoyed by strong performance across all metrics, including the top graduate prospects – with 94.9% employed in high-skilled work or furthering their studies within 15 months. Up 11 places this year, Edinburgh ties in fifth place overall with St Andrews, which has the highest entry standards of 213 UCAS points. Outside of Scotland, entry standards are highest at Cambridge (184 UCAS points) and tend not to reach the heights of some other subjects, with plenty of places available at under 144 points (equal to three As), including Southampton – which ranks 10th in the table and where entrants averaged 136 UCAS points. East Anglia, in =35th place overall, has the edge for research, the Research Excellence Framework 2021 results showed, followed by Bristol, which ranks second for research quality and 11th overall. In 51st place overall, Coventry outdoes all other institutions for student satisfaction with teaching quality and 31st-place Gloucestershire is top for students' evaluation of teaching quality, our National Student Survey analysis shows.

Geography at A-level or equivalent is a requirement for geography degrees. For environmental science, the leading universities look for two subjects from geology, maths, psychology, physics, geography, biology or chemistry. The demand for places varies between the disciplines, with human geography attracting the highest numbers (almost 16,000 and just under 3,000 enrolments in 2024) followed by physical geographical sciences (just under 14,000 and 2,365). Though still attracting a smaller cohort of students, applications to environmental science degrees have risen by a quarter since 2019 and in 2024 the subject attracted 7,535 applications and 1,375 new students gained places.

The subjects as a whole rank in the upper half of our employment table, in 33rd place, based on nearly seven in ten (67.9%) graduates employed in high-skilled work or furthering their studies within 15 months. Performance in achieving these outcomes varies considerably by institution, from Durham at 94.4%, down to 57.3% at Kingston (68th overall). Starting salaries compare less strongly, with the subjects in 43rd place out of 70.

Geography and Environmental Sciences	Teaching quality %	Student experience %	Research quality %	Entry standards (UCAS points)	Graduate prospects %	Overall score
1 Durham	90.9	86.6	68.8	167	94.4	100
2 Oxford	89.3	76.9	66	180	89	97.9
3 Cambridge	83.9	78.1	59.2	184	94	97.4
4 University College London	87.9	89.3	59.2	171	86.7	97.2
=5 Edinburgh	84.9	83.8	63.2	194	84.3	97.1
=5 St Andrews	87.1	82.7	48.2	213	83.7	97.1
7 London School of Economics	82.9	83.3	63	164	92.7	96.6
8 Loughborough	90.2	90.8	54.2	144	86.9	95.9
9 Sheffield	91.6	90.8	51	151	83.2	95.6
10 Southampton	87.5	84.6	67.5	136	87.2	95.4
11 Bristol	82.7	86.2	70	154	84.1	95
12 Dundee	88.4	85.4	46.2	169	83	94.8
13 Royal Holloway	89.6	87.1	64	120	84.6	94.3
14 Nottingham	86.9	87.7	58.5	143	81.4	93.9
=15 Birmingham	86.4	84	49.2	141	87.1	93.6
=15 Lancaster	82.7	80.5	68.2	142	84.8	93.6
17 King's College London	83.7	84.3	58.8	152	82.2	93.4
18 Reading	89.3	87.8	68.5	111	79.9	93.1
19 Glasgow	75	68.2	65.5	192	83.3	92.7
=20 Aberystwyth	91.6	88.3	47	112	83.2	92.6

Geography and Environmental Sciences cont.

	Teaching quality %	Student experience %	Research quality %	Entry standards (UCAS points)	Graduate prospects %	Overall score
=20 Exeter	83.9	85.5	67.2	146	75.9	92.6
=22 Leeds	79	80.6	66	145	83.9	92.5
=22 Manchester	85.3	83.8	49	147	82.1	92.5
=22 Stirling	88.4	81.8	45.8	175	73.5	92.5
25 Northumbria	94.7	92.2	49	119	74.2	92.3
26 Swansea	88.9	91.4	51.7	114	80.8	92.2
27 Aberdeen	84.5	83.1	41.5	171	77.8	92.1
28 Sussex	89.5	87.1	57.2	131	73.7	91.9
29 Newcastle	82.9	85.3	53.8	134	81.5	91.6
30 Liverpool	87.6	88.8	45.2	125	79.9	91.5
31 Gloucestershire	97.5	96.7	25.8	105	75	90.7
32 Queen Mary, London	87.2	85.9	52.5	129	73.6	90.6
=33 Queen's, Belfast	84.7	85.1	35.5	138	80.8	90.4
=33 York	79.8	79.3	65.5	132	78.1	90.4
=35 Bangor	84.7	81.4	67.5	116	73.5	90
=35 East Anglia	81.3	78.5	73.8	116	76.2	90
=35 West of England	95	93.1	40.8	113	68.3	90
38 Cardiff	85.3	87.3	38.2	126	78.5	89.9
39 Keele	89.1	83.8	35.2	105	82.4	89.7
40 Hertfordshire	96.9	91.1	42.5	121	62.4	89.6
41 Ulster	86.3	82.1	43	115	79.4	89.5
42 Warwick	80.5	78.2	-	162	92.6	89.3
43 Leicester	92.9	89.6	28.7	116	72.5	89.2
44 Liverpool John Moores	86.5	90.5	28.7	110	77.8	88.5
45 Leeds Beckett	90.6	89	24.5	104	-	88.1
46 Oxford Brookes	93.3	86.4	34.8	104	69.1	88
47 Manchester Metropolitan	84.9	83.2	44.8	106	74.7	87.9
48 Nottingham Trent	86.2	86.7	30.8	103	77.6	87.7
49 Salford	88.9	86.5	41	100	70.4	87.5
50 Northampton	93.2	83.6	12	92	80.3	87.2
51 Coventry	97.6	84.7	17	104	68.6	87
52 Bath Spa	85.6	84.4	19.2	110	76	86.3
53 Huddersfield	93	79.8	24	88	-	86.1
=54 Portsmouth	85.2	80.2	26.8	102	76.5	86
=54 York St John	90.4	80.6	14	100	76.1	86
56 Hull	83.6	75.8	42	97	75	85.9
57 Plymouth	84.6	83.2	31	110	70.7	85.8
58 South Wales	84.3	81.7	16.2	126	-	85.6
=59 Edge Hill	85.4	83.9	15.2	104	75	85.2
=59 Liverpool Hope	91.1	85.4	9.5	97	-	85.2
61 Brighton	90.4	83.9	31.8	100	62.3	84.9
62 Lincoln	81.1	84.8	14	105	77.8	84.8
63 Sheffield Hallam	92.5	86.4	-	107	67.3	84.3
64 SOAS, London	79.6	73.1	29.8	121	-	84.1

65 Chester		89.4	76.4	7.2	111	70	83.9
66 Bournemouth		84.9	82.3	31.2	100	60.9	83
67 Worcester		77.3	71.8	12.2	104	77.8	82.2
68 Kingston		84.1	78.7	17.2	101	57.3	80.3

Employed in high-skilled job	52%	Employed in lower-skilled job	19%
Employed in high-skilled job and studying	4%	Employed in lower-skilled job and studying	1%
Studying	11%	Unemployed	5%
High-skilled work (median) salary	£26,000	Low-/medium-skilled salary	£20,779

Geology

The study of how the earth was formed and shaped, geology degrees at the leading universities require any two subjects from: biology, chemistry, economics, further maths, geography, geology, maths, physics and psychology. "Geology is practical: discover your own fossil and mineral collection and make friends for life in small classes. Or, it's mathematical: for example, computer simulations of mining heat, and future climates. Relevant jobs in the UK and worldwide are in natural resources, energy supply, environmental protection, planetary exploration, and local and national government," explains Professor Stuart Haszeldine, School of Geosciences, University of Edinburgh.

Cambridge tops our Geology table for the sixth year running while St Andrews is runner-up for the third consecutive year. Imperial has gained a place to rank third and still has the lead for research, based on the results of the Research Excellence Framework. Exeter is down three places to rank sixth overall, but has the top rating for teaching quality for the second year in a row in our National Student Survey analysis. Cardiff is up eight places to rank 10th in the table, boosted by topping the ranking for student satisfaction with the broad undergraduate experience. Geology students in general tend to enjoy their degrees: even at the bottom end of the scale, Glasgow scores more than 71% for teaching quality.

Entry standards can be high; led by Cambridge – where entrants averaged 224 UCAS points – nearly half of the universities listed attracted over 144 points in the UCAS tariff (equivalent to AAA at A-level). Life after an undergraduate geology degree can often include postgraduate study, which over one in five graduates was engaged in either full-time or combined with a job 15 months on from their courses. More than half had already secured high-skilled full-time jobs. Overall, geology places 27th in our employment ranking of 70 subject areas. Rates of pay for those with a geology degree average at £26,000 and place =28th.

Geology	Teaching quality %	Student experience %	Research quality %	Entry standards (UCAS points)	Graduate prospects %	Overall score
1 Cambridge	85.5	82.1	79.5	224	94.3	100
2 St Andrews	89.6	80.8	68.2	210	100	99.9
3 Imperial College	86.8	85	81	176	87.2	96.8
4 Birmingham	89.2	83.4	74.8	149	95.3	96.6
5 Oxford	81.6	79.2	71.2	177	100	96.4
6 Exeter	93.1	82.2	69.8	134	92.9	95.5
=7 Aberdeen	92.7	84.4	41.5	190	-	94.5
=7 Durham	88.6	79.4	60.2	162	92.9	94.5

Geology cont.

	Teaching quality %	Student experience %	Research quality %	Entry standards (UCAS points)	Graduate prospects %	Overall score
9 Bristol	88.4	82.6	75.2	149	83.3	93.9
10 Cardiff	91.5	88.4	67.8	121	86.7	93.6
11 Edinburgh	81.1	77.4	63.2	188	89.1	93.4
12 Leeds	80.9	81.1	68.2	142	90.9	92.3
=13 Liverpool	90.6	82.9	57	130	87.7	92.1
=13 University College London	86.9	82.5	63	137	-	92.1
15 Leicester	90.6	81.9	50.5	126	92.7	92
16 Southampton	84.5	80.2	71	140	80.8	91.2
17 East Anglia	81.5	79.2	73.8	128	-	91.1
18 Manchester	86.4	83.8	69.8	144	75	90.9
19 Royal Holloway	92	79.3	42	115	83.9	88.5
=20 Hull	82.3	73.5	42	-	91.3	87.9
=20 Plymouth	86.5	84.8	40.8	118	83.9	87.9
22 Bangor	81.3	82.2	67.5	117	71.7	87.1
23 Keele	91.5	80	35.2	100	81.9	86.4
24 Glasgow	71.1	61.2	39.5	193	87.9	86.2
25 Portsmouth	89.7	88.3	40.8	105	64.8	84.4

Employed in high-skilled job	52%	Employed in lower-skilled job	13%
Employed in high-skilled job and studying	3%	Employed in lower-skilled job and studying	0%
Studying	18%	Unemployed	5%
High-skilled work (median) salary	£26,000	Low-/medium-skilled salary	£19,000

German

"Germany is the UK's biggest trading partner after the US and as such, German, which is spoken by millions worldwide, has been identified by the British Council as one of the five languages consistently most important to the UK's strategic interests," note Dr Mark Allinson, Dr Anna Havinga and Dr Benedict Schofield, Department of German, University of Bristol. Data from the Graduate Outcomes survey shows almost seven in ten (69.1%) German graduates were employed in high-skilled jobs and/or furthering their studies 15 months on from their degrees – outcomes that place the subject in the top half of our employment ranking of 70 (32nd). For average starting salaries it ranks =38th.

The small student numbers taking German degrees often create fluctuations in the table, as evidenced this year by Cambridge taking the lead from St Andrews, while Manchester is up four places to rank fourth. Bristol however is steady in third and remains in front for research quality in our analysis of the Research Excellence Framework 2021 results. In our National Student Survey analysis Cambridge is top for teaching quality and St Andrews leads for the broad experience. Students of German tend to enjoy their studies whichever university they attend – returning positive ratings for teaching quality which go no lower than 73.9% at Edinburgh.

Entry standards to German degrees are high: at 17 out of the 19 universities in our table German degree new students enrolled with over 144 UCAS points, on average (equivalent to three As at A-level). As with modern languages more broadly, demand for the subject has been in decline – although there was a slight upturn in 2024. German studies degrees are now grouped with Scandinavian studies within UCAS data, and although just 280 students started courses in the subjects in 2024 this represented an increase from 260 the year before, though this modest uplift has not reversed the many years of diminishing numbers of applications and new starters.

While no post-1992 universities feature in our table, there are still plenty of places to study German, either as a single honours degree or in combination with a wide range of subjects including law, film, accountancy and other languages. Most universities in the table offer German from scratch, as well as catering for those who took it at A-level.

German

	Teaching quality %	Student experience %	Research quality %	Entry standards (UCAS points)	Graduate prospects %	Overall score
1 Cambridge	92.5	70.6	61	198	91.5	100
2 St Andrews	90.7	90.9	51.5	208	-	99.9
3 Bristol	86.5	82.1	64	167	87	96.5
4 Manchester	92.1	85.6	59.5	155	-	96.4
5 Oxford	90	70.7	51.2	183	88.2	95.8
6 University College London	91.3	77.7	56	164	-	95.4
7 Warwick	92.3	87.4	46.2	155	84.8	93.7
8 Durham	87.2	77.1	46	173	85.6	93.2
9 Nottingham	83.6	79.2	62	148	-	92.9
10 Southampton	91.9	82.4	47.8	150	-	92.8
11 Newcastle	84.6	84.5	61.8	131	-	92.1
12 Birmingham	87.5	82.8	54.8	150	79.8	91.9
13 Exeter	84.3	80.6	50	151	82.8	91.1
14 Glasgow	85.1	77.9	25.5	202	-	90.3
15 King's College London	79.8	67	51.2	169	-	90.1
16 Leeds	84.3	67.7	52	148	-	89.7
17 Edinburgh	73.9	67.3	45.8	183	-	88.5
18 Cardiff	87.9	87.2	55.5	125	72	88.4
19 Bath	87.4	79.7	31.8	156	-	88.1

Employed in high-skilled job	56%	Employed in lower-skilled job		18%
Employed in high-skilled job and studying	2%	Employed in lower-skilled job and studying		1%
Studying	10%	Unemployed		4%
High-skilled work (median) salary	£27,000	Low-/medium-skilled salary		N/A

History

Among the reshuffles of our History table's top ten, LSE is up two places to occupy the runner-up spot, Cambridge is down three in sixth place and Durham has gained two places to rank fourth. Exeter has dropped six places to sit 16th and York has gained four to rank tenth this year. Unwavering, though, is St Andrews at No 1, Oxford in third place and University College London (UCL) fifth. St Andrews' position is strengthened by the highest entry standards – with the latest data showing its history entrants averaged 208 points in the UCAS tariff – and it is one of 22 universities out of 88 in the table where entry standards average over 144 points (equal to three As at A-level). The best job prospects are at the LSE, where 93% of history graduates were employed in professional-level jobs and/or further study 15 months after their degrees. Kent (in 18th place overall) leads for research quality, based on results of the latest Research Excellence Framework 2021, where it is followed by Leicester (ninth in the table) and UCL.

Tied with Liverpool, Royal Holloway and Stirling in joint 30th place, Hertfordshire is the highest-ranked modern university in the main ranking, although the post-1992 universities dominate on rates of student satisfaction: Derby (51st overall) and Lancashire (=38th) are first and second respectively for both teaching quality and the broad experience in our National Student Survey analysis.

Applications and enrolments to the subject showed a small downturn in 2024, compounding a longer-term downward flow in demand for history – in line with the pattern among the humanities – as university applicants look for greater career certainty in their undergraduate choices. But the lessening interest in history degrees seems confined to the lower- and medium-tariff institutions and in 2024 the subject still attracted 51,785 applications and 9,605 new undergraduates.

Graduate prospects vary considerably across the table, from those at LSE down to Essex, where only 53.5% of history graduates had secured the desired outcomes of a high-skilled job and/or postgraduate study 15 months after their degrees. Placing =55th out of 70 subjects for graduate prospects, history is not a degree with an immediate utilitarian use. When surveyed 15 months after their degrees less than four in ten graduates (37.1%) were employed full-time in high-skilled jobs, while around half that proportion had progressed to postgraduate study – either full-time or in conjunction with working. Meanwhile more than a quarter (25.9%) were working in jobs deemed "low-skilled". Graduate pay fares slightly better compared with other subjects; history ranking =46th and graduates in high-skilled jobs command £25,000 salaries.

"There are so many good reasons to study history," says Peter Frankopan, professor of global history, University of Oxford, and Unesco professor of Silk Roads studies, University of Cambridge: "First, learning how to handle, evaluate and understand complex sources is an important skill in its own right. Second, these days it is possible to investigate the past in ways that have never been possible before – from using climate archives and genomics to studying bone isotopes and big data. Third, approaches to history are more global and inclusive than they have ever been, which means there are wonderful questions to ask and answer."

Applications and enrolments to the subject showed a small downturn in 2024, compounding a longer-term downward flow in demand for history – in line with the pattern among the humanities – as university applicants look for greater career certainty in their undergraduate choices. But the lessening interest in history degrees seems confined to the lower- and medium-tariff institutions and in 2024 the subject still attracted 51,785 applications and 9,605 new undergraduates.

History	Teaching quality %	Student experience %	Research quality %	Entry standards (UCAS points)	Graduate prospects %	Overall score
1 St Andrews	91.8	88.2	62	208	82.9	100
2 London School of Economics	88.9	86.8	59.8	184	93	99.5
3 Oxford	86.9	74.4	61.3	186	89.1	97.3
4 Durham	86.5	75.9	59.2	183	88.6	96.8
5 University College London	86.9	79.2	67.8	168	85.4	96.5
6 Cambridge	88	70.2	54.5	199	83.4	96
7 Warwick	87.3	84.9	61.3	152	86	95.4

8 Strathclyde	91.2	89.5	49	199	70.5	94.9
9 Leicester	92.1	87.7	71.5	115	78.5	94.1
10 York	85.6	80.5	64.8	152	82	94
11 Queen Mary, London	90.6	84.9	67.2	138	76.2	93.9
=12 King's College London	84.9	74.6	62.7	163	80.2	93.5
=12 Loughborough	91.8	90.6	45	145	80.9	93.5
14 Birmingham	86	80.1	60.2	148	82.4	93.4
15 Bristol	83.4	81.6	56.5	165	81.6	93.3
16 Exeter	83.4	79.2	66	150	81.1	93.2
17 Sheffield	89.3	86.9	49	150	79.7	93
18 Kent	92.7	83.5	77.2	118	69.7	92.8
19 Glasgow	81.8	79.4	62.5	193	70.4	92.6
20 Cardiff	89.6	86.8	42.2	137	84.1	92.4
=21 Leeds	85.1	84.7	49.2	158	79.1	92.1
=21 Manchester	83.4	78.7	67	155	75	92.1
=21 Southampton	87	83.5	59.5	139	77.1	92.1
24 Aston	95.2	93.9	49	112	-	91.6
25 Nottingham	85.5	81.5	52.5	143	78.9	91.3
26 East Anglia	88.4	81.7	67.5	120	72.7	91.1
=27 Edinburgh	77.8	74.4	55.8	185	75	90.8
=27 Hull	94.7	90	60.8	100	69.8	90.8
29 Lancaster	86.9	83	51.7	139	75.5	90.7
=30 Hertfordshire	93	93.4	49	110	-	90.6
=30 Liverpool	88.7	87.9	52.8	129	73.3	90.6
=30 Royal Holloway	90.1	85.4	53.5	131	71.7	90.6
=30 Stirling	91.1	85.4	51.7	168	60.8	90.6
34 Roehampton	97	93.9	42.8	99	-	90.2
35 Sussex	86.3	84.9	62.7	125	70.2	89.9
36 Queen's, Belfast	87.8	83.3	54.2	143	67.3	89.6
37 Northumbria	91.8	86.3	49.5	120	69.8	89.5
=38 Aberdeen	86.9	80.3	38.5	165	70.2	89.3
=38 Lancashire	99.5	94.7	24.5	101	75	89.3
=40 Aberystwyth	92.2	89.7	36.8	116	74.4	89.1
=40 Teesside	98.4	93.4	49.2	87	66.7	89.1
42 Dundee	93.4	82.7	23.8	168	66.9	89
43 Reading	91.3	84.5	42.2	114	74.1	88.9
44 Bournemouth	91	89.5	47.2	101	72	88.6
45 Plymouth	92.4	92.1	42.8	106	68.7	88.2
46 Lincoln	85.7	72.3	66	106	68.9	87.5
=47 City St George's	89.6	87.4	40.8	111	-	87.4
=47 Worcester	92.1	80	30.2	107	76.4	87.4
=49 Coventry	92.6	85.9	33.2	111	70.6	87.3
=49 Swansea	89.1	86.4	45.2	120	65.6	87.3
51 Derby	100	98.1	-	96	78.4	87.2
52 Salford	93.9	88.7	51.7	107	58.3	87.1
53 Portsmouth	89.4	84.3	51.7	111	64	87
54 Oxford Brookes	93.2	89	28.2	107	70.7	86.9
55 De Montfort	88.5	87.5	37.5	103	71.6	86.5

History cont.

	Teaching quality %	Student experience %	Research quality %	Entry standards (UCAS points)	Graduate prospects %	Overall score
56 Birmingham Newman	95.3	93.8	15	107	71.4	86.4
57 SOAS, London	85.5	71.5	47.5	124	-	86.3
58 Ulster	91	92.3	34	108	65.9	86.2
59 Huddersfield	91	71.1	33.5	104	74.4	86
=60 Manchester Metropolitan	86.7	79.9	41	112	69.4	85.9
=60 Nottingham Trent	86.2	78.2	51.5	105	67.2	85.9
62 Edge Hill	89.3	87.1	27.8	101	73.6	85.8
63 Lincoln Bishop	97.7	94.1	16	93	-	85.6
64 Newcastle	80.5	79	33.5	139	71.8	85.5
=65 Bangor	93.4	89.3	33.2	106	60.8	85.2
=65 Gloucestershire	98	84.4	8.2	107	69.6	85.2
67 Liverpool Hope	92.9	89.7	24.2	96	67.9	85
68 Liverpool John Moores	88.9	87.9	19.8	114	67.9	84.3
69 York St John	93.7	87.2	18	105	64.7	84.1
70 Anglia Ruskin	85.6	85.1	47	86	64.4	83.9
71 Northampton	87.9	85.1	31.2	102	64.8	83.8
=72 Chichester	91.2	76.7	33	103	61.6	83.6
=72 Keele	89.2	82.6	41.5	110	55.8	83.6
74 Bath Spa	94.9	92.9	25	102	54.3	83.2
75 Leeds Beckett	94.6	88.5	13.8	104	61	83.1
76 Essex	87.2	80.6	40.2	121	53.5	82.9
=77 Brunel	92.5	73.2	-	95	77.4	82.6
=77 Wales Trinity St David	91.2	73.5	31	85	-	82.6
=79 Greenwich	91.5	85	25.5	99	58.2	82.3
=79 Wolverhampton	92.7	87.2	23.8	88	60	82.3
81 Sheffield Hallam	85	73.3	25.2	102	68.9	82.2
82 Goldsmiths, London	83.4	54.5	41.5	114	65.2	82.1
83 Winchester	87.4	67.6	18.8	100	64.9	80.6
84 Canterbury Christ Church	87.7	69.9	17.8	88	67.7	80.5
85 Chester	87.4	61.3	28.7	109	57.6	80.1
86 West of England	86.9	79.5	15	107	57.7	79.7
87 Brighton	73.8	64.9	44.2	98	-	78.4
88 Westminster	78.4	70.3	23	101	54.3	76.4

Employed in high-skilled job	37%	Employed in lower-skilled job		26%
Employed in high-skilled job and studying	4%	Employed in lower-skilled job and studying		2%
Studying	14%	Unemployed		5%
High-skilled work (median) salary	£26,000	Low-/medium-skilled salary		£20,000

History of Art, Architecture and Design

"Art history matters because art matters. Great works of art offer profound distillations of the human experience; they help us to understand our relationship with the world and with one another," says Professor Mark Hallett, Märit Rausing director, Courtauld Institute of Art,

"If you study art history you will be given the tools to analyse all kinds of art across all kinds of cultures. Art history will also provide you with the means to decipher the crowded visual environments we navigate every day. Finally, it gives you skills – of analysis, argument, presentation and collaboration – that will enable you to flourish in a wide variety of professions." In tenth place overall the Courtauld is a self-governing college of the University of London based in Somerset House and has previously topped our table – the only specialist institution to have done so in any ranking.

St Andrews returns to the lead in our new History of Art, Architecture and Design table, boosted by the top research quality rating along with entry standards outdone only by Cambridge and the second-best graduate outcomes. The university where the Princess of Wales studied history of art, St Andrews also features in the top five for rates of student satisfaction with teaching quality as well as the broader experience, measures derived from the National Student Survey. Cambridge has dropped 11 places to rank 12th overall this year due to poor results in the NSS, which put it bottom for both the student experience and teaching quality. Led by Lincoln, =19th in the table, Oxford Brookes (=16th) and Plymouth (22nd), modern universities are hitting the right notes with students whose positive feedback means they dominate these NSS-derived metrics.

Demand for places to study history of art, architecture and design degrees dipped in 2024, with applications down by around 6% (to just under 6,000) and around 8% fewer new starters (1,050) were accepted onto courses than in the year before. Oxford Brookes leads for graduate prospects, based on 74% being in high-skilled jobs or postgraduate study 15 months after their degrees. Career prospects for those with history of art, architecture and design degrees may not be immediately gratifying; the subject area ranks 65th of our employment index of 70 subjects, where its position is held back by the similar numbers of graduates employed full-time in high-skilled jobs (four in ten) as jobs deemed "low-skilled" (three in ten). The subject compares more favourably in our pay ranking, where starting salaries commanded by graduates rank it =54th.

History of Art, Architecture and Design	Teaching quality %	Student experience %	Research quality %	Entry standards (UCAS points)	Graduate prospects %	Overall score
1 St Andrews	90	88.2	78.2	190	71.4	100
2 University College London	89.4	88.5	64.7	166	-	95.6
3 Birmingham	86.6	83.7	70.2	164	-	95.1
4 Oxford	86.6	72.2	61.3	184	-	94.6
5 Bristol	87.6	84.9	59.8	150	69.7	92.9
6 Sussex	89.7	88.1	70	126	-	92.4
7 Leeds	88.7	87.1	54.8	160	66.9	92.3
8 York	81.4	76.3	77	146	67.3	92
9 Warwick	89.6	87.9	55	152	66.2	91.7
10 Courtauld	82	75.6	63.5	154	68.3	91.2
11 Manchester	81.3	79.8	70.8	144	-	91.1
12 Cambridge	72.7	45.1	65.8	198	-	90.2
13 Glasgow	89.2	81.3	68.8	167	54.3	89.9
=14 Goldsmiths, London	85.9	73.4	57.5	144	65.5	89.4
=14 Manchester Metropolitan	86.6	73.8	51.7	150	-	89.4
=16 Edinburgh	78.8	78.3	54	158	67.2	89.1
=16 Oxford Brookes	93.9	90.7	25.5	120	74	89.1

History of Art, Architecture and Design cont.	Teaching quality %	Student experience %	Research quality %	Entry standards (UCAS points)	Graduate prospects %	Overall score
18 Exeter	81.5	84.3	55.9	146	-	88.9
=19 Lincoln	95.3	95.8	43.8	113	-	88.6
=19 Nottingham	88.1	80.1	54.8	128	-	88.6
21 Brighton	85.3	80.8	53	113	-	85.8
22 Plymouth	92.3	89.5	26.5	116	-	84.1

Employed in high-skilled job	41%	Employed in lower-skilled job	31%
Employed in high-skilled job and studying	1%	Employed in lower-skilled job and studying	3%
Studying	7%	Unemployed	6%
High-skilled work (median) salary	£25,000	Low-/medium-skilled salary	£20,000

Hospitality, Leisure, Recreation and Tourism

Modern universities dominate the Hospitality, Leisure, Recreation and Tourism table, representing all but four of the 52 institutions tabled, but Birmingham – founded at the turn of the 20th century – is No 1 for the tenth year running. Helping secure its overall rank is the top-rated research in the area and second-highest entry standards in the UK. Ahead for entry standards is Stirling, where students arrived with an average of 167 UCAS points (Scottish universities benefitting from the favourable tariff conversion for Scottish secondary qualifications). The top 10 features most of the same universities this year as last, such as Surrey – up one place to rank third, Glasgow Caledonian (down four to sixth place) and Liverpool John Moores in seventh place (down four this year).

Robert Gordon University – in 30th place overall – has the top rates of student satisfaction with teaching quality, followed by Wolverhampton (19th) and Lancashire (38th), while for students' evaluation of the wider experience Wolverhampton leads the field, followed by Lancashire and Sunderland (43rd place overall). Conversely, students at Buckinghamshire New expressed the lowest rates of satisfaction with the wider experience and Anglia Ruskin is bottom for teaching quality, our National Student Survey analysis shows.

A wide variety of courses are incorporated in our Hospitality, Leisure, Recreation and Tourism table, all of them directed towards management in the leisure and tourism industries. They include degrees in international hospitality management, and adventure tourism management. Studying tourism takes a multidisciplinary perspective and equips students with core skills such as planning, logistics and marketing, while encouraging entrepreneurialism and leadership. An evolving industry, tourism is often at the forefront of adopting new technologies – especially related to sustainability, new trends and creating innovative and impactful experiences. Practical assessments are part of the student journey, setting them up to hit the ground running when they start work.

Winchester is top for career destinations, based on 74.1% of the university's graduates in the subjects employed in high-skilled jobs and/or further study 15 months after their degrees. As a whole, the subjects rank 61st out of 70 areas in our employment index, where they are held back by the high proportion (36.7%) of graduates working in jobs classified as "low-skilled". Salaries compare a little better: with hospitality, leisure, recreation and tourism ranked =56th out of 70, based on average graduate salaries of £24,000.

Hospitality, Leisure, Recreation and Tourism

		Teaching quality %	Student experience %	Research quality %	Entry standards (UCAS points)	Graduate prospects %	Overall score
1	Birmingham	86.6	83.6	73.2	153	-	100
2	Stirling	82.1	86.7	36.5	167	-	94.5
3	Surrey	89.4	86	57	131	65.2	93.1
4	Portsmouth	86.9	86.1	57.5	124	-	92.4
5	Leeds Beckett	90.8	89.3	49.2	116	71.1	92
6	Glasgow Caledonian	81.2	81.1	38.5	147	68.5	91
7	Liverpool John Moores	82	80.6	60.8	128	62.6	90.6
8	St Mary's, Twickenham	89.7	89.2	46	118	-	90.3
9	Manchester Metropolitan	87.8	85.2	42.8	124	65	89.7
10	Westminster	90.8	88.3	37.5	122	-	89.5
11	Falmouth	92.8	83.1	48.8	128	52.2	89.3
12	Staffordshire	93.2	89.9	38.8	111	63.9	88.9
13	Canterbury Christ Church	89.8	85.8	38	118	64.7	88.6
14	Plymouth	88.9	82.8	28.7	139	59.4	88.5
15	Edge Hill	89.9	91.9	32.5	119	-	88.3
16	Cardiff Metropolitan	84.8	79.9	43.8	120	65.4	88.2
=17	Sheffield Hallam	83	76.9	45.2	115	69.4	87.9
=17	York St John	93.9	88.9	27.5	118	-	87.9
19	Wolverhampton	96.2	97.2	25.2	107	-	87.3
20	Brighton	85.9	81.2	45.5	93	73.6	87.1
=21	Lincoln	83.8	81.3	30.8	123	66.7	87
=21	Winchester	87.4	90.4	20.8	110	74.1	87
=23	Hertfordshire	86.2	80.4	29	132	60	86.9
=23	Nottingham Trent	84.5	78.3	36.8	125	-	86.9
25	Ulster	92.4	89.5	45.8	108	51.2	86.7
=26	Edinburgh Napier	84.9	83.3	23.5	128	63.8	86.5
=26	London South Bank	83.3	83	32.2	-	66.7	86.5
=26	West of Scotland	93.3	90.2	29	-	54.8	86.5
29	Essex	91.2	87.4	32.5	108	-	86.1
30	Robert Gordon	98.2	90.1	-	123	60	85.1
31	Coventry	90.3	86.5	24.8	110	59.7	84.9
=32	Arts Bournemouth	82.1	71.2	23	138	-	84.8
=32	Northumbria	80.2	76.5	28.2	131	-	84.8
=34	Bournemouth	79.1	79.3	41.8	105	65.3	84.7
=34	Chichester	89.8	77	33.2	109	-	84.7
36	Gloucestershire	86.1	83.6	24.5	104	67.6	84.5
37	Birmingham City	90.9	87.8	-	119	67.7	84.4
38	Lancashire	96.1	94.7	19.2	116	45.7	84
39	Chester	81.3	71.3	25.2	120	64.8	83.8
40	West London	92.1	91.5	24.2	113	47.7	83.5
41	East London	91.8	89.7	-	106	68.8	83.2
42	West of England	86.7	86.8	-	114	68.3	82.8
43	Sunderland	93.7	92.5	22	114	42	82.6
44	Northampton	91.4	85.5	13.2	107	56.6	82.3

Hospitality, Leisure, Recreation and Tourism cont.	Teaching quality %	Student experience %	Research quality %	Entry standards (UCAS points)	Graduate prospects %	Overall score
45 Southampton Solent	83.6	82.8	18.5	100	64.6	81.9
46 Oxford Brookes	78.1	78.6	-	118	73.8	81.8
47 Wales Trinity St David	91.7	90.4	-	113	49.3	80.3
48 Buckinghamshire New	76.1	67.9	22.8	100	66.9	79.8
49 Greenwich	88.1	85.3	-	112	53.5	79.7
50 Derby	87.3	81.7	-	113	54.7	79.6
51 Bedfordshire	88.4	83.6	22	-	34.4	77.2
52 Anglia Ruskin	65	72.5	18.5	89	63.5	75.1

Employed in high-skilled job	45%	Employed in lower-skilled job		37%
Employed in high-skilled job and studying	2%	Employed in lower-skilled job and studying		1%
Studying	4%	Unemployed		6%
High-skilled work (median) salary	£25,000	Low-/medium-skilled salary		£21,300

Iberian Languages

York is up eight places to take the lead in our new Iberian Languages table. Its position is boosted by achieving the subjects' top results in the Research Excellence Framework 2021, along with high rates of student satisfaction: York ranks second for teaching quality and for the broad experience in our analysis of the latest National Student Survey (NSS). Surrey, which tables in fifth place overall, tops each NSS metric. Last year's No 1 Cambridge settles for runner-up this year but is in front for graduate prospects, with more than nine in 10 (91.5%) employed in high-skilled jobs or further study 15 months after their degrees. St Andrews, which led the table two years ago, is in third place. Such fluctuations are customary due to the small student numbers the languages of Spanish and Portuguese attract. Just three of the 32 institutions listed are post-1992 universities and entry standards tend to be high: at 19 universities tabled entrants averaged over 144 UCAS points (equal to three As at A-level).

"Studying Iberian languages (the languages of Spain and/or Portugal) allows students to communicate fluently in two major global languages, which means graduates can work across the world. It also introduces students to cultures that have a significant impact on our own. Students think critically about big questions affecting us all, from how the climate crisis is being addressed in different contexts to how sexes, genders and sexualities are thought about in diverse ways in other cultures," says Dr Eamon McCarthy, senior lecturer in Spanish and Latin American studies, University of Stirling.

In line with other modern language degrees, the demand for places to study Spanish and Portuguese continued to decline in the 2024 admissions cycle however, when Iberian studies attracted 4,340 applications and 810 new students (down from 4,505 and 820 respectively the year before and more than a third fewer than six years before in 2019). But there were still 59 universities and colleges offering Spanish on the UCAS website for 2026–27. Many students take Spanish as part of a broader modern language degree or paired with diverse subjects as part of a joint honours programme rather than as a single honours programme. Though no longer tracked individually by UCAS, Portuguese had been registering zero single honours students since 2012 – but it can still be studied, and 22 institutions were offering the language for 2026–27, mostly as part of joint honours degrees or combined modern or Latin languages courses.

Iberian Languages

	Teaching quality %	Student experience %	Research quality %	Entry standards (UCAS points)	Graduate prospects %	Overall score
1 York	94.2	92.1	74.8	156	-	100
2 Cambridge	92.5	70.6	61	198	91.5	98.9
3 St Andrews	91.5	83	51.5	200	-	97.4
4 Warwick	92.1	86.7	46.2	155	88.7	94
5 Surrey	94.4	96.6	63	111	-	93.7
6 Durham	87.2	77.1	46	173	85.6	92.5
7 Lancaster	83.8	77.4	68.5	137	-	92
8 Oxford	84.2	64	51.2	185	83.7	91.9
=9 Liverpool	87.7	81.9	59	136	-	91.5
=9 Manchester	87.4	78.4	59.5	146	80.2	91.5
=11 Birmingham	87.5	82.8	54.8	150	80.1	91.4
=11 Royal Holloway	92	88.1	60	111	-	91.4
13 Newcastle	83.4	84.3	61.8	134	83.1	91.3
14 Exeter	84.3	80.6	50	151	82.9	90.5
15 Bath	88.4	87.9	31.8	152	87.7	90.4
16 Southampton	92	78.3	47.8	138	-	90.1
17 Bristol	84.9	79.2	64	164	68.8	90
18 Nottingham	83.2	76.5	62	143	77.6	89.9
19 Queen's, Belfast	87	86.6	37	151	83.7	89.7
20 Leeds	87.1	81.2	52	140	78.7	89.6
21 Edinburgh	72.5	64.1	45.8	182	88.8	89.5
22 King's College London	79.6	75.1	51.2	162	80.4	89.3
23 Stirling	76.1	73.3	47.5	175	-	88.2
=24 Aberdeen	84	83.4	32.5	169	-	88
=24 Cardiff	87.5	84.8	55.5	134	70.5	88
26 Queen Mary, London	77.9	74.7	51.1	147	-	87.1
=27 Manchester Metropolitan	87.8	76.8	51.7	106	-	86.5
=27 University College London	72.8	60.1	56	164	-	86.5
29 Sheffield	88.3	83.4	35.8	-	73.8	85.9
30 Glasgow	80.3	75.1	25.5	215	61.7	84.1
31 Chester	77.4	76.2	31.2	101	87.5	83
32 Westminster	88.5	88.4	24.5	111	-	82.6

Employed in high-skilled job	49%	Employed in lower-skilled job	21%
Employed in high-skilled job and studying	4%	Employed in lower-skilled job and studying	0%
Studying	9%	Unemployed	8%
High-skilled work (median) salary	£26,900	Low-/medium-skilled salary	£23,000

Information Systems and Management

In a shake-up of our Information Systems and Management table, Glasgow is No 1, ousting University College London (UCL) into third place after four years at the top. Powering Glasgow's ascent are the highest entry standards – with students in the subject area averaging 190 UCAS points, the latest data shows. Runner-up Sheffield has the second-highest entry standards (171 UCAS points) and places in the top five for both metrics of student satisfaction: teaching quality and the broad experience. The top scorer in the Research Excellence Framework 2021, UCL remains in front for research quality. Northumbria, in fifth place overall, is top for student satisfaction with teaching quality as well as the broader experience in our National Student Survey analysis, where it is followed in both by Huddersfield. Fourth-place Ulster had the best-employed graduates when canvassed by the Graduate Outcomes survey, which showed more than four in five (82.6%) working in high-skilled jobs and/or enrolled in postgraduate study 15 months on from their degrees.

Our table includes all subjects to do with information curation and management. Formerly titled Librarianship and Information Management, this is the fifth appearance of our broadened and renamed subject grouping. The courses encompassed range from information systems, data management and curatorial studies to bioinformatics, museum studies and systems analysis and design. The ranking also still takes in librarianship, which requires some postgraduate training after a first degree to enter the profession and has practically disappeared at undergraduate level.

The subject group as a whole features in the upper half of our 70-subject employment, at 31st position. It compares even better on earnings (though pay is not an ingredient of our table) placing =21st, with graduates commanding salaries of £27,000, on average. At UCL, Edyta Kostanek, deputy programme director for BSc information management for business says "Students are equipped with cutting-edge knowledge that is supported by the latest research in innovation and entrepreneurship. With a curriculum that includes real-world projects and hands-on experience, graduates are ready to succeed in diverse sectors."

Information Systems and Management	Teaching quality %	Student experience %	Research quality %	Entry standards (UCAS points)	Graduate prospects %	Overall score
1 Glasgow	84.2	83.9	67.2	190	-	100
2 Sheffield	86.8	87.6	59.5	171	-	98.2
3 University College London	86.1	88.8	56.8	165	-	97.4
4 Ulster	83.3	80.5	45.8	122	82.6	94
5 Northumbria	95.1	95.1	25.8	-	76.7	92.7
=6 West London	83.9	84.6	45.5	120	-	91.1
=6 Westminster	83.3	84.3	50	113	-	91.1
8 Coventry	92.4	90.1	23.5	119	77.4	90.8
9 Portsmouth	86	83.6	32.8	-	74.6	89.3
10 Manchester Metropolitan	88.5	85.5	29	122	74.2	89
11 Huddersfield	81.2	90.2	26.5	129	74.2	88.4
12 Derby	83.3	80.4	24	126	-	87.9
13 De Montfort	84.6	76.5	24	103	-	85.8
14 East London	63.6	66.9	34.2	117	-	83.1

Employed in high-skilled job	62%	Employed in lower-skilled job		17%
Employed in high-skilled job and studying	4%	Employed in lower-skilled job and studying		0%
Studying	2%	Unemployed		8%
High-skilled work (median) salary	£27,000	Low-/medium-skilled salary		£23,000

Italian

To study Italian at undergraduate level, one modern language at A-level is required by the leading universities. Some require Italian specifically, while others allow it to be learned from scratch. Degree courses often include time spent abroad studying or teaching. Describing the merits of the subject, Katrin Wehling-Giorgi, professor in the School of Modern Languages and Cultures, Durham University says "Studying Italian will provide you with a plurilingual, intercultural mindset. You will become fluent in the language of a vibrant, top-ten world economy, the lingua franca of fashion, music and architecture. Have a taste of la dolce vita during your year abroad and be inspired by an unrivalled global cultural heritage that has shaped history for two millennia. Italy is the birthplace of lyric opera, Renaissance art, neorealist cinema, literary giants from Dante to Ferrante and a transnational diaspora, and studying Italian opens worldwide opportunities from the civil service to the cultural sector."

In a generally high-tariff subject and a table without any post-1992 universities, Glasgow ranks ninth overall and leads on entry standards, its new students averaging 200 UCAS points. No universities averaged below the 125 points at Cardiff. Cambridge retains its long held No 1 position in our Italian table overall, boosted by coming top for teaching quality in our National Student Survey analysis as well as having the edge for graduate prospects, with the Graduate Outcomes survey showing 91.5% in high-skilled jobs and/or further study 15 months after their degrees. Cardiff (tenth overall) is in front for student satisfaction with the wider experience. Based on results of the Research Excellence Framework 2021 Bristol (=6th in the table) leads for research quality. The small student numbers Italian degrees attract create volatility in the table – as evidenced by Durham slipping three places to rank fifth, University College London going from seventh last year to 11th, and Manchester climbing seven places to sit third.

There were 135 new students of Italian in 2024 – the same number of new starters as in 2023 but 27% fewer than five years before in 2019, following the downward trend in modern languages more widely. UCAS showed 37 colleges and universities offering 532 courses for 2026–27, many of them as part of joint honours degrees or as part of a wider modern languages programme and five offered Italian as a single honours degree.

Italian is close to the upper half of our 70 subject areas (39th place), based on 63.8% of those with an Italian degree working in high-skilled jobs and/or postgraduate study 15 months on. Average early career salaries of £25,715 rank the subject 37th.

Italian	Teaching quality %	Student experience %	Research quality %	Entry standards (UCAS points)	Graduate prospects %	Overall score
1 Cambridge	92.5	70.6	61	198	91.5	100
2 Warwick	92.3	87.4	46.2	155	85.6	94.8
3 Manchester	88.4	76.5	59.5	154	-	94.1
4 Oxford	86.5	65.9	51.2	189	-	93.8
5 Durham	87.2	77.1	46	173	85.6	93.7
=6 Birmingham	87.5	82.8	54.8	150	79.3	92.9
=6 Bristol	87.1	80.4	64	165	67.3	92.9
8 Exeter	84.3	80.6	50	151	82.8	91.7
9 Glasgow	87.9	81.4	25.5	200	-	91.6
10 Cardiff	88.5	87.9	55.5	125	70.2	90.2
11 University College London	83.4	71.7	56	143	-	89.8
12 Edinburgh	79.3	77.4	45.8	162	-	88.5

Employed in high-skilled job	45%	Employed in lower-skilled job	22%
Employed in high-skilled job and studying	5%	Employed in lower-skilled job and studying	1%
Studying	12%	Unemployed	6%
High-skilled work (median) salary	£26,000	Low-/medium-skilled salary	N/A

Land and Property Management

Cambridge's lead in the table remains unchallenged. Its land economy degree attracts the highest entry standards by far and the university leads the field in research quality too, based on results of the latest Research Excellence Framework (REF) 2021. Runner-up in the table for the fourth consecutive year, Manchester is second for entry standards and third for research. Fourth-placed Kingston also performed strongly in the REF 2021 and sits second to Cambridge for research quality. In a diverse subject grouping that includes programmes in woodland ecology, surveying and conservation, real-estate degrees are the biggest recruiters. In third place of the table Reading runs a Pathways to Property widening participation programme at its Henley Business School to attract greater numbers of state-school-educated applicants into studying real estate.

Graduate employment levels in land and property management are among the best of any subject group outside the health professions and engineering disciplines. The Graduate Outcomes survey showed almost 80% of graduates employed in high-skilled jobs and/or furthering their studies 15 months on, placing the subjects 13th in of our employment index's 70 areas. At Sheffield Hallam, which ranks fifth overall in our table, a perfect 100% of graduates achieved these outcomes. Average early career salaries of £26,265 also compare positively with other subjects albeit less strongly, in 27th place.

Anthony Goodier, principal lecturer in built environment, Sheffield Hallam University says: "This subject encapsulates diverse aspects of property and real estate. It can offer you an interesting, varied and rewarding global career. There are huge opportunities to work in the public and private sectors because land and property professionals have a crucial role to play in addressing the challenges we face, from meeting the housing need to improving the performance of urban and rural real estate as we progress towards net zero."

Land and Property Management	Teaching quality %	Student experience %	Research quality %	Entry standards (UCAS points)	Graduate prospects %	Overall score
1 Cambridge	83.8	63.4	74.8	201	-	100
2 Manchester	82.6	84.2	59.2	135	-	93.2
3 Reading	81.5	80.2	53.5	132	94.4	91.8
4 Kingston	84.8	77.9	63	95	-	90.2
5 Sheffield Hallam	79.2	66.3	43.2	118	100	89.5
6 Ulster	79.3	76.3	54.2	117	-	88.8
7 Birmingham City	86.6	86.5	34.8	111	-	88.6
8 Salford	83.4	84.3	43.5	-	82.8	87.1
9 Westminster	82.9	84.2	37.5	116	86	87
10 Nottingham Trent	83.6	83.5	38	110	85.7	86.7
11 Leeds Beckett	78.3	77.2	24.5	116	-	83.5
12 Liverpool John Moores	75.3	71.2	28.7	110	-	82.1
13 Royal Agricultural University	68	68.1	-	113	90.3	78.4

Employed in high-skilled job	68%	Employed in lower-skilled job	10%
Employed in high-skilled job and studying	9%	Employed in lower-skilled job and studying	0%
Studying	2%	Unemployed	4%
High-skilled work (median) salary	£26,500	Low-/medium-skilled salary	£20,000

Law

One of the most popular choices for higher education, law continues to attract record applications. In 2024, 163,325 applied to study law, 19% more than in 2019 after successive years of rising demand. Interest from 18-year-old applicants has seen the sharpest increase – of 33% between 2019 and 2024. The number of places available has risen too but has not kept pace with applications, and 29,830 law students were accepted onto courses in 2023 (up 14% since 2019). More encouragingly for school leavers, however, the number of places going to 18-year-olds has increased more steeply by 31% across the same timeframe.

There are not normally specific subject requirements for law, but A-levels of use include history, English, politics, classics and philosophy. Applicants are advised to read widely and to be curious about the law and its relationship with other areas of society. Entry standards reflect the fierce demand for places: four of the 104 universities tabled average more than 200 points in the UCAS tariff and nearly a third average over 144 points (equivalent to three As at A-level). Led by Glasgow, three Scottish universities (which benefit from the favourable tariff conversion for Scottish secondary qualifications) claim the highest entry tariffs among their law entrants. The highest entry standards south of the border are at Cambridge, which has returned to its customary No 1 spot in our table following University College London (UCL) taking the helm last year. But there are so many places to study law that there are still 14 universities where entrants averaged below 100 UCAS points.

The top 15 universities are largely consistent this year with last, albeit reshuffled – including London School of Economics and Political Science rising through the ranks to become runner-up (from fourth last year and ninth the year before), King's College London falling five places to rank 15th and Leeds gaining 16 places to sit 12th. In third place overall this year UCL's research quality within law is peerless, based on results of the latest Research Excellence Framework 2021, and it is followed by Kent (32nd place overall) and Bristol (tenth) for research quality. But Cambridge has the edge for graduate prospects – with 96.9% of graduates employed in high-skilled jobs and/ or postgraduate study within 15 months. In 20th place, Ulster is the top-ranked modern university in the table for the second consecutive year. The modern universities more broadly do best for students' evaluation of teaching quality, with our National Student Survey analysis showing Sunderland (=66th overall) in front, followed by Cumbria (81st) and Southampton Solent (=49th). In ratings of the broader experience post-1992 universities place first and second (Edge Hill and Sunderland respectively) followed by Russell Group member Sheffield (ranked eighth in the main table).

Law graduates who want to become solicitors in England progress to the legal practice course, while those aiming to be barristers take the bar vocational course. In Scotland, most law courses are based on the distinctive Scottish legal system, which also has different professional qualifications. About half of law graduates do not go into practice and, perhaps surprisingly, law ranks only 43rd out of the 70 subject areas in our employment ranking, with 63.1% of graduates in high-skilled work or postgraduate study 15 months on from degrees. Training contracts for those going into law keep pay in graduate-level jobs relatively austere, and the subject ranks a lowly 61st out of the 70 in our pay index. But the average starting salary of £23,500 earned by legal graduates across all universities bears little resemblance to the packets likely later down the line, and there is a strong case for the delayed career gratification posed by law.

Law

	Teaching quality %	Student experience %	Research quality %	Entry standards (UCAS points)	Graduate prospects %	Overall score
1 Cambridge	86.6	80.4	59.2	201	96.9	100
2 London School of Economics	87.2	85.5	61.3	199	87	98.5
3 University College London	81.8	75.9	74.5	182	93.1	98
=4 Durham	86	81.5	59.5	185	90.5	97.5
=4 Glasgow	76.2	74.6	66.8	232	88.7	97.5
6 Oxford	83.6	70	62	198	91.8	97
7 Strathclyde	87.7	87.5	45.8	205	84.4	96.9
8 Sheffield	87.3	89.4	55	155	91.7	96.7
9 Edinburgh	76.8	71.6	64.2	212	90.5	96.3
10 Bristol	80.2	80.9	67.5	173	88.4	95.7
11 Queen's, Belfast	78.3	83.7	62.3	169	91.8	95.5
12 Aberdeen	84.7	86.5	43.2	196	85.4	95.4
13 Leeds	81.2	85.8	66.5	167	83.3	94.9
14 King's College London	80.9	73.6	56.2	194	86.9	94.7
15 Queen Mary, London	82.5	82.8	57	163	86.9	94.4
16 Dundee	88.2	82.8	29.2	192	85.8	94.2
=17 Southampton	83.3	85	46.5	149	91.3	93.8
=17 Warwick	79.6	76.6	62	163	88.1	93.8
19 Nottingham	84.3	82.8	53.5	161	83.9	93.6
20 Ulster	86.9	82.5	55	132	87.5	93.5
21 Surrey	89.3	84.4	41.5	129	88	92.8
22 Exeter	77.3	77.7	54.8	158	90	92.7
23 Birmingham	77.1	77.2	61.5	152	88.4	92.6
24 Lancaster	86.4	86	48	145	81.9	92.5
25 York	80.7	81.7	49.2	154	85.9	92.2
26 Liverpool	79.4	83.2	51.5	146	85.4	91.7
27 Cardiff	74.4	78.8	60.5	149	87.3	91.6
28 Aston	85.7	87.7	43.5	122	84.7	91.3
=29 Manchester	79.9	76.4	40.8	159	86	90.8
=29 Newcastle	79	81.6	41.8	146	87.6	90.8
=29 Stirling	79.9	76.2	38.5	194	78.2	90.8
32 Kent	81.1	80.4	69.8	120	78.4	90.7
33 East Anglia	86.1	86.9	32.5	116	88.4	90.6
34 Royal Holloway, London	80.8	83.8	38	134	87.2	90.3
35 Northumbria	86.2	85.1	30.8	125	85.1	90
=36 Manchester Metropolitan	88.5	87.8	42.8	115	77.4	89.8
=36 Nottingham Trent	86.5	84.7	53	109	77.5	89.8
=36 Sussex	83.9	84.8	44.8	126	80.2	89.8
39 Leicester	81.7	82.9	32	132	86.1	89.4
40 Edinburgh Napier	86.4	85.8	5.5	168	82.4	89.2
41 Essex	83.1	83.5	56	118	74.6	89
42 Hertfordshire	88.6	87.3	29	117	78.9	88.7
43 South Wales	87.9	84	33.5	115	78.6	88.5
44 Kingston	89.6	87.9	27	102	80	88.2

Rank	University						
45	West of England	84.4	82.5	46.5	109	75.7	87.9
46	Plymouth	82.9	81.3	37.2	114	79.7	87.6
=47	Edge Hill	90	91.5	36	115	67.5	87.5
=47	Robert Gordon	84.9	80.3	-	148	87.2	87.5
=49	Abertay	85.3	84	5	-	87.8	87.4
=49	Gloucestershire	91.2	84.4	8.8	104	84.8	87.4
=51	Aberystwyth	86.8	86.1	34.2	121	71.3	87.2
=51	Glasgow Caledonian	78	75.5	25.8	184	74.2	87.2
=51	Swansea	79.8	82.2	27.8	123	83.2	87.2
54	City St George's	81.7	82.9	34.8	126	76	87
55	Reading	77.8	80.4	33.8	114	84	86.8
56	Southampton Solent	91.5	87.8	-	105	82.9	86.5
=57	Coventry	90	84.4	33.2	102	70	86.2
=57	Portsmouth	84.5	79.4	26.8	111	78.9	86.2
59	Winchester	88.3	85.3	11.5	108	79.3	86.1
=60	Greenwich	82.2	81.6	37	101	77.1	86
=60	Lincoln	81.9	85.2	32.8	104	77.2	86
=60	SOAS, London	66.7	63	58.8	130	84.6	86
63	Oxford Brookes	81.7	83	32.5	99	79	85.8
64	Brighton	86.5	83.9	28.5	102	73.2	85.6
65	Bournemouth	78	74.7	26	104	84.7	84.9
=66	Sunderland	92.8	90.3	-	113	71.1	84.8
=66	Wolverhampton	87.4	85.8	27.8	93	70.7	84.8
=68	Keele	77.1	78.9	29.5	106	80.3	84.7
=68	Worcester	87.2	83.4	12.8	111	74.4	84.7
70	Liverpool John Moores	83.1	84	9	123	76.8	84.6
71	Chester	89.7	86.3	12.8	117	67	84.3
72	Bangor	81.1	79.7	-	121	84	84.2
=73	Hull	84.8	82.8	11.2	106	76.6	84.1
=73	London South Bank	89	86	-	94	79	84.1
75	Salford	80.9	75	24.8	116	74.9	83.9
76	Leeds Beckett	85.8	87.5	11.8	108	71.2	83.8
77	Westminster	84.8	85.3	29	103	65.8	83.6
=78	Huddersfield	85	81.8	15.2	110	71	83.4
=78	York St John	88.4	78.1	-	105	77.6	83.4
80	De Montfort	85.8	84.4	13.5	84	75.9	83.3
81	Cumbria	92.6	86.9	-	97	68	82.8
82	Derby	86.2	80.2	-	102	75.7	82.4
83	Central Lancashire	85.1	81.8	13.2	111	66.5	82.3
84	West London	85.3	85.3	-	100	71.5	81.7
85	Liverpool Hope	79.3	71	-	102	84.1	81.6
86	West of Scotland	89.8	80.5	-	118	62.9	81.4
=87	Brunel	70.5	69.3	34.5	111	73.5	81.2
=87	Wales Trinity St David	89	80.8	-	92	69.8	81.2
89	Bradford	80.7	81.8	-	110	71.9	80.9
90	Middlesex	-	-	26	93	69.4	80.8
91	Buckingham	76.5	64.5	-	111	83.7	80.7
92	London Metropolitan	85.7	84.7	-	88	67.5	80.1

Law cont.

		Teaching quality %	Student experience %	Research quality %	Entry standards (UCAS points)	Graduate prospects %	Overall score
93	Birmingham City	78	79.2	9	110	67.1	79.8
94	Canterbury Christ Church	79.3	78.3	16.8	98	63	79.2
95	Northampton	79.4	81.2	-	81	73.5	79.1
96	East London	83.5	79.5	17.8	102	55.3	78.9
97	Anglia Ruskin	81.3	74.3	9.8	83	67	78.5
98	Bedfordshire	83.5	79.9	-	84	63.8	77.9
99	Staffordshire	73.3	67	18.2	108	65	77.7
100	St Mary's, Twickenham	72.1	64.5	-	89	80.5	77.5
101	Sheffield Hallam	73.2	62.1	-	113	73.8	77.4
102	Teesside	-	-	18.2	103	58.2	76.9
103	Roehampton	66.1	67	40.2	87	63.2	76.6
104	Greater Manchester	70.9	66.5	-	110	64.7	75

Employed in high-skilled job	45%	Employed in lower-skilled job	20%
Employed in high-skilled job and studying	6%	Employed in lower-skilled job and studying	2%
Studying	10%	Unemployed	5%
High-skilled work (median) salary	£24,500	Low-/medium-skilled salary	£20,000

Liberal Arts

Interdisciplinary by design, liberal arts degrees encompass the arts, humanities and social sciences, although there is no set formula. They provide undergraduates with opportunities to hone their analysis, communication skills and critical thinking. As students progress through the courses they begin to specialise in areas of particular interest. Dr George Legg, senior lecturer in liberal arts at King's College London says: "Studying liberal arts is vital for understanding key questions facing our world. Concerns around climate, technology, conflict and identity require multiple disciplinary perspectives if they are to be solved. To understand the Middle East, for example, requires knowledge of history, politics, geography, religion and languages, to name but a few of the subjects studied on a liberal arts degree. Rather than focusing on a single subject, students specialise – or major – in a certain discipline while also taking courses in other subject areas. This flexible thinking means liberal arts students are well equipped for the complex world that awaits them after graduation."

Now in its fifth edition, our Liberal Arts table features an extra two universities since last year, including Manchester in third place. But it is topped by Warwick, its inaugural No 1 boosted by peerless rates of student satisfaction with both teaching quality and the wider experience. University College London (UCL) is in second place after three years at the top, and still claims the leading research quality rating in the subject, the highest entry standards (185 UCAS points) and the best graduate outcomes, with 92.5% of liberal arts graduates in high-skilled jobs and/or postgraduate study within 15 months. Career paths include roles in the media, communications, PR, politics and art galleries. Job prospects for the subject as a whole rank 37th this year with 64.3% of graduates employed in high-skilled jobs and/or furthering their studies 15 months on. Salaries compare more favourably with other subject areas, with early career earnings of £27,000 per year placing the subject =21st out of 70 areas.

Liberal Arts

	Teaching quality %	Student experience %	Research quality %	Entry standards (UCAS points)	Graduate prospects %	Overall score
1 Warwick	95.6	94.5	61.3	172	-	100
2 University College London	77.9	79.8	67.8	185	92.5	98.6
3 Manchester	86.5	82.2	67	173	-	98.2
4 King's College London	79.7	73.3	62.7	179	90.3	96.1
=5 Birmingham	81	67.3	56.8	166	86.5	92.5
=5 Exeter	83.8	81.2	58.3	168	80.3	92.5
=7 Bristol	85.3	85.2	58.7	169	77.8	92.4
=7 Nottingham	84.3	79.4	58.2	152	83.8	92.4
9 Royal Holloway	94.9	85.9	53.5	127	-	92.1
10 Leeds	86.8	86.3	47	163	-	91.7
11 East Anglia	75.9	62.2	67.5	124	-	88.9
12 Sussex	78.9	75.2	61	123	-	88.8
13 Essex	89.4	85.1	40.2	118	-	85.7

Employed in high-skilled job	49%	Employed in lower-skilled job	22%
Employed in high-skilled job and studying	5%	Employed in lower-skilled job and studying	0%
Studying	10%	Unemployed	4%
High skilled work (median) salary	£27,500	Low-/medium-skilled salary	N/A

Linguistics

The scientific study of language, linguistics analyses how language is put together and how it functions, involving its form and meaning as well as how it works in context. "Linguistics is a frontier science that embodies psychology, sociology, neuroscience, computer science and many others. Studying linguistics will give you the skills to pursue many types of careers," says Dr Emma Nguyen, lecturer in child language acquisition, School of English Literature, Language and Linguistics, Newcastle University.

Within this category are some degrees in English language, and large numbers that pair linguistics with other subjects. The leading universities require English or English literature at A-level, while drama and theatre studies is also considered useful. There were 60 universities and colleges offering 631 courses in the subject for 2026–27. In 2024 there were, 3,195 applications to linguistics degrees and 565 students were accepted onto courses.

Retaining the lead in our new Linguistics table, Cambridge attracts the highest entry standards among its linguistics students and only Southampton does better on graduate prospects, with 92.1% employed in high-skilled jobs or postgraduate study 15 months on from their degrees. Ranked third overall University College London (UCL) has swapped places with Lancaster, which is this year's runner-up. Eighth-place York leads the field in research, based on results of the Research Excellence Framework 2021, while Oxford, formerly a regular incumbent at the top of the table now ranks 10th for the second year running. In fourth place, Queen Mary, London is up eight places – its overall rank improved by rates of student satisfaction that place it in the top four universities in our latest National Student Survey analysis. Leading the field on these metrics are Brighton – which is top for teaching quality, followed by Swansea. Westminster does best for the student experience, followed by UCL. In 15th place, Manchester Metropolitan remains the highest-ranked modern university, one of only four universities with post-1992 foundations in a subject ranking dominated by older universities.

The degree can lead to careers in speech therapy or in the field of teaching English as a foreign language. The subject ranks 57th in our employment index, based on 56% of graduates being in high-skilled jobs and/or further study within 15 months, and =56th in our pay scale.

Linguistics	Teaching quality %	Student experience %	Research quality %	Entry standards (UCAS points)	Graduate prospects %	Overall score
1 Cambridge	86.5	62.5	61	220	91.3	100
2 Lancaster	87.5	82.1	68.5	146	82.2	95.4
3 University College London	89.4	90.3	56	164	-	95.3
4 Queen Mary, London	94.7	89.1	51.1	-	83.3	94.7
5 Sheffield	88.6	87.3	62.3	146	-	94.6
6 Swansea	95.5	89.3	60	125	-	93.9
7 Southampton	91.7	78.5	47.8	140	92.1	93.4
8 York	83.6	82.7	74.8	139	72.4	93.1
9 Newcastle	88.7	79.6	61.8	140	-	93
10 Oxford	85.7	70	44	200	-	92.3
11 Westminster	95.1	93.1	55.5	105	-	90.8
12 Warwick	87.8	86	46.2	151	-	90.1
=13 Essex	90.4	81.4	65	138	62.7	89.9
=13 Reading	87.4	87.2	54.5	127	-	89.9
15 Manchester Metropolitan	90.8	67.3	61.8	108	78.8	89.6
16 Edinburgh	77.2	71.3	45.8	184	76.7	89
17 King's College London	86	80.2	51.2	136	-	88.8
18 Leeds	81.8	77.5	52	154	71.7	88.3
=19 Kent	86.2	79.6	57.5	108	-	87.6
=19 Manchester	82.3	76	59.5	148	64	87.6
21 Cardiff	80.9	80.8	55.5	123	-	87.2
22 Brighton	96.3	78.7	44.2	107	-	86.4
23 Bangor	91	85.3	42	110	-	85.3
24 Ulster	86.7	80.3	37	125	64.7	82.3
25 York St John	85	78.6	30.5	109	76.9	82
26 West of England	60	50.3	32.2	111	-	69.6

Employed in high-skilled job	38%	Employed in lower-skilled job	28%
Employed in high-skilled job and studying	3%	Employed in lower-skilled job and studying	1%
Studying	14%	Unemployed	6%
High-skilled work (median) salary	£25,000	Low-/medium-skilled salary	£20,000

Materials Technology

Cambridge's lead at the top of our Materials Technology table is ensured again this year, boosted by far the highest entry standards at 224 UCAS points on average – even in a subject where high grades are the norm among the leading universities. Cambridge is also one of five universities in the table where over 90% of graduates were employed in high-skilled jobs and/or postgraduate study 15 months on from their degrees. It is outdone on this measure by Imperial – where 100% of graduates had achieved the desired career outcomes, and Oxford (96.4%), and just ahead of Loughborough (93.1 %) and Sheffield (91.1%). The subject compares very well in the national salaries table, securing =5th place this year. It is 16th in our employment index, with nearly eight in ten graduates (78.2%) in professional level jobs and/or furthering their studies 15 months on.

"Materials are fundamental to anything that takes a physical form; understanding how to harness their full potential and manipulate them to enhance performance is one of the cornerstones to pushing the boundaries of technology and addressing issues such as climate change, sustainable energy solutions and the future of transportation. With graduate skills in materials technology you could be working on complex projects in space technologies, the future of aerospace advancements or medical applications," says Dr Leigh Fleming, head of the Department of Engineering, University of Huddersfield.

In second place overall, Imperial is in front for research quality in materials technology, based on results of the Research Excellence Framework 2021. For rates of student satisfaction Kingston, in fifth place overall, outdoes all others for teaching quality and the wider experience – metrics derived from the National Student Survey. Conversely, Queen Mary, London and Leeds come bottom for each respectively.

QS ranks Cambridge 4th in the world for materials science, with Oxford four places below it and Imperial =11th.

Materials Technology	Teaching quality %	Student experience %	Research quality %	Entry standards (UCAS points)	Graduate prospects %	Overall score
1 Cambridge	85.5	82.1	77.2	224	94.3	100
2 Imperial College	83.1	84.6	81	173	100	98.9
3 Oxford	85.9	79.6	77.5	186	96.4	98.4
4 Sheffield	90.4	85.9	66.8	156	91.1	96.1
5 Kingston	97.6	88.5	17.2	160	-	95
6 Leeds	88.8	69.1	64.8	146	-	93.4
7 Loughborough	81.9	77.5	46.5	143	93.3	91.6
8 Birmingham	80.1	79.6	63.7	148	87.3	91.4
9 Manchester	84.1	82.7	63	142	82.1	90.7
10 Queen Mary, London	78.1	75.6	66	127	-	89.9
11 Huddersfield	83.3	75.1	32.5	151	-	89.6
12 Swansea	81.8	80.4	48.8	104	84.6	87.5
13 Derby	82.9	80.9	14	127	-	86.7
14 Sheffield Hallam	78.5	73.3	30	103	-	84.2

Employed in high-skilled job	53%	Employed in lower-skilled job	10%
Employed in high-skilled job and studying	3%	Employed in lower-skilled job and studying	1%
Studying	21%	Unemployed	5%
High-skilled work (median) salary	£30,000	Low-/medium-skilled salary	N/A

Mathematics

More school pupils sit A-level maths than any other subject and the demand for places to study the subject at university increased in 2024, when more than 40,000 applied (up 8% year on year) and 7,330 new students were accepted onto undergraduate maths degrees (up 6%). The leading universities will usually look for extra maths as well as maths at A-level, or equivalent. Courses tend to combine pure and applied maths, but some universities allow for specialising in one or the other. The subject adds up to a promising career for most, ranking comfortably inside the top 25 of our employment table, with three-quarters (74.7%) of mathematics graduates in high-skilled employment or postgraduate study 15 months after finishing their degrees. Such expertise commands average graduate salaries of £29,000 – the 16th highest earnings in our pay index of 70 subject areas.

"Studying mathematics gives you a window into a fascinating world of ideas, ranging from exotic and beautiful pure maths through to some of the theory and concrete methods needed to tackle the biggest challenges facing humanity, including climate change and pandemics. Pursuing maths at university level will give you problem-solving and communication skills, critical and creative thinking, and analytical and data wrangling skills – and employers love a mathematician," say Professor Julia Gog, Claire Metcalfe and Rachel Thomas, Millennium Mathematics Project, University of Cambridge.

In a shake-up to the upper tier of our Mathematics table Oxford takes the lead, ousting Imperial into second place. Cambridge, which led the table two years ago, is down one place to rank third this time. In its latest global rankings by subject, QS puts Oxford third in the world for mathematics, Cambridge fourth and Imperial tenth. In a high-tariff table St Andrews has the top entry standards, its entrants averaging an extraordinary 230 UCAS points. Nine universities average 200 UCAS points or more and nearly half (29 out of of 61) universities tabled average 144 or higher (equal to three As at A-level). The high tariffs are due to the two maths A-levels – plus two or three others – taken by the most successful candidates at the top universities. But there are still plenty of places to be found with a broader spread of entry scores: 14 universities averaged 120 points or lower.

Oxford is in front for research, based on results of the Research Excellence Framework 2021 and also comes out top for graduate prospects – with 93.6% of its graduates employed in high-skilled jobs and/or postgraduate study 15 months after their degrees. In second place for graduate prospects is the London School of Economics and Political Science, with 92.2% of graduates achieving the desired outcomes within 15 months. Our analysis of the latest National Student Survey shows Aberystwyth (42nd in the main table) to have the maths students most satisfied with their teaching quality, followed by Manchester Met – which in =24th place is the top-ranked modern university. For the broad experience Aston (in =31st of the main table) comes top and Reading (=36th) follows it. Sheffield ranks in the top ten for both metrics, boosting it 11 places into this year's Mathematics top ten. At the opposite end of the scale Edinburgh (17th overall) takes the bottom place for teaching quality and Stirling (49th overall) finishes last for the broad student experience.

Mathematics	Teaching quality %	Student experience %	Research quality %	Entry standards (UCAS points)	Graduate prospects %	Overall score
1 Oxford	86.6	78.5	83.2	212	93.6	100
2 Imperial College	86.4	86.9	76.8	211	89.8	99.1

3	Cambridge	87.3	82.5	78	225	87.2	99
4	St Andrews	90.5	88.3	57.5	230	88.5	98.7
5	Heriot-Watt	88.5	88.4	66	190	90	97.6
6	Warwick	86	84.9	73.5	200	87.9	97.4
7	Bristol	82.6	80.5	77	188	91	96.6
8	Sheffield	90.6	90.3	59.2	154	85.9	94.8
9	Bath	81.3	83.2	61.5	189	90.2	94.7
10	Lancaster	88.3	83.3	70	160	83.7	94.5
11	Durham	85.3	79	48.8	204	88.9	94.3
=12	Birmingham	88.7	83.6	58.8	161	87	94.2
=12	London School of Economics	79.9	80.7	64	175	92.2	94.2
=14	Glasgow	76.3	73.5	74.5	216	84.6	93.9
=14	Manchester	83.8	84.2	66	172	85	93.9
16	University College London	83.4	84.7	57.5	176	87.4	93.6
17	Edinburgh	75.1	72.6	66	218	86.3	93
=18	Queen's, Belfast	87.9	80.3	44.5	169	88.2	92.8
=18	Strathclyde	86.4	85.1	43.2	210	80.5	92.8
20	Exeter	83.9	81.5	64.1	161	82.7	92.3
21	Nottingham	81.4	81.7	57.5	164	87.5	92.2
=22	Dundee	86.6	84.5	55.2	186	73.3	91.2
=22	Southampton	82.4	81	61.5	164	80.6	91.2
=24	Leeds	80.5	81.9	55.2	160	85.4	91.1
=24	Loughborough	84	85.3	46.5	162	83.8	91.1
=24	Manchester Metropolitan	93.7	92.3	45.5	124	79.2	91.1
=24	Swansea	87.9	87.2	58.2	117	82.7	91.1
=28	Aberdeen	87.2	84.8	40	170	-	91
=28	York	84	81.4	55	161	81.4	91
30	King's College London	83.6	83.8	59.5	169	75.8	90.7
=31	Aston	90.9	93.7	35.2	120	84.9	90.6
=31	Cardiff	82.5	85.5	45.5	141	88.2	90.6
=33	Leicester	82.7	78.9	51.7	119	91.8	90.5
=33	Newcastle	83.7	85.2	48	138	85.9	90.5
35	Sussex	89.4	91.9	50	131	76.5	90.2
=36	Nottingham Trent	87.4	88	59	108	80.4	90.1
=36	Reading	88.9	92.9	51.5	130	75.7	90.1
=38	Essex	90.7	92.6	29	141	80.1	89.6
=38	Hertfordshire	89.8	89	45.5	123	78.6	89.6
=40	East Anglia	86.6	87.6	44.5	136	78.8	89.2
=40	Surrey	85.1	85	33.5	141	85.5	89.2
42	Aberystwyth	95.8	90.7	22.5	118	79.2	88.7
43	Kent	83.5	80.7	46.5	136	80.9	88.5
=44	Plymouth	89.9	92.3	22.5	121	82.8	88.3
=44	Queen Mary, London	82.8	82.5	51.5	142	76.6	88.3
46	Liverpool John Moores	92.8	92.6	26	119	77.4	88.1
47	Coventry	-	-	36.8	130	83.6	88
48	City St George's	82.1	80.8	52	115	79.3	87.3
49	Stirling	75.7	64.9	41.8	174	84.2	87.1
50	Keele	89.5	79.6	27.3	131	74.7	86

Mathematics cont.

	Teaching quality %	Student experience %	Research quality %	Entry standards (UCAS points)	Graduate prospects %	Overall score
51 Liverpool	81.1	83.2	43.2	140	72.3	85.9
52 Royal Holloway	78	70.1	30.2	140	85.3	85.5
53 Portsmouth	91.9	86.3	37.2	112	66.1	85.4
54 Sheffield Hallam	93.1	83.1	-	110	81.5	84.9
=55 Brighton	93.3	82.1	32.5	-	63.8	84.8
=55 Brunel	82.4	84.2	32.2	105	78.2	84.8
57 Lincoln	89.4	81.6	17.5	117	75.2	84.6
58 Northumbria	85.4	85.1	49	121	61.5	84.3
59 West of England	89.7	76	32.2	117	65.4	83.4
60 Greenwich	86	88.6	28	93	69.4	83
61 Hull	89.2	71.5	-	110	79.2	82.2

Employed in high-skilled job	56%	Employed in lower-skilled job	11%
Employed in high-skilled job and studying	7%	Employed in lower-skilled job and studying	1%
Studying	11%	Unemployed	7%
High-skilled work (median) salary	£30,000	Low-/medium-skilled salary	£20,000

Mechanical Engineering

There is consistency in the top tier of our Mechanical Engineering table, with Imperial, Cambridge, Oxford and Sheffield leading a top four that is identical this year to last. At No 1 overall Imperial has the edge for research quality, based on results of the national Research Excellence Framework 2021 assessment, and it ties with Cambridge in claiming the highest entry standards – with mechanical engineering entrants averaging 222 UCAS points – in one of the highest-tariff subjects around: 25 universities in the table tallied over 144 UCAS points (equal to three As at A-level). Even so, there are places to be found with more modest qualifications, and at eight universities students arrived with under 100 UCAS points (Greenwich, in 54th place overall; Brighton, 50th; Wolverhampton, 69th; Bournemouth, 58th; De Montfort, 60th; Greater Manchester, 59th; Anglia Ruskin, 71st; and Northampton, 64th).

Mechanical engineering is the most popular strand of engineering by a clear margin, as reflected in the size of our table – which reaches to 71 universities. In 2024 the subject attracted over 38,700 applications and over 5,700 new undergraduates. UCAS showed 139 universities and colleges offering courses in mechanical engineering for 2026-27. Most of the leading universities require maths – preferably with a strong component of mechanics – and another science (usually physics) at A-level, or equivalent.

A top-15 rank in our employment table adds to the subject's appeal and graduates command starting salaries of £30,000 on average, which put mechanical engineering =5th in this year's pay index. "It is one of the most general of the engineering disciplines and you can take your career in a huge and diverse range of directions, including in the automotive industry, biomedicine, energy, acoustics, aerospace and robotics. You can quite literally engineer your future," says Dr Adrian Nightingale, lecturer in microfluidics and sensor design (mechanical engineering), University of Southampton.

Mechanical Engineering

	Teaching quality %	Student experience %	Research quality %	Entry standards (UCAS points)	Graduate prospects %	Overall score
1 Imperial College	88	89.2	81	222	96	100
2 Cambridge	80.4	80.8	77.2	222	97.2	97.3
3 Oxford	80.4	74.8	77.5	213	94	95.4
4 Sheffield	89.8	88.3	66.8	170	89.2	93.7
5 Bath	88.3	83	49.5	191	93	93
6 Bristol	80.7	78.9	68	176	93.3	92.3
7 Heriot-Watt	83.1	81.6	55.5	182	90.3	91.2
8 Southampton	83.4	81.1	70	168	85.8	91
9 Strathclyde	75.4	77.2	52.8	212	90.9	90.8
10 Leeds	80.7	82.4	64.8	174	87.5	90.7
11 Birmingham	79.1	81.8	63.7	149	94.4	90.3
12 Nottingham	82.1	82.1	59	148	93.6	90.2
13 University College London	79.9	77.2	70	179	83.2	89.9
14 Liverpool	89.9	83.7	57	143	86.4	89.7
15 Loughborough	82.5	82.8	46.5	157	94.4	89.6
16 Edinburgh	75.2	73.6	55.5	202	87.4	89.2
17 Surrey	88.2	84.3	55.2	130	88.7	89
18 Queen's, Belfast	80.7	80.9	51	158	89.7	88.4
19 Manchester	76	76.8	63	176	83.5	88.1
=20 Dundee	84	79.8	50.2	172	81.8	88
=20 Glasgow	65.6	61.5	61.5	211	90.9	88
22 Aberdeen	75.8	77.6	35.8	178	92	87.1
23 Lancaster	82.5	81.2	44.8	142	87.4	86.6
24 Queen Mary, London	75.8	79.2	66	146	82.3	86.5
25 Swansea	84.1	82.7	48.8	119	86.7	85.9
26 Bradford	96.1	84.1	27	120	-	85.8
27 Cardiff	73.2	74.5	54	141	90.6	85.7
=28 Nottingham Trent	84.1	78.3	59	104	85.3	85.5
=28 Robert Gordon	79.8	73	20.5	184	90	85.5
30 Leicester	85	80.6	39.8	120	88.4	85.3
31 Edinburgh Napier	82.5	85.2	22.8	147	88.2	84.9
32 Newcastle	69.7	71.5	58.5	132	89.3	84.3
=33 Exeter	74.2	76.3	47	147	84.8	84.2
=33 Sussex	78.5	81.4	29.5	134	90.8	84.2
=35 Northumbria	85.9	84.9	43	122	77.4	83.8
=35 Plymouth	86	79.8	32.5	118	85.6	83.8
37 Liverpool John Moores	80	83.4	45.5	114	82.4	83.4
38 Ulster	77	71.3	49.8	122	85.8	83.3
39 Hull	86.7	79.6	36.2	110	79.6	82.4
40 Kent	80.6	77.9	41.5	111	-	82
41 Manchester Metropolitan	86.1	80.1	45.5	120	69.7	81.7
=42 Coventry	87.4	84	23.5	104	80.4	81.4
=42 Teesside	94.1	90.3	18.8	116	70.8	81.4
44 Aston	78.2	71.7	35.2	120	81.7	80.8

Mechanical Engineering cont.

	Teaching quality %	Student experience %	Research quality %	Entry standards (UCAS points)	Graduate prospects %	Overall score
45 Glasgow Caledonian	78.8	77.3	12.8	154	80.3	80.6
=46 Derby	81.6	74.5	14	120	84.9	80.1
=46 West of Scotland	87.1	84.5	16.5	-	73.9	80.1
48 London South Bank	87.9	86.4	27.3	109	70.4	80
49 Lincoln	84.4	72.8	24	114	79	79.9
50 Brighton	70.6	67.9	36.5	98	90.2	79.6
51 Portsmouth	83.7	79	21	108	75.4	78.8
52 West of England	74.2	71.2	30.8	122	78.6	78.7
53 Birmingham City	86.6	85	17.5	121	67.5	78.5
54 Greenwich	80.4	71.5	31.5	98	-	78.3
55 Kingston	85.7	78	17.2	108	73.1	78.1
56 Oxford Brookes	77.5	70.6	18	113	81.5	77.9
57 Lancashire	78.8	73.6	23	124	71.4	77.4
58 Bournemouth	83.8	83.6	14	91	73.5	76.9
59 Greater Manchester	79.2	80.6	22	82	-	76.4
60 De Montfort	79.2	77	21.8	90	74.5	76.3
=61 Brunel	73.6	69.3	33	117	69.2	76
=61 Salford	70.4	67.5	33.2	120	72	76
63 Sheffield Hallam	72.7	68.1	30	109	71.1	75.3
64 Northampton	84.1	73.9	8.5	79	-	74.6
65 Chichester	74.5	65.9	12.5	117	-	74.4
66 City St George's	66.1	67.5	32.5	116	69	74
67 East London	85	89.2	21.2	109	48.1	73.6
68 Hertfordshire	68	65.2	33	105	68.6	73.4
69 Wolverhampton	73	66	18.2	97	-	73.2
70 Huddersfield	59.3	53.5	32.5	109	73.3	71.7
71 Anglia Ruskin	68.7	57.4	10	80	-	68

Employed in high-skilled job	68%	Employed in lower-skilled job	10%
Employed in high-skilled job and studying	4%	Employed in lower-skilled job and studying	0%
Studying	5%	Unemployed	6%
High-skilled work (median) salary	£30,000	Low-/medium-skilled salary	£24,000

Medicine

At just over 50,000, applications to study medicine fell for the second year running and were around 7% lower in 2024 than the year before, UCAS figures show, as numbers return to pre-pandemic levels. Commentators have also suggested the shift may be due to pay levels, highlighted by a series of strikes, and the gruelling depiction of doctors' working lives in memoirs and TV dramas. But despite the recent downturn, applications in 2024 were still around 12% higher than five years before in 2019. Reapplicants account for significant numbers, as would-be trainee doctors take a year out to improve their applications by doing more work experience, building on their personal statement and resitting the UCAT specialist aptitude test (see chapter 2). Such volume of demand is despite only four medical schools being allowed per application, with the fifth space left for a back-up subject – which most use for a related course requiring lower grades such as biomedical science.

The number of places available to study medicine remains capped by the government. A clutch of medical schools has opened since 2019 to increase capacity, including at Sunderland, Lincoln, Edge Hill, Kent/Canterbury Christ Church and Anglia Ruskin universities and 350 new spaces were added in 2025, taking the total number of medical school places to 8,326. Some schools are too new to have sufficient data to be included in our Medicine table yet. A pledge made by the previous Conservative government in 2023 to increase places to 15,000 a year by 2031–32 is still intact.

Nearly all schools demand chemistry and most biology. Physics or maths is required by some, either as an alternative or in addition to biology. Universities want to see a commitment to the subject through work experience in hospitals, GP surgeries, a hospice or similar medical setting. But noble aspirations will not help without a good UCAT score: each year about 37,000 candidates sit the computer-based test encompassing verbal reasoning, quantitative reasoning, and decision-making. Medical schools interview most candidates before making an offer. Undergraduates must be prepared to work long hours, particularly towards the end of the course, which will usually be five years long. Many students are now opting for the postgraduate route into the profession instead, though this is even longer.

Oxford's long reign at the top of our table remains unchallenged, and the university's strength in medicine was recognised with the Sunday Times Medical School of the Year 2026 award. Dundee is runner-up for the second consecutive year and Imperial is up one place to rank third in a top ten with little variation year-on-year. Boosted by the distinction of offering guaranteed work at the end of the course, the subject carries unique prestige. Medicine occupies second place in our graduate employment table, a step down from its usual first place – outdone by a hair's breadth by veterinary medicine on this occasion. Starting salaries of £35,000 on average are second only to those offered by dentistry degrees. Twelve medical schools report 100% graduate employment, and St Andrews, with the second-to-lowest rate, still reports 95% of medicine graduates in high-skilled jobs or further study after 15 months. Only Lancaster registered a lower proportion in high-skilled jobs or study, at 78.7%. The consistency of graduate prospects means we do not use the measure to help calculate our rankings to avoid small differences distorting positions (although the percentages are shown for guidance).

In such a compressed ranking, with just two medical schools scoring less than 80 points overall, success in our table's other four metrics is spread around. Our latest National Student Survey analysis shows Leicester – which places fourth overall – to have the highest rates of student satisfaction with teaching quality, followed by Keele (=14th overall). Imperial is third for teaching quality and top for students' evaluation of the wider experience, where Leicester ranks second again, and St Andrews (sixth in the table) sits third. At the opposite end of the scale, medical students at Edinburgh (18th overall) reported the lowest rates of satisfaction with teaching quality and the broad experience.

Occupying seventh place in the main table, Cambridge was the top scorer in the Research Excellence Framework 2021, followed by Bristol (ninth overall), University College London (=11th) and Leicester. The Scottish universities dominate our Medicine table's entry standards measure, led by Glasgow with 242 points in the UCAS tariff. Seven of the schools in the table average over 200 UCAS points.

Medicine

	Teaching quality %	Student experience %	Research quality %	Entry standards (UCAS points)	Graduate prospects %	Overall score
1 Oxford	90	85.3	67.5	204	99.4	100
2 Dundee	86.9	77.1	57	239	100	99.7
3 Imperial College	90.7	90.5	68.5	184	99.2	98.9
4 Leicester	91.7	88.4	70.2	172	99.6	98.1
5 Glasgow	77.5	63	68.5	242	99.6	97.9
6 St Andrews	88.9	87.5	45.5	222	95.7	97.5
7 Cambridge	77.7	64.5	76.2	220	99.5	97.3
8 Queen's, Belfast	85.4	79.6	66.2	193	100	96.5
9 Bristol	82.9	73.3	71.8	186	99.6	95.5
10 Hull-York Medical School	90.5	80.1	61.2	162	99.3	94.1
=11 Cardiff	85.2	79.4	55.5	189	100	94
=11 University College London	79.5	72.5	70.8	184	99.7	94
13 Aberdeen	84.9	78.2	30.5	238	98.8	93.9
=14 Keele	90.9	86.5	49	168	99.3	93
=14 Lancaster	87.5	81.4	55	172	100	93
=14 Swansea	80.1	66.3	66.8	-	98.9	93
17 Exeter	85.6	76.7	53.2	182	100	92.6
18 Edinburgh	66.2	55.1	64	225	100	90.9
19 Queen Mary, London	77.6	72.8	58	184	98.4	90.8
20 Manchester	81.2	69.2	61.3	170	99.4	90.7
21 East Anglia	82.2	74.8	50	179	99.4	90.4
22 Birmingham	79.2	75.1	59.8	168	99.4	90.3
23 King's College London	75.6	69.4	65.5	170	99.4	89.9
24 Sheffield	81.5	72.4	51	175	100	89.7
25 Liverpool	81.5	79.7	46.8	170	99.2	89.1
26 City St George's	80	64.6	48.8	178	99.3	88.4
27 Aston	83.8	73.6	46	162	-	88.2
28 Sunderland	89.8	85.8	30.2	160	-	88
29 Newcastle	78.1	69.6	50.7	172	99.2	87.9
30 Nottingham	77.4	57.7	54	177	99.6	87.7
31 Southampton	80.1	69.7	49.5	161	99.6	87.2
32 Sussex	85.7	78.4	32	164	100	86.8
=33 Leeds	77.1	65.3	39.5	173	99.1	85.1
=33 Plymouth	75.8	67.6	38.2	177	100	85.1
35 Warwick	82.2	73.4	23.2	-	99.5	82.3
36 Anglia Ruskin	77.3	63	33.8	155	-	81.9
37 Brighton	85.7	78.4	-	168	100	80.8
38 Buckingham	74.8	58	-	159	100	74.4
39 Lancashire	79.9	68.5	-	128	78.8	73.8

Employed in high-skilled job	81%	Employed in lower-skilled job	0%
Employed in high-skilled job and studying	8%	Employed in lower-skilled job and studying	0%
Studying	5%	Unemployed	0%
High-skilled work (median) salary	£35,000	Low-/medium-skilled salary	N/A

Music

Reflecting music's many contrasting genres, courses in our subject ranking vary considerably in style and content – from the practical and vocational programmes in conservatoires to the more theoretical degrees in older universities, via sonic arts, creative sound design and everything in between elsewhere. Applications rose for three years to 2022 but have cooled a little since and in 2024's admissions cycle music courses attracted just under 42,700 applications and just over 9,000 students were accepted onto courses.

"There's a reason we use words like 'play' for what musicians do. Music is about inventing and experimenting, creating order from aural chaos to express ourselves and connect with others. Studying music as a performer or creator means learning to be playful in your work every day. It means collaborating, problem-solving, listening – and really hearing. It means fast reactions and dedicated repetition. These are all skills associated with play, but also with the best of leaders," says Armin Zanner, vice-principal and director of music, Guildhall School of Music & Drama.

Cambridge's strength in undergraduate music provision is the most eminent for the second consecutive year, its rank buoyed by strong performance across all five metrics in our table without topping any of them individually. Manchester topped the table two years ago and ranks sixth this year. Durham, formerly a regular in the No 1 spot, is runner-up for the second year in a row. Royal Holloway, in seventh place overall, achieved the best results in music in the Research Excellence Framework 2021, while Westminster (44th in our main table) is not far behind it for research quality, followed by King's College London, which takes =12th place overall.

The Royal College of Music had the best-employed graduates when surveyed 15 months after their degrees, with 93.9% in high-skilled jobs and/or further study. It is one of eight specialist institutions in our table, which are led by Guildhall School of Music and Drama in 24th place, followed by the Royal Conservatoire of Scotland in 27th place, Royal Academy of Music (30th), Royal College of Music (35th), Rose Bruford College (39th), Royal Northern College of Music (=41st), Trinity Laban (47th), and Leeds Conservatoire (71st).

Entry standards tip over the 200 UCAS tariff point mark at three universities – Cambridge, Edinburgh and Glasgow – though there are also plenty of places to be found with a broad spectrum of entry standards, and admission to music courses rests largely on the strength of auditions. The Royal College of Music, for instance, is a highly competitive institution yet its entrants averaged only 91 UCAS points, the latest data shows.

In our analysis of the latest National Student Survey the best rates of student satisfaction with teaching quality were found at Kingston (=28th overall), followed by tenth-place Surrey. Sheffield, which ranks fifth in the main table, comes third for teaching quality and gets the best rates of student satisfaction with the wider experience, where it is followed by Surrey and Kingston. At the opposite end of the student satisfaction scale are the University for the Creative Arts (75th overall), Oxford (14th) and Plymouth (67th) at the foot of the ranking for the broad experience, while Plymouth (67th), Leeds Arts (79th) and Anglia Ruskin (60th) got the poorest feedback on teaching quality.

Music invariably ranks above the other performing arts in our employment table, as it does this year in 49th place. In the earnings table, music ties with art and design (and another four subjects) in =62nd place out of 70 subject areas.

Music

	Teaching quality %	Student experience %	Research quality %	Entry standards (UCAS points)	Graduate prospects %	Overall score
1 Cambridge	87.3	71	71	222	87.8	100
2 Durham	94.3	82.6	59.5	196	88.1	99.7
3 Bristol	93.1	83.9	64.2	180	86.6	98.6
4 Glasgow	88.7	78.6	60.5	214	78.4	97.2
5 Sheffield	94.4	90.3	57	166	-	97.1
6 Manchester	83	79.7	66.5	189	88.7	96.8
7 Royal Holloway	82.5	80.4	78.5	152	90.6	95.8
8 City St George's	91.8	80.4	66.5	146	-	94.4
9 Edinburgh	84.8	81	59.2	217	67.2	94.1
10 Surrey	94.6	89.4	43.8	159	79.3	94
11 Cardiff	91	84.7	50.5	148	84	93.5
=12 King's College London	80.4	78.6	72.2	166	-	92.9
=12 Nottingham	84.4	80.7	62.7	158	81.2	92.9
14 Oxford	80.4	57.9	49.2	193	88.7	92.3
15 Leeds	81.3	71.6	65.2	172	78.6	92
16 Birmingham	86.9	74.9	50.2	162	81.2	91.9
=17 Queen's, Belfast	89.9	85.8	46.8	162	71	91.2
=17 Southampton	86.8	79.9	58.8	156	73.3	91.2
19 Liverpool	88.9	86.8	43.8	155	76	91.1
20 Manchester Metropolitan	92.7	86.3	51.7	121	-	90.6
21 Bangor	86.2	88.2	42	146	80	90.5
=22 Huddersfield	84.8	79	71.5	122	77.6	90.4
=22 York	87.1	82.9	54.8	146	73.7	90.4
24 Guildhall School of Music and Drama	86	68.6	61.3	128	82	90.1
25 Birmingham City	91.8	76.4	46.5	138	75.8	90
26 Edinburgh Napier	92.5	88.7	8.5	196	68.6	89.6
27 Royal Conservatoire of Scotland	81.1	68.3	35.2	177	82.5	89.3
=28 Kingston	95.9	89.1	45	99	-	88.9
=28 Sunderland	93.7	77.9	49.8	113	-	88.9
30 Royal Academy of Music	81.7	74	20	156	92	88.7
31 Coventry	84.5	73.6	55.5	126	79.2	88.6
32 Aberdeen	89.1	77.3	31	181	64.4	88.3
33 Newcastle	83.9	75.6	59.2	144	68.4	88.2
34 De Montfort	93.3	86	45	126	65.3	88
35 Royal College of Music	83.2	75.8	45.5	91	93.9	87.8
36 West of England	90.6	88.7	48.2	122	65.2	87.6
37 Sussex	83.4	79.7	48	138	-	87.5
38 Goldsmiths, London	82.4	63.3	46.8	135	81.1	87.1
39 Rose Bruford	93.3	62.8	19	161	-	86.9
40 West London	88.2	84.2	32.2	125	74.6	86.8
=41 Royal Northern College of Music	84.5	78.3	34	111	82.8	86.2
=41 Ulster	81.8	75.7	49	129	72.9	86.2
43 Salford	84.2	75.9	30.2	128	78.4	85.7
44 Westminster	78.8	69.8	75.5	120	63.6	85.4

45	York St John	89.6	83.9	33.2	121	66.2	85.2
46	Falmouth	87.8	82.4	48.8	121	60	85.1
47	Trinity Laban	82.1	66.6	38	131	73.7	84.5
48	Bedfordshire	91.1	80.1	-	133	75	84.1
=49	Bath Spa	87.2	80.5	26	112	71.3	83.8
=49	Lincoln	88.3	79.7	37.2	115	62.9	83.8
=49	West of Scotland	87.7	82.6	19.2	163	55.7	83.8
=52	Hertfordshire	88.9	80.6	24.2	123	63	83.2
=52	Portsmouth	87	84.2	30.2	115	63.8	83.2
54	Bournemouth	86.4	74.8	38.5	112	62.5	82.7
55	Chichester	85.4	69.1	13.2	134	71.9	82.5
56	Greenwich	88	79.6	-	144	67	82.4
57	Chester	80.7	72.2	21	140	68.8	82.2
58	East London	84.2	65.3	13	150	67.4	82.1
59	Staffordshire	80.7	70	31.5	137	63.1	81.8
60	Anglia Ruskin	74.3	64.6	61.8	110	-	81.7
61	Nottingham Trent	85.9	82.9	-	123	72.5	81.6
62	Hull	82.1	76.7	35	102	67.3	81.5
=63	Northampton	88.3	74.9	12.2	121	-	81.4
=63	Wolverhampton	92.8	84.6	6.8	-	58.6	81.4
65	Canterbury Christ Church	82.8	72.6	38.5	102	65.3	81.3
66	Gloucestershire	80.4	74.5	23.8	116	69.6	81.1
67	Plymouth	70	58.9	49.8	143	-	80.8
68	Lancashire	90.7	74.5	19	111	59	80.7
69	Winchester	79.6	66.1	32.5	120	61.4	79.6
70	Brunel	79.5	68.1	38	101	-	79.4
71	Leeds Conservatoire	85.4	66.5	-	132	64.4	79
72	Worcester	83	75.9	5.8	124	-	78.8
73	Leeds Beckett	78.6	72	15.8	122	64.4	78.7
74	Edge Hill	84.2	79.8	-	129	57.4	78.2
75	Creative Arts	80.1	51.3	41.2	100	-	78
76	Southampton Solent	85.9	83	-	125	52.5	77.6
77	South Wales	74.9	62.1	35.8	93	66.7	77.5
78	Liverpool Hope	85	68.8	17.5	114	44.9	75.7
79	Leeds Arts	74.1	68.5	2.8	114	-	73.1

Employed in high-skilled job	49%	Employed in lower-skilled job	26%
Employed in high-skilled job and studying	4%	Employed in lower-skilled job and studying	1%
Studying	6%	Unemployed	6%
High-skilled work (median) salary	£25,000	Low-/medium-skilled salary	£20,000

Natural Sciences

Now in its fifth year, the Natural Sciences table is topped by Cambridge for the fifth time. In a convincing lead overall, Cambridge is first for research quality, entry standards and graduate prospects. Runner-up Exeter is in front for student satisfaction – topping the table for teaching quality and the wider experience in our latest National Student Survey analysis. Natural sciences attracts high grades throughout the ranking: entry standards are no lower than 152 UCAS points (at Loughborough). The subject's interdisciplinary approach provides a breadth of knowledge and practical skills likely to serve graduates well in their careers in industry or postgraduate research. Four of the 12 universities tabled had at least 90% of graduates employed in high-skilled jobs and/or further study within 15 months and none had less than 80% achieving these outcomes. As a subject, natural sciences ranks 14th out of the 70 groupings in our employment index and at =5th place for salaries, it compares more favourably still for earnings.

Natural sciences degrees give students the benefit of studying across different scientific disciplines as well as the flexibility to specialise in areas of specific interest as programmes progress. Some universities offer the opportunity to transfer to a single science after a year, if a student decides their interests lie in one particular direction. "As scientists we want to explore the universe and everything in it, but the universe isn't divided into biology, chemistry and physics," explains Professor Geoffrey Nash, head of natural sciences, University of Exeter, "Through studying natural sciences we look for the connections between areas of science, allowing us to harness their power to make a difference to people's lives, to make the world a better place. But studying science is also about beauty: it's an expression of our common humanity, a celebration of life."

Natural Sciences	Teaching quality %	Student experience %	Research quality %	Entry standards (UCAS points)	Graduate prospects %	Overall score
1 Cambridge	85.5	82.1	73.5	224	94.3	100
2 Exeter	95.6	91.3	59.3	180	90	96.5
3 Durham	89	84.5	53	206	89.4	95.4
4 Southampton	86.1	82	71	176	-	94.9
5 University College London	81	75.7	64	187	92.6	94.3
6 Nottingham	91.5	90.5	57.9	173	86.7	93.9
7 Lancaster	89.7	87	68.2	169	80	92.3
8 Leeds	80.6	78.1	50.2	177	91.7	91.5
9 Bath	82	83.7	49.2	190	85.3	91
10 York	82.3	69.2	66	181	83	90.9
11 Warwick	86.8	82.7	46.5	153	-	88.6
12 Loughborough	86.5	79.6	41	152	85	87.7

Employed in high-skilled job	50%	Employed in lower-skilled job		7%
Employed in high-skilled job and studying	6%	Employed in lower-skilled job and studying		0%
Studying	22%	Unemployed		6%
High-skilled work (median) salary	£30,700	Low-/medium-skilled salary		N/A

Nursing

Edinburgh has taken the lead in our Nursing table, ousting Glasgow into second place after three years at the top. Sheffield is in third place for the second consecutive year. Further down the table there has been more volatility, including Surrey falling 13 places to rank 20th and Keele down 11 places to 15th. Cardiff, which confirmed it would be retaining its nursing department after controversial plans to close it were shelved, has gained 12 places to rank 4th in the new Nursing ranking. Results of the Research Excellence Framework 2021 assessment show that King's College London (=21st overall) leads for research quality in nursing, followed by Manchester (=30th) and Southampton (=8th). In the QS World University Rankings by Subject, which focus on research and academic reputation and do not include measures for student satisfaction, King's College is top in the world for nursing.

Led by Glasgow, where nursing entrants averaged 192 UCAS points, Scottish universities tally the highest entry standards – benefitting from the favourable tariff conversion for Scottish secondary qualifications – while Cardiff has the highest outside Scotland, at 147 points, but the vast majority of universities (72) average fewer than 144 UCAS points (equal to three As at A-level). Ulster ranks =17th in the table and scores the highest with its students, placing top for teaching quality and the broader experience – based on their responses to the latest National Student Survey (NSS). Liverpool (=28th overall) is also in the top three for both. Conversely, Bradford comes bottom for teaching quality and South Wales got the poorest reviews for the broad experience.

After experiencing a boom during the pandemic years, applications to nursing and midwifery degrees in the UK fell for the fourth consecutive year, according to data released by UCAS for 2025-26 based on its January deadline. The picture varies by UK country; most starkly, England registered a 35% fall in the number of people applying to study nursing, with only 23,730 applications in 2025-26 compared with 36,410 in 2021. Royal College of Nursing general secretary and chief executive Professor Nicola Ranger called for a refocused recruitment drive by the government and said, "Today's broken model of education funding impoverishes students and saddles them with debt, and it is turning people away from the nursing profession. Low starting salaries make a bad situation worse." The number of nursing students accepted onto courses edged up by 0.6% between 2023 and 2024, but remained significantly down (-19%) on 2021.

But there are plenty of options available to those considering nursing courses – as evidenced by our Nursing table, which stretches to 80 universities – and the NHS Long Term Workforce pledge has set ambitious targets for student nursing intakes. "Nursing is about delivering safe, evidence-based care, which in the 21st century means student nurses will need a diverse range of skills and an ability to solve complex problems on an almost daily basis," says Susan Ward, head of nursing, School of Healthcare Sciences, Cardiff University.

As a degree, nursing offers a near guarantee of employment on graduation and three universities in our table – Birmingham, Edinburgh and Wrexham – record a perfect 100% rate of graduates being employed in professional-level jobs or postgraduate study within 15 months. No universities registered lower than the 80.9% of graduates achieving these outcomes at Anglia Ruskin. Nursing is third in the employment table of 70 subjects, behind only veterinary medicine and medicine. Pay, though not an ingredient of our subject ranking, is a topic of especially hot debate in nursing. Average graduate salaries of £25,665 rank the subject 41st out the 70 featured in our Guide, a big drop from 27th place three editions ago.

Nursing	Teaching quality %	Student experience %	Research quality %	Entry standards (UCAS points)	Graduate prospects %	Overall score
1 Edinburgh	84.1	82.1	55.2	189	100	100
2 Glasgow	81.9	75.8	63.5	192	97.2	98.8
3 Sheffield	90.9	89.7	63.7	139	97.5	96.8
4 Cardiff	89.9	87.4	58.8	147	96.4	96.3
=5 Leeds	83.5	81.2	65	141	98.1	95.7
=5 Queen's, Belfast	88.8	85.6	66.2	132	97	95.7

Nursing cont.

	Teaching quality %	Student experience %	Research quality %	Entry standards (UCAS points)	Graduate prospects %	Overall score
7 Hull	86.9	82.6	55.5	135	98.7	95.4
=8 Birmingham	81.5	71.9	55	144	100	95.3
=8 Southampton	84.7	80	69.8	141	96.3	95.3
10 Northumbria	85.7	84.4	53.5	134	98.9	95.2
=11 Dundee	84.3	77.3	60.8	130	99.7	95.1
=11 Glasgow Caledonian	84.1	80	61	136	98.2	95.1
13 East Anglia	89.5	86.8	55.5	130	97.1	94.9
14 Coventry	87.7	79	47.2	130	99.2	94.6
=15 Keele	87.4	76.5	66.2	114	99.4	94.5
=15 Queen Margaret, Edinburgh	91.7	91.9	36.5	162	92.3	94.5
=17 Exeter	87.4	70.5	54.5	135	-	94.4
=17 Ulster	94.8	94	53.5	120	95.4	94.4
19 Nottingham	82.5	75	66.8	136	96.6	94.2
20 Surrey	84.9	77.7	58	129	97.6	94.1
=21 Hertfordshire	87.1	84.6	48	120	98.8	93.9
=21 King's College London	86.5	82.6	76.2	134	92.7	93.9
=23 Bangor	78.1	70.6	59.8	137	98.7	93.8
=23 Edinburgh Napier	83.7	79.2	40.5	144	97.4	93.8
=25 Kingston	89.4	86.2	38.5	124	97.7	93.5
=25 Plymouth	84.2	76.1	39.5	138	98.1	93.5
27 Aston	87.7	87.5	46	120	-	93.3
=28 Liverpool	93.2	93.6	46.8	129	92.7	93.1
=28 Swansea	74.7	62.8	66.8	129	99.4	93.1
30 Manchester	80.1	76.1	71.2	137	93.7	92.9
31 Essex	87.5	82.9	28.5	133	97.3	92.8
=32 Oxford Brookes	91.9	85.5	37.8	113	97.3	92.7
=32 Portsmouth	89	85.6	41.2	111	98.2	92.7
34 York	79.3	72.7	65	133	95.2	92.6
=35 Lincoln	77.9	70.6	55.8	125	98.4	92.4
=35 Robert Gordon	81.7	70.7	24.5	138	99.7	92.4
37 West London	88.5	83.8	29.5	124	97.2	92.3
38 Stirling	74.6	68	44	136	98.9	92.1
=39 East London	88.8	85.9	25.5	-	96.1	91.9
=39 Nottingham Trent	85.1	76.8	43.5	121	-	91.9
41 Lancashire	83.7	75.2	35.5	135	96	91.8
=42 Staffordshire	83.2	77.4	30.8	120	98.9	91.7
=42 Sunderland	85.5	78.4	30.2	129	96.7	91.7
44 Derby	87.5	80.2	24	120	97.8	91.5
45 West of England	80.9	70.8	42.8	126	97	91.4
46 Birmingham City	77.5	69.3	37.8	135	97.4	91.3
=47 Liverpool John Moores	81.9	76.1	26.5	130	97.3	91.2
=47 Salford	81.1	70.2	37	127	97.3	91.2
=47 West of Scotland	84.9	74	30.8	134	95.3	91.2
=47 York St John	93.9	84.5	13.8	119	-	91.2

=51	Chester	81.1	70.1	31	126	98.1	91
=51	Teesside	82.8	75.4	35	126	96.3	91
=53	City St George's	80.7	69.8	58	122	94.4	90.9
=53	Middlesex	90.2	85.2	22.5	115	96.1	90.9
=55	Bournemouth	82.9	73.2	29.2	117	98.5	90.8
=55	Brighton	74	64.1	50.5	125	97.9	90.8
=55	Leeds Beckett	79.9	73.4	38	120	97.5	90.8
58	Greenwich	84.2	73.9	32.3	116	96.9	90.4
=59	Sheffield Hallam	75.4	65.8	29.8	124	99.5	90.3
=59	Wrexham	90.2	75.8	1.5	110	100	90.3
=61	London South Bank	86.4	78.8	34.5	118	93.9	90
=61	Wolverhampton	84.6	78.3	24.2	118	96	90
63	Bedfordshire	85.8	73.6	22.5	124	95.2	89.9
=64	Edge Hill	82.5	78.7	22.2	126	95.2	89.7
=64	Manchester Metropolitan	84.4	80.5	36	120	93.3	89.7
=66	Canterbury Christ Church	79.8	71.5	31.8	112	97.1	89.4
=66	Huddersfield	77.9	72.1	22.5	122	97.5	89.4
68	Northampton	85.4	78.4	5	132	94.7	89.2
69	Roehampton	91	86.7	37.5	83	-	89.1
70	South Wales	74.2	59.3	25.2	128	97.6	88.9
=71	Brunel	74.7	69.8	47.2	115	-	88.8
=71	Buckinghamshire New	91.1	85.6	16.8	102	94.6	88.8
73	Greater Manchester	82.5	74.2	2	124	97	88.7
74	Worcester	77.7	73.7	24.2	121	95.3	88.5
75	Suffolk	88.7	76.8	-	114	95.7	88.3
76	Bradford	72.6	63.4	33.8	132	94.2	88.1
77	De Montfort	76.6	68.1	20.8	110	96.3	87.3
78	Cumbria	76.2	72.1	18.5	115	94.1	86.7
79	Gloucestershire	75.3	60	16.2	117	95.2	86.4
80	Anglia Ruskin	85.3	79.8	33.8	104	80.9	82.5

Employed in high-skilled job	89%	Employed in lower-skilled job	2%
Employed in high-skilled job and studying	4%	Employed in lower-skilled job and studying	0%
Studying	1%	Unemployed	1%
High-skilled work (median) salary	£25,675	Low-/medium-skilled salary	N/A

Pharmacology and Pharmacy

Applications to pharmacology and pharmacy degrees have rocketed since before the pandemic. There were 7,605 applications to pharmacology in 2024 (up 81% since 2019) and over 18,600 applications to pharmacy (73% more than in 2019 when the subject received 10,800 applications). The numbers accepted onto courses have risen less steeply; in 2024, 2,630 new pharmacy students enrolled (up 22% since 2019) and 1,185 won places to study pharmacology (up 73%). The spike in interest is timely; the NHS Long Term Workforce Plan, published in 2023, has pledged to expand training places for pharmacists in England by 29% by 2028–29.

Solid career prospects are in store for graduates. The subjects are often in the top ten of our employment table, but rank 22nd out of 70 subject areas this year, based on three-quarters of those with pharmacology and pharmacy degrees being employed in professional-level jobs and/or furthering their studies within 15 months. Pay offers early career rewards: the subjects tie with veterinary science in third place of our pay index (behind only dentistry and medicine), based on average graduate salaries of £33,000.

No 1 for the fifth consecutive year, Strathclyde in Glasgow's eminence in our Pharmacy and Pharmacology table is secured by the highest entry standards (232 points in the UCAS tariff) along with strong performances across all other measures in our ranking. Strathclyde offers degrees in all three of the subjects encompassed in this grouping: pharmacology – which is a branch of medicine concerned with drugs, their uses, effects and how they interact with the human body; pharmacy – which trains and licenses individuals to dispense prescription medicines as pharmacists; and toxicology – which is similar to pharmacology but focuses on the toxic rather than healing properties of venoms, poisons and drugs. Most English universities offer only one or the other, and courses are evenly split among institutions.

King's College London (in 14th place overall) has the edge for research quality in our analysis of the Research Excellence Framework 2021 results. In our latest National Student Survey (NSS) analysis 30th-place East London achieves the highest rates of satisfaction with teaching quality and the broader experience, while Liverpool John Moores (25th overall) and third-place Queen's, Belfast follow it for the student experience. At the opposite end of the scale, the least satisfied students for both NSS-based measures were at Kent (46th overall).

The four-year MPharm degree is a direct route to professional registration as a pharmacist and the most popular option, or students can study three-year degrees in pharmaceutical science or as part of a broader degree. Pharmacology is available as a three-year BSc or as an extended course. Biology and chemistry are usually required by the leading universities, while maths, further maths and physics may also be useful.

"Cancer? Anxiety and depression? Diabetes? Most of us know people affected by one or more of these conditions. There are huge global challenges in pharmacology. Pharmacologists look for answers to viral pandemics, tropical diseases such as malaria and sleeping sickness, and venomous snake bites. Thanks to pharmacologists we can treat many conditions that used to be fatal. There are many more that still need research," explains Dr Andrew Fielding, senior lecturer in cancer research, Lancaster University.

Pharmacology and Pharmacy	Teaching quality %	Student experience %	Research quality %	Entry standards (UCAS points)	Graduate prospects %	Overall score
1 Strathclyde	87.3	85.5	65.8	232	93.1	100
2 Glasgow	84.7	90.2	63.5	218	-	99.7
3 Queen's, Belfast	91.3	92.1	66.2	162	97.7	98.3
4 Cardiff	90.1	82.1	58.8	158	97	95.9
5 Newcastle	87.1	81.3	65.8	139	97.5	95.1
6 Edinburgh	69.4	76.5	68.6	213	-	94.9
7 Ulster	86.7	72	53.5	179	95.8	94.7
=8 Dundee	85.1	79.1	60.8	184	88	93.5
=8 Nottingham	82.1	80.7	66.8	154	92.7	93.5
10 Manchester	80.1	71.9	71.2	160	91.1	92.9
=11 Bath	82.1	80.1	63.7	146	92.3	92.4
=11 Swansea	86.2	80.5	66.8	134	-	92.4
13 Liverpool	83.9	87.6	46.8	149	95.3	92.3
14 King's College London	81.3	80.6	76.2	147	85.8	91.7

15 Sunderland	91.5	84.3	30.2	124	100	91.3
=16 Brighton	82	76.1	50.5	142	94	90.6
=16 University College London	80.4	77.4	57.8	168	86.9	90.6
18 Leeds	82	77.7	52	158	-	90.5
19 Keele	86.2	74	66.2	125	88.5	90.4
=20 Aston	88.4	87.6	46	133	88.9	89.7
=20 Birmingham	81.7	80.3	55	142	89	89.7
=20 Bristol	83.6	75.2	57.5	151	86.4	89.7
=23 Aberdeen	85	86.1	30.5	174	-	89.6
=23 Glasgow Caledonian	89.9	87.9	61	147	79.3	89.6
25 Liverpool John Moores	89.6	92.8	26.5	145	91.1	89.3
26 Reading	83.3	76.5	54	125	90.9	89.2
27 Coventry	86.2	81	47.2	129	-	88.5
28 East Anglia	81.3	66.3	55.5	136	86.9	87.5
29 Queen Mary, London	89.4	88	54.8	138	76.7	87.1
30 East London	95	94.4	25.5	110	-	86.6
=31 City St George's	93.8	87	48.8	112	78.1	85.9
=31 Robert Gordon	68	60	24.5	193	92.1	85.9
33 Lincoln	73.8	68.6	55.8	131	86.3	85.8
=34 Bradford	72.7	67.4	33.8	155	88.8	84.9
=34 Huddersfield	83	77.9	22.5	131	89.5	84.9
36 Portsmouth	84.4	80	41.2	111	84.3	84.7
37 Kingston	82.3	77.5	38.5	127	84	84.6
38 Hertfordshire	78.1	75	48	126	81.8	84.1
39 Westminster	86.4	84.7	36.8	94	-	84
40 West London	88.4	85	29.5	98	-	83.6
41 Nottingham Trent	84.8	83.4	43.5	107	79.4	83.4
42 Wolverhampton	83.8	79.9	24.2	121	85.2	83.3
43 Lancashire	72	70.8	35.5	136	82.7	81.9
44 Greenwich	79.7	81.6	32.3	118	80.3	81.7
45 De Montfort	72.5	66.3	20.8	124	90	81.4
46 Kent	60.1	41.2	36.8	124	84.5	77.4
47 Anglia Ruskin	72.3	74	33.8	68	-	76.4

Employed in high-skilled job	59%	Employed in lower-skilled job	7%
Employed in high-skilled job and studying	7%	Employed in lower-skilled job and studying	0%
Studying	9%	Unemployed	6%
High-skilled work (median) salary	£33,000	Low-/medium-skilled salary	£20,500

Philosophy

The London School of Economics and Political Science (LSE) recorded a perfect 100% of graduates in professional jobs and/or further study 15 months after their degrees, helping secure the No 1 spot for LSE in our Philosophy table for the second year in a row. "Philosophy students go on to be politicians, lawyers, businesspeople, medical professionals, journalists and, more importantly, good parents, partners, citizens and friends," says Dr Michael T Stuart, lecturer in philosophy, University of York.

Students of philosophy engage with the ideas of great thinkers, examining their arguments and expressing their own opinions. Social science and humanities subjects (English, religious studies, psychology, politics, sociology) are useful in an application, while some of the leading universities may also look for maths – as degrees involve more mathematical skills than many candidates expect, especially when the syllabus has an emphasis on logic.

The upper end of our Philosophy table is remarkably stable year on year, other than minor reshuffles within it, and nine of this year's top 10 universities appeared in last year's top 10 too. Oxford, which led table five years ago and ranks third this year, attracts the highest entry standards – with entrants averaging 201 points in the UCAS tariff. More than half of the universities tabled average over 144 UCAS points (equal to three As at A-level), leaving almost as many with more accessible standards – such as Cardiff in 18th place overall and philosophy's top scorer in the Research Excellence Framework 2021, where entrants to the degree averaged 128 UCAS points. In our latest National Student Survey (NSS) analysis Newcastle (10th in the main table) outdoes the rest for the broad student experience and Oxford Brookes (21st) is unbeaten for teaching quality, followed by West of England (37th) and Hull (31st). Conversely, Edinburgh is bottom for both of these NSS-derived metrics, and ranks =29th overall.

"To do philosophy we examine the assumptions that underlie human pursuits such as physics, biology, psychology, theology, politics, art, mathematics and, of course, philosophy itself. And we attempt to characterise and explain some of the most important features of this world, like knowledge, justice, power, meaning, consciousness, beauty, gender, war, care and evil. Philosophy is honest, self-reflective and fresh. Its abstractness and rigour produce the most transferable skills of any university degree," explains Dr Stuart.

Overall, the subject places 51st out of 70 in our employment ranking of 70 subject areas, based on six in ten graduates (59.8%) being in high-skilled jobs and/or furthering their studies within 15 months. Graduate salaries compare more favourably in =38th place. The numbers of students starting courses have remained remarkably consistent across the past five years; there were 2,300 new philosophy undergraduates in 2024 out of just over 14,000 applications.

Philosophy	Teaching quality %	Student experience %	Research quality %	Entry standards (UCAS points)	Graduate prospects %	Overall score
1 London School of Economics	84.6	80.5	60	190	100	100
2 Warwick	90.7	89	55.8	168	88.7	98.1
3 Oxford	86.4	74.2	50.7	201	90.6	97.4
4 St Andrews	91.3	91.4	55	186	76.4	97.2
5 Cambridge	87.9	75.3	59	186	86.2	97.1
6 Birmingham	89.4	89.5	66	144	83	96.5
7 University College London	80.1	80.4	66.8	170	86.9	95.7
8 Durham	84	78.3	47.8	182	88.9	95.2
9 King's College London	83.1	79.4	52.2	176	87.1	94.9
10 Newcastle	91.6	91.9	61.8	136	76	94.7
11 York	84.1	78.2	66.2	147	83.7	94.3
12 Southampton	91.3	90.8	59	136	75	94
13 Glasgow	84.6	82	51	192	69.5	92.9
=14 Bristol	82.8	79.1	54.8	172	75	92.4
=14 Sheffield	85.7	86.3	45.5	146	81.9	92.4
16 Exeter	80.5	81.5	46.8	159	85.5	92.3
17 Nottingham	88.3	88.1	41.5	142	79.7	92.1
18 Cardiff	88	90.6	67.2	128	66.7	92

19	Loughborough	89.5	91.1	29.5	146	-	90.7
20	Essex	86.4	81.1	46.5	130	79.6	90.6
21	Oxford Brookes	97	91.6	28.2	106	80	90.5
22	Queen's, Belfast	89.2	81.2	33	149	-	90.1
23	Leeds	79.5	83.2	47	151	76.7	90
=24	Lancaster	85.6	82.8	49	142	70.2	89.8
=24	Manchester	82.1	75.7	55.5	156	69.8	89.8
26	Dundee	93.3	84.8	17.8	152	-	89.6
27	Liverpool	84.5	81.6	45.2	127	78.2	89.5
28	Swansea	91.7	90.5	31.5	120	-	89.4
=29	Edinburgh	76.8	72.1	49	171	72.3	88.8
=29	Sussex	83.9	83.3	49	124	72.8	88.8
31	Hull	94.1	89.1	31.5	105	-	88.7
32	Bangor	93.6	89.8	33.2	115	69.8	88.6
33	Stirling	84.1	77.2	36	142	-	87.7
34	Manchester Metropolitan	89.3	82.3	41	113	69.2	87.5
35	Aberdeen	80.5	79.8	22.8	172	-	87.2
36	Reading	83.2	82.3	36.2	119	73.3	86.6
37	West of England	96.1	89.3	35.2	108	53.6	85.7
38	Royal Holloway	83.8	80.5	26.5	123	70.7	85
39	East Anglia	81.3	73.1	38.2	114	69.6	84.3
40	Keele	89.6	87.1	9.5	113	-	83.8
41	Lincoln	92.7	85.5	-	100	74.1	83.5

Employed in high-skilled job	42%	Employed in lower-skilled job	22%
Employed in high-skilled job and studying	5%	Employed in lower-skilled job and studying	1%
Studying	11%	Unemployed	6%
High-skilled work (median) salary	£28,000	Low-/medium-skilled salary	£20,600

Physics and Astronomy

St Andrews has pipped Cambridge to first place post in our new Physics and Astronomy table. The two are separated by the narrowest of margins (0.1%) but the change of guard at the top ends a three-year reign for Cambridge. Stiff entry standards at the leading universities are a constant and the table attracts some of the highest in our Guide. Nine of the 48 universities tabled average over 200 UCAS points among entrants, led by St Andrews, where new undergraduates averaged an extraordinary 227 points. Only 20 universities averaged fewer than 144 UCAS points (equivalent to three As at A-level), although there are still five universities where this drops below 110 points, the equivalent of BBC at A-level. Most degrees in both physics and astronomy demand physics and maths at A-level, as well as good grades overall.

Famous physicists and astronomers from Galileo Galilei to Marie Curie, Albert Einstein to Stephen Hawking, have helped earn the subjects a reputation for being the rarefied preserves of boffins, but Dr Patrick Parkinson, UK Research and Innovation Future Leaders fellow in physics and astronomy, University of Manchester believes "Everyone is born a physicist – as babies we explore how things move, how things get hot or cold and periodic day and night," he says, "Studying physics and astronomy is the process of understanding and predicting our universe, from the smallest parts of matter to the start and end of time. It is a global pursuit using experiments and theory, along the way developing revolutionary technologies: transistors, the internet, GPS positioning, MRI scanners, fusion energy and quantum computing. Graduates apply the skills they learn in the fields of research, policy, engineering, computer science, finance and beyond."

Oxford is third in our rankings and third in the world for physics and astronomy according to QS, which also has Cambridge in fifth. Manchester (7th in the table) achieved the subjects' top scores in the Research Excellence Framework 2021, where it is closely followed by Sheffield (=18th overall) and Birmingham – in fourth place.

In our National Student Survey analysis St Andrews has outdone all other universities in the table for student satisfaction with teaching quality, with Loughborough (25th in the table) and Hull (36th) following it, while for the broad experience Salford (40th) is top, with St Andrews and Lancashire (34th) behind it.

At the opposite end of the scale, Imperial College London ranks bottom for teaching quality and fourth from bottom for the student experience – which hold back its overall ranking to 13th place, despite the second-best graduate prospects in the table. Oxford has the edge for graduate employment – with 97.1% in high-skilled jobs and/or furthering their studies within 15 months.

The subjects as a whole translate into positive career potential, ranking 21st in our employment index and 15th for pay.

Rising student numbers – in astronomy in particular – have been attributed at least in part to Brian Cox, the University of Manchester particle physicist, whose television work has injected some accessibility and cool into the field. Demand increased by around 14% in 2024, with over 3,810 applications to the subject and 810 students accepted onto courses. Physics – the much larger field – attracted 23,460 applications (up by about 9% year on year) and over 5,000 new undergraduates gained places (7% more than the year before).

Physics and Astronomy	Teaching quality %	Student experience %	Research quality %	Entry standards (UCAS points)	Graduate prospects %	Overall score
1 St Andrews	94.8	92.7	65.8	227	88.4	100
2 Cambridge	85.5	82.1	72.8	224	94.3	99.9
3 Oxford	87.6	67.7	66.5	210	97.1	98.5
4 Birmingham	89.4	84.7	73.2	179	91.3	97.8
5 Durham	88.2	85	57.2	216	89.7	96.7
6 Dundee	93.5	91.7	50.2	204	-	96.5
7 Manchester	80.9	79.5	74	191	89.5	95.7
8 Lancaster	91.4	88.1	58.5	163	91.2	95.6
9 Warwick	88.1	82.6	59.8	186	89.7	95.3
10 Bristol	83.2	78.6	70.5	180	87.7	94.5
=11 Bath	85.1	84.5	55.5	175	91.5	94.3
=11 Exeter	90	86	59.2	149	90.5	94.3
13 Imperial College	71.5	71.2	60.8	212	95.7	94.2
14 Glasgow	76.8	78.4	64.5	218	86.7	93.9
15 Strathclyde	86.9	74.5	63.2	202	83	93.5
16 Nottingham	87.9	79.6	68.8	162	84.5	93.4
17 Heriot-Watt	90.1	91.2	65.5	140	84.4	93.2
=18 Portsmouth	90.1	84.7	68.5	102	88.2	92.5
=18 Sheffield	86.9	90.8	73.8	156	78.2	92.5
20 Leeds	83.9	81.5	64.5	153	86.5	92.3
21 Cardiff	92.2	88.3	59.2	143	82.7	92.1

22 University College London	79.6	81.6	55.5	188	86.3	91.8
=23 Edinburgh	74.6	72.9	62.7	213	84.5	91.7
=23 Queen's, Belfast	86.7	83	46.8	161	88.8	91.7
25 Loughborough	94.7	92.4	39.2	150	83.5	90.8
26 York	83.1	75.6	62.7	154	84.2	90.7
27 Liverpool	88.3	86.4	61.5	133	81	90.4
28 Southampton	85.5	80.8	52.2	151	85.1	90.3
29 Surrey	84.6	81.3	45.5	128	91.2	90.1
30 Nottingham Trent	92.6	84.1	59	111	80.2	89.5
31 Leicester	93.2	91.5	44	127	81.2	89.2
32 Royal Holloway	90.3	86.4	48	138	80.2	88.9
33 West of Scotland	91.6	84	31	163	-	88.8
34 Lancashire	93.7	92.6	41.2	104	-	88.5
35 King's College London	77.1	72.5	49.2	156	86.4	88.1
36 Hull	94.3	91.6	45.5	102	78.3	87.5
37 Newcastle	76.1	71.6	48	138	88	87.3
=38 Aberdeen	84.7	65.1	40	173	-	87.2
=38 Swansea	83.8	85.5	46.5	117	83.1	87.2
40 Salford	94.1	94	33.2	114	80	87
41 Queen Mary, London	84.4	79.9	48.8	140	78.7	86.9
42 Keele	90.1	89.7	49.5	117	73.9	86.3
43 Northumbria	92.1	92.1	43	-	72	86
44 Sussex	80.3	78.4	55	132	77.1	85.8
45 Aberystwyth	89.9	88.5	21	120	81.1	84.6
46 Lincoln	85.4	84.4	28.2	100	-	82.5
47 Kent	76.8	77.8	32.5	116	77.4	81.2
48 Sheffield Hallam	81	68.9	-	107	87	79.4

Employed in high-skilled job	51%	Employed in lower-skilled job	10%
Employed in high-skilled job and studying	4%	Employed in lower-skilled job and studying	0%
Studying	20%	Unemployed	6%
High-skilled work (median) salary	£30,000	Low-/medium-skilled salary	£20,000

Physiotherapy

Physiotherapy's popularity has been gathering pace. UCAS figures show applications to be over a third higher in 2024 than they were in 2019. New student enrolments have increased more sharply – by around 45% across the same time frame – and in 2024 nearly 3,750 were accepted onto courses. Candidates need biology A-level, while physics, chemistry and maths are also useful, as are sociology and PE A-levels.

Lindsay O'Connor, senior teaching fellow in neurological physiotherapy, University of Southampton, says physiotherapists "work with individuals across the lifespan to achieve their goals and optimise function, from sitting up for the first time in critical care to rehabilitation after a sporting injury. Physiotherapists have the privilege of really getting to know the people we work with, understanding what matters to them to achieve the best outcome."

Led by Glasgow Caledonian at No 1 for the fourth consecutive year, modern universities feature prominently in our Physiotherapy table, occupying half of the top ten of the table that was formerly part of the "Subjects Allied to Medicine" grouping but is now in its 13th year as a standalone ranking. Students at runner-up Robert Gordon averaged an extraordinary 227 UCAS points – the highest in the table – and entry standards soar at the Scottish universities (which benefit from the favourable tariff conversion for Scottish secondary qualifications). South of the border, Essex leads on entry standards (185 UCAS points). For research quality in the subject, King's College London (12th place overall) leads the field, having achieved the best results in the field in the REF 2021, where it is followed by Southampton – a former No 1 in the table and fourth this year.

For student satisfaction, our analysis of the latest National Student Survey shows fifth-place Hull to be top for teaching quality, followed by Robert Gordon and Leeds Beckett (13th overall), while the same universities swap places for feedback on the wider experience – where Leeds Beckett leads, with Hull and Robert Gordon after it. At the opposite end of the scale, Buckinghamshire New's physiotherapy students reported the lowest rates of satisfaction with their teaching and the broad experience.

Graduate employment outcomes are reliably strong, and at three of the 44 universities listed 100% of physiotherapy graduates were employed in professional jobs and/or postgraduate study within 15 months. Only at two universities, London South Bank and East London, does this proportion fall below 90% and the subject ranks fifth in the employment table, behind veterinary medicine, medicine, nursing and radiography. For salaries, though not an ingredient of our ranking, physiotherapy compares less strongly but still features comfortably in the upper half of subjects, at =28th.

Physiotherapy	Teaching quality %	Student experience %	Research quality %	Entry standards (UCAS points)	Graduate prospects %	Overall score
1 Glasgow Caledonian	92.9	92.4	61	226	98.1	100
2 Robert Gordon	98	95	24.5	227	100	97.8
3 Queen Margaret, Edinburgh	90.4	90.4	36.5	208	-	96
4 Southampton	86.9	84.2	69.8	151	100	95.4
5 Hull	99.3	95.7	55.5	134	-	93.7
6 Liverpool	92.2	92.4	46.8	156	98.2	93.5
7 Ulster	88.4	83.3	53.5	160	97.9	93.4
8 Essex	89.9	86.7	32.5	185	97.5	93.1
=9 Cardiff	80	80.2	58.8	163	98.1	93
=9 Northumbria	90.1	88	60.5	138	97.9	93
11 Bradford	94.6	90.8	33.8	151	98.4	92.1
12 King's College London	81.8	74.5	76.2	156	93	91.9
13 Leeds Beckett	96.9	96.6	38	145	96.4	91.8
14 Brighton	92.6	86.7	50.5	140	96.4	91.7
15 Manchester Metropolitan	87.6	85.6	51.2	142	96	91
16 East Anglia	86	78.5	55.5	149	94.9	90.8
17 Keele	91.2	82.5	66.2	136	92	90.6
18 Birmingham	80.3	75.8	55	153	95.2	90.3
=19 Central Lancashire	90.2	90.3	35.5	143	96.3	90.1
=19 West of England	91.9	91.1	42.8	143	94.1	90.1
21 Hertfordshire	93	93.8	48	136	92.7	89.9
22 Plymouth	87.9	79	39.5	163	93.7	89.8
=23 Brunel	91.5	89	47.2	142	92.2	89.4

=23	Wolverhampton	86.5	73.7	24.2	145	100	89.4
=25	Nottingham	78.7	74.6	56	156	92.7	89.2
=25	Teesside	82.5	79.6	35	142	98	89.2
=27	Coventry	80.3	77.6	47.2	135	97	89.1
=27	Salford	96.2	94.4	37	142	91.7	89.1
=27	Sunderland	90.7	82.2	30.2	149	-	89.1
30	Worcester	96.6	93.4	24.2	121	97.7	89
31	Huddersfield	90.5	85.4	22.2	140	97.7	88.9
32	Bournemouth	87.1	81.1	29.2	136	97.4	88.6
33	York St John	96.4	90.3	13.8	147	94	87.8
34	Gloucestershire	85.6	73.6	24.5	156	-	87.4
35	Oxford Brookes	85.3	79.9	37.8	136	92.3	86.8
36	Sheffield Hallam	80	72.1	29.8	128	96.7	86.4
37	Leicester	95.9	93.3	-	130	94.4	85.4
38	Winchester	90.6	85.4	-	118	98.4	85.3
39	Cumbria	85.8	81.9	18.5	108	95.8	84.6
40	City St George's	79.2	74.2	-	123	97.9	83.4
41	East London	87.9	75.8	25.5	121	88.9	82.9
42	London South Bank	81	54.8	34.5	114	79.5	77
43	Greater Manchester	64.9	57.6	2	128	-	76.9
44	Buckinghamshire New	46.6	45	16.8	116	-	73.8

Employed in high-skilled job	87%	Employed in lower-skilled job	2%
Employed in high-skilled job and studying	4%	Employed in lower-skilled job and studying	0%
Studying	1%	Unemployed	3%
High-skilled work (median) salary	£26,000	Low-/medium-skilled salary	N/A

Politics and International Relations

Formerly the Politics table, our ranking's title has gained International Relations (IR) from this year and its contents reflect courses in both subjects – which are often offered in joint honours courses, as well as on their own. "There is no one way to study politics at university. You might have the chance to explore the inner workings of government, or ask why states come into conflict, or debate which rights should be considered universal. Whatever you decide to focus on, you'll confront some of the biggest challenges facing contemporary society and develop a set of skills, including critical thought, data analysis and self-expression, that can be applied to a wide range of career paths, such as in journalism, public service or the world of business," says Dr Rod Dacombe, reader in politics at the Department of Political Economy, King's College London.

The leading universities look for humanities and social sciences A-levels in general – English, economics, sociology and history among them – without demanding any specifically. "To get the most out of studying politics you need to find out what it is you really care about. Read about what is going on in the world, form opinions and be prepared to be challenged," advises Dr Dacombe.

The UK government has been led by four different prime ministers in the same timeframe that St Andrews – now in its seventh year at the top – has led our Politics ranking. Cementing its overall tenure in the table, St Andrews is boosted by the second-highest entry standards and third-best ratings for teaching quality and for graduate prospects. With entrants to its politics and IR courses averaging 202 UCAS points, Glasgow leads for entry standards in a table where more than a third of universities averaged 144 or higher (equal to three As at A-level).

There is stability at the upper end of the table more widely, with 14 of the top 15 featuring in successive annual tables – albeit reshuffled to an extent. The London School of Economics and Politics Science (LSE) is runner-up this year, swapping places with third-place Oxford. Sheffield has gained five places to rank fifth while Stirling has gained eight places to rank 15th. Strathclyde, fourth overall, was the top scorer in politics in the Research Excellence Framework 2021, where its results are followed by those of Royal Holloway (13th), Edinburgh (=16th) and the LSE.

Nottingham Trent – in =37th place – is the top-ranked modern university. Another two, Greenwich and Liverpool Hope (in 58th and 62nd place respectively, overall), share the top two ratings for student satisfaction – teaching quality and the wider experience – based on our analysis of the latest National Student Survey. In contrast, Edinburgh is bottom for teaching quality and Goldsmiths (71st in the table) is bottom for the wider experience.

Average starting salaries for politics and international relations graduates rank the subjects =28th in our pay index of 70 areas. In 45th place of the employment table they compare less favourably with other subject groupings. When surveyed 15 months after their degrees, 62.4% of graduates were employed in professional-level jobs and/or furthering their studies, but over a fifth were working in jobs classified as "low-skilled". These figures vary widely by institution – from Oxford, the LSE and St Andrews where more than 90% of graduates achieved the desired career outcomes within 15 months, down to four universities (West of England, Westminster, Canterbury Christ Church and Winchester) where under 60% had reached the same professional goals. Demand for the subjects boomed in the decade up to 2019, and after a dip in 2022 applications climbed again – to nearly 51,000 in 2024 – and almost 11,500 students were accepted onto courses (the biggest intake in around five years).

Politics and International Relations	Teaching quality %	Student experience %	Research quality %	Entry standards (UCAS points)	Graduate prospects %	Overall score
1 St Andrews	92.1	87.1	47	201	90	100
2 London School of Economics	84	83	65.8	188	91.4	99
3 Oxford	85.1	72.1	61.3	197	91.9	98.3
4 Strathclyde	85.8	81.9	70.5	193	75.6	96.8
5 Sheffield	88.6	87.1	58	152	84.6	96.3
6 University College London	79.9	78.3	64.5	176	89.5	96.1
7 Warwick	85.8	85.1	60.5	166	82.6	96
8 Durham	84.6	82.6	42.5	180	88.6	95.4
9 Cambridge	85	68.5	50.2	195	85.4	95.1
10 King's College London	84.6	81.8	52.2	179	81.9	94.9
11 York	85.3	81.4	57.5	151	85.3	94.8
12 Birmingham	83.9	82.7	51.5	146	87	94
13 Royal Holloway	84.9	80.6	67.2	122	82.7	93.6
14 Glasgow	78.7	74.3	50.2	202	80	93.1
15 Stirling	91.3	83.8	28.7	168	77.4	92.8
=16 Edinburgh	74.2	69.8	66.5	191	79.8	92.5
=16 Queen Mary, London	85.2	81.1	61.3	138	76.3	92.5
=18 Bath	82.8	84.6	31.8	166	85.6	92.4
=18 Bristol	81.2	80.1	50.7	167	79.4	92.4

=18 Exeter	80.1	78.9	57.5	152	82	92.4
21 Nottingham	85.1	83.2	46	146	79.3	92.1
22 Surrey	92.5	89.4	40.2	123	75	91.9
23 Manchester	81.1	78	60.5	155	74.7	91.6
24 SOAS, London	81.4	71.3	55.5	135	84.5	91.4
=25 Loughborough	87	88.3	29.5	137	81.9	91.3
=25 Reading	88.7	84.3	49.2	114	77	91.3
27 Aston	82.9	83	49	112	83.5	90.8
28 Northumbria	87.9	83.5	42	116	78.8	90.6
=29 Aberdeen	85.7	84.7	23.5	169	76.6	90.5
=29 Aberystwyth	91.2	86.1	42.8	111	73.4	90.5
=31 Leicester	89.5	89.1	36.8	112	76.6	90.4
=31 Newcastle	81.5	83.1	39.5	151	78.6	90.4
=33 Lancaster	82	76.7	49	136	79.1	90.3
=33 Sussex	85.7	83.3	55.7	127	70.2	90.3
35 Swansea	89.3	86.9	31.5	110	80.2	90.1
36 Essex	87.1	85.3	60.5	122	64.4	89.9
=37 Nottingham Trent	91.1	91.3	29.5	106	75.9	89.7
=37 Southampton	80.7	79.7	39.8	133	82.4	89.7
39 Liverpool	85.1	82.6	39.8	130	75.7	89.6
40 Queen's, Belfast	80.2	75.5	40.8	144	79.2	89.1
=41 Cardiff	80.2	78.3	49	137	74.7	89
=41 Leeds	79	78.9	35.8	154	78.8	89
=43 Bournemouth	86.9	76.8	47.2	87	77.6	88.4
=43 Brunel	91	81.5	35	95	74.2	88.4
=43 East Anglia	82	76.7	56.2	121	70.6	88.4
46 Salford	82.6	82	51.7	112	71.3	88.2
47 Lincoln	91	86.7	34	101	69.6	88.1
=48 Coventry	92	90.1	39.5	100	63.6	88
=48 Portsmouth	85.4	74.5	51.7	111	70.3	88
50 Plymouth	81.8	75.6	37.9	116	80.1	87.9
=51 Brighton	86.6	75.8	44.2	102	71.7	87.4
=51 City St George's	79.8	79.8	40.8	110	78.7	87.4
=53 Kent	84.1	78.8	41	109	69.8	86.6
=53 Oxford Brookes	88.1	86.9	27.5	109	67.7	86.6
55 Manchester Metropolitan	87.3	82.5	29	108	68.3	86.2
56 Ulster	84.7	73.9	53.8	116	60.4	86.1
57 Keele	90.5	81.1	28	107	64.8	86
58 Greenwich	93.7	92.5	-	100	71.4	85.9
59 West of Scotland	91.9	82.8	13.2	-	66.1	85.5
60 Westminster	88.3	84.7	41.5	99	57.8	85.3
61 Leeds Beckett	86.9	82.2	15.5	107	71.9	85.2
62 Liverpool Hope	93.1	94.1	5.5	98	63	84.6
63 West of England	86.5	85.9	35.2	107	56.9	84.4
64 Hull	86.9	82.2	11.2	107	69.9	84.3
65 Dundee	82.4	79.5	-	173	65.8	84.2
66 De Montfort	86.9	85	-	89	73	82.9
67 Sheffield Hallam	82	76.2	-	104	78.9	82.8

Politics and International Relations cont.	Teaching quality %	Student experience %	Research quality %	Entry standards (UCAS points)	Graduate prospects %	Overall score
68 Chester	81.9	81.1	12.8	110	-	82.5
69 Canterbury Christ Church	85.1	91.6	13.2	-	58.3	81.8
70 London Metropolitan	85.6	89	-	89	66.9	81.6
71 Goldsmiths, London	78.3	57.7	29	92	67.9	80.1
72 Northampton	84	80.4	1.2	90	-	79.9
73 Winchester	76.2	71.9	19.8	101	59.7	78.6

Employed in high-skilled job	46%	Employed in lower-skilled job	22%
Employed in high-skilled job and studying	5%	Employed in lower-skilled job and studying	1%
Studying	10%	Unemployed	7%
High-skilled work (median) salary	£27,500	Low-/medium-skilled salary	£20,352

Psychology

"Psychology students use the scientific method to study human behaviour in order to better understand our minds and brains," explains Professor Peter Fonagy, head of the Division of Psychology and Language Sciences, UCL. "Psychologists ask fundamental questions about consciousness, memory, language and other aspects of people that are not yet fully understood. They address mental health issues that pervade society, from day-to-day wellbeing to treatment of clinical disorders. They use their knowledge of how to change human behaviour to respond to global challenges such as climate change, pandemic disease and artificial intelligence. Whether you want to predict, measure or understand people, or just make them feel better, psychology is where to start."

The London School of Economics (LSE) is No 1 out of the 113 universities in our Psychology table. It is the fourth year running that LSE has topped the ranking, where its eminence is secured with the top research rating by a clear margin, based on our analysis of the Research Excellence Framework 2021. St Andrews, in second place overall, is top for graduate prospects and one of only 11 universities where at least 80% of graduates were in high-skilled jobs or postgraduate study 15 months after their degrees. While the older institutions dominate the upper ranks of the main table, a modern university has the most satisfied psychology students, our analysis of the latest National Student Survey shows: Wales Trinity St David outdoes all others for students' evaluation of teaching quality and the wider experience – ratings that have boosted its overall ranking by 14 places to =18th. Sheffield (16th overall) and Canterbury Christ Church (59th) come second and third for the student experience, while Lincoln Bishop (73rd) and Teesside (55th) occupy the same spots for teaching quality – while Goldsmiths (105th) and Edinburgh (26th overall) come bottom for each respectively.

Most undergraduate programmes are accredited by the British Psychological Society, which ensures that key topics are covered, but the clinical and biological content of courses varies considerably. Some courses require maths and/or biology A-levels among three high grade passes, while others are much less demanding. The contrast is evident in the table, with 36 universities averaging at least 144 points in the UCAS tariff (equivalent to three As at A-level) and another 32 falling below 110 points.

The numbers of psychology students accepted onto courses grew by 50% in the decade up to 2018. Even after demand cooling since 2021 there were still over 114,000 applications to the subject in 2024, and over 26,000 new students were accepted onto courses. Immediate career prospects are unlikely to be what is attracting so many students: psychology ranks 68th in our 70-subject employment table, based on only half of graduates being employed in professional-level jobs and/or studying within 15 months of finishing their degrees. The proportion working in "low-skilled" jobs at this point after graduation (31.9%) is not far below the proportion that had secured full-time professional jobs (34.2%). Explaining this, commentators within psychology suggest that graduates may benefit from a more gradual transition into complex psychological roles, such as those involving direct work with clients and service users, and that experience gained in non-graduate jobs can help to build confidence and serve as stepping stones to putting their university-acquired skills into practice. Average graduate salaries of £23,000 rank the subject =62nd out of 70.

Psychology	Teaching quality %	Student experience %	Research quality %	Entry standards (UCAS points)	Graduate prospects %	Overall score
1 London School of Economics	84.7	87.9	86.2	192	-	100
2 St Andrews	83.6	83.2	61.8	202	90.6	99.5
3 Cambridge	84.6	84.6	75	200	83.3	99.4
4 University College London	85.4	87.5	73.2	170	84.2	98.2
5 Glasgow	85.4	86.2	65.8	209	73.4	97.5
6 Strathclyde	84	84.4	65.8	198	76.4	96.9
7 King's College London	82.7	81.8	69	171	79.3	95.5
=8 Bath	83.4	90.4	37.2	176	83.4	95.3
=8 Durham	84	84.7	50	165	84.4	95.3
10 Exeter	81.1	84.2	62.7	168	81.4	95.1
11 Warwick	85	86.1	57.5	157	79.1	94.8
12 York	84.4	85	69.2	152	76.5	94.6
13 Royal Holloway	84.3	87.8	74	143	75.1	94.4
14 Loughborough	79.2	87.1	66.8	153	81.1	94.3
15 Birmingham	83.1	87.7	64	145	77.7	94
16 Sheffield	85.8	92	62.7	149	70.8	93.9
17 Surrey	85.4	87.5	58	135	76.6	93.3
=18 Bristol	82.8	78.6	57.8	169	74.9	93.2
=18 Wales Trinity St David	96.2	93.6	1.2	148	77.5	93.2
20 Cardiff	76.6	75.3	68.8	165	80.9	93
21 Southampton	86.8	88.7	60.5	147	66.6	92.6
22 Glasgow Caledonian	85.8	81.3	61	167	63.1	92
23 Liverpool	79.4	87.4	65.5	148	71.3	91.9
24 Reading	80.7	82.3	56.2	133	79.6	91.7
25 East Anglia	81.4	88.6	60.8	124	75.1	91.6
26 Edinburgh	72.5	75.2	76.8	192	68.4	91.5
=27 Aston	88.4	89.2	46	119	72.2	91.4
=27 Leeds	82.3	82.2	53.2	159	70	91.4
29 Queen's, Belfast	86.2	90	31	154	69.6	91.2
30 Nottingham	77.9	84.5	52.2	153	73.7	90.9
31 Newcastle	76.4	79.1	55.2	155	76.5	90.8
32 Chichester	89.9	86.5	8	112	84.9	90.7
33 Leicester	84.1	88.2	55	123	68.7	90.4

Psychology cont.

	Teaching quality %	Student experience %	Research quality %	Entry standards (UCAS points)	Graduate prospects %	Overall score
34 Heriot-Watt	80.3	85.5	13.5	155	81.8	90.3
35 Manchester	75.6	79.4	62.7	155	71.9	90.2
36 Sussex	81.2	83.6	59.5	133	68.2	89.9
=37 Stirling	83.1	77.9	47.2	161	65.6	89.8
=37 Ulster	85.3	87	41.8	121	71.1	89.8
=39 Dundee	83.1	79.6	39	176	61.7	89.5
=39 Essex	83.5	84.9	56	120	67.4	89.5
41 Edinburgh Napier	88.1	85.6	-	151	74	89.4
=42 Bangor	83.3	84.6	47	117	71.5	89.3
=42 Lancaster	77.7	77.3	48.8	145	74.2	89.3
44 Sunderland	89.8	81.9	30.2	112	71.4	89.1
45 Swansea	82.6	85.4	30	131	73	89
46 Staffordshire	89.1	82	30.8	114	70.7	88.9
47 Abertay	91	90.7	21	151	56.4	88.8
48 Aberdeen	79.6	80.9	49	163	61.7	88.7
=49 Lincoln	82.2	84.9	39.5	118	71.9	88.6
=49 Northumbria	84.8	89	28	124	69.3	88.6
51 Portsmouth	85.7	85.5	40.8	112	68.1	88.5
52 Oxford Brookes	85.2	85.1	39	114	68.1	88.3
53 Manchester Metropolitan	85.7	85.3	36	129	63.8	88.2
54 City St George's	84	86.5	36	122	65.4	87.8
55 Teesside	92.6	89	7.2	98	70.7	87.7
56 Suffolk	88.9	78.1	-	97	84	87.6
=57 Liverpool Hope	88.7	88.5	32	110	61.3	87.4
=57 Nottingham Trent	82.6	84.6	39.2	114	67.2	87.4
59 Canterbury Christ Church	89.2	91	24	102	64.1	87.3
60 Kent	75.9	75.6	50.7	116	73.6	87
61 Plymouth	80.2	78.9	40.5	120	68.5	86.8
=62 Coventry	83.6	78.9	47	111	63.4	86.7
=62 Lancashire	83.5	84.3	30	108	68.3	86.7
=62 West of England	81.5	82	35.2	122	66	86.7
65 Keele	79.5	83.7	35.2	115	69.6	86.6
=66 Aberystwyth	88.3	86.2	12.5	113	63.3	86
=66 Liverpool John Moores	84.7	87	16.2	123	63.2	86
68 Edge Hill	82	82.5	18.8	116	69.3	85.9
=69 Leeds Beckett	86.5	85.9	21.5	117	59.2	85.6
=69 South Wales	86.1	85.8	-	113	69	85.6
=69 York St John	85.1	81.4	20.5	119	63.6	85.6
72 West London	89.5	89.8	-	108	63.5	85.5
73 Lincoln Bishop	94.7	86.3	6.2	94	60	85.4
74 Hull	81	75.6	40.5	103	66.8	85.3
=75 East London	82.9	82.7	23.2	103	67.1	85.2
=75 St Mary's, Twickenham	84.9	86.3	-	107	70.4	85.2
=77 Birmingham City	83.9	84.6	18.2	119	61.6	85.1

Rank	University						
=77	Brighton	85.3	83.1	34	108	57.8	85.1
79	Middlesex	84.6	83.7	30.2	96	62.1	84.9
80	Hertfordshire	83	82.7	39.8	106	57.9	84.8
=81	Chester	85.2	83.4	13	117	60.8	84.6
=81	Derby	86.3	84.8	10.2	106	62.8	84.6
83	Leeds Trinity	84.4	78.2	9.2	111	67.4	84.5
84	Queen Margaret, Edinburgh	77.4	78.1	21	160	57.5	84.4
85	Anglia Ruskin	82.4	81.9	25	93	66.2	84.3
86	London South Bank	84.2	79.7	18	100	65	84.2
=87	Brunel	81.9	83	23.2	105	61.8	84
=87	Greenwich	78.5	79.6	32.3	105	64.4	84
=87	Roehampton	83.2	83.6	37.5	96	56.7	84
90	Winchester	86.1	83.6	16.2	107	57.7	83.9
91	London Metropolitan	88.4	87.4	-	92	62.5	83.8
92	Birmingham Newman	85.1	86.4	3.5	88	66.6	83.7
=93	Huddersfield	82.4	77.6	22	114	60.1	83.6
=93	West of Scotland	90.2	82.8	13.2	118	49.5	83.6
=95	Bournemouth	75.1	76.1	22.8	104	71	83.2
=95	Greater Manchester	84.1	74.3	1.8	99	69.9	83.2
97	Bath Spa	83	78.5	7.2	95	67.6	83.1
=98	Gloucestershire	79.9	76.9	5	111	67	82.7
=98	Queen Mary, London	77.2	77	-	147	61.8	82.7
=98	Sheffield Hallam	77.5	74.7	26.8	113	62.2	82.7
=98	Worcester	78.4	74.8	19.2	109	64.9	82.7
102	De Montfort	82.5	83.6	20.5	90	59.2	82.6
=103	Cumbria	84	78.2	-	110	61.9	82.4
=103	Salford	78.5	77	37	116	53.7	82.4
105	Goldsmiths, London	73.8	67.4	35.5	118	64.2	82.3
=106	Bradford	79	76.8	8.2	112	63	82
=106	Westminster	77.2	80.4	24.8	101	60.1	82
=108	Kingston	80.1	80.1	20.5	103	57.1	81.8
=108	Southampton Solent	87.3	80.7	-	104	55	81.8
110	Wolverhampton	83	75	12.5	95	58.8	81.2
111	Cardiff Metropolitan	80.4	78.2	-	122	53.7	80.4
112	Bedfordshire	76.2	72.7	-	96	63.8	79.2
113	Northampton	76.1	73.3	8.5	96	51.4	77.4

Employed in high-skilled job	34%	Employed in lower-skilled job	32%
Employed in high-skilled job and studying	5%	Employed in lower-skilled job and studying	2%
Studying	9%	Unemployed	5%
High-skilled work (median) salary	£24,800	Low-/medium-skilled salary	£20,000

Radiography

Coventry takes the lead in this year's Radiography table, its rank boosted by some of the subject's most satisfied undergraduates: our analysis of the latest National Student Survey shows Coventry to place first for the broad experience and second for teaching quality. De Montfort, in =11th place of the main table, comes top for teaching quality, and Portsmouth (=15th) is in the top three for both metrics. Conversely, Cardiff (18th in the table) comes bottom for the student experience and Salford (26th) is at the foot of the table for teaching quality.

After three years at the top, Glasgow Caledonian is runner-up of our dedicated ranking for radiography degrees, now in its 13th edition having previously been listed among "Subjects Allied to Medicine" in the Guide. Glasgow Caledonian's entry standards are second only to the those at Robert Gordon, where entrants averaged 187 points in the UCAS tariff. Another former No 1 for radiography, Leeds, is =7th this year. Strength in research is unbeaten at Keele (=11th overall), which achieved the top scores in the recent Research Excellence Framework 2021, followed by Leeds.

There are two radiography disciplines – diagnostic and therapeutic, explains Dr Jane Harvey-Lloyd, associate professor in diagnostic radiography, School of Medicine, University of Leeds: "Diagnostics uses a range of imaging modalities to diagnose illness and disease. Therapeutics uses methods like ionising radiation to treat mainly cancer. New technology is continuously emerging, providing new ways to diagnose and treat illness and disease. AI technology is already impacting the field, and increasing its use will allow radiographers to put person-centred care at the forefront of their practice. If you are considering a dynamic career that combines cutting-edge technology with caring for others, radiography is for you."

Diagnostic courses usually involve two years of studying anatomy, physiology and physics, followed by further training in oncology, psycho-social studies and other modules. Candidates need at least one science A-level, or equivalent, usually biology. Graduates of radiography can rest assured that professional-level work is on the horizon soon after university, with radiography invariably featuring in the top 10 of our employment ranking – where it ranks fourth this year. Exeter, Leeds, Robert Gordon, Canterbury Christ Church, Teesside and Derby achieved perfect 100% graduate prospects scores, due to every one of their radiography graduates being employed in professional jobs and/or postgraduate study within 15 months. Only one university, City St George's, had fewer than nine in ten graduates achieving these outcomes at the same point. For pay, radiography compares less strongly with other subjects, but is comfortably in the upper half of our 70-subject salaries index (26th).

Radiography	Teaching quality %	Student experience %	Research quality %	Entry standards (UCAS points)	Graduate prospects %	Overall score
1 Coventry	95.9	94.8	47.2	169	-	100
2 Glasgow Caledonian	89.4	87.7	61	183	95.9	99.6
3 Bangor	88.3	84.7	59.8	147	-	97.5
4 Robert Gordon	83.8	76	24.5	187	100	96.1
=5 Exeter	83	74.5	53.2	135	100	94.9
=5 Liverpool	86.9	79.7	46.8	143	98.5	94.9
=7 Leeds	66.3	60.1	65	151	100	94.8
=7 Queen Margaret, Edinburgh	84.5	82.6	36.5	163	-	94.8
9 Ulster	84.5	81.7	53.5	136	96.1	93.8
10 Bradford	89.3	87.1	33.8	147	97	93.7
=11 De Montfort	96.1	90.7	20.8	148	-	93
=11 Keele	72.1	71.4	66.2	131	-	93
13 Plymouth	89.6	85.6	39.5	132	-	92.7
14 Hertfordshire	89.1	87.0	48	123	94.8	92.5
=15 Canterbury Christ Church	88.9	80.5	31.8	119	100	92
=15 Portsmouth	95.5	91.4	41.2	114	95.5	92

17	West of England	89.4	84	42.8	125	95.3	91.9
18	Cardiff	67.1	56.6	58.8	143	96.7	91.7
19	Birmingham City	79.4	77.5	37.8	152	94.6	91.6
20	Teesside	73.9	73.6	35	120	100	90.2
21	Derby	79.4	66.9	24	130	100	90.1
22	Brighton	69	62.1	50.5	137	-	89.9
23	City St George's	87.3	85.2	58	124	87.8	89.8
24	London South Bank	89.4	82.3	34.5	127	90.9	88.8
25	Cumbria	84.4	74.2	18.5	119	98.2	88.6
26	Salford	66.2	65.4	37	136	95.2	88.2
27	Sheffield Hallam	87	81.9	29.8	126	90.7	87.8
28	Suffolk	89.6	84.4	-	112	98.6	87.2

Employed in high-skilled job	88%	Employed in lower-skilled job	3%
Employed in high-skilled job and studying	3%	Employed in lower-skilled job and studying	0%
Studying	2%	Unemployed	2%
High-skilled work (median) salary	£26,404	Low-/medium-skilled salary	N/A

Russian and Eastern European Languages

Unusually among our subject rankings, there are no post-1992 universities in the Russian and Eastern European Languages table, which is populated exclusively by institutions with older foundations, led by Cambridge. The subjects attract tiny student cohorts on single honours programmes, though many others learn Russian as part of a broader modern languages degree. Now grouped by UCAS as "Slavic studies", the languages attracted just 610 applications in 2024 (a step up from 480 in 2023) and 165 new students were accepted onto courses (ten more than the year before). Most undergraduates learn Russian or another Eastern European language from scratch, and while there are no required subjects for entry to degrees, a language is useful.

"Studying Russian opens up a world of amazing cultural diversity with a dramatic past," says Dr Ruth Coates, associate professor in Russian religious thought, Department of Russian, University of Bristol, "The country's devastating war against Ukraine has shown the extent of its will to strengthen its geopolitical position in the world. In this context, specialists familiar with Russia's language, politics, history and culture, who are able to provide context and interpret its actions, are more needed than ever. Studying Russian opens up a world of amazing cultural diversity with a dramatic past."

Cambridge's lead is confirmed for a second consecutive year, having also enjoyed an eight-year run at the top of the table until Bristol took over for two editions. Cambridge's rank is buoyed by the highest rates of student satisfaction with teaching quality and the top graduate prospects. Bristol's research in the field remains unsurpassed however, our analysis of the Research Excellence Framework 2021 shows, while Nottingham is not far behind it on this measure, and Cambridge ranks third.

Despite the small numbers, entry standards are high throughout the table, and in a tightly packed grouping they go no lower than 151 points at Birmingham (eighth overall). The latest data shows ninth-place Queen Mary, London attracted the highest average entry standards (204 UCAS points). Russian and Eastern European languages rank =52nd of our 70-subject employment ranking, based on six in ten graduates being in high-skilled jobs and/or further study within 15 months. They compare better in the pay index, at =28th.

Russian and Eastern European Languages	Teaching quality %	Student experience %	Research quality %	Entry standards (UCAS points)	Graduate prospects %	Overall score
1 Cambridge	92.5	70.6	61	198	91.5	100
2 Bristol	90.5	76.7	64	166	-	97.5
=3 Oxford	82.2	84.8	45.8	195	-	94.7
=3 University College London	89	68.5	51.2	178	-	94.7
5 Durham	84.6	81.9	56	156	91.3	94.5
6 Manchester	87.2	77.1	46	173	85.6	94.3
7 Exeter	85.7	80.8	59.5	152	-	93.7
8 Birmingham	84.3	80.6	50	151	82.8	92.4
9 Queen Mary, London	85.8	77.3	25.5	204	42.1	90.1

Employed in high-skilled job	42%	Employed in lower-skilled job	29%
Employed in high-skilled job and studying	8%	Employed in lower-skilled job and studying	2%
Studying	9%	Unemployed	3%
High-skilled work (median) salary	£26,500	Low-/medium-skilled salary	N/A

Social Policy

Social policy students analyse how societies respond to the challenges of social, demographic and economic change. "How effectively do societies ensure that everyone has what they need to lead a good life? How could we do better?" asks Kitty Stewart, professor of social policy, London School of Economics and Political Science (LSE), "Education, health, housing, employment, poverty and inequality are all core subjects for social policy students. We also think about the new challenges posed by migration, an ageing population and the climate crisis. Perhaps you've studied economics, politics or sociology at A-level and are most interested in the aspects of these disciplines that are about making a practical difference to people's lives. If so, social policy might be just what you are looking for." Many undergraduates take joint honours degrees – such as pairings with politics or modern languages – or within wider social sciences programmes.

The LSE occupies its accustomed place at the top of our Social Policy table this year, its rank helped by an established research strength in the field: LSE leads in our analysis of the Research Excellence Framework (REF) 2021, just as it did in the previous REF 2014 exercise. LSE is also in front for graduate prospects, with the latest data showing 85.2% working in high-skilled jobs and/or further study within 15 months. There has been plenty of movement elsewhere in the table: Bath, which toppled LSE from the No 1 spot three years ago and ranked third two years ago, is now in ninth place (up eight places since our previous edition). Seven-place improvements bring University College London into the runner-up spot and Edinburgh up to third; Bristol is up four places to joint fourth, while Glasgow is down four to rank sixth – but still averages the highest entry standards among social policy students, of 206 UCAS points. Eight universities averaged upwards of 144 UCAS points (equivalent to three As at A-level) and there are usually no required subjects for entry.

In our new National Student Survey analysis, Wales Trinity St David (=16th overall) ranks top for teaching quality, followed by Salford (14th) and Bedfordshire (13th), while for the wider experience Staffordshire (22nd), Coventry (11th and the highest-ranked modern university in the table) and Bristol occupy the top three places.

Having remained steady for around a decade or so, demand for the subject has dipped: in

2024 it attracted 5,250 applications with 1,305 undergraduates accepted onto courses.

Not all social policy graduates progress immediately into top careers, and the subject overall ranks 62nd in our employment table. When surveyed 15 months after their degrees, a third of social policy graduates were working full-time in jobs classified as "low-skilled" and not many more (40.1%) were employed in full-time professional-level jobs. The trend is reflected in our table, where at three universities (Northampton, Bedfordshire and West of Scotland) only a little over half of the graduates had found professional work or continued studying 15 months after their degrees. At one, Ulster, this proportion falls to 41.6%. Earnings compare more strongly with other subjects, ranking =56th in our pay index.

Social Policy	Teaching quality %	Student experience %	Research quality %	Entry standards (UCAS points)	Graduate prospects %	Overall score
1 London School of Economics	84.7	86.1	86.2	179	85.2	100
2 University College London	87.1	86.1	61.5	149	-	94.6
3 Edinburgh	84.5	78.5	55.2	184	-	94.5
=4 Bristol	83.7	87.3	77.8	141	66	93.3
=4 Strathclyde	83.3	81.8	43.8	201	69.1	93.3
6 Glasgow	76.3	73.2	62	206	71.7	93
7 Queen's, Belfast	86.2	85.9	56.5	140	-	92.7
8 Birmingham	83.2	81.5	61	143	73.1	92.1
9 Bath	84.1	75.6	59.5	153	-	91.8
10 York	81.6	77.6	58	133	77.9	91.1
11 Coventry	88	87.4	39.5	136	-	91
12 Plymouth	84.4	81.2	50.5	-	69.7	90.5
13 Bedfordshire	91.5	86	50.2	-	51.6	89.8
14 Salford	92	81.2	44.5	111	65.3	89.6
15 Cardiff	82.7	83.4	54	125	-	89.5
=16 Leeds	78.6	80	48.5	146	72.5	89.4
=16 Sheffield	84.1	86.1	36.8	136	69.9	89.4
=16 Wales Trinity St David	92.6	80.1	11.8	-	75	89.4
=19 Lancaster	85.7	77.2	51.5	110	-	88
=19 Stirling	76.5	78.3	47.5	157	-	88
21 Portsmouth	83.7	83.8	33	128	-	87.3
22 Staffordshire	90.1	89.2	18.2	92	69.1	86.7
23 Nottingham Trent	85.1	83.4	29.5	111	-	85.9
24 De Montfort	84	67.7	43.2	101	67.4	85.3
25 Edge Hill	86.1	86.8	17.5	108	-	84.9
26 West of Scotland	90.4	76.1	13.2	125	50	83.6
27 Hertfordshire	77.9	72	48	106	-	83.5
=28 South Wales	80.5	74.5	33.5	113	-	83.4
=28 Ulster	84.3	77.3	53.8	105	41.6	83.4
30 Bangor	80.2	70	33.2	120	-	83.1
31 Southampton Solent	86.1	84.1	9.5	100	-	82.6
32 Lincoln	74.5	75.2	51	96	-	82.2
33 Wolverhampton	80.1	74.5	12.2	98	-	79.1
34 Northampton	80.4	79.9	-	94	52.9	78.3

Employed in high-skilled job	40%	Employed in lower-skilled job	33%
Employed in high-skilled job and studying	4%	Employed in lower-skilled job and studying	1%
Studying	7%	Unemployed	5%
High-skilled work (median) salary	£25,000	Low-/medium-skilled salary	£21,000

Social Work

In a table often characterised by universities rising and falling in the rankings, an 11-place leap brings Essex to the No 1 spot, boosted by strong performance across the board – including top ten ratings for the student experience and teaching quality and the fifth-best graduate prospects. Lancaster is down three places to rank fourth this year and Queen's, Belfast is up four places in the runner-up position. Bristol, in eighth place overall, was the top scorer in the field in the Research Excellence Framework 2021, followed by Kent (last year's runner-up but down nine places to rank 11th this year) and then East Anglia (up 11 places to rank third overall).

In our latest National Student Survey analysis Teesside ranks =29th overall and outdoes all 72 other universities in the Social Work table for the broad undergraduate experience, where it is followed by London South Bank (=15th overall), while for students' feedback on teaching quality the same two universities swap places. At the opposite end of the scale, Wolverhampton (in 73rd) fares worst for both teaching quality and the broader experience.

Led by Glasgow Caledonian, which registered 97.7% of graduates in professional-level jobs and/or furthering their studies within 15 months, 19 universities had more than 90% of graduates achieving these looked-for career outcomes. The Frontline programme, modelled on Teach First, aims to attract graduates of other subjects to train in the profession, and degree apprenticeships offer another social work route (though these are not profiled here), but social work degrees are still the main pathway to careers. It comes as a surprise to some that graduate salaries for those with a social work degree compare very favourably with other subject areas. Average early career salaries of £29,885 rank social work 13th in our 70-subject pay index. It is comfortably in the upper half of the graduate table too, in 30th place. Added to the relative job security is a sense of purpose, as explained by Professor Anne Campbell, programme director of the master's in substance use and substance use disorders, School of Social Sciences, Education and Social Work, Queen's University Belfast: "Social work is 'a practice-based profession and an academic discipline that promotes social change and development, social cohesion and the empowerment and liberation of people' (International Federation of Social Workers, 2014). A career in social work will make a positive difference in the lives of children, young people, adults and older people. You will promote social justice in health and social care settings, and in education, criminal justice and the voluntary sector. You will be supported in practice and with continuous personal and professional development opportunities throughout your career." Applications and enrolments were up by around 4% in 2024, re-gaining some of the momentum lost the year before, but the demand for social work courses was at its second lowest for the past six years.

Social Work	Teaching quality %	Student experience %	Research quality %	Entry standards (UCAS points)	Graduate prospects %	Overall score
1 Essex	94.6	91.7	62.5	128	95.6	100
2 Queen's, Belfast	88.3	81.8	56.5	140	94.8	98.7
3 East Anglia	85.9	79.2	69.8	131	95.8	98.6
4 Lancaster	91.1	88.5	60.2	140	86.2	98.4

=5	Bath	81.6	86.3	59.5	145	92.1	98.2
=5	Dundee	90.6	82.6	28.5	158	94.3	98.2
7	Strathclyde	84.6	74.1	43.8	170	84.1	97.8
8	Bristol	80.2	83.5	77.8	146	80.8	97.7
=9	Bangor	92.1	89.9	59.8	119	-	96.4
=9	Nottingham	84.7	80.1	54	138	91.4	96.4
11	Kent	90.8	80.1	72.2	113	90.5	96.1
12	Salford	90.6	80.1	44.5	127	95.1	95.4
13	Glasgow Caledonian	91.4	88.4	26	131	97.7	95.1
14	Hull	94.1	88.5	53.8	127	79.5	94.8
=15	London South Bank	96.9	94.6	27.8	127	86.7	94
=15	Sussex	91.2	89.5	41	131	83.3	94
17	Hertfordshire	84	86.1	48	128	88.6	93.7
18	Lancashire	91.2	86.5	51.5	120	83.5	93.6
=19	Manchester Metropolitan	94.3	92	32.8	129	81.9	93.1
=19	Teesside	96.6	94.6	18.2	126	89.1	93.1
21	Keele	95.2	92	33.2	117	87	92.7
22	Ulster	89.1	86.1	53.8	119	80.3	92.5
23	Plymouth	81.4	82.9	50.5	125	85.7	92.2
24	Huddersfield	94.8	88.1	43.5	119	76.6	91.7
25	Brighton	89.4	77.9	34	117	92	91.4
=26	Staffordshire	87.9	85.6	18.2	123	94.7	91.1
=26	Suffolk	93.1	77.3	21.8	-	91.1	91.1
28	Portsmouth	89.7	92.4	33	111	88.3	90.9
29	Kingston	95.8	93.3	38.5	110	79.4	90.8
=30	Robert Gordon	92.1	91.9	-	129	93.1	90.7
=30	York	76.1	64.7	58	129	-	90.7
32	Northumbria	83.2	81.8	42	133	74.3	90.1
33	Birmingham City	87.7	84.6	25.8	129	80.3	89.8
34	Middlesex	88.7	82	27.8	107	92.8	89.5
35	Bournemouth	87.4	74.5	10.2	130	91.4	89.4
36	West London	87.7	84.4	39	124	73.3	89.3
37	Swansea	85.6	81.8	46.5	117	75.6	89
38	Southampton Solent	94	84.2	9.5	110	93.2	88.8
39	Lincoln	84.7	71.5	51	113	76.9	88.3
40	Liverpool Hope	89.5	84.3	21.2	112	85.3	88.1
41	West of England	70.7	68.4	35.2	118	96.4	87.9
42	South Wales	81.9	74.7	33.5	-	84	87.6
43	Goldsmiths, London	84.6	74.5	48	91	88.9	87.4
44	West of Scotland	90.6	81.3	13.2	116	83.5	87.1
=45	Anglia Ruskin	83.8	73.5	30	98	93.4	86.8
=45	East London	82.8	74.8	40	108	81.2	86.8
47	Chichester	92.4	84.1	3	117	83.7	86.7
48	Wrexham	89.1	80	20.5	-	79.3	86.6
49	Greenwich	88	80.8	17	118	78.4	86.3
50	Coventry	87.3	82.8	-	127	81.4	86
51	Nottingham Trent	86.9	75.6	29.5	110	75.5	85.5
52	Leeds Beckett	87.5	83	17.8	118	73.8	85.4

Social Work cont.

	Teaching quality %	Student experience %	Research quality %	Entry standards (UCAS points)	Graduate prospects %	Overall score
53 De Montfort	75.4	68.7	43.2	105	83.2	85.1
54 Chester	87.3	68.3	12.8	-	85	85
55 Sunderland	90.6	84.9	39.5	110	58.7	84.7
56 Liverpool John Moores	77.3	79.6	15.8	126	-	84.5
57 Cardiff Metropolitan	86.9	85.8	-	112	82.2	84
=58 Derby	90.4	78.2	25.5	109	64.8	83.4
=58 Edge Hill	81.4	70.7	17.5	118	75.4	83.4
=60 Canterbury Christ Church	82.7	72.9	31.8	110	69.6	83.3
=60 Sheffield Hallam	67.1	54.1	26.2	130	81.6	83.3
62 Gloucestershire	68.9	55.3	16.2	108	97.2	82.5
63 Leeds Trinity	94.5	91	-	100	70.7	81.8
64 Wolverhampton	86.2	79.8	12.2	108	69.1	81.6
65 Oxford Brookes	70.2	65.1	37.8	99	80.6	81.5
66 Winchester	83.5	67	16.5	112	70.1	81.3
67 Bedfordshire	92.1	87.2	50.2	81	52.7	81
68 Buckinghamshire New	89.4	81.3	12.5	101	63.7	80.2
69 Northampton	86.4	81	-	102	68.5	79.1
70 Greater Manchester	88.2	77.8	-	115	57.4	78.8
71 Birmingham Newman	96.1	92	13.8	83	52.5	77.5
72 London Metropolitan	80.7	75.1	-	95	65.6	75.6
73 Wolverhampton	57.7	50.5	8.2	108	-	70.6

Employed in high-skilled job	61%	Employed in lower-skilled job	19%
Employed in high-skilled job and studying	4%	Employed in lower-skilled job and studying	1%
Studying	4%	Unemployed	4%
High-skilled work (median) salary	£30,007	Low-/medium-skilled salary	£20,838

Sociology

The study of human social relationships and institutions, "Sociology encourages a profound and creative examination of the world," explains Professor Sam Friedman, professor of sociology, London School of Economics and Political Science, "It trains you to question assumptions that are taken for granted, delve beneath the surface and think critically about how society is organised and how we experience our lives. In particular it enables an exploration of the multiple forms of power and inequality that shape the world today, and how they affect the lives of all of us."

The most applied-to subject within the social sciences grouping (for now – economics is hot on its heels), sociology attracted over 67,200 applications in 2024 and nearly 14,200 new undergraduates were accepted onto courses. Such levels are despite a 12% year-on-year decline in applications and a 10% dip in new starter numbers – their fourth successive downturn. There are not usually any required subjects, though the leading universities look for a broad selection of humanities A-levels – from classics and ancient history to English and psychology.

With entry standards across our table of 87 universities ranging from 196 UCAS tariff points averaged by entrants at Oxford to 31 institutions where entrants averaged fewer than 110 points, there are broad options for applicants. Cambridge is the top-ranked university to study sociology for the sixth consecutive year; its overall rank boosted by the second-highest entry standards and graduate prospects that are just behind Durham – which registered 88.7% of sociology graduates in high-skilled jobs and/or further study within 15 months. Tenth-place Loughborough has the edge for research in sociology – based on results of the Research Excellence Framework 2021. Glasgow Caledonian is the top-ranked post-1992 university, in 25th place.

Our analysis of the latest National Student Survey (NSS) shows the best rates of student satisfaction with teaching quality to be found at West of Scotland (ranked 42nd in the table), followed by Brunel (=50th) and Liverpool Hope (68th). For students' evaluation of the broader undergraduate experience Loughborough is in front, with Manchester Metropolitan and Brunel close behind it. Goldsmiths finishes last for both of these NSS-based metrics, and ranks higher than only Anglia Ruskin in the main table.

Courses cover topics such as gender roles, multiculturalism, media and culture, and can include options to study criminology or social policy. The subject's academic breadth may be the source of its popularity, as it tends to offer little immediate gratification in terms of graduate prospects. In the new employment table, sociology ranks 66th out of 70 subject areas and it places =56th in our salaries ranking.

Sociology	Teaching quality %	Student experience %	Research quality %	Entry standards (UCAS points)	Graduate prospects %	Overall score
1 Cambridge	83.8	70.5	69.2	195	87	100
2 Oxford	85.9	75	70.5	196	-	99.8
=3 Durham	85.7	79.7	53	168	88.7	98.2
=3 London School of Economics	89.7	86.8	61	162	-	98.2
5 Lancaster	89.6	88.5	60.2	144	-	96.6
6 King's College London	86.8	81.9	57	146	82.6	96.3
7 Glasgow	80	75	62	188	75.7	95.8
8 Warwick	85.6	82.3	53.8	144	81.1	95.2
9 Bath	85.4	82.3	59.5	148	76.3	95
10 Loughborough	85.8	90.1	71.8	134	70	94.9
11 Surrey	91.3	87.2	48	126	76.9	94.5
12 York	85.1	83.6	68.5	140	70.4	94.2
13 Nottingham	86.6	86.1	54	135	74.2	93.8
=14 Exeter	83	83	46.8	150	75.8	93.2
=14 Queen's, Belfast	87.5	84	56.5	130	71.7	93.2
=14 Southampton	85.3	84.1	66.8	132	68.5	93.2
17 Sheffield	87	86.7	36.8	140	74.8	92.7
18 Essex	86.9	82.1	62.5	134	65.8	92.5
19 Aberdeen	83.6	83.3	37	168	69.1	92.3
20 Bristol	82.1	82.3	49	151	71	92.1
=21 Birmingham	81.2	84.3	61	137	68.8	91.9
=21 Swansea	87.4	87.3	46.5	126	-	91.9
=23 Aston	86.5	88.1	42.5	115	74.1	91.3
=23 Stirling	80.6	81.8	47.5	174	61.5	91.3
25 Glasgow Caledonian	86.8	84.6	26	165	65.5	91.2

Sociology cont.

	Teaching quality %	Student experience %	Research quality %	Entry standards (UCAS points)	Graduate prospects %	Overall score
26 Manchester	79.6	78.3	67.2	142	65.5	91.1
=27 Cardiff	82.7	83.3	54	135	67.3	90.9
=27 Sussex	84.8	79.9	55	127	68.3	90.9
29 University College London	83.9	83.6	-	151	85.7	90.8
30 Edinburgh	74.5	77.2	53.5	176	65.5	90.6
31 City St George's	81.3	82.5	64	115	68.9	90.4
32 Plymouth	83.4	80.4	50.5	112	74.6	90.3
33 Newcastle	84.7	86	42.5	148	60.6	90.2
34 Leeds	78.5	81	48.5	143	69.6	90
35 Liverpool	81.3	83.5	55	127	66.6	89.9
=36 Leicester	85.1	86	48	108	65.8	89
=36 Queen Margaret, Edinburgh	89.6	87.1	7.8	147	65.4	89
38 Portsmouth	84.4	84.5	33	112	71.3	88.6
=39 Nottingham Trent	86.6	83.6	29.5	103	73.6	88.5
=39 Royal Holloway	82.3	82.1	38	115	71.3	88.5
=39 Suffolk	86.7	78	21.8	110	77.6	88.5
42 West of Scotland	93.4	86.9	13.2	113	65	88.1
43 Northumbria	71.8	67.9	42	120	86.7	87.9
44 Liverpool John Moores	87.8	87.6	22.2	108	66.7	87.5
=45 Keele	86.5	82.3	33.2	125	59.5	87.4
=45 Kent	77	73.8	72.2	107	63.6	87.4
47 Canterbury Christ Church	89.8	86	13.2	-	64.2	87.2
48 Manchester Metropolitan	88.2	88.9	29	114	57	86.8
49 Huddersfield	84.6	81.8	43.5	102	61.7	86.7
=50 Brunel	91.5	88.6	30.8	106	53.8	86.6
=50 Roehampton	80.2	77.7	40.2	-	66	86.6
52 Ulster	86.7	81	53.8	106	52	86.5
=53 Oxford Brookes	85.3	83.4	27.5	106	65.2	86.4
=53 York St John	90.9	83.3	10	103	67.4	86.4
55 Chester	87.9	88.4	12.8	113	-	86.3
56 Coventry	85.2	77.6	39.5	96	63.4	85.9
=57 Abertay	85.6	79.8	13.5	-	68.2	85.8
=57 Bournemouth	82.3	79.4	10.2	108	76	85.8
59 Robert Gordon	88.5	85.4	-	136	59.3	85.7
60 Bangor	82.3	74.5	33.2	118	-	85.6
61 Derby	86.1	81.4	-	106	74.7	85.5
62 Edinburgh Napier	81.7	78.3	-	146	66.9	85.3
63 Hertfordshire	77.9	72	48	115	-	85.2
64 Worcester	88.7	83.2	12.8	104	-	85
65 Salford	81.2	80.9	44.5	112	54.2	84.8
66 Edge Hill	88	87.6	-	106	64.3	84.6
67 Kingston	83.2	84.1	27	97	-	84.3
68 Liverpool Hope	91.4	85.7	-	112	56.7	84.2
=69 Lancashire	87.1	80.4	-	107	66.8	84.1

=69	Teesside	88.5	80.2	18.2	92	-	84.1
=69	West of England	82.1	79	35.2	115	54	84.1
72	Birmingham City	86.2	84.9	21	110	52.6	83.8
73	Greenwich	82.5	81.5	-	103	70.3	83.4
74	Leeds Beckett	81.4	83.2	17.8	101	62	83.3
75	Sheffield Hallam	85.4	79	-	103	62.7	82.4
=76	East London	81.2	75.8	26.8	106	55.4	82.3
=76	Westminster	85.8	84.3	-	103	58.7	82.3
78	Gloucestershire	79.6	68.5	24.5	95	65.2	82.1
79	Brighton	84.1	80.7	34	101	44.9	81.8
80	Winchester	81.9	77.8	-	93	67.1	81.4
81	Bath Spa	83.1	82.6	-	100	58.9	81.1
82	South Wales	82.6	74.7	-	111	56.9	80.5
83	Middlesex	85.6	82	-	103	50.7	80.3
84	Lincoln	77.8	79.8	-	104	59.8	79.8
85	Northampton	79.1	78.8	4.2	95	58.2	79.5
86	Goldsmiths, London	65.9	54.7	52.5	107	58.6	79.2
87	Anglia Ruskin	76.1	60.9	35.5	78	50.7	77.1

Employed in high-skilled job	36%	Employed in lower-skilled job	32%
Employed in high-skilled job and studying	4%	Employed in lower-skilled job and studying	1%
Studying	9%	Unemployed	7%
High-skilled work (median) salary	£25,500	Low-/medium-skilled salary	£21,000

Sports Science

The best university sports facilities do not always equate to top outcomes in the academic discipline of sport science – but they can help, such as the laboratories in which performance, endurance and recovery are closely monitored. Loughborough, the most famous name in university sport, podiums in fourth place of our table overall. Though not an ingredient of our ranking, Loughborough's superb facilities are the training hub for countless elite sportspeople, and with Loughborough-linked athletes returning home from the Paris 2024 Olympics with 16 medals, if Loughborough University were a country, it would have outperformed nations including Brazil, Austria and South Africa.

Fittingly, sports science is one of our more competitive subject rankings, with ranks changing hands regularly. Success in this context is universities' performance in sports degree courses and research, rather than the standard of their sports facilities or their teams' victories. Having finished second to Glasgow for the past five years, Bath lifts the cup in our new Sports Science table – its third No 1 since 2017, during which period the table has also been led by Birmingham, Exeter and Loughborough. Bath benefits from a top ten rate of student satisfaction with the broad undergraduate experience and a top 20 finish for teaching quality as well as graduate prospects and research quality ratings that rank in the top four universities. Fifth-place overall, Exeter leads the field for research in sports science by a clear margin, based on results of the Research Excellence Framework 2021. Following it for research quality are King's College London (sixth in the table) and Bangor (11th). Nottingham has placed second to Loughborough in the British Universities and Colleges Sport (BUCS) points table for the four years up to 2024-25. But it has pipped its rival to the post in our academic ranking, boosted by a three-place rise that places Nottingham third this year.

In our new National Student Survey analysis Greater Manchester (=52nd overall), Northampton (66th) and Lancaster (19th) are the top three universities for teaching quality, in descending order. For the wider experience Greater Manchester takes the lead again, followed by Aberdeen (14th) and Coventry (=12th).

Dr Adam Brazil, lecturer in sports biomechanics, University of Bath, says sports science connects learning to real world settings and "provides an exciting framework to explore scientific disciplines such as human physiology, biomechanics and psychology, knowledge of which you may have the opportunity to apply during a professional work placement."

Sport and exercise sciences have been one of the big growth areas of UK higher education over the past 15 years or so. Applications increased to 66,750 for 2024 entry and new student enrolments were over 16,000, despite a second consecutive dip. Many courses involve more science and less physical activity than some candidates expect, and the leading universities look for the sciences and maths at A-level. Sports science ranks 46th out of the 70 subjects in our employment table, based on 62.1% of graduates being in high-skilled jobs and/or furthering their studies within 15 months. Early career salaries stack up less favourably, in =56th place.

Sports Science	Teaching quality %	Student experience %	Research quality %	Entry standards (UCAS points)	Graduate prospects %	Overall score
1 Bath	91.6	92.8	73.2	161	84.7	100
2 Glasgow	81.5	70.4	68.5	211	-	98.2
3 Nottingham	90.2	92.9	61	156	82.8	97.6
4 Loughborough	82.4	85.4	66.8	162	86.6	97
5 Exeter	82.3	86.3	84	152	81.2	96.6
6 King's College London	85.4	82.8	80.2	150	-	96.5
7 Surrey	92.7	92.5	58	127	84.4	96.2
8 Durham	91.1	89.6	61	164	75.5	96.1
9 Swansea	93.9	93.5	48.2	128	83.8	95.6
10 Birmingham	83.9	83.4	73.2	144	78.7	94.4
11 Bangor	91	92.9	73.8	136	69.5	94
=12 Coventry	94.8	94.2	24.8	118	87.3	93.8
=12 Newcastle	90.2	86.8	50.7	145	77.5	93.8
14 Aberdeen	90.9	94.4	30.5	153	-	93.7
15 Chichester	90.7	84.2	33.2	124	87.6	93.2
=16 Liverpool John Moores	88	85.6	60.8	133	76.8	93.1
=16 Manchester Metropolitan	85.2	83.4	51.2	132	83.9	93.1
18 Strathclyde	93.5	94	-	204	70	92.9
19 Lancaster	95.2	91.1	55	121	72.7	92.8
20 Edinburgh	80.4	78.3	55	186	70.8	92.3
21 Salford	93	86	37	135	75.8	91.9
=22 Brighton	89	86.1	45.5	119	79.5	91.6
=22 Cardiff Metropolitan	87	84.1	43.8	132	79.2	91.6
24 Edge Hill	88.8	86.8	32.5	132	80.3	91.5
=25 Leeds Beckett	87.8	86.4	49.2	128	75.3	91.2
=25 Portsmouth	86.5	84.3	57.5	119	76.8	91.2
=27 Brunel	85.7	86.4	50.5	117	79.5	91.1
=27 Stirling	83.4	80.9	36.5	172	73.2	91.1

29 St Mary's, Twickenham	85.5	83.1	46	113	83.1	91
30 Northumbria	82	80.6	60.5	137	74.5	90.8
31 Teesside	92.8	85.9	35	112	78.6	90.7
32 Worcester	91.4	86.6	15.2	119	84.1	90.6
33 Essex	88.9	89.7	32.5	155	68.6	90.5
34 Canterbury Christ Church	93.3	89.8	38	112	74.6	90.4
=35 Abertay	91.5	89.3	19.8	148	72.5	90.3
=35 Leeds	67.2	72.2	65.8	146	84.5	90.3
=35 Roehampton	90.9	92.3	37.5	95	80.5	90.3
=38 Lincoln	92.3	90.6	30.8	117	75.4	90.2
=38 Sheffield Hallam	86.4	80.7	45.2	125	77.1	90.2
40 Oxford Brookes	90.6	82.4	37.8	114	78	90.1
=41 Buckinghamshire New	95	89.7	22.8	97	80.5	89.8
=41 Gloucestershire	91.7	85.2	24.5	111	80.7	89.8
=41 South Wales	88.3	80.7	45.8	117	75.9	89.8
=44 Hertfordshire	83.5	80.6	48	118	77.7	89.4
=44 Nottingham Trent	88	88.3	36.8	116	75.5	89.4
=46 Robert Gordon	90.4	87	-	166	72	89.2
=46 York St John	91	85.2	27.5	119	75.5	89.2
=48 Bournemouth	82.7	81.4	41.8	122	78.2	89.1
=48 Liverpool Hope	91.1	85.6	13.8	129	76.9	89.1
=48 Ulster	81.5	75.1	43.2	137	76.6	89.1
51 Hull	95	89.4	47.2	117	62.7	88.9
=52 Greater Manchester	98.4	95.4	-	125	71.8	88.8
=52 Greenwich	87.2	74.1	32.3	104	83.9	88.8
=52 Lancashire	91.4	88.9	19.2	123	74	88.8
=52 West of Scotland	89.3	87.5	29	142	67.9	88.8
56 Southampton Solent	92.8	90.9	18.5	117	73.1	88.5
=57 Bedfordshire	93.6	89.2	22	82	80.2	88.2
=57 Hartpury	90.5	85.3	15.8	122	75.6	88.2
59 London South Bank	89.3	89.6	32.2	101	-	87.7
=60 Staffordshire	90.4	83.4	30.8	124	67.8	87.5
=60 Winchester	88.5	82.3	20.8	118	75.3	87.5
62 Plymouth Marjon	89	86.5	20	126	70.1	87.3
63 Edinburgh Napier	76.5	75	23.5	156	75.4	87.1
=64 Derby	92.2	89.1	-	114	75.4	86.9
=64 Wolverhampton	90.4	85	25.2	106	72.1	86.9
66 Northampton	96.1	93.2	5	108	69.7	86.7
=67 Chester	83.3	77.6	15.8	126	75.8	86.1
=67 Kingston	88.4	90.3	38.5	114	61.8	86.1
69 Birmingham City	90	86.9	-	123	70.8	85.6
70 Suffolk	87.4	83	-	112	76.9	85.4
71 Leeds Trinity	79.9	73.8	18	105	81.9	85.2
72 Aberystwyth	81.8	77.1	48.8	95	-	85.1
73 East Anglia	88.8	88.2	-	129	67.4	84.9
74 Middlesex	87	83.8	16	104	71.4	84.8
75 Sunderland	84	76.7	22	135	63.6	84.2
76 Kent	82.9	80.5	37.2	119	62	84.1

Sports Science cont.

	Teaching quality %	Student experience %	Research quality %	Entry standards (UCAS points)	Graduate prospects %	Overall score
77 Anglia Ruskin	89.9	86.5	18.5	104	63.5	83.9
78 Huddersfield	82.4	73.2	22.2	111	70.9	83.6
79 Wales Trinity St David	86.2	74.3	11.8	102	70.6	82.9
80 East London	89	83	-	120	57.3	81.1
81 Birmingham Newman	82.5	80	13.2	84	-	80.1
82 Cumbria	83.5	79.6	-	106	61.1	79.4

Employed in high-skilled job	46%	Employed in lower-skilled job	24%
Employed in high-skilled job and studying	5%	Employed in lower-skilled job and studying	1%
Studying	9%	Unemployed	3%
High-skilled work (median) salary	£25,000	Low-/medium-skilled salary	£20,500

Subjects Allied to Medicine

A wide range of degrees is encompassed within the Subjects Allied to Medicine table. They include audiology, complementary therapies, counselling, health services management, health sciences, nutrition, occupational therapy, optometry, ophthalmology, orthoptics, osteopathy, podiatry and speech therapy. Physiotherapy and radiography have rankings of their own. Not all the universities that feature in this table offer all of the subjects that fall under the broad "allied to medicine" heading, and performance in our ranking is naturally influenced by which specialisms are offered.

In a top three of Scottish universities Glasgow Caledonian takes the lead, ousting Strathclyde into second place, while Glasgow is down one to rank third this year. Led by Glasgow – where entrants averaged 221 UCAS points – the same three universities have the highest entry standards, driven in part by Scottish universities benefitting from the favourable tariff conversion for Scottish secondary qualifications. A two-place rise brings Cardiff into fourth place, and the highest-ranked university south of the border.

The post-1992 universities represent more than half of the table, but only Glasgow Caledonian places in the top 10. King's College London sits =12th overall but its strength in research is unsurpassed, based on results of the Research Excellence Framework 2021. Manchester (fifth overall), Southampton (11th) and 17th-place Bristol follow it for research quality.

In our National Student Survey (NSS) analysis, Glasgow Caledonian is rated top for teaching quality and the wider experience by its students, in rankings that see Edinburgh Napier (15th in the table) and West of Scotland (=43rd) fill second and third places respectively for teaching quality. For the wider undergraduate experience, Strathclyde and St Mary's, Twickenham (=57th in the main table) are second and third. Conversely, Brunel comes bottom for both for the second consecutive year, and ranks =81st overall.

For entry in 2024, a second consecutive increase brought applications to ophthalmics degrees near to 5,600, and after a one-year dip in demand for counselling, psychotherapy and occupational therapy courses the subjects regained momentum, attracting almost 7,700 applications (up 4%). Applications to nutrition and dietetics degrees remained almost the same year on year (around 4,700 – 15% fewer than two years ago), and in complementary and alternative medicine (1,845 applications in 2024). The best rates of graduate employment are found jointly at Buckinghamshire New and Wrexham – where 97.4% of graduates were in high-skilled work or postgraduate study within 15 months – while 31 universities in total had at least nine in 10 graduates achieving the same outcomes. At just three, Middlesex, East London and Roehampton, this proportion falls below 70%. Their generally solid job prospects rank the subjects allied to medicine 10th in our 70-subject employment table (up from 24th last year) though pay falls outside the top half of subjects – with average graduate salaries of £25,655, placing the subjects 42nd.

Subjects Allied to Medicine	Teaching quality %	Student experience %	Research quality %	Entry standards (UCAS points)	Graduate prospects %	Overall score
1 Glasgow Caledonian	97.6	95	61	185	91.6	100
2 Strathclyde	86.5	90.9	65.8	196	87.4	97.5
3 Glasgow	80.5	81.4	63.5	221	86.9	97
4 Cardiff	87	86.2	58.8	156	97.1	95.4
5 Manchester	87.4	86	71.2	143	90.4	94.1
=6 Lancaster	89.5	88.1	55	147	91.1	93.5
=6 University College London	81.4	79.8	57.8	172	91.8	93.5
8 Swansea	89.8	85.2	66.8	136	89.3	93.3
9 Dundee	86.1	83.8	60.8	181	78.3	92.8
10 East Anglia	87.7	85.8	55.5	132	94.5	92.5
11 Southampton	82	79.7	69.8	142	90.9	92.2
=12 City St George's	86.8	81.1	58	135	93.7	92.1
=12 King's College London	80.8	80.6	76.2	166	79.8	92.1
14 Robert Gordon	87.8	87	24.5	171	92	91.9
15 Edinburgh Napier	93.6	90.4	40.5	139	86	91.2
16 Northumbria	91.3	86.6	53.5	134	84.6	91
17 Bristol	78.7	76.2	68.7	171	80.5	90.9
18 Nottingham	84.8	79.8	57.9	149	84.8	90.7
=19 Exeter	82.4	81.1	53.2	143	90	90.5
=19 Newcastle	80	78.8	61.8	151	86.8	90.5
=21 Aston	87.5	87.5	46	128	91	90.4
=21 Leeds	79.6	79.7	65	156	83	90.4
=23 Queen Mary, London	83.7	81.3	54.8	146	85.1	90
=23 West of England	86.1	80.3	42.8	132	93.9	90
=25 Plymouth	86.3	81.6	39.5	138	91.2	89.7
=25 Surrey	85.2	80.7	58	127	87.9	89.7
=25 Ulster	83.9	80	53.5	138	87.3	89.7
28 Birmingham	79	77.1	59.8	152	85.1	89.6
29 Sheffield	86.4	86.8	63.7	148	73	89.5
30 Liverpool	83.6	80.7	46.8	132	90.8	89.2
=31 Bradford	86.2	81.5	33.8	149	87.3	89.1
=31 Essex	87	82.3	28.5	145	90.1	89.1
33 Queen Margaret, Edinburgh	79.4	73.1	36.5	170	87.6	88.9
34 Hertfordshire	90.4	85.3	48	126	82.4	88.8
34 Hull	90.1	80.3	55.5	109	87	88.8
36 Reading	84.2	79.7	56.2	125	86.5	88.7
=37 Lincoln	86.1	80.1	55.8	112	85.4	87.8

Subjects Allied to Medicine cont.

	Teaching quality %	Student experience %	Research quality %	Entry standards (UCAS points)	Graduate prospects %	Overall score
=37 South Wales	90.9	81	25.2	127	89.5	87.8
=39 Brighton	84.8	82.3	50.5	121	84.7	87.7
=39 Salford	89.4	84.1	37	123	85.3	87.7
=39 Sussex	84.5	83.9	54.2	129	80	87.7
42 Leicester	81.1	76.2	62	126	83.3	87.6
=43 Oxford Brookes	84.5	76.3	37.8	117	93	87.3
=43 West of Scotland	93.1	88.4	30.8	139	75.4	87.3
45 Canterbury Christ Church	85.4	78.3	31.8	114	95	87.2
46 Bangor	86.5	84.7	59.8	119	76	87.1
47 Wrexham	85	80.5	20.5	118	97.4	87
48 Keele	83.4	85.5	66.2	123	72.5	86.7
49 Edge Hill	86.9	80.9	22.2	123	90.5	86.5
50 Coventry	78	73.8	47.2	133	86.1	86.3
51 Portsmouth	84.9	79.3	41.2	120	84.2	86.2
=52 London South Bank	82.2	76.3	34.5	108	93.9	85.9
=52 West London	87.1	88	29.5	117	-	85.9
54 Sunderland	84.6	75.2	30.2	132	84.7	85.6
=55 Buckinghamshire New	85.8	75.5	16.8	108	97.4	85.5
=55 Northampton	87	85.3	7.5	106	97.3	85.5
=57 Cardiff Metropolitan	79.4	77.8	20.5	134	90.9	85.3
=57 St Mary's, Twickenham	92.7	90.5	-	112	90.2	85.3
59 Huddersfield	80.5	76.1	22.5	127	91	85.1
=60 Gloucestershire	90.3	87	16.2	118	-	84.9
=60 Leeds Beckett	87.2	87.1	38	115	76.3	84.9
62 Staffordshire	79.7	73.5	30.8	116	91.8	84.8
63 Teesside	79	72	35	120	89.3	84.7
64 St Mark and St John	89.4	81.8	-	122	90.8	84.6
65 Bournemouth	82.2	80.6	29.2	109	88.1	84.4
66 Worcester	83.1	78.2	24.2	127	83.3	84.2
=67 Liverpool John Moores	83.5	76.8	26.5	132	80	84.1
=67 Manchester Metropolitan	85.2	84.5	36	126	73.2	84.1
=67 Westminster	87.2	87	36.8	-	71.2	84.1
70 Greenwich	81.3	73.1	32.3	117	84.5	83.7
=71 Derby	91.3	88.1	24	115	73.5	83.6
=71 Sheffield Hallam	76.9	70.4	29.8	119	90.1	83.6
=71 Suffolk	81.9	81.4	-	126	92.3	83.6
74 Nottingham Trent	78.1	75.6	43.5	118	80.3	83.4
=75 Central Lancashire	78.5	74.2	35.5	123	81.9	83.3
=75 York St John	84.4	79.6	13.8	115	86.8	83.3
77 Birmingham City	80.1	79	37.8	129	72.6	82.7
78 Kent	77.1	79.1	50	104	77.2	82.4
79 Anglia Ruskin	77.7	73	33.8	99	86.3	81.9
80 Cumbria	75.6	68.4	18.5	123	88.7	81.8
=81 Brunel	57.1	49.4	47.2	135	94.1	81.3

=81	Chester		72	73.5	31	117	84.1	81.3
83	Bedfordshire		72.7	62.8	22.5	116	89.9	80.8
84	De Montfort		87.1	85.7	20.8	105	70	80.5
85	Bolton		84.6	76.1	2	120	75.1	79.4
86	Wolverhampton		80.4	72.2	24.2	112	73	79.3
87	London Metropolitan		78.7	76.3	23.8	-	71.2	78.2
88	Middlesex		80.2	69.6	22.5	108	69.9	77.7
89	Roehampton		79.3	86.3	37.5	96	60.7	77.6
90	East London		83.8	74.4	25.5	101	62.2	77

Employed in high-skilled job	74%	Employed in lower-skilled job		8%
Employed in high-skilled job and studying	4%	Employed in lower-skilled job and studying		1%
Studying	4%	Unemployed		3%
High-skilled work (median) salary	£26,000	Low-/medium-skilled salary		£20,000

Theology and Religious Studies

Risen from the runner-up spot, Durham takes the lead of the new Theology and Religious Studies table. It is boosted by the best career prospects in the ranking, with 92.3% of graduates employed in professional-level jobs and/or postgraduate study 15 months after their degrees, as well as performing strongly across the board. Second-place Cambridge is held back from its former top spot on the table by middling rates of student satisfaction with teaching quality and the wider experience, derived from our new National Student Survey (NSS) analysis – metrics topped by Exeter, which is tied with Bristol in sixth place overall. Positive reviews in the NSS from students at St Andrews put it second for teaching quality and the student experience. Exeter also leads the field for research, based on results of the Research Excellence Framework 2021, where it is followed by Birmingham and King's College London. Entry standards do not reach the heights of some other subjects, but at over half of the universities tabled, new entrants averaged more than 144 tariff points (equal to three As at A-level). Even so, there are still four universities that look for less than 110 points.

Examining how different beliefs have influenced society historically and their roles within the contemporary world, theology and religious studies courses draw on students' critical thinking and textual analysis, encouraging intellectual curiosity and articulate communication. There are usually no required subjects and it is not necessary to be a religious believer but it helps to have experience of essay-writing subjects such as history, English or politics – in which balancing arguments and analysing texts are to the fore.

By no means do all who take theology or religious studies degrees go on to work for the Church; other career routes include the civil service, law, international development, the arts, banking, investment, teaching, research, the media and communications. But the vocation is among the career pathways that contribute to the subjects ranking 38th out of 70 in our employment table. For pay they place =46th.

The pattern of applications and enrolments in theology and religious studies – which has been following a similar pattern to the size of congregations filling church pews on Sundays – has staged a minor resurrection in the past two years, with the number of students accepted onto courses increasing for two years running. For entry in 2024 there were 910 new undergraduates out of 3,400 applications, the most in four admissions years, the highest demand in four years. There are 42 universities and colleges offering degrees in theology and religious studies in 2026-27, often as part of combined honours courses.

Theology and Religious Studies

	Teaching quality %	Student experience %	Research quality %	Entry standards (UCAS points)	Graduate prospects %	Overall score
1 Durham	92.7	85.1	55	168	92.3	100
2 Cambridge	88.6	77.3	58.5	182	87.2	98
3 Glasgow	89.6	83.2	62.5	190	79.3	97.2
4 Oxford	90.7	82.8	44.8	171	87.6	97
5 St Andrews	94.7	93.2	36.5	161	-	96.6
=6 Bristol	87.1	92	48.5	156	86.2	96
=6 Exeter	95.7	96.5	75	144	71.8	96
8 Birmingham	89.4	84.3	67.2	147	81.2	95.7
9 Cardiff	93.8	85.3	42.2	118	86.1	93.9
10 Nottingham	91.2	89.2	51.5	129	76.9	92.5
11 Manchester	88.9	81.4	39.5	142	-	92.2
12 King's College London	78.3	74.7	67	148	80.9	92.1
13 Edinburgh	82.3	79.3	51.2	161	78.4	91.9
14 Leeds	79.8	84.7	52	138	-	91.1
15 Chester	91	72.5	44.5	103	79.4	89.4
16 Liverpool Hope	87.8	90.5	30.5	107	-	88.7
17 Birmingham Newman	93.6	83	8.8	103	-	86.4
18 St Mary's, Twickenham	83.1	75.2	31	114	-	86.1
19 York St John	88.2	83.1	15.8	101	-	85.5

Employed in high-skilled job	49%	Employed in lower-skilled job	21%
Employed in high-skilled job and studying	5%	Employed in lower-skilled job and studying	2%
Studying	10%	Unemployed	4%
High-skilled work (median) salary	£25,500	Low-/medium-skilled salary	£19,000

Town and Country Planning and Landscape

Leeds is No 1 in this year's table, ousting Loughborough after a year at the top. Helping it to the top, Leeds' students report the highest rates of satisfaction with teaching quality and the broader undergraduate experience in our new National Student Survey analysis. Loughborough's record on graduate employment is unbeaten and it also leads for research quality, based on its performance in the Research Excellence Framework 2021, where it is closely followed by Sheffield (=4th overall). Averaging 177 points in the UCAS tariff, University College London attracts the highest entry standards and ranks third overall, down from the No 1 position it last held two years ago. Cambridge, another former leader of the table, is now absent from it due to its land economy degree being included in our Land and Property Management table instead.

Courses under the rubric of town and country planning and landscape studies include urban studies, sustainable development and rural enterprise land management. "If you're interested in sustainability, cities and making the world a better place, town and country planning could be the degree for you," advises Dr Andy Inch, senior lecturer at the School of Geography and Planning, University of Sheffield, "Good planning is vital for tackling many of the 21st century's biggest challenges, from climate change and nature depletion to housing, health and inequality. A professionally accredited planning degree will push you beyond understanding the big issues to asking what can be done about them, opening up a range of exciting future careers. And one of the best things about studying planning is that you can learn by visiting interesting places and think about the ways they're changing."

Positive career outcomes place the subjects 18th out of 70 in our employment table, with the latest figures showing that more than three-quarters of graduates had secured professional-level jobs and/or postgraduate study within 15 months. Pay is promising too: average early career salaries of £26,265 are in the top 25.

There were 3,620 applications to planning courses in 2024 and 775 students were accepted onto degrees (20 fewer than the year before and the fourth consecutive decline). Landscape design degrees attract smaller numbers – 180 new students in 2024 – although these have risen for two years in a row.

Town and Country Planning and Landscape	Teaching quality %	Student experience %	Research quality %	Entry standards (UCAS points)	Graduate prospects %	Overall score
1 Leeds	98.3	98.1	64.8	141	-	100
2 Loughborough	85.5	83.4	72	142	92	99.3
3 University College London	83.2	83.8	61	177	88.9	97.8
=4 Edinburgh	82.3	72.5	59	167	-	96.9
=4 Sheffield	88.8	86.6	71.8	145	87.3	96.9
6 Queen's, Belfast	97.3	96	36.5	137	-	96.8
7 Heriot-Watt	84.4	78.2	59	162	88.2	96.4
=8 Birmingham	89.3	86.5	49.2	138	-	96.1
=8 Manchester	81.9	86.2	59.2	143	-	96.1
10 Liverpool	87.2	91.9	45.2	122	89.7	95.5
11 West of England	91.9	88.7	40.8	120	-	94.8
12 Reading	85.1	79.2	53.5	126	-	94.7
=13 Cardiff	80.1	86.8	38.2	121	89.4	93.6
=13 Ulster	83.1	80.8	54.2	112	-	93.6
15 Newcastle	79.2	79.1	56	120	87.8	93.3
16 Leeds Beckett	94.5	91.4	24.5	112	86.7	92.5
17 London South Bank	88.2	82.7	35	107	-	92.4
18 Oxford Brookes	91.2	82.7	33.2	83	87.2	91.3
19 Greenwich	83.5	80.4	30	109	-	91.1
20 Gloucestershire	83.1	57.6	24	104	-	88.9

Employed in high-skilled job	66%	Employed in lower-skilled job		12%
Employed in high-skilled job and studying	4%	Employed in lower-skilled job and studying		1%
Studying	6%	Unemployed		4%
High-skilled work (median) salary	£27,000	Low-/medium-skilled salary		£21,500

Veterinary Medicine

Glasgow returns to the top of the Veterinary Medicine table, while Liverpool takes second place. Entrants to Glasgow's veterinary medicine degree averaged an eye-watering 239 points in the UCAS tariff – the top entry standards in a high-tariff table. But Liverpool has the edge for research in the subject, based on results of the Research Excellence Framework 2021, where it is followed by Glasgow. A new entry to the table this year, ninth-place Harper Adams and

Keele vet school has the most accessible entry standards, with its trainee vets entering with an average of 152 points in the UCAS tariff. Nottingham ranks sixth overall but scores the best ratings from students in our analysis of the latest National Student Survey – where it comes top for teaching quality and the wider experience. Nottingham also has the edge for graduate prospects, with 97.9% of graduates employed in high-skilled jobs and/or postgraduate study 15 months after their degrees. But employment scores are so tightly bunched, going no lower than 93.1% achieving the same outcomes at Edinburgh, that they do not form part of the calculations that determine universities' positions. Veterinary medicine tops our 70-subject employment table this year. For graduate salaries, it ties in third place with pharmacy and pharmacology.

Veterinary medicine student numbers are centrally controlled, and the subject is offered by very few universities; none of them in Northern Ireland and only one in Wales, at Aberystwyth – which is too new to have sufficient data for our table yet. The same goes for the UK's 11th vet school, which launched at Central Lancashire in 2023. But the joint vet school at Harper Adams and Keele, which opened in 2020, has established enough statistics to populate the metrics in our table – which it joins for the first time this year, bringing the list to nine vet schools.

The norm for veterinary medicine degrees is five years, but the Cambridge course takes six and Bristol, Nottingham, the Royal Veterinary College and Harper and Keele offer a gateway year. Edinburgh, Bristol and the Royal Veterinary College also run four-year accelerated courses for graduates.

Some veterinary schools demand high grades in chemistry and biology, while others require chemistry and one or two additional science subjects, such as biology, maths or physics. Applicants to institutions including Cambridge and the Royal Veterinary College may also be required to take an admissions test, while Surrey uses an online questionnaire. All vet schools require candidates to have proven their commitment to the course by completing some form of relevant work experience before applying. Ever a competitive subject, in the 2024 admissions cycle there were 11,705 applications for 1,785 places. The deadline for applications is October 15th, earlier than for most other subjects to allow extra time to process the high demand for courses.

Veterinary Medicine	Teaching quality %	Student experience %	Research quality %	Entry standards (UCAS points)	Graduate prospects %	Overall score
1 Glasgow	86.4	74.4	64.8	239	97.3	100
2 Liverpool	92	86.3	68.2	174	96.9	97.8
=3 Cambridge	91.2	77	60.2	198	96.1	97.4
=3 Edinburgh	90.7	85.2	50.2	210	93.1	97.4
5 Surrey	91.2	81.4	58	168	96.4	94.6
6 Nottingham	94	89.3	52	157	97.9	94.4
7 Bristol	84.1	73.8	60.2	182	96.1	93.2
8 Royal Veterinary College	82.3	73.2	55	183	97.4	91.8
9 Harper Adams	79	65.2	19.5	152	-	80.8

Employed in high-skilled job	92%	Employed in lower-skilled job		1%
Employed in high-skilled job and studying	2%	Employed in lower-skilled job and studying		0%
Studying	1%	Unemployed		2%
High-skilled work (median) salary	£33,000	Low-/medium-skilled salary		N/A

11 Applying to Oxbridge

Known collectively as Oxbridge, a term coined in 1850 by William Makepeace Thackeray in his novel *Pendennis* (he briefly attended Trinity College, Cambridge), the two ancient universities of Oxford and Cambridge continue to bring academic prestige on a scale unparalleled by other UK universities. This is despite their duopoly at the top of our league table – which was unbroken for nearly three decades – ending five years ago when St Andrews first pipped them to the post. Since then, only Oxford has placed No 1 (three years ago), and Cambridge has ranked no higher than third. This year, they both tie in fourth place; the first time that neither university has featured among the top three in our league table's 32-year history.

In global rankings however, which do not include student reviews among their metrics and factor research profiles more significantly, Oxbridge's dominance is enduring: Oxford has been placed first in the world by Times Higher Education (THE) every year from 2017 to 2026, and it is fourth in the QS World University Rankings 2026. Cambridge also excels on the global stage – placed joint third by THE and sixth by QS. In the 2025 Academic Ranking of World Universities by ShangaiRanking, Cambridge is in fourth place and Oxford sixth.

But it is their admissions arrangements, rather than their reputations, that warrant a separate chapter in our *Guide*. Oxford and Cambridge are part of the UCAS system but there are three significant peculiarities to the process of applying to them:

1. The deadline for applications is October 15 at 6pm – three months earlier than for other universities for entry in 2027 or deferred entry in 2028.
2. You can only apply to one or the other university in the same year, so you need to choose between the two.
3. Selection is in the hands of the colleges rather than the university centrally. Most candidates apply to a specific college, although open applications can be made if you are happy to go to any college.

What are the chances of getting in?
For anyone with Oxbridge in their sights this is the starter for ten. Competition for admission is intense each year and Oxbridge continues to broaden its intake. Cambridge typically receives about six applications per place on average across all subjects, while Oxford receives around seven per place. But these ratios vary noticeably by subject, as the tables on

pages 275–277 show. Each university publishes an admissions statistics report annually on its website, providing the latest entry figures by indices including college, subject, ethnicity, type of school and eligibility for free school meals. Oxford's, though, has become more focused on individual criteria rather than a broader brush encapsulating college-wide figures. But in general, some of the oldest and richest colleges – such as St John's, Oxford, and Trinity, Cambridge (both old colleges with big endowments) – attract the highest numbers of applications. Combine this with a popular subject, such as economics and management or computer science, and the odds of securing an offer can seem even more formidable. In theory, though, all colleges are equally hard to get into, as Oxbridge "pools" students who they like but do not have space for, allowing other colleges to snap them up.

Other than pandemic-induced fluctuations, applications and enrolments are fairly consistent from year to year. Cambridge received 22,153 applications in 2024 (up 3.3% from 2023), made 4,760 offers (an increase of 4.5% from 4,238), and accepted 3,632 new undergraduates (an increase of 1.1% from 3,557). Oxford received 23,061 applications in 2024 (down from 23,211 in 2023), made 3,793 offers (up from 3,721) and admitted 3,245 new undergraduates (up from 3,219).

China was by far the biggest provider of students from outside the UK in 2024, with Cambridge taking 252 students from China and Oxford 191. At Cambridge this was followed by Singapore and Hong Kong and at Oxford by Singapore then the United States. However, applications from both EU students and the rest of the world had fallen from last year at Oxford. Cambridge said that applications from EU students fell slightly but increased from the rest of the world.

Entry standards are famously formidable. While three A grades is Oxford's minimum standard offer, many courses – particularly in the sciences – require at least one A* grade. At Oxford, 54.1% of applicants, 77% of offers and 85.7% of students admitted were awarded A*AA or better at A-level, while 45.5% achieved three A* grades or better. The picture is very similar at Cambridge, where the typical conditional A-level offer is A*AA or A*A*A. Of home students accepted to Cambridge in the 2024 cycle, 94.7% achieved the equivalent of A*AA or better, counting only their best three A-levels, excluding general studies and critical thinking. Such statistics should not put bright, academically driven students off from applying. What is the worst that can happen? One wasted option out of five on a UCAS form, perhaps.

One thing to be mindful of, though, is that selectors have to be confident that applicants will cope with the demands of an undergraduate course at Oxbridge. At only eight weeks long, Oxbridge terms are intensive. Admissions tutors are looking for genuine interest in the chosen subject, very high levels of academic ability and outstanding examination results, along with a capacity for hard work, independent learning and intellectual flexibility.

Student satisfaction?

Feedback in the latest National Student Survey (NSS) hints of discontent among Oxbridge students: in our new NSS analysis Oxford places 124th and Cambridge is 117th for the broad undergraduate experience. And although they do much better for students' evaluation of teaching quality, both universities rank lower this year than last – with Oxford down 25 places to 44th, and Cambridge sitting =59th, a 29-place decline. These outcomes have contributed significantly to the universities' overall declines in our main league table. Tepid rates of student satisfaction among research-intensive universities have long been an issue, but others – among them the London School of Economics and Political Science, St Andrews and Durham – have received positive feedback in successive recent editions of the NSS, following

2025 Tompkins Table

The 2025 Tompkins table ranks by college the results of all Cambridge students in their end-of-year Tripos examinations each summer.

2025	2024	College	Score (%)	Firsts (%)	2025	2024	College	Score (%)	Firsts (%)
1	1	Trinity	74.58	42.44	16	4	Pembroke	69.15	31.79
2	2	Christ's	72.96	37.26	17	16	Magdalene	68.82	29.02
3	5	Selwyn	72.78	39.09	18	20	Sidney Sussex	68.55	30.56
4	6	Churchill	72.43	36.97	19	19	Trinity Hall	67.65	27.49
5	7	Queens'	71.48	34.45	20	17	Robinson	66.65	25.66
6	11	Downing	71.04	35.07	21	21	Fitzwilliam	66.59	25.73
7	9	Emmanuel	71.01	34.46	22	23	Lucy Cavendish	66.42	24.3
8	14	St John's	70.34	34.26	23	29	Hughes Hall	66.19	25.42
9	12	Clare	70.2	32.26	24	13	St Edmund's	65.98	25.98
10	15	Peterhouse	70.16	33.8	25	27	Newnham	65.63	23.13
11	10	Gonville and Caius	70.13	32.1	26	26	Murray Edwards	64.72	21.82
12	8	St Catharine's	69.69	32.32	27	24	King's	64.72	21.5
13	22	Wolfson	69.68	32.63	28	28	Girton	64.21	21.03
14	18	Jesus	69.36	30.8	29	25	Homerton	62.28	18.08
15	3	Corpus Christi	69.28	32.7					

Based on degree classifications: 1st = 5pts; 2:1 = 3pts; 2:2 = 2pts, 3rd = 1pt.

their efforts to improve student-facing issues such as marking, feedback and student services. Oxbridge only has up to date results for these metrics in our guide for the past two years, due to the universities' students' five-year boycott of the NSS that began in 2017. The reason for Oxbridge's lacklustre showing in the NSS, some argue, is due to the high expectations of its students, which they are disappointed to find were not entirely met.

Of the two tables which rank the colleges of Cambridge and Oxford respectively according to the proportions of students with the best degrees, only the Tompkins Table (above) at Cambridge survives; the Norrington Table having been discontinued at Oxford in 2024. A spokesperson for the Conference of Colleges at Oxford said: "It was judged that the Norrington Table does not encapsulate the added value given by college teaching. Nor does it relate to differences at the level of specific degree courses."

The career landscape looks promising for those with Oxbridge degrees. Remarkably, both universities have the same score for graduate prospects in our current analysis and rank joint third, with 90.4% of graduates employed in high skilled jobs or engaged in postgraduate study 15 months on from their degrees.

Diversity

Progress to widen access to Oxbridge has accelerated in recent years – including by ethnicity and indices of social deprivation. But in 2024 admissions to Oxford from state schools were at the lowest since 2019, falling from 67.6% in 2023 to 66.2% in 2024 while private school intake increased from 32.4% to 33.8%. Of UK students at Cambridge, 71% came from state schools in autumn 2024, down from 72.6% in 2023, while the proportion from independent schools increased from 27.4% to 29%. Even so, there are improvements over the longer term: our records show that as far back as 2002, Oxford's intake from state schools was 54.3% and at Cambridge it was 55.5% in the same year. Dr Martin Thompson, director of undergraduate admissions at Cambridge, said the university remains committed to widening participation and that the figures came after a period of rapid growth in state school admissions and remained above pre-Covid levels, when the state school intake was 68.7%. Both universities said the pandemic had affected their state school intake in recent years. Cambridge said its long-term trend remained positive and Oxford said it had taken more pupils on free school meals.

Our own *Good University Guide* social inclusion index measures admissions from non-selective state schools only – not including state grammars, which are highly selective. The latest available data shows Oxford recruited 51.6% of its intake from non-selective state schools – ranking it 111th for this metric out of the 114 universities in England and Wales tabled. Cambridge fares more poorly still, in 115th place, and is one of three universities where less than half of the intake came from non-selective state schools (49.9%). The universities compare better with others on ethnic diversity: the proportion of the intake of students from ethnic minorities ranks Oxford 61st (28.3%) and Cambridge 51st (34%). Cambridge has shown improvement in the years since the Stormzy Scholarship was introduced in 2018 and expanded in 2021. More than 40 black British students have benefitted so far from the £20,000 award, covering tuition fees and a maintenance grant. Thirty scholarships are being offered from 2024–26 through a partnership between Stormzy's #Merky Foundation and HSBC UK.

The universities continue to work hard to dispel their "champagne set" connotations and attract bright students from a broad range of backgrounds, admitting more students from the least advantaged backgrounds than ever before (14.5% in 2024 at Oxford, 16% at Cambridge). Each university has launched a foundation year: Oxford's Astrophoria Foundation Year for UK state school students launched in 2023 and offers up to 50 places per year, while the Cambridge Foundation Year in arts, humanities and social sciences launched in 2022 and accepted 48 students in 2024. Designed for students who have experienced educational disadvantages, the one-year courses are fully funded, with fees and living costs covered by the universities, and entry requirements are lower than for undergraduate programmes. Foundation year students who achieve the required level may progress to a full degree. Oxford has also grown its bridging programme, Opportunity Oxford and OppOx Digital, which supported 490 UK offer-holders in 2024 in their transition from school or college to the university. Among other outreach activities, Cambridge works with social mobility charities such as the Sutton Trust and Target Oxbridge, while individual colleges have links with different areas with low records of sending students to Russell Group universities.

While Oxbridge is making progress, overall the universities continue to prop up the nether regions of our social inclusion index of universities in England and Wales – which looks at nine measures of social inclusion: state school entrants (non-grammar); ethnic minorities; black attainment gap; white working-class males; low participation areas; low participation areas dropout gap; first-generation students; disabled students; mature students. Oxford ranks 108th (up from 111th) and Cambridge has gained two places to rank 113th.

Stating the case: public or private

Since taking over as Cambridge's vice-chancellor in 2023, Deborah Prentice (formerly provost of Princeton University in the US) has reassured private school applicants who may "fear discrimination" that "we are open to talent from absolutely everywhere and it's more competitive because we're trying to get the applicant numbers up but there's no discrimination". Her leadership follows that of Professor Stephen Toope, who made major efforts on widening access, overseeing the creation of the university's foundation year and stating: "We have to keep making it very, very clear we are intending to reduce over time the number of people who are coming from independent school backgrounds into places like Oxford or Cambridge."

At Oxford, Irene Tracey, the university's first state-educated vice-chancellor and the former warden of its Merton College refuted claims of a conspiracy against privately educated pupils, telling *The Times* in 2023: "I've done admissions for 25 years so I can absolutely speak at the coalface about how we do it. There are no quotas. There are no biases, it's so thorough and fair, and we work our socks off to make sure that we've got the best kids. Inevitably, as we've opened up and done so much more on engagement, you're going to have more competition and that's going to be reflected in the numbers. That's the reality".

Oxford applications and acceptances by course

Arts	Applications			Acceptances			Success rate %		
	2024	2023	2022	2024	2023	2022	2024	2023	2022
Ancient and modern history	101	98	81	27	20	14	26.7	20.4	17.3
Archaeology and anthropology	123	125	101	27	22	20	22.0	17.6	19.8
Asian and Middle Eastern studies	113	109	168	45	35	48	39.8	32.1	28.6
Classical archaeology and ancient history	169	152	67	37	25	19	21.9	16.4	28.4
Classics	287	313	293	121	100	123	42.2	31.9	42
Classics and English	56	60	30	18	13	8	32.1	21.7	26.7
Classics and modern languages	24	23	23	11	10	8	45.8	43.5	34.8
Computer science and philosophy	135	129	31	15	12	9	11.1	9.3	29
Economics and management	1517	1542	1192	93	83	84	6.1	5.4	7
English language and literature	869	975	1142	237	212	240	27.3	21.7	21
English and modern languages	102	91	117	26	35	18	25.5	38.5	15.4
European and Middle Eastern languages	30	40	28	15	13	8	50.0	32.5	28.6
Fine art	248	255	189	33	28	28	13.3	11.0	14.8
Geography	290	339	371	98	70	77	33.8	20.6	20.8
History	951	958	1029	248	214	246	26.1	22.3	23.9
History and economics	131	158	99	17	18	13	13.0	11.4	13.1
History and English	97	104	89	19	12	7	19.6	11.5	7.9
History and modern languages	87	72	87	25	18	16	28.7	25.0	18.4
History and politics	340	381	279	53	48	39	15.6	12.6	14
History of art	98	107	137	18	14	12	18.4	13.1	8.8
Law	1872	1858	1302	216	192	196	11.5	10.3	15.1
Law with law studies in Europe	331	341	317	34	26	31	10.3	7.6	9.8
Mathematics and philosophy	173	163	90	17	19	16	9.8	11.7	17.8
Modern languages	357	309	573	174	145	189	48.7	46.9	33
Modern languages and linguistics	89	91	72	42	39	27	47.2	42.9	37.5
Music	212	169	221	94	81	70	44.3	47.9	31.7
Philosophy and modern languages	54	56	51	23	21	13	42.6	37.5	25.5
Philosophy and theology	154	146	118	32	25	28	20.8	17.1	23.7
Physics and philosophy	154	139	146	16	12	16	10.4	8.6	11
Philosophy, politics and economics (PPE)	1774	1864	1640	270	229	232	15.2	12.3	14.1
Theology and religion	132	116	91	44	46	28	33.3	39.7	30.8
Religion and Asian and Middle Eastern studies	14	3	4	3	1	1	21.4	33.3	25
Total Arts	**11084**	**11,286**	**10,178**	**2,148**	**1,838**	**1884**	**19.4**	**16.3**	**18.5**

Oxford applications and acceptances by course cont.

Sciences	Applications			Acceptances			Success rate %		
	2024	2023	2022	2024	2023	2022	2024	2023	2022
Biochemistry	886	875	399	121	100	90	13.7	11.4	22.6
Biology	731	742	428	130	109	111	17.8	14.7	25.9
Biomedical sciences	494	490	193	49	41	33	9.9	8.4	17.1
Chemistry	1070	1015	638	214	175	180	20.0	17.2	28.2
Computer science	881	866	147	66	52	23	7.5	6.0	15.6
Earth sciences (Geology)	172	163	116	42	34	34	24.4	20.9	29.3
Engineering science	1137	1031	720	204	163	157	17.9	15.8	21.8
Experimental psychology	402	379	212	69	43	50	17.2	11.3	23.6
Human sciences	161	193	155	34	26	31	21.1	13.5	20
Materials science	211	148	79	46	44	33	21.8	29.7	41.8
Mathematics	1959	1807	917	205	179	161	10.5	9.9	17.6
Mathematics and computer science	610	593	119	68	51	28	11.1	8.6	23.5
Mathematics and statistics	-	142	172	-	3	22	-	2.1	12.8
Medicine	1500	1712	1471	170	149	149	11.3	8.7	10.1
Physics	1518	1494	1011	184	174	173	12.1	11.6	17.1
Psychology and philosophy (PPL)	245	275	161	43	38	29	17.6	13.8	18
Total Sciences	**11,977**	**11,925**	**6,938**	**1,645**	**1,381**	**1314**	**13.7**	**12.7**	**18.7**
Total Arts and Sciences	**23,061**	**23,211**	**17,116**	**3,793**	**3,219**	**3,198**	**16.55**	**14.5**	**18.6**

Of the 90 UK schools which received at least six Oxford and at least six Cambridge offers in 2024, 37 were private and 53 were in the state sector – including grammars, sixth-form colleges, and comprehensives. The vast majority of Britons are educated in state schools: 94% of the population and 83% of those who take A-levels. Although their share has fallen, the number of places occupied by private school pupils is still disproportionately large.

Choosing the right college

Undergraduates at Cambridge are admitted to 29 colleges, each with its own distinctive history, atmosphere and location. It is worth visiting before applying to help you decide on a college that most suits, though it is possible to make an open application. Oxford has 30 colleges that accept undergraduates, and applicants should likewise do their research. That said, both universities work to find a college for those who either make an open application or who are not taken by their first choice. At Oxford, subject tutors put candidates into bands, using the results of admissions tests as well as exam results and references. Applicants may not be seen by their preferred college if the tutors think their chances are better elsewhere.

Cambridge interviews around 80% of applicants, whereas Oxford interviews around 40% to 45% of candidates. The tables on pages 275–76 and 277 give an idea of the levels of competition for a place in different subjects. But only individual research will help you uncover where you will feel most at home.

Cambridge applications and acceptances by course

Arts, Humanities and Social Sciences	Applications			Acceptances			Success rate %		
	2024	2023	2022	2024	2023	2022	2024	2023	2022
Anglo-Saxon, Norse and Celtic	65	62	54	27	19	22	41.5	30.6	40.7
Archaeology	79	82	60	22	32	21	27.8	39.0	35
Architecture	526	522	583	64	60	66	12.2	11.5	11.3
Asian and Middle Eastern studies	111	124	160	38	60	54	34.2	48.4	33.8
Classics	115	126	123	53	50	53	46.1	39.7	43.1
Classics (four years)	79	106	97	34	29	37	43.0	27.4	38.1
Economics	1571	1336	1513	161	162	151	10.2	12.1	10
Education	164	190	268	37	34	41	22.6	17.9	15.3
English	719	756	776	182	187	185	25.3	24.7	23.8
Geography	437	524	491	101	99	96	23.1	18.9	19.6
History	599	607	580	174	164	171	29.0	27.0	29.5
History and modern languages	94	88	125	31	31	30	33.0	35.2	24
History and politics	260	342	335	57	67	49	21.9	19.6	14.6
History of art	103	87	96	35	31	20	34.0	35.6	20.8
Human, social and political sciences	1259	1436	1482	174	166	168	13.8	11.6	11.3
Land economy	614	629	487	71	71	64	11.6	11.3	13.1
Law	1604	1580	1845	236	230	217	14.7	14.6	11.8
Linguistics	120	119	143	43	26	31	35.8	21.8	21.7
Modern and medieval languages	218	254	336	117	128	144	53.7	50.4	42.9
Music	130	140	153	64	51	71	49.2	36.4	46.4
Philosophy	288	306	308	50	50	51	17.4	16.3	16.6
Theology and religious studies	128	105	107	41	37	43	32.0	35.2	40.2
Total Arts, Humanities and Social Sciences	9283	9521	10122	1812	1784	1785	19.5	26.6	17.6

Sciences	2024	2023	2022	2024	2023	2022	2024	2023	2022
Computer science	1863	1583	1,625	141	121	136	7.6	7.6	8.4
Engineering	2654	2410	2,672	321	333	344	12.1	13.8	12.9
Mathematics	1840	1588	1,515	260	258	252	14.1	16.2	16.6
Medicine	1791	1754	1,971	271	273	271	15.1	15.6	13.7
Medicine (graduate course)	489	548	529	30	40	37	6.1	7.3	7
Natural sciences	2529	2444	2,695	569	547	568	22.5	22.4	21.1
Psychological and behavioural sciences	837	891	939	72	81	87	8.6	9.1	9.3
Veterinary medicine	336	333	402	67	73	64	19.9	21.9	15.9
Total Science and Technology	12,339	11,551	12,348	1,731	1,726	1,759	14.0	14.2	14.2
Total	21,622	21,072	22,470	3,543	3,510	3,544	16.75	20.4	15.8

The application process
Historically, the application process has been viewed as one shrouded in myth and conspiracy, but both universities have worked hard to demystify it. Cambridge requires most applicants to take a written pre-interview admission assessment at the beginning of November. Some subjects administer tests at interview and some applicants are asked to submit examples of their written work. The Cambridge website lists the pre-interview assessments, which may include a reading comprehension and problem-solving test, or a thinking skills assessment, in addition to a paper on the subject itself. Applicants to Oxford must also take an admissions test for many courses, and written work submissions may be a requirement. Those who are shortlisted are invited to interview in early to mid-December. These tests are described by those in the know as "the pathway to interview", which applicants are advised to prepare for as they would an A-level exam. Applicants to Cambridge must also complete an online Supplementary Application Questionnaire (SAQ) by October 23 (6pm UK time) in most cases. The interviews for Cambridge may be online or in person; for Oxford they were all online for 2026 entry. Applicants receive either a conditional offer or a rejection in the new year. For more information about the application process and preparing for interviews, visit **undergraduate.study.cam.ac.uk** and **ox.ac.uk/admissions/undergraduate**.

Oxford College Profiles

Balliol

Oxford OX1 3BJ 01865 277 777 balliol.ox.ac.uk
Undergraduates: 414 Postgraduates: 397 undergraduate@balliol.ox.ac.uk

The alma mater of many prominent post-war politicians, from Harold Macmillan to Yvette Cooper, the college is named after John de Balliol, who was ordered by the Bishop of Durham to perform a substantial act of charity in 1263. His widow, Dervorguilla, formally established Balliol – making it the oldest academic site cofounded by a woman in the English-speaking world – and her statue is at Master's Field. Balliol poses a triple "threat" (to study) of a student-run bar infamous for its blue cocktail, its popular café and a major player in the university drama scene – the Michael Pilch Studio. The JCR (junior common room, the term for the undergraduate student union at most Oxbridge colleges) is well known for its "bops" (big organised parties). Historically a regular in the Norrington table's top ten (whose college rankings were discontinued in 2025), academic excellence and social commitment are Balliol hallmarks. Students and tutors inhabit rooms on its central Broad Street campus in both the beautiful Front Quad and the Garden Quad. Undergraduates are guaranteed accommodation for all years of their course, while postgraduate students are lodged in Holywell Manor or in new accommodation at Master's Field, where Balliol has its own sports facilities. The impressive medieval library houses 70,000 books and friendly librarians can buy any text required for the college's 33 undergraduate courses. They also host a popular quiz and ghost story evenings. Offering gong-baths, floristry workshops and visits to the City Farm, Balliol is keen to enhance students' wellbeing. The college runs three sustained contact programmes, which are open to year 11 students at state schools and *Try Before you Buy* days for under-represented year 12 students. In 2024, Balliol awarded over £1.8 million to students in scholarships, prizes, grants, bursaries and hardship awards.

Brasenose

Oxford OX1 4AJ 01865 277 822 bnc.ox.ac.uk
Undergraduates: 365 Postgraduates: 255 admissions@bnc.ox.ac.uk

Looking onto the Radcliffe Camera and Hawksmoor's quadrangle at All Souls, Brasenose is tucked in the heart of historic Oxford. The Brazen Nose knocker, after which the college is named, was removed from the front door and placed on the dining-hall wall in 1890, where it hangs above the high table. Renowned as a friendly, diverse, medium-sized college it admits 111 new undergraduates each year across 18 STEM and humanities subjects. More than 80% of UK entrants were drawn from state schools in the three academic years from 2022 to 2024 (the third-highest proportion among Oxford colleges) and the college has links with schools and colleges in East Berkshire and North Yorkshire. Students run a lively range of clubs, societies and social events, such as the Brasenose Arts Week, yoga sessions, dog walks and music recitals. Welfare and academic support services for students are well-resourced and detailed in the 'Blue Book' student handbook. Formal dining is offered in Brasenose's 16th century hall three times a week and students are offered accommodation for all years of undergraduate study. Rooms and food are subsidised by the college. Postgraduate students can apply for accommodation across two central Oxford sites: Hollybush Row and the St Cross Annex. Brasenose is redeveloping Frewin Hall, where in 2022 archaeologists discovered the remains of the "lost" St Mary's College underneath the site. The college has strong teams and facilities for many sports including football, cricket, rugby, netball, rounders and lacrosse, while the Brasenose boat club, founded in 1815, is one of the oldest in the world.

Christ Church

Oxford OX1 1DP 01865 286 583 chch.ox.ac.uk
Undergraduates: 455 Postgraduates: 225 admissions@chch.ox.ac.uk

Nicknamed "The House" by its students, Christ Church cuts an imposing silhouette on the Oxford skyline and boasts the city's largest quadrangle. Its grandeur, water-meadow stocked with Highland cattle and illustrious history attract prospective students, academics and tourists in swathes. Founded by Cardinal Thomas Wolsey in 1525, the college houses the Cathedral of the Oxford diocese. The Very Reverend Professor Sarah Foot was installed as Dean of Christ Church in July 2023 – the first woman appointed to the role in the college's 500-year history. Bowler-hatted porters, wooden-panelled "sets" (double rooms) and a Picture Gallery collection of old masters characterise an opulent feel; this is the college Evelyn Waugh's fictitious Sebastian Flyte attended in *Brideshead Revisited*. Accommodation covers all four years and ranges from the 1960s brutalism of Blue Boar (for first-years), to the neoclassical Peckwater sets (for second-years) and the elegant Meadows and Old Library rooms (mostly for third- and fourth-years). UK students from lower-income households are eligible for up to 50% subsidy on accommodation and dining – held in the Great Hall, recognisable as the *Harry Potter* set for Hogwarts, which serves two sittings every evening: formal and informal. Students can buy wine from The Buttery or visit "The Undie" student bar from Wednesday to Saturday. The Art Room is a well-loved creative space open to students of all subjects. Representing more than a third of the intake from 2022 to 2024, Christ Church had the highest intake of students from Black, Asian, and Minority Ethnic groups at Oxford. It awards over £1 million in graduate funding annually and opened Oxford Edge, the Centre for Entrepreneurship and Innovation in 2025. Extracurriculars include an impressive choir, which serves the cathedral, as well as music and drama societies. Competitive in university rowing, Christ Church's women's eight held a podium position for the third year running in the 2025 summer competition whilst the men finished fourth.

Corpus Christi

Oxford OX1 4JF 01865 276 693 ccc.ox.ac.uk
Undergraduates: 258 Postgraduates: 102 admissions.office@ccc.ox.ac.uk

Nestled between Christ Church and Merton, its secluded garden and terraces are described as an 'inspiring oasis' for study and friendship. Progressive principles distinguished Corpus's foundation in 1517 by Richard Fox, Bishop of Winchester – whose coat of arms shows a pelican in a selfless act of charity. Fox's focus on humanist learning had a strong influence on the college's impressive 16th-century library. The original bookstacks sit alongside the newly opened Spencer Building, which provides a modern library and workspace containing 70,000 volumes. Recent exhibitions have showcased Corpus's own Magna Carta and King James Bible manuscripts. Academic expectations are high with medicine, English literature, Classics and PPE particularly well-represented. The college provides one of Oxford's most generous bursary schemes, which bestows travel, book and vacation grants to complement its students' academic interests. A welfare programme offers gardening, dog-walks and counselling to students. Quirky extracurriculars include a popular new Wine Society, which invites connoisseurs to present eight wines from the Corpus cellars to curious novices for £10. The airy Al Jaber Auditorium hosts concerts, shows, screenings and art exhibitions throughout the year. Corpus's drama society, the Owlets, is highly regarded, while its sports clubs pair up with other small colleges to make composite teams such as the highly successful Corpus-Somerville women's rugby team. In 2024, Corpus celebrated the 50th anniversary of its famous tortoise fair, an annual summer gathering in the college gardens where university pet tortoises race for a lettuce prize – won in recent years by Aristurtle of St Peter's.

Exeter

Oxford OX1 3DP 01865 279 668 exeter.ox.ac.uk
Undergraduates: 364 Postgraduates: 349 admissions@exeter.ox.ac.uk

Exeter has been situated on Turl Street since 1315, one year after it was founded, and boasts, arguably, *the* Oxford view from the Fellows' Garden, overlooking Radcliffe Square. Its newly restored Jackson library blends Victorian Gothic architecture with 21st century facilities and the college's prominent chapel spire is juxtaposed with a striking Antony Gormley sculpture, which looks down onto Broad Street. Exeter's modern Cohen Quad is located ten minutes away on Walton Street. Sustainability is to the fore: recent carbon-saving initiatives include double glazing in students' rooms. Undergraduates are guaranteed three years of college accommodation and Exeter's new on-course support programme is designed to ease the transition from school to university. The college is linked with the Southwest of England region but works with state schools across the UK. Its Exeter Plus six-month programme is for Year 12 students interested in applying to Oxford, while the ExVac student-run charity operates holiday camps for children in need of a break. A new scholarship for refugee students launched in 2025. A welfare officer coordinates student wellbeing activities on site. A sporty college, Exeter regularly fields four teams in football and rowing and there are plans for padel courts, golf simulators and cricket nets. A wide range of festivals is celebrated in the college's Jacobean dining hall and a very active JCR organises nearly annual summer balls. Arts-based extracurriculars are particularly strong, with the annual Turl Street Arts Festival shared with neighbours Lincoln and Jesus, regular DJ nights in the college bar and amateur garden productions put on in the summer. Exeter counts many prominent 20th century writers among its alumni, including Martin Amis, Philip Pullman and JRR Tolkien.

Harris Manchester

Oxford OX1 3TD 01865 271 009 hmc.ox.ac.uk
Undergraduates: 110 Postgraduates: 160 admissions@hmc.ox.ac.uk

The inscription on Harris Manchester's clocktower, 'it is later than you think, but it is never too late' is apt for Oxford's only college exclusively for mature students (aged over-21). It was originally founded in Manchester in 1786 to provide education for non-Anglican students. Following spells in York and London it settled in Oxford in 1889, moving to its current central site in 1892 where it enjoys beautiful red-brick buildings and grounds just off Holywell Street. In 1996, Harris Manchester received its Royal Charter as a College of the University of Oxford. The college is known for its friendly atmosphere where all members of the MCR (middle common room, for postgraduate students) are also members of the JCR – which has a student-run bar. Close to the Bodleian, Harris Manchester's own library is extensive and boasts the best student-to-book ratio of any college. All accommodation is on the main site and students can typically "live in" for at least the first and final years of their course. Meals are included in the fees, meaning self-catering is not an option for students living in college, but Harris Manchester has a reputation for excellent food. Students dress in academic gowns at formal dinners on Monday and Wednesday evenings. Due to its small size, the college offers a more limited range of degree courses. Many sports teams join up with other smaller colleges and all students have free membership of the Iffley Road gym.

Hertford

Oxford OX1 3BW 01865 279 400 hertford.ox.ac.uk
Undergraduates: 410 Postgraduates: 319 undergraduate.admissions@hertford.ox.ac.uk

The college is one of the most centrally located, nestled in a corner of Radcliffe Square next door to the Bodleian library. A skyway linking the Old and New Quads across New College Lane is one of Oxford's iconic landmarks: Hertford Bridge, also known as the Bridge of Sighs. A pioneer of access in the 1960s, Hertford celebrated 50 years of admitting women in 2024 and its outreach programme for state school students has been operating since the 1960s. The college continues to accept among the highest intakes of state school students at the university and in the three years from 2022 to 2024, 78.5% of UK undergraduates came from the state sector. Hertford has a generous bursary scheme for undergraduates as well as scholarships for graduate students. College-owned accommodation is available across all years, and subsidised meals (including the popular weekend brunch) can be enjoyed in the historic dining hall. Known as DTB – Down the Bar – Hertford's bar is open nightly during term. Extracurriculars are plentiful, including a wide range of sports, a music society and chapel choir, subject societies, and a thriving JCR and MCR. Welfare, health and wellbeing support is available 24 hours a day, as are study and academic skills sessions.

Jesus

Oxford OX1 3DW 01865 279 700 jesus.ox.ac.uk
Undergraduates: 380 Postgraduates: 280 admissions.officer@jesus.ox.ac.uk

Founded in 1571 by Queen Elizabeth I at the request of a group of Welshmen, Jesus is the only Elizabethan college of Oxford. The college's first members were mostly Welsh lawyers, resulting in Jesus being known for centuries as Oxford's "Welsh college". It continues to provide a programme of financial support and outreach for prospective Welsh students, leading the Oxford Cymru consortium. Known for being a friendly college, it is situated on a small site off Turl Street in the historic heart of the city and students are a few minutes' walk from main university libraries. Jesus' Cheng Yu Tung Building opened in 2022 and combines postgraduate facilities with open-plan teaching and research spaces, the Cheng Kar Shun Digital Hub and a café, gym, exhibition space and multifaith room. College academics are engaged in interdisciplinary research in fields from climate change, astrophysics and medical research to medieval history, classics and law. Off site, Jesus has squash courts and extensive playing fields with hockey, cricket, football and rugby pitches, grass tennis courts, netball courts, a boathouse and a sports pavilion. The lively JCR is housed in modern accommodation and runs a diverse programme of student events throughout the year, including the annual Turl Street Arts Festival. Jesus holds a shared summer ball with Somerville every three years.

Keble

Oxford OX1 3PG 01865 272 708 keble.ox.ac.uk
Undergraduates: 465 Postgraduates: 525 admissions@keble.ox.ac.uk

One of Oxford's largest and most visually striking colleges, Keble's Victorian Gothic polychromatic brick façade looks onto University Parks. Its "holy zebra" stripy brickwork was intended to mark the college out from its predecessors and attract attention and funding. Keble's dining hall stands out of the crowd too: it is the longest in Oxford. Its epic proportions reflect Keble's foundational premise that students should eat together regularly. It is hung with an exhibition of photographic portraits showcasing individuals who represent resilience and tenacity. The chapel is decorated with fine art including William Holman Hunt's *The Light of the World*. Café Keble moonlights as the college bar and opens throughout term. Student productions run from the O'Reilly Theatre every fortnight, making Keble one of the best places for drama. Each year, students run a lively Arts Week as well as the acclaimed Early Music Festival. Undergraduate accommodation is provided for three years; some students choose to live out in their second or third year. Its vibrant community spirit provides Keble students with a covetable social life. The graduate community is based a short distance from the main site at the HB Allen Centre with 250 new rooms. Keble's sporting facilities are excellent, with gyms on both sites, a sports ground for football, cricket, netball and tennis 15 minutes away, as well as shared squash court and a boat house. College-branded maroon track-tops worn by sports teams out on the town are an Oxford nightlife staple.

Lady Margaret Hall

Oxford OX2 6QA 01865 274 310 lmh.ox.ac.uk
Undergraduates: 432 Postgraduates: 365 admissions@lmh.ox.ac.uk

Lady Margaret Hall (LMH) began in October 1879, when nine women arrived at the college and became the first females to receive an Oxford education. Co-educational since 1978, LMH continues to widen access: it was the first college to establish a foundation year for students from under-represented groups and paved the way for the Astrophoria Foundation Year, the university-wide scheme. It recently launched a Chemistry Bursary. LMH's location in North Oxford allows the college an enviable expanse of green space compared with more central colleges. Elegant gardens back onto the Cherwell River and the grounds include a punt house, tennis and pickleball courts and a football pitch. The college is close to the university's new £185m Schwarzman Centre for the Humanities, which opened in 2025. LMH has a strong reputation in PPE with Nobel Peace Prize laureate Malala Yousafzai among its recent graduates. Its art scene is supported by extensive library collections in the arts and humanities. The library is spread across three floors and contains 75,000 books. Music is well supported: there is a music recording studio, a chamber choir, several student-run ensembles, and visits by guest artists. Most recently, a student DJ collective, Martian Moves, has emerged from the college. Accommodation is guaranteed for first, second and third-year students and includes more modern rooms in Pipe Partridge, a graceful neoclassical building with 64 en-suite bedrooms that also houses the Simpkins Lee Theatre. LMH was one of the first colleges to appoint a head of student wellbeing, along with a dedicated study skills support team.

Lincoln

Oxford OX1 3DR 01865 279 836 lincoln.ox.ac.uk
Undergraduates: 325 Postgraduates: 321 admissions@lincoln.ox.ac.uk

An ivy-covered medieval front court distinguishes Lincoln – due to mark its 600th anniversary in 2027. Centrally located on Turl Street it neighbours Exeter, Jesus and Brasenose. On Ascension Day each year, a small door connecting Lincoln and Brasenose opens for 10 minutes – allowing undergraduates through to toast their colleges' friendship with ivy-flavoured ale. A strong performer in the now discontinued Norrington table, Lincoln prides itself on academic excellence and is known for being an unpretentious and friendly smaller college. It boasts one of the most beautiful libraries in Oxford: a converted Queen Anne Church looking onto the High Street. Lincoln's supportive environment includes a welfare coordinator, college counsellor and nurse. Its environmental efforts were recognised with a second Beyond Gold Green Impact Award in 2025. The college's West Midlands access programme, Pathfinders, launched in 2022 and works with pupils eligible for free school meals. This may shift the dial on Lincoln's intake of students from state schools, which at 57% across the three years from 2022 to 2024 was among the lowest of all Oxford colleges. The dining hall serves three meals a day during term time – a rarity among older colleges. Deep Hall, the college bar, is popular with undergraduates and serves lighter bites. Lincoln offers a wide range of student bursaries and grants: in 2024-25 it awarded over £225,000 in non-repayable bursaries to undergraduates. City-centre accommodation is guaranteed either on the main site or on Bear Lane or Little Clarendon Street nearby. Drama and music are popular: the Oakeshott Room in the refurbished Garden Building is well-used for screenings and performances, especially during the Turl Street Arts Festival.

Magdalen

Oxford OX1 4AU	01865 276 063	magd.ox.ac.uk
Undergraduates: 385	Graduates: 279	admissions@magd.ox.ac.uk

Magdalen's beautiful grounds – complete with deer park, water-meadow, and Addison's Walk river path – are said to have inspired C. S. Lewis, who taught at the college for three decades, to dream up Narnia while strolling around them. The choir sings from the college bell tower at 6am to mark May Morning. Magdalen is also the majority owner of the Oxford Science Park, which is known for its medical and life science technology firms. Magdalen historically placed within the top five of the now discontinued Norrington Table. Around a quarter of students receive financial support from the college, from travel grants to funding for creative projects. Students can also access counselling and mentoring. The Magdalen Monday Movies film club hosts screenings in the Grove Auditorium and strength in drama is on show at the Magdalen Players' production in the gardens each summer. The Florio Society (poetry) and Atkin Society (Law) are among extensive extracurriculars. Attractive in-college rooms are charged at a flat rate for undergraduates and have long been a big draw. Magdalen hosts the main punting station in Oxford and its boat club is the college's oldest sporting club.

Mansfield

Oxford OX1 3TF	01865 270972	mansfield.ox.ac.uk
Undergraduates: 245	Postgraduates: 145	registrar@mansfield.ox.ac.uk

"Tell me what it is you plan to do with your one wild and precious life?" Mansfield principal Helen Mountfield asks freshers when they arrive, quoting the poet Mary Oliver. Opened in 1886, the college's original purpose was to educate nonconformist ministers. It continues to cultivate intellectual autonomy and freedom, valuing diversity and difference. Most students come from state schools: 93.7% between 2022 and 2024 – the highest state-sector intake of all Oxford colleges – but this "isn't a quota", points out Mountfield, "we take people wherever they come from, we look at them on merit, and we try to find the people we think will most make best use of a place here and benefit from it most". Located on a leafy street near University Parks, Mansfield is a short walk from major STEM departments and central Oxford libraries. The college has extensive facilities considering its size, including the popular Crypt café and unusual chapel-dining-hall. A well-stocked library and three specialist reading rooms (for law, PPE and theology) are open 24 hours a day. All undergraduates are housed in college accommodation, either on the main site (where all first-years live) or in college-owned accommodation elsewhere in Oxford. The Hands Building is home to the law faculty's Bonavero Institute of Human Rights, providing a lecture space and additional accommodation. The college hosts Mansfield Public Talks, renowned in the city and free for all. It has a holistic approach to student wellbeing, emphasising the importance of friendship at university and fostering an atmosphere that is relaxed and close-knit. With Somerville, Mansfield became the first Oxford University College of Sanctuary in 2021.

Merton

Oxford OX1 4JD	01865 286 316	merton.ox.ac.uk
Undergraduates: 323	Postgraduates: 296	undergraduate.admissions@merton.ox.ac.uk

Merton is Oxford's oldest college and one of its most prestigious, founded in 1264 by Walter de Merton, then Lord Chancellor of England. It houses Europe's oldest academic library in continuous use and offers a wide range of subjects for study. Its luminous alumni reflect the college's curricular breath, from writer T. S. Eliot and physicist Sir Antony Leggett, to Naruhito, Emperor of Japan, former Prime Minister Liz Truss, and mathematician Sir Andrew Wiles.

Merton regularly topped the Norrington table until the ranking system was discontinued in 2024, meriting its rarefied academic reputation as well as the moniker "where fun goes to die" – a catchphrase rebuffed by the college's fortnightly bops, biennial white-tie winter ball and annual Merton Society Garden Party. Since 1971, students perform the "Time Ceremony" where Mertonians walk backwards around Fellows' Quad on the last Sunday in October during the transition from British Summer Time to Greenwich Mean Time. The college is located close to the city centre, with beautiful gardens and easy access to meadows leading down to the river. Some of the cheapest accommodation across Oxford colleges is guaranteed for all years of undergraduate degrees, alongside generous bursaries and grants. Merton's extracurriculars include sport, music, poetry, drama, and subject societies. Facilities span two libraries, music practice rooms, a multi-faith prayer room, bar and games-room, as well as an on-site gym, and a boathouse on the River Isis. The chapel choir is renowned, with its Girl Choristers drawn from the local Oxfordshire community.

New College

Oxford OX1 3BN 01865 279 272 new.ox.ac.uk
Undergraduates: 434 Postgraduates: 314 admissions@new.ox.ac.uk

Do not be fooled by the name: New is one of Oxford's oldest colleges and serves as the architectural template for many more modern college foundations. Founded by William of Wykeham, New was the first college built as an integrated complex in 1379. The high medieval city walls shelter luxuriant gardens and are unique to New. The sprawling grounds are the setting for its white-tie commemoration ball, held every three years. The college's charms have made on-screen appearances in *Mamma Mia 2*, *His Dark Materials* and *Harry Potter*. But within the college's grand design lives a relaxed and diverse community. New held an impressive academic record until the Norrington was discontinued in 2024, rarely leaving the top ten colleges for undergraduate performance in finals. A commitment to outreach work led to the college's Step-Up access programme, in operation since 2017, and New is a part of the Oxford Cymru outreach programme, which aims to increase the intake of students from Wales. Music, drama and sport are prominent and are all aided by excellent facilities. The Clore Music Studios provide state-of-the-art practice facilities while the Chapel and Antechapel host regular classical concerts and performances by the world-renowned New College Choir. The college houses most undergraduates in college accommodation – recently expanded to include the new Gradel Quadrangles: a two-minute walk from the main college site.

Oriel

Oxford OX1 4EW 01865 276 555 oriel.ox.ac.uk
Undergraduates: 333 Postgraduates: 323 admissions@oriel.ox.ac.uk

The fifth-oldest college at Oxford, Oriel is celebrating the 700th anniversary of its royal foundation in 2026. Known for its immaculate Jacobean front quad and striking portico, Oriel enjoys a central location on the south side of High Street, directly across from the University Church of St Mary. In just the last century, it has produced two Nobel Laureates, at least ten Olympic medallists and numerous luminaries in arts and culture. Nicknamed "Toriel" due to its Conservative reputation, the college's controversial statue of alumnus Cecil Rhodes now includes a plaque describing him as a "committed British colonialist" who exploited the "peoples of southern Africa". Oriel offers over 20 merit-based scholarships across a range of subjects and its outreach work includes a link with Generating Genius – a charity that aims to bridge the diversity gap in STEM subjects. A welfare team can be reached 24 hours a day. Oriel has a reputation for 'strong crew spirit' due to its historic success rowing on the Isis. There is also a sports ground, multiple gyms and squash courts. A former winner of the now defunct Norrington Table, Oriel is known as brainy as well as sporty. Accommodation is guaranteed for the duration of study, tiered from A* to D class with corresponding rates of rent. All year groups live, eat and socialise together and the college's small size helps create a friendly atmosphere. The recently renovated Hall, with its Gothic hammerbeam roof, serves (optional) formal dinner six days a week. Students put on a summer play in Oriel's quad – where mallards also nest, despite the college's landlocked location, and their ducklings are escorted safely to the river.

Pembroke

Oxford OX1 1DW   01865 276 412   pmb.ox.ac.uk
Undergraduates: 390   Postgraduates: 245   admissions@pmb.ox.ac.uk

Pembroke sits in a quieter corner of the city centre, tucked away off St Aldates opposite Christ Church. Blending traditional and modern architecture, its four quads – Old, Damon Wells Chapel, North and Rokos – span five centuries. Known for its relaxed and inclusive atmosphere, Pembroke promotes a down-to-earth approach at the same time as nurturing an ambitious intellectual community. With a focus on interdisciplinary learning, there are talks and panels with high-profile figures, as well as weekly opportunities for Pembroke's own academics and students to share their research. Undergraduate courses include joint honours – from PPL (psychology, philosophy and linguistics) to European and Middle Eastern languages. History is both a strong subject and a strong presence around college: founded by King James I in 1624, Pembroke celebrated its 400th anniversary in 2024. The McGowin Library is open 24/7 and its special collections include works by alumnus Samuel Johnson. Pembroke's outreach programmes include initiatives targeting pupils from the north of England, and West London. The college offers a wide variety of extracurriculars, from planting and maintaining an orchard, to its successful rowing club and other sports teams. The student-led JCR Art Committee manages an art collection and gallery. Almost all undergraduates live in college accommodation and share meals in the dining hall and onsite café, Farthings. The Sir Geoffrey Arthur accommodation annexe on the banks of the River Thames has recently expanded to provide more rooms and facilities for students and new academics. Nearly half of the college estate is served by decarbonised energy.

Queen's

Oxford OX1 4AW   01865 279 161   queens.ox.ac.uk
Undergraduates: 347   Postgraduates: 231   admissions@queens.ox.ac.uk

Queen's impressive neoclassical buildings and bell tower create a grand entrance on Oxford's main thoroughfare to the college's supportive and stimulating community. The New Library includes a fully accessible underground extension to one of the largest libraries in Oxford, comprising three reading rooms from the 17th, 19th and 21st centuries. The Upper Library is renowned as one of the most beautiful reading rooms in Oxford. Academically, Queen's is strong in a range of subjects and offers diverse degrees – including fine art, Asian and Middle Eastern studies, biomedical sciences and psychology. The college's Translation Exchange works with link schools to boost language-learning among pupils and potential applicants, running the Think Like a Linguist Project and the Anthea Bell Prize. Queen's also partners with the Access Project to support young people from three schools in Cumbria and Blackburn with Darwen. An annual budget of around £90,000 per year funds grants and loans awarded by a student finance committee. Music awards (including choral, organ and instrumental) are given to offer holders following auditions. Classic FM recognised the mixed-voice chapel choir at Queen's as "one of the world's most renowned choirs". College facilities are excellent, with accommodation offered throughout undergraduate courses at the main site (a third of them en-suite) and in annexes around central Oxford. Queen's is fully catered, providing three subsidised meals a day. The lecture theatre is used for concerts and screenings. Sport and drama are also important to college life with the garden play a major highlight of the summer term. Queen's has a popular beer cellar and ample JCR facilities with free afternoon tea a big hit with students. Alumni include cricketer Claire Taylor (the first woman to be named a Wisden Cricketer of the Year), Rowan Atkinson and Tim Berners-Lee (the masterminds behind Mr Bean and the World Wide Web respectively).

St Anne's

Oxford OX2 6HS 01865 274 840 st-annes.ox.ac.uk
Undergraduates: 472 Postgraduates: 468 admissions@st-annes.ox.ac.uk

True to its motto: *consulto et audacter* (purposely and boldly), St Anne's is bold and forward-looking. It gained full college status in 1952 but has been widening access since 1879, when it was founded as the Society of Oxford Home-Students – allowing women to study in affordable halls without having to pay for college membership. The Schwarzmann Centre for the Humanities opened in 2025 across the road from St Anne's, making the college very convenient for both humanities and the Science Park. The college's Bevington Road redevelopment of 82 undergraduate rooms launches in 2026. The outreach scheme Aim for Oxford works with students from St Anne's link region, the North East of England, and the college runs a Women and Non-Binary People in STEM programme. It also supports the COSARAF scholarship for underprivileged Muslim students, as well as two Tikvah Scholarships – for a Jewish student and an Israeli student of any or no faith. Each year St Anne's funds 40 "Study Abroad" visiting students and it is the only college to offer paid internships for its students – based in the UK, India, Serbia and Japan. Rooms are decided by ballot and accommodation is guaranteed over three-year courses. The welfare team's Be Well, Do Well programme aims to help students succeed at Oxford. The new library on the Woodstock Road is a point of pride, adding 2,000 books a year. St Anne's musical tradition prevails in student-led ensembles and a termly showcase, while its new "All-Steinway School" status should enhance its appeal to music applicants. The St Anne's / St John's Rugby Football Club (The Saints) is a pillar of sport at both colleges. Many students cycle to the university sports ground on Iffley Road, although there is an on-site gym and nearby sports field.

St Catherine's

Oxford OX1 3UJ 01865 271 700 stcatz.ox.ac.uk
Undergraduates: 510 Postgraduates: 415 admissions@stcatz.ox.ac.uk

Established in 1962, "Catz" is Oxford's youngest college and its modernist design by Arne Jacobsen sets it apart from the rest. Occupying a spacious site, it offers a vast 36 undergraduate subjects and has the most undergraduate students. Rooms – small but warmer than in older colleges – are available on site for first, second and third years. Positioned next to the Social Science faculty, Catz is characterised by an open, laid-back atmosphere but achieves excellent academic results, consistently ranking in the Norrington table's top 10 until the table's discontinuation in 2024. The airy Wolfson and College libraries house more than 60,000 books and study spaces. Extensive facilities include a theatre, on-site boathouse, squash courts, a water garden, an amphitheatre, gym, and – rare among Oxford colleges – a car park. A progressive JCR compounds the less traditional feel and with the largest bar in Oxford, Catz has a social reputation, hosting "bops" throughout the year. Welfare support includes a college counsellor and a fund for gender expression. Catz ran 97 outreach events for over 3,000 students in the 2024–25 academic year, continuing its sustained Catalyst Programme with linked areas in Wales, London and Teesside. High student numbers and generous budgets translate into success on the sports pitch and onstage at Catz. Men's rugby and women's football are particularly strong, while the annual Cameron Mackintosh Chair of Contemporary Theatre has seen visiting professorships held by Arthur Miller and Sir Tom Stoppard. Catz students also take active roles in writing and directing their own productions.

St Edmund Hall

Oxford OX1 4AR   01865 279 009   seh.ox.ac.uk
Undergraduates: 413   Postgraduates: 334   Visiting students: 27   admissions@seh.ox.ac.uk

Known as "Teddy" Hall, the college claims to be "the oldest surviving academic society to house and educate undergraduates in any university". It is among the oldest Oxford colleges, first recorded in 1317, though Edmund of Abingdon (declared a saint after his death) taught at a house on its site in the 1190s. Located off the High Street on picturesque Queen's Lane, the college library is housed in the church of St Peter-in-the-East and its medieval crypt is an architectural jewel. The college's blog showcases St Edmund Hall academics' research, allowing students to engage with the latest thinking. Emphasising learning outside undergraduate study, the college hosts programmes such as the Centre for the Creative Brain, Access Hall Areas, and the Geddes Memorial Prize and Lecture – the latter awarding £6,500 of journalism prizes to university students annually. Adding to its literary slant, the college hosts a Writer in Residence, offers writers' workshops and publishes in-house magazines and circulars. Outreach is focused on the East Midlands, and the college offers in-school talks as well as visits. The St Edmund Hall community is known for being social, creative and vigorously sporty. A two-part college bar houses The Buttery, a hub for sports teams or societies and the lively Well Bar. Food is excellent with formal dinners twice a week (Sunday is black-tie) and celebratory dinners to mark diversity events and religious festivals. Undergraduate accommodation is offered for two years, with first-years housed in medieval quads a stone's throw from the Bodleian library. Offsite accommodation is on Norham Gardens, close to University Parks, which is being redeveloped into three buildings: the Villa, West House and Park House due to open in October 2026.

St Hilda's

Oxford OX4 1DY   01865 286 620   st-hildas.ox.ac.uk
Undergraduates: 400   Postgraduates: 350   admissions@st-hildas.ox.ac.uk

Founded in 1893 as an all-female college, Hilda's started admitting men in 2006 and now has an equal gender split. Its riverside position just beyond Magdalen Bridge and into Cowley creates a campus feel, and the college boasts beautiful gardens as well as college-owned punts and kayaks. Hilda's exceptionally well-stocked library has reading rooms and a specialist law library. The JCR-run student bar is one of the busiest in the city and student societies book Hilda's impressive Jacqueline du Pré Music Building and panoramic rooftop bar. The modern Anniversary Building, complete with 52 student bedrooms and a music recording studio, add to the college's amenities. The purchase of the former site of St Benet's Hall in 2022 on St Giles means Hilda's can now house undergraduates for the duration of their studies. Professor Dame Sarah Springman, appointed Principal in February 2022, is focusing on developing the "whole person" in students and extra-curriculars are encouraged whether artistic, musical, sporting, political or humanitarian. Sport is particularly strong, with excellent hockey, football, and cross-country teams competing successfully in intercollegiate "Cuppers" competitions. The college's Rugby Football Club, Hildabeasts RFC, is also well-known across the university. The college prides itself on inclusivity: a "class liberation officer" represents those who self-identify as working class and Hilda's has its own multifaith room. Outreach initiatives focus on schools in Hampshire and Surrey, Hilda's link regions. An extensive range of scholarships, bursaries, and grants supports students. Hilda's College Ball in early summer is one of the university's most affordable. Round tables in the dining hall, unique among Oxford colleges, encourage conversation and a convivial atmosphere.

St Hugh's

Oxford OX2 6LE   01865 274 910   st-hughs.ox.ac.uk
Undergraduates: 415   Postgraduates: 438   admissions@st-hughs.ox.ac.uk

At its 14-acre north Oxford site down the Banbury Road, Hugh's has a modern and progressive outlook and a thriving culture across the arts, humanities, sciences, and social sciences. There is a campus feel at the large site, where green spaces and Edwardian red-brick buildings combine with contemporary facilities such as the Dickson Poon China Centre building, where students have access to the KB Chen Library to consult holdings of the Bodleian without leaving college. There is also the Howard Piper Library in an elegant 1930s art deco building, housing over 85,000 books and open 24/7. Though out-of-the-way compared to some colleges, a 15-minute walk or short bike ride brings students to the city centre. A network of academic assistance and an in-house college counsellor have helped foster a welcoming atmosphere in recent years. There are scholarships and prizes for undergraduates, graduates, and prospective applicants including financial support for travel, academic projects and hardship funds. Linked with Kent, Hugh's outreach team runs the length of the Kentish coast every year, stopping at around 25 schools to deliver talks and subject taster sessions. Accommodation is guaranteed to undergraduates for the duration of their first degree. Rent is lower than average with several rooms specially designed for the use of students with accessibility issues. Postgraduate accommodation is also available. The subsidised food is well-known for its quality with regular formal dinners a highlight of college life. There is also a popular café, the Wordsworth Tea Room, on site. Excellent extracurricular facilities include music rooms, a gym, a boathouse, and a sports ground shared with Keble.

St John's

Oxford OX1 3JP   01865 277 317   sjc.ox.ac.uk
Undergraduates: 446   Postgraduates: 261   admissions1555@sjc.ox.ac.uk

St John's enjoys a prime spot – a few minutes' walk from the Bodleian and the High Street on St Giles. One of the wealthiest Oxford colleges, it was reputedly possible at one time to walk from St John's, Oxford to St John's, Cambridge without leaving college land. In real terms, its finances enable cheaper rent and food for students, along with access to generous academic prizes and book grants. College buildings combine traditional limestone quadrangles (the Front and Canterbury Quads) with modern accommodation blocks (Kendrew Quad and Beehive Building) and a spacious new Library & Study Centre. Founded by London cloth merchant Sir Thomas White in 1555, the college traditionally produced Anglican clergymen. In its early history, John's prioritised the teaching of medicine and law, but it expanded into the arts and humanities over the past half-century. John's has a reputation for academic and sporting success, finishing eighth in the final iteration of the Norrington Table in 2024 and fielding a long list of college teams. Students compete in rowing, football, rugby, netball, badminton, squash, tennis, cricket, croquet, ultimate frisbee, and darts – helped by two gyms, a boathouse, two squash courts and a large sports ground off the Woodstock Road. A chapel choir, drama society and full orchestra make use of practice rooms and the state-of-the-art auditorium, and St John's has a busy cultural programme of exhibitions, concerts and lectures.

Outreach initiatives include the Inspire Programme of pre- and post-GCSE support for non-selective state-school applications. Student welfare and wellbeing support includes an in-house psychotherapist, free yoga sessions and a "College Cat Stakeout" where students hunt the grounds for resident felines.

St Peter's

Oxford OX1 2DL   01865 278900   spc.ox.ac.uk
Undergraduates: 375   Graduates: 255   admissions@spc.ox.ac.uk

St Peter's is known for its friendliness, informality and excellent relations between students and tutors. Founded as St Peter's Hall in 1929 to offer an Oxford education to students with limited financial means, it was granted full college status in 1961. A smaller college, Peter's admits around 100 undergraduates and 100 postgraduates a year. Located in the heart of Oxford off George Street, it is close to most central university departments and libraries but also convenient for the bus and railway stations. All freshers live in college and Peter's can accommodate up to half of its second-year students; the rest "live out" in private accommodation. Third- and fourth-year students can live in college rooms including in the recently completed annexes next to Oxford Castle. The dining hall caters for different diets and twice a week puts on an affordable formal dinner. The student-run college bar is loved by Peter's students and is legendary across the university for its buzzy atmosphere and lethal five-shot cocktail, the Crossed Keys. The beautiful college library and dedicated law library are open 24 hours a day. Particularly strong for rowing, five St Peter's students and alumni represented Oxford in the Boat Race 2025. Mark Carney, Prime Minister of Canada, is among the college's illustrious alumni. The college's Summer Garden Play and Garden Party are highlights of the Trinity term. Its intake of UK students from state schools (61.9% from 2022–2024) is among the lowest at Oxford colleges. Peter's employs a full-time access and outreach coordinator, however, working with schools, teachers, parents and carers in the college's dedicated link regions in Enfield, Waltham Forest, Merseyside and the Isle of Man. Welfare support includes tailored resources for students.

Somerville

Oxford OX2 6HD   01865 270 619   some.ox.ac.uk
Undergraduates: 454   Postgraduates: 280   academic.office@some.ox.ac.uk

Located just off St Giles, Somerville takes its name from pioneering scientist and writer, Mary Somerville. It was founded in 1879 as the second women's college at Oxford and was the university's first non-denominational college. Men have been admitted since 1994. Somerville stands near many of the university's faculty buildings – including the new £185m Schwarzman Centre for the Humanities, which opened in 2025. Somerville continues to expand on its promise to "include the excluded" through one of the strongest portfolios of scholarships and early career support at Oxford. Its scholarships and early fellowships create greater access to academia for undergraduates and postgraduates, and improve career opportunities for aspiring academics. Travel grants are generous, too. Somerville also takes part in the university's Astrophoria Foundation Scholarships and offers sanctuary scholarships for refugee students as well as scholarships for students from marginalised communities. In 2024, Somerville launched the RISE Campaign, which aims to galvanise the college community around four goals: resilience, inclusivity, sustainability and academic excellence. The centrepiece of RISE is the Ratan Tata Building for interdisciplinary study, which begins construction in Spring 2026 to Passivhaus standards. Eminent Somervillians include Nobel laureate Dorothy Hodgkin, novelist AS Byatt, and former Prime Minister

Margaret Thatcher. The college has a 100,000-volume library and funds a busy Arts Week programme. Somervillians are particularly well represented in student journalism and drama. Extracurriculars include an excellent chapel choir, a baking society and a boat club. College rooms on the central site provide accommodation for all undergraduates and some first-year postgraduates. Somerville is one of Oxford's most international colleges and has particularly strong links with India through the Oxford India Centre for Sustainable Development, which it hosts. Having tended to fall towards the bottom of the academic rankings historically, Somerville made an impressive rise in the final Norrington table, reaching the top ten.

Trinity

Oxford OX1 3BH   01865 279 900   trinity.ox.ac.uk
Undergraduates: 330   Postgraduates: 155   admissions@trinity.ox.ac.uk

With gates onto Broad Street, St Giles and Parks Road, Trinity is nestled in the heart of Oxford, near the Sheldonian Theatre and Bodleian Libraries. Its long drive, pristine lawns and picturesque walk give the impression of a countryside stately home. The new Levine Building has brought modern facilities, however, including the de Jager Auditorium, five teaching rooms, 46 student bedrooms, an informal study space and a popular café. A landscaping project has restored a woodland garden and created a new one in Library Quad. Students have 24-hour access to the library of nearly 60,000 books. First and second years live in college, with covetable grand "sets" (shared double rooms) among the accommodation. Third and fourth years mainly live out, either in college-owned properties on Staverton Road and the Woodstock Road or in privately rented properties. Trinity's food is famously good with Monday's steak-and-brie night especially popular and the head chef's recipes published on the college Instagram. Formal Hall is held three times a week, though new student kitchens provide spaces for informal dining. Trinity's annual programme of public lectures and performances attracts high-profile musicians and speakers. Many students volunteer for the paid student ambassador programme, which supports the college's outreach work in Oxfordshire, while it also focuses widening participation on its link regions of Milton Keynes and the Northeast of England. An in-house psychotherapist is available twice a week. Trinity's new president, Sir Robert Chote, began his tenure in 2025.

University College

Oxford OX1 4BH   01865 276 677   univ.ox.ac.uk
Undergraduates: 415   Postgraduates: 240   admissions@univ.ox.ac.uk

Known as "Univ", the college is as central you can be in Oxford, located on the High Street opposite All Souls. Its founding history is a subject of great debate. Legend has it that Univ was founded by King Alfred in 872, but it is more likely that Univ owes its origins to William of Durham, who died in 1249. Either way, the college can claim to be the oldest in Oxford or Cambridge. Its ancient roots belie a forward-thinking college; Univ's Opportunity Programme, launched in 2016, paved the way for a university-wide Opportunity Oxford scheme supporting offer-holders from under-represented backgrounds in the transition to university. Its Beacon Programme bursaries benefit students from widening access backgrounds and further financial help includes travel grants for study trips abroad. Baroness Valerie Amos LG, the Labour life peer and former United Nations official, became Oxford's first black head of house in 2019, and the second black woman to lead an Oxbridge college. In-college accommodation is provided for first and third years – in flats, sets or single rooms – with second years housed in a modern annexe on Staverton Road. Two 24-hour libraries and the Bodleian a stone's throw away make Univ ideal for book lovers. There is an excellent chapel choir, and students stage an annual garden play. Univ's boathouse towers above other colleges' facilities, and rowing excels. College members have access to a chalet in the foothills of Mont Blanc in summer, shared with Balliol and New College.

Wadham

Oxford OX1 3PN   01865 277 545   wadham.ox.ac.uk
Undergraduates: 482   Postgraduates: 242   admissions@wadham.ox.ac.uk

Wadham occupies an impressive and attractive site opposite Trinity on Parks Road and offers one of the largest selections of course combinations at Oxford. The college is known for its leftist politics and social activism, and Wadham prides itself on a liberal and inclusive laid-back atmosphere. At the recently opened Back Quad development – comprising the William Doo Undergraduate Centre and the Dr Lee Shau Kee Building – the Locke Access Centre is the first university building purpose-built for outreach work, reflecting Wadham's extensive widening access programmes that have engaged with over 37,000 pupils across around 1,000 events over the past seven years. The college does not run any gowned formal dining, but weekday dinners are served in the 17th century hall at a competitive price. The McCall MacBain Graduate Centre has a kitchen for students to make their own meals. First and final year undergraduates are guaranteed on-site rooms, others are offered more modern off-site accommodation on Iffley Road or in Summertown. The JCR and MCRs have combined to form a student union at Wadham. They organise some of the best events in the Oxford social calendar: Queerfest, the largest queer event at the university on an invariably wet November night and Wadstock, which kicks off the Trinity term in 60s style. The beautiful Holywell Music Room is the oldest purpose-built music room in Europe. Wadham's sixth warden, John Wilkins, helped to found the Royal Society during the English Civil War. Other Wadhamite alumni have gone on to win Nobel prizes and Oscars.

Worcester

Oxford OX1 2HB   01865 278 391   worc.ox.ac.uk
Undergraduates: 450   Postgraduates: 270   admissions@worc.ox.ac.uk

Before the dissolution of the monasteries, 15 abbeys had lodgings in Gloucester college, which was re-founded as Worcester College after the benefaction of Sir Thomas Cookes (a Worcestershire baronet) in 1714. One of Oxford's most popular and oversubscribed colleges, Worcester also takes pride in an inclusive ethos and diverse intake of students: between 2022 and 2024, 85.6% of offers went to state school students. It boasts beautiful grounds – perfect for activities including croquet, ultimate frisbee or lounging in the sun – and the only lake within a college site. Undergraduates live in college for three years and Worcester is unique to have sports fields on site. The famous neoclassical Hall and Chapel, with interiors by James Wyatt and William Burges, remain in daily use and the older buildings and cottages continue to house students and the JCR. The Sultan Nazrin Shah Centre contains lecture theatres, rehearsal spaces, a dance studio and a water garden. Arts and humanities students love the Worcester Arts Week, regular concert programme, music lesson scheme, and summer performances of Shakespeare plays by the Buskins dramatic society. Worcester has three libraries housing 65,000 volumes within the 24-hour access modern reading rooms, specialist Law Library, and venerable Old Library – home to important European manuscripts, special collections, prints, architectural drawings and early printed books. The college's Commemoration Ball every three years is a hot ticket, which students have attempted to break into via inflatable dinghy. Good food is served at Formal Hall three nights a week and the Cellar Bar downstairs is famously fun.

Cambridge College Profiles

Christ's

Cambridge CB2 3BU   01223 334 900   christs.cam.ac.uk
Undergraduates: 440   Postgraduates: 304   admissions@christs.cam.ac.uk

Christ's is considered very academic, even by Cambridge's standards. It regularly tops the Tompkins Table (although Trinity has beaten it into second place for the past two years), and a Christ's team won University Challenge for the first time in 2025. The main site is right in the city centre, which is convenient for accessing many university departments (and many nightclubs). The college holds 150 of its alumnus Charles Darwin's letters, and a garden is named after him. Concealed by trees is a 17th century outdoor swimming pool and pavilion. Upon completing their final exams of the summer, Christ's students jump in the water fully-clothed. Christ's is one of very few colleges where academic performance affects how accommodation is allocated. A few enviable rooms are reserved for students who achieve a first in their first or second year. About 60 undergraduates live in houses on Jesus Lane and King's Street. The rest live on-site – along with the college cats, Finch and Baines. Some buildings date back to 1505. More modern accommodation is on offer in the brutalist New Court, and the newly-opened Yusuf Hamied Court. Washing machines and powder are free. Construction work will begin in summer 2026 on a new library and expanded cafeteria.

Churchill

Cambridge CB3 0DS   01223 336000   chu.cam.ac.uk
Undergraduates: circa 449   Postgraduates: circa 396   admissions@chu.cam.ac.uk

Churchill's Brutalist buildings stand out from the cobblestones and timber framing of Cambridge. Beyond the imposing concrete entrance is the largest single site of any college. The campus has 42-acres of playing fields and 1,000 trees. Churchill also boasts an art studio, squash and tennis courts, a dance studio and a music centre with a recording studio. The college also has some of the best provisions for students with families, including 45 larger flats and maisonettes, and a children's playground. The modern buildings reflect the college's atmosphere. Students can walk on the grass and gowns aren't needed at formals. Churchill collaborates with the Welsh government organisation Seren, which assists Welsh sixth-formers with applications to Oxbridge and other Russell Group universities. The college was founded to champion science and technology and by statute, 70% of students must take STEM subjects. Churchill's large size means arts students are still in good company, although the college does not offer every humanities undergraduate course. The college is set back from the city centre, neighbouring the mathematics department, and its sports pitches are opposite the newly-developed Cambridge West Innovation District.

Clare

Cambridge CB2 1TL   01223 333200   clare.cam.ac.uk
Undergraduates: 497   Postgraduates: 300   admissions@clare.cam.ac.uk

Dating from 1326, Clare is Cambridge's second-oldest college and offers garden views leading out onto the Backs and the River Cam. After extensive building work, many formal spaces in Clare's Old Court are now fully accessible. The new River Room café has stunning views of the grounds, which back onto the river. Students perform a play in the picturesque Fellows' Garden at the end of each Easter term. If students wish to take off on the river, the college's four punts are free to book. Clare students are especially proud of the Cellars – a bar in an old crypt beneath the chapel, the site of parties hosted by generations of students. Clare's jazz and sound engineering societies also use the space for events. Postgrads have a separate, somewhat calmer bar. First-year students live together in Memorial Court, across the river and a road from the main site. A handful of undergrads obtain rooms in the historic Old Court, but many live across the city on the Castle Court site. Clare has a prestigious choir and strong rowing teams. Despite Clare's extensive outreach programmes, the proportion of incoming state-educated students decreased from a high of 75.2% in the 2022 admissions cycle to 68.5% in the 2024 cycle – one of the lowest in Cambridge. Sir David Attenborough is an alumnus and an Honorary Fellow.

Corpus Christi

Cambridge CB2 1RH   01223 338 000   corpus.cam.ac.uk
Undergraduates: 315   Postgraduates:181   admissions@corpus.cam.ac.uk

Corpus Christi College is signposted by the unusual Chronophage clock, which is often ringed by tourists. The small central site corners King's Parade, so is conveniently close to the city centre. Some students stay in truly historic rooms, full of charm but rarely en-suite. Old Court was built in 1352 and is said to be the oldest continually inhabited court at either Cambridge or Oxford. Many first-years live in hostels near the main site, including the more modern Beldam building. The newly renovated Modford Lodge provides accommodation for undergrads near the Sidgwick Site. The Corpus Playroom is one of the most-used theatres by students of all colleges. A mile west of the original college buildings are the sports facilities and Leckhampton, a campus for postgraduates. Corpus has its own gym, tennis and squash courts and playing fields. Students join with those from Christ's and King's to form "CCK" sports teams. The cosy Taylor Library has over 100 desk spaces. Corpus is also home to the Parker Library, which boasts a famed collection of rare medieval manuscripts. Pelican Bar, which doubles up as a café during the day, lies beneath Library Court.

Downing

Cambridge CB2 1DQ   01223 334 800   dow.cam.ac.uk
Undergraduates: 465   Postgraduates: 441   admissions@dow.cam.ac.uk

Downing's grand neoclassical buildings encircle immaculate lawns. The college was originally founded in 1800 to champion the study of law and natural sciences, and it maintains strong reputations in both subjects. The site is next-door to the Old Addenbrooke's Site and the Downing Site, which are home to many natural science departments. Downing boasts some of the most comfortable accommodation in Cambridge, featuring plenty of double beds, en-suite bathrooms and practical kitchens. A few students live within the college boathouse at the edge of Midsummer Common. Washing machines are free for students to use. Downing teams are formidable opponents on sports pitches and on the River Cam. There are also opportunities for students to engage with the arts, through shows at the 160-seat Howard Theatre, an annual literary magazine, and contemporary art exhibitions at the Heong Gallery. Students work on the giant sofas in the Lord Butterfield Cafe and Bar during the day, then attend live music events in the evenings. The college aims to raise £40 million by 2027 for its Downing 360 campaign, so it can hire more fellows and update more accommodation. The refurbishment of Bene't Place was completed in 2024. The building has modern rooms for supervisions and a multi-faith space.

Emmanuel

Cambridge CB2 3AP   01223 334 200   emma.cam.ac.uk
Undergraduates: 468   Postgraduates: 313   admissions@emma.cam.ac.uk

Emmanuel's pale neoclassical entrance contrasts the bustling Grand Arcade shopping centre over the road. The tranquil grounds include a 1740s pool for the students to swim in, and two ponds for the ducks and moorhens. A lawn called the "Paddock" has plenty of picnic tables. Undergraduates usually live on-site. A subterranean passageway connects the accommodation across the street in North Court to the main college buildings. The college also has more than 150 rooms for postgraduates, both on-site and around Cambridge and there is a shop for provisions by the cafeteria. The chapel was designed by Christopher Wren, and hosts some of the Emmanuel College Music Society's many concerts. Music is a popular pastime here and the college owns numerous pianos, a three-manual organ and a double-manual harpsichord. Students refer to their college as "Emma" – and appreciate its proximity to Cambridge's only Wetherspoon's pub. Although an increasing number of colleges allow students to use washing machines for free, Emmanuel remains the only college with staff who actually do students' laundry for them as part of their rent.

Fitzwilliam

Cambridge CB3 0DG   01223 332 000   fitz.cam.ac.uk
Undergraduates: 490   Postgraduates: 481   admissions@fitz.cam.ac.uk

Fitzwilliam was founded in 1869 to make the university more accessible to those who could not afford to join a college. It relocated to a larger site north of the city centre in 1963, and gained full college status in 1966. Fitzwilliam maintains this mission of inclusivity: 84.3% of UK students accepted in 2024 came from state schools – the second highest proportion of any Cambridge college. "Fitz" adopted the billy goat as its mascot and there are two wicker goat sculptures adorning the gardens – which are known to wander into students' corridors during parties. Strewn among lush gardens is a quirky variety of buildings, ranging from an 1813 manor house and an airy modern library to the uniquely shaped dining hall. What the on-site accommodation blocks lack in traditional appearance, they make up for with practicality. Nearly all are en-suite or semi en-suite. Large kitchens include ovens – a rarity in Cambridge. Second-year undergrads often choose college-owned houses between the main site and the sports pitches. Fitz consistently sits in the middle section of the Tompkins Table. Extra-curricular societies are livelier than at many other colleges. Students can join a wide variety of music groups, and sports teams perform well in inter-college contests. Fitz has a strong claim to being the best college for football, as it boasts seven Cuppers victories from the last eight years. The college has begun a £40 million "Future Fitz" project, which entails 130 en-suite student rooms, more energy-efficient buildings, and even more sports facilities.

Girton

Cambridge CB3 0JG   01223 338 999   www.girton.cam.ac.uk
Undergraduates: 529   Postgraduates: 375   admissions@girton.cam.ac.uk

Girton began as a college only for women, but began admitting men in the 1970s. The head of the college retains the title of "Mistress", regardless of their gender. The college is closer to Girton village than to Cambridge's city centre. It can take upwards of 45 minutes to walk from King's Parade to the entrance. However, the distance gives the campus a more tranquil feel. The 50-acre site includes orchards, a museum, two bars, three gyms, abundant sports courts and pitches, and the only indoor heated swimming pool of any Cambridge college. The meadows and woodland are inhabited by enigmatic black squirrels. In recent years, Girton has stayed near the bottom of the Tompkins Table. It ranked 28th out of the 29 undergraduate colleges in both 2024 and 2025. Some undergrads stay in the original red-brick Victorian buildings or more modern en-suites in Ash Court. Others live in the eco-conscious Swirles Court site, a 15-minute walk away. Girton has received awards for energy efficiency and has an environmentally friendly green roof. A corridor of bedrooms in the main building is only for women and nonbinary students. Each year, the drama society pulls together a rather Girton-specific musical in Freshers' Week and pantomime ahead of Christmas.

Gonville & Caius

Cambridge CB2 1TA   01223 332 413   cai.cam.ac.uk
Undergraduates: 584   Postgraduates: 254   admissions@cai.cam.ac.uk

Caius is pronounced "keys" – an Elizabethan founder decided the Romanised spelling of his name was more fashionable, and thus confused tourists for centuries to come. The college's main site, Old Courts, tops King's Parade. The historic Gate of Honour leads straight to the university's Senate House – although legend has it that if students use it before their graduation, they'll be graded a third. Caius claims to have the oldest purpose-built chapel in Cambridge, as some walls date back to 1390. All first-year undergraduates live in modern en-suite rooms on West Road, next to the Sidgwick Site humanities departments. Some undergrad students do snag rooms in the main site's medieval court, but many live in different accommodation across central Cambridge. Building works for the "Decarbonisation Project" are scheduled to be completed by mid-2026 and should make the older buildings more efficient to heat. Caius is one of only two colleges where three-course Formal Hall dinners are served each night, in addition to an earlier cafeteria-style meal. Caius students must pay in advance for 31 meals each term. This academically strong college has a particular reputation for medicine. The proportion of UK freshers who attended state schools has risen from 55.4% to 72.8% over the last five years.

Homerton

Cambridge CB2 8PH   01223 747 111   homerton.cam.ac.uk
Undergraduates: 609   Postgraduates & PGCE: 848   admissions@homerton.cam.ac.uk

Homerton is the newest Cambridge college. The institution used to specialise in training teachers, then achieved full college status in 2010. All undergraduate subjects are now offered, but Homerton has an excellent reputation for its education course. The library's unusual Children's Literature Collection boasts nearly 20,000 volumes. Homerton is further from the city centre, but conveniently close to the Faculty of Education, the Biomedical Campus at Addenbrookes and the railway station. The spacious 25-acre site centres on the gothic 19th century buildings. A new £8 million dining hall and buttery, modern Porter's Lodge and auditorium have opened in recent years. 90 per cent of rooms are en-suite, making Homerton the best Cambridge college for bathrooms. Meadow-style planting gives the grounds a more informal feel than the rectangular lawns of central colleges. Homerton owns an orchard, where students can use a barbecue. The college produces juice from the apple trees and honey from beehives. Homerton has its own on-site gym. Other sports facilities are shared with St Mary's School, and the boathouse is also used by the City of Cambridge Rowing Club. Homerton ranked last in 2025's Tompkins Table.

Hughes Hall

Cambridge CB1 2EW   01223 334 898   hughes.cam.ac.uk
Undergraduates: 75   Postgraduates: 747   ugadmissions@hughes.cam.ac.uk

This college for mature students is based east of Christ's Pieces, in a different area of Cambridge to many other colleges. Hughes Hall undergrads enjoy being surrounded by fewer tourists. The college sits by Mill Road – a lively spot for cafés, restaurants and vintage clothes shops. The science departments of the Downing Site are a short walk or cycle away. The 269 rooms on the college site range from a grand Victorian building, to sets shared between two people, to modern en-suites in Gresham Court. Many rooms have views of the university's tennis courts and cricket grounds. Students gather on the two roof terraces on the Fenner's Building. The college has another 123 rooms in houses across the local area. Hughes Hall lacks the sports facilities, performance venues or chapels boasted by other colleges. However, its rowing and rugby teams regularly rank near the top of "bumps" and "cuppers". In 2023, the college launched a Pathways Programme to improve students' skills for academics, personal development and the workplace. Hughes Hall is unusual for not offering the undergraduate medicine course.

Jesus

Cambridge CB5 8BL   01223 339 339   jesus.cam.ac.uk
Undergraduates: 539   Postgraduates: 422   undergraduate-admissions@jesus.cam.ac.uk

Jesus is close to the city centre, yet has acres of lawns and on-site sports pitches. The grounds feature over 20 sculptures, including works by honorary fellow Antony Gormley, and a large bronze horse, which students are forbidden from sitting on. First-year undergraduates are housed on-site. Many students choose to live nearby in the college's picturesque terraced houses. Washing machines are free to use. The college recently renovated the bar, common room and dining hall. It has just added another staircase of postgraduate student rooms and is refurbishing more accommodation ahead of the next academic year. The sports teams have a great track record, but Jesus also caters for the more artistic. Students run the annual John Hughes Arts Festival and Jesus's West Court Gallery often hosts impressive exhibitions. Students can borrow certain pieces from an art collection to decorate their bedrooms, for a deposit. The huge May Ball is popular among students from all colleges. Ella Henderson headlined the event in 2025, and Tinie Tempah in 2024. University legend has it that Jesus's drinking society started the infamous C-Sunday tradition (when once a year, thousands of Cambridge students drink from dawn to dusk on Jesus Green).

King's

Cambridge CB2 1ST   01223 331 100   kings.ac.uk
Undergraduates: 451   Postgraduates: 398   undergraduate.admissions@kings.cam.ac.uk

The college chapel on King's Parade is known for being the most photographed building in Cambridge. In summer, students stroll through a wildflower meadow that has stunning views of the River Cam and cows. Approximately half of undergraduates stay on-site, and others live in "hostels" nearby. Bedrooms in the older buildings still have quirky architectural features. Two blocks were refurbished in 2021, and have en-suite shower rooms. There are plenty of extra-curricular activities to keep students busy, such as the art studio, the allotments and a lively politics society. Once a term, a cellar opens up for a music event called King's Bunker. The Christmas Eve carol service is televised annually – although the chapel choir is the last of any college's to not admit women. The parties have rather unique themes, such as "Ye Olde Bunker" and "Laundry Day". May Balls in the 1970s reached a level of rowdiness that concerned local police, so now the college runs an alternate event called King's Affair. Guests wear theatrical fancy dress instead of white tie. King's partnered with the charity IntoUniversity to open a new education centre in Middlesbrough in March 2025. The facility provides academic support and mentoring for young people.

Lucy Cavendish

Cambridge CB3 0BU   01223 332 190   lucy.cam.ac.uk
Undergraduates: 455   Postgraduates: 638   admissions@lucy.cam.ac.uk

Lucy Cavendish was founded in 1965 for female mature students aged 21-plus, and took in its first cohort of 18-year-old female undergraduates in 2020. It opened up to students of all genders and ages in 2021. In 2024, 63% of successful applicants were women. "Lucy" is guided by the aim of widening access to Cambridge. The college admits the highest proportion of state-educated UK students – 94.3% from 2024. No other Cambridge college reached 90%. The college's Academic Attainment Programme supports 1,000 high-achieving pupils at UK state schools over two years. The main college site is tucked between St Edmund's College and the grounds of St John's. Lucy aims to house all undergrads and first-year postgrads, and it has invested money into accommodation over the last few years to cater to the changing student population. A new eco-conscious accommodation site opened in 2022, featuring a bright café and bar. The majority of the 72 new rooms have double beds, and all are en-suite. Some students stay in halls on-site, or at their Histon Road site. The college also puts students in houses in the local area. All of Lucy Cavendish's electricity comes from renewable energy sources. Students socialise in a communal conservatory with views of the gardens. Lucy does have its own gym and some sports teams, but lacks some of the drama or sport facilities boasted by older colleges. Students can practice instruments or participate in yoga in the Music and Meditation Pavillion. There is also a popular sewing and knitting society.

Magdalene

Cambridge CB3 0AG 01223 332 100 magd.cam.ac.uk
Undergraduates: 375 Postgraduates: 258 admissions@magd.cam.ac.uk

The college sticks to the 15th century pronunciation of its name: "Maudlin". The spelling was only finalised in the 18th century, so the postal service could distinguish it from Magdalen College at the University of Oxford. Magdalene was the last all-male college standing until it accepted women in 1988. It boasts the longest river frontage of any college. In summer, students sunbathe along a riverbank nicknamed "the beach". The Junior Common Room (JCR) maintains punts for students to use. Some students live on the main site or in college-owned houses, but many pick rooms in the buildings across Magdalene Street known as "the Village". The active theatre society holds productions at Cripps Auditorium. Magdalene shares sports pitches with St John's College and a boathouse with Queens' College. It is the only Cambridge college to have its own Eton Fives court. The chapel was built in the 1470s. The college is currently restoring its Grade I-listed Pepys Building, which includes a library housing 3,000 of Samuel Pepys's manuscripts and books. The spacious New Library opened in 2021, along with an art gallery and archive centre.

Murray Edwards

Cambridge CB3 0DF 01223 762100 murrayedwards.cam.ac.uk
Undergraduates: 383 Postgraduates: 227 admissions@murrayedwards.cam.ac.uk

"Medwards" is one of the two remaining all-female colleges at Cambridge. The college was founded in 1954 under the name New Hall, then renamed in 2008. Its uniquely Modernist campus is just north of the city centre, close to Fitzwilliam and Churchill. Meals are served in a dining hall with a large concrete dome. The library is a bright and airy space for study. Medwards students can walk on the grass – as well as sunbathe and picnic. The gardeners encourage students to pick flowers for their rooms and herbs for their cooking. Medwards houses more than 600 works of modern and contemporary art by women – featuring pieces by Tracey Emin and Barbara Hepworth. First-years are housed together on-site. Their kitchens boast some of the very few freezers in Cambridge college accommodation. The three-storey Art Café/Bar is adorned with artwork, and overlooks a large fountain. AstraZeneca partnered with the college to launch the Murray Edwards Enterprising Women programme, to assist female students and recent graduates from across the university with becoming entrepreneurs. The

Gateway programme aims to prepare students for the workplace. Medwards is also the alma mater of television presenter Claudia Winkleman.

Newnham

Cambridge CB3 9DF   01223 335 700   newn.cam.ac.uk
Undergraduates: 386   Postgraduates: 265   admissions@newn.cam.ac.uk

Newnham is one of two remaining women's colleges at Cambridge. Alumnae include Diane Abbott, Clare Balding, Sylvia Plath and Emma Thompson. The college is across the road from the Sidgwick Site. Humanities students from other colleges frequent Newnham's airy Iris Café to study between lectures, or to sample the extensive selection of pastries. Newnham has sports pitches and tennis courts on-site. The 18-acre grounds are a beautiful backdrop for the JCR's annual May Week garden party. Undergraduates live in the modern Dorothy Garrod Building, or one of five 18th century blocks. Many bedrooms have balconies or window seats overlooking the gardens. The rent for every room is the same – regardless of size, en-suite bathroom or kitchen facilities. Newnham is the only college not to offer the undergraduate course in economics, and it lacks a chapel or multi-faith space. Its library is exceptionally well-stocked with 100,000 volumes – including 6,000 rare books. Students can perform in weekly music recitals in the old laboratories. Newnham's outreach programmes include the Essay Writing Masterclass Programme – a free, 12-week course for female Year 12 students interested in pursuing humanities or social sciences at university.

Pembroke

Cambridge CB2 1RF   01223 338 100   pem.cam.ac.uk
Undergraduates: 453   Postgraduates: 288   admissions@pem.cam.ac.uk

Cambridge's third-oldest college is conveniently located in the midst of several university science departments. The picturesque main site features a small orchard, 1350s buildings, and a chapel designed by Christopher Wren. Bathrooms and kitchen facilities are in scant supply within the on-site accommodation. However, Pembroke is developing the Mill Lane site across the road, which will create 110 new en-suite rooms and more spaces for students to socialise. Pembroke also accommodates students in Selwyn Gardens near the Sidgwick Site, or Lensfield Road near the station. The college owns elegant terraced houses on Fitzwilliam Street, which are popular among third-year students. Pembroke is particularly proud of its alumnus Ted Hughes. The college houses many of his manuscripts, has stained glassed windows decorated with his quotes, and displays his desk. A strong reputation for drama is upheld by the Pembroke Players theatre society, one of the largest in Cambridge. Actors Naomie Harris and Tom Hiddleston attended Pembroke. In 2024, 59.5% of the undergraduates accepted to Pembroke were women – the highest proportion beyond the women's colleges and Lucy Cavendish. Many students from Pembroke claim that their college's brunch is the best in Cambridge.

Peterhouse

Cambridge CB2 1RD   01223 331 403   pet.cam.ac.uk
Undergraduates: 301   Postgraduates: 203   admissions@pet.cam.ac.uk

Peterhouse is the oldest Cambridge college, dating to 1284. It is also the smallest, and does not offer every subject. It is the only college not to accept undergraduates for geography or psychology. The centuries-old main site sits opposite Pembroke College, and the colleges share sports grounds. Peterhouse also has its own gym and squash court. The Deer Park has not been home to an actual herd of animals since 1935, although in summer plenty of students roam onto the grass from the nearby bar. Undergraduates are accommodated in historic courts or terraced houses nearby. Freshers mostly live on the other side of the Fitzwilliam Museum, either in St Peter's Terrace – grand Georgian houses on Trumpington Street – or an eight-storey 1960s high-rise building next-door. Peterhouse has two libraries: the Perne and the larger Ward, which previously housed the university's Museum of Classical Archaeology. Three-course Formal Hall dinners are lit by candles in the wood-panelled hall each evening. The atmospheric 17th-century chapel features a recently rebuilt organ and has a strong tradition of music. In 2022, a 16th century brewhouse was converted into new music practice and recital spaces.

Queens'

Cambridge CB3 9ET   01223 335 511   queens.cam.ac.uk
Undergraduates: 542   Postgraduates: 546   admissions@queens.cam.ac.uk

The apostrophe in Queens' College was not used consistently until 1831, and is often not used consistently by students today. Tradition has it that the college was founded in 1448 by the Lancastrian leader Margaret of Anjou, then her Yorkist rival Elizabeth Woodville refounded the college 17 years later out of spite. The college site is split across the River Cam. The east half features medieval courts, a timber-framed long gallery, and two libraries. Across the iconic Mathematical Bridge is a less cohesive set of buildings. Freshers live together in the 1970s Cripps Courts. Several undergraduates share twin-bedded sets. The city centre and the Sidgwick Site are both a short walk away. Students can pick from an extensive selection of societies. The sports teams range from climbing to water polo. The Bats drama club often puts on shows in the college gardens. Queens' Arts Festival is the largest annual college event of its kind. Students display their work and attend a week of performances, workshops, panels and DJ nights. The annual Medieval Outreach Day aims to engage high-achieving sixth-form students with history and culture.

Robinson

Cambridge CB3 9AN   01223 339 143   robinson.cam.ac.uk
Undergraduates: 398   Postgraduates: 280   apply@robinson.cam.ac.uk

Robinson primarily consists of red bricks. The college takes pride in its distinctive look – students drink in the Red Brick Café Bar and perform with the Brickhouse Theatre Company. Robinson is opposite the University Library, close to the Sidgwick Site's humanities departments. Students needn't cycle far to the shops in the city centre, but the college's café also sells some groceries. The university-subsidised U bus stops outside Robinson, and helps students travel to further-flung sites. The River Cam runs through extensive gardens, where students can walk all over the grass and play croquet in the summer. Freshers' rooms mostly have balconies overlooking the lawns, and en-suite bathrooms. In later years, many students share houses scattered among the grounds. The state school intake has gradually increased from 47.4% to 63.2% over the last ten years. A dedicated wellbeing centre opened in October 2022. The cafeteria-style Garden Restaurant serves a variety of meals. Robinson's campus features an auditorium, a modern chapel, an outdoor theatre and a space devoted to the college's fortnightly "bop" parties.

Selwyn

Cambridge CB3 9DQ   01223 767 839   sel.cam.ac.uk
Undergraduates: 375   Postgraduates: 322   admissions@sel.cam.ac.uk

Selwyn neighbours the Sidgwick Site – ideal for humanities students who love a lie-in. The faculties of economics and divinity overlook part of the grounds. Red brick Gothic Revival buildings border grass courts. Selwyn has rapidly risen up the Tompkins table in recent years, from 14th place in 2022 to third in 2025. After extensive fundraising, many facilities have been upgraded over the last few years. The new Ann's Court includes an auditorium and a library with 100 study spaces. A final piece of building work is planned to link two parts of Ann's Court and create a community space. First-year students get en-suite rooms over the road in Cripps Court. Sports facilities are a ten-minute walk away on Fulbrooke Road and are also used by King's students. Selwyn shares a boathouse with King's and Churchill. The college's teams tend to prioritise participation over achievement. Selwyn's drama society puts on Shakespeare plays in the gardens. The chapel choir has recorded albums and toured internationally. Instead of a May Week ball, Selwyn organises an annual Snowball event in December each year. The college runs a bridging programme for freshers from under-represented backgrounds ahead of their first term.

Sidney Sussex

Cambridge CB2 3HU   01223 338 800   sid.cam.ac.uk
Undergraduates: 370   Postgraduates: 320   admissions@sid.cam.ac.uk

Sidney is situated in the centre of Cambridge, opposite the supermarket most frequented by students. The university's ADC student theatre is around the corner. Accommodation for undergraduates is mostly on the main site and spills over to the surrounding streets. The college's Sid Bar is one of the last still run by students. The space is popular for its cheap pints and signature Cambridge-themed drinks – including a cocktail named after Sidney alumna Carol Vorderman. Free wellbeing activities, such as meditation and yoga classes, also take place in the bar. The Rococo dining hall is an atmospheric setting for the thrice-weekly formal dinners. Sidney shares the St John's College sports facilities. The gym is free for students, staff and Fellows to use. For a smaller college, Sidney has an exceptionally active choir. The group tours internationally and performs three times a week in the chapel, including at candlelit Vespers. The EQUIP programme aims to prepare students for life after Cambridge, and a new strand offers extra support for first-gen students. On summer evenings, students sit at picnic tables scattered throughout the immaculate gardens. Oliver Cromwell's head is buried in a secret location beneath the grounds.

St Catharine's

Cambridge CB2 1RL   01223 388 300   caths.cam.ac.uk
Undergraduates: 439   Postgraduates: 391   undergraduate.admissions@caths.cam.ac.uk

St Catharine's – nicknamed "Catz" – is just beyond King's Parade. The compact campus lacks large gardens, but the college recently spent £30 million renovating many facilities and accommodation blocks. Alumnus Sir Ian McKellen opened a new dining hall, gym, music room and prayer room in 2022. The college aims to achieve net zero carbon emissions by 2040, and so has installed six air source heat pumps. Freshers live in courts on the main site, known as the "Island" site. Most second-year students share flats at the St Chad's Site on Grange Road, near the University Library. These newer accommodation blocks have fully-equipped kitchens. Catz has several successful sports teams, as well as some more unique extra-curriculars. Students run societies devoted to bubble tea, cheese and wine, and yarn handicrafts. The college does not accept undergraduates for architecture, education, linguistics, or history of art. Law, medicine and veterinary medicine are not on offer to applicants who already have a degree. During the 2024 to 2025 academic year, St Catharine's engaged 3,822 participants in outreach activities, hosted 20 visits from schools, and sent representatives to 34 schools. The college recently introduced a new bursary for Scottish undergraduate students.

St Edmund's

Cambridge, CB3 0BN 01223 336 250 st-edmunds.cam.ac.uk
Undergraduates: 225 Postgraduates: 701 admissions@st-edmunds.cam.ac.uk

"Eddies" only accepts students aged 21 or older. The 10-acre site is a short walk north-west of the city centre. Students enjoy picnics and barbecues in the leafy grounds. Eddie's boasts a large student-run bar, which opens into the gardens. Plenty of open-mic nights are held there. The central 1896 building includes 60 rooms for students. Many undergrads choose to live in the 262 en-suite rooms and flats of the recently-built Mount Pleasant Halls. The college offers accommodation to students with children and the St Teddy's Club organises events for families. St Edmund's was originally founded as a space for Roman Catholic students. Although students of all faiths and none are now welcome, Eddie's remains the only Cambridge college with a Catholic chapel and Dean. Cambridge traditions take a backseat here – Fellows don't sit at a high table during formal dinners. St Edmund's has a strong reputation for sport and 17 alumni have competed at the Olympic Games. The Isaac Newton Trust recently gave funding to St Edmund's and the two other mature colleges – Hughes Hall and Wolfson – for outreach programmes at UK further education colleges.

St John's

Cambridge CB2 1TP 01223 338 703 joh.cam.ac.uk
Undergraduates: 609 Postgraduates: 347 admissions@joh.cam.ac.uk

St John's has developed a reputation of being one of Cambridge's most traditional and academically rigorous colleges – hence the origins of the chant "We'd rather be at Oxford than St John's". The proportion of privately educated students has decreased in recent years, although only 61.8% of UK students accepted in 2024 came from state schools – one of the lowest figures in Cambridge. St John's is the second-wealthiest college after Trinity, so can afford a range of grants and awards for students. The college is piloting a ground-breaking Free Places scheme. Subject to fundraising, St John's will start to pay the full tuition and maintenance costs for some UK undergraduate students with challenging financial circumstances in the 2028/2029 year. Some undergraduates live in shared "sets" with rather unusual layouts. Food is a big feature of St John's. Formal dinners in the atmospheric 16th-century hall take place several times each week. Students can eat other meals in the stylish buttery, or café, or bar. A dazzling array of breakfast dishes and baked goods are available at weekend brunch. St John's students love to remind people their May Ball was once named the seventh-best party in the world by Time magazine.

Trinity

Cambridge CB2 1TQ 01223 338 422 trin.cam.ac.uk
Undergraduates: 707 Postgraduates: 315 admissions@trin.cam.ac.uk

Henry VIII founded Trinity in 1546 by merging two earlier colleges. Trinity remains a place of extremes. It is by far the wealthiest Oxbridge college, reporting net assets of £2.413 billion for the year ended 30th June 2024. Trinity topped the Tompkins Table in both 2025 and 2024. The college can also claim the most undergraduates, the most University Challenge victories, and the most British prime ministers among its alumni of any Cambridge college. However, in the 2024 admissions cycle, Trinity accepted the lowest proportion of female students. Only 36.5% of freshers were women. Excluding the mature colleges, Trinity also admitted the fewest UK state school students – just 54.4%. The outreach team is starting school visit days in autumn 2025. The college can afford plenty of bursaries and travel grants for students, including extra funding for graduates to support projects during the summer holidays such as internships, language courses and volunteer work. Through the Trinity Maintenance Grant, eligible students can receive up to £3,000 per year, paid on top of the main Cambridge University Bursary to total £7,500 per year in bursary funding. Undergraduates are housed in the 750 on-site rooms. In later years, students can apply to share a set with a friend. The gym, sports pitches and tennis courts are across the River Cam, near the university's library. Trinity's famous alumni include Francis Bacon, A. A. Milne, Sir Isaac Newton and King Charles III. Lord Byron kept a bear called Bruin in his room while he studied at Trinity.

Trinity Hall

Cambridge CB2 1TJ   01223 332 535   www.trinhall.cam.ac.uk
Undergraduates 361   Postgraduates 225   admissions@trinhall.cam.ac.uk

Trinity Hall actually pre-dates its larger neighbour Trinity College by about 200 years. The main site is compact but charming, with an elegant 18th century court and a riverside terrace. The modern Jerwood Library overlooks the Cam, so students watch punters glide past the windows. "Tit Hall" is close to the bustling cafés of King's Parade. Humanities students can commute quickly to the Sidgwick Site by cycling over Garret Hostel Bridge. About 107 undergraduates get to live on the main campus. The rest are split among Tit Hall's other sites across Cambridge. The Thompson's Lane site is a short walk away, and offers rooms with double beds and en-suite bathrooms. The Wychfield Site is further afield, beyond the "hill colleges" on Storey's Lane. Undergrads and postgrads can choose between a range of rooms there, and have easy access to the college's extensive sports facilities. Trinity Hall has its own squash and tennis courts, plus grounds for football, hockey, rugby, cricket and netball. The WongAvery Music Gallery was added to Avery Court in 2022, and received a regional award from the Royal Institute of British Architects. The college has also planned construction works to make the central site more efficient to heat and eco-friendly.

Wolfson

Cambridge CB3 9BB   01223 335 918   www.wolfson.cam.ac.uk
Undergraduates 173   Postgraduates 1,072   ugadministrator@wolfson.cam.ac.uk

The majority of Wolfson students are postgraduates, but the college accepts approximately 50 new undergraduates aged 21 or older each year. The site is in the west of Cambridge, beyond Newnham and Selwyn. The college was founded in 1965, but the intricate gardens pre-date the buildings. Many students live on-site, in accommodation varying from single en-suite rooms, to flats for families, to shared sets. Wolfson is one of Cambridge's most international communities – students come from 99 different countries. The WolfWorks programme and Wolfson Writing Centre host frequent workshops to boost students' academic skills. Wolfson shares the Old Combined Boathouse with Corpus Christi, Girton and Sidney Sussex. The rowing teams often excel in inter-college competitions. The college recently completed a multi-million refurbishment of its dining spaces. In a break from Cambridge tradition, there is no high table for Fellows at Formal Hall. Wolfson has a strong tradition of poetry. Students and staff can contribute writing to the annual WolfWords anthologies. Each year, the college hosts a poetry night with plenty of wine and cheese. The large May Balls have a calmer atmosphere – and much cheaper tickets – than events dominated by teenage undergrads.

12 University Profiles

This chapter provides profiles of all 130 universities that feature in The Times and Sunday Times league table. It also has profiles of the Open University, which supplies the greatest number of the country's part-time degrees; Birkbeck, University of London, which specialises in evening courses; and the University of the Highlands and Islands. Because of their special course or geographical circumstances, none of these appear in our main ranking. We do not have separate profiles for specialist colleges, such as the Royal College of Music (www.rcm.ac.uk) or institutions that only offer postgraduate degrees, such as Cranfield University (www.cranfield.ac.uk). This is not a reflection on their quality, it is simply due to their particular roles. A number of additional institutions with degree-awarding powers are listed at the end of the book, along with their contact details.

Dating back to 1836, the federal University of London (www.london.ac.uk) is Britain's biggest conventional higher education institution by far, with a total of more than 240,000 students. The majority study at its 17 self-governing colleges in the capital. Further afield it also offers degrees at the Institute in Paris, and its global prestige attracts more than 40,000 students in 190 countries to take University of London degrees via distance learning. Its School of Advanced Study comprises eight specialist institutes for research and postgraduate education (details at www.sas.ac.uk).

The following University of London colleges have their own entries in this chapter: Birkbeck, Brunel, City St George's, Goldsmiths, King's College London, London School of Economics and Political Science, Queen Mary, Royal Holloway, SOAS, and University College London. Contact details for its other constituent colleges are given on page 439.

Guide to the profiles

Valuable information about each university is contained in their profiles. These benefit from our extensive survey of UK universities, which inform the detailed, up-to-date synopses in this chapter. The latest campus developments, results from the National Student Survey, trends in application and social data, financial help available to undergraduates, research reputation and findings from the government's Teaching Excellence Framework inform their content. You can also find contact details for admission enquiries along with postal addresses and open day information.

We also include data under the heading "The Social Inclusion Index" in Chapter 6. This is taken from our latest table on social inclusion that gives details of student recruitment and the socioeconomic and ethnic mix of each institution. The methodology for its data can be found on pages 90–101.

In addition, each profile provides information under the following headings:

» **The Times and Sunday Times rankings:** For the overall ranking, the figure in bold refers to the university's position in the 2027 *Guide* and the figure in brackets to the previous year. All the information listed below the heading is taken from the main league table. (See Chapter 1 for explanations and the sources of the data).
» **Undergraduates:** The number of full-time undergraduates. The figures are for 2020-21 and are the most recent from the Higher Education Statistics Agency (HESA).
» **Accommodation:** The information was obtained from university accommodation services, and their help is gratefully acknowledged.

Tuition fees

Details of tuition fees for UK students in 2025-26 are given. At the time of going to press, universities had not published their 2026-27 tuition fees for UK students, but the government had confirmed they would increase from £9,535 in line with inflation. For international students, tuition fees for 2026-27 are given wherever possible, although some universities had not confirmed their fees at the time of going to press. In these cases, the fees for 2025-26 are given. It is of the utmost importance that you check university websites for the latest information. Every university website gives details of the financial and other support available to students, from scholarships and bursaries to study support and hardship funds. Some of the support will be delivered automatically but most will not, and it is up to applicants to explore the details on university websites, including methods of applying and deadlines, to get the greatest benefit. In addition, in England the Office for Students (**www.officeforstudents.org.uk**) publishes "Access and participation plans" for every English university on its website. Each agreement outlines the university's plans for fees, financial support and measures being taken to widen access to that university and to encourage students to complete their courses.

University of Aberdeen

The granite city's university has a justifiably solid reputation thanks to its ancient lineage (dating to the 15th century) and academic clout (it boasts association with five Nobel laureates). This is backed up by high undergraduate satisfaction: the university ranks =25th for student experience and =44th for teaching quality this year.

Aberdeen has 12 teaching schools and offers almost 400 degrees, with the opportunity for students to switch and mix subjects as their interests broaden. Some of the university's best results in the latest Research Excellence Framework (REF 2021) were in theology and religious studies, Earth systems and environmental sciences, and public health. However, Aberdeen has slipped to =63rd in our research quality ranking.

Longstanding links with Aberdeen's offshore oil and gas industries include a partnership with the National Decommissioning Centre in Newburgh, though MEng courses in civil and mechanical engineering with subsea technology, and mechanical engineering with biomechanics are being discontinued from 2026. New for 2025 are degrees in sport and exercise science, and physics with astrophysics; new from 2026 is an LLB in international law and comparative law, and a MEng in electrical and electronic engineering with robotics.

Entry requirements for medicine are AAA at A-level or AAAAB in Scottish Highers, while other degrees ask for BBB to BBC at A-level. Contextual offers are available under a broad range of criteria, and about 12% of entrants in 2024 gained their places through clearing. Improving 19 places from last year, Aberdeen ranks 28th for graduate outcomes, with work placements and internships helping 82.2% of leavers find highly skilled jobs or further study within 15 months of completing their studies.

The Old Aberdeen Campus houses the imposing King's buildings as well as a modern library and the £35 million Science Teaching Hub. Life sciences and medical students share Europe's largest health campus with NHS Grampian. The medical school has benefitted from recent upgrades, and there is a new Centre for Zoology and Osteoarchaeology. The Hillhead Student Village includes an outdoor gym and a community garden with plants from the Cruickshank Botanic Garden.

Among more than 100 societies and 50 clubs, the university boasts the oldest shinty club in the world, established in 1861. Alongside the Aberdeen Sports Village, there is a boathouse on the River Dee, and a climbing bothy. The King's College Chapel provides a 16th-century backdrop for chamber concerts and houses a three-manual organ. For lovers of the great outdoors, the region has 150 miles of coastline and the university is within striking distance of the Cairngorms National Park and the Glenshee Ski Centre.

Students have access to a free counselling service. All first-years are guaranteed a room if they apply by the deadline. Accommodation ranges from £103 to £178 a week, and is free for the first year for students from the most deprived Scottish postcodes. Aberdeen is 3rd among Scottish universities for its proportion of black and ethnic minority students (17.3%) but ranks 7th for its achievement gap. Means-tested and merit-based financial awards are offered according to whether applicants are from Scotland, the rest of the UK, or abroad.

King's College Aberdeen AB24 3FX
study@abdn.ac.uk
abdn.ac.uk
ausa.org.uk

Overall ranking =23
(last year 15)

Accommodation
University provided places 2,184
Self-catered £103–£178 per week

Student numbers
Undergraduates 9,170
Applications per place 5.8:1
Overall offer rate 82.6%

Fees
Scots fees £0–£1,820
International fees £20,800–£24,800
RUK fees £9,535
Medicine £50,100

abdn.ac.uk/study/open-days/undergraduate-open-day/
abdn.ac.uk/study/undergraduate/finance

Abertay University

Dundee is the UK's only Unesco city of design and, having launched the world's first computer games degrees in 1997 and an ethical hacking course in 2006, Abertay University has now opened Scotland's only dedicated virtual production film studio to sit alongside its competitive games lab and Cintiq (digital arts) lab. There are also plans for a new national malware analysis centre.

Centrally located in Dundee, Abertay makes an asset of its small size, with 4,000 students who report high rates of satisfaction to go with the city's community feel, sitting in =37th place in the wider student satisfaction measure. For teaching quality, it ranks 27th. Abertay has expanded into transnational education, and students in more than 20 countries can study for an Abertay degree. Abertay also introduced Scotland's first accelerated degrees, taking three years to complete rather than the usual four.

There are two new degrees available from 2025: environmental management and sustainability, and engineering management. Courses fall within two academic faculties: Social and Applied Sciences, and Design, Informatics and Business. All games students become members of UK Interactive Entertainment, the games business trade body. Abertay made a relatively small submission to the most recent Research Excellence Framework (REF 2021) across eight subject areas, with its strongest performances coming in art and design, engineering, food science and psychology.

Applicants can expect offers ranging from BBC to CCC at A-level, or AABB to BBBC in Scottish Highers. Abertay accepted more than 1,000 students from about 5,000 applications in 2024 – 12% of them through clearing and more than a third through contextual offers. Most courses have a work placement built in; there is an annual student internship with the V&A Dundee; and a scheme backed by Santander provides 15 work placements for students during the summer. But in our analysis of the Graduate Outcomes survey, Abertay has fallen 29 places to rank 98th.

At the city-centre campus, a £1.2 million library revamp will provide new social spaces for students and improved facilities for Abertay Students' Association. The broader environment in Scotland's fourth-largest city is vibrant and affordable, and student life includes a range of societies and a gallery space hosted by The School of Design and Informatics. There is a free and confidential counselling and mental health service, while a pilot wellbeing clinic, run by trained and paid student interns under academic supervision, launched in 2025. About 600 study rooms are available from £129 a week. Places are prioritised for entrants from outside the Dundee area postcode, students with disabilities and those who have left care.

Abertay places 2nd in our Scottish social inclusion league table. Abertay also accepts qualifications from a further education college, and there are evening classes for those without formal qualifications who have been away from study for at least three years. Financial support includes a bursary of £1,750 a year for students from England, Northern Ireland or Wales; subject-specific scholarships for games/computing/cyber courses; the Baillie Gifford Scholarship for Women studying forensic science or ethical hacking; and foundation bursaries worth £2,500 a year for students from low-income households.

Kydd Building Bell Street Dundee DD1 1HG
sro@abertay.ac.uk
abertay.ac.uk
abertaysa.com

Overall ranking 62
(last year 74)

Accommodation
University provided places 600
Self-catered £129–£202 per week

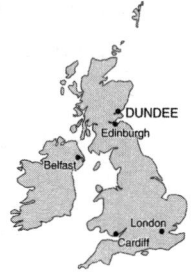

Student numbers
Undergraduates 3,485
Applications per place 4.7:1
Overall offer rate 87%

Fees
Scots fees £0–£1,820
International fees £15,000–£15,500
RUK fees £9,535

abertay.ac.uk/visit/open-days
abertay.ac.uk/study-apply/money-fees-and-funding/tuition-fees

University of Aberystwyth

Maybe it's the sea air, but Aberystwyth is home to Wales's most contented students. It sits =12th (down from 2nd last year) in the wider student experience rankings, and 10th for teaching quality. Welsh University of the Year in 2024, Aberystwyth is awarded University of the Year for Sustainability 2026, jumping up from =109th to rank 29th in the People & Planet league table thanks to ambitious carbon neutrality targets and leading teaching and research on climate change.

Many courses can be studied wholly or partially in Cymraeg (Welsh), but you do not have to be a Welsh speaker to study here. The university features in the upper half of our table for research quality (=62nd) thanks to strong results in agriculture, food and sports science, and Celtic studies in the latest Research Excellence Framework (REF 2021).

Aberystwyth's School of Veterinary Science has welcomed its fifth cohort of Bachelor of Veterinary Science (BVSc) students in collaboration with the Royal Veterinary College (RVC) in Hertfordshire. New for 2025 are courses in biomedical science, electronics, intelligence and international security, equine and veterinary bioscience, and zoology. Course entry requirements range from 96 to 144 UCAS tariff points, with contextual offers at the lowest end applicable to all courses except veterinary science. Demand for places rose by about 14% in 2024, with 2,000 out of 10,500 applicants accepted, about 10% through clearing.

Each academic department has links with employers and more than 40 undergraduate programmes include an integrated year in industry or professional practice. The university also offers opportunities to study abroad. It ranks 90th in our analysis of graduate outcomes.

The gothic Old College on the seafront was the original campus until operations moved to Penglais, a 32-hectare site perched between Cardigan Bay and the Cambrian Mountains. The National Library of Wales is next door, the Lluest Equine Centre nearby houses a purpose-built teaching facility, and a £40.5 million Enterprise Campus (AberInnovation) is at the university's Gogerddan site. The university plans to turn the Old College building into a cultural and creative centre to improve flexible working. Excellent sports facilities include a 40m x 23m air dome, a self-powered gym and stabling for students' horses.

Students find a sense of safety on a small-town campus and more than 100 clubs and societies in which to spread their wings. Aberystwyth is often considered the cultural capital of Wales, and the university has its own boutique cinema and theatre. Support for mental health includes one-to-one and daily drop-in sessions with the wellbeing service. First-years are guaranteed one of more than 3,000 accommodation places and students can choose mixed or gender-specific flats.

Aberystwyth has dropped out of the top 50 to rank 62nd for social inclusion. It runs the Access All Aber residential visit for year 12 students from Wales who meet the criteria, leading to enhanced contextual offers for those who successfully complete the programme. Just under a third of new undergraduates receive financial aid, including merit-based entrance scholarships; awards for care leavers, young carers and students estranged from family; Welsh-medium scholarships; and subject-specific awards.

Penglais Campus Aberystwyth SY23 3FL
ug-admissions@aber.ac.uk
aber.ac.uk
abersu.co.uk

Overall ranking 42
(last year 48)

Accommodation
University provided places 3,106
Catered £220 per week
Self-catered £119–£205 per week

Student numbers
Undergraduates 5,405
Applications per place 5.0:1
Overall offer rate 94.4%

Fees
UK fees £9,535
International fees £18,170–£20,715

aber.ac.uk/en/study-with-us/open-days
aber.ac.uk/en/undergrad/before-you-apply/fees-finance/tuition-fees

Anglia Ruskin University

Opened by the influential art critic John Ruskin in 1858 as the Cambridge School of Art, Anglia Ruskin University (ARU) now occupies four campuses encompassing a range of specialisms tailored to a population of more than 30,000 undergraduates. ARU has long been the main provider of health and social care graduates in the east of England. Ranking 39th in our social inclusion index, widening access is ingrained at the university, and about half of students are aged over 21 when they enrol. It also offers degree apprenticeships for roles including medical doctor, physiotherapist, social worker, data scientist, civil engineer and police constable.

In the Research Excellence Framework (REF 2021), nine subject areas were judged to have made a world-leading impact, and ARU's music therapy research for patients with dementia was recognised with the presentation of a Queen's Anniversary prize in 2022. ARU took a step up in the Teaching Excellence Framework (TEF 2023), replacing its overall silver award with a gold, although in our National Student Survey (NSS) analysis it has dropped to =99th from =37th for teaching quality and to 109th from 73rd for the wider student experience. ARU's relatively low continuation rate of 85% also hampers its overall ranking in our main league table, although this is often a consequence of a diverse student community.

ARU is offering 24 new degrees in 2025 and 2026, spanning the fields of science and engineering, business and law, education, and game design. A contextual offer scheme operates in most subjects, including medicine. Unusually, Anglia Ruskin does not require a maths A-level for some of its engineering programmes as part of its diversification strategy. Many courses offer a year in industry, shorter-term work experience opportunities, or live briefs from industry partners. ARU Temps is an on-site recruitment agency that arranges paid temporary work and internships that fit around students' studies. Even so, ARU remains outside our top 100 for graduate prospects, based on 69% of graduates being in skilled employment 15 months after their degrees.

The £30 million Peterborough Campus opened its newest teaching building in 2024, featuring specialist labs for microbiology studies and engineering suites. In Cambridge, facilities include simulated hospital wards, lifelike crime-scene rooms and the law clinic, where lawyers work beside students to provide legal advice to the community. In Chelmsford, the riverside base hosts the £20 million medical school, and ARU Writtle is the university's 370-acre campus in the Essex countryside. ARU also has an outpost in London Docklands, mainly for business and law students.

Sports and leisure facilities vary by campus. Cambridge is geared up for undergraduates, offering student nights at pubs and bars. A counselling and wellbeing service offers one-to-one support, workshops and podcasts, and students are trained as peer wellbeing mentors. First-years who have firmly accepted an offer for a full-time place in Cambridge and Chelmsford are guaranteed accommodation, but there is no similar assurance for Peterborough or Writtle.

Financial aid includes the ARU Bursary of up to £300 for those where the household income is less than £42,875 and help with travel and laptop purchase for those whose incomes are under £25,000. Sport and merit-based scholarships are also available.

Bishop Hall Lane Chelmsford CM1 1SQ
answers@aru.ac.uk
aru.ac.uk
angliastudent.com

Overall ranking 123
(last year 130)

Accommodation
University provided places 1,119
Catered £131–£190 per week
Self-catered £126–£227 per week

Student numbers
Undergraduates 15,530
Applications per place 4.0:1
Overall offer rate 76.9%

Fees
UK fees £9,535
International fees £16,700–£19,500

aru.ac.uk/study/open-day
aru.ac.uk/study/tuition-fees

Arts University Bournemouth

The place to be creative by the seaside, Arts University Bournemouth (AUB) is a small institution with big ambitions. Since becoming a university in 2012, it has developed a broad spectrum of creative fields within four schools, including the largest film school outside London. With a range of integrated foundation years set to launch in autumn 2026, and the promise of interdisciplinary courses, AUB has earned the runner-up spot for Specialist University of the Year 2026. Its research profile is on an upward trajectory, climbing to 103rd in our research quality index, with more than 12% of submissions classified as world-leading or internationally excellent in 2021. Architecture and history of art and design were among the strongest subjects.

AUB was rated silver overall in the Teaching Excellence Framework in 2023, with campus facilities found to be "exceptional". However, in our analysis of the latest National Student Survey (NSS), AUB remains 82nd for teaching quality and has slipped to 105th for the wider experience. AUB is among many preparing for redundancies across its academic, technical and professional services teams, with the university stating that "the financial outlook remains difficult" in May 2025.

New for 2025 are BAs in business of games; content creation with marketing; fashion management and strategy; games narrative; and media, marketing and advertising. A degree in movement and creative practice will be introduced in 2026. Course requirements start at BBB at A-level (reduced to BCC for those eligible for a contextual offer), or ABB for architecture. All courses, except architecture, now offer a one-year work placement and the AUB Innovation Studio runs a free six-month incubator programme to graduates ready to start their own business. Despite this, however, institutions with an art and design focus tend to occupy the lower ranks of our graduate prospects table: AUB ranks 127th.

Teaching is based on a single site and students are encouraged to work together across disciplines. Facilities include the CRAB drawing studio designed by Sir Peter Cook, and the restored art deco Palace Court Theatre. New fine art studios utilising north-facing light are under construction, while a new research centre for plastics innovation and curation opened in 2025. AUB does not have its own sports facilities, but students share Bournemouth University's extensive gym, classes and courts at a subsidised rate. There is a rolling programme of lunchtime and evening music concerts and AUB's gallery hosts exhibitions and panel discussions.

More than 200 staff have been trained in mental health first aid and the university has teamed up with the NHS, Bournemouth University and local charities to offer a range of intervention and support services. Although AUB does not guarantee accommodation, there is enough space for all first-years to live in.

The university runs outreach schemes for all ages. Those who complete All Access AUB qualify for additional consideration from the admissions team and a reduced conditional offer up to two grades lower than standard. AUB ranks 81st in our social inclusion index, up two places. About a fifth of entrants receive some form of financial assistance, including pre-enrolment support to help with travel costs to offer-holder days and transition events.

Wallisdown Poole BH12 5HH
admissions@aub.ac.uk
aub.ac.uk
aubsu.co.uk

Overall ranking =73
(last year 78)

Accommodation
University provided places 1,131
Self-catered £174–£244 per week

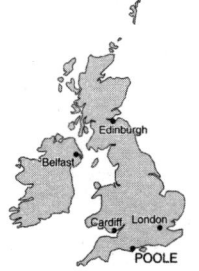

Student numbers
Undergraduates 3,570
Applications per place 5.0:1
Overall offer rate 75.2%

Fees
UK fees £9,535
International fees £19,950

aub.ac.uk/open-days
aub.ac.uk/fees

University of the Arts, London

The capital's home for creative courses has a reputation for producing Turner Prize winners, and has ranked 2nd in the global QS index for art and design for seven years running, driving record demand to study at the arts institution. A university since 2003, University of the Arts London (UAL) is made up of six colleges, each with its own identity, offering students unrivalled access to the city's rich cultural life.

UAL made by far the largest submission for art and design in the latest Research Excellence Framework (REF 2021) to rank in the top 50 (47th) in our research quality index. 85% of its work was judged to be world-leading or internationally excellent. A new site in Shepherd's Bush for pre-degree and foundation programmes has freed up the space to accommodate 3,000 more students at the university, which is already the largest in Europe in its specialism. The 2025 launch of UAL Online, offering online, part-time degrees with multiple entry points throughout the year and no campus attendance, should raise student numbers further still.

However, UAL slipped from silver to bronze overall in the latest national Teaching Excellence Framework (TEF 2023). Student outcomes were graded silver and the student experience bronze, correlating with tepid feedback from undergraduates in the National Student Survey (NSS). Student feedback has improved this year, and UAL has risen to =89th and 97th in our rankings for teaching and student experience respectively.

Two new courses in sound arts welcomed their first students this year at London College of Communication. UAL asks for 64–136 UCAS tariff points and applicants may need to submit a portfolio. After a bumper recruitment year in 2024, only 5% of entrants secured a place through clearing, but almost half benefitted from UAL's contextual admissions process. UAL is working hard to improve notoriously tough employment rates for creative graduates through an in-house temp agency, placements and project work with global brands, but only manages 124th in our graduate prospects ranking.

Facilities across the six colleges include the £200 million Central Saint Martins Campus at King's Cross and the £216 million London College of Fashion in east London. Student societies proliferate under the Arts SU banner, covering interests across culture, faith, creativity and academia, and the university runs a rolling programme of exhibitions, seminars, workshops and more. The sporting calendar culminates in varsity competitions against Goldsmiths, University of London.

In-person and online counselling sessions are available and there is a 24-hour mental health support line, as well as urgent care for emergencies. Expensive London rents mean the cheapest twin room costs £167.50 a week, with some accommodation costing £393 a week. First-year international students on a full-time course are guaranteed accommodation, and under-18s and disabled students are prioritised. All other rooms are allocated on a first-come, first-served basis.

There is a £1,400-a-year bursary for those receiving a full maintenance grant, as well as various donor-funded course-related scholarships and a hardship fund. In spite of an extensive outreach programme including Saturday clubs for year 10 students, this year UAL has plunged to 86th from 48th in our social inclusion ranking.

---

272 High Holborn London WC1V 7EY
admissions@arts.ac.uk
arts.ac.uk
arts-su.com

Overall ranking 53
(last year =40)

Accommodation
University provided places 3,814
Self-catered £168–£393 per week

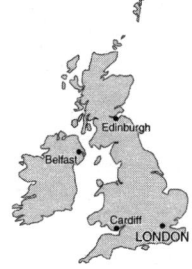

Student numbers
Undergraduates 16,105
Applications per place 6.0:1
Overall offer rate 48.4%

Fees
UK fees £9,535
International fees £29,990

arts.ac.uk/open-days
arts.ac.uk/study-at-ual/fees-and-funding

Aston University

Almost half of Aston's students are based at the highly rated business school building on the city-centre campus. The pioneer of degree apprenticeships in the UK, Aston had 1,250 enrolments in 14 undergraduate programmes at the last count in 2024, and a work placement in the UK or abroad is a compulsory element of most degrees. New initiatives aim to equip students for success in AI, entrepreneurship, leadership and environmental sustainability, and Aston remains in the top 25 in our analysis of the Graduate Outcomes survey.

The university achieved the best possible results in the Teaching Excellence Framework (TEF 2023), with triple gold for student experience, student outcomes and overall grades. In our analysis of the National Student Survey (NSS), Aston has fallen from 16th to =47th for student experience, and is =83rd for teaching quality, down nine places. In the latest Research Excellence Framework (REF 2021), 79% of the team's work was assessed to be world-leading or internationally excellent. The university hosts research centres in bioenergy, photonic technologies, neuroscience and forensic linguistics, and the new Digital Futures Institute is a hub for machine learning, AI and the Internet of Things.

This autumn, the Aston University Mathematics School opens. Also new for 2025 are degrees in nursing studies (mental health), AI and robotics, and media and communication. From 2026 Aston will offer a BA in aerospace engineering and pharmacology (subject to approval). Four courses have been withdrawn: chemistry, applied chemistry, transport management, and product design and management.

Aston's medical school requires grades of A*AA, while the lowest requirement for other courses is CCD. Qualifying students can expect a contextual offer reduction of one or two grades. Applications to study at Aston have soared to more than 23,600 in 2024. The number of places available has also increased, though not at the same rate.

The 60-acre campus is close to the centre of the buzzing city of Birmingham. The new Woodcock Street building will house the business and law faculties and have its own restaurant, exhibition and study spaces when it opens in 2025-26, while pockets of greenery provide places to relax among outdoor sculptures. The UK's second city, Birmingham, is home to five universities and offers student-friendly nightlife by the bucketload, as well as rich cultural diversity.

The £10 million Students' Union stages gigs and open-mic nights, and there are more than 20 sports clubs. Women-only sessions are available at the gym. Counsellors are available to provide support and students can use the 24/7 Togetherall online service. There is also a multi-faith chaplaincy, disability services and residential support.

First-years who meet Aston's criteria are guaranteed student accommodation in Aston Student Village. One of the better-performing pre-1992 universities in our social inclusion index, Aston has placed 2nd in England for three successive years in the Higher Education Policy Institute's social mobility rankings. In our analysis, Aston ranks =34th for social inclusion. Nearly half of entrants in 2025 benefitted from some form of financial assistance, including scholarships for study and placement costs.

Birmingham B4 7ET
ugadmissions@aston.ac.uk
aston.ac.uk
astonsu.com

Overall ranking 41
(last year 35)

Accommodation
University provided places 1,333
Self-catered £158–£164 per week

Student numbers
Undergraduates 12,330
Applications per place 5.5:1
Overall offer rate 73.3%

Fees
UK fees £9,535
International fees £21,500
Medicine £47,000

aston.ac.uk/open-days/undergraduate
aston.ac.uk/study

Bangor University

Research-led teaching comes with a hard-to-beat outdoors setting in Bangor, on the doorstep of the Eryri (Snowdonia) mountains and overlooking the Menai Strait. In 2024 Bangor launched the North Wales Medical School in collaboration with Betsi Cadwaladr University Health Board, and its newest addition is the first pharmacy school in north Wales, launching in September 2025. As for many courses at Bangor, elements of the pharmacy programme can be studied in Welsh as well as English.

Bangor sits in the top 40 of our research quality index, with 85% of its submission to the latest Research Excellence Framework (REF 2021) assessed to be world-leading or internationally excellent. Research facilities informing undergraduate teaching include an oceanic research vessel, the Prince Madog, as well as 18 hectares of botanic gardens, animal care facilities, aquariums and greenhouses. Bangor is working towards cutting its carbon dioxide equivalent emissions by 25%, and ranks in the top 20 in the People & Planet league table.

Welsh universities did not take part in the latest Teaching Excellence Framework (TEF 2023), but in the assessment six years earlier Bangor was rated gold. Our latest NSS analysis shows improvement after last year's dramatic fall in student satisfaction: Bangor now sits =51st for teaching quality and =71st for the wider experience. The university is launching 11 courses for 2025 in subjects including literature, film and languages and 2026 will welcome dental therapy, criminology, and psychology. Entrants averaged 123 UCAS tariff points in 2024, putting Bangor firmly mid-range among UK universities for its entry standards. In most cases its contextual admissions scheme offers a one-grade reduction in entry requirements.

Almost all undergraduates can choose to take a year's work placement at the end of their second year. Studying abroad or volunteering options are also offered. There are close links with employers such as ZipWorld, the NHS, Santander, BBC Cymru and Welsh Rugby Union. Despite these efforts Bangor sits only =94th in our graduate prospects table, with 71.6% of leavers in highly skilled jobs or further study within 15 months.

The university buildings form a compact coastal hub within walking distance of the city centre. The Pontio arts centre has several theatres and a 200-seat cinema hosting an eclectic programme of entertainment seven days a week. More than 150 free clubs and societies make use of facilities including a sports centre named after the cycling coach Sir Dave Brailsford, who grew up nearby. The university's wellbeing services range from individual counselling and emotional resilience workshops to support groups, mindfulness training and wellbeing drop-ins.

All first-years who apply before the advertised deadline are guaranteed accommodation in one of the two student villages, St Mary's and the larger Ffriddoedd. In our social inclusion index, Bangor ranks 52nd, helped by the relatively high proportion of white working-class boys. The university offers both sport and merit-based scholarships, and students from the UK – but excluding Wales –may qualify for a £500 or £1,000 Bangor bursary, payable over three years. There are also bursaries for student carers, those who have been in care and students who are estranged from their families.

College Road Bangor LL57 2DG
applicantservices@bangor.ac.uk
bangor.ac.uk
undebbangor.com

Overall ranking 59
(last year 64)

Accommodation
University provided places 2,611
Self-catered £99–£245 per week

Student numbers
Undergraduates 5,910
Applications per place 4.7:1
Overall offer rate 82.5%

Fees
UK fees £9,535
International fees £18,000–£21,000

bangor.ac.uk/openday
bangor.ac.uk/studentfinance/new-undergraduates

University of Bath

Secure in our top ten since 2021, Bath more than holds its own, without being a member of the Russell Group, and each year brings another record-breaking number of applications – over 38,000 hopefuls applied in 2024, with 4,820 accepted. It is University of the Year in the Southwest 2026 and Highly Commended in our University of the Year 2026. Its world-class sports facilities, which contributed to medals at the Paris Olympics and Paralympics, along with its highly-rated sports science degrees, have earned Bath Sports University of the Year 2026.

The leafy self-contained campus at Claverton Down on the outskirts of the Unesco world heritage city provides a well-equipped community environment for school-leavers. Among its legions of purpose-built academic facilities is the £70 million School of Management, and the Institute for Advanced Automotive Propulsion Systems. Bath's renowned work placement scheme is taken up by around two thirds of students, and our analysis puts Bath 6th for graduate outcomes, continuing its top ten record.

In the latest Research Excellence Framework (REF 2021), 92% of Bath's submissions were rated world-leading or internationally excellent, placing Bath 31st in our research quality index. Some of its best results were in engineering; pharmacy and pharmacology; and sport and exercise sciences. The 2025 QS rankings put Bath =12th in the world for sport, and in the top 10% overall. Bath earned triple gold in the Teaching Excellence Framework (TEF 2023), and Bath students agree: in our analysis of the National Student Survey (NSS), it ranks 11th for the wider student experience, although it has tumbled 32 places to 65th for teaching quality.

Bath is regularly among the top universities for accounting and finance in our annual subject tables, and a BSC course in finance will begin in 2026. Bath practises what it preaches too: the university has continued to register a surplus in its accounts while others are struggling. Entry requirements range from A*A*A to ABB, and it strengthened its contextual offer scheme to drop down two grades from 2025, with the exception of computer science and joint degrees in maths and physics. In 2024, the university accepted 16% of students through the scheme, with guaranteed offers for applicants who complete one of Bath's access schemes.

Alongside the Olympic-standard Sports Training Village (STV), students can keep fit at the Team Bath Gym and Fitness Centre. The Edge is the campus cultural hub, where more than 180 student groups offer the chance to participate in creative interests. Bath and its accessible nightlife is in easy reach. To aid mental health and wellbeing, there are support groups, specialist one-to-one counselling, and social prescribing, recommending art, yoga, gardening and exercise.

First-years who apply by the deadline are guaranteed a room, with some part- and fully-catered options available. Social inclusion is a work in progress, with Bath ranking 107th. Students from ethnic minorities make up just under a quarter of the Bath intake and just 2.3% are over 21. Almost a third of Bath's entrants benefitted from scholarships or bursaries in 2025, with some awards worth up to £5,000 a year.

Claverton Down Bath BA2 7AY
admissions@bath.ac.uk
bath.ac.uk
thesubath.com

Overall ranking 7
(last year 8)

Accommodation
University provided places 4,500
Catered £271–£316 per week
Self-catered £155–£280 per week

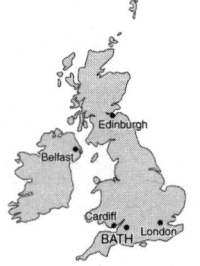

Student numbers
Undergraduates 15,030
Applications per place 7.9:1
Overall offer rate 62.7%

Fees
UK fees £9,535
International fees £24,200–£30,500

bath.ac.uk/topics/undergraduate-open-days
bath.ac.uk/topics/tuition-fees

Bath Spa University

Visitors to Bath Spa's main Newton Park campus would be forgiven for thinking they've taken a wrong turn into a National Trust property, with its gardens designed by Capability Brown and a Georgian manor house owned by the Duchy of Cornwall. Student-facing facilities, though, are fit for the 21st century. Twenty years on from becoming a university, Bath Spa has made significant upgrades to its resources for music, criminology and law. Other campuses include Locksbrook Road for arts and design and Sion Hill for fashion and textiles, both in Bath city centre, and Hackney, east London, for business and management, and health and social care courses.

Bath Spa recorded its best results yet in the most recent Research Excellence Framework (REF 2021), increasing the scale of its world-leading research by 60% and bringing it up to 88th in our research quality index. In the government's Teaching Excellence Framework (TEF 2023) Bath Spa was awarded triple silver, while our analysis of the National Student Survey (NSS) ranks Bath Spa 17th for teaching quality and 36th for the wider student experience – a vast improvement on =66th and 109th respectively last year.

Environmental sustainability is a contemporary theme at the university, which is ranked in the top 20 greenest institutions in the country by People & Planet. From 2025 the expanding curriculum gains undergraduate programmes in music (performance), and primary education (5–11) with QTS; from 2026 it will offer computer science. Degrees in pharmaceutical science and textile design are being discontinued.

Bath Spa is a medium-tariff university with a standard offer of BBC, or 120 UCAS tariff points, for all courses. Contextual admissions reduce this demand to BCC. The university received more than 14,500 applications for 2024 entry, enrolling nearly 5,750 students, less than 10% of which came through clearing. A professional placement year is offered on most courses, as well as help for students seeking internships, but in our analysis of the Graduate Outcomes survey, Bath Spa remains in the bottom 15.

The university has more than 30 sports societies and clubs, many of which compete in the British Universities and Colleges Sport (BUCS) league. Art and culture lovers gravitate to the Michael Tippett Centre, which has a 50-seat auditorium and two recording studios; the university's main theatre, with capacity to seat 186 people; and an outdoor amphitheatre.

First-years who apply by the deadline are guaranteed accommodation. Bath Spa offers layered and flexible wellbeing services from mental health practitioners, to disability advisers and a chaplain. Students may also find it helpful to spend time with the university's 15 accredited care dogs. There are free food larders at Newton Park and £1 soup at the Students' Union. Period products are available for free on campus.

It was the University of the Year for Social Inclusion in our 2024 guide, thanks in part to the greater diversity at its London campus. However, the university has dropped out of the top 30 to rank =68th. The Bath Spa bursary of £1,050 a year aims to remove financial barriers to higher education for students from under-represented groups, while there are also merit-based scholarships and a laptop fund.

Newton Park Newton St Loe Bath BA2 9BN
admissions@bathspa.ac.uk
bathspa.ac.uk
bathspasu.co.uk

Overall ranking 77
(last year 76)

Accommodation
University provided places 1,853
Self-catered £145–£311 per week

Student numbers
Undergraduates 5,730
Applications per place 2.5:1
Overall offer rate 78.6%

Fees
UK fees £9,535
International fees £16,460–£18,380

bathspa.ac.uk/open-days
bathspa.ac.uk/students/student-finance

University of Bedfordshire

The University of Bedfordshire, formed by the 2006 merger of the University of Luton and De Montfort University's Bedford Campus, has teaching campuses in Luton, Bedford, Aylesbury and Milton Keynes. Real-life simulated settings sharpen the vocational focus of this modern university; Annie Brewster Square at the Luton Campus features a mock street with flats and houses, a police custody suite, hospital ward and community clinic. In 2025-26, Bedfordshire will open a new, immersive security operations centre, which will enable students to get into the head of a cyber-attacker.

In the latest Research Excellence Framework (REF 2021), creative writing and English were among the top-scoring subjects, with 60% of the university's research assessed as world-leading or internationally excellent, putting Bedfordshire =84th in our research quality index. It is one of only seven universities in our table awarded bronze overall in the Teaching Excellence Framework (TEF 2023), but our latest analysis of student satisfaction shows a much brighter picture; teaching quality is up 32 places to =28th and the wider experience up 18 places to =60th.

Amid falling applications, in 2025 the university announced plans to make redundancies and merge faculties and schools to cut spending and ensure its long-term sustainability, but stated students would not be affected. Bedfordshire remains under "enhanced monitoring" by the Office for Students after a 2024 report raised concerns around student engagement and low continuation rates. More positively, Bedfordshire has earned the top spot in the 2024-25 People & Planet league thanks to refurbished buildings, sustainable food and a reduction in water use.

New honours degree courses include social media content creation; applied professional practice in contemporary policing and criminal investigation; and marketing data analytics. Degrees in professional policing, photography, and education studies with English have been withdrawn. Bedfordshire demands between 96 and 120 UCAS tariff points. Individual skills and background are considered, though contextual data is not part of the admissions process.

Bedfordshire aims to boost graduate careers through professional accreditations, paid internships and lived experience projects. Physical education teaching students can gain behind-the-scenes experience with Luton Town football club and Bedford Blues rugby union club. However, Bedfordshire remains in the bottom 20 of our graduate outcomes analysis at 112th.

The university markets its proximity to London as a big draw, although the social scene is lively enough closer to home. The university-owned gyms in Luton and Bedford have high-quality equipment, and shuttle buses take students to the playing fields and a multipurpose sports hall. Bedfordshire has been a member of the University Mental Health Charter since 2021 and offers one-to-one counselling and workshops. Many students live at home, but first-years who apply in the main cycle are guaranteed a room.

Bedfordshire is in the top ten for first-generation students (7th) and state-school recruitment (=10th). All students can benefit from some form of financial assistance, from subsidised lunches and free gym membership to merit-based scholarships of £2,500 a year.

University Square Luton LU1 3JU
study@beds.ac.uk
beds.ac.uk
bedssu.co.uk

Overall ranking =118
(last year 129)

Accommodation
University provided places 1,085
Self-catered £117-£236 per week

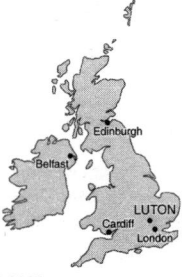

Student numbers
Undergraduates 6,455
Applications per place 4.4:1
Overall offer rate 73.0%

Fees
UK fees £9,535
International fees £16,800

beds.ac.uk/open-days
beds.ac.uk/howtoapply/money

Birkbeck, University of London

Based in leafy Bloomsbury, Birkbeck is in the University of London heartland, close to University College London and SOAS, and to Senate House library. Birkbeck stands out from its academic neighbours due to the hours it keeps: known as London's night university, it has long offered part-time study through evening classes on campus, playing a vital role in making higher education accessible to students who are combining work or childcare with their studies. London's culture and opportunity is on the doorstep, and the non-traditional learners of all ages and backgrounds that Birkbeck attracts create a diverse student body.

A college of the University of London since 1920, Birkbeck's research profile is in step with its peers. It withdrew from our league table in 2019 on the grounds that our measures place a heavily part-time university at a disadvantage. We continue to include it in our listings because of its unique place in British higher education.

The university ranks within the top 350 universities globally in the Times Higher Education 2025 league table, and it is up 20 places in the latest QS global rankings, at =388th. Birkbeck achieved only bronze in the latest Teaching Excellence Framework (TEF 2023), having held silver in the previous assessment six years earlier, and it is among the universities that have cut jobs to cut costs in recent years, as it addressed a £2.2 million financial deficit in 2022-23.

The largest subject areas, for both full- and part-timers, are business and management, and psychology; and law is the most popular subject for full-time students. New options for 2025 are computer science (with or without AI); data science; environment, culture and communication; environmental geoscience; mathematics and computer science; theatre studies; and psychological studies. Foundation years are offered on all new courses.

The college welcomes applications from people without standard qualifications and continues to attract non-traditional learners of all ages and backgrounds. Those who have taken A-level or recent equivalents are made offers based on the UCAS tariff; others are assessed on the basis of interviews and/or short tests. Micro-placements give students work experience on defined projects and Birkbeck hosts CV clinics, mock interviews and career assessments.

At the Malet Street headquarters in Bloomsbury, Birkbeck has resources that include its own library, science laboratories, and student services. A 15-minute walk away, Birkbeck has opened a Euston Road teaching facility, housing its largest lecture theatres, new classrooms, and a co-learning space. Wellbeing services at Birkbeck offer practical support, rather than therapeutic interventions, to assist students to progress through their studies. To help students finance their studies, the university offers budgeting workshops, a monthly food pantry and guidance in navigating the student loans system.

Most Birkbeck students live at home, but a housing team can help to find places in University of London intercollegiate halls. Diverse university-funded awards include cash bursaries of up to £800 to help with study costs, awarded to students from low-income households. Those who qualify under a needs-based assessment may receive up to £4,000 a year through the Birkbeck Financial Support Scheme, while hardship fund payments of up to £1,000 also help to make ends meet.

Malet Street Bloomsbury London WC1E 7HX
my.bbk.ac.uk
bbk.ac.uk
birkbeckunion.org

Overall ranking N/A
(last year) N/A

Accommodation
University provided places

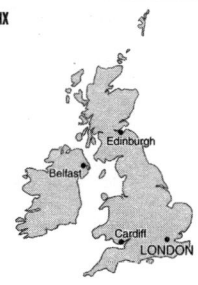

Student numbers
Undergraduates N/A
Applications per place 4.6:1
Overall offer rate N/A

Fees
UK fees £9,535
International fees £18,500

bbk.ac.uk/prospective/open-days/undergraduate-and-postgraduate-information

bbk.ac.uk/student-services/fee-payment/fees

University of Birmingham

The Birmingham student experience offers the best of both worlds: life on a leafy 26-acre campus in suburban Edgbaston combining modern and historic buildings, but within easy reach of the UK's second city. A research-led member of the Russell Group, Birmingham's enviable record on employability earns it Highly Commended in our University of the Year 2026 category.

The university achieved superb results in the national Research Excellence Framework (REF 2021) and ranks tenth in our research quality index thanks to scores in physics; Earth systems and environmental sciences; philosophy, theology and religious studies; and sport and exercise sciences. Birmingham aims to become a global top-50 university, and has climbed to 76th and =93rd in the QS and Times Higher Education global rankings respectively. A global outlook is ingrained in all courses and the university has more than 225 international exchange agreements.

Birmingham was rated silver overall in the latest Teaching Excellence Framework (TEF 2023) but achieved gold for student outcomes. Birmingham's results climbed to 88th for satisfaction with teaching quality and =47th for the wider experience in our latest National Student Survey (NSS) analysis, and recent investments should help lift this further. Among 28 new courses being launched are AI and public policy; politics, philosophy and economics (PPE); and energy engineering. Entry requirements range from BBB to A*A*A, with contextual offers typically one grade lower than standard, or two grades below through the Pathways to Birmingham access programme. 20% of entrants benefitted from these two schemes, with a further 10% entering via clearing. Birmingham attracted a record 57,625 applications in 2024, accepting more than 8,500 new undergraduates.

Birmingham's careers network, with more than 300 leading employers each year, including Lloyds Banking Group, Jaguar Land Rover, PwC and Goldman Sachs, has helped make Birmingham the most targeted university in the UK by the largest number of top graduate employers. About 9,000 students a year step into graduate jobs, internships and work placements. In our analysis of the latest Graduate Outcomes survey, Birmingham ranks 16th.

A £600 million-plus decade of development has produced energy-efficient student townhouses at Pritchatts Park and new teaching space for STEM subjects. The Centre for Anatomy, Surgical and Clinical Skills is due to open in 2026 at Birmingham's Health Innovation Campus near the Edgbaston Campus. The Selly Oak Campus hosts drama courses, and the BBC Drama Village offers student placements.

With more than 350 student groups, there is something for everyone. Off campus, galleries, museums, concert venues and student-friendly nightlife abound.

To support students, there are wellbeing officers in every academic school, and a no-wait mental health and wellbeing drop-in service. Rooms in halls are guaranteed for first-years who apply in time. As with other research-intensive universities, Birmingham tends to occupy the lower reaches of our social inclusion index, ranking 100th in our latest analysis.

About four in ten of 2024's new entrants received financial support, which includes a £2,000-a-year award for those who meet widening participation criteria.

Edgbaston Birmingham B15 2TT
admissions.bham.ac.uk/newenquiry
birmingham.ac.uk
guildofstudents.com

Overall ranking 16
(last year 22)

Accommodation
University provided places 4,267
Catered £153–£258 per week
Self-catered £99–£205 per week

Student numbers
Undergraduates 23,755
Applications per place 6.7:1
Overall offer rate 69.6%

Fees
UK fees £9,535
International fees £22,850–£31,050
Medicine £31,390–£50,360

birmingham.ac.uk/study/undergraduate/open-days
birmingham.ac.uk/study/undergraduate/fees-funding

Birmingham City University

The vibrant metropolis of Birmingham has a well-founded reputation as a leading student destination. Birmingham City University (BCU) occupies some prime spots with its campuses and specialist institutions, which include the Royal Birmingham Conservatoire and the Jewellery School, founded in 1890, in the city's Jewellery Quarter. It has poured £5 million into specialist facilities for sports and exercise degree courses, but offers a broad curriculum of more than 150 undergraduate courses.

In the latest Research Excellence Framework (REF 2021) BCU more than doubled its submission, compared with the previous national assessment in 2014. Creative writing and English produced the best results, while land and property management, building, and town and country planning also did well. Under its Strategy 2030 plan, the university announced a move towards having a greater focus on teaching, and it is one of the bigger providers of degree apprenticeships, offering 13 programmes with around 1,300 students enrolled to train as nurses, social workers, chartered surveyors and paramedics. In the Teaching Excellence Framework (TEF 2023), BCU won silver overall, and gold for student experience. Results from the latest National Student Survey (NSS) show rising satisfaction with both teaching quality (up 13 places to =69th) and the wider experience (up 12 to =64th).

Several new gaming technology degree courses launched in September 2025, and from 2026, BCU will offer new degrees in creative writing, electrical and electronic engineering, and human biosciences. It has withdrawn courses in American legal studies, biomedical engineering, digital forensics, digital media computing, and secondary science (biology) with QTS. Music technology will stop recruiting from September 2026. UCAS point requirements for entry range from 136 for Architecture to 32 for music. Contextual offers (up to four grades below standard) are available for applicants to all three-year degrees, except acting and music.

BCU has about 50 recognised professional accreditations for a range of its courses, and students can also build experience through the Graduate+ range of extracurricular employment-related activities. There are opportunities to gain work experience through mentoring schemes, industry visits and year-long placements, but BCU ranks only 100th in our analysis of the Graduate Outcomes survey.

City Centre and City South are the main campuses, with facilities designed to encourage collaboration between arts, science, technology, engineering and maths sectors. Extra sites throughout Birmingham are equipped to provide students with hands-on learning experiences, from television and film studios to mock law courts, and a 500-seat concert hall at the Royal Birmingham Conservatoire. Students have access to top sports facilities across Birmingham for free or at reduced membership fees.

Pre-entry appointments are available for any students who want to discuss mental health support. Full-time first-years are guaranteed accommodation if they apply in time, though most students commute from home. Students from low-income households who enrol via the Accelerate programme can qualify for a £1,000 scholarship in the first year, while the High Achievers' Scholarship is worth £1,000.

Curzon Building 4 Cardigan Street
Birmingham B4 7BD
admissions@bcu.ac.uk
bcu.ac.uk
bcusu.com

Overall ranking 113
(last year =107)

Accommodation
University provided places 2,294
Self-catered £105–£206 per week

Student numbers
Undergraduates 21,580
Applications per place 4.2:1
Overall offer rate 78.3%

Fees
UK fees £9,535
International fees £17,690–£27,500

bcu.ac.uk/student-info/open-days
bcu.ac.uk/student-info/finance

Birmingham Newman University

A close-knit atmosphere and a peerless record on widening participation are trademarks of Birmingham Newman, which is The Times and Sunday Times University of the Year for Social Inclusion 2026. A former teacher training college, this small Catholic institution in southwest Birmingham welcomes a diverse range of students of all faiths or none, and opens the door wide to higher education.

Birmingham Newman's biggest recruiting subjects are within education, health and social care, and psychology, but its academic focus has diversified and new facilities have been added. Nevertheless, it is still one of the smallest universities in our guide, with just under 3,000 students. This personal touch is reflected in superb rates of student satisfaction, with Birmingham Newman =15th for students' evaluation of their broad experience and 16th place for their teaching quality in our analysis of the latest National Student Survey (NSS). The university was rated silver in the government's Teaching Excellence Framework (TEF 2023).

Birmingham Newman describes itself as "teaching-led". In the latest Research Excellence Framework (REF 2021) it doubled the size of its academic submission compared with the previous national assessment in 2014, but it sits near the bottom in our research quality index (=124th). Harming its overall ranking is a relatively low continuation rate.

Entry tariffs range from 48 to 120 UCAS points and demand for places is at record levels, with contextual offers undercutting the standard ask by eight UCAS points for eligible students. Every full-time degree has a work placement module, which students complete with public, private and third-sector organisations. Through its teacher training heritage the university works with educational institutions across the West Midlands, and since the opening of its nursing and physiotherapy department in 2023, it has built relationships with healthcare trusts. Our analysis of the latest Graduate Outcomes survey puts Birmingham Newman 78th.

The modern campus has had £20 million of investment, including labs for paramedic science, occupational therapy and physiotherapy at the recently expanded School of Nursing and Allied Health. A mock law court, computer science laboratory and a careers and employability hub have also been added. Wellbeing and mental health advisers help students navigate emotional challenges. A disability and inclusion team provides advice and practical support and offers free ADHD screenings. First-year students are guaranteed a space in halls if they apply by the end of July.

Birmingham Newman's No 1 rank in our social inclusion index is boosted by its intake from under-represented groups, including those who are the first in their family to go to university (72.8%), pupils from non-selective state schools (99%), and those from low participation areas (24%). Birmingham Newman supports parents of first-generation applicants to understand the higher education processes, as well as providing pupils with activities that encourage an aspirational approach to their learning.

One Sanctuary Scholarship is awarded each year to forced migrant students and the Newman University Support Fund provides up to £1,750 a year for those experiencing hardship.

Genners Lane Bartley Green
Birmingham B32 3NT
admissions@newman.ac.uk
newman.ac.uk
newmansu.org

Overall ranking 107
(last year =90)

Accommodation
University provided places 276
Self-catered £107–£215 per week

Student numbers
Undergraduates 2,345
Applications per place 5.9:1
Overall offer rate 85.5%

Fees
UK fees £9,535
International fees £12,500

newman.ac.uk/study/open-days
newman.ac.uk/study/student-finance/undergraduate-finance-information

Bournemouth University

Sea, sand and work experience add to the charms of this south coast university, which straddles two campuses in the seaside town: Talbot (the main site) and Lansdowne (where most accommodation is based). A big draw for students at Bournemouth University (BU) is its work placement pledge: every undergraduate degree course brings an opportunity for students to gain hands-on experience with an employer either in the UK or abroad. Situated close to seven miles of sandy blue-flag beaches, BU is also noted for its commitment to environmental sustainability and ethical practices, coming 11th in the People & Planet table.

Out of 100 degree programmes and 17 subject areas, BU has become renowned for degrees in media, production and tourism, and hosts the National Centre for Computer Animation. Research in communication, cultural and media studies, and leisure and tourism was well regarded in the latest Research Excellence Framework (REF 2021). However, BU dropped to 79th in our research quality rating, against stronger gains at other universities.

BU was awarded silver overall in the Teaching Excellence Framework (TEF 2023), but only bronze for the student experience. In our analysis of the latest National Student Survey, the university has fallen to =122nd for teaching quality and =103rd for the wider experience. There are four new courses from 2025 spanning robotics, law, business and communications. However, as part of efforts to plug a £20 million funding shortfall, Bournemouth is suspending a dozen or so degrees, and applicants should check the university website for any further course changes.

With an average of 108 UCAS tariff points among new entrants, Bournemouth ranks =114th for entry standards. Applications dipped by about 9 per cent in 2024, and just under 4,000 new students enrolled on courses. Those who meet the AccessBU criteria may find their offer reduced by up to 16 UCAS tariff points. Despite its ambitious work placements and professional accreditations for several courses, BU is 60th in our analysis of graduate outcomes.

At the Talbot Campus the Poole Gateway Building has industry-standard TV studios and a motion-capture studio for animation. The faculty of health is based at Lansdowne, where the Bournemouth Gateway Building provides health students with simulation suites replicating an operating theatre, hospital wards, and an ambulance. Sport and fitness opportunities include yoga, boxercise and Zumba, as well as surfing and kayaking. For BU's creative students, there are three art spaces to show their work. An out-of-hours welfare duty officer ensures that round-the-clock care is available and BU has launched a Dorset universities suicide prevention strategy in partnership with the NHS.

First-years who select BU as their first choice by the deadline are guaranteed one of 3,759 study bedrooms. BU has climbed seven places in our social inclusion table to 63rd overall. It is in the top 25 for its proportion of white working-class male students, and nearly half of new students in 2024 were the first in their family to go to university. Care leavers' bursaries, and maintenance bursaries for students from low-income households, provide £800 a year. Scholarships reward academic excellence, musical or sporting talent, and there is a dedicated scholarship awarded to female students of cybersecurity.

Fern Barrow Poole BH12 5BB
futurestudents@bournemouth.ac.uk
bournemouth.ac.uk
subu.org.uk

Overall ranking =79
(last year 82)

Accommodation
University provided places 3,759
Self-catered £139–£239 per week

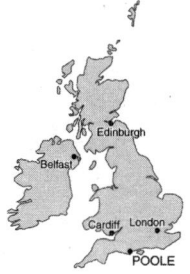

Student numbers
Undergraduates 12,395
Applications per place 5.1:1
Overall offer rate 81.8%

Fees
UK fees £9,535
International fees £18,700–£19,700

bournemouth.ac.uk/study/undergraduate/open-days
bournemouth.ac.uk/study/undergraduate/undergraduate-fees-funding

University of Bradford

With social inclusion at its heart, Bradford works hard to support under-represented groups to access higher education. Located minutes from the centre of the UK's City of Culture 2025, it is well placed to make the most of the area's new and refurbished facilities. On the self-contained campus, biodiversity is given a boost through edible gardens, buildings made from hemp and beehives tended by student keepers. Facilities are also forward-looking; its Digital Health Enterprise Zone was the site of one of the first Covid-19 mass vaccine trials.

The Research Excellence Framework (REF 2021) highlighted strengths in archaeology, engineering, accounting and allied health subjects. With 73% of work judged to be world-leading or internationally excellent, Bradford's gains were not enough to prevent a 25-place drop to 87th in our research quality index. In the Teaching Excellence Framework (TEF 2023) Bradford was awarded triple silver, but our analysis of the latest National Student Survey (NSS) shows declining satisfaction with teaching quality (up six places to 119th) and the wider undergraduate experience (110th).

The Peace Studies and International Development department recently celebrated its 50th anniversary, while the three-year-old Bradford-Renduchintala Centre for Space AI is tasked with advancing the region's capabilities within automation and communications. As part of a £13 million cost-saving, courses in film and television, and chemistry will stop accepting new students. New for 2025 are degrees in computer science for artificial intelligence, sustainable process engineering, and legal theory and solicitors practice.

Courses require 136–164 UCAS tariff points. About a third of students in 2024 entered through clearing, and about half of new undergraduates join via access or foundation courses or Btec qualifications. Bradford is comfortably in the upper half of UK universities for graduate prospects, placing 51st in our analysis, a notable achievement in the fifth most "income-deprived" local authority in England. Many courses offer opportunities for work experience or placements and are designed with input from a range of industry partners.

The City Campus has facilities for accommodation, entertainment and sport, as well as teaching and learning. Specialist developments and additions include the Lady Hale Moot Court, which opened in 2020, and the Wolfson Centre for Applied Health Research at Bradford Royal Infirmary. The sports park is a five-minute walk from campus and has a full-size football pitch, tennis courts and a conditioning suite. There is a peer-support wellbeing scheme, plus counselling and mental health appointments.

Allocation of the 1,002 rooms available at the student village, endorsed by the university, is on a first-come, first-served basis, although the majority of students live at home and commute. Bradford is top in England and Wales for first-generation students, and for students from black and ethnic minority backgrounds. It has been the UK's No 1 university for social mobility for four years running in the Higher Education Policy Institute's annual ranking, but is =35th in our social inclusion index, down from 15th last year. More than 3,000 cash bursaries are awarded to students from households with an income of less than £30,000, as well as a number of country-specific scholarships.

Bradford BD7 1DP
enquiries@bradford.ac.uk
bradford.ac.uk
bradfordunisu.co.uk

Overall ranking 86
(last year 111)

Accommodation
University provided places 1,002
Self-catered £75–£128 per week

Student numbers
Undergraduates 7,800
Applications per place 4.9:1
Overall offer rate 82.9%

Fees
UK fees £9,535
International fees £20,538–£24,456

bradford.ac.uk/study/open-days
bradford.ac.uk/money/fees

University of Brighton

There's seaside charm in spades at this south coast university, newly consolidated on three campuses in student-friendly and diverse Brighton. An ambitious overhaul includes the Brighton Cricket Academy, the UK's largest indoor facility for the sport, which opened in October 2025. The Brighton and Sussex Medical School is run in a longstanding partnership with the University of Sussex and accepts about 200 trainee doctors each year, who are based at Falmer.

One of the most successful post-1992 universities for research, Brighton rose to 54th in our research quality index based on its results in the Research Excellence Framework (REF 2021). Its best subjects were hospitality and tourism, nursing, and architecture and building. In the Teaching Excellence Framework (TEF 2023), Brighton's overall silver award reflected strong student outcomes, but the university was handed bronze for student experience. In our latest analysis of the National Student Survey (NSS), Brighton has fallen again for satisfaction with teaching quality (=103rd) but climbed eight places for the wider experience (102nd).

Nine programmes are new for 2025 including three joint honours business management degrees (with events, law or tourism). From 2026, students can enrol on degree courses in pharmaceutical sciences, and civil with structural engineering. Brighton also fields a diverse portfolio of 13 degree apprenticeships including teaching, civil engineering, social work, and nursing.

Demand for places dipped steeply in 2024, with applications and enrolments falling 14% and 13% respectively in a year. Contextual offers were introduced in 2024, reducing the course requirements by at least two A-level grades or 16 UCAS tariff points for those who meet the criteria. Brighton is 84th for graduate prospects in our analysis, with 73.3% of graduates in highly skilled jobs or further study. Santander funds £1,050 summer internships at small and medium-size businesses, and the university also provides scholarships and mentoring programmes in partnership with employers.

On the biggest campus, Moulsecoomb, the School of Business and Law is based at Elm House, a landmark building with ceramic tiles designed to evoke flocks of seagulls. Humanities and social sciences are also based at Moulsecoomb and there are five new halls of residence. Falmer is home to the new sports facilities, and the School of Education, Sport and Health Sciences. The university's School of Art and Media is based at the City Campus, a pebble's throw from Brighton Pier, with design spaces and dance studios for students.

Besides the sea air, gritty coastal culture and club scene, students can make use of ample sports facilities. For students in need, Brighton provides counselling, pastoral support and financial advice. Brighton's 2,420 spaces are sufficient for all first-years who apply in time to be guaranteed a randomly allocated space. All campuses have accommodation on site, and there is free student parking on campus for those who are not in halls and live 30 miles away or 45 minutes away by public transport.

Brighton has risen five places in our social inclusion index, now ranking 57th. A fifth of new admissions in 2025 qualified for one of Brighton's financial awards, which include accommodation support, bursaries for care leavers and those from low-income households, and merit-based and sports scholarships.

Mithras House Lewes Road Brighton BN2 4AT
enquiries@brighton.ac.uk
brighton.ac.uk
brightonsu.com

Overall ranking =90
(last year 71)

Accommodation
University provided places 2,420
Self-catered £169–£260 per week

Student numbers
Undergraduates 11,870
Applications per place 6.6:1
Overall offer rate 79.1%

Fees
UK fees £9,535
International fees £17,250
Medicine £47,700

brighton.ac.uk/studying-here/visit-us/open-days
brighton.ac.uk/studying-here/fees-and-finance

University of Bristol

The combination of a leading research university and a charming cosmopolitan city, that's within easy reach of most of the country, makes Bristol one of the most consistently popular destinations for students. The main campus's Georgian buildings and green spaces will be reframed from September 2026, with the £500 million Temple Quarter Enterprise Campus (TQEC) opening next to Temple Meads railway station. The site will include cyber teaching rooms, a financial trading computer room and a makerspace.

The latest Research Excellence Framework (REF 2021) reinforced Bristol's research pedigree: 94% of work across 28 subject areas was rated world-leading or internationally excellent, with notable achievements in engineering, medicine, law and chemistry. The university ranks 6th in our research quality index. Climbing three places in the QS World University rankings year-on-year, Bristol was rated the 51st in the 2026 edition, and has broken into our top ten overall. In the Teaching Excellence Framework (TEF 2023) Bristol achieved silver overall and silver for student experience.

Among the 27 new courses for 2025 and 2026 are four new AI programmes, following its crowning as AI University of the Year in 2024. At the same time, the single-honours French, Spanish, Russian, Italian, German and Portuguese courses are being discontinued, to be replaced by a restructured modern languages programme. Links with more than 150 universities allow students to study abroad for a semester or year, and scholarships for summer schools and shorter programmes are also offered.

Last year, a record of more than 63,000 applicants chased fewer than 7,500 spots. Entry grades range from A*A*A to BBC, though contextual offers accounted for more than 40% of entrants in 2024. Few Russell Group universities have undergone similar expansions of student numbers following the lifting of the cap on student recruitment a decade ago. The university was the fifth most targeted institution by top employers in the latest High Fliers graduate market report, and our analysis of graduate outcomes puts Bristol =17th.

Alongside the expanding teaching facilities, the campus's Richmond building houses the Students' Union (which runs more than 300 sports and arts societies), two theatres and one of the city's largest gig venues. The botanic garden in Stoke Bishop has more than 4,500 plant species. Students are well served by pubs and clubs, and with job opportunities on the doorstep, many graduates find no reason to leave.

Bristol guarantees accommodation to first-years who apply by the end of June. An induction module covers issues including sexual consent, freedom of speech, drugs and alcohol, and the university has invested £5 million a year in wellbeing services. Efforts to diversify the intake include gateway programmes for medicine, dentistry and veterinary science degrees. After recent modest gains in our social inclusion index, Bristol slips to 110th this year. About 30% of the intake qualifies for some form of financial award, from bursaries of up to £2,500 per year of study, to the Vice-Chancellor's Scholarship for exceptional talent in sport, music, or the performing arts. The university has dropped ten places in the latest People & Planet league table to sit at =26th, fifth among its Russell Group peers.

Beacon House Queens Road Bristol BS8 1QU
choosebristol-ug@bristol.ac.uk
bristol.ac.uk
bristolsu.org.uk

Overall ranking 10
(last year 11)

Accommodation
University provided places 7,057
Catered £182–£326 per week
Self-catered £116–£284 per week

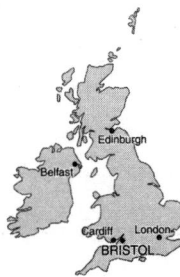

Student numbers
Undergraduates 23,015
Applications per place 8.4:1
Overall offer rate 67.6%

Fees
UK fees £9,535
International fees £24,800–£48,300
Medicine £44,500

bristol.ac.uk/study/undergraduate/visits/open-days
bristol.ac.uk/study/undergraduate/fees-funding

Brunel University London

Named in honour of the engineering genius Isambard Kingdom Brunel, the west London institution became the latest to join the University of London federation in 2024. Many of its courses include professional qualifications, though the original focus on STEM, education and management has expanded to include the performing arts, humanities, health, sport sciences and business. 2025 marks the medical school's second intake of 50 UK students.

Brunel's self-contained campus is a big draw for freshly fledged undergraduates. Everything is in one place – from academic buildings and excellent sports facilities to student support services and social hangouts, along with accommodation. It is also a haven for woodland and wildlife, and has held Green Flag status for eight years running.

In the Research Excellence Framework (REF 2021), good results in sport and exercise science, anthropology and allied health subjects were enough for 71st place in our index. In the Teaching Excellence Framework (TEF 2023) the university is one of only seven with a bronze overall rating, and in our National Student Survey (NSS) analysis it has fallen from 61st to =91st for student experience, although satisfaction with teaching quality has improved five places to =105th.

Educational developments in 2024 should put Brunel on stronger footing, including the move to a more student-friendly semester structure and a new attendance system to monitor progress more effectively. Brunel has attracted some well-known figures to the academic teaching staff over the years, including the author Will Self and the performance poet Benjamin Zephaniah.

New from 2025 are degrees in engineering with business, computer systems engineering (artificial intelligence), and degree apprenticeships for registered nurse (child health), and registered nurse (mental health). Degrees in environmental sciences, and flood and coastal engineering have been withdrawn.

Grade requirements range between AAB and CDD. Brunel's contextual offers usually lop off two grades from the standard requirement, but this benefitted only 5% of 2024's entrants. Brunel is a pioneer of sandwich degrees and the university's Professional Development Centre nurtures relationships with businesses locally and nationally. According to our analysis of the Graduate Outcomes survey, however, job prospects have been declining, and the university falls to =102nd this year.

Brunel's Indoor Athletics Centre is the centrepiece of sports provision and some of Britain's best athletes use its facilities. Team Brunel was the first to introduce a branded sports hijab and the Sports Centre has a women-only gym. The Students' Union hosts more than 100 sports clubs and societies, and an on-campus nightclub (The Venue) has capacity for 600 revellers.

Accommodation on campus is guaranteed for all first-years who apply by the end of August, though a large proportion of Brunel students live at home and commute. One of the more successful pre-1992 universities in our social inclusion index, Brunel draws the fourth-highest proportion of students from black and ethnic minority backgrounds in England and Wales. More than 300 means-tested bursaries are worth £6,000 over three years, and merit-based scholarships reward strength in sport, engineering and the physical sciences, among other subjects.

Kingston Lane Uxbridge UB8 3PH
admissions@brunel.ac.uk
brunel.ac.uk
brunelstudents.com

Overall ranking 117
(last year =107)

Accommodation
University provided places 4,155
Self-catered £180–£382 per week

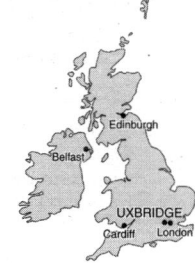

Student numbers
Undergraduates 8,565
Applications per place 6.5:1
Overall offer rate 73.4%

Fees
UK fees £9,535
International fees £20,400–£24,795
Medicine £49,395

brunel.ac.uk/study/open-days/undergraduate-open-days
brunel.ac.uk/study/undergraduate-fees-and-funding

University of Buckingham

Britain's first private university, founded in 1976 and opened by Margaret Thatcher, the University of Buckingham offers two-year degrees condensed into 40-week academic years, which Buckingham believes allows graduates to hit the world of work with a head start on their peers. The course offering matches the range at other UK universities despite Buckingham's bijou size of only 1,600 undergraduates. The expense of private tuition fees – £27,750 in total for the two-year degree for UK students living on campus – is higher than mainstream institutions, but offset by saving a year's living costs.

Three years ago, Buckingham was the highest riser in our league table and it was shortlisted for University of the Year 2024. Small class tutorials are a feature of its face-to-face teaching and it was rated silver overall in the Teaching Excellence Framework (TEF 2023). However, our analysis of the latest National Student Survey (NSS) shows satisfaction with teaching quality down to 125th and the wider undergraduate experience to 130th. As a private institution, Buckingham does not take part in the national Research Excellence Framework, but it does put a high priority on research and students can expect to be taught by academics who are active in their field.

The university has been plagued by rumours of infighting between current and previous academics during the past couple of years. The vice-chancellor Professor James Tooley was suspended in October 2024 pending an investigation into "serious allegations" about his conduct. He was reinstated three months later and the university said the claims were "not substantiated".

A new BA in secondary education (maths and Send) was added to the curriculum for September 2025, and Buckingham's Centre of Heterodox Social Science has dived into the culture wars with a 15-week online course studying progressive illiberalism. Some foundation programmes ask for DD, or 48 UCAS tariff points, while at the upper end you'll need ABB (128 points) to get into medicine. Buckingham has fallen to =57th in our Graduate Outcomes survey analysis. A micro-internship scheme connects students with industry partners to complete short, paid, flexible projects, and the university runs two well-supported degree apprenticeships.

The original riverside campus is set across three repurposed sites in leafy Buckingham, where recent upgrades include simulated GP surgeries. All courses will soon be taught in Buckingham, with the medicine and health sciences campus in Crewe due to close by 2026. The main campus has a bar, fitness facilities and a refurbished refectory with social learning spaces. Student-led clubs and societies cover academic, sport, cultural, medical and religious interests. The brighter lights of Milton Keynes are a 20-minute drive away.

Undergraduates have regular meetings with their personal tutor for academic support and guidance, and can access counselling and mentoring advice through the wellbeing department. First-years who apply by the deadline are guaranteed a room in halls of residence. Buckingham is in the top 30 for its proportion of black and ethnic minority students and has risen from 114th to 88th in our social inclusion index for England and Wales. Financial support includes the High Achiever scholarship of £2,000, and the University of Buckingham Bursary, which is worth up to £9,500.

Hunter Street Buckingham MK18 1EG
admissions@buckingham.ac.uk
buckingham.ac.uk
su.buckingham.ac.uk

Overall ranking 128
(last year 114)

Accommodation
University provided places 550
Catered £225–365 per week
Self-catered £140–£235 per week

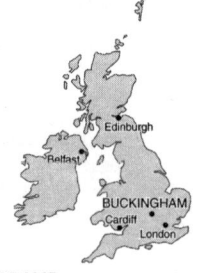

Student numbers
Undergraduates 1,520
Applications per place 4.3:1
Overall offer rate N/A

Fees
UK fees £9,250–£13,875
International fees £14,800–£23,040
Medicine £45,000

buckingham.ac.uk/study/visit-us/open-days
buckingham.ac.uk/admissions/fees

Buckinghamshire New University

More than £100 million of investment at Buckinghamshire New University (BNU) is improving its facilities for hands-on teaching in healthcare with a range of simulated environments. A new engineering school has launched courses designed to meet skills needs, and BNU is growing its stable of degree apprenticeships. Film and television students are taught at the nearby Pinewood Studios; those taking travel and aviation courses have the chance to study for a pilot's licence; and BNU has worked with Thames Valley police for more than 15 years to deliver policing programmes.

BNU climbed five places in our research quality rankings to 118th following the results of the latest Research Excellence Framework (REF 2021), with some of the best performances from art and design, history of art, geology, and sports sciences. Overall, 44% of BNU research was judged to be world-leading or internationally excellent. The university achieved triple silver in the Teaching Excellence Framework (TEF 2023), and has enjoyed upbeat rates of student satisfaction with teaching quality ranked 8th and the wider undergraduate experience up 31 places to =15th in our latest National Student Survey (NSS) analysis.

BNU has been reducing its partnership agreements with other colleges following a 2024 report by the Office for Students (OfS) raising concerns about business and management courses. A dozen degrees are also being discontinued, including textile design, aviation management for professionals, and psychology and criminology. Degrees in computer science (blended), and mechanical engineering are launching, along with a degree apprenticeship in civil engineering. Entry requirements start at 88 UCAS tariff points, rising to 144, and BNU makes contextual offers where applicable. About 3,000 students enrolled in 2024, more than a fifth of them through clearing.

Despite its proactive industry links and practical slant to courses, BNU remains in the bottom 30 in our analysis of the Graduate Outcomes survey (=105th) with 69% of leavers finding highly skilled work, or returning to study within 15 months of graduating.

The main High Wycombe Campus's Gateway Building is a focal point in the town, while the historic Brunel Engine Shed, opposite the railway station, is being converted into a community space and public art gallery. A second base in west London hosts most of BNU's healthcare students, and a third in Aylesbury is home to nursing, business, law and apprenticeship courses. BNU funds free sports and recreational activities, for which facilities include a swimming performance centre, approved by Swim England, and a three-lane running track with 3D motion-capture technology.

Students can self-refer to the counselling service to access integrative or cognitive therapy, and mental health advisory sessions. Most BNU students live at home, allowing the university to guarantee a space for all first-years who want a room, of which almost half cost the minimum rate of £99 a week. BNU performs well in our social inclusion table but it has seen a dip in the past year, down 16 places to 37th. More than 10% of entrants received financial support this autumn, including up to £500 a year for those from low-income households, and £1,100 a year for students from Gypsy, traveller, Roma, showman and boater communities.

High Wycombe Campus Queen Alexandra Road High Wycombe HP11 2JZ
admissions@bnu.ac.uk
bnu.ac.uk
bucksstudentsunion.org

Overall ranking 120
(last year 122)

Accommodation
University provided places 920
Self-catered £99–£206 per week

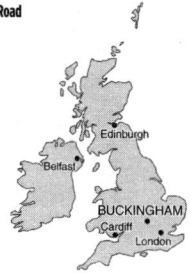

Student numbers
Undergraduates 5,150
Applications per place 3.3:1
Overall offer rate 74.7%

Fees
UK fees £9,535
International fees £15,150–£21,050

bucks.ac.uk/study/undergraduate/open-days
bucks.ac.uk/study/fees-and-funding

University of Cambridge

The University of Cambridge, our University of the Year in the East 2026, balances eight centuries at the forefront of academic excellence, research and innovation with a continuous drive into the future. Cambridge offers a more intimate setting than Oxford, but has its fair share of medieval courts and grand Tudor entrances. The city encompasses 31 colleges, six academic schools, over 150 departments, 100 libraries and nine specialist museums, all within beautiful buildings and sprawling green spaces.

Globally, Cambridge placed sixth in the 2026 QS rankings; fifth in the 2025 Times Higher Education rankings; and fourth in the 2024 Shanghai Ranking. The university's research pedigree is confirmed by the latest Research Excellence Framework (REF 2021), which rated 93% of its work as world-leading or internationally excellent, earning Cambridge 2nd in our research ranking. Cambridge also comes top in 19 of our subject tables, more than any other university.

Most lectures are delivered in person, as are its small group supervisions, and Cambridge was awarded triple gold in the government's Teaching Excellence Framework (TEF 2023). Our analysis of the latest National Student Survey (NSS) shows fairly high rates of satisfaction with teaching quality (=59th), but it places 117th for the wider undergraduate experience. The three-year BA in architecture is being replaced with a four-year integrated Master of Architecture, while the innovative four-year Design Tripos degree welcomed its second cohort in October 2025.

Admissions are in the hands of the colleges and applicants can choose a specific college or make an open application, while a "pool" system gives the most promising rejected candidates a second chance. Offers are usually A*A*A or A*AA at A-level. Cambridge does not enter clearing or make contextual offers, but the fully funded Cambridge Foundation Year in arts, humanities and social sciences is designed for disadvantaged students and requires BBB at A-level. Completion allows progression to a range of undergraduate degrees. Typically, Cambridge receives six applications per place but there is huge variation between courses.

Cambridge graduates rank =3rd in the UK for graduate prospects. The university holds ten sector-specific careers fairs each year, and its career development platform, Handshake, advertises vacancies and internships.

A demanding academic schedule is crammed into eight-week terms, requiring a concerted effort from students. Undergraduates can enjoy the social side too, with more than 700 societies and sports clubs at both university and college level. The colleges have differing characteristics, including their levels of diversity. Overall, the university has made strides in widening participation, with state sector admissions reaching 71% in 2024 and ethnic diversity aided by initiatives like the Stormzy Scholarship.

Cambridge launched a Student Mental Health and Wellbeing Plan, and each college also has a senior tutor, nurse and wellbeing adviser. Most students are guaranteed a room in college or college-owned flats and houses for three years, some for four. Basic kitchen facilities are available along with communal café-style meals, and three-course dinners known as formal halls. The Cambridge Bursary pays up to £3,500 a year to students with household incomes below £62,215. There are also about 500 academic scholarships awarded annually.

Cambridge Admissions Office
Student Services Centre New Museums Site
Cambridge CB2 3PT
admissions@cam.ac.uk
www.undergraduate.study.cam.ac.uk
cambridgesu.co.uk

Overall ranking =4
(last year 4)

Accommodation
Colleges websites provide accommodation details.

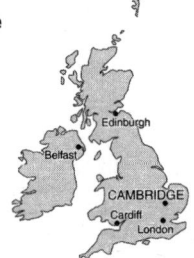

Student numbers
Undergraduates 13,090
Applications per place 6.3:1
Overall offer rate 24.5%

Fees
UK fees £9,535
International fees £27,024–£41,124
Medicine £70,554

www.undergraduate.study.cam.ac.uk/events/cambridge-open-days
www.undergraduate.study.cam.ac.uk/fees-and-finance
See chapter 11 for individual colleges.

Canterbury Christ Church University

The curriculum is increasingly broad at this former teacher training college, where courses span creative arts and industries, nursing, law and social sciences. From 2025, Canterbury Christ Church University (CCCU) has brought in modules focusing on life beyond the classroom, tackling contemporary issues, and connecting with local communities and employers. Foundation years are offered as a way into a number of degree courses and CCCU has a successful record on widening participation, remaining in the top 30 of our social inclusion index at 27th. The university remains a Church of England foundation but admits students of all faiths and none.

Canterbury scored triple silver in the Teaching Excellence Framework (TEF 2023), and between 2014 and 2021, it more than doubled the proportion of world-leading work in the national Research Excellence Framework. The university scrapes into the top 100 in our research quality index at 99th. In our analysis of the latest National Student Survey (NSS), CCCU has leapt 72 places to rank sixth for teaching quality, and 105 places to be =5th for the wider experience. However, poor continuation rates continue to hold CCCU back in our main academic table.

There were 200 degree apprentices at the last count, in fields such as manufacturing engineering, occupational therapy and policing. New from 2025 are several degrees across engineering, sport, music and policing. Grade requirements range from DDE at A-level (64 UCAS tariff points) for a foundation year to ABB (128 points) for physiotherapy degrees. Almost three in ten students entered through clearing in 2024.

CCCU ranks =67th in our analysis of graduate employment, and the university teams up with industry and local businesses to keep courses up to date with required skills.

The campus in the cathedral city has undergone a £150 million redevelopment, including new buildings for STEM subjects and the Daphne Oram Creative Arts Building, which has facilities for drones, motion capture and XR (extended reality). The Medway Campus houses teacher training courses and a simulated hospital setting for health students. CCCU courses are also delivered at Global Banking School campuses in Greenford, west London, Birmingham and Manchester, and there is a postgraduate centre in Tunbridge Wells.

The Students' Union is at the main Canterbury site, and the sports centre and playing fields are a mile away at Stodmarsh. Cricket, hockey and tennis facilities are at Polo Farm Sports Club, two miles from the main campus. Mental health services include counselling, drop-ins and workshops, and students can seek support at the chaplaincy. The Safezone app alerts security staff if a student needs urgent assistance.

Canterbury is richer in real ales than raves, but provides a charming backdrop to student life, where those attending three universities mingle in the cobbled streets or make forays to the seaside at Whitstable or Margate. All CCCU's accommodation is off campus, but university-approved rooms are guaranteed for first-years who apply by the end of July. CCCU pays a university grant of up to £600 a year to undergraduates whose household incomes are under £25,000, doubled to £1,200 a year for care leavers. Academic, sport and music scholarships are also available.

North Holmes Road Canterbury CT1 1QU
courses@canterbury.ac.uk
canterbury.ac.uk
ccsu.co.uk

Overall ranking 81
(last year 109)

Accommodation
University provided places 1,280
Self-catered £124–£200 per week

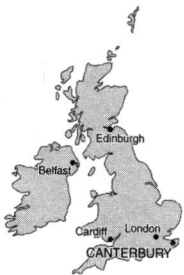

Student numbers
Undergraduates 6,860
Applications per place 0.5:1
Overall offer rate 82.4%

Fees
UK fees £9,535
International fees £15,500
Medicine £49,700

canterbury.ac.uk/study-here/applying/visit-us
canterbury.ac.uk/study-here/fees-and-funding/ug-fees-funding-and-student-finance

Cardiff University

Wales's top-ranked institution and our Welsh University of the Year 2026 is the only Russell Group university in Cymru, coupling academic clout with a hard-to-beat student location. A new overseas site in Kazakhstan offers four-year programmes with foundation years in computer science, civil engineering, exploration geology and business management. The main action remains around Cardiff's city centre campus, where a £600 million upgrade has boosted the undergraduate experience. Its charms are evident in UCAS figures, which show applications to Cardiff tipping over 46,000 for the past three years.

Cardiff achieved glowing results in the Research Excellence Framework (REF 2021), with 90% of its submissions rated world-leading or internationally excellent, particularly in philosophy, communication, education and architecture. It has risen to 21st for research in our rankings, but has received lukewarm responses in the National Student Survey (NSS). In our new analysis it has risen to =99th for teaching quality and to =51st for the wider undergraduate experience.

Under its first female vice-chancellor, Professor Wendy Larner, Cardiff is investing £5.4 million in five new research and innovation institutes in technology, science and social science. In early 2025, Larner announced plans to merge several schools and cut course provision in response to the university's "precarious financial position". She later backtracked on planned course closures, and Cardiff has committed to retaining its nursing and music courses, but will discontinue German, Italian, religious studies and ancient history in 2026.

Offers range from A*AA to BBC and contextual offers of one grade lower are received by about 28% of UK entrants. In 2024, 13% entered through clearing. Cardiff ranks =12th for graduate prospects, based on 85.1% of leavers in highly skilled work or further study 15 months after graduating.

The Centre for Student Life opened in 2021, bringing study space and a lecture theatre under the same roof as support services. Other new and modernised buildings house teaching for maths and computer science, and an architectural robotics laboratory. The healthcare sciences share a 53-acre campus with the University Hospital Wales. There are more than 200 student societies and 60 sports teams, and Cardiff's live music scene and relative affordability create an upbeat student vibe. Adventures on the coast and Bannau Brycheiniog (Brecon Beacons) national park are not far away.

Students can access a range of counselling, support and self-help resources. All first-years who apply in the main UCAS cycle as a firm applicant and meet the deadlines are guaranteed a single occupancy room, where rents start at £126 a week.

In our social inclusion index, Cardiff has slipped to 106th. Widening participation work experience bursaries of £2,000 are available, alongside the main Cardiff University bursary for students from lower-income households. There is also targeted support for students who are unpaid carers, have served in the armed forces, are leaving care, or who are estranged from their families. The Cowrie Foundation scholarship benefits financially disadvantaged black British students.

Cardiff CF10 3AT
enquiry@cardiff.ac.uk
cardiff.ac.uk
cardiffstudents.com

Overall ranking =28
(last year 32)

Accommodation
University provided places 6,365
Catered £156–£179 per week
Self-catered £126–£177 per week

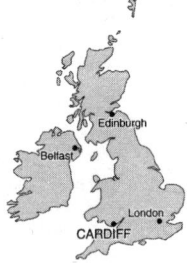

Student numbers
Undergraduates 22,475
Applications per place 5.8:1
Overall offer rate 73.4%

Fees
UK fees £9,535
International fees £23,700–£29,450
Medicine £45,450

cardiff.ac.uk/study/open-days-and-visits/undergraduate
cardiff.ac.uk/study/undergraduate/tuition-fees

Cardiff Metropolitan University

Former winner of our Welsh University of the Year award (2021) and Runner-up for the 2024 title, Cardiff Metropolitan (Met) is known for fielding a strong sporting tradition on the pitch as well as in the lecture hall. The Cyncoed campus to the north of the student-friendly city is the base for sports governing bodies such as Welsh Athletics and Team Wales, which prepares athletes for competition in the Commonwealth Games. Comprehensive facilities include the £7 million National Indoor Athletics Centre and physiotherapy and sports medicine facilities.

More than 40 degrees have been added in the past six years, branching out into technology from its previous areas of art and design, education, sport and health sciences, and management. New degrees for 2025 include electrical and electronic engineering, health and wellbeing (top-up), and psychology and criminology, while in 2026, Cardiff Met will introduce a foundation course in sport.

In light of the latest Research Excellence Framework (REF 2021) the university has climbed to 78th in our research rankings, with the strongest results coming from sport, and art and design. Though Cardiff Met is aiming for net zero carbon emissions by 2030, and encourages students to use the Taff Trail, part of a popular national cycle route, it has dropped from 6th place to 12th in the People & Planet league table. Our latest National Student Survey (NSS) analysis ranks the university 66th for teaching quality and =66th for the wider undergraduate experience. Student numbers have risen, but Cardiff Met is among the many UK universities seeking to make cost savings, and potential job losses have been reported.

Entry requirements range from 128–96 UCAS tariff points, or 64–32 points for foundation courses. Contextual admissions benefitted 70% of undergraduates in 2024, and almost a fifth enrolled through clearing. The academic schools have links with industry partners, facilitating courses that align to skills requirements. In our analysis of graduate outcomes, Cardiff Met's recent charge up our table has been arrested; it has fallen 11 places to =74th.

Cardiff Met's two campuses are close to the city centre, with the Cyncoed Campus the main site for student housing and sport. Llandaff is home to the Cardiff School of Technologies and the School of Art and Design, which hosts ceramics and fabric workshops as well as augmented reality technology.

From Students' Union activities to high-level sport competition, there is no shortage of opportunities to get involved. Cardiff Met has Welsh Premier League sides in men's and women's football, and 12 rugby teams. To support mental health, there are psychoeducational workshops, one-to-one counselling and online resources. During the summer, Cardiff Met runs transition events for new students with tips on dealing with neurodiversity or mental health issues.

First-years are guaranteed a room if they make Cardiff Met their firm choice and apply in time. A compulsory halls induction course covers sexual consent, alcohol and drugs. Cardiff Met has slipped from the top 30 in our social inclusion index four years ago to =54th. About a fifth of students qualify for financial assistance, including performance and elite sports scholarships as well as awards worth up to £3,000 for those studying in Welsh.

Western Avenue Llandaff Cardiff CF5 2YB
askadmissions@cardiffmet.ac.uk
cardiffmet.ac.uk
cardiffmetsu.co.uk

Overall ranking 71
(last year =66)

Accommodation
University provided places 2,178
Catered £203–£228 per week
Self-catered £137–£168 per week

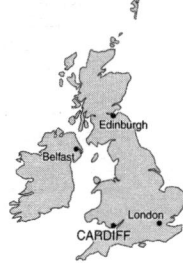

Student numbers
Undergraduates 8,255
Applications per place 3.7:1
Overall offer rate 86.2%

Fees
UK fees £9,535
International fees £16,000

cardiffmet.ac.uk/study/opendays/
cardiffmet.ac.uk/support/fees-and-finance

University of Chester

Chester is just the right size for most students, with cosy pubs and quirky bars among the cobbled streets. At the university's main 32-acre Exton Park Campus, the new School of Education includes a practical forest school teaching area. First established as a teacher training college in 1839, Chester retains a focus on teaching courses, although undergraduate options are broadening. New for September 2025 are 20 single honours courses and nine joint honours programmes across performing arts, data science, languages, sociology and politics.

Theology, health subjects and sports and exercise science produced some of Chester's best results in the latest Research Excellence Framework (REF 2021), boosting the number of submissions judged world-leading or internationally excellent from 31% to 51%. However, Chester slipped to 109th in our research quality index against even bigger gains at other universities. Triple silver in the Teaching Excellence Framework (TEF 2023) is at odds with a dip in student satisfaction. Results from the latest National Student Survey (NSS) trigger a fall of 22 places to =101st for teaching quality and 19 places to 120th for the wider experience.

Foundation years are being added to 24 degree programmes, offering access with fewer UCAS tariff points (72) than required for direct entry to a degree course, most of which demand 112–120. Contextual offers may be considered, and Chester accepts a wide range of different qualifications and entry points. The university's Future Skills curriculum, introduced in 2025, is shaped around social learning, digital skills and continuous assessment, while its flagship work-based learning scheme has offered second-year placements for more than 25 years. According to our analysis of the latest Graduate Outcomes survey, Chester ranks in the upper half of universities, in 58th place.

Exton Park is one of five main sites. The Queen's Park Campus houses Chester Business School, and the Wheeler building, overlooking the River Dee, is the base for the university's medical, nursing and midwifery courses. Next to Chester crown court is the School of Law and Social Justice, with its own moot court. There are also university centres in Birkenhead, Nantwich and Warrington. Sports facilities include tennis and squash courts, a swimming pool and a fitness studio. Chester students also have access to rented facilities at Grosvenor Rowing Club, Chester Rugby Club, and West Cheshire Athletics Club.

First-years are guaranteed a room and nearly a quarter of hall spaces are catered, though many students live at home and commute. Students can self-refer to the university's counselling service, and take part in low-intensity cognitive behavioural therapy or wellbeing sessions such as a men's mental health group. A signatory of the Recovery Friendly University Pledge, Chester is committed to supporting students and staff rebuilding their lives after a struggle with addiction.

Chester succeeds in recruiting more than a fifth of students from low-participation areas (16th) but has slipped slightly in our social inclusion index overall to 21st. Financial help ranges from travel bursaries for taster events to awards of £1,500 for carers, care leavers, and those who are estranged from their families – as well as for students from Gypsy, Roma, traveller, showman and boater communities.

Parkgate Road Chester CH1 4BJ
admissions@chester.ac.uk
chester.ac.uk
chestersu.com

Overall ranking 109
(last year 89)

Accommodation
University provided places 1,380
Catered £200–£205 per week
Self-catered £115–£179 per week

Student numbers
Undergraduates 7,745
Applications per place 5.8:1
Overall offer rate 72.4%

Fees
UK fees £9,535
International fees £10,750–£14,450

chester.ac.uk/study/visit-us/open-days/
chester.ac.uk/student-life/fees-and-finance

University of Chichester

Renowned for its close-knit atmosphere, this small West Sussex university folds seaside charm and countryside comforts into the academic timetable. A former teacher training college, Chichester became a university in 2005 and has an industry-led curriculum on its two campuses – one in the historic cathedral city and another by the sea at Bognor Regis. Teacher training remains an established strength and was rated outstanding by Ofsted in May 2023, while the university is also known for its performing arts, social sciences and sports provision.

Overall, the university holds a gold rating in the Teaching Excellence Framework (TEF 2023), and student satisfaction has also rallied considerably in our analysis of the latest National Student Survey (NSS). Chichester has climbed 16 and 20 places respectively to rank 12th for teaching quality and =87th for the wider experience. Chichester gained the power to award research degrees in 2014, and in the latest Research Excellence Framework (REF 2021) its submissions in sport, history, and English and creative writing produced the best results. Against stronger performances elsewhere, however, Chichester fell 32 places in our research quality index to 113th.

There are four course additions in September 2025: biomedical science, children's health and wellbeing, law with business, and psychology of esports. From 2026 a degree in speech and language therapy will join the curriculum. The university has a growing portfolio of degree apprenticeships with 500 students enrolled on programmes including accounting finance, digital technology solutions, and data science.

Courses demand grades from ABB to CCC with contextual admissions reducing these by up to two A-level grades. Admissions through clearing made up 11% of the intake in 2024.

Chichester ranks =70th in our analysis of the Graduate Outcomes survey. Its degree apprenticeship programme draws on the expertise of businesses such as Rolls-Royce and the energy supplier SSE, and most of Chichester's degree programmes provide work placements.

The Bishop Otter Campus in Chichester includes a music block and the School of Nursing and Allied Health, next to St Richard's Hospital. Students have access to mock wards and simulation suites to develop their clinical skills, and an environmental climate chamber to simulate extreme heat, cold and altitude. The Bognor Regis Campus, linked to the city site by a bus service, has a new community diagnostic centre as well as the flagship Tech Park.

Halls of residence are found at both campuses and a third of the accommodation places are catered. First-years are guaranteed a room if they apply in time. The student-led Sports Federation fields competitive teams and organises more than 25 clubs for those who are in it for fun and fitness. Services provided by wellbeing, mental health and disability support teams include short-term counselling, and access to specialists in neurodiversity and specific learning difficulties.

Chichester has fallen 35 places to 94th in our social inclusion index, though a tripling in disabled recruitment to 29% puts the university in the top 10. Chichester awards £1,000 over three years to students who previously received free school meals, and a £400 gifted athlete programme provides performance analysis, psychology, nutrition and physiotherapy, and kit.

Bishop Otter Campus College Lane
Chichester PO19 6PE
admissions@chi.ac.uk
chi.ac.uk
ucsu.org

Overall ranking 54
(last year 62)

Accommodation
University provided places 2,136
Catered £188–£213 per week
Self-catered £144–£202 per week

Student numbers
Undergraduates 4,530
Applications per place 5.3:1
Overall offer rate 74.1%

Fees
UK fees £9,535
International fees £16,800–£18,180

chi.ac.uk/study/open-days-and-campus-tours/open-days
chi.ac.uk/study/undergraduate/fees-finance

City St George's, University of London

The recent merger of City, University of London and St George's has created a new powerhouse in UK higher education. The newly branded City St George's, University of London is a multi-campus institution in the capital, combining St George's world-renowned health and medical expertise with City's professional focus on business, law, communications and technology. With more than 27,000 students, the larger, unified university is poised for greater investment in its facilities, research and student experience.

Both legacy institutions brought with them formidable research profiles. In the latest Research Excellence Framework (REF 2021), City ranked 37th for research quality, with 86% of its work rated world-leading or internationally excellent. St George's ranked similarly at 42nd, with its historic achievements in cardiac pacemakers and IVF.

Our analysis ranks the newly combined university 40th. The MBA from Bayes Business School is ranked 7th in the UK by the Financial Times (2025). St George's, England's second-oldest medical school, pioneered the four-year graduate-entry medicine (MBBS) programme and now trains a wide range of healthcare professionals. Despite "outstanding" student continuation rates and achieving silver overall in the Teaching Excellence Framework (TEF 2023), St George's rated bronze for student experience. In our analysis of the National Student Survey (NSS), City St George's ranks =75th for student experience.

New for September 2025 are maths with business, English with creative writing, and English with publishing.

A-level requirements range from CDD to AAA. A contextual offer scheme can reduce this by up to two grades, with a third of applicants receiving such an offer in 2024. Despite the competitive nature of many courses, both former institutions used clearing extensively, with 28% of St George's intake and 32% of City's coming through this route.

Both universities had strong records on graduate prospects last year, ranking 3rd (St George's) and 45th (City) based on the proportions of graduates in highly skilled work or postgraduate study within 15 months of finishing. Combined, they are ranked 14th, with 84.9% going into high-skilled work or postgraduate study. St George's courses are intrinsically linked with healthcare employers such as the NHS.

The university's London campuses offer distinct environments. The main Clerkenwell Campus has benefitted from more than £140 million in development. The Tooting Campus is integrated within St George's University Hospital, immersing students in a busy, real-world healthcare environment from day one. Specialist facilities include anatomy suites, paramedic science labs, clinical skills rooms and the Museum of Human Diseases.

Around 1,000 self-catered rooms are available. Accommodation is guaranteed for first-year students who firmly accept their offer and apply on time and who reside outside London zones 1-6.

Ethnic minority intake is high, at 80.1%, making it 5th on the list – it is =5th nationally for closing the black awarding gap. A dedicated Office for Institutional Equity and Inclusion was launched in 2023.

In 2023-24, City St George's provided more than £2 million in support for students from under-represented backgrounds.

Northampton Square London EC1V 0HB
enquiries@citystgeorges.ac.uk
citystgeorges.ac.uk
csgsu.co.uk

Overall ranking 48
(last year 49)

Accommodation
University provided places 1,000
Self-catered £220-£309 per week

Student numbers
Undergraduates 16,705
Applications per place 5.5:1
Overall offer rate 61.5%

Fees
UK fees £9,535
International fees £11,970-£29,250

citystgeorges.ac.uk/prospective-students/open-events-and-fairs
citystgeorges.ac.uk/prospective-students/finance

Coventry University

A three-time winner of our Modern University of the Year award (2014–16) and shortlisted for University of the Year in 2021, Coventry's latest innovation is to implement six entry points a year for students, with modules taught one at a time to give an in-depth understanding of a subject area before moving on to another. The institution has become one of the UK's biggest recruiters of students from abroad, with an expanding network of global hubs from Brussels to Beijing, Dubai and Singapore. The group's remarkable global connections earned it the Queen's Award for Enterprise in 2022.

Coventry achieved a gold rating overall in the Teaching Excellence Framework (TEF 2023). However, Coventry has slipped to 39th for satisfaction with teaching quality and =60th for the wider undergraduate experience in our new National Student Survey (NSS) analysis. The university has expanded its research centres, increased research and doctoral staff and developed purpose-built facilities, which has paid off with a jump from =108th to 72nd in our research rankings, based on the results of the latest Research Excellence Framework (REF 2021). The best outcomes were in architecture, education, linguistics, and communication and media studies.

Demand for places has been declining, and its risk-taking strategy has left Coventry more exposed than other institutions to the financial challenges facing all UK universities. Its accounts in 2023-24 revealed a pre-tax deficit of £59.3 million, though the university's vice-chancellor and chief executive, John Latham, is confident in Coventry's adaptability and cash reserves.

From September 2026, the curriculum will swell to include 43 new courses, among them ecology and conservation, politics with philosophy, and events management. The university's London campus is launching degrees in digital marketing and analytics, and international finance and accounting.

Entry requirements range from 128 to 96 UCAS tariff points. Contextual offers tend to reduce the required grades by up to 24 points, and last year 13% of new students entered through clearing. Coventry's focus on technical skills, and its mentorship and work experience partnerships, are intended to create graduates ready to hit the workplace. In our analysis of the Graduate Outcomes survey, Coventry ranks =74th with 74.4% of leavers finding highly skilled jobs or returning to study within 15 months. It offers 34 degree apprenticeship programmes, with 3,000 students enrolled.

The main campus is located in a city that was flattened by bombing during the Second World War and rebuilt with lashings of concrete, though recent building and renovation projects abound. Other bases are in Scarborough, Dagenham and Greenwich. First-years who make Coventry their firm choice are guaranteed a space in halls, and support for students includes the 24/7 Spectrum.Life platform, which delivers "in the moment" help and up to six sessions of counselling.

Coventry has risen five places this year to be ranked 32nd in our social inclusion index overall, and its flexible start dates are designed to fit around personal and work commitments and make higher education accessible for more students. Care leavers can apply for fully funded accommodation in halls for a maximum of four years, and there is a range of scholarships available.

Priory Street Coventry CV1 5FB
ukadmissions@coventry.ac.uk
www.coventry.ac.uk
yoursu.org

Overall ranking 78
(last year 54)

Accommodation
University provided places 1,880
Self-catered £145–£220 per week

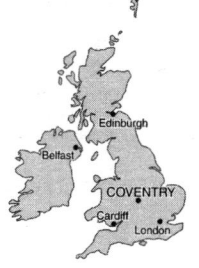

Student numbers
Undergraduates 18,520
Applications per place 5.3:1
Overall offer rate 88.1%

Fees
UK fees £9,535
International fees £16,800–£27,400

www.coventry.ac.uk/opendays
www.coventry.ac.uk/study-at-coventry/finance

University for the Creative Arts

One of the seven specialist arts universities in our league table, the University for the Creative Arts (UCA) puts creativity into the commuter belt. Its courses range from fine art to virtual and immersive reality, interior design to silversmithing and, as of this autumn, a degree in body art. Highly specialist facilities support students to further their creative education, such as at UCA's Canterbury School of Architecture, or on set at Maidstone Television Studios, where TV production students experience hands-on learning.

UCA's performance in the latest Research Excellence Framework (REF 2021) far outdid its results in the previous national assessment in 2014, triggering a 57-place rise in our research quality index to 55th. The submission included entries relating to sculpture, ceramics, photographic collections, films, essays and books. However, declining rates of student satisfaction have contributed to a decline in its overall performance – UCA has fallen to =120th for teaching quality and to 127th for the wider student experience, according to our analysis of the National Student Survey (NSS). UCA was also downgraded from gold to silver overall in the most recent Teaching Excellence Framework (TEF 2023).

Exam results are only part of the picture for winning a place at UCA; portfolios and auditions also play a key role. Standard requirements vary between 32 UCAS tariff points for entry to integrated foundation-year courses, to 128 points for architecture. About 4% of entrants gained their place through clearing in 2024. A concerted effort to boost employability means all undergraduates have a guarantee of work placements lasting from a fortnight to a year. Despite industry links with the National Theatre, Spotlight and Equity UK, UCA is at the bottom of our graduate prospects index.

Farnham, with its market-town charm and student-friendly pubs, is home to the new School of Communications and the School of Games and Creative Technology. Facilities include a virtual production studio, a green screen and filming studios, and a stop-motion animation studio. The Epsom campus is the closest to London and has more of the city buzz about it, while historic Canterbury has a large student population (including those of neighbouring Kent and Canterbury Christ Church universities). The latter hosts degree courses in architecture, fine art, interior design, graphic design, and illustration and animation.

Besides the numerous arts and cultural facilities, clubs and societies include cheerleading, football and rugby (though there are no sports facilities). A 24/7 service offering help with mental health issues via WhatsApp and an online Report + Support platform are available. There are 1,238 beds across its three campuses – not quite sufficient for it to guarantee accommodation to all first-years, but students who apply before the deadline should expect to secure a place.

The university has a network of industry professionals and creative workshop tutors who run activities for schools and colleges, and UCA ranks =8th overall for social inclusion, up from 12th last year. One student on each course is picked to win the UK Excellence Scholarship, which covers £1,500 of the first year's tuition fees. Further financial support includes the Grenfell Tower Scholarship, offering a full fee waiver to survivors of the 2017 fire in London.

Falkner Road Farnham GU9 7DS
admissions@uca.ac.uk
uca.ac.uk
ucasu.com

Overall ranking 127
(last year 87)

Accommodation
University provided places 1,238
Self-catered £158–£198 per week

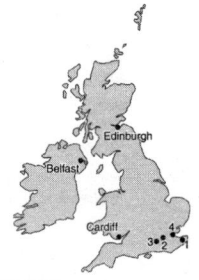

Student numbers
Undergraduates 4,075
Applications per place 5.7:1
Overall offer rate 96.7%

Fees
UK fees £9,535
International fees £16,950–£17,500

uca.ac.uk/study-at-uca/opendays
uca.ac.uk/study-at-uca/fees-finance

University of Cumbria

Cumbria is one of the UK's youngest universities, gaining university status in 2007, but what it may lack in history it makes up for in career-focused futures. The Pears Cumbria School of Medicine builds on Cumbria's existing strength in training nurses, midwives and allied health professionals, and its first medical students begin their graduate studies this year, in partnership with Imperial College London. There is also a new campus in Barrow-in-Furness linked to the nuclear submarine-capable shipyard, and another in Carlisle city centre is in the pipeline. Cumbria has been making impressive gains in our social inclusion index, where it sits 25th, and its integrated foundation years are among its initiatives to help to widen participation in higher education.

Cumbria occupies 123rd place in our research rankings, based on the results of the latest Research Excellence Framework (REF 2021), which, combined with low proportions of firsts and 2.1s and faltering student satisfaction, contributes to a low ranking in our league table. In our analysis of the latest National Student Survey (NSS), Cumbria remains near the bottom for teaching quality (127th) and the wider undergraduate experience (128th). It was rated silver overall in the latest Teaching Excellence Framework (TEF 2023) and silver for student outcomes, but bronze for student experience.

New courses available from 2025 include a range of ecology and conservation degrees, criminology and forensic investigation, mechanical engineering, and computer science. Degrees in tourism and visitor economy management, environmental science, and sociology will launch the following year. Courses in animal conservation science, and marine and freshwater conservation are being discontinued. 25% of 2024 entrants received a contextual offer and more than 20% gained their places through clearing. Demand for places has been declining, however, and in 2024 there were 40% fewer enrolments than a decade before.

The university fosters links between its courses and local, regional and national organisations across industry to provide opportunities for students. For graduate prospects, Cumbria is in the middle reaches of our table, with 74.8% of leavers in highly skilled work or further study 15 months after finishing their degree. The university offers 17 degree apprenticeships, with partners including the nuclear site Sellafield, BAE Systems and the NHS, and has about 2,300 students enrolled.

Students are based at seven campuses, stretching from the Lake District to Canary Wharf in east London. Most courses are based at the main campus in Lancaster, set in parkland a short walk from the city centre, or one of two sites in Carlisle. Ambleside near Windermere offers the UK's biggest programme of outdoor education courses, plus conservation and forestry degrees, while Canary Wharf hosts health, education and business degrees.

Cumbria is the only British university whose mental health team offers climbing therapy, in addition to the more traditional talking therapies and workshops. Fitness suites and sports halls are available at the Lancaster and Carlisle Campuses, and Ambleside has a gym and on-site fitness classes. About a fifth of new students live on site and accommodation is guaranteed for first-years.

Fusehill Street Carlisle CA1 2HH
enquirycentre@cumbria.ac.uk
cumbria.ac.uk
ucsu.me

Overall ranking 129
(last year 128)

Accommodation
University provided places 619
Self-catered £88–£141 per week

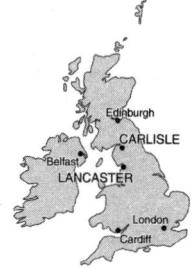

Student numbers
Undergraduates 5,265
Applications per place 3.9:1
Overall offer rate 75.4%

Fees
UK fees £9,535
International fees £14,900–£16,900

cumbria.ac.uk/events/open-days
cumbria.ac.uk/study/student-finance

De Montfort University

Not too big, not too small – Leicester's size and relative affordability are a draw for the city's large student population. Although it has outposts in Whitechapel and overseas, this university is rooted in Leicester, and it offers guaranteed work experience with nearby industrial partners for all of its undergraduates. It follows a block teaching model in which students focus on one subject at a time, rather than multiple exams at once.

In the latest Research Excellence Framework (REF 2021) more than 60% of DMU's work was judged as world-leading or internationally excellent, but this was not enough to prevent a 28-place fall in our research quality rankings to 95th. It has also dipped in the government's Teaching Excellence Framework (TEF 2023) from gold in 2017 to silver overall, with only bronze for the student experience. Feedback from undergraduates in the latest National Student Survey (NSS) ranks De Montfort =83rd for teaching quality and =78th for the wider student experience.

The university has a target of net-zero carbon emissions by 2032 and took 2nd place in the People & Planet league table for 2024–25. Despite a strong financial footing, with surpluses of £12.6 million and £22.4 million in recent years, it is among many now making staff cuts to reduce costs.

Eight course closures include media and communication with French, English language with Spanish, and visual effects, though 12 additions are being made for 2025, including fashion marketing, and politics with Mandarin. Entry standards range from 56 to 128 UCAS tariff points. One third of offers in 2024 were contextual, and nearly 20% of students entered through clearing. Travel bursaries help students get to interviews or employers' open days and there is lifelong careers support available for graduates. In spite of this, DMU only manages 105th in our analysis of the Graduate Outcomes survey.

Unusually for a campus university, DMU is located in the city centre. Investment of £136 million has upgraded teaching and learning spaces, with a £6.5 million Digital Hub the latest addition to the campus. Enhanced media facilities include a virtual production studio and VFX lab. There is also a simulated trading floor for students of accounting, economics and finance courses, and a mock pharmacy. A free bus service gets students around the city and to the university sports facilities. There is an Islamic prayer space, a chapel and a multi-faith room.

The online Healthy DMU hub provides first points of contact for students seeking support for their mental health, and there is special provision for autistic students. 442 spaces in halls of residence are sufficient for the university to guarantee a space to first-years who apply by the June deadline, though many students live at home. Nearly 70% of DMU's students are from black, Asian and ethnic minority backgrounds, and it ranks 30th in our social inclusion index overall. In 2023, it was the first British university to win a silver award in the Race Equality Charter. A range of financial awards largely benefits those from low-income backgrounds, or who have left care or are estranged from their families. The Stephen Lawrence Professional Scholarship is open to first-year students of degrees including law, journalism and architecture.

The Gateway Leicester LE1 9BH
enquiry@dmu.ac.uk
dmu.ac.uk
demontfortsu.com

Overall ranking 108
(last year 113)

Accommodation
University provided places 422
Self-catered £95–£161 per week

Student numbers
Undergraduates 16,605
Applications per place 3.2:1
Overall offer rate 89.3%

Fees
UK fees £9,535
International fees £16,250–£17,250

dmu.ac.uk/study/undergraduate-study/open-days
dmu.ac.uk/study/fees-funding

University of Derby

The University of Derby has launched an accelerated two-year degree in international business and AI, designed in partnership with Rolls-Royce, and it also offers apprenticeships in engineering, manufacturing, and business through the Nuclear Skills Academy. It spans four sites in the East Midlands city and has a campus for nursing students in Chesterfield.

Derby is rated gold in the government's Teaching Excellence Framework (TEF 2023). Students are happy with teaching quality, with Derby ranking =22nd for this measure in our analysis of the latest National Student Survey (NSS), though it has slipped to =4th for the wider student experience. In the latest Research Excellence Framework (REF 2021), education and geology produced some of the best results, helping to raise the university seven places in our research quality index to =110th. Derby has just opened a £17.6 million bioscience research facility, and its scientists lead in sustainability research to restore damaged coral reefs, but the threat of job cuts faced by senior academics at Derby has attracted criticism from the University and College Union.

New from 2025 are degrees in international business and AI, dance and movement for wellbeing, and business management and sustainable practice. From 2026, the curriculum gains an Internet of Things degree, and joint honours courses combining psychology and counselling. The university's grade requirements range from 128 to 96 UCAS tariff points, reduced by 16 points, or two grades, for a contextual offer. Lower tariffs apply to degrees with an integrated foundation year. According to our analysis of the Graduate Outcomes survey, Derby has been improving, and sits =82nd this year. Students can be mentored by employers to help them to build a network, bolstered by the university's business links with organisations such as JCB, Aldi, and HMRC.

Kedleston Road, the largest of the four city campuses, hosts most teaching subjects as well as the Students' Union, a multi-faith centre, the main sports facilities, and the new state-of-the-art Bioscience Superlab. The university's new business school building will give students access to a trading floor and immersive learning in a Google-style creativity lab. Other hands-on learning opportunities include a crime-scene house for forensic science students, a replica crown court, a Bloomberg financial markets laboratory and an NHS-standard hospital ward.

Derby has its own live-music venues and student-friendly nightlife, but those in search of brighter lights can seek out Nottingham or Sheffield. The £10.8 million sports centre at Kedleston Road is home to more than 30 sports clubs, some of which compete in the BUCS (British Universities and Colleges Sport) league. Students in crisis can seek help from counsellors and mental health practitioners, and have access to 24/7 support through the TalkCampus app.

For three years running the halls were voted the best UK university housing in the Global Student Living Awards (2022 to 2024). There are enough spaces to guarantee a spot to all first-years who apply by the end of July. Derby is sixth for recruitment of students from deprived areas and 19th overall in our social inclusion index. Almost a third of students receive some financial help, with bursaries worth up to £1,000 and sports scholarships up to £3,000.

Kedleston Road Derby DE22 1GB
askadmissions@derby.ac.uk
derby.ac.uk
derbyunion.co.uk

Overall ranking 96
(last year 77)

Accommodation
University provided places 1,962
Self-catered £115–£183 per week

Student numbers
Undergraduates 11,745
Applications per place 4.3:1
Overall offer rate 86.4%

Fees
UK fees £9,535
International fees £14,900–£16,900

derby.ac.uk/open-days/undergraduate
derby.ac.uk/study/fees-finance

University of Dundee

Dundee's main campus is two minutes from the centre of the student-friendly city. The university is renowned as a centre of research in life sciences, which has helped to propel Dundee to rank =38th in our research quality index. With more than 200 undergraduate courses, the options range from creative art (at its highly rated Duncan of Jordanstone College of Art and Design) to accountancy, law, and dentistry.

Academic activities are organised within eight schools, while Dundee's many research institutes are guided by three overarching themes of population health and wealth, climate action and net zero, and equity and inclusion. The Scottish universities did not take part in the latest Teaching Excellence Framework 2023, but Dundee was rated gold in the previous assessment six years earlier. Rates of student satisfaction have been patchy in recent years, but in our latest analysis of the National Student Survey (NSS), Dundee has climbed to =20th for teaching quality and =60th for the student experience. The Education Academy was created in 2023 to focus on improving the student experience and employability.

Dundee's troubled finances have been much reported, and in 2025 the Scottish government pledged £62 million in two bailout payments to secure its future.

Degree course requirements range from AAA to CC at A-level, or AAAAB to CCC in Scottish Highers. In 2024, nearly 13% of entrants received a contextual offer, which included a guaranteed interview, reduced grades and a place at the university's access summer school. In 2024, the university attracted more than 16,600 applications and about 2,500 new students were accepted. Promising graduate careers have long been a strength at Dundee, not least in the biomedical sector. The university ranks in the top 20 in our analysis of the Graduate Outcomes survey, with 83% of leavers in highly skilled work or postgraduate study within 15 months.

Dundee's self-contained city campus has benefitted from about £200 million of redevelopment. The medical school has its own 20-acre (81,000-sq m) site, while nursing and midwifery students are 35 miles away in Kirkcaldy. All full-time first-years are guaranteed accommodation if they apply by the deadline, and Dundee strives to create balanced residences. There are excellent sports facilities on campus including a swimming pool and recently refurbished 400 sq m fitness and conditioning suite. A thriving music society is among more than 240 such groups for students to choose from. Off campus, the university is a founding partner of the striking V&A Dundee museum, and students get free access to the botanic garden overlooking the River Tay.

A peer-to-peer buddying system helps new students to settle in and specialist provision for student wellbeing includes counselling, mental health nurses and a listening service. The university's outreach programmes engage with more than 2,000 potential entrants a year, with strong recruitment from deprived areas and of disabled students, putting Dundee 7th out of the 15 Scottish institutions in our guide for social inclusion overall. Scottish students do not pay tuition fees, and qualify for funding from the Scottish government. The Rest of UK (RUK) bursary is worth £2,000 in the first year, and there are also academic awards available.

Nethergate Dundee DD1 4HN
dundee.ac.uk/contact
dundee.ac.uk
dusa.co.uk

Overall ranking =23
(last year 36)

Accommodation
University provided places 1,587
Self-catered £154–£231 per week

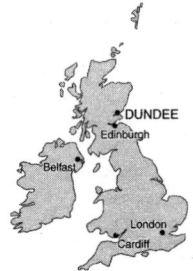

Student numbers
Undergraduates 9,620
Applications per place 6.6:1
Overall offer rate 65.5%

Fees
Scots fees £0–£1,820
International fees £21,600–£27,400
RUK fees £9,535
Medicine £53,370

dundee.ac.uk/open-days
dundee.ac.uk/collections/tuition-fee-guidance

Durham University

Durham is one of Britain's most historic and competitive universities, and this academic big hitter is The Times and Sunday Times University of the Year 2026. Given its collegiate structure and high entry requirements, comparisons with Oxbridge are hard to ignore. But unlike at Oxford and Cambridge, admissions are centralised, as is Durham's teaching.

Up two places to rank 3rd in our main academic table, Durham is also =94th in the QS World University Rankings 2026. In our UK research quality index, based on the latest Research Excellence Framework (REF 2021) results, Durham is 23rd, with its best results in education and geography, archaeology, and forensic science. Classics and ancient history, theology, and sports science also did well. Teaching is all in-person rather than online, and the latest Teaching Excellence Framework (TEF 2023) rated Durham gold for student outcomes. Feedback from Durham students in the latest National Student Survey (NSS) 2025 is positive, ranking =24th for teaching quality and 46th for the wider experience. Durham needs to save £20 million over the next two years to ensure a "sustainable financial base" after an £8 million deficit, with two hundred job cuts forecast in professional services roles.

Durham's entry requirements are A*A*A to ABB. The university attracted almost 35,000 applications for 2024 entry for just 5,580 places, though there is strong variance between subjects. A fifth were eligible for contextual offers, which reduce the standard entry requirements by two grades. The university is in the top ten of our graduate prospects measure (5th) and the top ten universities targeted by the largest number of top graduate employers, according to High Fliers 2025.

Durham is not a campus university, but the city's small size creates a campus-like atmosphere. Buildings range from the historic to the contemporary across the colleges. Durham has poured about £75 million into the Faculty of Science, adding a new Mathematics and Computer Science Building and more laboratories for the Department of Psychology. Societies include more than 30 theatre companies, a similar number of music groups, student radio and a newspaper. These, along with university-wide balls, and sport, are the backbone of social life. Durham has twice been crowned our Sports University of the Year, and has invested £35 million in its Sports and Wellbeing Park. There are 15 boathouses, a five-lane cricket centre, six grass rugby pitches and five full-size indoor sports courts.

Students can self-refer for mental health and wellbeing support. College facilities vary, but all offer accommodation for first-years who apply by the deadline, with more than 7,600 places available. A new code of practice between the university and letting agents has been devised to improve a chaotic and expensive private housing system.

Durham is one of only three universities with more than half its intake from selective schools. About 20% of students receive some form of financial help, and the main source of bursary provision, the uncapped Durham Grant Scheme, costs the university £80 million a year.

The Palatine Centre Stockton Road Durham DH1 3LE
durham.ac.uk/study/askus
durham.ac.uk
durhamsu.com

Overall ranking 3
(last year 5)

Accommodation
University provided places 7,660
Catered £179–£198 per week
Self-catered £175–£198 per week

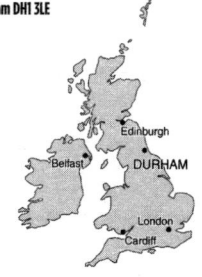

Student numbers
Undergraduates 16,900
Applications per place 6.2:1
Overall offer rate 67.6%

Fees
UK fees £9,535
International fees £26,750 – £29,250

durham.ac.uk/visit-us/open-days
durham.ac.uk/study/undergraduate/fees-and-funding

University of East Anglia

The University of East Anglia (UEA) campus covers 360 acres on the outskirts of Norwich combining modernist architecture with fens and meadows. A strong tradition of research at the university includes the world-leading Tyndall Centre for Climate Change Research, and another jewel in UEA's crown is its creative writing course, whose alumni include Ian McEwan, Tracy Chevalier and Sir Kazuo Ishiguro.

In the latest Research Excellence Framework (REF 2021), 91% of the university's submission was classified as world-leading or internationally excellent, pushing it up 15 places to 17th in our research quality index. Highlights included agriculture, food and veterinary sciences, development studies, and social policy and social work. A triple silver rating in the Teaching Excellence Framework (TEF 2023) highlighted the university's "outstanding" physical and virtual learning resources. However, UEA's finances have struggled, and in 2023 the university made staff cutbacks of 400 positions, equivalent to 10% of the workforce.

Three courses confirmed as closing from 2025 are American literature with creative writing, business information systems, and society, culture and media with a year abroad. Placement years, study abroad and foundation years are also being added to a wide range of courses. Standard offers range from AAA to BBB. Nearly a quarter of 2024's UK-based entrants benefitted from UEA's nuanced approach to contextual offer-making, which includes a gateway year for medicine. Nearly one in five entrants gained their place through clearing.

The university offers careers support to its students from day one and throughout their first three years as a graduate, utilising links with organisations such as Aviva, BT, National Trust and the National Centre for Writing. It has however fallen 11 places since 2022 to =35th in our analysis of the Graduate Outcomes survey.

Facilities on the spacious campus include Productivity East, a £7.4 million interdisciplinary hub for engineering, technology and management, and the opening of the £30 million New Science Building in 2020. Six wildlife trails and a sculpture trail encourage students to get close to nature. The campus also has two live music venues as well as the Sainsbury Centre for visual arts, while sports facilities include an Olympic-size swimming pool, a fitness centre, five sports halls and a climbing wall. Crafts and pottery are among more than 250 clubs and societies in which students socialise and grow their interests.

There is support available in the form of wellbeing advisers, talking therapists, advisers specialising in finance, help with visas and learning enhancement tutors to improve study skills. Accommodation prices start at £100.03 a week for students sharing a twin room, and first-years who apply by the deadline are guaranteed accommodation. UEA is ranked 78th in our social inclusion index, but has performed better in its work to close the black achievement gap. Bursaries of £1,600 or £3,000 are awarded to students from low-income households (less than £20,000 a year) or who have left care, respectively. Merit-based scholarships are available in music, sport, social sciences, medicine, the arts and the sciences.

Norwich Research Park Norwich NR4 7TJ
admissions@uea.ac.uk
uea.ac.uk
ueasu.org

Overall ranking 40
(last year 33)

Accommodation
University provided places 3,615
Self-catered £100–£215 per week

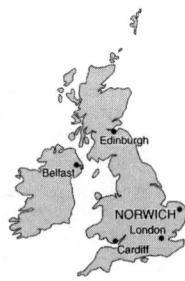

Student numbers
Undergraduates 11,920
Applications per place 4.1:1
Overall offer rate 81.7%

Fees
UK fees £9,535
International fees £23,100–£29,300
Medicine £47,700

uea.ac.uk/visit/uni-open-days
uea.ac.uk/study/fees-and-funding#tuition

University of East London

The University of East London (UEL) has two campuses in Stratford and one in Docklands. Practice-based, immersive-style settings have been brought on stream, such as mock wards and an operating theatre for healthcare students. Investments in the student experience appear to be working. Based on our National Student Survey (NSS) analysis, the university soared 77 places up our teaching quality index to rank 12th last year – earning it our teaching award. It remains in the upper reaches in this year's analysis for teaching quality (=20th) but drops slightly to =53rd for the wider experience. A silver rating overall in the Teaching Excellence Framework (TEF 2023) was a step up from bronze six years earlier.

A 2021 study by the Institute for Fiscal Studies (IFS) showed UEL to be a significant engine of social mobility with more than three times the national average number of graduates from the lowest-income households going on to "impactful" careers, though a completion rate of 87.5% places it 115th in the UK. In the latest Research Excellence Framework (REF 2021), the best results came in computer science, allied health, and social work and social policy. Against sector-wide gains UEL fell from 76th to 104th in our research rankings.

An expanding curriculum will add programmes in paramedic science and three new nursing specialisms. UEL's portfolio of degree apprenticeships spans 16 areas from podiatry to digital technology. UEL does not make contextual offers, but it does apply a holistic approach to admissions and accepts a wide range of professional qualifications, as well as portfolios, interviews and auditions.

Among UEL's career-boosting initiatives is the Professional Fitness and Mental Wealth programme, and an entrepreneurship scheme offering funding and mentoring to student start-ups. In time, such efforts may shift the dial on graduate outcomes. For now, UEL ranks 119th overall for graduate prospects, with 63.6% of graduates in highly skilled work or postgraduate study within 15 months.

When the Docklands base was completed in 1999, as London's first new campus for 50 years, its striking architecture was described as "poetry". More than £20 million is being invested into the three campuses through the UEL Connected Campus programme. As well as laboratories for health and primary care teaching, a mock courtroom, a trading floor and a Harvard-style lecture theatre are among innovations. Westfield Stratford City could not be more conveniently located, while the Docklands Light Railway provides easy access to the rest of the capital. Students get free off-peak membership of SportsDock, a multimillion-pound facility on the Docklands Campus.

A wellbeing service provides access to appointments with counsellors in person, and by video or phone calls. UEL has two distinctive waterside halls of residence on campus, and first-years are guaranteed a room if they meet the eligibility criteria and apply by the deadline.

34.6% of undergraduates are at least 21 on entry and the university offers the option of starting courses in January as well as September. It is =44th overall in our social inclusion table. Around half of students receive some financial help, with the largest award being the merit-based vice-chancellor's scholarship of up to £28,605.

Docklands Campus University Way London E16 2RD
study@uel.ac.uk
uel.ac.uk
eastlondonsu.com

Overall ranking 114
(last year 126)

Accommodation
University provided places 1,160
Self-catered £176–£232 per week

Student numbers
Undergraduates 8,460
Applications per place 3.7:1
Overall offer rate 74.4%

Fees
UK fees £9,535
International fees £15,560–£16,800

uel.ac.uk/study/undergraduate/undergraduate-open-days
uel.ac.uk/study/fees-funding

Edge Hill University

On a 160-acre plot of prime northwest England landscape outside the market town of Ormskirk, Edge Hill University has been blazing a trail as one the UK's leading modern universities, since it gained university status in 2006. Students warm to its inclusive campus atmosphere, and a growing curriculum keeps academic ambitions on track with the lovely setting. Its green spaces have won Green Flag status for 13 years running and Edge Hill is perhaps the only university in the UK with its own man-made beach. The university's medical school offers a foundation year pathway to entry targeting budding doctors from widening participation backgrounds, and Edge Hill introduced broader "fair entry criteria" in 2025. The 2022 winner of our Modern University of the Year award, Edge Hill has experienced a remarkable return to form in student satisfaction. Our latest National Student Survey (NSS) analysis places it 17th for the wider undergraduate experience (up from =104th) and =32nd for teaching quality (up from 119th). The new NSS findings are in keeping with those of the government's Teaching Excellence Framework (TEF 2023), in which the university gained silver overall and gold for student experience.

Edge Hill's best results in the latest Research Excellence Framework (REF 2021) came in hospitality, leisure, and information systems and management. However, against stronger performances elsewhere, Edge Hill fell 20 places in our research quality index. New courses joining the portfolio in the next two years include chemistry, law and business, and psychology with forensic perspectives, as well as a degree in global infectious disease run in partnership with the Liverpool School of Tropical Medicine. Nine courses are closing in 2025 and 2026, including television, English literature with creative writing, and religion. Entry requirements range from 104 UCAS tariff points up to 144 for medicine, and most courses publish a UCAS tariff point range. Less than 10% of the circa 3,600 first-years came through clearing in 2025. Edge Hill is just above the middle ground of UK universities at =54th in our analysis of the Graduate Outcomes survey, and in the 2024–25 academic year it hosted more than 270 employers at graduate and departmental careers fairs.

Edge Hill's spacious site includes the £27 million Catalyst building, which houses student support services, the university library and study spaces. The departments of media and computing feature studios for television, animation, sound, photography and radio. Performance facilities include two theatres, where student productions are supported by professional teams of front-of-house and technical staff. Students have more than 100 clubs and societies to choose from and access to a £30 million sports centre. Characterful Ormskirk is a ten-minute walk away, or those in search of brighter lights can get to Liverpool by train in 30 minutes.

Edge Hill's Campus Connectors team are students employed to offer informal peer support, and the university offers counselling and disability support. Accommodation prices start at £90 a week, rising to £165, and first-years who apply by the housing deadline are guaranteed a room.

Edge Hill is ranked 22nd overall for social inclusion. Several scholarships and bursaries of up to £2,000 are available with different eligibility criteria.

St Helens Road Ormskirk L39 4QP
admissions@edgehill.ac.uk
edgehill.ac.uk
edgehillsu.org.uk

Overall ranking 63
(last year =84)

Accommodation
University provided places 2,592
Self-catered £90–£165 per week

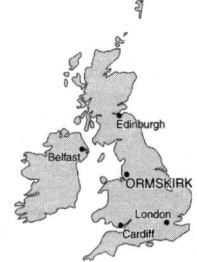

Student numbers
Undergraduates 9,550
Applications per place 4.2:1
Overall offer rate 79.4%

Fees
UK fees £9,535
International fees £17,000

edgehill.ac.uk/study/visit-us/open-days
edgehill.ac.uk/study/fees-and-funding

University of Edinburgh

An ancient university with a cutting-edge outlook, Edinburgh is a big-hitter in the UK for research, and a top-50 university in the QS global rankings. Its academic fields extend across almost 400 degree programmes – with about the same number of social and sports clubs and societies. The Old Royal Infirmary has been converted from its former use to house the Edinburgh Futures Institute, where the focus is on data, financial and public services. The university also hosts the £79 million national supercomputer, Archer2.

Edinburgh is 11th in our research quality index, and in the latest Research Excellence Framework (REF 2021), 96% of its submission was assessed as world-leading or internationally excellent. Some of the best results were in psychology, English, anatomy, and computing. In a push to achieve net-zero carbon emissions by 2040, Edinburgh has completed its divestment from fossil fuels – a substantial undertaking, given it has the third-largest endowment fund of any UK institution. In the 2024-25 People & Planet rankings the university was placed =107th.

Rates of student satisfaction remain low, and students have reported particular difficulty obtaining feedback from lecturers. In our new National Student Survey analysis, Edinburgh is second from bottom for teaching quality and 119th for the wider experience. Though not in deficit in its most recent financial return, Edinburgh is looking to save £140 million from its annual budget. Job cuts have been made and there may be more to come.

The first students of a new biological sciences degree began in September 2025, and from 2026 a new degree in religion, culture and society will replace religious studies. Physiology and oral health sciences degrees are being withdrawn, and the landscape architecture degree is revised. Entry requires A-level grades from BBB up to A*A*A*, or Scottish Highers of BBBB to AAAAA. Edinburgh was an early convert to contextual admissions, benefitting about 20% of 2024 entrants. Just 2.5% entered through clearing. Fieldwork and industry placements are embedded in Edinburgh's courses, and the High Fliers graduate market report puts it in the top 15 universities targeted by leading employers, but the university sits 33rd in our analysis of graduate outcomes.

There are five main campuses across Edinburgh and at Easterbush. More than 100,000 students converge on the city, and the nightlife is lively without being overwhelming. The city itself is a famous cultural hub from festivals to fixed art collections. The university's sporting programmes and facilities are among the best in the UK, producing several Olympic champions. For welfare, same-day counselling appointments and a 24/7 chaplaincy listening service are available. There are free period products, and the university employs an intercultural and anti-discrimination adviser.

There are 10,460 residential places reserved for undergraduates and all first-years who come from outside Edinburgh's city limits are guaranteed a room. The university is near the bottom of our Scottish social inclusion index, ranking 14th. Its Access Edinburgh Scholarship for UK students is received by more than a quarter of entrants and worth up to £5,000, and there are several subject-specific and merit-based awards.

Old College South Bridge Edinburgh EH8 9YL
futurestudents@ed.ac.uk
ed.ac.uk
eusa.ed.ac.uk

Overall ranking 25
(last year =17)

Accommodation
University provided places 10,460
Catered £200–£350 per week
Self-catered £151–£266 per week

Student numbers
Undergraduates 25,170
Applications per place 9.0:1
Overall offer rate 43.6%

Fees
Scots fees £0–£1,820
International fees £28,000–£36,800
RUK fees £9,535
Medicine £51,961

ed.ac.uk/studying/undergraduate/open-days-events-visits/open-day
registryservices.ed.ac.uk/student-funding

Edinburgh Napier University

One of four universities in the Scottish capital, Edinburgh Napier University (ENU) has gained eight places in our academic league table, nearly breaking into the top 50. The undergraduate degree in cybersecurity and forensics was the first in the UK to be fully certified by the National Cyber Security Centre, and hands-on learning facilities dotted around the three main campuses train students in wide-ranging specialisms from nursing and midwifery, to film production. ENU takes the majority of its undergraduates from Scotland, but for those from the rest of the UK and Ireland, tuition fees are waived in the fourth year and there are merit bursaries of £1,000 per year of study for those who achieve at least BBB at A-level, or equivalent qualifications.

The university boosted its research reputation in the latest Research Excellence Framework (REF 2021), achieving one of the sector's biggest improvements to reach =73rd in our research quality index. Some of the best results were in building, land and property management; and town and country planning. But rates of student satisfaction took a dive in the latest National Student Survey (NSS), and ENU ranks =92nd for satisfaction with teaching quality and =85th for the broad undergraduate experience.

New from September 2025 are degrees in international hospitality management, international tourism and airline management, and accounting (all at nearby partner colleges). Scottish Highers entry requirements range from AABB to BBC. The university publishes two offer levels for courses, standard and minimum, with the latter being two to three grades lower. About 12% of students were admitted through clearing in 2024. Analysis of the Graduate Outcomes survey puts Edinburgh Napier in 41st place in our graduate prospects table, with 80% of graduates in highly skilled jobs or further study within 15 months. A career focus is evident in ENU's stable of eight graduate apprenticeships (equivalent to degree apprenticeships in England and Wales).

Campuses are spread across one of Britain's leading student cities, packed with culture and known for its warm welcome. Merchiston hosts creative arts subjects; engineering and the built environment; and computing. Facilities there include soundproofed music studios and a broadcast journalism newsroom at Screen Academy Scotland. The Craiglockhart campus hosts the Business School, while Sighthill is the base for the schools of nursing, midwifery and social care.

Arts and culture are well supported at ENU, with 12 music practice rooms, plus studios, editing suites and design workshops. Sports include American football, cricket, football, golf, gymnastics and rugby. A team of three mental health advisers work closely with academic staff to meet students' needs, and workshops help with sleep, handling change, loneliness or procrastination. Student accommodation is at three halls of residence and the university can guarantee a space to all first-years from outside Edinburgh who apply by the deadline.

The university's drive to increase the numbers from under-represented groups continues, and ENU stays steady in 6th place in our Scottish social inclusion index. While undergraduates from Scotland are eligible for the national scheme for financial help, about 80% of students from the rest of the UK are likely to be eligible for some form of university-funded financial help.

Sighthill Court Edinburgh EH11 4BN
ugadmissions@napier.ac.uk
napier.ac.uk
napierstudents.com

Overall ranking 51
(last year 59)

Accommodation
University provided places 1,300
Self-catered £124–£209 per week

Student numbers
Undergraduates 9,315
Applications per place 5.7:1
Overall offer rate 71.4%

Fees
Scots fees £0–£1,820
International fees £17,520–£20,310
RUK fees £9,535 (£28,605 max, 4yrs)

napier.ac.uk/study-with-us/undergraduate/meet-us/open-days
napier.ac.uk/study-with-us/undergraduate/fees-and-finance

University of Essex

Founded on the vision to integrate living alongside learning, Essex is a campus university in the historic setting of Wivenhoe Park. The much-reduced footfall of EU undergraduates since Brexit has been felt keenly at Essex, but the university remains determined to keep up its European links. As a member of the Young Universities for the Future of Europe alliance of ten research-intensive universities – including Maastricht and Bremen – students have opportunities to study across the continent.

Social sciences are Essex's longstanding academic strength, and the university ranks =72nd for sociology in the 2025 QS World University Rankings. In the most recent Research Excellence Framework (REF 2021), 83% of Essex's research was rated world-leading or internationally excellent, but bigger gains elsewhere meant that Essex dropped 16 places to 41st in our research quality index. Essex was rated triple silver in the government's Teaching Excellence Framework (TEF 2023). Its recent National Student Survey results have been variable in our overall rankings, but our latest analysis puts it in the top 35 for teaching quality and the top 25 for the student experience.

A freeze on staff promotions was introduced in 2024 to help prevent a financial deficit, and job cuts have been reported. Twenty-five undergraduate degrees have been withdrawn from 2025, including courses in politics, journalism, and economics, and a further 17 are temporarily suspended. However, the curriculum has gained new degrees in stage management, microbiology, urban sustainability studies, and international affairs. A new degree apprenticeship in biomedical science joins a roster of seven programmes with more than 400 students enrolled.

Most courses require BBC or BBB and Essex's contextual admissions policy undercuts standard offers by up to two A-level grades or equivalent. The Knowledge Gateway is home to more than 90 businesses, many of which offer internships or employment, but Essex sits outside the top half of our graduate prospects table, ranking =91st.

Upgrades to the university's academic facilities in Colchester include modern skills laboratories and simulation equipment at the School of Health and Social Care, and an experimental facility studying improvements in crop photosynthesis. A modern seaside campus at Southend has courses in business, health and the arts, and the third campus, Loughton, is home to Essex's acting school. The Students' Union includes a revamped bar and common room, and there are more than 100 student-led societies. Sport is well supported, with recent top 30 results in the British Universities and Colleges Sport (BUCS) table, and partnerships with Essex County Cricket Club and Colchester Rugby Club.

Counselling is available on all three campuses, and students can access online cognitive behavioural therapy. Antiracism training is run for students and staff, and all new students must complete mandatory online sexual consent and bystander training. The university guarantees accommodation to first-years who make Essex their firm choice and meet application deadlines.

Essex has ambitious outreach programmes with their succcess reflected in a student population more diverse than most pre-1992 universities. It ranks =35th in our social inclusion index. At least half of new entrants qualify for one of Essex's financial awards.

Wivenhoe Park Colchester CO4 3SQ
admit@essex.ac.uk
essex.ac.uk
www.essexstudent.com

Overall ranking 44
(last year =46)

Accommodation
University provided places 6,084
Self-catered £102–£296 per week

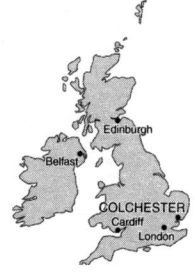

Student numbers
Undergraduates 9,460
Applications per place 5.4:1
Overall offer rate 79.4%

Fees
UK fees £9,535
International fees £20,475–£30,275

essex.ac.uk/visit-us/open-days
essex.ac.uk/student/money

University of Exeter

Exeter has built a strong reputation for world-class research, on a famously leafy campus 20 minutes from Devon's stunning coastline. Recent developments include facilities for computing, engineering, data science and AI programmes; a new multifaith centre; and expanded wellbeing services. As part of its Strategy 2030, Exeter is throwing its academic weight behind tackling global challenges such as climate change, healthcare, and social justice, including the UK's first "net-zero in operation" research centre for water and waste. This has earned Exeter a top ten spot in the People & Planet league, and it is Runner-Up for Sustainable University of the Year 2026.

Results from the latest Research Excellence Framework (REF 2021) confirm Exeter's place at 18th in our research quality index. It was awarded gold in the latest Teaching Excellence Framework (TEF 2023) for its undergraduate provision, but its performance in the National Student Survey (NSS) has seen a dip, with our analysis placing it 109th for teaching quality and =60th for the wider student experience.

More than 60 courses join the curriculum from 2025, including robotics and artificial intelligence, physics with biophysics, and multiple engineering streams. Many of these can include a year abroad or an industrial placement. A global sustainability degree joins the roster in 2026, while courses in nutrition, flexible combined honours (Penryn), and mathematics and physics have been withdrawn. Exeter has 3,000 students enrolled across its 11 undergraduate and eight postgraduate degree apprenticeships.

Offers for undergraduate degrees range from A*AA to BBB. A contextual admissions policy undercut this by two or three grades for 25% of the 7,600 entrants in 2024, while 8% entered through clearing. Historically strong for graduate outcomes, Exeter has slipped to rank 31st in our index this year. In the Graduate Market 2025 report by High Fliers, Exeter is ranked the 8th most targeted university by leading employers, and more than 4,600 students embark on work placements as part of their course.

The university guarantees a room for all first-years who meet the deadline. The main Streatham Campus is an attractive hillside site bordering the city centre. Fewer than two miles away, the St Luke's Campus houses the medical school, the Graduate School of Education and programmes in sport and health sciences. The Penryn Campus, in Cornwall, is shared with Falmouth University and hosts the Renewable Energy Engineering Facility (Reef). A former winner of our Sports University of the Year title, Exeter was fourth in the 2024-25 British Universities and Colleges Sport (BUCS) league table and has some of the best facilities in the country, with Penryn also making use of one of the best locations in the UK for water sports. Cultural venues include the Northcott Theatre and the Bill Douglas Cinema Museum, and there is a campus sculpture walk.

Exeter ranks bottom for social inclusion in our latest data, but is working with schools and supporting national schemes such as IntoUniversity and the Sutton Trust's Pathways to Law to widen access. The Access to Exeter bursary, worth up to £2,200 a year, is available for students from households with an income of less than £35,000, alongside sport, choral and organ scholarships.

Northcote House The Queen's Drive Exeter EX4 4QJ
exeter.ac.uk/about/enquiry
exeter.ac.uk
exeterguild.org; thesu.org.uk

Overall ranking 14
(last year 13)

Accommodation
University provided places 6,639
Catered £193–£310 per week
Self-catered £132–£235 per week

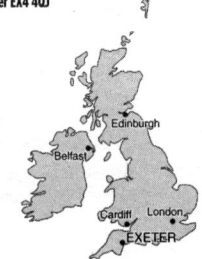

Student numbers
Undergraduates 22,995
Applications per place 5.8:1
Overall offer rate 85.1%

Fees
UK fees £9,535
International fees £24,700–£30,900
Medicine £47,500

exeter.ac.uk/open-days/undergraduate
exeter.ac.uk/undergraduate/fees

Falmouth University

A hotbed of creativity on the Cornish coast, Falmouth University offers a unique student experience in a setting of stunning beaches, independent coffee shops and eclectic bars. Founded as the Falmouth School of Art in 1902, today its degrees span film, fashion, music, and theatre, alongside business, marketing, game development, and architecture. Teaching is practice-based, taking place in studios and workshops flooded with natural light from the university's famous subtropical gardens. Students benefit from sharing with the University of Exeter a campus and Students' Union in nearby Penryn, creating a larger, more diverse community.

In the Research Excellence Framework (REF 2021) 63% of Falmouth's art and design submissions were rated world-leading or internationally excellent, a result that saw the university leap 52 places in our research quality rankings. Triple silver in the Teaching Excellence Framework (TEF 2023) is at odds with declining student satisfaction; in our analysis of the latest National Student Survey (NSS), Falmouth ranks =95th for teaching quality and 118th for the wider experience.

From 2025 the curriculum gains a combined arts online degree. Entry requirements typically start from 104 UCAS tariff points but interviews, auditions, or portfolio reviews are required for most courses, and all offers are contextual and tailored to the individual. Students across all academic departments have opportunities to work on real projects in collaboration with industry partners, and some courses are accredited by professional organisations. That has yet to translate to high rates of graduate employment, however. In common with fellow arts specialists, Falmouth struggles in our graduate prospects analysis, sitting second bottom at =128th.

Teaching facilities at the Falmouth campus include an in-house photo agency that takes on live industry projects. At the purpose-built Penryn Campus nearby, performing arts students have access to a motion-capture studio, video-editing suites with specialist animation software, fully sprung dance floors, rehearsal studios, and theatre space. The student-friendly social scene consists of pop-up bars, beach bonfires and festivals on farms, all within walking distance. Students have their pick of more than 140 clubs, from surfing to LGBTQ+ groups. The Sports Centre on Penryn Campus has a gym, sports hall and an outdoor orienteering route, and the local area provides the setting for activities such as wild swimming and water sports. Part-time jobs in the tourist trade help with living costs.

Mental health support includes one-to-one appointments and same-day drop-ins on campus with therapists, as well as Spectrum Life, a free and confidential service available 24/7 online, by phone or by text. A place in university accommodation is guaranteed to all first-years who apply by the deadline. Students can opt to have meals included at the Glasney Student Village, and 7% of rooms are catered.

Just inside the top 90 of our social inclusion index (89th), Falmouth's outreach activities target schools and colleges in areas across the UK where progression rates to university are low. About a quarter of entrants in 2024 qualified for financial assistance in the form of means-tested bursaries, international scholarships or hardship awards. Care-leavers are eligible for a bursary of £1,000 per year of study.

Woodlane Falmouth TR11 4RH
futurestudies@falmouth.ac.uk
falmouth.ac.uk
thesu.org.uk

Overall ranking =87
(last year 73)

Accommodation
University provided places 1,452
Catered £200–£249 per week
Self-catered £144–£256 per week

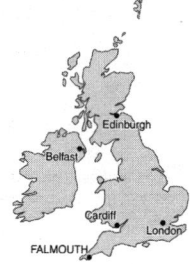

Student numbers
Undergraduates 5,050
Applications per place 3.2:1
Overall offer rate 67.1%

Fees
UK fees £9,535–£11,100
International fees £6,935–£19,950

www.falmouth.ac.uk/experience/open-days
www.falmouth.ac.uk/study/tuition-fees

University of Glasgow

Students can mingle between medieval quads and modern laboratories at this ancient and ambitious institution. Glasgow's main Gilmorehill Campus, famed for the Gilbert Scott building's iconic bell tower, is at the heart of the city's fashionable West End. A £1 billion campus redevelopment is currently under way, adding 14 acres and flagship facilities. It's no surprise that students arrive with top grades – in our entry-standards metric, Glasgow is on a par with Cambridge.

It is one of two Russell Group universities in Scotland and won our Scottish University of the Year title for 2024. Glasgow also holds a top 100 spot in the QS World University Rankings 2026. Its prestige is confirmed by the latest Research Excellence Framework (REF 2021), our analysis of which ranked the university 12th in the UK, with particular success in the fields of medicine, veterinary studies, and life sciences. Degree options are broad and flexible across 70 subject areas, and students can study or work abroad without adding to the standard four-year length of courses. However, the university has fallen to 126th in our latest National Student Survey (NSS) analysis for teaching quality, and 116th for wider student experience.

Standard offers range from AAA to CCC at A-level and AAAAAA to BBBB in Scottish Highers. The university makes contextual offers with reduced requirements for eligible students, and a small number of places (9% in 2024) are secured through clearing. Glasgow ranks in the top third nationally (27th) for graduate prospects, and the careers department partners with more than 150 organisations annually to provide in excess of 300 exclusive – and mostly paid – internships.

The university occupies three sites around Glasgow. The redeveloped Gilmorehill Campus now features a new learning hub and the £116 million Mazumdar-Shaw Advanced Research Centre (ARC). Four miles away, the spacious Garscube Campus hosts the veterinary school and outdoor sports pitches. Liberal arts and teaching courses are delivered in Dumfries, where more than £13 million has been spent on sporting and social facilities. The city is Scotland's biggest metropolis, known for its friendly atmosphere and relative affordability, as well as its excellent music scene. There are purpose-built sports facilities on the Gilmorehill Campus and at the Garscube site.

The university's SafeZone app helps students who are lost, need to report an emergency or require first aid. Students also have access to a confidential advice line, plus one-to-one sessions with counsellors, cognitive behavioural therapists, psychologists and mental health advisers. Nearly 5,400 accommodation spaces are available for 2025–26, with a room in halls guaranteed for first-years who apply by the July deadline. Off-campus housing can be in short supply with five universities in the city.

The university runs several pre-entry schemes to widen participation from priority postcodes, but it ranks bottom in Scotland in our social inclusion index. Typically students from England, Wales and Northern Ireland will have their fourth-year tuition fees waived. They are also eligible to claim access bursaries of £1,000 to £3,000 a year if they are from a low-income household. The university provides about £12 million in undergraduate scholarships for academic excellence and about 13% of entrants in 2025 received some kind of financial assistance.

University Avenue Glasgow G12 8QQ
gla.ac.uk/study/enquire/
glasgow.ac.uk
guu.co.uk; qmunion.org.uk

Overall ranking 22
(last year 16)

Accommodation
University provided places 5,539
Catered £204–£225 per week
Self-catered £121–£234 per week

Student numbers
Undergraduates 21,190
Applications per place 5.5:1
Overall offer rate 66.5%

Fees
Scots fees £0–£1,820
International fees £26,580–£31,800
RUK fees £9,535
Medicine £58,890

gla.ac.uk/explore/visit/undergraduate/opendays
gla.ac.uk/undergraduate/fees

Glasgow Caledonian University

Glasgow Caledonian University (GCU) has reached new heights in our academic league table this year, where it secures Runner-Up for Modern University of the Year 2026. Nicknamed Cally (with various spellings) by its students, its mission is to be the "university for the common good". More than half of its undergraduate programmes are accredited by professional bodies and most include a work placement. GCU is Scotland's leading provider of graduate apprenticeships (equivalent to degree apprenticeships in England), including civil engineering, cybersecurity and accountancy. It is also one of the largest providers of graduates to NHS Scotland. Based mainly on a single campus in the centre of one of the UK's busiest student cities, GCU also has a postgraduate campus in London.

GCU ranks 36th this year, buoyed by the 18th highest entry standards and 34th best graduate prospects in the UK. Also helping to fuel its league table ascent is its research profile, with nursing and allied health subjects producing some of its best work in the Research Excellence Framework (REF 2021). The latest National Student Survey (NSS) puts the university at =55th for overall student experience. Upgrades to the campus, including student accommodation and teaching facilities, came on stream from the start of the 2025 academic year.

Courses are organised within three schools, and the School of Computing, Engineering and Built Environment is one of Britain's leading teaching centres for building and surveying. Biological sciences is no longer recruiting from September 2025. Offers for undergraduate degrees range from 147 to 96 UCAS tariff points, equivalent to AAA to CCC at A-level, or Scottish Highers of BBCC up to AABBB. Minimum entry requirements apply for those eligible for contextual offers, which were made to about a fifth of new entrants in 2024. Clearing accounted for 5% of admissions in 2024. An enhanced Employment on Campus service opens in 2025-26 to support students looking for paid work, while the Careers Centre advertises graduate jobs, internships, placements and part-time work.

The Heart of the Campus building is the centrepiece of GCU's site, near Queen Street station. Standout facilities include the Sir Alex Ferguson Library, a virtual hospital, the Vision Centre for optometry students, and the Fashion Factory. Glasgow offers a hard-to-beat music scene and student-centric fun. The university has waived membership fees for students' use of the ARC health and wellbeing centre, which has three gyms and two large sports halls.

The student wellbeing team comprises counsellors, wellbeing and mental health advisers, and a disability service. Caledonian Court student accommodation is fresh from an upgrade, though only 70% of applicants can be housed in halls.

GCU ranks 3rd for the number of students from non-selective state schools and 2nd for ethnic minorities, but it has dropped four places to 8th overall in Scotland. Financial support includes a £6,000 cash-back bursary for Rest of the UK (RUK) students, and more than 10% of students receive direct financial assistance from the university.

Cowcaddens Road Glasgow G4 0BA
studentenquiries@gcu.ac.uk
gcu.ac.uk
gcustudents.co.uk

Overall ranking 36
(last year 44)

Accommodation
University provided places 655
Self-catered £125–£148 per week

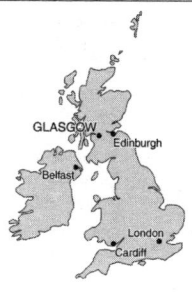

Student numbers
Undergraduates 12,685
Applications per place 4.1:1
Overall offer rate 68.5%

Fees
Scots fees £0–£1,820
International fees £15,200
RUK fees £9,535

gcu.ac.uk/study/opendays
gcu.ac.uk/study/tuitionfees

University of Gloucestershire

Adding a high street twist to higher education, the University of Gloucestershire has transformed a former Debenhams into a new city centre campus. The development also contains an arts, health and wellbeing centre delivered in partnership with the NHS, and a new public library. Students can get the best of town and country living in Cheltenham and Gloucester on the edge of the Cotswolds Area of Outstanding Natural Beauty, and the county hosts more than 45 music, arts and science festivals each year.

Gloucestershire earned triple silver in the Teaching Excellence Framework (TEF 2023). Reflecting the institution's history as a teacher training college, Gloucestershire is one of only four universities in the southwest to receive full accreditation from the Department for Education to this professional route at undergraduate and postgraduate level. Its primary and secondary teacher training courses are rated "good" by Ofsted. However, rates of student satisfaction are mixed: in our latest National Student Survey analysis, Gloucestershire has climbed 11 places to =79th for teaching quality, but dropped to 122nd for the wider experience.

Its Countryside and Community Research Institute is one of the largest rural research centres in the UK and produced some of Gloucestershire's best results in the latest Research Excellence Framework (REF 2021). Overall, 47% of the university's submission was rated as world-leading or internationally excellent and it climbed one place to =110th in our research rankings. Among eight new degrees launching are crime and criminal investigation, three sociology degrees, and film and TV production. Offers range from 48 UCAS tariff points for an integrated foundation year up to 136 for physiotherapy. Experience is taken into account for mature students.

Mentoring, placements and keynote speakers are part of the careers and employability services on offer. A proportion of 76.4% of graduates in high-skilled jobs or further study 15 months on from their degree ranks the university =57th in our table.

There are four campuses in Cheltenham and Gloucester. The main Park Campus has refreshed facilities for creative and digital programmes, including new studio and workshop spaces for fine art and photography. Teaching courses and humanities subjects are based at Francis Close Hall, which combines ivy-clad buildings with a new biomedical laboratory, architecture studio and community teaching space. The purpose-built Oxstalls Campus caters for business, healthcare, sport and exercise sciences. The new City Campus in Gloucester focuses on psychology, education and social work-related programmes.

The university's sporting tradition is supported by facilities at Oxstalls Sports Park and in Cheltenham, including tennis courts, international-standard 3G pitches for rugby and football, fitness suites and a sports hall. Students can access advisers online and by phone across wide-ranging issues. One-to-one counselling and a chaplaincy are also available.

Gloucester guarantees accommodation to all first-years in halls on or near campus. It has climbed 32 places in our social inclusion rankings, rating highly for its intake of white working-class boys, and 5th for its proportion of disabled students. One in five new entrants received a scholarship or bursary in 2025, including awards targeted at first-year students progressing from partner schools.

The Park Campus The Park Cheltenham GL50 2RH
admissions@glos.ac.uk
glos.ac.uk
yourstudentsunion.com

Overall ranking =84
(last year =90)

Accommodation
University provided places 1,778
Self-catered £132–£240 per week

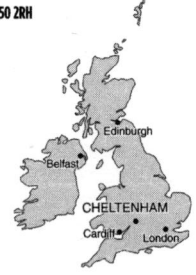

Student numbers
Undergraduates 5,420
Applications per place 4.1:1
Overall offer rate 88.9%

Fees
UK fees £9,535
International fees £17,425
RUK fees £9,535

glos.ac.uk/visit-us/open-days/undergraduate-open-days
glos.ac.uk/finance/fees-and-loans

Goldsmiths, University of London

Progressive, creative and rooted to its original southeast London campus in the increasingly hip New Cross neighbourhood, Goldsmiths offers degrees across the creative arts, as well as social sciences and humanities, management, law, and computing. The QS World University Rankings 2025 place it =26th for performing arts, and 37th for art and design. The alumni list reads like a Who's Who of the creative industries, from designer Mary Quant to film director Sir Steve McQueen. In the latest Research Excellence Framework (REF 2021), 79% of work submitted by Goldsmiths was rated world-leading or internationally excellent. Despite slipping 13 places, Goldsmiths is comfortably in the top half of our research ranking at 49th.

However, Goldsmiths has been significantly affected by the financial challenges facing UK universities, with a £16 million budget deficit in 2023 leading to job cuts and a marking boycott. Students threatened legal action over course and module closures and the sense of unrest is reflected in a bronze rating from the latest Teaching Excellence Framework (TEF 2023). It is also the only university in our guide to be told by the Office for Students that its provision requires improvement. A restructuring into two academic faculties promises an enhanced student experience, and the university has made some modest improvements in student satisfaction. In our new National Student Survey analysis it is 116th for teaching quality and 126th for the wider undergraduate experience.

New for 2025 are integrated degrees in English, history, politics and international relations, sociology, journalism, promotional media and social work. Ending in 2025 are BA courses in politics, and anthropology and sociology. Applicants are expected to achieve ABB to CCC at A-level, though Goldsmiths takes applicants' educational backgrounds into account and will consider those without the standard entry requirements based on their work experience, creative portfolio or audition. Just under 1,700 new students were accepted on to courses in 2024, a 40% drop since 2017. The university ensures students gain experience in industry by teaming up with partners from multinational companies to local art collectives. But in our analysis of graduate outcomes, the university ranks 111th.

All Goldsmiths' undergraduate teaching and support is based on a single campus in southeast London, where facilities range from a gallery, 200-seat theatre, and digital video and audio-editing equipment to the university's own yarn shop. Goldsmiths Students' Union runs a variety of activities, and societies on offer include athletics, anime, pole dancing, yoga and debating. Some sports are based on-site, and at Loring Sports Ground, half an hour away.

Students can seek help from counsellors, financial advisers and wellbeing support officers, and the Students' Union runs workshops on keeping safe. All accommodation is within a 30-minute commute. First-years are prioritised and international students who apply by the deadline are guaranteed a space. Goldsmiths has risen from 55th to 43rd in our social inclusion index, with outreach initiatives including drop-in classes for ex-offenders and those who have struggled with addiction and mental health. A fifth of entrants received a scholarship or bursary in 2025, including full fee waivers for students from the borough of Lewisham.

New Cross London SE14 6NW
course-info@gold.ac.uk
gold.ac.uk
goldsmithssu.org

Overall ranking =87
(last year 80)

Accommodation
University provided places 1,392
Self-catered £176–£389 per week

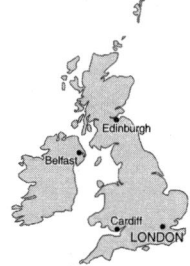

Student numbers
Undergraduates 4,650
Applications per place 5.9:1
Overall offer rate 73.9%

Fees
UK fees £9,535
International fees £20,650–£28,900

gold.ac.uk/open-days
gold.ac.uk/ug/fees-funding

University of Greater Manchester

The university formerly known as Bolton adopted its University of Greater Manchester name in December 2024, reflecting its growing footprint across the northwest. This change is accompanied by a new learning model, The Greater Manchester Way, where students study in intensive five-week blocks, designed to fit around their lives. Widening participation is a guiding tenet at this institution, which is known for its supportive approach and strong record on social inclusion, helped by the lower living costs in Bolton, a short train ride from Manchester's bright lights.

A focus on student support was recognised in the Teaching Excellence Framework (TEF 2023), where the university earned gold for student experience, leading to an overall silver rating. However, the panel awarded it bronze for student outcomes, reflecting a higher-than-average dropout rate. Our latest National Student Survey analysis shows a recent downturn, with a big drop in rankings for both teaching quality (to =59th) and the wider student experience (to 101st). More significantly, in May 2025 the vice-chancellor and two other staff members were suspended amid a police investigation into "allegations of financial irregularities". Research strengths include the National Centre for Motorsport Engineering, but in our analysis of the latest Research Excellence Framework (REF 2021), the University of Greater Manchester fell 16 places to 128th.

An expanding curriculum has gained about 24 new degrees over the past three years – among them a number of psychology-based courses, artificial intelligence and practical creature and character effects. The latest additions are in commercial surface design and contemporary art practice (both offered with or without a foundation year). The university is highly accessible, and in 2024 almost a third of new students (32%) gained their place through clearing. Getting students ready for work is a key focus. The university ranks 71st for graduate prospects, with nearly 75% of leavers in high-skilled jobs or further study after 15 months. Its degree programmes have exceptional industry links, and the university also owns one of the northwest's largest apprenticeship training providers.

The main Deane Campus houses the £31 million Bolton One health, leisure and research centre and the Greater Manchester Business School. At the £40 million Institute of Medical Sciences at the Royal Bolton Hospital site, virtual queueing and electronic check-in platforms are among the high-tech fixtures. Bolton has also established an outpost in Salford through a training partnership. On-campus facilities include a multisport hall, climbing wall and a sports and spinal injuries clinic, as well as a 25m competition swimming pool and a hydrotherapy pool. At the Life Lounge, a team of mental health professionals provides support, supplemented by a 24/7 online service and therapeutic counselling.

Rooms are available in the privately-owned, university-endorsed Orlando Village, though the majority of students live locally and commute to their studies. Some 65.2% are the first in their family to go to university, 21.1% are from deprived areas, and 63% are mature students. The university offers targeted financial support to students who have served in the armed forces and care leavers. Progression scholarships are also available for students from partner colleges.

Deane Road Bolton BL3 5AB
admissions-team@greatermanchester.ac.
greatermanchester.ac.uk
ugmsu.com

Overall ranking 126
(last year 119)

Accommodation
University provided places 383
Self-catered £139–£199 per week

Student numbers
Undergraduates 5,385
Applications per place 4.7:1
Overall offer rate 65.5%

Fees
UK fees £9,535
International fees £17,500–£22,515
Medicine £45,000

greatermanchester.ac.uk/open-days
greatermanchester.ac.uk/student-life/fees-and-funding

University of Greenwich

Student life is shipshape at Greenwich's historic Dreadnought building, which houses resources ranging from the Students' Union, bar and gym to the university radio station, all on a world heritage site. Originally one of the UK's first polytechnics, and becoming a university in 1992, in September 2025 Greenwich announced a new chapter in its history: a partnership with the University of Kent to form a new "super-university", the London and South East University Group. It is scheduled to be established for the 2026/2027 academic year, subject to due diligence.

Greenwich can boast two recent Nobel laureate associations, in peace prize winner Abiy Ahmed and physics winner Charles Kao. The latest Research Excellence Framework (REF 2021) helped it climb one place to =73rd in our research rankings, and it has gained government accreditation as an Academic Centre of Excellence in Cyber Security Research. Its Natural Resources Institute has also been recognised for its work tackling causes of famine and disease. Greenwich was rated gold overall in the government's Teaching Excellence Framework (TEF 2023), a step up from its previous silver rating. However, student satisfaction has waned and it sits in the lower half of the table, at =79th for teaching quality and =72nd for student experience.

A broad course offering gained 18 new options in 2025, including civil and construction engineering, entrepreneurship and innovation, digital marketing and advertising, and primary education studies. Standard offers range from 128 to 104 UCAS tariff points, lowered by 16 points for those eligible for contextual offers. In 2024, 8,600 out of 29,000 applicants were accepted. Professional placements are built into some courses, but graduate prospects remain one of Greenwich's weaker suits. It ranks 100th in our rankings based on the proportion of graduates in high-skilled jobs or further study 15 months after leaving.

The Stockwell Street development in Greenwich has a landscaped roof terrace, large architecture studio, model-making workshop and television and sound studios. At the nearby Avery Hill Campus, facilities include three clinical skills laboratories and a library. The Medway Campus is shared with the University of Kent and Canterbury Christ Church University. More than 50 of Greenwich's courses now include sustainability modules, and it is decarbonising its campuses as part of a drive to be net-zero by 2030. There are gyms and student centres at all three campuses including an indoor 3G training facility shared with Charlton Athletic FC. Known for its cute market and the Cutty Sark ship, Greenwich is also packed with bars, clubs and restaurants, and the O2 arena is nearby. First-years are guaranteed a room in halls of residence if they apply before the June 30 deadline.

Wellbeing services include one-to-one counselling and a chaplaincy. Greenwich scores highly for its proportion of ethnic minority students and those from low-participation areas, but it has dropped 13 places to 33rd in our social inclusion table. Around four in ten new entrants received a financial award from Greenwich in 2025, ranging from means-tested support and commuter bursaries, to awards for those who complete access programmes, and choral scholarships for auditioned members of the choir.

Old Royal Naval College Park Row
Greenwich SE10 9LS
courseinfo@gre.ac.uk
gre.ac.uk
greenwichsu.co.uk

Overall ranking 100
(last year 102)

Accommodation
University provided places 2,733
Self-catered £140-£373 per week

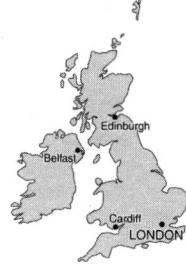

Student numbers
Undergraduates 15,640
Applications per place 3.4:1
Overall offer rate 79.0%

Fees
UK fees £9,535
International fees £17,500-£22,700

gre.ac.uk/events/opendays
gre.ac.uk/finance

Harper Adams University

Agricultural courses are attracting new interest from applicants who have grown up watching *Clarkson's Farm*, according to Britain's farm-based universities. Land management, in particular, is having a moment at Harper Adams, with fans inspired by "Cheerful Charlie" Ireland on Jeremy Clarkson's hit series about the trials and tribulations of rural life. A working pig, dairy and arable farm of about 500 hectares in the Shropshire countryside has been the centre of the university's academic operations for nearly 125 years. The university's first off-campus site, the Quad in Telford, was opened in October 2024 and will host about 300 students a year alongside start-up businesses.

Ranked 99th in the world by QS for agriculture and forestry in 2025, Harper Adams continues to diversify, including new courses in brewing, distilling, and viticulture. 60% of the university's work submitted to the latest Research Excellence Framework (REF 2021) was rated world-leading or internationally excellent, though its research ranking has fallen to 115th. The university's Hands Free Farm continues to test the potential of robots used in farming, and at the innovative Future Farm, paludiculture – or wet peat farming – is an emerging research focus. Harper Adams was rated gold overall in the Teaching Excellence Framework (TEF 2023), but the latest National Student Survey (NSS) hints at discontent, with the university plunging to 107th for satisfaction with teaching quality.

From 2025, courses are being introduced in applied data science, robotics, automation, and mechatronic engineering, digital business management, agriculture with policy and environment, and an accelerated two-year degree in veterinary bioscience. The highest demand of 136 UCAS points is for integrated master's degrees in engineering, while foundation courses require 72 points. Applicants from a low-participation area or who have spent time in care are eligible for a contextual offer (one grade lower). The curriculum is developed in collaboration with industry and all students have a work placement in their penultimate year. Harper Adams ranks 77th for graduate prospects, and is top among the three land-based specialist universities.

The Barn Students' Union venue and the Welly Inn pub are the main hangouts on campus and clubs cater to wide-ranging interests, from beer brewing to astronomy. Sports facilities include a shooting ground and a heated outdoor pool, and there's a rowing club on the River Severn in nearby Shrewsbury. Harper Adams was rocked by a report in August 2024 into claims of physical and sexual abuse during rugby club "hazing" initiation rites. A spokesman said the university had introduced new powers for the Students' Union to stop funding clubs and exclude members involved in "unacceptable behaviours". The wellbeing team includes a counsellor, mental health adviser, sexual violence liaison officer, and chaplain.

Accommodation on campus is guaranteed for those from abroad, disabled students or care leavers. The university is almost always able to accommodate all first-years and just over half the rooms are catered. Only the Royal Agricultural College is less diverse than Harper Adams. However, it is placed 11th for recruitment of disabled students. Scholarships from philanthropic and industry donations totalling more than £650,000 were awarded to 152 students in 2024-25.

Edgmond Newport TF10 8NB
admissions@harper-adams.ac.uk
harper-adams.ac.uk
harpersu.com

Overall ranking =79
(last year 53)

Accommodation
University provided places 774
Catered £125–£193 per week
Self-catered £83–£146 per week

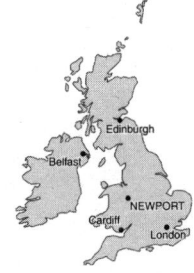

Student numbers
Undergraduates 2,590
Applications per place 4.5:1
Overall offer rate 82.5%

Fees
UK fees 9,535
International fees £16,500–£19,760

harper-adams.ac.uk/study/991/open-days
harper-adams.ac.uk/apply/finance

Hartpury University

Hartpury University's first chancellor, the actor Martin Clunes, runs a 130-acre farm, presents animal documentaries and is involved with horse charities – so he's at home at a university where the first degree programme was equine science. Students can bring their own horse to campus, which features indoor and outdoor arenas for horse trial and dressage events. Today, the curriculum covers a broad selection of land-based and sports courses, as well as equine and veterinary nursing. Founded in 1948 as an agricultural institute, Hartpury became a university in 2018. In only its fifth appearance in our league table, it has climbed 15 places and earns our Specialist University of the Year award.

The university's Agri-Tech Centre is part of a ten-year vision to turn its commercial Home Farm into a pioneer in increasing productivity and profitability through advances in robotics and other emerging technologies. Its first submission to the national Research Excellence Framework (REF 2021) focused on sport and exercise science, with an emphasis on equestrian sport and the use of water treadmills. Hartpury received triple gold in the Teaching Excellence Framework (TEF 2023), and champions face-to-face teaching, an approach that places it 13th for satisfaction with teaching quality in our analysis of the latest National Student Survey (NSS). However, for the wider student experience, it ranks lower at =72nd.

New courses from September 2025 include a degree in sports performance, with top-up courses in animal training and veterinary physiotherapy coming in 2026.

Undergraduate offers range from ABB (128 UCAS tariff points) to DDD (72). Contextual offers are eight or 16 points lower (equivalent to up to two grades) for eligible students. The university received almost 3,500 applications for 2024 entry and accepted 850 new students. Partnerships with more than 3,000 employers in agriculture, animal, equine, sport, and veterinary nursing provide opportunities for field trips, career events, work placements and live briefs. Despite these efforts, Hartpury ranks towards the bottom of our graduate prospects table at 124th.

Hartpury occupies five sites spanning 360 hectares. The main Home Farm covers 72 hectares and has dairy and beef calf rearing units. Recent investments include the £12.75 million University Learning Hub. Newer still is the Veterinary Nursing and Technical Skills Centre, with laboratories and a clinical skills centre with animal simulators. Students enjoy country life to the full in an area of outstanding beauty. Sports facilities are also central to university life, including the championship-level Hartpury University RFC and Gloucester-Hartpury Women's RFC. The £10 million Sports Academy is surrounded by pitches, a golf driving range, and a floodlit rugby stadium. Wellbeing officers offer daily drop-ins and one-to-one appointments until 10:30pm while therapeutic services include counselling and a 24/7 student assistance programme.

There are 370 on-site student bedrooms and 236 off-campus, and first-years are guaranteed a place. Hartpury ranks =58th in our social inclusion index, down one place from last year. About 15–20% of students qualify for some form of financial assistance, with bursaries targeted at those from households with incomes up to £42,000, and care leavers and students estranged from their parents.

Gloucestershire GL19 3BE
admissions@hartpury.ac.uk
hartpury.ac.uk
hartpurysu.co.uk

Overall ranking 101
(last year 116)

Accommodation
University provided places 606
Self-catered £166–£225 per week

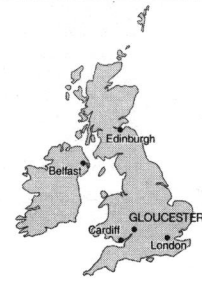

Student numbers
Undergraduates 2,145
Applications per place 4.1:1
Overall offer rate N/A

Fees
UK fees £9,535
International fees £18,150

hartpury.ac.uk/university/open-days
hartpury.ac.uk/university/student-life/fees-finance

Heriot-Watt University

Steeped in Scottish heritage, Heriot-Watt's story can be traced to Robert the Bruce, who in 1315 was recorded as giving the land that is now used for the main Riccarton Campus as a dowry for one of his daughters. The university is known for its strength in engineering, science and design; a degree in data science has been added for the 2025 entry, and from 2026 physics will run with an industrial placement. It is Runner-Up for Scottish University of the Year 2026.

A 12-place rise brings the university into our main academic ranking's top 40 this year, and represents an impressive 25-place jump up across the past two years. It now hosts the UK's first purpose-built National Robotarium, which opened at its Edinburgh site in 2022. Physics did well in the latest Research Excellence Framework (REF 2021), and joint submissions with the University of Edinburgh in mathematical sciences, architecture, engineering, built environment and planning also excelled. The university is comfortably in the upper half of UK universities in our research quality index.

The university's improved overall ranking is boosted by the 12th-highest entry standards in the UK and top-25 graduate prospects. However, our analysis of the National Student Survey (NSS) shows student satisfaction rates remain low – the university is outside the top 100 for teaching quality and has dropped to 98th for the wider student experience.

Courses demand from BCC to AAA at A-level and in Scottish Highers from BBBC up to AAAB. Contextual offers provide a minimum course requirement or a one- to two-grade reduction. In 2024, nearly 1,700 first-years were accepted, 10% of them through clearing. Many degree programmes include industry placements or projects, and carry professional accreditation, which is reflected in buoyant rates of graduate employment.

Riccarton, on 380 acres of parkland, is the academic headquarters where a £6 million library refurbishment increased capacity to more than 1,000 study spaces. The Borders Campus at Galashiels hosts courses in textiles, fashion and design, while the postgraduate Orkney centre specialises in renewable energy. Student life benefits from a musical slant – with plenty of opportunities to join choirs, bands and groups, such as the Heriot-Watt pipe band. Six indoor courts have been added to the Oriam Indoor Tennis Centre, which opened in 2024, and the university also has a hydro pool and gym facilities. In Edinburgh, ranked the seventh best student city in Europe by QS Best Student Cities 2026, populations of four universities converge to create a student-centric vibe in a city renowned for fun, festivals and culture.

Daily drop-ins, workshops and one-to-one counselling are provided by the wellbeing team. With almost 2,000 university-owned rooms, accommodation is guaranteed to all first-years from outside of the city who apply by the housing deadline. Ranking fifth in Scotland for social inclusion, Heriot-Watt's Global College is among its efforts to widen participation by providing courses at foundation and pre-master's levels. Students from England, Wales and Northern Ireland receive a £1,500 Travel Home Bursary in their first year. Awards of up to £3,100 a year also help towards living costs for students from low-income homes.

Edinburgh EH14 4AS
studywithus@hw.ac.uk
hw.ac.uk
hwunion.com

Overall ranking 39
(last year 51)

Accommodation
University provided places 1,986
Self-catered £182–£259 per week

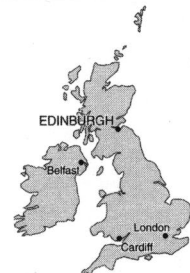

Student numbers
Undergraduates 6,595
Applications per place 5.6:1
Overall offer rate 82.8%

Fees
Scots fees £0–£1,820
International fees £19,456–£25,008
RUK fees £9,535

hw.ac.uk/visit-us/open-days-and-events/edinburgh-open-days
hw.ac.uk/study/fees-and-funding

University of Hertfordshire

Hertfordshire is rising through the ranks of our league table – up 16 places to enter the top 70 – and will open a new medical school in 2026. Its new five-year undergraduate medicine degree adds to the university's strong health portfolio, which already includes nursing, midwifery and pharmacy.

Originally a technical college focused on mechanical and aeronautical engineering, the university's engineering courses are now based in the Automotive Centre, and many of its graduates have gone on to work in Formula One teams. The university rose one place to rank 59th in our research quality index, with 78% of its submissions rated world-leading or internationally excellent in the latest Research Excellence Framework (REF 2021). In the nationwide Teaching Excellence Framework (TEF 2023), Hertfordshire achieved silver overall. Our analysis of the National Student Survey (NSS) shows improved student satisfaction, with the university ranking =27th for the wider student experience and =51st for teaching quality, placing it in the upper half of the table for both.

Degrees in automotive technology, and psychology in education have been withdrawn. From 2025, a new top-up degree in applied computing and artificial intelligence is being offered and from September 2026, degrees in business and French, management, and business analytics and artificial intelligence will be added. Hertfordshire's new medical degree will initially only be for international students, though there are plans to open the course to UK students soon. Entry requirements range from 144-104 UCAS tariff points, or 48 points for foundation degrees. Contextual offers provide an eight-point reduction for eligible students.

Many courses include professional accreditations and offer work placements. Students can also study abroad under partnerships with 150 universities in more than 35 countries, and Hertfordshire offers 24 degree apprenticeships, with data science a recent addition. The university ranks 85th in our analysis of the Graduate Outcomes survey, based on the number of graduates in highly skilled jobs or further study within 15 months.

Modern facilities are a hallmark of Hertfordshire's two main campuses in Hatfield, which are linked by a free shuttle bus, footpaths and cycle lanes. The Spectra building, home to the School of Physics, Engineering, and Computer Science, is the latest addition, equipped with technology for robotics and cybersecurity research and hands-on learning. The university's Bayfordbury Observatory also boasts one of the largest telescopes available to students in the UK. The £15 million Hertfordshire Sports Village on the de Havilland Campus caters to all abilities, and the Institute of Sport has a biomechanics laboratory with a rare Gait Real-Time Analysis Interactive Lab (Grail) system.

The university provides counselling, mental health and disability support, as well as a 24-hour helpline. All first-years who meet the deadline for applications are guaranteed a study bedroom on campus. Hertfordshire has dropped from 27th last year to 51st in our social inclusion index. Outreach includes GCSE booster workshops and summer schools to encourage wider participation. The university's undergraduate bursary is worth £1,000 in the first year of study to students from households with incomes under £30,000. Students who have left care, are displaced from their country or who are adult carers are eligible for further support.

College Lane Hatfield AL10 9AB
ask@herts.ac.uk
herts.ac.uk
hertssu.com

Overall ranking 67
(last year 83)

Accommodation
University provided places 4,700
Self-catered £129–£277 per week

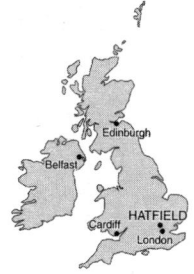

Student numbers
Undergraduates 11,090
Applications per place 5.9:1
Overall offer rate 66.0%

Fees
UK fees 9,535
International fees £15,965–£23,200
Medicine £42,000

herts.ac.uk/study/open-days-and-events
herts.ac.uk/study/fees-and-funding

University of the Highlands and Islands

Deeply rooted in the communities of some of the most remote parts of Scotland, offering jaw-dropping scenery and a unique student experience, the University of the Highlands and Islands (UHI) is unlike any other in our rankings. It encompasses 12 colleges and research institutions and more than 70 local learning centres spread out across hundreds of miles, stretching from the Isle of Skye – where programmes are provided in Gaelic – to Shetland in the far northeast of Scotland, and Campbeltown in the southwest.

UHI's disparate sites, with a large number of part-time staff and further education students, make comparisons with other universities a challenge. The course portfolio reflects local needs near each campus, including collaboration with conservation and energy organisations. Widening participation is a founding principle; more than half the students are aged over 21 at the start of their courses and more than 3,000 undergraduates study part-time. Blended learning has been a necessary means of teaching for more than 20 years, mixing online delivery with fieldwork and self-study. In 2025, UHI launched the Centre for Rural Health Sciences, based at its Inverness and Stornoway Campuses, and dedicated to improving health and wellbeing in the Highlands and Islands, with an emphasis on community engagement.

Three newly launched courses are HNDs in acting and performance, and social science, and an integrated master of optometry with independent prescribing. From September 2026 the university plans to offer programmes in drama and filmmaking in the Highlands and Islands, and engineering systems, as well as a master of accounting graduate apprenticeship. Entry ranges from 114 UCAS tariff points to 42 points, and a contextual admissions policy formalises UHI's inherently inclusive approach to admissions. All students and graduates have access to Future Me, UHI's online platform to plan a career path.

Colleges vary in size, from the bigger outposts in towns such as Perth, Elgin and Inverness to smaller research bases on the islands. A £9.5 million Life Sciences Innovation Centre opened in 2023 on the UHI Inverness campus. A clinical simulation suite there provides nursing and healthcare students with a real-world clinical care environment. Redevelopment at the Outer Hebrides Campus has brought facilities including a Future Energy Lab for training in energy transition sectors, such as hydrogen and renewables. At UHI Perth, there is the Academy of Sport and Wellbeing, and there are sports halls at Inverness and Moray, as well as outdoor and water sports facilities at Fort William. At the Moray School of Art, students have an exhibition space.

UHI's "green button" online counselling service provides support via webcam, instant messaging, telephone or email. Most students live locally but the university offers rooms at eight of its locations. Priority goes to first-years, international students and those who are care-experienced, estranged, or have physical or mental impairments. Despite its widening access remit, UHI ranks bottom in Scotland for its recruitment of students from deprived areas (3.9 per cent), which contributes to a six-place decline in our social inclusion for Scotland, to 9th place. More than 40 scholarships, bursaries and discretionary funds target diverse groups, including several subject-specific awards.

UHI House Perth Road Inverness IV2 3JH
info@uhi.ac.uk
uhi.ac.uk
hisa.uhi.ac.uk

Overall ranking N/A

Accommodation
University provided places 453
Self-catered £114–£195 per week

Student numbers
Undergraduates 5,256
Applications per place 1.7:1
Overall offer rate 65.1%

Fees
Scots fees £0–£1,820
International fees £14,988–£16,950
RUK fees £9,535

uhi.ac.uk/en/studying-at-uhi/open-days
uhi.ac.uk/en/studying-at-uhi/how-much-will-it-cost

University of Huddersfield

Courses relating to the allied health professions are the most popular at Huddersfield. An ambitious £250 million National Health Innovation Campus is under development, and the first of seven specialist centres opened in 2024. Huddersfield attracts high numbers of students who live at home and commute to purpose-built facilities either side of the Huddersfield Narrow Canal, in a town known for its friendliness and relatively low cost of living.

The university maintained its triple gold record in the government's Teaching Excellence Framework (TEF 2023). However, a 24-place fall in our main academic ranking this year leaves Huddersfield outside the top 100, largely due to depleted rates of student satisfaction. In our analysis of the latest National Student Survey (NSS), Huddersfield has fallen to 113th for teaching quality and 115th for student experience. The dip in morale may be related to job cuts on campus, with cost-saving redundancies having an impact on several departments.

Ten courses ended in September 2025: journalism, broadcast journalism, film-making, film studies, education, special educational needs, disabilities and inclusion, childhood studies, fashion design, and early childhood and education. Up to 20 new courses are beginning in 2025 and 2026, including courses in crime and forensics, radiography, dental hygiene, and media and film studies. New entrants average 118 UCAS points and the university is in the lower half of UK universities for its entry standards (=80th). Huddersfield does better for graduate prospects, ranking 69th thanks to a curriculum developed in collaboration with employers, as well as work placements and internships.

A decade of development has improved the Queensgate Campus. The £31 million Joseph Priestley Building for science subjects and the £30 million Barbara Hepworth Building are the headline additions. The Oastler Building houses music, humanities and media while the Yorkshire Film and Television School has a 300 sq m film studio as well as music and sound production facilities. The university is also one of many to open branch campuses in London, offering business-focused postgraduate courses.

At the £22.5 million Student Central building, sports facilities include an 80-station gym, two multi-purpose studios, a physiotherapy treatment room and a double sports hall. The Jo Cox More in Common Centre provides a 200-capacity community hall, Muslim, Christian and multifaith prayer rooms and a community lounge. Students can find willing listeners among the university's team of wellbeing and mental health advisers and counsellors. Societies cover a wide range of interests and help to build community spirit among undergraduates. The Students' Union works with independent halls of residence and private landlords, but the university does not own any accommodation.

Huddersfield has dropped 21 places to =41st in our social inclusion index but it has gone up one place to 12th for recruitment of students who are the first in their family to go to university. Eligibility for financial support is not decided before a student enrols. Instead, those who actively engage with their nominated student support coach under the Enhanced Support Team may qualify for awards up to £1,000 if they have a mental health condition or meet other eligibility criteria.

Queensgate Huddersfield HD1 3DH
study@hud.ac.uk
hud.ac.uk
huddersfieldsu.co.uk

Overall ranking 102
(last year =78)

Accommodation
University provided places 0

Student numbers
Undergraduates 10,655
Applications per place 5.0:1
Overall offer rate 80.0%

Fees
UK fees £9,535
International fees £16,500–£22,000

hud.ac.uk/open-days/undergraduate
hud.ac.uk/study/fees

University of Hull

Everything is within a ten-minute walk on Hull's leafy, self-contained campus, where a £200 million investment project is improving resources, accessibility and energy efficiency. Hull is a member of the Turing University Network for research in data science and AI, and has been awarded £11 million to establish a world-leading centre for research into addiction and mental health. Other projects include a partnership with the Salvation Army focused on modern slavery, and an official partnership with Team GB that will include the Milano-Cortina 2026 Winter Olympics, and the Los Angeles Olympics in 2028.

Steady in 60th place of our main academic ranking for two years in a row, Hull was rated gold overall in the government's Teaching Excellence Framework (TEF 2023). Student satisfaction rates have shot up in our analysis of the National Student Survey (NSS), reflecting Hull's consolidation of support services into a single location on campus, coming 18th for teaching quality and 41st for the wider experience. In the Research Excellence Framework (REF 2021), 82% of Hull's submissions were assessed as world-leading or internationally excellent, raising the university two places in our research quality index to 51st.

Degrees in games design and creative writing, mathematics with data science, and philosophy with politics began in September 2025. Hull has also launched an accelerated two-year degree in diagnostic radiography and degrees in secondary teaching (biology or psychology). From 2026, civil engineering, and psychology with sports psychology join the course offering, while degrees in chemistry are ending. Entry grades range from 128 to 104 UCAS tariff points for most degrees. Contextual offers can reduce this by up to 16 points, and 10% of students entered through clearing in 2024. Hull consistently occupies a middling position in our table for graduate prospects, now ranking 61st, with work placements including the Westminster-Hull internship programme for politics students, as well as partnerships with the Royal Philharmonic Orchestra and Opera North.

A Formula One-standard racing car simulator is among the specialist facilities for engineering, and the Hull York Medical School is based at Hull's £28 million health campus. The university has also established a postgraduate centre in central London, offering courses in business-related fields. Other resources include a collection of turn-of-the-century art and a versatile 400-seat cultural venue on campus, as well as world-class sports facilities including an indoor arena. The city has a vibrant nightlife and the university's own nightclub, Asylum, has had a glow-up. Students who are struggling can turn to the mental health and wellbeing team for support, including time with a therapy dog.

First-years are guaranteed a room if they apply by July 31 and there's a guarantee for clearing entrants too, if they apply by September 1. Based in a region with comparatively low participation in higher education, Hull performs well in our social inclusion index, where it ranks 40th overall. About 11% of entrants in 2025 qualified for a financial award, including a full fee waiver granted to ten undergraduates in any subject each year, and a scholarship for LGBTQ+ students funded by Attitude Magazine.

Cottingham Road Hull HU6 7RX
study@hull.ac.uk
hull.ac.uk
hulluniunion.com

Overall ranking 60
(last year 60)

Accommodation
University provided places 2,170
Self-catered £130–£299 per week

Student numbers
Undergraduates 9,135
Applications per place 4.1:1
Overall offer rate 79.6%

Fees
UK fees £9,535
International fees £17,500–£20,000
Medicine £47,000

hull.ac.uk/choose-hull/study-at-hull/visit-us/open-days
hull.ac.uk/study/undergraduate/fees-and-funding

Imperial College London

Pushing boundaries is in Imperial College London's DNA. Britain's only higher education specialist in STEMB (science, technology, engineering, medicine and business) is a global leader in interdisciplinary research, and counts 14 Nobel laureates among its alumni. The direct involvement of a high concentration of leading researchers in undergraduate teaching is a big draw. It tops our table for graduate prospects and takes the prize for University of the Year for Graduate Employment 2026.

The university is first in our research quality rating, beating the University of Cambridge to the top spot, with 55% of its work assessed as world-leading in the latest Research Excellence Framework (REF 2021). Imperial's global influence is underlined by its second-place ranking in the QS World University Rankings 2026, behind only Massachusetts Institute of Technology, and it was rated gold overall in the government's Teaching Excellence Framework (TEF 2023). In our analysis of the National Student Survey (NSS), Imperial has tumbled 28 places to 98th for teaching quality, although it has remained steadier for the wider student experience (=37th).

Imperial's first graduate-entry medicine students began their courses in September 2025, and from 2026 it will offer integrated master's programmes in biochemistry, biological sciences, and biotechnology. It is suspending its integrated master's degree in chemical engineering with nuclear engineering and withdrawing materials with management from 2025. In 2024, almost 33,000 applicants chased 3,255 places.

Minimum A-level entry requirements are AAA, with standard offers between A*A*A and AAA, but in reality many competitive courses demand higher grades. Imperial does not use UCAS tariff points or recruit through clearing, but there is a reconsideration pool in August.

The main South Kensington Campus is home to the Dyson School of Design Engineering, while the new 23-acre White City Campus hosts the School of Public Health as well as innovation and collaboration space. The Faculty of Medicine is one of Europe's largest in terms of staff and student numbers and Imperial has teaching bases at four central and west London hospitals. Imperial students find themselves in the beating heart of London, which was rated the world's best student city by QS for six years in a row until last year. More than 340 student-run clubs and societies make use of facilities including the Blyth Centre for Music and Visual Arts, the Ethos sports centre and Harlington Sports Ground. Imperial's Ash Music Scholarships come with free lessons (instrument or voice) at the Royal College of Music.

Health and wellbeing services on campus include confidential counselling and a multifaith centre for worship, as well as help for living with conditions including autism and ADHD. All first-years who apply by the deadline are guaranteed a space in halls, with prices ranging from £145 to £390 per week. The university has the lowest state school intake in England and Wales at 42.3% and ranks 105th in our social inclusion index. Four in ten new UK students receive some form of financial support, which includes the Imperial Bursary for undergraduates with annual household incomes up to £70,000. This is a much higher income threshold for bursaries than at other universities.

Exhibition Road South Kensington London SW7 2AZ
imperial.ac.uk/study/apply/
imperial.ac.uk
imperialcollegeunion.org

Overall ranking 6
(last year 6)

Accommodation
University provided places 2,978
Self-catered £145–£235 per week

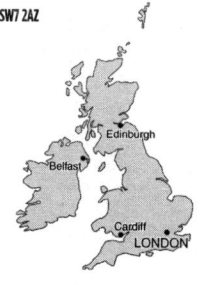

Student numbers
Undergraduates 12,045
Applications per place 10.1:1
Overall offer rate 32.8%

Fees
UK fees £9,535
International fees £21,650–£40,700
£43,300–£55,800

imperial.ac.uk/study/visit/undergraduate/open-days
imperial.ac.uk/study/ug/fees-and-funding

Keele University

Keele has been a champion of interdisciplinary scholarship since it was founded in 1949. The university is now streamlining its combined honours degrees into integrated single-honours programmes to be more responsive to the job market. However, it continues to fly the flag for a broad-based higher education with its Global Challenge Pathways, which are elective study options that can be taken alongside a core degree. Students have everything they need on the largest campus in the country, from sports and cultural facilities to a bank, pharmacy and Marriott hotel. Bursting the 600-acre Keele bubble, a new teaching space has opened in nearby Newcastle-under-Lyme, bringing the university to the town centre for the first time.

Keele is comfortably in the upper half of our research quality index. 80% of its submission was rated world-leading or internationally excellent in the latest Research Excellence Framework (REF 2021), with some of the best results in allied health, dentistry, agriculture, and communication and media studies. The university's veterinary school, a joint venture with Harper Adams, opened in October 2021. Rising rates of satisfaction hint at contentment, with our National Student Survey (NSS) analysis ranking Keele 40th for the student experience and 54th for teaching quality. Keele was rated gold overall in the Teaching Excellence Framework (TEF 2023), repeating its success from six years earlier.

In May 2025, Keele joined the many universities announcing job cuts, after it said the UK sector was facing "unprecedented financial challenges". Twelve new courses in 2025 include sport and exercise science, neuroscience with psychology, and occupational therapy. From September 2026, these will be joined by social sciences, and a course in philosophy, politics and economics. Standard offers range from A*AA to BBC, and the university has broadened the eligibility criteria for its contextual offer scheme. More than a fifth of new entrants in 2024 gained their places through clearing. Keele is =46th for graduate prospects, based on the proportion of leavers in highly skilled jobs or further study 15 months on. The university collaborates with employers like Müller, the Ironbridge Gorge Museum, Petrostate and the NHS to provide placements and internships.

A busy Students' Union and more than 200 clubs and societies contribute to the social scene. Off campus, Newcastle-under-Lyme is the main student hub, while Stoke-on-Trent is nearby. Sports facilities include a bouldering wall, sports halls and a gym. Keele's "whole community" approach to mental health support includes joining the disability and dyslexia services with the counselling and mental health team. A 24/7 student assistance programme provides another source of help. First-years who apply by the end of June deadline are guaranteed a place in halls of residence on campus.

Keele outperforms many other pre-1992 universities in our social inclusion index, where it places well inside the upper half of UK universities at 61st. It is 21st for recruitment of students from deprived areas. Undergraduates may be eligible for up to £1,500 Access and Success awards. Care leavers and those estranged from their families qualify for £1,000 a year grant, plus a £500 graduation bonus.

Keele ST5 5BG
enquiries@keele.ac.uk
keele.ac.uk
keelesu.com

Overall ranking 43
(last year =57)

Accommodation
University provided places 2,695
Self-catered £117–£223 per week

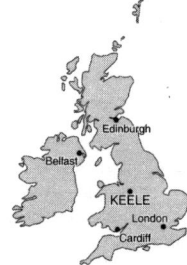

Student numbers
Undergraduates 8,665
Applications per place 5.9:1
Overall offer rate 65.5%

Fees
UK fees £9,535
International fees £16,600–£24,900
Medicine £46,700

keele.ac.uk/study/opendays/undergraduateopendays
keele.ac.uk/study/undergraduate/tuitionfeesandfunding

University of Kent

Kent listened to student feedback to bring in timetable changes from September 2025, introducing a three-term academic year instead of two and spreading deadlines throughout the year so that Christmas and Easter breaks are study-free. Founded in the 1960s, Kent's original low-rise Canterbury campus is set on 300 acres and is one of Britain's few collegiate universities. Each college has its own academic and residential facilities, serving as the social hub for students, especially in their first year.

Kent is partnering with the University of Greenwich to create the London and South East University Group – bringing both institutions under one structure whilst enabling each university to retain its name, identity and local presence. A strong performance in the latest Research Excellence Framework (REF 2021) moved Kent up to =32nd in our research quality index, with some of the best results coming in architecture, classics, law, philosophy, and theology. In the Teaching Excellence Framework (TEF 2023), Kent was rated silver overall, losing its gold burnish from TEF 2017. It has also fallen in our latest analysis of the National Student Survey (NSS), to =114th for teaching quality and 107th for the wider student experience.

Rounds of cost-cutting might have dampened spirits on campus as the university seeks £20 million savings, with more than 50 undergraduate programmes closing from September 2025. These include health and social care, music and audio technology, philosophy and religious studies, English literature, and art history. The lowest entry criteria is CCC (96 UCAS tariff points) while the highest is AAB (136 points) for law, reducible by up to 16 UCAS points for contextual offers. Last year 4,000 out of 20,200 applicants were accepted, including 18% through clearing. Kent holds more than 800 career-related events a year and works with both large employers and local small and medium-size enterprises. However, in our Graduate Outcomes analysis it ranks =90th.

Recent campus developments include upgraded facilities for natural sciences, computing and forensic science. Architecture and planning students have also been given more studio space. The Kent and Medway Medical School opened in 2020 on the outskirts of Canterbury in collaboration with Canterbury Christ Church University. The Medway Campus, also shared with other universities, houses Kent's School of Pharmacy, music technology facilities and the refurbished Business School.

There are plenty of student-centric venues among Canterbury's cobbled streets and the seaside charms of Whitstable and Margate are not far away. The sports centre on campus draws about 150,000 student visits a year to its gym, three sports halls, and training areas for boxing and martial arts. As well as offering wellbeing services including counselling, Kent has targeted support for disabled and neurodivergent students. Practical responses to the cost of living crisis include £3 meal deals and a campus pantry. There are 2,252 rooms on campus and 1,488 off campus, and Kent guarantees a place to all first-years who apply by the June deadline.

Ranking =71st overall in our social inclusion index, Kent is 31st for ethnic diversity. The Kent Financial Support Package provides £1,000 per year to eligible UK students from households with incomes up to £30,000. Merit-based scholarships are also offered.

Canterbury CT2 7NZ
information@kent.ac.uk
kent.ac.uk
ksu.co.uk

Overall ranking 56
(last year =40)

Accommodation
University provided places 6,090
Self-catered £275–£306 per week

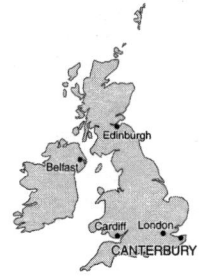

Student numbers
Undergraduates 12,880
Applications per place 5.1:1
Overall offer rate 90.7%

Fees
UK fees £9,535
International fees £19,300–£23,500
Medicine £49,700

kent.ac.uk/courses/visit/open-day-dates
kent.ac.uk/courses/fees-and-funding

King's College London

King's College London (KCL) is enshrined in the capital, and its students are in the thick of all the city has to offer. Four of its five campuses are within a square mile of each other, close to the banks of the Thames. The recent redevelopment of the Strand Quad created new subterranean square footage for the Department of Engineering and a pedestrianised area above ground. The Pears Maudsley Centre for Children and Young People is charged with revolutionising mental health research and care for young people, and the new Net Zero Centre coincides with KCL ranking 18th in the People & Planet league table.

A member of the research-led Russell Group of universities since 1998, KCL counts 14 staff and alumni who have been awarded the Nobel prize. The university ranks 8th in our research quality index after 55.1% of the work submitted to the latest Research Excellence Framework (REF 2021) was judged to be world-leading, and is up 9 places to 31st in the QS global rankings this year. It is rated silver overall in the Teaching Excellence Framework (TEF 2023), and won gold for student outcomes. Student satisfaction, often a problem with London universities, is improving based on our analysis of the National Student Survey (NSS).

New for 2025 are degrees spanning AI, international law, psychology, criminology and healthcare. Politics and international affairs will replace European politics from 2026. Courses demand from BBC up to A*A*A, and contextual admissions of one or two grades lower are made to students who meet widening participation criteria. These accounted for 20% of the 7,800 new students (from 68,500 applications) last year, and around 9% of students gained their places through clearing. KCL graduates do well in the job market, and more than 350 employers visit King's each year. It places =12th in our analysis of the Graduate Outcomes survey.

The Strand and Waterloo Campuses house most of the university's non-medical departments. Bush House, the former headquarters of the BBC World Service and another historic London building, houses KCL's business school, the Faculty of Social Science and Public Policy and some student services. Denmark Hill, in south London, is the base for the Institute of Psychiatry, Psychology and Neuroscience and dentistry teaching facilities. KCL's cultural life is enriched by the King's Culture programme of free exhibitions, talks and workshops. Sports grounds at Honor Oak Park and New Malden in south London have facilities for all the main sports, as well as rifle ranges.

Support for students' welfare ranges from guided self-help and workshops to specialist support groups around race, sexuality and gender. KCL's halls of residence are spread out across the capital, with accommodation guaranteed to all first-years who apply by the deadline. KCL was the top-ranked Russell Group university in the Social Mobility Index 2023, and it is 87th in our social inclusion ranking for England and Wales. About a third of entrants in 2025 received some form of financial assistance, including a range of merit-based scholarships and the King's Living Bursary, which is open to UK students from households with incomes up to £42,875.

Strand London WC2R 2LS
newstudents@kcl.ac.uk
kcl.ac.uk
kclsu.org

Overall ranking 19
(last year =24)

Accommodation
University provided places 5,590
Catered £284–£385 per week
Self-catered £155–£375 per week

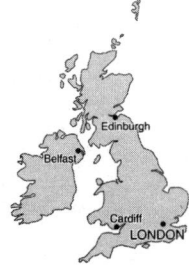

Student numbers
Undergraduates 21,835
Applications per place 8.8:1
Overall offer rate 44.3%

Fees
UK fees £9,535
International fees £12,100–£58,200
Medicine £53,000

kcl.ac.uk/study/undergraduate/events/open-days
kcl.ac.uk/study/undergraduate/fees-and-funding

Kingston University

At Kingston, contemporary thinking meets a riverside setting. The university is pioneering the Future Skills model of education, which embeds careers-focused training in undergraduate courses to prepare students for an increasingly AI-influenced job market. Students are based at four campuses in southwest London, with a focus on recent investment at its Penrhyn Road site, including the Royal Institute of British Architects (RIBA) Stirling prize-winning Town House building.

Creative courses are among its most successful, with strong results in the Research Excellence Framework (REF 2021), where Kingston now ranks 70th. The university also performed well in the Teaching Excellence Framework (TEF 2023), earning triple gold ratings (up from bronze). Student satisfaction is in the upper half nationally for both teaching quality (=61st) and overall experience (=51st) in our National Student Survey (NSS) analysis.

Nine new degrees will be available from September 2025, including interaction design, historic building conservation, and nursing. Kingston is closing its humanities department, with no new admissions to degrees in English or philosophy. The Kingston Language Scheme's short courses in modern languages are also being withdrawn. Offers typically range from 96 to 144 UCAS tariff points. Last year, nearly 6,000 new undergraduates were accepted, with about a quarter coming through clearing. The Future Skills programme works with partners like John Lewis and the Civil Aviation Authority. The university is also expanding its portfolio of degree apprenticeships in healthcare.

Despite these efforts, Kingston is ranked 114th for graduate prospects, based on the proportion of graduates in highly skilled work or further study after 15 months.

The university has four campuses: Penrhyn Road and Knights Park near the town centre, Kingston Hill and Roehampton Vale. The new Town House building has an auditorium, informal learning spaces, a studio theatre and a library, whose special collections include Iris Murdoch and Stephen Sondheim archives. The Penrhyn Road main building has upgraded social spaces, a kitchen for commuting students and a careers hub. The Kingston School of Art has benefitted from a £29 million investment in creative teaching space and workshops, while Roehampton Vale's aerospace degrees benefit from the university's own Learjet and flight simulator. Three miles from the main campus, Tolworth Court provides outdoor sports facilities including 12 football pitches, two rugby pitches, and three tennis courts. Cultural facilities include the Stanley Picker Gallery at the Knights Park Campus, and a standout music facility with a live room stocked with instruments and rare recording equipment.

Students can access both remote and in-person appointments with the disability and mental health service and counselling team. There are just less than 2,300 spaces available in halls, and first-year full-time students are given priority. The student population is one of the most ethnically diverse, and more than half of its recruits are the first in their family to go to university. Financial support includes the £2,000 Kingston Bursary for at least 500 entrants from low-income households. Students who are carers, care leavers or estranged from their families are also eligible for support.

Holmwood House Grove Crescent
Kingston upon Thames KT1 2EE
Ukenquiries@kingston.ac.uk
kingston.ac.uk
kingstonstudents.net

Overall ranking 94
(last year 97)

Accommodation
University provided places 2,300
Self-catered £130–£408 per week

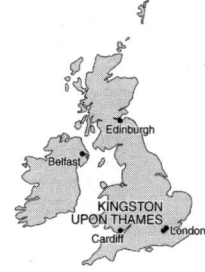

Student numbers
Undergraduates 12,750
Applications per place 4.7:1
Overall offer rate 83.3%

Fees
UK fees £9,535
International fees £17,700–£19,500

kingston.ac.uk/study/open-days
kingston.ac.uk/fees-funding-and-payments

University of Lancashire

It has dropped "central" from its name, but the University of Lancashire is still rooted to its home county with its main campus in Preston and one in Burnley, alongside sites in Cumbria and overseas in Cyprus. Its curriculum ranges from astronomy to zoology, and it is a leader in degree apprenticeships. For students, the friendly city of Preston offers a lower cost of living than nearby Manchester or Liverpool.

Lancashire's research profile is on the rise, with particular strengths in physics and allied health, with links to NASA bolstering its aerospace credentials. Two thirds of Lancashire's submissions to the latest Research Excellence Framework (REF 2021) were rated world-leading or internationally excellent, and the university sits at =81st in our research quality index. Rated silver overall in the Teaching Excellence Framework (TEF 2023), Lancashire has held roughly steady in our National Student Survey (NSS) analysis with a rise of three places to =47th for teaching quality balanced by a drop of nine places to =75th for student experience.

The university is updating its course portfolio for 2025, launching programmes in artificial intelligence, data science and financial technology. At the same time, it is closing 56 courses, including several modern languages and English-related degrees. Typical entry requirements range from 96 to 144 UCAS tariff points. Foundation years are available for most courses, and the university's contextual offer scheme applies to all degrees, except some dental and pharmacy courses. In 2024, nearly three in ten new students benefitted from this policy.

Work placements and strong industry links with partners such as the NHS, BBC and Lancashire Constabulary boost graduate employability. In our analysis of the Graduate Outcomes survey, Lancashire places 76th, with nearly three-quarters of graduates in highly skilled jobs or further study 15 months after leaving the university.

Under a £200 million masterplan at the Preston Campus, Lancashire has opened a new Engineering Innovation Centre and a student centre with a rooftop garden. At the Burnley Campus, Lancashire is converting a vacant mill into teaching and social space. The Westlakes Campus focuses on nursing and other health subjects, and at Larnaca in Cyprus there is space for about 1,000 students studying sports, business, law, and English. The Sir Tom Finney Sports Centre at the Preston Campus and the UCLan Sports Arena two miles away have grass and artificial pitches, floodlit tennis/netball courts, an eight-lane athletics track and a 1.5 km cycle circuit. The PR1 Gallery exhibits collections year-round, and the university cinema's programme includes free film festivals.

The wellbeing service provides extended hours and students can access support that includes one-to-one counselling, course-specific workshops and emergency accommodation if needed. There are over 1,500 student rooms in total, and accommodation is guaranteed for first-years on the Preston campus. The university has gone up nine places to 17th in our social inclusion index and remains highly committed to access, with 96% of its students coming from non-selective state schools. Around a quarter of new students receive financial support from 22 scholarships and bursaries, including fully-funded medical scholarships for students from the northwest.

Preston PR1 2HE
cenquiries@lancashire.ac.uk
lancashire.ac.uk
uclansu.co.uk

Overall ranking 93
(last year 96)

Accommodation
University provided places 1,616
Catered £205 per week
Self-catered £87–£149 per week

Student numbers
Undergraduates 15,960
Applications per place 4.2:1
Overall offer rate 70.9%

Fees
UK fees £9,535
International fees £17,325–£39,000
Medicine £49,000

lancashire.ac.uk/open-days
lancashire.ac.uk/study/fees-and-finance

Lancaster University

Founded in 1964, research-led Lancaster achieved strong results in the latest national assessment with 91% of its work rated as world-leading or internationally excellent in the Research Excellence Framework (REF 2021). Linguistics and mathematics produced some of the university's best results.

Lancaster is a regular among the top 150 universities in the world according to QS, although it dips to 157th in the rankings for 2026. Lancaster outperforms seven Russell Group universities in our research quality index, ranking 19th and it takes the title of University of the Year in the Northwest 2026. An international perspective is integral at the university, with five joint campuses around the world in Beijing, Indonesia, Ghana, Malaysia and Leipzig in Germany.

Crucially, student satisfaction is high compared with its peers. In our National Student Survey (NSS) analysis, Lancaster ranks =27th for student experience and =51st for satisfaction with teaching quality, placing it comfortably ahead of most research-intensive rivals. This is reinforced by a gold overall rating in the Teaching Excellence Framework (TEF 2023), which praised its "supportive learning environment" and "outstanding rates of successful progression". The university continues to expand its global reach, opening its latest overseas campus, in Indonesia, in February 2025.

Lancaster is streamlining its portfolio, closing around 160 course pathways from 2026, primarily affecting some humanities, arts, and language subjects.

Looking ahead, the university is launching new future-focused degrees, including pharmacology and language sciences, from 2025. From 2026, it will introduce degrees in neuroscience, creative industries, and a unique BSc in mathematics, AI and real-world systems. Foundation years have also been added to 15 subjects, broadening access to fields such as engineering and physics.

Standard requirements range from A*AA to BBB, with foundation year courses requiring CCC. All courses are included in the university's contextual offer scheme (except medicine) with offers reduced by two A-level grades for eligible applicants. In the top third (29th) for the proportion of graduates in highly skilled work or further study after 15 months (82.1%), Lancaster has sector-leading industry engagement. The university helps secure paid placements and internships with top employers, and offers opportunities for paid summer internships for science and technology students and graduates. The average graduate salary is £26,000.

Lancaster has invested more than £220 million in its Bailrigg Campus since 2013. Recent additions include the Margaret Fell lecture theatre, a second engineering building with state-of-the-art labs, and an InfoLab which has been upgraded into a semi-immersive "data cyber quarter".

Lancaster students belong to a college, where they sleep, study and socialise. There are eight for undergraduates and one for postgraduates; each has a 24/7 porter. First-years who meet the deadline are guaranteed a place.

The university ranks 90th overall for social inclusion. About a third of its students are first-generation students (29.6%). About a third of UK undergraduates receive financial support. There is an annual bursary of £1,000 for students with a household income below £30,000 and a £2,000 scholarship for those with top grades (AAA or equivalent).

Bailrigg Lancaster LA1 4YW
ugadmissions@lancaster.ac.uk
lancaster.ac.uk
lancastersu.co.uk

Overall ranking 15
(last year 12)

Accommodation
University provided places 6,700
Catered £264–£65 per week
Self-catered £130–£230 per week

Student numbers
Undergraduates 12,485
Applications per place 5.3:1
Overall offer rate 86.8%

Fees
UK fees £9,535
International fees £24,700–£29,820
Medicine £47,120

lancaster.ac.uk/study/open-days/undergraduate-open-days
lancaster.ac.uk/study/fees-and-funding

University of Leeds

As a leading university in one of the UK's best student cities, the University of Leeds is an enduring frontrunner on UCAS applications. Its research-led pedigree underpins a broad course offering, while a £32 million investment programme in 2025 aims to create vibrant and welcoming student spaces for learning and wellbeing at the classic redbrick campus, which is only a ten-minute walk from the city centre.

A member of the elite Russell Group, Leeds's research standing is world-class. In the latest Research Excellence Framework (REF 2021), 90% of its research was rated world-leading or internationally excellent, helping it secure a top 20 spot in our research quality index (20th). It is consistently in the top 100 in the QS World University Rankings (86th for 2026) and closing in on Times Higher Education's top 100 (123rd in 2025).

Student satisfaction shows a mixed but improving picture. While our National Student Survey (NSS) analysis shows a 26-place gain to =66th for the overall student experience, the university ranks lower (=114th for teaching quality). Similarly, the latest Teaching Excellence Framework (TEF 2023) awarded Leeds silver overall (down from gold in 2017). The panel commended its "outstanding rates of continuation and completion" for students.

Leeds is halfway through Curriculum Redefined, a decade-long review of the courses it offers and how well it prepares graduates for work and life. New degree programmes for 2026 reflect a focus on future-facing skills, with courses in primary education and computer science. Two new courses combine chemistry or physics with AI, taught as bachelor's or integrated master's degrees, with or without a year in industry or abroad.

Courses ask for grades from A*AA to CDD. Contextual offers reduce entry requirements by up to two grades, accounting for a fifth of entrants in 2024. To be eligible, applicants must come from deprived postcodes or have completed the university's access scheme. Just over 10% of nearly 8,500 new students were accepted through clearing. A vast network of over 320 global university partners and hundreds of employers underpins excellent graduate prospects. Leeds ranks =35th in our analysis of the Graduate Outcomes survey of the proportion of graduates in highly skilled work or further study after 15 months (81%). The average graduate salary is £27,500.

Extensive sports facilities start with the Edge, which has a swimming pool. Premium gym membership at the Edge is included in student rent on campus. The university also houses the £5 million Brownlee Centre, the UK's first purpose-built triathlon training base, named for its famous Olympic alumni, Alistair and Jonny Brownlee.

Leeds guarantees a room to first-years who meet the deadline. Much of the accommodation is further from the city centre than the campus. The university ranks 109th in our social inclusion index. More than a quarter of its students come from selective schools, while about a third (31.8%) are the first in their family to attend university. More than a quarter of new entrants receive financial help. The Leeds Bursary offers up to £2,000 a year for students from low-income households.

Woodhouse Lane Leeds LS2 9JT
study@leeds.ac.uk
leeds.ac.uk
luu.org.uk

Overall ranking 26
(last year 29)

Accommodation
University provided places 8,483
Catered £200–£262 per week
Self-catered £118–£222 per week

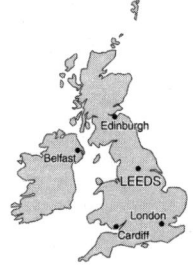

Student numbers
Undergraduates 25,980
Applications per place 8.0:1
Overall offer rate 59.9%

Fees
UK fees £9,535
International fees £26,000–£51,750
Medicine £47,000

leeds.ac.uk/undergraduate-open-days
leeds.ac.uk/undergraduate-fees/doc/fees-undergraduate-fees

Leeds Arts University

Leeds Arts University is a small specialist institution with about 2,000 undergraduates. It was rated triple silver in the Teaching Excellence Framework (TEF 2023), with praise for its "physical and virtual learning resources that are tailored and used effectively to support outstanding teaching and learning", which were deemed an "outstanding-quality feature".

Students are generally content, with the university ranking in the upper half of UK universities for teaching quality (=32nd) and overall student experience (=66th) in our analysis of the National Student Survey (NSS). The university has been building a research culture, making its first submission to the Research Excellence Framework (REF 2021). Although it entered at the foot of our research rankings (129th), some work in the history of art, design, and architecture was recognised as world-leading.

Courses demand from 104 to 120 UCAS tariff points (average 139), and nearly 800 new undergraduates were accepted on to courses in 2024 out of close to 5,400 applications.

The university hosts a roster of career-focused events – creative industry employers have included Paramount+, Overdue for Paris Fashion Week, Hallmark, and Clothsurgeon of Savile Row – and a well-established guest speaker programme features figures like artist Jake Chapman and screenwriter Russell T Davies. Job prospects soon after graduation can be challenging for art and design specialisms. Our analysis shows Leeds Arts is fourth from the bottom among UK universities for graduates in highly skilled work or postgraduate study after 15 months (126th, 59.4%).

Facilities on the Blenheim Walk Campus include studios for film, music and photography, a 230-seat auditorium, and a specialist arts library. Students have access to professional-standard equipment, including large-format digital printers and industrial-grade machinery for working with wood and metal. The university has focused on improving facilities for cyclists and increasing the number of trees on campus.

Student societies have an arts and cultural slant, including life drawing and zine making. Although Leeds Arts does not have its own sports facilities, students can use nearby leisure centres. The university offers fitness classes and a running club, and has football and netball teams that compete in local leagues. Its small size fosters a close-knit atmosphere and a holistic approach to student support. Students can access one-to-one meetings with welfare advisers and counsellors. A place at Carr Mills or the Leather Works accommodation is guaranteed to first-years who firmly accept their place and book by June 11.

Leeds Arts ranks 70th in our social inclusion index, with 94% of the intake from non-selective state schools. The university's commitment to widening participation is shown through its Creative Pathways Programme with partner schools and free after-school art clubs. More than a third of new entrants receive some form of financial aid. The Skin's Chancellor Scholarship (named in honour of the university's first chancellor, Skin – the lead singer of Skunk Anansie) of £3,000 a year is awarded to two UK students and one international student. The Creative Practice Support Bursary provides up to £1,600 to those from low-income households, and care leavers qualify for a bursary of £1,500 a year.

Blenheim Walk Leeds LS2 9AQ
admissions@leeds-art.ac.uk
leeds-art.ac.uk
leedsartsunion.org.uk

Overall ranking 103
(last year 92)

Accommodation
University provided places 592
Self-catered £127–£193 per week

Student numbers
Undergraduates 2,025
Applications per place 6.8:1
Overall offer rate 61.1%

Fees
UK fees £9,535
International fees £18,000–£18,600

leeds-art.ac.uk/apply/open-days/undergraduate-open-days
leeds-art.ac.uk/apply/undergraduate-fees-and-finance

Leeds Beckett University

Academic breadth extends across nine schools at Leeds Beckett University, which has two campuses: a spacious site in the Headingley suburb and a City Campus in the heart of Leeds. Arts, law, business, and engineering are among its disciplines, but the university's forte is sport. The world-class Carnegie School of Sport has been a "power behind the podium" for athletes. Beyond sport, students enjoy multicultural Leeds, a city with legendary nightlife and relative affordability.

Leeds Beckett edged into the top 100 in our research quality index, moving up three places to 97th (26.7%) based on 53% of work submitted to the latest Research Excellence Framework (REF 2021) being rated world-leading or internationally excellent. The university's best results were in sports sciences, followed by allied health and building subjects.

However, Leeds Beckett was rated only bronze overall in the Teaching Excellence Framework (TEF 2023), down from silver. Its relatively low rates of continuation and professional-level graduate careers hold it back. For the student experience, the TEF panel awarded Leeds Beckett silver, commending "a supportive learning environment". In our analysis of the latest National Student Survey (NSS), it is 39th for the overall student experience and 56th for teaching quality.

Ending in 2025 are degrees in health and exercise science, broadcast media technologies, creative media technology and sport development. Hospitality business management with marketing closes in 2026. New for 2026 is an integrated master of architecture degree, as well as degrees in content creation, music business, and fashion communication and content.

Students need a minimum of 104 UCAS tariff points, up to 136 points (average 115). Contextual offers are available on many undergraduate programmes for students who meet widening participation criteria.

Collaborations with more than 4,000 organisations support the university's ambition. The rugby league team Leeds Rhinos are a strategic partner of the Carnegie School of Sport, and the university has a longstanding partnership with Disney. Our analysis of the Graduate Outcomes survey puts Leeds Beckett in 98th place (70.8%) for the proportion of leavers in highly skilled work or postgraduate studies 15 months after finishing their degree.

Leeds Beckett guarantees accommodation to all first-years who make the university their first choice and apply by the deadline, although more than half of undergraduates live at home and commute. Investment in sports facilities continues with two new 3G football pitches and a 3G rugby pitch. The Athletic Union has 40 sports clubs with more than 80 teams. An app allows students to book facilities and track fitness. New multi-faith facilities have been created at both campuses. A multidisciplinary team offers counselling and mental health support, and students can be assigned a specialist mentor.

Ranking 64th in our social inclusion index, Leeds Beckett is =23rd for its proportion of white working-class male students (6.2%), an under-represented group in higher education. About 10% of new entrants receive financial help, such as bursaries for students from low-income and other disadvantaged backgrounds.

City Campus Leeds LS1 3HE
admissionenquiries@leedsbeckett.ac.uk
leedsbeckett.ac.uk
leedsbeckettsu.co.uk

Overall ranking 83
(last year 88)

Accommodation
University provided places 2,400
Self-catered £144–£245 per week

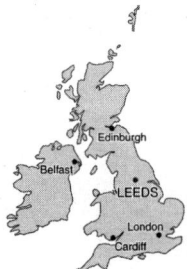

Student numbers
Undergraduates 15,260
Applications per place 4.7:1
Overall offer rate 77.0

Fees
UK fees £9,535
International fees £14,850–£16,350

leedsbeckett.ac.uk/undergraduate/open-days
leedsbeckett.ac.uk/undergraduate/financing-your-studies

Leeds Trinity University

Leeds Trinity has a reputation for having a close-knit atmosphere, helped by its small size and a self-contained campus in suburban Horsforth. This is backed up by superb feedback in the latest National Student Survey (NSS), where it ranks 2nd in the UK for teaching quality and the wider experience. This campus culture has been replicated in a more urban setting since the new City Campus opened last October at Trevelyan Square. The academic focus here is on business, computer science, construction, criminology, investigation and policing, and law.

The university has its roots in two Catholic teacher training colleges from the 1960s, and teacher training is still its strongest suit. In the latest Research Excellence Framework (REF 2021), theology produced the best results. Leeds Trinity research takes 121st place in our research quality rankings (15.1%). Rated triple silver in the government's Teaching Excellence Framework (TEF 2023), Leeds Trinity drew praise for its "content and delivery that effectively encourage students to engage in their learning". Student satisfaction has improved since last year.

Leeds Trinity has launched degrees in digital media production and accounting and finance. A new degree in nursing (child) will begin in January 2026, and from September 2026, the curriculum gains degrees in psychology with occupational, business, and marketing perspectives, as well as health perspectives.

Degrees require 96-120 UCAS tariff points. Students eligible for a contextual offer may have their entry requirements undercut by up to two A-level grades. In 2024, the university attracted nearly 7,800 applications and accepted 1,815 new students, a 20% decrease from the previous year.

The majority of degrees include professional work placements, and volunteering at home or abroad is also credited. Our analysis of the Graduate Outcomes survey ranks Leeds Trinity in =86th place, based on the proportion (73%), in highly skilled work or postgraduate study 15 months on from finishing a degree course.

At the main campus in Horsforth, a health and life sciences building opened recently, joining psychology-teaching facilities and a 3G football pitch. The City Campus includes a trading room, a law court, and specialist labs for computer science and construction. Halls of residence on the Horsforth Campus have space for all students who apply by the UCAS deadline, though Leeds Trinity stops short of making an accommodation guarantee. The majority of students live at home and commute.

Students with no family history of university make up 64.8% of undergraduates and Leeds Trinity is 18th overall in our social inclusion index. Initiatives to widen participation include foundation years, pre-16 support and, for local Year 12 students, taster days and a summer school. Students entering with AAB or the equivalent qualify for a £1,000 academic achievement award in their first year. The Leeds Trinity Bursary (£500) is awarded to students from low-income backgrounds in their second year. The university also extends financial support to students who have been in care or are estranged from their families. There are a limited number of sanctuary scholarships per year for those from forced migrant backgrounds, providing a full tuition fee waiver.

Brownberrie Lane Horsforth Leeds LS18 5HD
admissions@leedstrinity.ac.uk
leedstrinity.ac.uk
ltsu.co.uk

Overall ranking =90
(last year 112)

Accommodation
University provided places 749
Self-catered £113–£161 per week

Student numbers
Undergraduates 3,375
Applications per place 4.3:1
Overall offer rate 74.3%

Fees
UK fees £9,535
International fees £12,000–£14,500

leedstrinity.ac.uk/undergraduate/open-days
leedstrinity.ac.uk/study/fees-and-finance

University of Leicester

The stars are in sight in more ways than one at Leicester. The research-intensive East Midlands university hosts the £100 million Space Park, opened by the astronaut Tim Peake in 2022, complete with a rooftop observatory. It is also investigating how the final frontier is shaping our lives at the Leverhulme Centre for Humanity and Space.

In the latest Research Excellence Framework (REF 2021), 89% of its work was assessed as world-leading or internationally excellent. It maintained its position of =26th in our research quality index. Vice-chancellor Nishan Canagarajah has aspirations for the university to join the Russell Group. Leicester also received a gold rating in the latest Teaching Excellence Framework (TEF 2023).

Soaring rates of student satisfaction are added to Leicester's credentials: in our analysis of the National Student Survey (NSS), Leicester ranks 9th for student satisfaction, with the wider undergraduate experience up 53 places across the past two years. It also ranked =41st for teaching quality (up 13 places, year-on-year).

Degree courses require A*AA to BCC at A-level for a foundation STEM subject. Contextual offers, which provide a discount of up to two A-level grades, were offered to 5% of 2024's entrants. Leicester welcomed a record number of undergraduates for 2024 entry, more than 5,000 for the first time. Three in ten gained their places through clearing.

The university seeks to include work experience opportunities for students in all its degree courses. Leicester's endeavours to boost employability help it to rank =35th, in our analysis of the Graduate Outcomes survey, based on the proportion (81%) in highly skilled jobs or postgraduate study within 15 months of graduation.

The compact campus, located a mile south of the city centre, is in the second phase of a £500 million modernisation project. The Georgian architecture of the Fielding Johnson Building contrasts with modern academic and residential blocks. At the satellite Brookfield Campus, the School of Business has lecture theatres and a trading room.

Leicester guarantees all students who apply before September 1 a space in university-managed halls. Prices range between £82 and £273 a week.

The city is home to one of the biggest Diwali celebrations outside India. On campus the university's award-winning Students' Union is the only one in the country with its own O2 Academy. There are more than 200 clubs and societies. Both the university's sports centres have a gym, swimming pool, spa and studio. Students who need help have access to a wellbeing team and a 24-hour phone line.

Black and ethnic minorities represent 68.8% of students, placing the university 13th in our social inclusion index for this measure. The achievement gap with white peers is closing. Leicester ranks 77th for social inclusion overall in England and Wales. To widen access, there is a range of progression programmes such as Pathways to Law and AccessLeicester. About 30% of new entrants receive a financial award. The Citizens of Change scholarship awards fee discounts of £2,500 a year. Students from low-income households qualify for the £1,000-a-year Leicester Bursary. There are also two sanctuary scholarships each year covering fees and support for asylum seekers.

University Road Leicester LE1 7RH
admissions@le.ac.uk
le.ac.uk
leicesterunion.com

Overall ranking =28
(last year =27)

Accommodation
University provided places 3,739
Self-catered £82–£273 per week

Student numbers
Undergraduates 13,230
Applications per place 5.3:1
Overall offer rate 74.3%

Fees
UK fees £9,535
International fees £18,950–£25,900
Medicine £29,000–£47,000

le.ac.uk/open-days
le.ac.uk/study/undergraduates/fees-funding

University of Lincoln

In an attractive city with a cathedral and a castle, the University of Lincoln is at the vanguard of modern higher education. A £400 million investment over the past two decades has transformed a former industrial site into the modern waterfront Brayford Pool Campus, offering wide-ranging specialist resources.

Lincoln's academic ambitions have been similarly evolutionary. Its School of Engineering was the first in the UK in more than 20 years when it opened, and a medical school which has operated jointly with the University of Nottingham becomes independent of its partner from September 2026. Lincoln is home to the world's first Centre for Doctoral Training in Agri-Food Robotics, and the National Centre for Food Manufacturing.

The university joined an elite group when it was awarded triple gold in the government's Teaching Excellence Framework (TEF 2023). Assessors praised its outstanding course content, delivery, and resources, as well as its "supportive learning environment". More than three quarters (79%) of Lincoln's research was judged to be internationally excellent or world-leading in the latest Research Excellence Framework (REF 2021). History, social policy, allied health professions and computer science produced some of the best results and it rose one place to 66th in our research rating.

Eight degrees have been withdrawn, seven of them with immediate effect, including sport development and coaching, robotics, and chemistry with education. Public health and human behaviour has replaced health and social care. Lincoln's own medicine degree will be introduced from 2026, and its medicine with a gateway year began in September 2025. New degrees in computer science, sport coaching, and media and communications have also been launched.

Ninety-six points in the UCAS tariff is sufficient for entry to some degrees, while requirements can be as high as 136 points for pharmacy. Medicine degrees call for AAA. Contextual offers are eight UCAS points lower for students from areas with lower rates of progression to higher education. In 2024, 14% of entrants were accepted through clearing.

The TEF panel praised Lincoln for its "highly effective" approaches to helping students after graduation. However, Lincoln ranks 89th in our analysis of the Graduate Outcomes survey, with 72.9% in highly skilled jobs or postgraduate study 15 months after graduating.

The £6 million Lincoln Arts Centre has a 450-seat theatre and three large studio spaces. Students can access a wellbeing hub via drop-ins, phone or email. The university's WOW (Wellbeing Orientation Welcome) summer school is a two-night experience for students with autism or other conditions that may make the transition to university more challenging. Gym members have access to weekly classes. A space in halls is guaranteed to first-years who apply before August 1.

Lincoln has dropped to =58th in our social inclusion index but has a high share of white working-class male students, ranking 18th. Most new full-time undergraduate students (85–90%) received some financial support in 2025. The University of Lincoln scholarship, worth £500 per year for up to three years, is awarded automatically to full-time UK undergraduates with household incomes of less than £25,000.

Brayford Pool Lincoln LN6 7TS
admissions@lincoln.ac.uk
lincoln.ac.uk
lincolnsu.com

Overall ranking =64
(last year 56)

Accommodation
University provided places 3,299
Self-catered £99–£199 per week

Student numbers
Undergraduates 11,545
Applications per place 4.7:1
Overall offer rate 84.5%

Fees
UK fees £9,535
International fees £16,600–£17,900
Medicine £46,700

lincoln.ac.uk/studywithus/opendaysandvisits/undergraduateopendays/
lincoln.ac.uk/studywithus/undergraduatestudy/feesandfunding/

Lincoln Bishop University

The best things come in small packages, and this adage fits Lincoln Bishop University. With a population of less than 1,500 full-time undergraduates, it consistently comes in for some of the best feedback in the National Student Survey (NSS). In our latest analysis, it ranks 3rd in the UK for satisfaction with teaching quality and 7th for the wider student experience.

Based on a leafy site a few minutes' walk from Lincoln Cathedral, the university was founded in 1862 as an Anglican teacher training college, gaining university status in 2012. It adopted its new name, Lincoln Bishop University, this year, having previously been known as Bishop Grosseteste University. A 12-place ascent of our main academic ranking brings Lincoln Bishop inside the top 75, boosted by high scores for theology in the latest Research Excellence Framework (REF 2021). The university was also awarded triple silver in the Teaching Excellence Framework (TEF 2023), with the panel praising its "highly effective teaching, assessment and feedback practices".

Applicants need 96 to 112 UCAS tariff points. Contextual offers are applied to all subjects at undergraduate level, undercutting the standard offer by up to 32 UCAS tariff points. Lincoln Bishop specialises in vocational placements for teacher training and counselling, as well as short-term experiences for subjects including education and health and social care, and the university's business centre provides support for start-ups. The focus on career-building is paying off, and the university ranks 54th in our analysis of graduate prospects.

One of Lincoln Bishop's two on-campus halls of residence also houses modern learning facilities, thanks to a £2.2 million extension. The library also has teams to provide student advice and learning development. Facilities for archaeology have been boosted by more than £427,000 from the Arts and Humanities Research Council. The Ermine Library and Community Hub nearby is run by Lincoln Bishop with the support of volunteers, where recent investment has improved the community space, by installing a suite of computers and adding an outdoor learning area.

Lincoln Bishop is one of two universities in the quaint, historic city, making for a lively student vibe. Facilities include a sports hall, fitness suite and acres of outdoor fields. Students can stay active with fitness classes, indoor tennis, hockey, volleyball and rugby. Cultural activities fall under the auspices of the chaplaincy and range from a weekly discussion group to trips to the Royal Shakespeare Company.

A student advice team offers counselling and mental health support, and students have access to a 24/7 mental health app. The campus grounds offer a sense of calm, and students can take time out in the Peace Gardens. First-years who apply by the deadline are guaranteed a place in halls.

Lincoln Bishop has a strong record in our social inclusion index, jumping four places to 5th overall. In 2025, 10% of undergraduate students qualified for some form of financial support. Bursaries of £1,000 a year are awarded to students from low-income households who also qualify under a range of personal circumstances, including parents, care-leavers and student carers.

Longdales Road Lincoln LN1 3DY
courseenquiries@lincolnbishop.ac.uk
lincolnbishop.ac.uk
lbusu.co.uk

Overall ranking 74
(last year 86)

Accommodation
University provided places 548
Self-catered £123–£205 per week

Student numbers
Undergraduates 1,365
Applications per place 2.7:1
Overall offer rate 93.4%

Fees
UK fees £9,535
International fees £10,790–£14,380

lincolnbishop.ac.uk/open-days

lincolnbishop.ac.uk/apply-now/fees-and-funding

University of Liverpool

A venerable university in an iconic city, the University of Liverpool has always had a lot to recommend it, and now it can add soaring student satisfaction to its list of attractions. In our new National Student Survey analysis, Liverpool has jumped into the UK top ten for student experience (10th) – a remarkable turnaround from =100th only two years ago. The main campus is about five minutes on foot from the city centre, putting students at the heart of Liverpool's legendary culture, nightlife and sport. Liverpool's global reach allows students on most courses opportunities to study abroad at one of more than 100 partner institutions – from America to South Korea.

Liverpool claims to be the original "redbrick" university. Impressive results in the latest Research Excellence Framework (REF 2021) triggered a 16-place rise in our research quality index to 24th, with 91% of its work rated world-leading or internationally excellent, led by veterinary science, chemistry, psychology, and modern languages. Its Interdisciplinary Centre for Sustainability Research launched in 2024. Liverpool was upgraded to gold overall in the government's Teaching Excellence Framework (TEF 2023), and also rated gold for student outcomes, with silver for the student experience.

Liverpool has introduced graduate entry law from 2025, and will add a year in industry to its economics degrees from 2026.

Standard undergraduate degrees ask for up to AAA at A-level, with foundation options available. Contextual offers, received by about 10% of new entrants in 2024, can reduce the standard grade requirements by up to two A-level grades for eligible students.

The university is highly popular, receiving more than 43,000 applications and accepting its largest-ever intake of more than 7,300 new undergraduates in 2024.

A top 30 ranking (30th) in our analysis of the Graduate Outcomes survey – based on leavers in highly skilled jobs or further study 15 months after finishing their degrees – is powered by strong industry links with leading employers such as AstraZeneca, Unilever and Airbus. The university offers students paid internships, work experience and long-term schemes. The Sir Peter Rigby Centre for Enterprise, which opened in 2024, provides co-working spaces and a podcast studio to help student entrepreneurs develop their ventures.

Most teaching takes place at the main city Knowledge Quarter Campus. Modern university facilities include the £12.7 million Digital Innovation Facility (DIF), which opened in 2022. Recent campus improvements have revamped lecture theatres and introduced a gaming suite and two new computer suites.

A place in university halls is guaranteed for all first-year students – including those who come through clearing or as an insurance choice – provided they apply by the deadline.

Liverpool is 104th overall in our social inclusion index and the university runs an extensive range of outreach activities. The Liverpool Scholars programme, for example, supports students from under-represented backgrounds and can lead to a reduced A-level offer.

More than a quarter of UK undergraduates receive financial support. The Liverpool Bursary offers up to £2,000 per year for students from households with an income up to £35,000.

Liverpool L69 7ZX
ug-recruitment@liverpool.ac.uk
liverpool.ac.uk
liverpoolguild.org

Overall ranking 18
(last year 23)

Accommodation
University provided places 5,312
Catered £242 per week
Self-catered £105–£248 per week

Student numbers
Undergraduates 22,040
Applications per place 5.9:1
Overall offer rate 73.2%

Fees
UK fees £9,535
International fees £24,100–£48,550
Medicine £47,600

liverpool.ac.uk/undergraduate/open-days-and-visits
liverpool.ac.uk/study/fees-and-funding/tuition-fees

Liverpool Hope University

Liverpool Hope University springs four places up our main academic league table this year (=90th). This improvement is spurred by glowing reviews from its undergraduates in the latest National Student Survey (NSS), where it ranks 5th for teaching quality and 23rd for the wider undergraduate experience. Students are based at the original Hope Park Campus, in a leafy suburb, and at the Creative Campus near Liverpool Lime Street station. A new i3 Building has opened at Hope Park with high-tech resources, including a simulation lab with virtual reality hardware. As one of the UK's smaller universities, Liverpool Hope maintains a close-knit vibe within easy reach of the city's epic student appeal.

Formed by the 1980 merger of teacher training colleges, Liverpool Hope became a university in 2005. Its founding colleges were of both Catholic and Anglican faiths, making it Europe's only ecumenical university. In the latest Research Excellence Framework (REF 2021), the university dropped to 105th in our research quality index, though theology and education produced some of its best results.

Liverpool Hope received triple silver in the Teaching Excellence Framework (TEF 2023), with praise for its "outstanding teaching, feedback and assessment practices". However, the university is held back in our main ranking due to its performance on graduate prospects and continuation rates, which are outside the top 100 for both metrics.

Offers range from 120 to 104 UCAS tariff points. The university attracted more than 11,500 applications in 2024, and nearly 1,700 entrants were accepted. Some 16% entered through clearing.

Liverpool Hope aims to boost employability through industry links with local organisations. However, graduate prospects remain weak. The university sits 115th in our Graduate Outcomes survey analysis (65.2% in highly skilled jobs or further study after 15 months).

The Hope Park Campus is the university's biggest site, with more than £40 million in new buildings and facilities over the past six years. Recent improvements include a moot courtroom for the School of Law and a simulation suite for social work students.

Creative life has space to thrive at the university's Arts Centre. The Capstone Theatre hosts performances and festivals. Access to all Liverpool Hope's sports facilities and classes is £30 a year. The £5.5 million sports complex has a sports hall, squash courts, dance studio, artificial pitches and outdoor courts. The university is an accredited Duke of Edinburgh Gold Award provider and has an outdoor education centre, Plas Caerdeon, at Eryri National Park in Snowdonia. A student life team provides services such as counselling, mental health support, and learning support.

Accommodation is at three sites: Hope Park, Creative Campus and Aigburth Park. There is usually a space for all entrants who apply through the main admissions cycle.

Liverpool Hope recruits the 7th-highest proportion (8.1%) of white working-class male students, the most under-represented group in higher education, and draws a fifth of its students from deprived areas. It ranks 24th overall in our social inclusion index.

Ten Access to Hope scholarships of £3,000 per year are available, and aid is offered for care leavers. Merit-based performance scholarships reward talent in dance, drama, music, or sport.

Hope Park Taggart Avenue Liverpool L16 9JD
courses@hope.ac.uk
www.hope.ac.uk
www.hopesu.com

Overall ranking =90
(last year =94)

Accommodation
University provided places 1,146
Self-catered £95–£130 per week

Student numbers
Undergraduates 4,035
Applications per place 6.8:1
Overall offer rate 85.5%

Fees
UK fees £9,535
International fees £14,500

hope.ac.uk/opendays
hope.ac.uk/undergraduate/feesandfunding

Liverpool John Moores University

Liverpool John Moores University (LJMU) is Merseyside's main modern university, with two campuses, City and Mount Pleasant, supporting about 27,000 students. The two are connected by the Copperas Hill development, which regenerated a disused site into a facility for the Student Life Building and Sports Building. Named after Sir John Moores, who was a philanthropist and the founder of the Littlewoods retail and football pools company, LJMU is a pioneer in degree apprenticeships, with a diverse range of 32 programmes and 1,600 students enrolled. Four new options join the earn-while-you-learn roster from September 2025.

LJMU gained its royal charter in 1992, but its heritage traces back to the Liverpool Mechanics' School of Arts, founded in 1823. The university commemorated its bicentenary with a gold rating for student outcomes in the government's Teaching Excellence Framework (TEF 2023). The TEF panel identified the standout feature of the student experience to be the university's "outstanding engagement with its students, leading to continuous improvement". Results of the latest National Student Survey (NSS) show an enhanced appreciation for the broad experience, with the university ranking 18th in our analysis and in the top 50 for teaching quality (41st).

Research is a point of pride for LJMU, which submitted work from more than 600 academic staff in the latest Research Excellence Framework (REF 2021). Of the submission, 73.1% was rated world-leading or internationally excellent. Astrophysics, sport and exercise sciences, and engineering produced some of the best results. Among its areas of expertise is the Football Exchange at the School of Sport and Exercise Sciences.

LJMU has launched degrees in business with finance and economics, criminology and international relations, and policing, psychology, and investigations. A suite of computer science degrees launches in September 2026.

LJMU's requirements range from 72 UCAS points for foundation degrees up to 128 points. Reduced offers of up to 16 points below standard requirements are made to students who have engaged with outreach activities or meet other widening participation criteria.

Undergraduate courses include work-based learning opportunities. Law undergraduates can gain pro bono experience from their first year at the Legal Advice Centre. LJMU is outside the upper half nationally (79th) for graduate prospects, based on the 73.7% proportion employed in high-skilled jobs or further study 15 months after their degrees.

Specialist facilities at the City and Mount Pleasant campuses include the six-storey, £27 million John Lennon Art and Design Building. Further afield, in the Canary Islands, LJMU owns and operates the Liverpool Telescope – the world's largest fully robotic telescope.

With 3,800 residential spaces in the city, LJMU guarantees accommodation to first-years – including those who secure their places via clearing. There are 250 rooms at the lowest end of the rent scale (£90 a week).

Ranking 54th in our social inclusion index, LJMU is in the top ten in England and Wales for the recruitment of white working-class male students – the most under-represented group in higher education.

Student Life Building Copperas Hill
Liverpool L3 5AH
applicantsupport@ljmu.ac.uk
ljmu.ac.uk
jmsu.co.uk

Overall ranking 61
(last year =66)

Accommodation
University provided places 3,800
Self-catered £90–£179 per week

Student numbers
Undergraduates 20,255
Applications per place 4.5:1
Overall offer rate 84.2%

Fees
UK fees £9,535
International fees £17,750–£18,250

ljmu.ac.uk/study/undergraduate-students/visit-us/undergraduate-open-days
ljmu.ac.uk/discover/fees-and-funding-finance

London Metropolitan University

London Metropolitan University is guided by the principle of opening the doors wide to higher education. Mature students (over 21) account for more than two thirds of undergraduates, and only one other university has a higher proportion of students who went to non-selective state schools (99%). The university ranks 16th in our social inclusion index for England and Wales and is Runner-Up for University of the Year for Social Inclusion 2026.

London Met was ahead of the curve when it formed through the UK's first university merger in 2002. In the Research Excellence Framework (REF 2021), it places 89th in our research quality index, with 60% of its research assessed as world-leading or internationally excellent. Maths produced the best result. The university has edged up three places in our main academic ranking (=124th) but has never broken into the top 100. Student satisfaction has cooled this year, with London Met ranked =83rd for teaching quality (a 60-place drop) and 84th for the wider experience (a 48-place drop) in our analysis of the latest National Student Survey (NSS). The Teaching Excellence Framework (TEF 2023) awarded the university gold for student experience, underpinning a silver award overall.

However, continuation rates remain a sticking point; only 81.7% of undergraduates are projected to carry on to their second year, which is an improvement on 79.1% last year. London Met has moved up ten places for this metric, to =119th.

In September 2025, the university launched BEng degrees in AI and robotics, and biomedical engineering, as well as BSc courses in mental health nursing, building surveying, and real estate. A new CertHE in business management is also available.

London Met is at the bottom of the table for entry standards with an average entry of 94 UCAS tariff points. If applicants fall short on their first choice, the university will consider an application for an alternative course.

London Met has ambitions to expand its nursing provision and provide 1,500 healthcare workers by 2028, after a £5.8 million boost from the Office for Students. The university's Careers Education Framework enhances employability. London Met ranks 120th in our graduate prospects table, with 63.4% of graduates in highly skilled jobs or further study within 15 months.

Among facilities at Holloway Road is the Science Centre's superlab, one of the largest teaching laboratories in Europe. The School of Art, Architecture, and Design is in Aldgate, while Accelerator, a business start-up hub, is in Shoreditch. Most London Met students live at home and commute. The university does not own halls of residence but points students towards private halls with affordable rooms if needed.

The university runs a range of outreach activities to widen participation from under-represented and disadvantaged students. London Met has an ethnically diverse student population, with more than half of students (65.3%) from ethnic minority backgrounds.

Bursaries of £1,500 a year benefit students who have left care, and the university offers grants to help offers grants to help those with children, or who have disabilities or adult dependants. Sanctuary scholarships are also offered, providing a full fee waiver, maintenance loan, and mentorship. There are also a limited number of bursaries for social work students that are not means-tested.

166–220 Holloway Road London N7 8DB
courseenquiries@londonmet.ac.uk
londonmet.ac.uk
londonmetsu.org.uk

Overall ranking =124
(last year 127)

Accommodation
University provided places N/A

Student numbers
Undergraduates 6,770
Applications per place 6.6:1
Overall offer rate 85.2%

Fees
UK fees £9,535
International fees £19,500–£21,000

londonmet.ac.uk/events/undergraduate-open-days
londonmet.ac.uk/applying/funding-your-studies

London School of Economics and Political Science

The London School of Economics (LSE) has topped the league table for the second year in a row and is our University of the Year for Academic Performance 2026, Russell Group University of the Year 2026 and University of the Year in London 2026, not to mention joint Runner-Up for University of the Year for Graduate Employment 2026. Investment in its campus in the heart of London has resulted in a spectacular turnaround in rates of student satisfaction. Our analysis of students' feedback in successive National Student Surveys (NSS) ranked LSE 112th for the broad experience as recently as six years ago – now it is =12th. A busy Students' Union delivers more than 3,000 events, and more than 250 societies and sports clubs.

In 1895, LSE's Fabian Society founders dreamt of an institution to get at the "concrete facts of industrial life and the actual working of economic and political relations". Today the curriculum has more than 40 undergraduate programmes, and LSE is a global leader in social sciences and management. In the QS World University Rankings, it was ranked 6th in the world for these subjects in 2025. A new degree in economics and data science is being introduced in 2026.

In the latest Research Excellence Framework (REF 2021), 93% of LSE's submission was judged as world-leading or internationally excellent, placing it 3rd in the UK for research in our analysis. The best results were in economics, anthropology, social policy, health policy, and media and communications. The university was also upgraded from bronze to silver in the government's latest Teaching Excellence Framework (TEF 2023).

Competition to study here is fierce – and global. LSE is one of the few universities not to enter clearing. Offers range from A*AA to AAB. Contextual offers, which are usually one to two grades lower than standard, are made to eligible UK applicants, such as those from deprived areas, leaving care or taking part in an LSE or Sutton Trust Pathways access programme.

The future is bright for those armed with a degree from LSE and the university continues to innovate on employability, ranking 2nd in our analysis of the Graduate Outcomes survey. Fifteen months after finishing their degree, 92.5% of its graduates are in highly skilled jobs or postgraduate study. There are more than 3,845 university-owned or endorsed rooms, about 40% of them catered, and accommodation is guaranteed to first-years who apply by the June deadline. Prices range from £137.55 a week for a bed in a triple room to £469 a week for a single studio.

LSE aims to attract the most capable students from a wide range of backgrounds and it has the 21st-highest level of ethnic diversity but it has dropped a place to =101st overall in our social inclusion index.

About a quarter of the intake claim some form of financial aid. Awards include means-tested bursaries, which have increased in value from 2025-26 to range from £1,250 to £4,250 a year, awarded on a sliding scale to students with household incomes up to £50,000.

Houghton Street London WC2A 2AE
lse.ac.uk/ask-LSE
lse.ac.uk
lsesu.com

Overall ranking 1
(last year 1)

Accommodation
University provided places 3,845
Catered £138-406 per week
Self-catered £140-£469 per week

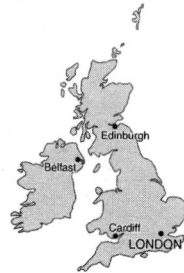

Student numbers
Undergraduates 5,645
Applications per place 14.5:1
Overall offer rate 21.0%

Fees
UK fees £9,535
International fees £27,500–£34,000

lse.ac.uk/study-at-lse/meet-visit-and-discover-LSE/experience-lse/undergraduate-open-day
lse.ac.uk/study-at-lse/Undergraduate/fees-and-funding

London South Bank University

A university since 1992, London South Bank University (LSBU) is underpinned by its civic mission to provide "industrial skill, general knowledge, health and wellbeing" to the people and businesses of south London. A professional, practical accent to course provision ranges from the technology and baking science degrees delivered by its National Bakery School (the world's oldest baking institution, founded in 1894), to courses at LSBU's business and healthcare campus in Croydon, which opened in 2022.

The Research Excellence Framework (REF 2021) rated 68% of research submitted by LSBU as world-leading or internationally excellent (up 14 percentage points compared with the previous REF), and LSBU ranks 91st in our research quality index.

LSBU maintained a silver rating overall in the government's Teaching Excellence Framework (TEF) 2023, underpinned by a silver for student outcomes, but only bronze for the student experience. Assessors highlighted LSBU's "very high continuation and completion rates, with outstanding outcomes for some student groups and subject areas". However, our data shows that across all areas the LSBU students' projected continuation rate of 84.6% is relatively poor, placing the university 114th for this metric.

Rates of student satisfaction improved last year but have dipped according to our analysis of the latest National Student Survey (NSS): LSBU ranks =89th for students' evaluation of teaching quality (down 19 places) and =103rd for satisfaction with the wider experience (a 14-place decline). The discontent may be related to financial struggles at the university, which reported a budget deficit of £16.4 million and announced job cuts in 2024.

New degree offerings are available in acting for stage and screen, pharmaceutical science, cyber security, computer science (conversion), data science, applied artificial intelligence, product design and technology, engineering product design, architectural technology (with foundation year), civil engineering (with foundation year), architecture (with foundation year), education, and apprenticeships in building services engineering and civil engineering.

Some of LSBU's most competitive courses require 128 UCAS tariff points, but most need at least 112. The TEF 2023 found that more than half of full-time students enter with Btecs, access or foundation courses, or "none, unknown or other entry qualifications", rather than with A-levels.

LSBU has made the most of its London location by cultivating links with more than 1,500 organisations, including the National Theatre, NHS, Unilever and Lidl. In our analysis of the Graduate Outcomes survey, tracking the proportion in highly skilled work or further study after 15 months, LSBU ranks =64th (75.4%). In 2023-24, 7.4% of first-years lived in LSBU's halls. There is no specific accommodation guarantee but the university says it can house all students who need it.

Nearly three-quarters (72.7%) of the intake are from ethnic minority backgrounds (the 8th highest nationally) and 96.9% from non-selective state schools (15th), putting LSBU in 31st place in our social inclusion index (up from 34th last year).

There are bursaries of £1,000 a year for care leavers, students estranged from their families, and young carer students. The Lawrence Burrows Education Trust funds ten bursaries of £3,000 for students with a West Indian or Asian background.

---

103 Borough Road London SE1 0AA
lsbu.ac.uk/contact-us/enquiry-form
lsbu.ac.uk
southbanksu.com

Overall ranking 111
(last year 100)

Accommodation
University provided places 1,338
Self-catered £194–£268 per week

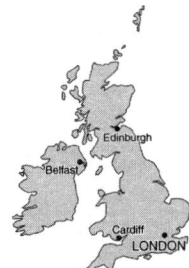

Student numbers
Undergraduates 10,930
Applications per place 4.8:1
Overall offer rate 62.6%

Fees
UK fees £9,535
International fees £15,500–£17,600

lsbu.ac.uk/study/study-at-lsbu/open-days
lsbu.ac.uk/study/undergraduate/fees-and-funding

Loughborough University

Students can get used to coming in first place at Loughborough – not only in elite sports competitions but in the academic race too. Strong results across the board, from research to student satisfaction and graduate employment, keeps Loughborough in the top 20 (12th) in our rankings.

The course offering covers a wide range from engineering and computer science, to fine art and finance. For sports-related degrees, however, Loughborough is peerless, leading the QS World University Rankings for sport for the ninth consecutive year in 2025. It is Runner-Up for Sports University of the Year 2026 in the UK. The university's 523-acre single-site campus is known for having the UK's largest concentration of world-class sports facilities and is the base for six national sporting bodies, including British Athletics and England Netball. Less well known is that Loughborough has won its eighth consecutive Green Flag Award in 2025. Sporting dominance is Loughborough's calling card. The university topped the British Universities and Colleges Sport (BUCS) table in 2024-25 for the 44th consecutive time.

Studies on sport and exercise science also got exceptional results in the latest Research Excellence Framework (REF 2021) in which 91% of Loughborough's work was rated world-leading or internationally excellent. Greater gains elsewhere, however, meant that the university fell four places to 34th in our research quality index.

Loughborough's academic excellence was confirmed with a rare triple gold in the government's latest Teaching Excellence Framework (TEF 2023), earning the highest rating for student experience, student outcomes, and overall quality.

While student satisfaction remains high, a dip in the National Student Survey (NSS) puts it in 14th place for the wider student experience (down from third) and =67th for teaching quality (down from 32nd).

Standard offers range from A*AA to BBC at A-level. A contextual offer scheme can reduce this by up to two grades for eligible applicants and 10% of entrants benefitted in 2024.

Loughborough's deep-rooted industry links translate into outstanding graduate outcomes and two thirds of its undergraduates are on degree programmes that include a placement year. This focus on employability helps it rank 11th in our analysis of the Graduate Outcomes survey, with 86.3% of graduates in highly skilled work or postgraduate study 15 months after finishing their degree.

Loughborough has more than 6,000 rooms across 17 halls of residence and more than half are catered – a rarity on UK campuses. The university guarantees accommodation to all first-years who apply by the July deadline.

Loughborough is in the lower ranks of the top 100 (97th) for social inclusion overall, with just 66.5% of students drawn from non-selective state schools (103rd). It has improved the share of ethnic minority students to 29.6% (56th).

The Loughborough University Bursary pays £1,000 a year, plus a £500 pre-placement grant, to students from households with incomes up to £30,000. Up to 50 students a year receive £3,000 each year if they complete certain access scheme requirements. Women in Science bursaries have been introduced. Scholarships are available for those who show talent in a range of sports, paying up to £5,000 to applicants competing at junior international level.

Epinal Way Loughborough LE11 3TU
admissions@lboro.ac.uk
lboro.ac.uk
lsu.co.uk

Overall ranking 12
(last year 10)

Accommodation
University provided places 6,492
Catered £163–244 per week
Self-catered £120–230 per week

Student numbers
Undergraduates 14,915
Applications per place 6.4:1
Overall offer rate 72.3%

Fees
UK fees £9,535
International fees £24,700–£33,000

lboro.ac.uk/study/undergraduate/visit-us/open-days
lboro.ac.uk/study/undergraduate/fees-funding

University of Manchester

Manchester's Cosy Campus initiative has added new, welcoming spaces, along with the surprising adjective, to one of Britain's biggest universities. Introduced in response to the rising cost of living, the scheme puts a human touch into spaces for working and socialising, installing kitchenettes, comfy seating and carpeting to make students feel more relaxed on the large city centre campus. With 500 undergraduate programmes, Manchester is the UK's most applied-to university, attracting 92,500 applications in 2024.

Founded in 1824 as England's first civic university, Manchester has educated or hired a mass of influential individuals across two centuries, from the suffragette, Christabel Pankhurst, and the founder of modern computing, Alan Turing, to the comedian and writer, Meera Syal, and the actor, Benedict Cumberbatch. In 2004, a merger with the University of Manchester Institute of Science and Technology (UMIST) created a research powerhouse ranked 35th in the world in the 2026 QS list.

A member of the Russell Group of research-led universities, Manchester received a £17.4 million increase in funding by Research England for 2022-23. In the latest Research Excellence Framework (REF 2021), 93% of the university's research was rated world-leading or internationally excellent, placing Manchester 7th in our research quality index. The university gained a silver rating overall in the Teaching Excellence Framework (TEF 2023).

While student satisfaction has historically been low, our analysis of the National Student Survey (NSS) shows real improvement: it has climbed out of the bottom ten for teaching quality (117th) and broken into the top 100 (96th) for the wider student experience.

A degree in fashion product innovation was introduced in 2025.

Entry starts from BCC and goes up to A*A*A*. Contextual offers for eligible students are usually one grade below standard requirements, but those who enter through one of the university's access programmes may qualify for an extra grade reduction on top.

The university was the second most targeted university by the UK's top employers in 2024-25. However, in our analysis of the Graduate Outcomes survey it ranks 39th, with 80.8% of graduates in highly skilled jobs or postgraduate study 15 months after finishing their degree.

The fully refurbished Manchester Aquatics Centre reopened in 2024, complete with two 50m pools and diving springboards. There are both indoor and outdoor facilities at the Armitage Sports Centre. The university owns and operates almost 8,700 rooms. All full-time first-years who apply by the end of August are guaranteed a space.

Manchester is =91st in our social inclusion index overall, fourth among its 21 Russell Group peers in England and Wales. It ranks 47th for students from ethnic minority backgrounds, with 37.3%, but its selective school contingent is relatively high at 69.7% (101st).

The Manchester Bursary contributes £1,300 for those with a household income below £35,000, and £2,600 for those with less than £25,000. Further support is available to students who have left care or who are estranged from their families. There are two Raheem Sterling Foundation Scholarships that pay tuition fees for the duration of a degree plus an £8,000-a-year maintenance bursary to black students from Manchester.

Oxford Road Manchester M13 9PL
manchester.ac.uk/connect/contact-us
manchester.ac.uk
manchesterstudentsunion.com

Overall ranking 27
(last year =27)

Accommodation
University provided places 8,688
Catered £164-227 per week
Self-catered £112-£267 per week

Student numbers
Undergraduates 30,480
Applications per place 9.3:1
Overall offer rate 57.7%

Fees
UK fees £9,535
International fees £25,000-£38,000
Medicine £38,000-£58,000

manchester.ac.uk/study/undergraduate/open-days-visits/open-days
manchester.ac.uk/study/undergraduate/fees-and-funding

Manchester Metropolitan University

Powering into the top 40 (38th) of our main academic ranking, Manchester Metropolitan University (MMU) is a big university with big ambitions to combine a top student experience with degrees that are in step with employers' demands. Its efforts are reflected in its award for Modern University of the Year 2026. Rising rates of student satisfaction show it is on the right track with undergraduates, whose responses in the latest National Student Survey (NSS) put MMU in the top 20 (=19th) for the student experience and top 25 (=24th) for teaching quality.

The All Saints Campus, located near the city centre, has been upgraded to the tune of more than £400 million over the past decade, with improvements ranging from wildflower areas boosting biodiversity to the £115 million Dalton Building to advance STEM education and research.

The university is a pioneer of degree apprenticeships and partners with more than 700 employers to link apprentices with places to earn while they learn, and it ranks 50th in our research quality index. MMU is awarded The Times and Sunday Times Modern University of the Year 2026. Plus, it's been in the top five most sustainable and ethical universities for five years running according to People & Planet.

It was awarded a gold rating overall in the Teaching Excellence Framework (TEF 2023), underpinned by gold for the student experience and silver for student outcomes. In the latest Research Excellence Framework (REF 2021), 30% of its work was considered world-leading.

The Manchester School of Architecture, run in collaboration with the University of Manchester, ranks 5th for architecture and the built environment in the 2025 QS World University subject rankings. According to independent analysis, the university delivers an estimated £1.4 billion to Greater Manchester.

Coming in 2026 are degrees in textiles, business psychology, international hospitality and tourism, business management, and user experience design. Closing in 2025 are courses in French, Spanish interpreting and translation; and various part-time English courses. Check the University website for planned course closures in 2026.

With new entrants averaging 127 UCAS points, MMU is in the upper half of UK universities for its entry standards (=53rd). It is also in demand: MMU attracted nearly 59,500 applications in 2024, and admissions hit a new high – with more than 11,500 new students accepted on to courses.

Students can access work placements or internships with large companies. For now though, MMU ranks only =93rd in our graduate prospects measure, based on 71.6% of its graduates in high-skilled jobs or further study 15 months on.

Accommodation allocation is on a first-come, first-served basis. An accommodation guarantee applies to full-time first-years who make MMU their firm choice and pay a deposit before the end of July.

Half of Manchester Metropolitan's recruits are the first in their family to go to university (49.9%) and 94.1% went to non-selective state schools. Overall, MMU ranks =54th in our social inclusion index, up from 64th last year. The awarding gap for black students is relatively low, at 17.5% (ranking 31st).

The Success Fund will pay eligible applicants between £200 and £1,500 a year.

Ormond Building Lower Ormond Street Manchester M15 6BX
mmu.ac.uk/contact-us/course-enquiry
mmu.ac.uk
theunionmmu.org

Overall ranking 38
(last year =46)

Accommodation
University provided places 3,165
Self-catered £154–£231 per week

Student numbers
Undergraduates 28,625
Applications per place 5.2:1
Overall offer rate 78.7%

Fees
UK fees £9,535
International fees £20,000–£31,500

mmu.ac.uk/study/open-days/undergraduate
mmu.ac.uk/study/undergraduate/funding-your-studies

Middlesex University

Practice-based learning is the theme at Middlesex University. Law students, for example, use chambers inside Hendon Town Hall as a mock courtroom. Not far from the northwest London campus, Middlesex has a £23 million centre of simulation-based learning in the West Stand of the StoneX Stadium – the home ground of Saracens Rugby Club. The facility provides hands-on learning facilities to students enrolled on Middlesex's sports science, nursing and midwifery, and healthcare sciences programmes.

The university's flexible course system offers a January start on some programmes and under its 2031 learning framework, timetables are organised to help students to manage their studies alongside work, caring and other responsibilities.

In the Teaching Excellence Framework (TEF 2023) it was awarded silver overall, while rated bronze for the student experience and silver for student outcomes. In our analysis of the National Student Survey (NSS) 2024, Middlesex is =40th for satisfaction with teaching quality but the university has dropped 51 places to =80th for the student experience.

The university's earn-while-you-learn route is flourishing. Its apprenticeship programmes are expected to attract about 1,350 enrolments by 2026, with students training for a career in fields such as teaching, social work and policing.

Middlesex submitted work in a dozen subject areas to the latest Research Excellence Framework (REF 2021). Although Middlesex recorded an improvement in the REF 2021, rival institutions did better, and the university slipped down our research quality ranking to =81st. Overall, Middlesex picks up 116th place in our academic league table.

The university closed its master's course in theatre arts in 2025, and there are no new course introductions in 2025-26.

Courses demand from 120 to 96 UCAS tariff points, with applicants' work experience and portfolio also taken into consideration.

More than 1,000 partners worldwide contribute to developing Middlesex's courses and research including Warner Bros Discovery, Ogilvy and PwC. Despite such efforts, Middlesex ranks only =117th for graduate prospects, based on our analysis of the Graduate Outcomes survey, which tracks the proportion of those going on to highly skilled jobs or further study within 15 months (64.7%).

On the main campus, a £200 million investment programme has consolidated library services and added two academic buildings at the business school. Facilities include a dance theatre and studios, music, radio and television studios; fashion and textiles workshops and dedicated facilities for animation, graphic design and illustration.

Full-time first-years get priority in halls, but there is no guarantee. However, all first-years who applied in 2024-25 were housed.

Middlesex rises 13 places in our social inclusion index to reach our top 20 (19th). More than 70% of students are from black, Asian or ethnic minority backgrounds, and six in ten are the first in their family to go to university (60.1%). Community-based outreach initiatives and the Make Your Mark programme break down barriers to higher education.

Loans of laptops and tech are available to all students. The Professor Malcolm Sargeant Scholarship (£2,900) is open to first-year students of any subject. There are also ten £1,000 law bursaries and two £1,000 bursaries for nursing and midwifery students.

The Burroughs Hendon London NW4 4BT
mdx.ac.uk/about-us/get-in-touch/ask-a-question
mdx.ac.uk
mdxsu.com

Overall ranking 116
(last year 117)

Accommodation
University provided places 976
Self-catered £165–£220 per week

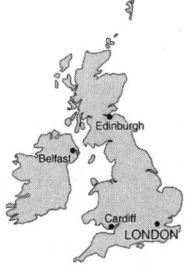

Student numbers
Undergraduates 9,335
Applications per place 6.0:1
Overall offer rate 70.0%

Fees
UK fees £9,535
International fees £16,000–£16,600

mdx.ac.uk/study/open-days/open-day
mdx.ac.uk/study/fees-and-funding/undergraduate-finance

Newcastle University

As a founding member of the Russell Group, Newcastle's research power is internationally recognised. In the latest Research Excellence Framework (REF 2021), 42% of its work was assessed as world-leading, led by English language and literature, to rank =26th in our research quality index. It holds a strong position in the top 150 of the QS World University Rankings. However, student satisfaction has recently waned. Our analysis of the National Student Survey (NSS) shows a drop in its rankings for both student experience and teaching quality.

This is echoed in the latest Teaching Excellence Framework (TEF 2023), where the university received a silver rating overall (down from gold), with bronze for student experience. Despite this, the TEF panel highlighted Newcastle's "very high quality academic experience for students".

The university is also navigating financial headwinds, confirming in 2025 that it is looking to reduce staff costs by £20 million after a shortfall in international student enrolment.

From 2025, courses set to launch include ancient history and history, computing and mathematics, finance, modern languages and international relations, pharmacology MSci, and a physiological sciences MSci, with aerospace engineering taking off in 2026.

Standard entry requirements are from AAA to CCC. Newcastle's contextual offers are two grades lower than the standard requirement across all subject areas. Applications for 2024 entry rose for the third year running, at more than 36,800. More than 6,700 new students were accepted onto courses, with 11% through clearing.

Newcastle excels in preparing students for the world of work, ranking 26th in the UK for graduate prospects. An impressive 82.4% of its graduates are in highly skilled jobs or further study within 15 months of finishing their degrees.

The campus blends historic redbrick architecture with cutting-edge modern facilities. Recent developments include the upgraded Stephenson Building for engineering, featuring a "makerspace" for interdisciplinary collaboration, and the £350 million Newcastle Helix site, which houses two national innovation centres for ageing and data. The university also boasts off-campus facilities including commercial farms and a seagoing research vessel for its marine science programmes.

Newcastle's ambitious plans for a health innovation neighbourhood have been given consent, and will be built on the 29-acre former site of Newcastle General Hospital.

Newcastle teams keep pace with the big hitters in university sport, ranking 8th in the latest British Universities and Colleges Sport (BUCS) points table. The School of Arts and Cultures provides a creative seam to university life from fine art to DJing.

Newcastle guarantees accommodation to first-year students who make it their firm choice and apply by the end of June.

Like most Russell Group universities, Newcastle places well outside the top 100 in our social inclusion index, at 111th of 114. About two thirds of its students are drawn from non-selective state schools but it is making progress in its efforts to widen participation from under-represented groups.

More than a fifth of new students qualify for financial aid. This includes means-tested Opportunity Scholarships worth up to £2,000 per year for students from households with incomes up to £35,000.

Newcastle upon Tyne NE1 7RU
apps.ncl.ac.uk/contact-us/general-enquiry
ncl.ac.uk
nusu.co.uk

Overall ranking 34
(last year =30)

Accommodation
University provided places 5,444
Self-catered £98–£220 per week

Student numbers
Undergraduates 20,500
Applications per place 5.5:1
Overall offer rate 80.2%

Fees
UK fees £9,535
International fees £23,800–£30,600
Medicine £46,000

ncl.ac.uk/study/meet/undergraduate-open-day
ncl.ac.uk/undergraduate/fees-funding

University of Northampton

On the banks of the River Nene, Northampton's £330 million Waterside Campus has been the university's home since 2018. Courses have a practical, industry-focused edge and the university aims to banish digital poverty by giving all full-time UK undergraduates entering in 2025 a free laptop.

Everyone gets £500 credit to spend on campus catering too, or the same amount discounted from their accommodation costs. Added to that, Northampton students won't miss a compulsory course trip due to expenses – because the university picks up the bill for their travel and accommodation.

A seven-place improvement in our main academic ranking to =118th is helped by a higher proportion of Northampton students achieving 2:1 or a first in their degree, and much improved student satisfaction with teaching quality – with Northampton up 30 places to =51st in our analysis of the National Student Survey (NSS). This is matched by a triple silver rating in the Teaching Excellence Framework (TEF 2023). It fares less positively for the broad student experience however (=94th, a ten-place decline), and Northampton's continuation rate remains a sticking point, with only 84.3% of new students still studying one year later (116th).

Even though the university increased the size of its submission to the latest Research Excellence Framework (REF 2021), it fell into the bottom ten in our research quality rating (122nd), against bigger gains at other universities.

Apprenticeship versions of nursing, physiotherapy and management degrees are new for 2025, as well as courses in physiotherapy; acting for stage and screen; graphic design; and hospitality management. A BA in criminal justice begins in 2026.

Courses typically ask for BBB to BCC. Contextual offers, typically DDD, are made to applicants who meet widening participation criteria, applied to about 10% of admissions in 2024. Approximately 17% of new starters arrived through clearing.

Each year, 3,500 students undertake a placement as part of their course with over 800 organisations. In our analysis of the national Graduate Outcomes survey, Northampton is 101st, based on 69.7% of leavers in highly skilled jobs or postgraduate study within 15 months.

The Northampton Employment Promise guarantees an internship of at least three months or a postgraduate course to any graduates who have not found full-time work within a year of graduating with at least a 2:2 degree or Higher National Diploma.

The university's sports dome is used for teaching as well as recreation. Student sports clubs are free. The Active Campus initiative features a mile-long trim trail, table tennis tables, table football, and lawn games.

All new full-time students are guaranteed a room in halls, either on or within five minutes' walk of the campus in the town centre or, for those who prefer, about five miles away with a shuttle bus link.

Northampton is joint 18th for its high proportion of students from non-selective state schools (96.4%) and joint 41st overall in England and Wales.

About two thirds (67%) of new entrants qualify for some form of financial assistance. Awards include fully funded accommodation for students who have left care or who are estranged from their families, and £1,500 scholarships to undergraduates from the area.

University Drive Northampton NN1 5PH
admissions@northampton.ac.uk
northampton.ac.uk
northamptonunion.com

Overall ranking =118
(last year 125)

Accommodation
University provided places 2,250
Self-catered £88–£195 per week

Student numbers
Undergraduates 7,945
Applications per place 4.1:1
Overall offer rate 86.3%

Fees
UK fees £9,535
International fees £15,700–£18,200

northampton.ac.uk/about-us/contact-us/open-days
northampton.ac.uk/study/fees-and-funding

Northumbria University

The northeast's top-ranked modern university is taking a giant leap in the space race. Powered by investments from the UK Space Agency and Lockheed Martin UK Space, Northumbria's £50 million North East Space Skills and Technology (NESST) centre on the City Campus is due to open in 2026. The future-facing hub for space skills, research and technology is designed to provide a talent pipeline for the UK's space industry. Northumbria's undergraduate degrees in aerospace and satellite engineering are ready for take-off in September 2026.

The biggest university in the northeast, Northumbria rose six places in our research quality index to 58th, based on our analysis of the latest Research Excellence Framework (REF 2021). Sport and exercise science, English language and literature, and geography and environmental studies did best.

When awarding Northumbria a silver rating overall in the Teaching Excellence Framework (TEF 2023), the judging panel reserved gold for the student outcomes aspect of the assessment, along with another silver for the student experience.

In our analysis of the latest National Student Survey Northumbria lost ground for teaching quality, at =83rd (down 15 places) but improved for students' evaluation of the wider experience (up 13 places to =42nd).

From 2026, with the opening of NESST, the university will offer a BEng/MEng in aerospace satellite engineering, as well as courses in financial mathematics, football coaching and performance, and electrical engineering top-up.

Most degree courses require 112 UCAS tariff points, with a small number needing up to 128 points. Contextual offers, made to just over a quarter of applicants in 2024, typically reduce this by 16 points.

More than 60% of Northumbria graduates progress into jobs in the northeast, cementing the university's proud record of producing more highly skilled employees in the region than any other university. It has committed to give all on-campus undergraduates access to experiential learning by the end of its Strategy 2030 period. Almost four in five (78.4%) graduates were in high-skilled jobs or postgraduate study 15 months after leaving, according to our analysis of the Graduate Outcomes survey.

In the heart of Newcastle, the City campus has had a £200 million upgrade over the past decade. There is a £30 million Sport Central facility, and nearly 30 competitive teams compete in British Universities and Colleges Sport (BUCS) fixtures, where their successes put Northumbria 23rd in the overall points table for 2024-25. Accommodation is guaranteed for all undergraduates who apply by June 30. About 35% of first-years live on campus.

Located in a region with among the lowest take-ups of higher education in the UK, Northumbria's recruitment of white working-class males (the most under-represented group in higher education) places it =23rd. The university draws 14.6% of its intake of students from areas of low participation and ranks 48th overall in our social inclusion index.

UK students may qualify for one of up to 40 Northumbria Undergraduate UK scholarships, worth £4,000 in the first year. There are a similar number of subject-specific scholarships worth £2,000-£3,500. There are also awards and bursaries of £2,000 for care leavers, carers and estranged undergraduates.

Sutherland Building Newcastle upon Tyne NE1 8ST
bc.applicantservice@northumbria.ac.uk
northumbria.ac.uk
mynsu.co.uk

Overall ranking 47
(last year 43)

Accommodation
University provided places 3,827
Self-catered £100-£206 per week

Student numbers
Undergraduates 18,810
Applications per place 3.9:1
Overall offer rate 91.2%

Fees
UK fees £9,535
International fees £19,350-£21,250

northumbria.ac.uk/study-at-northumbria/visit-northumbria/university-open-days
northumbria.ac.uk/study-at-northumbria/fees-funding

Norwich University of the Arts

Norwich University of the Arts – known as Norwich Arts – became a university only in 2012, evolving out of the Norwich School of Design, founded in 1845. Degrees in esports, electronic music and sound production, marketing, and computer science are among the new undergraduate options at Norwich University of the Arts. Fresh facilities have come on stream too, including an immersive visualisation laboratory and a virtual production studio. Redevelopment of Bank Plain, the university's 12th campus building, is partly complete. The grade-II-listed, high-ceilinged former Barclays Bank has room for student services and social spaces, and the final phase will realise ambitious plans for a flagship new library and archive.

With fewer than 3,000 students, Norwich Arts was still able to make an impact in the Research Excellence Framework (REF 2021), in which 71% of its work in art and design was assessed as world-leading or internationally excellent. This was a huge improvement compared with REF 2014, sending Norwich Arts 26 places up our research quality table to rank 61st.

The university was awarded triple gold – with the top rating overall, as well as for student experience and outcomes – in the latest Teaching Excellence Framework (TEF 2023). But rates of student satisfaction have been erratic, and have taken a steep dive this year. In our analysis of the latest National Student Survey (NSS), Norwich Arts falls 35 places to rank 111th for satisfaction with the undergraduate experience. Satisfaction with teaching quality has also evaporated (down 54 places to 108th). The faltering scores have contributed to a 23-place decline in our main academic ranking (to 104th) and the university finishes fourth out of the five specialist arts institutions this year.

Entry requirements range from 120 to 80 UCAS tariff points and offers also depend on the strength of an applicant's portfolio and their responses to questions during the admissions process. Norwich Arts does not make contextual offers.

Norwich Arts fosters wide-ranging industry collaborations to ensure that its courses are professionally relevant and students are supported in securing internships and placements. Our analysis of the Graduate Outcomes survey shows that 61.9% of graduates were in highly skilled jobs or postgraduate study 15 months after leaving Norwich Arts – which puts Norwich Arts above all other arts universities for graduate prospects, albeit in 121st place in our table.

The university has 650 rooms available and guarantees accommodation to first-years who want to live in the city.

Overall, Norwich Arts ranks 23rd in our social inclusion index for England and Wales. It leads a regional outreach network and succeeds in recruiting 19% of undergraduates from low-participation postcodes (23rd). It is in the top ten for its relatively low awarding gap between black and white students (-9.7%).

About 40 to 50% of entrants qualified for financial support in 2025. For students with a household income below £25,000, there is a contribution towards the cost of materials, equipment and other expenses. The university offers £1,000 a year to undergraduates who are in care or estranged from their parents. Scholarships include the Chancellor's Scholarship Fund, worth £9,250 per year, open to students of black or mixed black heritage.

Francis House 3–7 Redwell Street Norwich NR2 4SN
admissions@norwichuni.ac.uk
norwichuni.ac.uk
norwichsu.co.uk

Overall ranking 104
(last year 81)

Accommodation
University provided places 650
Self-catered £117–£234 per week

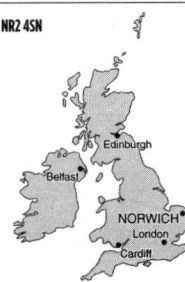

Student numbers
Undergraduates 2,665
Applications per place 3.7:1
Overall offer rate 79.9%

Fees
UK fees £9,535
International fees £18,500

norwichuni.ac.uk/courses/open-days/undergraduate-open-days
norwichuni.ac.uk/courses/undergraduate/fees-and-funding-ug/fees-funding

University of Nottingham

With nearly 9,000 new starters at Nottingham last year, this East Midlands institution is a powerhouse. As a founding member of the Russell Group, research continues to be a strong suit at the university where magnetic resonance imaging (MRI) scans were invented in the mid-1970s. For today's undergraduates, its broad choice of courses adds to its appeal – as do the 400 student-led societies on its beautiful 330-acre campus.

Nottingham is investing £16 million in creating a clinical teaching centre, and by September 2026, students will have access to eight new simulation suites including an operating theatre. Halls of residence are having an overhaul too.

Nottingham is especially hard to ignore for sporty students: the university takes second place in the latest British Universities and Colleges Sport (BUCS) league and access to its £40 million David Ross Sports Village is free as part of a university accommodation package.

In the latest Research Excellence Framework (REF 2021) the university's submission within pharmacy and health sciences, and economics did especially well: the university is 22nd in our research quality index.

Nottingham was rated silver overall in the Teaching Excellence Framework (TEF 2023), achieving silver for the student experience and gold for student outcomes.

Our analysis of the latest National Student Survey (NSS) shows growing contentment with the wider undergraduate experience, at =72nd (and 23 places higher than two years ago). However, students' evaluation of teaching quality has dipped seven places to 97th, based on the latest National Student Survey.

Thirteen new courses are planned for 2026 – five in mechanical engineering, and the remainder in modern languages, art history and music disciplines. However, more than 40 courses are being closed or suspended.

Entrants need from A*AA to BBB for undergraduate degree courses, and BBB-BCC for integrated foundation courses. About a third of new students each year qualify for Nottingham's contextual offer scheme, generally one A-level grade lower, or two for those entering through an access scheme. Almost a fifth (18.5%) entered through clearing in 2024.

Nottingham has long been a favourite recruiting ground for large employers. The High Fliers graduate market report placed it third in 2024-25. In our graduate outcomes analysis, Nottingham secures a top 20 result (19th) – based on 83.3% being in highly skilled jobs or further study within 15 months.

More than 8,500 rooms are available, 3,800 of them owned or managed by the university, including catered and self-catering accommodation. First-years who apply by the August deadline are guaranteed a space. About 40% of first-year students live on campus.

More than a third of Nottingham's students come from selective schools and less than a third are the first in their family to go to university – factors that anchor the university near the bottom of our social inclusion index (103rd). More than one third of Nottingham students come from ethnic minority backgrounds (49th) and the black awarding gap (-21.8%) is in the upper half nationally (52nd). About 30% of UK undergraduates qualify for assistance. A core bursary, where annual household income is less than £35,000, is worth £1,400 a year, with a further £1,000 award if other criteria are met.

University Park Nottingham NG7 2RD
nottingham.ac.uk/help-and-support/home/contact-us.html
nottingham.ac.uk
su.nottingham.ac.uk

Overall ranking 30
(last year =30)

Accommodation
University provided places 8,566
Catered £233-331 per week
Self-catered £129-£300 per week

Student numbers
Undergraduates 26,870
Applications per place 5.8:1
Overall offer rate 70.1%

Fees
UK fees £9,535
International fees £23,000-£38,400
Medicine £46,700

nottingham.ac.uk/open-days
nottingham.ac.uk/studywithus/what-next/fees-and-funding.aspx

Nottingham Trent University

Nottingham Trent University (NTU) has a burgeoning research profile and enjoys an unwavering position as the top-ranked modern university in the British Universities and Colleges Sport (BUCS) league where it eclipses all but eight universities.

A postgraduate centre opened in 2024, and NTU's focus on research is reflected in its 53rd place in our analysis of the latest Research Excellence Framework (REF 2021). Law, engineering, nursing and pharmacy were among the top performers, each with at least 98% of their submissions rated world-leading or internationally excellent.

In the latest Teaching Excellence Framework (TEF 2023), NTU achieved gold ratings overall and for the student experience, with silver for student outcomes.

In our analysis of the latest National Student Survey (NSS), NTU shows consistency, taking 30th place for satisfaction with teaching quality and =25th for satisfaction with the wider undergraduate experience.

There are more than 20 new BA and BSc courses on offer from 2025, including several in business management, economics and accounting, as well as computer science (games technology); and sport therapy and rehabilitation. Also new are BMus degrees in songwriting and vocal performance, and popular music performance; a BEng top-up in aerospace engineering; and HNC/HND in computing for England (netswork engineering).

Applicants need 128–96 UCAS tariff points (72–64 points for foundation year courses). NTU's contextual offers typically lower the A-level requirements for eligible applicants by two grades. About a quarter of new entrants benefitted from contextual offers in 2024. Over a fifth (22.7%) of the 2024 intake took up places through clearing.

Every course includes 240 hours of work experience, and a dedicated employment team can help students to find international opportunities. The university ranks 95th in our graduate prospects measure, based on the proportion of leavers in high-skilled jobs or postgraduate study 15 months after finishing their degrees.

Students are based at three sites in and around Nottingham, plus one in Mansfield and another in east London. The main City Campus combines revamped historic buildings with cutting-edge facilities, including mock law courts. The Clifton Campus occupies 32 hectares and features purpose-built facilities such as the Health and Allied Professions Centre and the Medical Technologies Innovation Facility. Clifton is also the base for NTU's extensive sports provision and the Dryden Enterprise Centre for start-ups. NTU Mansfield offers foundation degrees in partnership with Vision West Nottinghamshire College. Further afield in Whitechapel, east London, NTU has expanded into a new hub for digital arts, production and performance.

All first-year undergraduates are guaranteed accommodation in university-owned or partner-owned residences, with rooms allocated on a first-come, first-served basis.

More than a third of students are from ethnic minorities and 15.7% are from deprived areas (both in the top 50), but overall NTU sits outside the upper half of our social inclusion index, in 79th place. About a quarter of students received some financial assistance in 2024-25. Support includes a £750-a-year bursary and £170 opportunity bursary for students from households with incomes under £27,500.

---

50 Shakespeare Street Nottingham NG1 4FQ
enquiries@ntu.ac.uk
ntu.ac.uk
trentstudents.org

Overall ranking 46
(last year 42)

Accommodation
University provided places 4,943
Self-catered £117–£221 per week

Student numbers
Undergraduates 29,750
Applications per place 4.2:1
Overall offer rate 90.8%

Fees
UK fees £9,535
International fees £17,500–£18,250

ntu.ac.uk/study-and-courses/open-days
ntu.ac.uk/study-and-courses/undergraduate/fees-and-funding

The Open University

The Open University (OU) was founded in 1969 to promote educational opportunity for all and is still the model for distance learning around the world. More than 2.3 million students worldwide have benefitted from an OU education since its inception, and the OU attracts the biggest student numbers in the UK today. It has more than 100,000 undergraduates, and nearly 70% of OU students are already in work, balancing their careers with studying.

Tutorials, day schools or online forums and social networks allow students to keep in touch with each other and work is monitored by continual assessment, examination or assignment.

Our rankings do not include the OU as it does not easily compare with campus-based universities. But where comparisons can be made, it tends to perform well. In the latest Research Excellence Framework (REF 2021) 76% of the OU's research was rated world-leading or internationally excellent.

In the Teaching Excellence Framework (TEF 2023), the OU celebrated gold overall, with silver for the student experience and gold for student outcomes. The TEF panel commended "very high-quality teaching, assessment and feedback practices" that were "effective in supporting its students' learning, progression and attainment".

In line with the government and employers' demand for upskilling and retraining workers, the OU has expanded into Higher Technical Qualifications and is broadening the provision of continued professional development courses. More than 90 courses already include business agility, digital marketing and transformation to AI, counselling and design thinking.

Enrolments for degree apprenticeships have increased to more than 9,000, up from just over 7,000 a year ago. The OU offers a full range of undergraduate degree courses with no formal entry requirements and cheaper tuition fees (£7,784 per year) – opening doors to higher education that traditional campus-based institutions cannot. All students are classified as part-timers, regardless of whether they study at full-time intensity or not, which allows them to complete their studies without any of their benefits being affected. New courses include degrees in business and economics, business and law, and computer science with artificial intelligence.

The university is a major producer of educational media, maintaining an enduring partnership with the BBC since the 1970s, co-producing major series like Planet Earth III.

The OU's headquarters at Walton Hall in Milton Keynes serve as the base for about 1,200 full-time academics and about 250 postgraduates. The university employs 4,000 associate lecturers. Significant investment has boosted laboratory space by nearly 50% since 2016.

Despite the potential for isolation as a distance learner, the OU provides substantial support. This includes the OU Wellbeing app, the TalkCampus peer-to-peer platform, and Shout, a 24/7 text messaging service. Students also connect through online forums, social networks, and student association activities.

The OU provides extensive financial aid through fee reductions and targeted scholarships. In 2025-26, 2,409 Access module students were expected to gain a free place.

Walton Hall Milton Keynes MK7 6AA
general-enquiries@open.ac.uk
open.ac.uk
oustudents.com

Overall ranking N/A

Accommodation
Not applicable

Student numbers
Undergraduates 133,265
Applications per place N/A
Overall offer rate N/A

Fees
UK fees £7,784
International fees £8,184

open.ac.uk/courses/what-is-distance-learning/open-days
open.ac.uk/courses/fees-and-funding

University of Oxford

Oxford has slipped from 3rd to 4th in our table, where it ties with its ancient rival, Cambridge. The university is unsurpassed for its good honours, with 93% of students gaining firsts or 2.1s (1st nationally). Oxford is 4th in our research quality index, with a stellar set of results in the latest Research Excellence Framework (REF 2021), which rated 91% of its submissions world-leading or internationally excellent. In global rankings, which take account of the research profile but not student reviews, Oxford has been ranked 1st in the world by Times Higher Education (THE) every year from 2017 to 2025. In THE's subject rankings, Oxford has reigned unbeaten in computer science for seven years and has held the crown for clinical, pre-clinical and health subjects for 14 years – it earns the title of Medical School of the Year 2026.

The university achieved triple gold in the Teaching Excellence Framework (TEF 2023). However, feedback in the latest National Student Survey (NSS) hints of discontent: our new analysis puts Oxford in 124th place for the broad undergraduate experience. Although it does much better for teaching quality, it has dropped 25 places to 44th.

Oxford averaged the fifth-highest entry standards, with 197 UCAS points. The university does not make contextual offers but, like Cambridge, its admissions process takes an applicant's background into account. Oxford invites only the strongest contenders to interview and does not enter clearing. For 2024 entry, Oxford had 23,061 applications, and 3,245 undergraduates were accepted. Typically, it gets seven applications per place, though this varies significantly per course.

The university ties with Cambridge in =3rd place in our Graduate Outcomes survey analysis, based on 90.4% of graduates being in highly skilled work or postgraduate study 15 months after finishing their course. Oxford's careers service works with more than 500 industry partners, generating over 1,900 exclusive work experience opportunities each year.

Oxford is part of the UCAS system but there are significant peculiarities to applying. The deadline is much earlier than for most other universities: October 15. You can apply to either Oxford or Cambridge in any one year, but not both. Selection is in the hands of individual colleges, not the university.

Oxford's short eight-week terms mean that student life may be likened to a series of sprints. The university expects all students to study for at least 40 hours a week.

Students live in college accommodation. Most can be housed for at least two years, if not the full duration of their degree. Rents vary by college, and while meals are taken in the dining hall, most colleges allow students to opt out and have basic self-catering facilities.

The number of applicants accepted from state and independent schools is an enduring hot topic. In 2024, 66.2% of Oxford's UK undergraduates came from state schools (including selective grammars). Our social inclusion figures consider only the proportion from non-selective schools (51.6%, placing Oxford 111th in England and Wales for social inclusion). It does better with its proportion of students from ethnic minorities (28.3%, 61st) and its black awarding gap has narrowed to -7.6%, sending it into 7th place.

About one in four students receives funding.

University Offices Wellington Square
Oxford OX1 2JD
ox.ac.uk/undergraduate/ask
ox.ac.uk
oxfordsu.org

Overall ranking =4
(last year 3)

Accommodation
University provided places

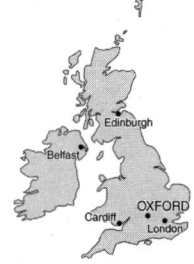

Student numbers
Undergraduates 12,265
Applications per place 7.3:1
Overall offer rate 20.3%

Fees
UK fees £9,535
International fees £32,260–£59,260
Medicine £46,600

ox.ac.uk/admissions/undergraduate/open-days-and-visits
ox.ac.uk/admissions/undergraduate/fees-and-funding/course-fees

Oxford Brookes University

From creative beginnings as the Oxford School of Art in 1865, the university is named in honour of the artist, craftsman and educator John Henry Brookes and gained university status in 1992. It was awarded silver in the government's Teaching Excellence Framework (TEF 2023), with a silver rating for student outcomes but only bronze for the student experience.

More than 400 researchers in 15 subject areas were entered for the latest Research Excellence Framework (REF 2021) and 70% of work was judged to be world-leading or internationally excellent. However, Oxford Brookes dropped 18 places in our research quality index, to =75th.

Rates of student satisfaction are on the way up. In our analysis of the latest National Student Survey (NSS), Oxford Brookes ranks =47th for satisfaction with teaching quality (up from 58th), and =53rd for the wider student experience (up 14 places).

Oxford Brookes falls out of the top 50 in our academic standings overall, slipping 19 places to 69th - not least because of a falling continuation rate (=70th) and low proportion of students gaining firsts and 2:1 degrees (65.6%, 121st).

An international focus has led to teaching partnerships with Metropolitan College Greece, and the Chengdu University of Technology, and 39 new courses are being added, including accounting options with a foundation year, history of art, Japanese, and electric motorsport. Eight apprenticeship programmes will be available from 2025, with 340 training places including nurses, architects and town planners.

The university does not make entry requirements public, but it does have a contextual admission policy. January starts, as well as the usual September entry, are offered for some courses.

In our analysis of the Graduate Outcomes survey, nearly four in five (77.8%) graduates had high-skilled jobs or had returned to study 15 months after their degrees ended.

A decade-long £220 million investment programme at Oxford Brookes is approaching its final stages. Under the Oxford Campus Vision, new student rooms are being built and teaching and library services are being pulled back from Harcourt Hill to consolidate operations at Headington.

The nightlife in halls, at the Students' Union - and in the wider, student-friendly city - is lively enough for most, if a little on the pricey side.

Sports facilities include a 25m swimming pool, multiple gyms, and Brookes Climb - Oxfordshire's leading climbing wall. The Oxford Brookes University Boat Club (OBUBC) is renowned for its triumphs at the Henley regatta, and at the Paris 2024 Olympic Games.

The university has 4,547 accommodation spaces and a room is guaranteed for all except those who enter via clearing. However, over the past five years, even those who came through clearing have been given a place.

Oxford Brookes has risen nine places in our social inclusion index this year, to 76th. Two thirds of the student population is over 21, putting Oxford Brookes in the top 10 for mature students. Just under a quarter (24%) of undergraduates received financial support in 2023-24. This is likely to grow in 2025-26, as the minimum household income threshold for low-income bursaries (£1,000-£1,250 a year) will rise from £35,000 to £45,000.

Headington Campus Oxford OX3 0BP
admissions@brookes.ac.uk
brookes.ac.uk
brookesunion.org.uk

Overall ranking 69
(last year 50)

Accommodation
University provided places 4,547
Self-catered £134-£225 per week

Student numbers
Undergraduates 10,420
Applications per place 1.8:1
Overall offer rate 83.9%

Fees
UK fees £9,535
International fees £16,750-£18,950

brookes.ac.uk/open-days
brookes.ac.uk/study/fees

University of Plymouth

A 12-place rise up our main academic rankings brings Plymouth into the top 60 (58th). The university earned triple gold in the government's Teaching Excellence Framework (TEF 2023) – overall and for the student experience and student outcomes. Assessors commended its "wide and readily available range of outstanding quality academic support ensuring a supportive learning environment for students". Based on our analysis of the latest National Student Survey (NSS), Plymouth ranks just outside the top half of UK universities for student satisfaction with teaching quality, and has risen ten places to =87th for their evaluation of the wider undergraduate experience.

The university has won three Queen's Anniversary awards for its research on microplastics and marine litter, and for widening access. Verified as a carbon neutral university in 2023, the University of Plymouth is pushing towards net zero and its environmental and ethical performance puts it =23rd in the 2024-25 People & Planet University League table.

Across all subjects, more than three quarters of its work submitted to the latest Research Excellence Framework (REF 2021) was rated world-leading or internationally excellent, and the university ranks 64th in our research quality index.

In May 2025 Plymouth announced job cuts to save costs amid the financial challenges facing UK universities. A spokesperson for the university said: "Plymouth is well placed to weather the storm, but we've seen increases to costs that are outside of our control, combined with a 10% drop in income, so we must act now to cut budgets."

Degree courses in marine conservation, music and sound production, and acting for screen, stage and future media are planned for 2026.

Courses require between 144 and 104 UCAS tariff points, excluding medicine and dentistry, where typical offers are as high as 152 points (A*AA). A contextual admissions policy allows "appropriate flexibility" to offer some places with lower tariff points than advertised.

Plymouth is in the top 50 (43rd) in our analysis of the Graduate Outcomes survey, with 79.7% of its graduates in highly skilled jobs or further study within 15 months. The university seeks employers' input to the curriculum and for careers support, while the Cube aims to inspire student and graduate entrepreneurs.

Plymouth has transformed its City Campus, adding a new design and engineering building; a moot court and a cold case unit; an updated Bloomberg suite is among resources at the Business School; and a brain research and imaging centre opened in 2021 at Plymouth Science Park.

A place in halls (or an accredited private alternative) is guaranteed to those who make Plymouth their first choice and apply by the deadline.

Plymouth is among the top 30 universities for its recruitment of white working-class male students (5.9%), one of the most under-represented groups in higher education. Overall, the university slipped slightly from 72nd place to 83rd in our social inclusion index. There are more than 20 bursaries and scholarships. Extra help is extended to students who have left care, are carers themselves, are estranged from their families or are from Gypsy, Roma and traveller communities.

Drake Circus Plymouth PL4 8AA
admissions@plymouth.ac.uk
plymouth.ac.uk
upsu.com

Overall ranking 58
(last year 70)

Accommodation
University provided places 1,917
Self-catered £134-£239 per week

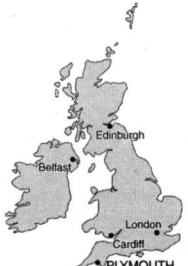

Student numbers
Undergraduates 13,820
Applications per place 5.2:1
Overall offer rate 78.3%

Fees
UK fees £9,535
International fees £17,600-£18,650
Medicine £40,700

plymouth.ac.uk/study/open-days
plymouth.ac.uk/study/fees

Plymouth Marjon University

Plymouth Marjon University students are well-placed for coast and countryside at the university's self-contained campus a few miles north of Plymouth. The campus offers sea views on a clear day, easy access to local sandy coves as well as Plymouth, and is on the doorstep of Dartmoor National Park.

A former teacher training college, Marjon is a consistent top-scorer for teaching quality and comes joint 8th in the UK for students' evaluation of their teaching in our analysis of the latest National Student Survey (NSS). It is also in the top 30 for the wider undergraduate experience.

Marjon was awarded a gold rating overall in the Teaching Excellence Framework (TEF 2023), underpinned by gold for the student experience and silver for student outcomes. Ofsted rated its early-years provision outstanding, with training for primary and secondary age rated good.

Marjon benefitted in our rankings from its decision to enter the Research Excellence Framework (REF 2021), after opting out in 2014, although it placed towards the bottom of our research quality index, at 118th. The university is also held back in our main academic table by its continuation rate (placing 97th), with only 86.8% of students projected to carry on from the first to the second year of their studies – although this is often a side-effect of diverse student populations.

Marjon operates franchise programmes in colleges elsewhere in the southwest of England in subjects ranging from business management to professional golf. It also has a partnership with Bristol School of Acting.

Courses in football performance coaching and community football coaching will begin in September 2026. There were no planned course closures at the time of writing.

Entry requirements range from 120 to 64 UCAS tariff points, and a contextual offer system will begin for 2026 admissions. In 2024, 16% of entrants gained their places through clearing.

Marjon's vocationally focused courses have close links with local employers in relevant fields. The university is 62nd in our analysis of the Graduate Outcomes survey, with 75.7% of its graduates in highly skilled jobs or further study 15 months after leaving university.

A new Health Education and Community Wellbeing Hub has opened on campus, thanks to £5.8 million of funding from the Office for Students. The facility includes clinical skill, diagnostic and simulation laboratories, supporting the university's launch of clinical programmes such as nursing and allied health professions.

The thriving sports science courses have access to a rehabilitation clinic and a sports science laboratory with a climate chamber and an anti-gravity treadmill.

First-years holding a firm offer take priority in the allocation of the 400 self-catered rooms, although there are no accommodation guarantees.

Widening participation is deeply ingrained, and Marjon ranks 12th in our social inclusion index. Based in an area with low take-up of higher education, Marjon succeeds in recruiting the fifth-highest proportion (8.7%) of under-represented white working-class male students, and the joint seventh-highest proportion of disabled students (29.2%).

Grants of £2,000 a year are available for care leavers and students who are estranged from their families. Sports performance scholarships include in-kind support worth up to £4,000 a year.

Derriford Road Plymouth PL6 8BH
admissions@marjon.ac.uk
marjon.ac.uk
marjon.ac.uk/msu/

Overall ranking 70
(last year 75)

Accommodation
University provided places 400
Self-catered £115–£139 per week

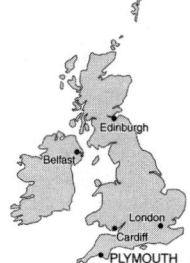

Student numbers
Undergraduates 1,495
Applications per place 3.6:1
Overall offer rate 76.6%

Fees
UK fees £9,535
International fees £14,600

marjon.ac.uk/courses/open-days
marjon.ac.uk/courses/fees-and-funding

University of Portsmouth

The University of Portsmouth's low dropout rates among undergraduates help the university climb three places in our main academic ranking. It is also among a minority of universities to reach the top half of our main academic table (52nd) while achieving a similar ranking in our social inclusion index (46th).

Portsmouth has links with London – it has a campus in Walthamstow, while a partnership with King's College London (KCL) enhances dental clinical experience. Under the same partnership, the second cohort of Portsmouth medical students enrolled in autumn 2025 on a four-year graduate-entry course with a medical degree awarded by KCL.

Portsmouth earned gold overall in the Teaching Excellence Framework (TEF 2023), underpinned by gold for the student experience and silver for student outcomes. The TEF panel said Portsmouth showed outstanding tailored "approaches that are highly effective". Students concur. Their feedback keeps Portsmouth in the upper reaches of our latest National Student Survey (NSS) analysis, despite a dip in form this year which leaves Portsmouth =41st for teaching quality (down from =28th) and =32nd for the broad experience (a nine-place decline).

A growing focus on research paid off in Portsmouth's results in the Research Excellence Framework (REF 2021), which moved the university into the top half of our research quality index (61st). Physics led the way with 100% of its REF submission rated world-leading or internationally excellent.

Four new courses are planned for 2026: musical theatre, humanities and social sciences, counterterrorism, intelligence and cybercrime, and marketing management.

Portsmouth did not supply up-to-date figures for admissions or entry offers, citing commercial sensitivity. In 2023-24, new entrants averaged 114 UCAS points, putting Portsmouth just inside the top 100 for entry standards (=91st). After a ten-year downward trend in applications, 2024 had an uplift of 1,525 applicants, taking the total to 21,450.

Entrants benefit from Portsmouth's new "connected degrees" approach, which allows students to take a work placement year before their final year, or after to explore options. Based on three-quarters (75.1%) of leavers being employed in highly skilled jobs or postgraduate study 15 months after finishing their degree, Portsmouth ranks =67th for graduate prospects.

A £250 million development programme is set to transform the main City Campus over the next decade. Much of the recent investment is in simulation facilities to give students hands-on training. The university's facilities at the Ravelin Sports Centre include a ski simulator as well as squash courts and a 175-station fitness centre.

New students who apply by the June deadline and make Portsmouth their firm choice are guaranteed accommodation. About 60% of first-years live in halls.

The university has entered the top 50 in our social inclusion index (46th) and performs strongly in the numbers of disabled students (22nd), white working-class males (26th) and those from low-participation areas (=29th).

Financial support includes a £500 annual bursary for all students with a household income of less than £25,000 and a care leaver bursary worth £1,700 a year. Sport scholarships worth between £2,000 and £6,000 are awarded to about 20 talented athletes a year.

University House Winston Churchill Avenue
Portsmouth PO1 2UP
admissions@port.ac.uk
port.ac.uk
upsu.net

Overall ranking 52
(last year 55)

Accommodation
University provided places 3,851
Catered £159-£206 per week
Self-catered £110-£191 per week

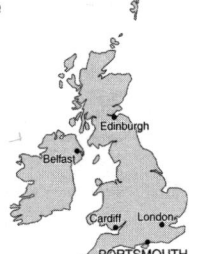

Student numbers
Undergraduates 15,110
Applications per place 4.2:1
Overall offer rate 83.9%

Fees
UK fees £9,535
International fees £17,200-£19,200

port.ac.uk/study/open-days/undergraduate-open-days
port.ac.uk/study/undergraduate/undergraduate-fees-and-student-finance

Queen Margaret University, Edinburgh

Students can sample a smorgasbord of careers at Queen Margaret University (QMU) through a scheme that pairs them with four mentors. It is the latest employment-focused innovation from the university, which was founded in 1875 as a cookery school and named after St Margaret, the 11th-century wife of King Malcolm III of Scotland. QMU moved to its purpose-built campus in 2007 (the same year it gained university status) on the southeastern side of Edinburgh.

QMU's ambitions are big but the university remains relatively small, with fewer than 5,000 full-time students at the campus – creating a close-knit community feel.

QMU has recorded one of the biggest improvements in our main academic table year-on-year, gaining 39 places to rank 66th. It is a return to form, fuelled in part by improved feedback in the latest National Student Survey (NSS), which puts it =47th for teaching quality (up 54 places) and =91st for the wider student experience (a 29-place gain) in our analysis. There has also been an upturn in good honours putting QMU in the top 20 (19th) for this metric.

QMU ranks 96th on the basis of the latest Research Excellence Framework (REF 2021). Some world-leading or internationally excellent work was identified in seven research areas. The best results were found in communications, cultural and media studies; speech and language science; and nursing and allied health professions.

Students are also able to work towards QMU qualifications at partner institutions in Kathmandu in Nepal, Tashkent in Uzbekistan, and Colombo in Sri Lanka.

A BA in digital and graphic design begins in 2026.

Nearly all UK entrants are from Scotland and apply with Highers. Entry requirements for those sitting A-levels range from AAB to CCC. Contextual offers are typically two grades lower than standard.

A mentoring scheme, an entrepreneur in residence and a new internship scheme offering students paid summer placements at the university are designed to boost graduate skills. But for now, with only 67% of graduates in highly skilled work or further study 15 months after leaving, QMU is 111th in our analysis of the Graduate Outcomes survey.

Facilities for living and learning are on QMU's self-contained campus. The library has been upgraded and there is a new Outdoor Learning Hub especially useful for trainee primary teachers, but all students are welcome to connect with the natural world.

With 800 spaces, the university does not guarantee accommodation, but it prioritises disabled and care-experienced students, as well as those from outside the EH postcode. Just less than half of first-years (44.7%) live on campus.

The university ranks 3rd out of 15 in our social inclusion index for Scotland. It has the second-highest proportion of both disabled students (7.6%), and of those who are the first in their family to go to university (49.5%).

In 2024, 13 of QMU's 36 undergraduates from the rest of the UK (not including Scotland, which has its own funding system) qualified for university bursaries of £500–£2,000 a year. QMU also supports eight undergraduates to access the Robertson Trust Scholar Scheme, via match funding of up to £4,250 a year.

University Drive Musselburgh Edinburgh EH21 6UU
admissions@qmu.ac.uk
qmu.ac.uk
qmusu.org.uk

Overall ranking 66
(last year =105)

Accommodation
University provided places 800
Self-catered £145–£176 per week

Student numbers
Undergraduates 3,500
Applications per place 6.6:1
Overall offer rate 62.3%

Fees
Scots fees £0–£1,820
International fees £9,725–£17,325
RUK fees £9,535

qmu.ac.uk/open-days-and-meeting-us/undergraduate-open-days
qmu.ac.uk/study-here/fees-and-funding

Queen Mary, University of London

The "elite Eastender", Queen Mary University of London (QMUL) combines its Russell Group status with a deep-seated mission to improve lives through education. With nine Nobel laureates among its alumni and former staff, its research ranks 16th in the UK. Yet it is equally known for its trailblazing work on social mobility, making it a rare institution that excels in both academic league tables and social inclusion.

In the latest Research Excellence Framework (REF 2021), 92% of QMUL's submission was assessed as world-leading or internationally excellent, with drama and film departments producing some of the best results, along with politics and international studies, engineering, economics and history. This academic power is reflected in its 35-place climb in the QS World University Rankings over the past two years.

Its historic 18th-century roots in London's East End give it a distinctive focus on social justice. In the modern era, it was the first Russell Group university to deliver degree apprenticeships, a provision now rated as "outstanding" by Ofsted.

The latest Teaching Excellence Framework (TEF 2023) awarded QMUL silver overall, praising its "very high rates of continuation and completion." However, it received bronze for student experience, which aligns with its historically mixed results in the National Student Survey (NSS) where it has tended to yo-yo up and down the lower reaches. In our analysis of NSS 2025, QMUL is =91st (down seven places) for satisfaction with the wider undergraduate experience but has gained ground on satisfaction with teaching quality (up nine places to 112th).

Standard offers range from A*AA to BBB at A-level. An excellent contextual offer scheme can reduce entry requirements by up to three grades for eligible students. Demand is high, with applications passing 42,000 for the first time in 2024, when more than a fifth (22%) of new students were accepted through clearing.

QMUL ranks in the top 50 (=46th) for graduate prospects. Almost four in five graduates (78.6%) are in highly skilled work or further study 15 months after completion according to our analysis of the Graduate Prospects survey. This is supported by about 150 annual employer events, a "micro-internship" programme connecting students with London businesses, and funding for full internships, many of them with local organisations.

Accommodation is guaranteed either on or near campus to first-years who have a firm offer and apply by June 30.

QMUL has the sixth-highest intake of students from black and minority ethnic backgrounds (77.1%). Crucially, it also has the narrowest black awarding gap in England and Wales (-3%), demonstrating its outstanding commitment to ensuring students from all backgrounds can succeed. Extensive outreach schemes help, such as Access to Queen Mary, an 18-month programme helping to prepare students for higher education. There is targeted information for families who are supporting their student in progressing to university, and travel bursaries for prospective applicants who receive free school meals. More than a third of undergraduates are expected to receive financial support, with the majority qualifying for the Queen Mary Bursary, worth up to £1,700 a year depending on household income.

---

327 Mile End Road London E1 4NS
admissions@qmul.ac.uk
qmul.ac.uk
qmsu.org

Overall ranking 35
(last year 39)

Accommodation
University provided places 3,167
Self-catered £165–£416 per week

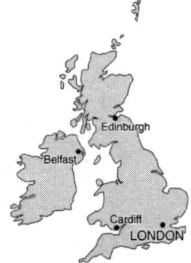

Student numbers
Undergraduates 17,190
Applications per place 8.9:1
Overall offer rate 64.5%

Fees
UK fees £9,535
International fees £25,000–£29,950
Medicine £49,950

qmul.ac.uk/undergraduate/openday
qmul.ac.uk/undergraduate/feesandfunding

Queen's University, Belfast

The number one university in Northern Ireland is on the cusp of the UK top 20 this year, boosted by a five-place rise in our main academic league table. Students are based at Queen's University Belfast's (QUB) historic campus on the south side of the city, where investment of £700 million over two decades is keeping this Russell Group university up to speed with fellow research heavyweights. Improved feedback in the National Student Survey (NSS) has, in our analysis, lifted it by 42 places in two years to rank =32nd for the student experience.

In the latest Research Excellence Framework (REF 2021), Queen's submissions in agriculture, food and veterinary science; health and biomedical sciences; law; and engineering produced the best results. Overall, the university is 35th in our research quality rating. It is 199th in the QS World University Rankings 2026.

The university won a seventh Queen's Anniversary prize for higher education in 2020 for its pioneering work to facilitate collaboration between schools of different faiths. Queen's and University College Dublin signed a memorandum of understanding in 2022 to enhance co-operation in research and innovation in areas of mutual strength, and Queen's is involved in 43 of the 62 projects to be funded by the Irish government's €37.3 million North-South Research Programme.

Queen's is not closing any degrees in 2025 or 2026 and there are no new courses planned for 2026. The first education studies students enrolled in 2025.

Entry grades range from A*AA for medicine and for actuarial science with risk management, to BBC/BCC for nursing and midwifery degrees. Students who meet widening participation criteria are eligible for the Pathways Opportunity Programme, which undercuts a conditional offer by up to two grades. Queen's is consistently in demand, with applications nearing 30,000 in the 2024 admissions cycle and around 5,000 new students accepted onto courses.

The university nurtures links with business and industry partners to create opportunities for internships, placements and graduate roles. Queen's ranks 9th in the UK for graduate prospects, based on our analysis of the Graduate Outcomes survey, showing that 87.1% of its undergraduates had found high-skilled jobs or were engaged in postgraduate study 15 months after finishing their degrees.

There are more than 200 student clubs and societies, and the campus is a 15-minute walk to Belfast city centre and its nightlife. However, the social scene is centred around the Students' Union, which forms part of the £42 million One Elmwood student centre. The arts are well supported on campus, where there is an arthouse cinema, a gallery and a studio theatre as well as the new writing centre.

First-years are guaranteed accommodation as long as they meet the deadline at the end of June.

Most undergraduates come from Northern Ireland, two thirds from grammar schools, which educate a much larger proportion of the province's population than elsewhere in the UK. This is why we cannot include the Northern Ireland universities in our social inclusion index.

About three in ten undergraduates receive some form of financial support.

University Road Belfast BT7 1NN
admissions@qub.ac.uk
qub.ac.uk
q-su.org

Overall ranking 21
(last year 26)

Accommodation
University provided places 4,160
Self-catered £89–£225 per week

Student numbers
Undergraduates 16,590
Applications per place 6.0:1
Overall offer rate 73.5%

Fees
UK fees £4,855 (NI/ROI)
International fees £22,400–£26,600
RUK fees £9,535
Medicine £50,180

qub.ac.uk/Study/Undergraduate/open-days
qub.ac.uk/Study/Feesandfinance

University of Reading

There's space to breathe on Reading's 300-acre Whiteknights Campus, which has a lake, a meadow and woodlands, as well as academic facilities to support the university's broad course offering.

The university has been recognised for its award-winning research and teaching in climate change. The new Global Sustainability Leaders Scholarship provides a generous £6,000 per year to up to 400 students (300 in 2025) with AAA at A-level (or AAB for contextual offer-holders). Scholars will also benefit from sustainability leadership and development opportunities and career support. Reading is the inaugural Times and Sunday Times University of the Year for Scholarships and Bursaries 2026.

Archaeology, art and design, and earth systems and environmental sciences contributed some of the university's best results in the latest Research Excellence Framework (REF 2021). Overall, however, Reading fell nine places in our research quality index to =38th, because gains were greater at other institutions. Reading is in the top 200 universities in the world for the second year running, at 194th in the QS World University Rankings 2026.

Reading was rated silver in the government's Teaching Excellence Framework (TEF 2023). Assessors commended its "use of research in relevant disciplines, scholarship, professional practice and employer engagement". A year ago, it took our Sustainable University of the Year award, and is 4th in the UK for its environmental and ethical performance, ranked by People and Planet 2024-25. In our analysis of the latest National Student Survey (NSS), the university is 50th for the broad experience and 94th for satisfaction with teaching quality.

From 2026, Reading will offer biomedical engineering with professional experience; and environmental science with a study year abroad. Reading requires AAA for its integrated master's course in applied psychology. The lowest requirements of CCD apply to agriculture and foundation courses. Contextual offers – typically two grades lower – made up a third of all offers in 2024. Reading's employer partnerships provide internships, placements, and live projects across sectors such as finance, technology, health and sciences, and construction. Links with key organisations include Enterprise Mobility, EY, Teach First, PepsiCo, and the Environment Agency. The university is in the top 40 (40th) in our analysis of the Graduate Outcomes survey, with 80.4% of Reading graduates being employed in highly skilled work or further study within 15 months of finishing their degrees.

New undergraduates who apply by the end of August are guaranteed accommodation.

More than 40% of students are from black and ethnic minority backgrounds, putting Reading in the top half of UK universities for the diversity of its intake. It also has a relatively high proportion of disabled students (22%, 32nd). Overall the university ranks =91st in our social inclusion index for England and Wales.

In addition to the Global Sustainability Leaders Scholarship, there are 100 Vice-chancellor Global Scholarships awarded every year to international students, each worth £4,000, as well as sports scholarships of up to £2,000. The Reading Bursary, offered to students from low-income households, is worth up to £1,500.

Whiteknights PO Box 217 Reading RG6 6AH
reading.ac.uk/question
reading.ac.uk
readingsu.co.uk

Overall ranking 33
(last year =24)

Accommodation
University provided places 4,982
Catered £173–£294 per week
Self-catered £158–£347 per week

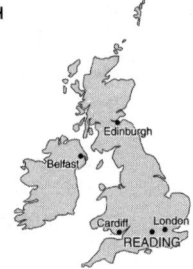

Student numbers
Undergraduates 12,880
Applications per place 5.4:1
Overall offer rate 86.4%

Fees
UK fees £9,535
International fees £25,850–£30,650

reading.ac.uk/ready-to-study/visiting-and-open-days/opendays
reading.ac.uk/ready-to-study/study/fees-and-funding

Robert Gordon University

Named after the Aberdeen-born merchant trader and philanthropist, Robert Gordon University (RGU) has more than 275 years' history of education. Awarded university status in 1992, it was formerly our leading modern institution for graduate employment, placing in the top 20 for graduate prospects during some of the peak years of North Sea oil and gas production (and is still in the top 40). RGU is up 11 places to rank 50th overall in our main academic league table.

Much as Aberdeen itself has shifted its focus to opportunities in decommissioning and renewable energy, so too has the university adapted: its National Subsea Centre, opened in 2023, is working in the North Sea and worldwide to develop smart digital and engineering technologies to enable a faster and more sustainable transition to a net zero energy basin.

RGU's best results in the latest Research Excellence Framework (REF 2021) were in computer science and engineering. Our analysis of the National Student Survey (NSS) puts RGU =28th in the UK for teaching quality, although there has been a dip in form for the broad experience this year, with RGU in =78th place (down from =36th).

Entry standards are high – an average of 157 UCAS tariff points. At the highest end, courses ask for AAB at A-level; at the lowest, CC. For Scottish Highers it's BCC and AABBB. About one in ten offers are contextual. Applications rose by 3.4% year-on-year in 2024, and 10.8% of entrants joined through clearing. Three part-time online BSc courses are closing in 2025-26, to be replaced by BEng degrees: electronic and electrical engineering; mechanical engineering; and renewable energy engineering. More than four in five (81.6%) graduates were working in highly skilled jobs or enrolled in postgraduate study 15 months after earning their degree. RGU has risen nine places in our graduate prospects index to rank 32nd.

At the Garthdee Campus on the banks of the River Dee, where all teaching is based, the landmark green-glass library tower symbolises the university's ambitions after £120 million of investment. A digital laboratory space with capacity for 200 students has opened above the library, for teaching or independent study and with laptops to borrow. There is a drilling simulator that replicates real-life settings, while at the Energy Transition Institute students have access to drilling and advanced rig training using 3D graphics and a control cabin complete with drillers' chairs.

All students are entitled to free RGU Sport membership, with three gyms, a swimming pool, badminton courts, bouldering and climbing facilities, and a sports hall available.

All first-year students can be accommodated, although the university stops short of a guarantee and rooms offered may not be in the first choice of location. About three in ten first-years live on campus.

RGU has risen from tenth to fourth place out of the 15 universities in our Scottish social inclusion index this year. It has a relatively low proportion of students from minority ethnic backgrounds (13.4%, 9th), but has the lowest awarding gap of any Scottish university.

About half of students receive some financial support. A small number of access scholarships are offered to students who meet widening participation criteria.

Garthdee House Garthdee Road Aberdeen AB10 7AQ
admissions@rgu.ac.uk
rgu.ac.uk
rguunion.co.uk

Overall ranking 50
(last year 61)

Accommodation
University provided places 903
Self-catered £99–£184 per week

Student numbers
Undergraduates 8,180
Applications per place 4.5:1
Overall offer rate 76.1%

Fees
Scots fees £0–£1,820
International fees £17,670–£27,650
RUK fees £7,220

rgu.ac.uk/study/visit-us/open-days
rgu.ac.uk/study/finance-funding

University of Roehampton

A campus university in the capital, Roehampton occupies 54 acres in southwest London, between Putney and Richmond upon Thames. A future-facing approach to higher education prevails at this former teacher training college, which gained university status in 2004. A Sustainable Engineering and Technology Centre opened on campus this term to support newly-launched degrees in the subject area, and Roehampton was an early adopter of esports courses. Roehampton launched the UK's first esports scholarships and Europe's first Women in Esports scholarships, both worth £2,000 a year.

Roehampton is in our top 50 for research – the highest ranking for a non-specialist modern university. In the Research Excellence Framework (REF 2021) more than three-quarters of the university's research across 11 subject areas was rated as world-leading or internationally excellent, especially in the arts and humanities. Dance, drama and education had some of the best results.

The university earned triple silver in the Teaching Excellence Framework (TEF 2023), and the assessors noted that "exceptional support for staff professional development and excellent academic practice [was] embedded" across the university. Overall, Roehampton has slipped further outside our top 100, falling six places to =124th. It is held back by relatively low entry standards (129th), first and 2:1 degrees (63.2%, 125th) and graduate prospects (=128th). But positive student feedback about the broader undergraduate experience put Roehampton in the upper half of our analysis of the results of the latest National Student Survey (NSS) (=55th).

New degrees from 2026: fashion management; fashion marketing; and nutrition and dietetics. Education courses remain a focus for the university, which has partnerships with over 700 schools. Training for primary school teachers was rated outstanding by Ofsted in 2023, while secondary school teacher training was rated good.

New entrants averaged 95 UCAS points and applicants eligible for a contextual offer are afforded flexibility on the standard requirements. Student numbers have fallen: in 2024 just under 1,400 first-years started courses at Roehampton, down 46% compared with a decade ago.

With only 58.1% of graduates in high-skilled jobs or further study 15 months after finishing their degree, Roehampton is =128th for graduate prospects.

Roehampton prides itself on having the friendly atmosphere of a traditional campus, yet it's only 20 minutes away from central London. The parkland site houses the £13 million Sir David Bell Building, opened as a digital media hub in 2020, where students have access to industry-standard film studios, editing suites and newsrooms, with facilities for photography and sound production. With more than 1,600 rooms on campus, first-years who apply by the deadline are guaranteed accommodation.

Roehampton has broken into the top 10 in our social inclusion index (=8th). Almost 60% of students are the first in their family to attend university (59.4%, 17th) and 97.6% are from non-selective state schools (=10th). Just over 70% of students are from black and ethnic minority backgrounds (11th) and the black awarding gap has closed in a year from 25.6% (77th) to 14.5% (22nd).

The £1,000 Roehampton Bursary is awarded in the first year to students who receive the full maintenance loan.

**Grove House Roehampton Lane
London SW15 5PJ**
ug.information@roehampton.ac.uk
roehampton.ac.uk
roehamptonstudent.com

Overall ranking =124
(last year 118)

Accommodation
University provided places 1,675
Self-catered £146 per week

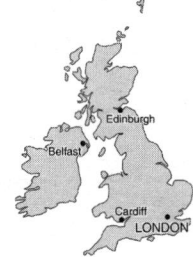

Student numbers
Undergraduates 5,905
Applications per place 4.9:1
Overall offer rate 81.7%

Fees
UK fees £9,535
International fees £16,950–£19,500

roehampton.ac.uk/study/open-days
roehampton.ac.uk/study/fees-and-funding

Royal Agricultural University

Established in 1845 after a meeting of the Fairford and Cirencester Farmers' Club, concerned at a lack of government support for agricultural education, the RAU gained university status in 2013. Today the institution makes the most of its international reputation as the first high-level agricultural college in the English-speaking world. The RAU has six research clusters – sustainability, regeneration and biodiversity in agriculture; livestock health and welfare; food policy, quality and security; equine science; rural economy; and cultural heritage.

Half of the work submitted by RAU to the Research Excellence Framework (REF 2021) was considered world-leading or internationally excellent, leading to 101st place in our research index. While rated triple silver in the government's Teaching Excellence Framework (TEF 2023), feedback from undergraduates in the latest National Student Survey (NSS) was less favourable. The RAU is in last place (130th) in our teaching quality rankings and 125th for the wider undergraduate experience. The poor rates of student satisfaction contribute to RAU's overall rank in our main academic league table, again in final place (130th). Compounding its position, only 66.9% of students achieved first-class or 2:1 degrees (118th).

The RAU launched the first undergraduate programmes at the International Agriculture University (IAU) in Tashkent as part of a long-term partnership with the Uzbekistan Ministry of Agriculture. A degree in bloodstock and equine performance management is new from September 2025. In 2026, rural land and property management joins the portfolio.

Two degrees are closing in 2025 (environment, food and society; applied farm management) and two in 2026 (applied equine science and business; international equine and agricultural business management).

Requirements range from 104 to 96 UCAS points for BSC degrees, and 64 to 56 for FdSc courses. Contextual offers reduce these by 8 points.

Students can spend a sandwich year in industry as part of their degree, and entrepreneurial activity is encouraged. However, with only 68.7% of graduates in high-skilled jobs or further study 15 months after their degrees, RAU is in the bottom 25 (109th) in our analysis of graduate prospects.

Set on a bucolic 25-acre campus, facilities include Farm491, an agritech incubator and innovation space focused on the future of farming and food systems. There is also an equestrian centre providing stabling and livery facilities as well as teaching space.

Accommodation is allocated on a first-come, first-served basis. To date, all first-years wanting to live in have been accommodated, but there are no guarantees.

The RAU has entered the top 100 of our latest social inclusion index, after an impressive 16-place improvement. Spurring its rise is RAU's unsurpassed proportion of disabled students among its intake (39.4%). It also does relatively well on the recruitment of white working-class male students (3.6%, ranking RAU =58th).

Efforts to broaden its appeal include two Next Generation scholarships, which pay £6,000 a year to eligible students from a minority ethnic community. About one in 11 students in 2024 qualified for some form of financial help.

Stroud Road Cirencester GL7 6JS
admissions@rau.ac.uk
rau.ac.uk
rau.ac.uk/student-life/social/students-union

Overall ranking 130
(last year 131)

Accommodation
University provided places 270
Catered £203–£270 per week
Self-catered £201–£270 per week

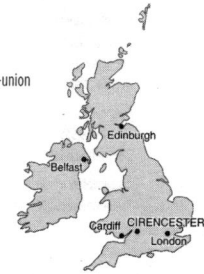

Student numbers
Undergraduates 780
Applications per place 4.5:1
Overall offer rate n/a

Fees
UK fees £9,535
International fees £16,950

rau.ac.uk/courses/open-days-and-events
rau.ac.uk/student-life/undergraduate-funding

Royal Holloway, University of London

Pioneering from the outset, Royal Holloway, University of London, was formed from two colleges, both among the first places in Britain where women could access higher education (the novelist George Eliot was an alumna). Royal Holloway is pushing boundaries in the UK's film, TV, and performance industries as the lead partner for the CoStar (convergent screen technologies and performance in real time) National Lab for research and development in the creative industries – a £75.6 million investment by the UK government. It is also a centre of excellence in cybersecurity research.

In an impressive performance by Royal Holloway in the latest Research Excellence Framework (REF 2021), 88% of its work was assessed as world-leading or internationally excellent, led by success in music, communication and media studies, and geography, ranking the university =26th in our research quality rating. There are 55 research centres across wide-ranging academic fields, from the Centre for Algorithms and Applications to the Centre for Workplace Research in Asian Societies. Royal Holloway gained triple silver in the Teaching Excellence Framework (TEF 2023) and won praise for "the use of research in relevant disciplines, innovation, scholarship, professional practice and employer engagement". Rising rates of student satisfaction, based on our analysis of the latest National Student Survey (NSS), rank Royal Holloway =30th (up 18 places) for the broad experience and =83rd (up ten places) for satisfaction with teaching quality.

A two-year Diploma of Higher Education in health studies and a one-year Certificate of Higher Education in health and social care are new for 2025, and a BSc in marketing is in development for 2026 entry. Thirty-six BA and BSc courses have been discontinued (check the university website for further details).

Standard offers range from AAA to CCC with a contextual offer policy up to two grades lower for applicants who qualify under a range of widening access criteria.

Royal Holloway's Skills for Choice and Opportunity framework aims to support students in building 12 key skills required by employers. Responses to the Graduate Outcomes survey place the university in the top half (45th) for the proportion of graduates in professional-level jobs or further study 15 months after finishing their degree.

Royal Holloway has its own observatory and recently opened a £2 million hangar as part of the Omnidrome Research and Innovation Centre, which has 895 sq m space for the development and testing of specialist air, land, and water drones.

There are 2,867 study bedrooms for undergraduates and 20% of the spaces are catered. Entrants are guaranteed a place as long as they make Royal Holloway their firm choice and meet the application deadline.

Nearly half of Royal Holloway's student population is from an ethnic minority background (32nd) and 26% of new undergraduates entered with a contextual offer in September 2024. The university is =71st overall in our social inclusion index, up 11 places compared with our previous edition.

More than three in ten UK undergraduates qualified for bursaries in 2025. Payments range from £500 a year to £3,000 a year for those from low-income households, care leavers and mature students.

Egham Hill Egham TW20 0EX
royalholloway.ac.uk/applicationquery
royalholloway.ac.uk
su.rhul.ac.uk

Overall ranking 32
(last year 34)

Accommodation
University provided places 3,099
Catered £123–216 per week
Self-catered £139–£220 per week

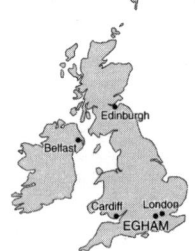

Student numbers
Undergraduates 10,260
Applications per place 5.1:1
Overall offer rate 87.5%

Fees
UK fees £9,535
International fees £21,400–£28,900

royalholloway.ac.uk/student-life/visit-royal-holloway/open-days
royalholloway.ac.uk/studying-here/fees-and-funding/

University of St Andrews

Prince William praised the sense of community he found at the University of St Andrews and this feedback is echoed by students two decades later at Scotland's top university, which retains its 2nd place in our rankings. It is 4th in the UK for student experience and 7th for teaching quality in our latest National Student Survey (NSS) analysis. The university and its diverse international student body dominate the small Fife seaside town – accounting for more than half of the population – and students benefit from plenty of direct contact with leading academics.

There are four faculties: arts, divinity, medicine and science. A flexible four-year degree structure is a big draw, allowing students to take multiple subjects before specialising. This academic breadth is supported by formidable research power. In the latest Research Excellence Framework (REF 2021), 88% of its work was assessed as world-leading or internationally excellent, earning it 25th place in our research quality index.

Through its £300 million Making Waves campaign, the university is increasing funding for bursaries and scholarships and investing in new academic posts to attract leading researchers, which will directly benefit undergraduates through expert mentorship.

The first students began a new five-year medical degree in September 2025. The programme focuses on community healthcare and clinical training will be in NHS settings across Fife. The university has also broadened its joint honours offerings, allowing undergraduates to combine disciplines such as Arabic, comparative literature, and management.

The lowest A-level entry requirements are ABB, rising to A*A*A (or BBBB to AAAAB for Scottish Highers). As part of its efforts to widen participation, the university offers three levels of entry requirements (standard, minimum and gateway) depending on an applicant's circumstances.

St Andrews ranks an impressive 7th in the UK for graduate prospects, with more than 87% of its graduates in high-skilled jobs or postgraduate study 15 months after finishing their degrees. The university facilitates career growth through alumni networking, international internships, and tailored work experience programmes in America and China. Four miles from the main campus, the university's Eden Campus houses an entrepreneurial ecosystem that supports university start-ups and spin-out companies.

The university is the town – perhaps more than anywhere else in the UK. Its ancient buildings are woven into the fabric of St Andrews, about 50 miles northeast of Edinburgh, alongside state-of-the-art new facilities. A fundraising appeal for the university's 600th anniversary, in 2013, supported by the Prince of Wales, raised £100 million for scholarships and student support and to improve the university's facilities.

All first-years who apply by the June deadline are guaranteed a place in one of the university's halls of residence, more than half of which are catered.

St Andrews presents a paradox in social inclusion. While it has the most ethnically diverse student body of any Scottish university, it ranks at the bottom for other key measures, admitting the smallest proportion of students from non-selective state schools (64.1%) and the fewest who are the first in their family to go to university (18.1%).

College Gate North Street St Andrews KY16 9AJ
admissions@st-andrews.ac.uk
st-andrews.ac.uk
yourunion.net

Overall ranking 2
(last year 2)

Accommodation
University provided places 4,398
Catered £208–£317 per week
Self-catered £171–£236 per week

Student numbers
Undergraduates 8,720
Applications per place 9.7:1
Overall offer rate 30.0%

Fees
Scots fees £0–£1,820
International fees £31,670–£36,366
RUK fees £9,535
Medicine £37,730

st-andrews.ac.uk/study/meet-us/in-st-andrews/ug
st-andrews.ac.uk/study/undergraduate/fees

St Mary's University, Twickenham

St Mary's is a haven of sports grounds, where facilities include the Sir Mo Farah Athletics Track, named after the Olympian long-distance runner and St Mary's alumnus, a new esports arena which is kitted out with 60 high-performance gaming machines, a stage and a 217-inch video wall as part of a £3 million investment in computer science facilities.

The university was founded in 1850 to train teachers, and its School of Education maintains that ethos – holding Ofsted's top rating since 2011. St Mary's was awarded silver overall in the Teaching Excellence Framework (TEF 2023), with gold for the student experience and silver for student outcomes.

The university ranks 87th in the latest Research Excellence Framework (REF 2021), with sport and theology the leading subject areas. A relatively low proportion of students achieving firsts and 2:1s (67.9%) holds the university back in our main academic ranking, as do its lower entry standards.

Student satisfaction is typically St Mary's strongest suit, but feedback cooled in the latest National Student Survey (NSS). The university has gone from ranking 9th for feedback on teaching quality to =36th, and from =16th for the wider experience to =58th, based on our analysis of the survey.

It moved to a three-faculty structure from 2023, focusing on business and law; education, theology and the arts; and sport, technology and health sciences. St Mary's is offering psychology with counselling from September 2025, and from 2026 will welcome students (initially international only) to its new school of medicine. No courses have been listed for withdrawal.

Applications and enrolments to St Mary's have been fairly consistent over the past decade with entry requirements averaging 108 UCAS tariff points. Our analysis of the Graduate Outcomes survey shows 79.8% of St Mary's graduates were in highly skilled jobs or postgraduate study 15 months after finishing their degrees, which puts it in the top 50 (42nd). Students benefit from a range of collaborations with industry and it has partnerships with the Chelsea Football Club Foundation and the Royal Ballet Company.

At the Teddington Lock Sports Campus, the university's facilities are used for fixtures organised by British Universities and Colleges Sport (BUCS) as well as lectures. A postgraduate facility in Edinburgh offers programmes in theology and education.

First-years who apply before the June deadline are guaranteed a room.

St Mary's draws 94.9% of its students from non-selective state schools, putting it 38th on that metric, and 33.2% are from ethnic minority backgrounds (53rd). More than half (55.3%) are aged over 21 when they enrol. But with relatively few students from low participation areas, and a black awarding gap that ranks it =89th, St Mary's has fallen outside the upper half of our social inclusion index, to 82nd place.

The St Mary's Bursary is worth £2,000 a year for students from low-income households, and those who have been in care or are estranged from their families are eligible for a £3,000 annual bursary. Sport scholarships are in three tiers depending on an applicant's competition level: gold for senior international; silver, junior international/national; or bronze, county/regional. They are worth up to £2,000 and include free gym membership, and nutrition and psychology support.

Waldegrave Road Twickenham TW1 4SX
apply@stmarys.ac.uk
stmarys.ac.uk
stmaryssu.co.uk

Overall ranking 68
(last year 52)

Accommodation
University provided places 662
Catered £178–£300 per week
Self-catered £-

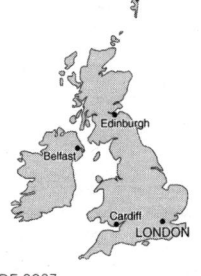

Student numbers
Undergraduates 3,125
Applications per place 5.0:1
Overall offer rate 85.7

Fees
UK fees £9,535
International fees £17,100–£18,150

stmarys.ac.uk/open-events/undergraduate.aspx
stmarys.ac.uk/tuition-fees/about.aspx

University of Salford

Salford students are based at three campuses – Peel Park (the main base), Frederick Road and MediaCity. Courses prioritise work experience placements and incorporate live briefs from experts to boost employability. The institution is =54th in our graduate prospects index.

Salford is in 72nd place of our main academic ranking for the second year in a row. There was a strong performance in the latest Research Excellence Framework (REF 2021) in which 78% of its submissions were rated world-leading or internationally excellent – helping the university to reach 67th place in our research quality index.

Sustainability is embedded in its campus developments and Salford ranks 8th in the UK for its ethical and environmental performance in the People & Planet 2024–25 university league table.

Salford moved up in the latest Teaching Excellence Framework (TEF 2023), where it earned silver overall (up from bronze in the previous assessment) underpinned by silver ratings for the student experience and student outcomes. Rates of student satisfaction are improving too: in our analysis of the latest National Student Survey (NSS), Salford ranks =71st for teaching quality (up 11 places). It has lost ground on the wider experience, however, where satisfaction has slipped 18 places to leave Salford only just inside the top 100 (=98th).

Eighteen new courses join the curriculum for 2025–26 including automation and instrumentation, business analytics, construction project management, creative digital media, data science, digital and software technology, social media content creation, business with management, and occupational therapy. Reopening are adult nursing at Bury College and psychology at Salford City College. In 2026, Salford will offer CertHE and DipHE courses in motion capture for the creative industries.

Courses demand from 128 to 64 UCAS tariff points for courses with a foundation year. Contextual offers are up to two grades below the standard requirement.

Our analysis of the Graduate Outcomes survey showed that 76.6% of students were employed in high-skilled jobs or had returned to postgraduate study 15 months after the end of their course.

Salford developed the Old Fire Station opposite its Peel Park Campus into its own micro-brewery (beer labels designed by a student) and in-house bakery. On campus there is a swimming pool with sauna and spa, five fitness suites and a 3G pitch, which is the site of Salford's British Universities and Colleges Sport (BUCS) football and rugby league fixtures.

The counselling and wellbeing service offers in-depth wellbeing sessions, therapeutic groups and counselling.

First-years are not guaranteed a room, but 1,300 of the 2,111 rooms available to Salford students are ringfenced for new undergraduates, which has been enough in the past.

Breaking into the top 30, Salford is up 17 places to rank 28th in our social inclusion index. Its proportion of students from non-selective state schools (96.3%) is in the top 20. Salford recruits 17.8% of students from areas with low participation in higher education (=26th).

Financial support includes the Salford Inspire Fund, which gives most undergraduates £150 a year to spend at the Inspire online store on learning resources. Low-income students may qualify for an extra £350.

Maxwell Building The Crescent Salford
Greater Manchester M5 4WT
enquiries@salford.ac.uk
salford.ac.uk
salfordstudents.com

Overall ranking 72
(last year 72)

Accommodation
University provided places 2,111
Self-catered £121–£191 per week

Student numbers
Undergraduates 17,220
Applications per place 4.7:1
Overall offer rate 74.9%

Fees
UK fees £9,535
International fees £14,500–£19,000

salford.ac.uk/undergraduate/open-days
salford.ac.uk/undergraduate/fees-and-funding

University of Sheffield

The Yorkshire university located in a city famed for steel is forging a path up our academic league table, up one place to 13th overall. This rise is powered by outstanding student satisfaction, earning it the title of University of the Year for Student Experience 2026. It is also 19th for teaching quality in our latest survey analysis, bucking the trend among Russell Group universities. Runner-up for The Times and Sunday Times University of the Year in our previous edition, the 1905-founded university evolved from three 19th-century institutions – Sheffield Medical School, Firth College and Sheffield Technical School.

Sheffield's reputation for research is world-class. It ranks 15th in our research quality index, with 92% of its work rated world-leading or internationally excellent in the latest Research Excellence Framework, and recently broke into the top 100 of the QS World University Rankings. Its academic clout is underlined by six Nobel prize-winners and its highly regarded Advanced Manufacturing Research Centre (AMRC).

In the Teaching Excellence Framework (TEF 2023), Sheffield gained silver overall, with assessors highlighting its "outstanding quality academic support" and a supportive learning environment.

An integrated master's degree in pharmacy (MPharm) launched in September 2025, offered with an optional preparatory year. The university has withdrawn its degrees in urban studies and aerospace engineering (private pilot instruction) from 2025. Sheffield's BA politics degree will accept its final intake of students in 2026, however the university will still be offering its BA in International Relations and Politics.

Degree courses demand grades from A*AA to BBB at A-level. In 2024, about 17% received a contextual offer up to two grades lower, or three grades lower for entrants who have completed a widening access summer school. The university attracted more than 43,000 applications in 2024 and more than 5,600 new students were accepted onto courses. Of these, 9% got a place through clearing.

Sheffield is a go-to destination for top employers, ranking among the top 20 most-targeted universities in the UK according to the High Fliers report 2024-25. It places 22nd in our analysis of the Graduate Outcomes survey, with 82.9% of leavers in highly skilled jobs or postgraduate study.

Sheffield is in the top 30 (28th) in the latest British Universities and Colleges Sport (BUCS) overall points table. Excellent sports facilities near the main precinct include an upgraded 180-piece gym, six floodlit synthetic turf pitches, a swimming pool and a sports hall. Outdoor pitches for rugby, football and cricket are a bus ride away.

Accommodation is guaranteed to all first-years who apply by the deadline, with rents from £106 a week.

Amongst Russell Group universities, only Cardiff and Queen Mary University of London recruit more students from non-selective state schools than Sheffield (78.4%), which ranks 93rd overall in our social inclusion index.

Financial support is generous and accessible. The number of bursaries is not capped, and around three in ten new students are expected to qualify for an award. Students from households with an income of £40,000 or less are eligible for bursaries of up to £1,000 a year, with extra support available for those from low-progression areas, care leavers and student carers.

Western Bank Sheffield S10 2TN
study@sheffield.ac.uk
sheffield.ac.uk
su.sheffield.ac.uk

Overall ranking 13
(last year 14)

Accommodation
University provided places 5,980
Catered £190 per week
Self-catered £106–£204 per week

Student numbers
Undergraduates 20,335
Applications per place 7.7:1
Overall offer rate 77.7%

Fees
UK fees £9,535
International fees £23,810–£30,570
Medicine £45,310

sheffield.ac.uk/undergraduate/visit/open-days
sheffield.ac.uk/undergraduate/fees-funding

Sheffield Hallam University

A large, modern university of more than 34,000 students – nearly 24,000 of them undergraduates – Sheffield Hallam University has a reputation as an engine of social mobility. Its success at widening participation in higher education has propelled it to 7th place overall in our social inclusion index. No university does better than Hallam at recruiting white working-class male students, one of the most under-represented groups in higher education, and nearly a quarter (24.3%) come from areas with low participation rates at university. A degree from Hallam offers solid employment chances, landing it in the top half of our table for graduate prospects (63rd).

Founded in 1843 as the Sheffield School of Design, Hallam gained university status in 1992. In the latest Research Excellence Framework (REF 2021), 72% of its submission was rated world-leading or internationally excellent. Some of the best results were in sport, art and design, and the built environment and planning.

Hallam earned gold overall in the Teaching Excellence Framework (TEF 2023), with silver for the student experience and gold for student outcomes. It is in the top half of UK universities (=64th) for its continuation rate – based on 89.7% of students projected to carry on from the first to the second year of their studies.

However, student satisfaction holds Hallam back in our main academic league table. Our latest National Student Survey (NSS) analysis shows year-on-year declines in satisfaction with teaching quality, for which Hallam ranks =122nd (down 15 places) and with the wider undergraduate experience, at 123rd – an 11-place dip.

For 2026 new additions are: business management and AI; data science (with foundation year); and computer science for games (top-up).

The highest entry requirements are 136–128 UCAS tariff points, and the lowest offers are typically 120–112 points. A contextual offer scheme reduces the requirements for eligible students, usually by 8–16 points.

The university teams up with more than 1,000 organisations to promise work experience to undergraduates in every year of their degree. Employers also have a hand in course design, and many courses are accredited by professional bodies. Three quarters of leavers are in highly skilled jobs or further study within 15 months, according to our analysis of the Graduate Outcomes survey.

Most teaching facilities are at the City Campus. Hands-on learning resources include the largest PlayStation teaching laboratory in the world, developed in partnership with Sony, and a 3D virtual radiography room for healthcare students.

The university has about 4,000–5,000 rooms. All first-years who apply by the beginning of August are guaranteed a place in halls of residence.

Sheffield Hallam's mission is to transform lives and open doors to higher education, offering support at the application stage and during the transition to student life. It does well across all metrics within our social inclusion index and has gone up from 13th last year to rank 7th overall.

Sheffield Hallam invested £3.67 million in financial support in 2023-24 and awarded the Student Success Scholarship (between £600 and £2,100) to more than 3,900 first-years – just over 20% of new entrants.

Howard Street Sheffield S1 1WB
shu.ac.uk/study-here/ask-a-question
shu.ac.uk
hallamstudentsunion.com

Overall ranking 95
(last year =84)

Accommodation
University provided places 4,500
Self-catered £85–£210 per week

Student numbers
Undergraduates 20,545
Applications per place 4.0:1
Overall offer rate 76.8%

Fees
UK fees £9,535
International fees £17,155

shu.ac.uk/visit-us
shu.ac.uk/study-here/fees-and-funding

SOAS University of London

Founded in 1916, the School of Oriental and African Studies (SOAS) University of London has turned its original academic focus on its head, evolving from its roots in Britain's imperialist projects, when its purpose was to train colonial administrators to run the empire's colonies, to debating those founding aims. The SOAS development studies course ranks fifth in the 2025 QS World University Rankings. More than 40% of undergraduate programmes include the opportunity to spend a year studying in another country and all have the option to learn a non-European language alongside their degree programme.

SOAS climbed ten places in our research quality index, to 36th, thanks to a strong performance in the latest Research Excellence Framework (REF 2021). Of the research that it submitted, 87% was ranked world-leading or internationally excellent, with particular success in law, anthropology and music. It has relaunched the SOAS Middle East Institute (formerly the London Middle East Institute) and opened the Centre for Pan-African Studies last year, to promote interdisciplinary research, policy dialogues and public engagement on issues related to the African continent and its diaspora. SOAS anthropologists have been awarded nearly £8 million from Research England to help address inequalities in access to mental health care.

Two years ago, SOAS entered our top 30 and was shortlisted for our Specialist University of the Year title. However, a double-digit fall last year has been compounded by another ten-place decline in our new academic ranking, bringing SOAS to 75th. Poor student satisfaction has contributed to its fall: it ranks in the bottom three for students' evaluations of both teaching quality and the wider experience in our analysis of the latest National Student Survey (NSS), and in the Teaching Excellence Framework (TEF 2023), it received only a bronze rating for student experience.

Its entry requirements go up to AAA, though contextual offers benefitted one in eight applicants last year – undercutting the standard rate by up to two A-level grades. SOAS attracted a record number of applications in 2024 (more than 6,400) and nearly a quarter of entrants in 2024 gained their places through clearing.

SOAS ranks =64th according to our analysis of the national Graduate Outcomes survey, based on 75.4% of graduates working in high-skilled jobs or engaged in further study 15 months after finishing their degrees.

SOAS has a discrimination charter outlining its abhorrence of racism, antisemitism and all forms of cultural, ethnic and religious chauvinism. New students are required to take part in consent and active bystander training sessions.

Counselling is offered in person or online and in one-to-one, group or workshop settings.

First-years who apply during the main cycle are guaranteed accommodation. Prices range from £162 to £387 a week.

With students from ethnic minority backgrounds making up 81.2% of its admissions, SOAS has the third most ethnically diverse student body in the UK. It ranks 85th overall in our social inclusion index for England and Wales.

Awards include the SOAS bursary (£4,500), as well as the University of London Scholars Programme and Rahim Lalji '14 Development Studies Bursaries.

---

10 Thornhaugh Street Russell Square
London WC1H 0XG
study@soas.ac.uk
soas.ac.uk
soasunion.org

Overall ranking 75
(last year 65)

Accommodation
University provided places 1,481
Catered £205–£359 per week
Self-catered £162–£387 per week

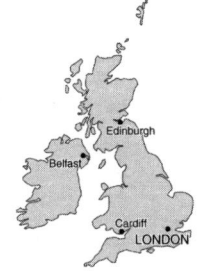

Student numbers
Undergraduates 4,030
Applications per place 3.8:1
Overall offer rate 92.6%

Fees
UK fees £9,535
International fees £22,870

soas.ac.uk/visit/soas-open-days
soas.ac.uk/study/fees-and-funding

University of South Wales

A modern university guided by the vision "to change lives and our world for the better", University of South Wales (USW) offers more than 300 courses and has an emphasis on equipping students with work-ready skills and experience. It is made up of three campuses in Cardiff, Newport and Pontypridd, but its heart lies in the Valleys. Calon (Welsh for heart) is the university's new Computing, Engineering and Technology building at Pontypridd. Calon has a flight simulator and a robotics lab among 40 new innovative teaching, learning and research spaces due to open for students in 2026.

The Cardiff Campus, in the city centre, houses USW's creative courses in the Atrium building. Courses at the £35 million Newport base include cybersecurity, education and psychology. Its three campuses are united by USW's upward trajectory in our league tables – after three years of climbing steadily, it places =82nd in our main academic ranking.

An improved performance in the Research Excellence Framework (REF 2021), compared with 2014, triggered a rise for USW to 94th in our research quality index. Some of the best results were produced by sport and exercise sciences, social work and social policy, music, drama, dance, performing arts, film and screen studies, and allied health subjects.

The proportion of students who continue their course after the first year has been a sticking point for USW, but it has boosted its overall position by gaining 20 places to rank =72nd for continuation rates. Feedback in the latest National Student Survey (NSS) has cooled, with USW =61st for teaching quality (a 20-place decline) and 108th for the student experience (down 11 places).

USW ranks =80th for its entry standards, based on new entrants across all courses arriving with an average of 118 UCAS tariff points. Employability is built into all courses, such as cybersecurity students having opportunities to take part in live projects with real companies. In our analysis of the Graduate Outcomes survey, 71.1% of USW students were in highly skilled jobs or further study 15 months after finishing their degree (96th).

As well as Students' Union events, every campus has coast and countryside adventures nearby, while Cardiff has a well-earned reputation as a student city that's hard to beat. Students can book a 45-minute appointment with a wellbeing adviser, who may then refer them for workshops, short courses, activities, mental health advice or counselling.

USW has been able to accommodate all first-year, full-time students who have requested to live in halls, but demand changes annually.

USW has shot up 16 places in our social inclusion index to rank 15th, successfully recruiting the 13th highest proportion of students from areas with low participation rates in higher education. Around four in ten USW undergraduates are aged 21 and above when they enrol.

Financial packages include the USW Gwent Bursary of £1,000 for students who meet contextual offer criteria and who are resident at a NP (Newport) postcode at the time of applying. There is extra support for students who have left care, are estranged from families and who are carers.

---

1 Lantwit Road Treforest Pontypridd CF37 1DL
equiries@southwales.ac.uk
southwales.ac.uk
uswsu.com

Overall ranking 82
(last year =94)

Accommodation
University provided places 1,442
Self-catered £115–£230 per week

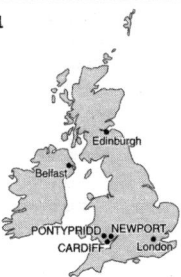

Student numbers
Undergraduates 11,235
Applications per place 4.2:1
Overall offer rate 90.9%

Fees
UK fees £9,535
International fees £15,850–£16,200

southwales.ac.uk/open-days
southwales.ac.uk/money

University of Southampton

There is a spotlight on the University of Southampton, the first global top 100 university to open a branch campus in India, offering courses in computer science, business, economics and accountancy. This ambitious move, with its first students enrolling in September 2025, joins an existing overseas campus in Malaysia, cementing the university's international outlook. At home, the university, a founding member of the Russell Group, is in the midst of a £600 million campus investment, adding new STEM and health facilities and recruiting more than 100 new academics across its five faculties.

A top 20 UK university, Southampton's research performance is outstanding. It ranks 14th in our research quality index, with 90% of its work rated world-leading or internationally excellent in the latest REF. It sits comfortably in the world's top 100 in the QS rankings. Engineering and computer science produced some of its best research results. The university also holds a solid triple silver rating in the Teaching Excellence Framework (TEF 2023).

Crucially, student satisfaction is on a strong upward trend. Our latest National Student Survey (NSS) analysis shows the university has made significant gains, ranking 45th for the overall student experience (a 29-place gain).

From 2025, new launches include degrees in business management and human resource management, and physics with artificial intelligence. Earth sciences and microbiology will join the course offering from 2026, while programmes in population science are closing.

Typical entry requirements range from A*AA to BBB at A-level. Southampton's contextual offers can reduce the standard requirement by up to two grades for eligible students. Demand is high, with more than 43,400 applications in 2024, and 13% of new undergraduates gained places through clearing.

Southampton is one of the UK's most sought-after universities by top employers, ranking 12th in the country for employer targeting. It places 15th in our graduate prospects index, with 84.3% of its graduates in high-skilled jobs or postgraduate study 15 months after finishing.

The vastly extended Jubilee Sports Centre on the main campus features a 200-station gym and a 25m pool. Making the most of its location, the university has three water sports centres. Southampton teams finished 25th in the latest British Universities and Colleges Sport (BUCS) league.

Consent training is mandatory, and counsellors and solution-focused wellbeing advice are available. A "Welcome to Southampton" module supports the academic transition to higher education, and the Student Hub runs engagement activities.

The university guarantees accommodation in a single room for all applicants who apply by the July 1 deadline. Options include a quieter lifestyle, alcohol-free and LGBTQ+ accommodation.

An eight-place uplift in our social inclusion ranking takes Southampton to 98th overall. It is in the top half of universities for the proportion of students from ethnic minority backgrounds, who represent a third of the intake.

Around a quarter of UK undergraduates receive a bursary of £1,000 or £2,000 per academic year, based on household incomes of £36,200 or less. A number of merit-based scholarships are also available.

University Road Highfield Southampton SO17 1BJ
enquiry@southampton.ac.uk
southampton.ac.uk
susu.org

Overall ranking 17
(last year 19)

Accommodation
University provided places 6,250
Catered £219–265 per week
Self-catered £153–£228 per week

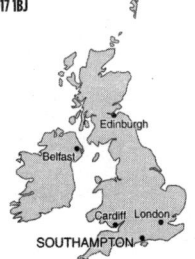

Student numbers
Undergraduates 16,170
Applications per place 7.6:1
Overall offer rate 76.5%

Fees
UK fees £9,535
International fees £23,400–£30,500
Medicine £30,500–£59,400

southampton.ac.uk/open-days/undergraduate
southampton.ac.uk/courses/fees/undergraduate.page

Southampton Solent University

Student life is shipshape and fashionable at this modern university, which gained its status in 2005 after earlier mergers between the College of Nautical Studies at Warsash, Southampton College of Art and the College of Technology. Southampton Solent has sailed up our main academic league table lately, rising 22 places to rank 76th. The university has been investing in practice-led, real-world teaching facilities including the UK's largest ship and port simulation centre at its Warsash Maritime School, a Human Health Lab replicating a medical ward and an Anatomage table, and virtual production stage equipment for courses across CGI, computer gaming and the digital arts. Solent's Certificate in Practical Artificial Intelligence qualification is a new provision, which students achieve via a free course bringing them up to speed on how to get the best out of AI.

In the Research Excellence Framework (REF 2021), 34% of the work submitted for assessment by Solent achieved the top ratings of world-leading or internationally excellent. Though modest, the scores prompted a one-place improvement in our research quality index.

The university was resoundingly endorsed by a gold rating overall in the government's Teaching Excellence Framework (TEF 2023), underpinned by golds for the student experience and student outcome – making Solent one of a small group of universities to gain the prestigious TEF "triple gold". Its approach goes down well with students, whose feedback in the latest National Student Survey (NSS) put Solent =24th for teaching quality in our analysis.

New offerings for 2025 are maritime engineering; sports coaching and physical education; and event management; as well as both HNC and integrated master's courses in renewable energy engineering, electronic engineering and mechanical engineering.

Degrees require 120 to 104 UCAS tariff points. The 2024 intake saw 10% of applicants receive contextual offers reducing requirements by 16 points (or 32 points for those meeting two or more criteria).

Solent Creatives provides students with access to funding for freelance and start-up business ideas. There are partnerships for work experience too, including with Southampton FC and its charity, Saints Foundation. For now, Solent is outside the top 100 for graduate prospects (114th), based on two-thirds of graduates being employed in highly skilled jobs 15 months on from their degrees, or engaged in further study.

Solent's main East Park Terrace Campus is close to the city centre, with the £33 million Spark building at its heart with space for 1,500 students. Recent developments on campus have added an attractive quad and a replica law court.

The university has just over 1,000 rooms. First-year full-time students who apply by the end of June are guaranteed a room, and 45% live on campus.

Ranked 14th in our social inclusion index overall, Solent excels in its recruitment of under-represented white working-class male students, which at 8.3% of entrants is among the top six proportions in England and Wales. More than a fifth of students are drawn from deprived areas, and around four in ten students are aged over 21 when they enrol.

Bursaries (up to £1,500) target students who have left care, are local, estranged from their families or who are carers.

East Park Terrace Southampton SO14 0YN
admissions@solent.ac.uk
solent.ac.uk
solentsu.co.uk

Overall ranking 76
(last year 98)

Accommodation
University provided places 1,021
Self-catered £126–£165 per week

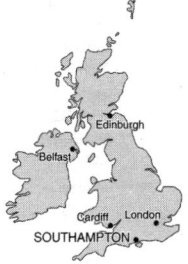

Student numbers
Undergraduates 6,535
Applications per place 4.9:1
Overall offer rate 95.0%

Fees
UK fees £9,535
International fees £17,750

solent.ac.uk/open-days
solent.ac.uk/finance

Staffordshire University

This institution with an eye for innovation introduced computer games degrees more than 20 years ago and, in 2018, Staffordshire became the first UK university to introduce esports as a degree. It has a competitive esports arena featuring player desks and audience seating, networked with a broadcast studio. A leading provider of earn-while-you-learn programmes, Staffordshire's Catalyst building is its base for apprenticeship and skills training, supporting nearly 3,000 trainees following higher and degree apprenticeships in fields including biomedical science, paramedicine, social work and teaching.

A 14-place improvement returns Staffordshire inside the top 100 of our main academic league table, at =8th. The university performed strongly in the Research Excellence Framework (REF 2021), with 68% of its submissions rated world-leading or internationally excellent. In our research quality index, Staffordshire ranks =84th.

It was rated triple silver in the government's Teaching Excellence Framework (TEF 2023) overall and for the student experience and student outcomes. At the time of the TEF assessment, the most popular subjects were computing, followed by creative arts and design, and nursing and midwifery. In our analysis of the latest National Student Survey (NSS), a 25-place improvement moves it up to =89th for undergraduates' evaluation of teaching quality and it has also edged up to 112nd for their feedback on the wider experience. Rounds of redundancies at the university may have contributed to discontent on campus.

Ending in 2025 are degrees in security and intelligence; sports journalism; surface pattern and textile design; and working with children, young people and families. Staffordshire is introducing degrees in sport business management and a top-up in business management in 2025. From 2026, it will offer law combinations with business, marketing, management, criminology, criminal investigation and psychology; as well as psychology and criminology; and psychology and forensic investigation.

Staffordshire's UCAS tariff band ranges from 48 UCAS tariff points (for entry to foundation year courses) up to 128 points. Our analysis of the Graduate Outcomes survey shows 73.7% of Staffordshire graduates in high-skilled jobs or further study 15 months on from their degrees, putting the university =80th for graduate prospects.

The main campus in Stoke-on-Trent is where you will find the Catalyst building, for apprenticeship and skills training. A new simulation suite replicates community settings such as living rooms, a bedsit and a custody suite. These join the simulated hospital wards on the campus. University-owned halls at the Stoke-on-Trent Campus are not far from the teaching and sport facilities, and students who make Staffordshire their firm choice, and apply before the end of August, are guaranteed a room.

Staffordshire takes 2nd place in our social inclusion index. It recruits more than a quarter of its intake from neighbourhoods with low rates of participation in higher education, and 59.2% of its entrants are the first in their family to go to university.

More than 1,000 new entrants accessed some type of financial help in 2024. Bursaries include the Horizon Fund, which provides ten £1,500 awards to local students from low-income households.

College Road Stoke-on-Trent ST4 2DE
enquiries@staffs.ac.uk
staffs.ac.uk
staffsunion.com

Overall ranking =87
(last year 101)

Accommodation
University provided places 1,227
Self-catered £113–£162 per week

Student numbers
Undergraduates 10,575
Applications per place 3.3:1
Overall offer rate 82.5%

Fees
UK fees £9,535
International fees £16,750–£19,000

staffs.ac.uk/visit/undergraduate-open-day
staffs.ac.uk/student-life/fees-and-finance

University of Stirling

A campus community awaits students at the only university with its own loch and castle. The University of Stirling was established in the 1960s, but its setting is unique – stretching across a 330-acre site beneath the Ochil Hills, with facilities dotted round Airthrey Loch. The Pathfoot Building, designed by John Richards and now listed, was the original heart of the campus and opened in 1967. Now Campus Central, a £23 million project opened in 2021, provides a gateway to academic life.

Stirling has some of the best university sports facilities in Scotland and the campus is home to the National Tennis Centre as well as the National Swimming Academy, both open for undergraduates to use.

Stirling's research record remained consistent in the latest Research Excellence Framework (REF 2021), in which almost 80% of the submission was rated world-leading or internationally excellent. Some of the best results were in agriculture; veterinary and food science; geography and environmental science; and social work and social policy. The university ranks 49th in our research quality index. The Institute of Aquaculture stands out for its pioneering work in the world's fastest-growing food production sector.

An eight-place rise to 55th in our main academic league table is driven by an improved continuation rate, and entry standards that rank Stirling =14th, with new entrants averaging 171 UCAS points. But Stirling's feedback in the annual National Student Survey (NSS) continued to worsen in 2025, and our analysis puts the university 111st for teaching quality (down eight places) and 106th for the broad experience (down from =92nd).

The standard entry requirements differ by course, with offers based on grades rather than tariff points. For a small proportion of eligible students, contextual admissions take the pressure off by two Higher grades. Applications went up 4% in 2024, and 7% of new students gained places through clearing.

With just over two thirds of leavers in high-skilled jobs or further study 15 months after finishing their degree, Stirling is 66th for graduate prospects.

Performance sport is a focus, with eight Stirling athletes having competed at the 2024 Paris Olympics. Sports facilities are extensive and include a gym, cycle studio, and fitness studios, and outdoors, artificial pitches for sports such as hockey, football, rugby, Gaelic football and an all-weather athletics track.

The mental health, wellbeing and counselling service offers services including one-on-one therapy and a sensory room in the wellbeing suite.

First-year undergraduates who live more than 20 miles from campus are guaranteed a room in halls, as long as they confirm their place and meet the housing application deadline.

Stirling maintains its 11th place in our latest Scottish social inclusion ranking. Only 6.4% of the intake had an ethnic minority background in the latest figures (14th). Stirling has the highest proportion of disabled students (8.8%) of any university in Scotland. Students from the rest of the UK (who do not qualify for Scotland's funding system) are eligible for the new Stirling Success Scholarship, worth up to £5,000. There are 18 sports scholarships available, worth £2,000 a year. The Reid Family Scholarship of £9,000–£21,525 helps Scottish students who meet the criteria for widening participation.

Stirling FK9 4LA
admissions@stir.ac.uk
stir.ac.uk
stirlingstudentsunion.com

Overall ranking 55
(last year 63)

Accommodation
University provided places 2,565
Self-catered £97–£219 per week

Student numbers
Undergraduates 8,355
Applications per place 5.9:1
Overall offer rate 82.6%

Fees
Scots fees £0–£1,820
International fees £18,400–£22,400
RUK fees £9,535

stir.ac.uk/study/visit-us/undergraduate-open-days
stir.ac.uk/study/fees-funding

University of Strathclyde

Students succeed with a smile at the University of Strathclyde, the highest of the three Glasgow universities in the National Student Survey (NSS), and the winner of our Scottish University of the Year 2026 title.

Strathclyde has made an impressive nine-place leap up our main academic ranking, placing it 11th in the UK. Strathclyde wins our Runner-Up University of the Year 2026 award. It has the fourth-highest entry standards in the UK and the biggest engineering faculty in Scotland.

Strathclyde tops our new subject tables three times – for communication and media studies, creative writing, and for pharmacology and pharmacy. Students benefit from its prime spot in the middle of Glasgow, where Strathclyde has just come to the end of a £1 billion campus investment. Known as "StrathLife" by insiders, the university experience involves about 200 societies and nearly 50 sports clubs.

The university performed strongly in the latest Research Excellence Framework (REF 2021), with almost 90% of its research rated world-leading or internationally excellent. It ranks 30th in our research quality index. Feedback from undergraduates in the National Student Survey 2025 reflects positive experiences, with Strathclyde ranking =36th for teaching quality and =19th for the broader student experience in our analysis.

From 2025 there is direct entry to the BSc chemistry course, which was previously open to students transferring from the integrated master's degree.

Almost all undergraduates are from Scotland, with English students the biggest cohort from the rest of the UK. Students arrive highly qualified, but there is some concession afforded to those eligible for a contextual offer, which applies a one A-level grade concession in a non-essential subject.

Strathclyde ranks =20th in the UK for graduate prospects, based on 83% being in highly skilled jobs, or postgraduate study, 15 months after the end of their degree. It has links with businesses such as Rolls-Royce and GlaxoSmithKline that can provide opportunities for internships and graduate roles.

Strathclyde's campus overhaul includes a £60 million Learning and Teaching building, which houses student support and the students' association.

Counselling is available Monday to Friday and a 24/7 phone line is manned by counsellors.

Rooms in halls include sports centre membership. Priority goes to those living more than 25 miles away. There's no accommodation guarantee but everyone who applied in 2024-25 got a room.

With 16.3% of students from ethnic minority backgrounds, Strathclyde ranks 6th in Scotland on that metric. Nearly nine out of ten students were state-educated and the university ranks 10th overall in our Scottish social inclusion index.

The Strathclyde Access Bursary provides up to £3,000 to students from England, Wales, Northern Ireland and the Republic of Ireland, and an accommodation bursary adds another £1,000 to those from the rest of the UK.

---

16 Richmond Street Glasgow G1 1XQ
study-here@strath.ac.uk
strath.ac.uk
strathunion.com/

Overall ranking 11
(last year 20)

Accommodation
University provided places 2,021
Self-catered £129–£175 per week

Student numbers
Undergraduates 13,285
Applications per place 5.7:1
Overall offer rate 57.1%

Fees
Scots fees £0–£1,820
International fees £19,850–£30,300
RUK fees £9,535

strath.ac.uk/studywithus/openday
strath.ac.uk/studywithus/feesfunding/fees

University of Suffolk

This small, modern university in the east of England has gone up 27 places in our main academic league table while rolling out a raft of new developments to lift the student experience. Sports facilities have been added at Suffolk's waterfront campus in Ipswich Marina, as have teaching laboratories for dental therapy courses and a Bloomberg lab for business and finance programmes.

Students give glowing reviews in the latest National Student Survey (NSS), putting Suffolk at the top in our analysis – and earning it two Runner-Up University of the Year 2026 awards – for teaching quality and student experience. Suffolk has the highest intake of mature students in England and Wales (89.2%), among other metrics which keep it in the top ten of our social inclusion index for a second year.

The university made its first submission to the Research Excellence Framework in 2021, in social work and social policy, 68% of which was rated world-leading or internationally excellent. This places Suffolk above 23 other universities in our research quality index in its first entry. It also earned an overall silver rating in the Teaching Excellence Framework (TEF 2023), underpinned by silver ratings for student experience and student outcomes, improving on its previous bronze award.

While its record in our social inclusion index is commendable, Suffolk's continuation rate is a sticking point, with only 80.3% of students projected to continue from the first to second years of their studies, putting it second from bottom.

New programmes in September 2025 are esports (plus a course with professional placement), and accounting and finance. Courses require from 96 to 120 UCAS tariff points. Contextual offers usually undercut the standard rate by one A-level grade or equivalent.

Suffolk's close relationships with businesses including BT, support students in accessing internships, placements and graduate jobs. In 2024, it became a primary partner of Ipswich Town Football Club. Suffolk's healthcare provision includes the Integrated Care Academy and a Dental Community Interest Company. But based on 72% of graduates being employed in highly skilled jobs or further study 15 months after their degrees, Suffolk ranks only 92nd for graduate prospects.

The modern waterfront campus has a £13 million Health and Wellbeing Building that is used by students, practice partners and the community. There is counselling and computerised cognitive behavioural therapy available, as well as specialist mentoring and workshops. Ipswich offers a waterside town experience within easy reach of Suffolk's stunning countryside.

Many students live at home, so Suffolk's 655 university-endorsed rooms are usually enough to go around, although there is no formal accommodation guarantee.

The university is making strides on social mobility, drawing 27% of its intake from deprived areas (the 7th highest proportion), and 61.3% of students are the first in their family to go to university (10th).

About 30% of students qualify for assistance, including means-tested annual bursaries of £500 and the Ipswich Award of £1,000, as well as £500 bursaries for care leavers and estranged students. Subject-specific awards are also available for students of esports and accounting and finance.

Waterfront Building 19 Neptune Quay
Ipswich IP4 1QJ
admissions@uos.ac.uk
uos.ac.uk
uosunion.org

Overall ranking 97
(last year 124)

Accommodation
University provided places 655
Self-catered £110–£207 per week

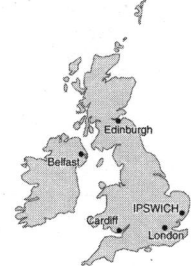

Student numbers
Undergraduates 2,450
Applications per place 3.0:1
Overall offer rate 57.2%

Fees
UK fees £9,535
International fees £15,090–£18,380

uos.ac.uk/life-at-suffolk/visit-us/open-days
uos.ac.uk/life-at-suffolk/funding-your-studies/undergraduate-study

University of Sunderland

The northeast university with capital ambition opened its £11.4 million Canary Wharf Campus in March 2025. The majority of students are based not by the River Thames, but by the River Wear. The University of Sunderland's first cohort of medical doctors graduated in 2024, and Sunderland's School of Pharmacy and Pharmaceutical Sciences recently opened a new drug discovery and development research institute.

Sunderland is at the forefront of social mobility. Its intake of students includes the second-highest proportion of students from deprived areas (28.5%) and eighth-highest proportion of students whose parents did not go to university (63.1%).

A triple silver rating in the government's Teaching Excellence Framework (TEF 2023), overall and for the student experience and student outcomes, commended the university for its engagement with students. Our analysis of the latest National Student Survey (NSS) shows that rates of student satisfaction soared; the university is 14th for students' evaluation of teaching quality (up from =38th) and it has gained 19 places to rank =42nd for their feedback on the broad experience.

In the Research Excellence Framework (REF 2021) more than 70% of the work it submitted was rated as either world-leading or internationally excellent. Some of the best results were in art and design, and English. Overall, Sunderland gained one place in our research quality indicator, to rank 80th.

Sunderland has made up some ground on its continuation rate and now ranks 108th (from 122nd last year) with 85.1% of students projected to carry on from their first to second year of their studies.

The physiological sciences degree is no longer recruiting from September 2025, but new courses in audiology and cardiac physiology are being offered.

New students average 124 UCAS tariff points to rank in the upper half of our table.

New esports, mock law-courts and business and management facilities are now open, complementing external improvements to the St Peter's riverside campus. In recent years, nearly £80 million has gone into student-facing facilities such as a £5 million Anatomy Centre, a Centre for Graduate Prospects and enhanced study facilities. Sunderland's simulation facilities include a £1.4 million midwifery suite with a full maternity ward. The campus in Canary Wharf, London, offers business, healthcare, tourism and hospitality courses at undergraduate level. The CitySpace Fitness facility on the City Campus includes a 50m swimming pool and a seven-metre climbing wall. Students can learn to ski at a dry slope near campus, and the snow sports team competes nationally.

Mental health and welfare support includes the Shine a Light project, which targets ethnic minority students. With 688 places available, an accommodation guarantee applies to first-years who meet the appropriate deadlines. Many students live at home and commute to university.

The university just dropped out of the top ten in our social inclusion index of England and Wales, placing 13th. Sunderland also has particularly strong representation from first-generation students (63.1%, ranking 8th) and white working-class males (7.4%, =13th).

University of Sunderland bursaries last for three years and range in value from £500 to £3,000. Priority is given to students with low household incomes and those from groups not well-represented in higher education.

Edinburgh Building Chester Road Sunderland SR1 3SD
student.helpline@sunderland.ac.uk
sunderland.ac.uk
sunderlandsu.co.uk

Overall ranking 105
(last year =105)

Accommodation
University provided places 688
Self-catered £85–£180 per week

Student numbers
Undergraduates 10,710
Applications per place 3.2:1
Overall offer rate 67.8%

Fees
UK fees £9,535
International fees £16,500–£20,000

sunderland.ac.uk/open-days
sunderland.ac.uk/fees-funding-support/tuition-fees

University of Surrey

Founded in 1891 as Battersea Polytechnic Institute, before a move to Surrey in 1962, the most recent addition to the University of Surrey is a School of Medicine, whose first 34 government-funded places for UK medical students start this autumn.

Surrey has dropped ten places from last year, ranking 31st in our main academic table. Its research pedigree is excellent, placing it 29th for research quality, with 41% of its work assessed as "world-leading" in the latest Research Excellence Framework (REF 2021). Economics produced some of the best results. Its hospitality and tourism courses are a magnet for students worldwide, judged to be top in Britain and 16th in the 2025 QS World University Rankings. The university secured a triple silver rating in the Teaching Excellence Framework (TEF 2023), where assessors commended its "effective engagement with students". This is reflected in the National Student Survey (NSS), where Surrey consistently ranks in the upper tiers for student satisfaction, placing it in the top 25 this year for teaching quality (=22nd) and the overall student experience (=21st).

New courses include games design, international airline and airport management, criminology and psychology, politics and international relations, and a law (environmental and sustainability pathway) LLB.

The minimum requirement is CCC; the highest is AAA. Surrey's contextual admissions policy, introduced for 2022 to widen participation, has proved successful, with almost a third (32%) of its students qualifying for a two-grade reduction in A-level entry requirements.

The university's longstanding focus on producing work-ready graduates pays off. Based on our analysis of the Graduate Outcomes survey, Surrey is at =17th for graduate prospects, with 83.7% of its graduates in highly skilled jobs or further study 15 months after finishing their degrees.

Surrey's campus is packed with modern facilities including the £45 million School of Veterinary Medicine and the Kate Granger Building, which houses clinical simulation suites for training nurses, midwives and paramedics. The £36 million Sports Park offers world-class facilities, including an Olympic-sized swimming pool and a 120-station gym. On the arts scene, more than 20 productions are staged annually across four university theatres.

MySurrey Dots hubs provide spaces for study, clubs, socialising and events. The Centre for Wellbeing offers virtual, phone and in-person appointments from Monday to Friday.

First-years who have chosen Surrey as their firm choice and apply by the deadline are guaranteed a place in halls of residence, with some costing less than £100 a week.

Ranking 84th in our social inclusion index, Surrey is among the country's more ethnically diverse institutions, with 47.1% of its students from black, Asian or minority ethnic backgrounds. Its contextual admissions policy has also proven successful, with almost a third of students qualifying for a two-grade A-level reduction.

Around 10% of UK undergraduates receive the main bursary, worth £3,000 a year, for students from households with incomes of less than £25,000 and in areas with low university participation. Support is also available for care leavers and those estranged from their families.

Guildford GU2 7XH
admissions@surrey.ac.uk
surrey.ac.uk
surreyunion.org

Overall ranking 31
(last year 21)

Accommodation
University provided places 6,130
Self-catered £86–£215 per week

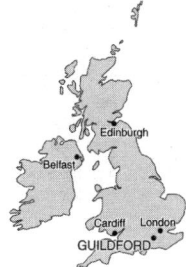

Student numbers
Undergraduates 11,095
Applications per place 6.9:1
Overall offer rate 68.8%

Fees
UK fees £9,535
International fees £14,000–£41,500
Medicine £46,300

surrey.ac.uk/open-days
surrey.ac.uk/fees-and-funding

University of Sussex

Progressive since its 1961 foundation, the University of Sussex broke the mould of single-discipline academic departments by organising research and teaching within interdisciplinary schools of study. The research powerhouse on the edge of the South Downs continues to make academic strides, and in 2024 became one of only a handful of universities to hold a Black Studies library collection, housing more than 750 rare and/or unique items related to black British history and culture.

Excellent results were recorded in the latest Research Excellence Framework (REF 2021). Some of its strongest work was recorded in anthropology and development studies; communication, cultural and media studies; sociology; art and design, and education. Overall, 89% of the submission was rated world-leading or internationally excellent (=32nd).

At Sussex's 12 Centres of Excellence for research, academics are addressing a range of societal challenges such as genome-damaging diseases, quantum computing and AI. Development studies is the university's standout strength: for the ninth consecutive year, Sussex is ranked top in the QS World University subject rankings for 2025.

Undergraduates can work towards a single or joint honours degree, or choose a major/minor course, spending 75% of their time on their core subject and 25% on another. The university was rated silver overall in the Teaching Excellence Framework (TEF 2023), with silver for student outcomes and bronze for student experience. Satisfaction with teaching quality has fallen nine places to =74th. However Sussex comes out well in our analysis of the latest National Student Survey (NSS), ranking 29th for satisfaction with the wider undergraduate experience.

Standard requirements range from A*AA to BBC at A-level. Contextual offers are generally two grades lower. Sussex's four-year degrees with an integrated foundation year typically require CCC.

Undergraduates are encouraged to take work placements, study abroad and learn a language, and can make use of the university's mentoring and internship schemes. But Sussex ranks only =86th in our analysis of the Graduate Outcomes survey, with 73% of graduates in highly skilled jobs or postgraduate study after 15 months. The 22-place fall is a factor in dragging down the university's overall academic ranking, down seven places to 45th.

Sussex has almost 5,000 residential spaces for students, nearly all on campus – enough to guarantee a room to all first-years who apply by the deadline.

The university has acted to help students out with the cost of living with the £2 Sussex Saver meal deal in catering outlets, and a new Health and Wellbeing Centre is due to open at the heart of the campus in 2026.

The university is 89th overall in our social inclusion index. For ethnic diversity, its performance is around the middle of the pack (57th) while the proportion of students who are the first in their family to go to university (36.3%) places Sussex 84th. Students drawn from selective state and independent schools represent 17.5% of the intake, according to the latest data (80th).

A third of students qualify for financial assistance, which includes the Sussex Bursary of £1,000 in the first year to students from low-income households and £500 in subsequent years.

Sussex House Falmer Brighton BN1 9RH
ug.enquiries@sussex.ac.uk
sussex.ac.uk
sussexstudent.com

Overall ranking 45
(last year 38)

Accommodation
University provided places 4,849
Self-catered £123–£215 per week

Student numbers
Undergraduates 13,280
Applications per place 5.3:1
Overall offer rate 92.7%

Fees
UK fees £9,535
International fees £22,575–£26,250
Medicine £46,700

sussex.ac.uk/study/visit-us/undergraduate/open-days
sussex.ac.uk/study/fees-funding

Swansea University

At the edge of the sand, with its own seafront promenade, Swansea University's £450 million Bay Campus marks the eastern end of Swansea Bay. Singleton Park, the main campus, established in 1920, is at the other end. Our Runner-Up Welsh University of the Year 2026 is only nine places behind Cardiff, although the gap has widened by four places in a year.

In the latest Research Excellence Framework (REF 2021), 86% of the university's work was rated world-leading or internationally excellent, with some of the best results produced by medicine and life science subjects, mathematics and geography (45th). Swansea is on the march in the global rankings. Since 2021 it has advanced 183 places, reaching 292nd in the QS World University Rankings 2026.

Rates of student satisfaction are on the way up, too. In our analysis of the latest National Student Survey (NSS) the university ranks =56th for satisfaction with teaching quality (up 20 places) and =32nd (up 32 places) for positive feedback on the wider undergraduate experience.

New courses in 2025 offer a degree pathway with and without a foundation year in applied medical science; medical pharmacology; microbiology and immunology; and population health and medical sciences.

Entry requirements range from AAB to CCC at A-level. Under Swansea's guaranteed offer policy, there is flexibility on grades for applicants who have firmly accepted a conditional offer. Swansea ranks =35th for graduate prospects with 81% of graduates employed in highly skilled jobs or further study 15 months on. The Swansea Employability Academy helps students to secure paid internships and co-ordinates programmes for career development. Swansea also offers many of its degrees as four-year courses with a year spent in industry or abroad.

The 65-acre Bay Campus doubled the size of the university and hosts the £32.5 million Computational Foundry, as well as the School of Management and the Great Hall. The £20 million Sports Park has an indoor athletics and hockey centre as well as an outdoor athletics track, grass and all-weather pitches, tennis courts and gym. Its own university teams compete successfully in the British Universities and Colleges Sport (BUCS), where Swansea ranks 26th in the latest overall points table.

The wellbeing and disability service offers cognitive behavioural therapy and emotional freedom techniques, and a 24/7 digital mental health service with trained clinicians.

The university has more than 4,200 residential spaces – enough to guarantee accommodation to all first-years who apply by the deadline.

The university is in 75th place overall in our social inclusion index for England and Wales. It is not among the most diverse universities, although the proportion of students from ethnic minorities has risen from 17% (82nd) to 23% (70th) in a year. However, the degree awarding gap between black and white students (-18%) ranks Swansea 35th. More than 92% of students went to non-selective state schools (=55th).

Excellence Scholarships of £3,000 are paid over three years and are awarded automatically to all UK students who achieve AAA at A-level, or equivalent results. Merit scholarships of £2,000 are awarded to entrants with AAB grades, or equivalent.

Singleton Park Swansea SA2 8PP
admissions@swansea.ac.uk
swansea.ac.uk
swansea-union.co.uk

Overall ranking 37
(last year 37)

Accommodation
University provided places 4,284
Catered £165–£171 per week
Self-catered £144–£183 per week

Student numbers
Undergraduates 14,700
Applications per place 3.8:1
Overall offer rate 79.0%

Fees
UK fees £9,535
International fees £17,400–£27,050
Medicine £46,050

swansea.ac.uk/open-days
swansea.ac.uk/undergraduate/fees-and-funding/tuition-fees

Teeside University

At Teesside University's evolving campus, a £300 million investment is rolling out a masterplan of modern resources, reflecting the institution's proud history of removing barriers to higher education. Following the £36.9 million BIOS health and science building, the Digital Life building is the latest addition, featuring cybersecurity and smart labs, digital art studios and one of the world's largest fully immersive simulation suites. Three in ten of its intake of undergraduates come from areas of socioeconomic deprivation – no university recruits a higher proportion.

Almost two thirds of Teesside's submission to the Research Excellence Framework (REF 2021) was rated world-leading or internationally excellent, and it sits in 93rd place in our research quality index. The research environment has become more stimulating with the recent opening of a £5 million postgraduate hub and a £13.1 million Net Zero Industry Innovation Centre.

Teesside has leapt 20 places up our main academic ranking into =84th place, helped by much-improved feedback in the latest National Student Survey (NSS), ranking 31st for teaching quality (up 28 places) and 71st for the wider experience (a 19-place gain) in our latest analysis. The positive reviews from students echo those of the government's Teaching Excellence Framework (TEF), in whose assessment Teesside swept the board with gold. The university is one of an elite group to gain the TEF's top rating overall and for both underpinning factors: student experience and student outcomes.

There was praise from Ofsted for Teesside's apprenticeship provision, which was rated "outstanding" in a 2025 inspection.

The university is a leading provider of the earn-while-you-learn route and has more than 2,500 students enrolled on 40-plus apprenticeships.

Courses require from 128 to 80 UCAS tariff points, and more students enter with Btecs or access courses than A-levels. Foundation years are offered as a route into university for students who have grades significantly below the minimum entry tariff.

Teesside is in 44th place in our graduate prospects index, based on 79.2% of graduates being in highly-skilled jobs or further study 15 months on.

The Olympia sports complex on campus incorporates a sports hall with capacity for 500 spectators, a climbing wall and a gym.

Personalised support is the goal for Teesside's mental health service, which has one-to-one counselling and runs workshops to promote a healthy lifestyle.

There are 912 rooms, which are allocated on a first-come, first-served basis although first-years and students with medical conditions receive priority. In 2024–25 about 90% of accommodation applicants got a place in halls.

In tenth place in England and Wales in our social inclusion index (down from second last year), Teesside draws a high proportion of students from deprived areas, but its dropout rate for this group (3.4%) ranks it only =89th. The majority of Teesside students (61.5%, ranking 9th) are the first in their family to go to university and its recruitment from non-selective state schools (98.4%) is the fifth-highest.

There are valuable subject-specific scholarships encompassing arts and media, business, computer games, computing, engineering, nursing and health, and science – worth from £2,000 to as much as £27,000.

Middlesbrough TS1 3BX
enquiries@tees.ac.uk
tees.ac.uk
tees-su.org.uk

Overall ranking =84
(last year 104)

Accommodation
University provided places 912
Self-catered £100–£175 per week

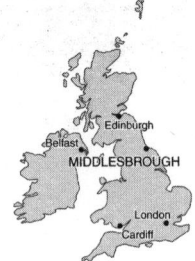

Student numbers
Undergraduates 9,620
Applications per place 3.6:1
Overall offer rate 78.6%

Fees
UK fees £9,535
International fees £17,000

tees.ac.uk/opendays
tees.ac.uk/sections/fulltime/funding

Ulster University

Ulster University has a hands-on approach to higher education at its three campuses in Belfast, Coleraine and Derry-Londonderry. In Belfast, it has opened Studio Ulster, a £75 million virtual production facility that builds on Northern Ireland's emergence as a leading film and television centre by plugging the skills gap in visual effects.

At Derry-Londonderry, medical students have access to expanded teaching and research facilities on campus and at Altnagelvin Hospital. At Coleraine, the new Centre for Food and Drug Discovery is a "one-stop shop" for innovation, where specialists from academia, industry and healthcare collaborate to address global challenges and maximise productivity.

Ulster is 44th in our research quality index: 87% of its submission to the Research Excellence Framework (REF 2021) was rated world-leading or internationally excellent, with the strongest results in allied health subjects; and 97% of the university's research had "outstanding" or "very considerable" impact.

Most teaching is in-person, but Ulster is also a pioneer of blended learning and its online recordings – provided for every module for more than 20 years – are popular with students. Feedback from students remains positive although it has cooled lately. Ulster is in the top half for satisfaction with teaching quality (38th) and the wider experience (=42nd), although both have slipped from the top 25 in our latest analysis of the National Student Survey (NSS). With 81.2% of Ulster students graduating with a first or 2:1 degree, Ulster ranks =63rd.

In September 2026, the university will welcome students on courses in liberal arts; sports therapy and rehabilitation; and software engineering, all based at Derry-Londonderry.

Ulster's asking grades are AAA to CCC (or CC for foundation programmes) and the university does not make contextual offers. Applications are at record levels and rising year on year, up 11.5% in 2024.

The university works with 1,000 industry partners to offer more than 4,000 professional practice placements. More than three-quarters of Ulster graduates were in high-skilled work or further study 15 months after finishing their degrees, according to our analysis of the latest Graduate Outcomes survey (=51st).

Ulster's £363.9 million Belfast Campus in the city centre was one of the biggest academic projects in Europe and opened in 2022. It created a "campus community within a building" with space for 15,000 students, putting learning and research facilities under the same roof as student services and social spaces. There is a two-storey library, a student-run restaurant and training kitchens, and the campus is the base for the Belfast School of Art, as well as a wide range of other courses.

The Belfast site has opened a new gym and studio, and Coleraine has its own sports facilities. Counselling services (run by an outside provider) are complemented by a 24/7 online support hub.

One of Ulster's 2,900 rooms is guaranteed for all first-years who apply by the July 7 deadline. About 30% of first-years live on campus.

Financial support targets those from households with incomes of less than £19,203 and includes access bursaries of 10% of fees (£485 a year).

Cromore Road Coleraine BT52 1SA
study@ulster.ac.uk
ulster.ac.uk
uusu.org

Overall ranking 49
(last year 45)

Accommodation
University provided places 2,943
Self-catered £103–£235 per week

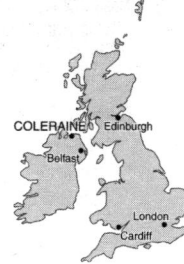

Student numbers
Undergraduates 17,660
Applications per place 6.0:1
Overall offer rate 83.1%

Fees
UK fees £4,855 (NI/ROI)
International fees £17,490
RUK fees £9,535
Medicine £39,630

ulster.ac.uk/study/undergraduate/open-days
ulster.ac.uk/student/fees/tuition-fees

University College London

A research heavyweight on a global scale, University College London (UCL) has secured its top 10 rank in the QS World University Rankings for the 14th year running. Proud to be the home of "disruptive thinking" since 1826, UCL now wants to lead the discussion in academia and the wider community on "disagreeing well".

UCL is the biggest component of the University of London Federation with about 40,000 students. Thirty Nobel laureates have developed their expertise at UCL and its research continues to make a global impact. The university is fifth in our research quality index, based on the latest Research Excellence Framework (REF 2021), in which 93% of its work was rated world-leading or internationally excellent.

UCL was the Sunday Times University of the Year two years ago. It was awarded silver overall in the Teaching Excellence Framework (TEF 2023), with silver for student experience and gold for student outcomes. Yet students have given UCL mixed reviews in successive National Student Surveys (NSS) – a common trend at research-led, big city universities. UCL falls seven places to =66th for the wider experience, although there is a four-place recovery for satisfaction with teaching quality to 110th place.

The A-levels to aim for to get a place on a degree course range from AAA to ABB. Foundation years have lower requirements and contextual offers are typically one to two grades lower than standard, benefitting about a third of new entrants. Just 5% of undergraduates gained a place through clearing.

UCL is 8th according to our analysis of the Graduate Outcomes survey, with 87.5% of leavers in highly skilled jobs or further study within 15 months. The university is a top recruiting ground for large employers and its free extracurricular entrepreneurship programme provides student start-ups with a springboard.

The Main Building on UCL's quad, facing Gower Street in central London, fits the image of an academic heavyweight with its grand portico and cloisters. UCL has 16 specialist libraries and a new student centre with 1,000 extra study places. Finance students practise on a virtual trading floor. UCL's medical school is one of the largest in Europe.

There are 450 sports clubs, societies, volunteering projects and community networks. Indoor sports and fitness facilities are on campus but outdoor pitches are a free coach ride away in Hertfordshire.

UCL's free mental health support includes counselling, psychiatric support and workshops.

First-years who apply in time have priority for more than 8,000 residential places. Self-catering rent starts at £145 a week. UCL guarantees university accommodation to students aged under 18, care-leavers and those with additional needs for the duration of their studies.

An ethnically diverse intake puts UCL 22nd and it has climbed 27 places to 80th overall in our social inclusion index, earning it Highly Commended for University of the Year for Social Inclusion 2026. About three in ten UK undergraduates receive some financial aid. UCL's main undergraduate bursary – £1,000 to £3,000 – is awarded to those with household incomes below £42,875.

Gower Street London WC1E 6BT
ucl.ac.uk/prospective-students/
undergraduate/admissions-enquiries
ucl.ac.uk
studentsunionucl.org

Overall ranking 9
(last year 7)

Accommodation
University provided places 8,247
Catered £225–412 per week
Self-catered £145–£486 per week

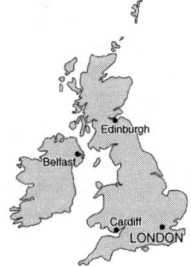

Student numbers
Undergraduates 23,033
Applications per place 8.6:1
Overall offer rate 35.2%

Fees
UK fees £9,535
International fees £27,500–£43,500
Medicine £53,400

ucl.ac.uk/prospective-students/open-days/
undergraduate-open-days
ucl.ac.uk/prospective-students/graduate/tuition-fees

University of Wales Trinity St David

The third-oldest university in England and Wales, after Oxford and Cambridge, with a royal charter from 1828, University of Wales Trinity Saint David (UWTSD) was founded in 1822 as St David's College, later became the University of Wales Lampeter, and took its present form in 2010 through a merger with Trinity University College. Three years later it absorbed Swansea Metropolitan University. The flagship Swansea School of Art (now Swansea College of Art) is the oldest art school in Wales.

Students on the outdoor education degree at UWTSD combine on-site learning with practical applications. "Nature's campus" includes the Cynefin outdoor education centre just outside Carmarthen, Bannau Brycheiniog (Brecon Beacons National Park), the Gower Peninsula and the Cambrian mountains.

An improved performance in the latest Research Excellence Framework (REF 2021) prompted a 13-place rise in our research quality index since REF 2014, with UWTSD just outside the top 100. Its best results were in art and design, education, Celtic languages and literature, theology, and psychology.

UWTSD is 4th for student satisfaction with teaching quality, based on our analysis of the latest National Student Survey (NSS) (up four places) and takes our University of the Year for Teaching Quality 2026 award. UWTSD fares nearly as well in students' evaluation of the broad experience (as it does for teaching quality), with a 12-place improvement ranking it 8th. Across both measures of student satisfaction UWTSD outdoes all other Welsh universities.

Courses require from 120 to 80 UCAS tariff points. Four in ten applicants were eligible for a contextual offer in 2024, with 3% of students securing a place through clearing.

There are opportunities to gain professional qualifications, work placements and internships with partner organisations such as Jaguar Land Rover, South Wales police and Marriott Hotels. But UWTSD is in the bottom ten of our graduate prospects ranking (125th), based on 59.6% of its graduates being in highly skilled jobs or further study 15 months after finishing their degrees.

Those studying for UWTSD's motorsport engineering degree learn in advanced workshops and laboratories at the SA1 Waterfront Campus in the city's maritime quarter. Humanities students, of subjects such as archaeology and ancient civilisations, have moved from Lampeter to the Carmarthen Campus, but still benefit from access to UWTSD's special collections and archives. Small class sizes and community spirit are constants, and the university hosts bases in Cardiff, Birmingham and London. Wellbeing team services include counselling and 24/7 safeguarding for students struggling with mental health, finances and relationships.

Only the Carmarthen Campus offers an accommodation guarantee, for first-years applying by the end of July, but other campuses provide help to first-years to get a place in purpose-built or private accommodation.

UWTSD has climbed to 4th place in our social inclusion index for England and Wales. Almost all its undergraduates come from non-selective state schools (98.5%, ranking 4th) and almost two in three (65.1%, ranking 5th) are the first in their family to go to university. Yet it is one of the least ethnically diverse universities. Almost a fifth (18%) of students receive financial assistance.

Carmarthen Campus College Road Carmarthen SA31 3EP
admissions@uwtsd.ac.uk
uwtsd.ac.uk
uwtsdunion.co.uk

Overall ranking 99
(last year 110)

Accommodation
University provided places 288
Self-catered £102–£139 per week

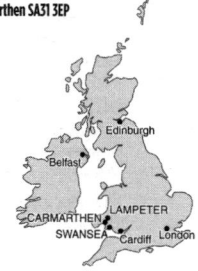

Student numbers
Undergraduates 9,580
Applications per place 2.9:1
Overall offer rate 78.5%

Fees
UK fees £9,535
International fees £15,525

uwtsd.ac.uk/open-days
uwtsd.ac.uk/study/fees-and-finance

University of Warwick

An academic powerhouse celebrating its 60th anniversary, the University of Warwick has always had epic ambitions, from its 750-acre campus to its Venice palazzo and its base in The Shard. A £425 million Science and Engineering Precinct is now being created to combine disciplinary excellence with interdisciplinary working – the biggest single investment since its foundation. A fixture in our top ten since 1998, this year it is Highly Commended in Russell Group University of the Year 2026 and wins the title of University of the Year Midlands 2026.

Research-led since its foundation, Warwick achieved impressive results in the Research Excellence Framework (REF 2021), ranking 13th in our research quality index with 92% of its work rated world-leading or internationally excellent. Economics, classics, computer science, and business and management produced some of its best results. Warwick is 74th in the 2025 QS World University Rankings. The biggest subjects are economics, maths, engineering and politics.

The university received top honours in the government's Teaching Excellence Framework (TEF 2023), one of 26 institutions out of 228 to achieve a rare triple gold for its overall grade, student experience and student outcomes. The TEF panel wrote that the university's "use of research, innovation, scholarship and professional practice contribute to an outstanding academic experience". Our latest analysis of the National Student Survey (NSS) shows healthy levels of student satisfaction, despite a dip in form this year, with teaching quality =47th and the wider undergraduate experience =23rd. These results outdo many of Britain's research heavyweights.

Standard entry requirements range from AAA to ABB at A-level. Contextual or differential offers can reduce this by one or two grades for eligible applicants.

Warwick is a primary target for top graduate employers and ranks just outside the top ten in our analysis of the Graduate Outcomes survey, with 86.4% of leavers in highly skilled jobs or further study 15 months after finishing.

Substantial investment in the campus between Coventry and Warwick has delivered world-class facilities for arts and sciences. The £60 million Faculty of Arts Building (FAB) includes an antiquities room, screening rooms and drama studios. The Marsh Observatory, opened in 2023, has a 40cm telescope and digital imaging technology to train the astronomers of tomorrow.

The £49 million Sports and Wellness Hub offers a 200-station gym, 25m swimming pool and climbing walls. University teams finished 13th in the latest British Universities and Colleges Sport (BUCS) overall points table. A wellbeing support team oversees disability, funding and mental health services, while a community safety team is available 24/7.

The university has nearly 7,000 rooms in halls. First-years who make Warwick their firm choice are guaranteed accommodation if they apply by the August deadline.

Warwick ranks =101st in our social inclusion index and admits relatively few students who are the first in their family to go to university, or are from non-selective state schools (59.9%).

The Warwick Bursary (£500–£2,500 a year) is awarded to students with household incomes under £42,875.

Coventry CV4 7AL
ugadmissions@warwick.ac.uk
warwick.ac.uk
warwicksu.com

Overall ranking 8
(last year 9)

Accommodation
University provided places 6,700
Self-catered £121–£245 per week

Student numbers
Undergraduates 18,960
Applications per place 7.5:1
Overall offer rate 70.8%

Fees
UK fees £9,535
International fees £26,290–£33,520
Medicine £30,670–£53,460

warwick.ac.uk/study/undergraduate/opendays
warwick.ac.uk/study/undergraduate/studentfunding/course-costs

University of the West of England

First founded as a merchant navigation school in 1595, the University of the West of England (UWE Bristol) gained university status in 1992. With more than 25,500 undergraduates on the register, it is now the southwest's biggest university. UWE Bristol has ploughed £300 million into boosting facilities that keep pace with its popularity. Its creative City Campus is spread across four sites in the heart of Bristol, one at Bower Ashton and three of them contemporary art centres: Spike Island, Arnolfini and Watershed.

More than three-quarters (76%) of the work it submitted for assessment in the Research Excellence Framework (REF 2021) was rated as world-leading or internationally excellent. The best results were in architecture, built environment and planning, allied health subjects, communication and media studies, engineering, and law.

UWE Bristol holds a silver rating overall from the Teaching Excellence Framework (TEF 2023), underpinned by a gold award for the student experience and silver for student outcomes. Assessors commended it for "embedding outstanding teaching, feedback and assessment practices", for inspiring students and for stretching their "knowledge and skills to the fullest potential". Results of the latest National Student Survey (NSS) show the university is heading in the right direction towards its pre-pandemic heights of student satisfaction, when it ranked in the top 10 for broad experience and 11th for teaching quality. In our new NSS analysis, it is =69th for teaching quality (up 27 places from 2024) and =75th for the wider experience (an 11-place improvement).

It has also gained ground in our main academic ranking where it is up 11 places to re-enter the upper half of the table and rejoin the top ten modern universities.

Courses require from 144 to 104 UCAS tariff points. A contextual offer policy gives eligible students a 16-point reduction in the standard requirements, or an eight-point reduction for foundation year courses. Eligibility has been widened and about 40% are now contextual.

Work placements range from a full "sandwich" year to shorter or part-time opportunities of 60 to 100 hours with organisations such as Disney, the NHS, Nike and PwC. More than three quarters of graduates (76.2%) were in highly skilled jobs or further study 15 months after leaving UWE Bristol, according to our Graduate Outcomes survey analysis, placing it as 59th for graduate prospects.

Training for sports, including football, American football and rugby teams, is held at the £4.5 million Hillside Gardens complex a few miles away, where there are artificial and grass pitches and covered spectator seating. There is a walled garden to relieve mental fatigue and UWE's wellbeing service includes access to counselling, a chaplain and an out-of-hours team.

UWE Bristol is 49th overall in our social inclusion index. Only 8.6% of its students come from grammar or independent schools and the university ranks in the top 30 for its recruitment of white working-class males (5.9% of the intake). Nearly a quarter (23.5%) are from ethnic minority backgrounds.

The £500 low-income bursary is paid every year of study, subject to annual assessment. There is support for students who are parents or carers, or who have left care or are estranged from their families.

Frenchay Campus Coldharbour Lane Bristol BS16 1QY
admissions@uwe.ac.uk
uwe.ac.uk
thestudentsunion.co.uk

Overall ranking 57
(last year 68)

Accommodation
University provided places 5,661
Self-catered £115–£286 per week

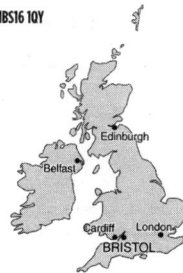

Student numbers
Undergraduates 24,170
Applications per place 4.8:1
Overall offer rate 75.2%

Fees
UK fees £9,535
International fees £16,000

uwe.ac.uk/courses/open-days
uwe.ac.uk/courses/fees

University of West London

The University of West London (UWL) is the poster university for reinvention, having staged an extraordinary turnaround over the past 20-plus years, transforming from the former Thames Valley University (which finished bottom of our league table in 2001) into today's top-70 institution (top-50 two years ago).

UWL reached our top 100 for research (92nd), based on the results of the Research Excellence Framework (REF 2021) in which nearly 80% of its submission was rated world-leading or internationally excellent.

UWL ranks 11th for satisfaction with teaching quality and joint 5th for positive feedback about the wider undergraduate experience in our latest National Student Survey (NSS) analysis. It was 1st for both only two years ago. Assessors from the government's Teaching Excellence Framework (TEF 2023) rated the university silver overall. Their report commended "outstanding teaching, feedback and assessment practices that are highly effective and tailored to support students' learning, progression and attainment". The TEF panel awarded UWL gold for the student experience, but bronze for student outcomes. Our analysis also shows the university ranks =103rd for its continuation rate (85.4%). However, the TEF report highlighted "educational gains that are relevant to students' ambitions, and consistent with the institution's goals as an engine for social mobility".

Degree courses demand from 120–96 UCAS tariff points (BBB-CCC at A-level). Foundation years have lower requirements. Applications are welcome from those who meet the entrance criteria through experience rather than academic qualifications.

An employer-led curriculum and career-focused activities are central to UWL's work-ready drive. Yet in our graduate prospects index, UWL is outside our top 100 at =102nd, based on 69.4% of graduates who were in high-skilled jobs or further study 15 months on from finishing their degree.

As well as the Ealing and Brentford sites – which are linked by a free shuttle bus – UWL has the Berkshire Institute for Health in Reading, a base for nursing and midwifery students in the city centre. At the recently opened School of Medicine and Biosciences, a research-driven approach is focused on reducing inequalities and delivering hyper-local social and care initiatives. The university's £13.8 million leisure centre in Gunnersbury Park is one of London's largest outdoor sports facilities. Students can find support for their mental wellbeing via UWL's counselling service, which has no waiting list, where students are able to speak to a counsellor, often within 24 hours of registering for the service.

There are 621 spaces in halls. The university guarantees a place to those who want one.

UWL ranks =68th overall in our social inclusion index, a big drop from 32nd last year due largely to UWL's relatively low record on recruitment and retention of students from deprived areas (7.8% and =84th), and of white working-class male students (=103rd). However, its recruitment of ethnic minority students remains a strength (56.5%, the 28th-highest proportion), and around four in ten undergraduates are aged 21-plus when they enrol (a top-25 proportion of mature students).

About half of full-time undergraduates qualify for financial assistance, which includes £1,000-a-year undergraduate bursaries for those from low-income households.

St Mary's Road Ealing London W5 5RF
undergraduate.admissions@uwl.ac.uk
uwl.ac.uk
uwlsu.com

Overall ranking =64
(last year =57)

Accommodation
University provided places 621
Catered £374–£456 per week
Self-catered £234–£316 per week

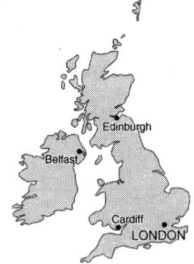

Student numbers
Undergraduates 8,000
Applications per place 6.4:1
Overall offer rate 67.6%

Fees
UK fees £9,535
International fees £16,250

uwl.ac.uk/whats-on
uwl.ac.uk/study/undergraduate/funding-bursaries-and-scholarships/undergraduate-tuition-fees

University of the West of Scotland

With a focus on practice-based learning environments and real-world experience, the University of the West of Scotland (UWS) stops off at four campuses along Scotland's west side, and one in London. The modern university is up 11 places in our main academic table, boosted by rates of student satisfaction with teaching quality, ranking it 15th in the UK, based on our analysis of the latest National Student Survey (NSS). Headquarters are at the Paisley site near Glasgow and there's a riverside campus in a coastal setting at the Ayr Campus. The smallest UWS base, Dumfries, is in an 85-acre parkland site. UWS Lanarkshire is characterised by its high-tech facilities for healthcare students. Across all sites, UWS is Scotland's leading university for access, and it tops our Scottish social inclusion index again this year.

Sport and exercise sciences, leisure and tourism, and physics led the way for UWS in the Research Excellence Framework (REF 2021), with 71% of the submissions assessed as world-leading or internationally excellent. The university's Institute of Clinical Exercise and Health Science is responsible for some of its leading research.

In our NSS 2025 analysis, UWS has risen 32 places, to 15th, as a result of feedback on teaching, and it is up 19 places (to =85th) for satisfaction with the wider undergraduate experience. However, UWS remains held back by its continuation rate (often an issue for universities with a diverse intake) and with only 77.7% of students projected to continue past their first year, it is at the foot of the table.

Standard entry requirements range from 80 UCAS tariff points on nursing courses to 112 points for the education degree. Care-leavers are guaranteed an offer if they come through one of the university's recruiting programmes, or are guaranteed an interview/audition for courses that require them. In 2024, 7.2% of new students enrolled via clearing.

Employability initiatives at UWS include academic, professional and personal development modules built into undergraduate programmes. UWS ranks 81st for graduate prospects in our analysis of the numbers in highly skilled jobs or further study 15 months after finishing a degree.

Most courses leave Wednesday afternoons free to encourage students to take part in sport and social activities, and membership to gym and fitness facilities at the four Scottish campuses is free of charge. Paisley and Ayr campuses have 696 beds between them, with allocation on a first-come, first-served basis. In 2024–25, all first-years who requested a place got one.

The UWS Foundation Academy works with 33 schools across the west of Scotland to pave the way to university for eligible pupils. Its free programme includes a campus visit, online training in academic skills and a reduced offer. UWS, which remains the most socially inclusive institution in Scotland overall, recruits the most students who are the first in their family to go to university (50.8%) and no Scottish universities have a higher intake of mature students (55.8%).

UWS provides practical financial help to support students in need. In 2023–24, it awarded £1.75 million in total through Discretionary and Childcare Funds – the latter helps eligible student-parents to meet costs that may otherwise stand in their way of attending university.

Paisley Campus Paisley PA1 2BE
ask@uws.ac.uk
uws.ac.uk
uwsunion.org.uk

Overall ranking 110
(last year 121)

Accommodation
University provided places 696
Self-catered £98–£173 per week

Student numbers
Undergraduates 10,100
Applications per place 3.7:1
Overall offer rate 71.2%

Fees
Scots fees £0–£1,820
International fees £15,500–£21,250
RUK fees £9,535

uws.ac.uk/study/open-days-info-sessions
uws.ac.uk/money-fees-funding

University of Westminster

Powered by a pioneering spirit as the UK's first polytechnic institution, founded in 1838, the University of Westminster champions diversity and opportunities for all. Most of its campuses are in the thick of London's West End – to the extent that the capital itself becomes a campus of sorts, providing an urban university experience like no other.

Westminster's wide-ranging course options are organised within 12 schools across three colleges (College of Design, Creative and Digital Industries, College of Liberal Arts and Sciences and Westminster Business School).

Art and design produced the university's best results in the latest Research Excellence Framework (REF 2021), keeping pace with many leading institutions. Overall, Westminster places in the upper half of UK universities in our research quality index (58th).

Westminster achieved triple silver in the Teaching Excellence Framework (TEF 2023), up from bronze in the previous assessment six years earlier. Feedback in the National Student Survey (NSS) is improving. Westminster has risen 14 places to rank =32nd for satisfaction with the student experience in our analysis. For satisfaction with teaching quality, it has risen 12 places to =95th. The scores have spurred a five-place rise in our main academic ranking. However, relatively low numbers of students achieving firsts and 2:1s hold Westminster back (it ranks =112th for this metric), as do its graduate prospects and continuation rate.

Several courses have been withdrawn and it is worth checking the website. New courses include: tourism management; international event management; creative computing; international communication and international business; fashion accessories design; fashion manufacturing; fashion sustainability; advanced legal research; games art/design; immersive media design; applied artificial intelligence; and environmental sustainability and data science.

Entry starts from EE at A-level and ranges up to ABB. The university does not make contextual offers. Westminster is in the bottom ten for graduate prospects (122nd), based on analysis of the Graduate Outcomes survey showing only 61.2% of graduates working in highly skilled jobs or furthering their studies 15 months after their degree. Its new Centre for Employability and Enterprise may bring a renewed focus when it opens in 2026.

Membership of all university sports facilities and teams has been free since 2023, including the Regent's Street gym and Quintin Hogg Memorial Sports Ground in Chiswick, west London, overlooking the Thames, where there are extensive grounds for football, rugby, hockey, lacrosse, cricket, tennis and netball. Westminster is a member of the Mental Health Charter programme. Students are provided with one-to-one sessions with wellbeing advisers, counsellors, mentors and mental health practitioners.

Allocation in halls is first-come, first-served – there's no guarantee of a place in one of the 804 rooms but priority is given to new students who apply by June 1, and those with a disability or medical condition. A high proportion of students live at home.

Westminster is in the top 40 in our social inclusion index (38th) and its student population in London reflects the city's diversity.

There were 479 means-tested Westminster Bursaries of £700 per year of study given to new students in 2024-25.

---

309 Regent Street London W1B 2HW
course-enquiries@westminster.ac.uk
westminster.ac.uk
uwsu.com

Overall ranking 115
(last year 120)

Accommodation
University provided places 804
Self-catered £191–£266 per week

Student numbers
Undergraduates 15,955
Applications per place 5.0:1
Overall offer rate 81.8%

Fees
UK fees £9,535
International fees £17,000

westminster.ac.uk/study/open-days-and-events
westminster.ac.uk/study/fees-and-funding

University of Winchester

Known as King Alfred College until 2004, its university charter was granted in 2005. The University of Winchester has since expanded into a multi-faculty, modern institution, encompassing humanities and social sciences, education and the arts, business and digital technology, law, crime and justice, and health and wellbeing. Musical students are well catered for, with about 17 music groups such as the King Alfred Singers Choir and Chapel Music Group, and students can access group or individual tuition through the music school.

In the latest Research Excellence Framework (REF 2021), Winchester tripled its proportion of world-leading work compared with the previous assessment in 2014 but fell 24 places to 106th in our research quality index against bigger gains elsewhere. Theology was among the strongest subjects.

Awarding Winchester triple silver overall, for student experience, and student outcomes in the government's Teaching Excellence Framework (TEF 2023), assessors were impressed by the "excellent academic practice embedded across the [university]". Teacher training remains a significant strength at Winchester, which is rated "outstanding" by Ofsted for its primary and secondary provision in all areas.

However, dramatically lower rates of student satisfaction have contributed to a fall of three places in our main academic league table this year, compounding an 18-place tumble in our last edition to leave Winchester ranked 106th. Our analysis of the latest National Student Survey (NSS) suggests growing discontent on campus: feedback on teaching quality places Winchester =92nd (down ten places) and for satisfaction with the wider undergraduate experience 113rd (12 places lower).

New for 2025, the Discover Winchester scheme will provide contextual offers one grade (8 points) below standard entry requirements. Degree courses demand between 128 and 88 UCAS tariff points. Foundation year entry, available on selected degrees, requires 48 UCAS points.

Winchester fosters links with employers such as Southern Health and Hampshire Hospitals NHS Foundation Trusts.

Winchester is outside the top 100 for graduate prospects – 69% of graduates were in high-skilled jobs or postgraduate study 15 months after finishing their degree, according to the Graduate Outcomes survey.

A ten-minute walk from the cathedral city, the campus is divided into the King Alfred and the West Downs quarters. The majority of students live and study on the King Alfred quarter. Specialist facilities include psychology and sports labs, a performing arts studio and recording suite.

Free fitness classes are a perk at the university gym on the King Alfred Campus. Students have access to counselling, mental health mentors and therapeutic groups.

First-years who apply by the June deadline are "usually guaranteed" one of 1,589 residential spaces. About 80% live on campus.

Winchester is 53rd in our social inclusion index for England and Wales, its overall rank boosted by a relatively high proportion of disabled students (28.7%, 12th). Most of the intake (94.1%) is drawn from non-selective state schools (=43rd).

Winchester offers a new Widening Participation Bursary, worth £1,000 a year, to students from under-represented backgrounds.

Sparkford Road Winchester SO22 4NR
admissions@winchester.ac.uk
winchester.ac.uk
winchesterstudents.co.uk

Overall ranking 106
(last year 103)

Accommodation
University provided places 1,589
Catered £212 per week
Self-catered £152–£204 per week

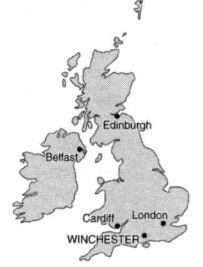

Student numbers
Undergraduates 5,745
Applications per place 4.7:1
Overall offer rate 89.8%

Fees
UK fees £9,535
International fees £16,700

winchester.ac.uk/News-and-Events/On-Campus-Events/Open-Days
winchester.ac.uk/student-life/Students-and-money

University of Wolverhampton

A spirit of social mobility runs through the University of Wolverhampton, the West Midlands institution that has been transforming its campuses as part of its mission to transform lives. Wolverhampton has introduced new facilities in healthcare, created a Screen School for creative and digital students and upgraded pharmacy teaching spaces. The university is a key provider of health sector staff including nurses, midwives, paramedics and social workers for the Black Country. Its efforts make waves: research by the Higher Education Policy Institute think tank puts the university in the UK's top ten for social mobility.

More than half of Wolverhampton's submission to the Research Excellence Framework (REF 2021) was judged as world-leading or internationally excellent (109th).

The most recent Teaching Excellence Framework (TEF 2023) rated Wolverhampton bronze overall and for both underpinning aspects of student experience and student outcomes (down from silver in the previous assessment). Despite the rating, TEF assessors did pay credit to Wolverhampton, saying it "fosters a supportive learning environment". Our latest National Student Survey (NSS) analysis shows Wolverhampton is doing better than bronze for student satisfaction; it is up ten places to =44th for students' evaluation of teaching quality. It has also made ground on feedback regarding the wider undergraduate experience, edging up six places to =80th. The university has in turn edged a couple of places up our main academic ranking to 121st.

Degree courses demand 120-96 UCAS tariff points (equivalent to BBB-CCC at A-level). A contextual admissions policy applies to most courses and 31% of students were recruited through clearing in 2024.

Wolverhampton's courses are developed in consultation with industry practitioners. Wolverhampton is =82nd for graduate prospects, based on our analysis of the Graduate Outcomes survey, which shows that 73.4% of leavers were in highly skilled jobs or had returned to further study 15 months after finishing their degree.

The university has invested in new facilities for healthcare, nursing and paramedic students based at Walsall and City Campuses. In Telford, the new Centre for Health and Social Care trains key workers.

The Walsall Campus is the base for high-quality sports facilities including a new Active Wellbeing, Rehabilitation and Performance Centre, funded by the Office for Students. It has extensive sports facilities including grass and 3G pitches, outdoor courts for tennis and netball, a gym and strength facility and a 200m running track. The recently opened £120 million site in Springfield regenerated an old brewery into Europe's largest specialist construction and built environment campus, hosting the £45 million School of Architecture and Built Environment.

Wolverhampton's halls are among the UK's most pocket-friendly, with rooms starting at £96 a week. Allocations of the 1,081 rooms are made on a first-come, first-served basis, and there is space for about 85% of first-years who request it.

In 11th place of our social inclusion index overall (down from 6th last year), continuing outreach work by the university aims to raise aspirations and attainment among young people in the region. The university provided 834 awards worth a total of almost £500,000 in 2024-25.

Wulfruna Street Wolverhampton WV1 1LY
admissions@wlv.ac.uk
wlv.ac.uk
wolvesunion.org

Overall ranking 121
(last year 123)

Accommodation
University provided places 1,081
Self-catered £96–£114 per week

Student numbers
Undergraduates 11,245
Applications per place 5.4:1
Overall offer rate 72.8%

Fees
UK fees £9,535
International fees £15,995–£17,000

wlv.ac.uk/news-and-events/open-day
wlv.ac.uk/apply/funding-costs-fees-and-support/fees-and-costs

University of Worcester

The University of Worcester is building a burgeoning reputation in higher education. It has flourished since gaining its charter in 2005 and there is now a broad subject mix across eight academic schools including arts and humanities, psychology, business, and since 2023, the Three Counties Medical School, which offers a four-year graduate entry medical degree.

Climbing one place further up our main league table, Worcester ranks 98th this year, partly driven by a top-ten performance in our sustainability metric, based on People & Planet's university league, which assesses environmental and ethical performance.

In the latest Research Excellence Framework (REF 2021), one third of Worcester's submission was rated world-leading or internationally excellent, with some of its best results in art and design, history, and sport and exercise science. However, it fell out of the top 100 (121st) compared with its performance in the previous national assessment in 2014. Worcester's Three Counties Medical School was allocated 62 places for UK students to begin in the 2025-26 academic year – 12 more than its original 50.

Triple silver – overall, for student experience and student outcomes – greeted Worcester in the Teaching Excellence Framework (TEF 2023). Rates of student satisfaction are showing signs of recovery, having been slow to return to pre-pandemic form. In our analysis of the latest National Student Survey (NSS), Worcester ranks =61st for feedback on teaching quality (up 29 places year-on-year). However, at =82nd for satisfaction with the wider undergraduate experience it has lost eight places. Further campus investment may help to shift the dial.

New for 2025 are computer science and football performance and coaching, to be joined in 2026 by forensic science and operating department practitioner courses. There are no planned closures.

New entrants to Worcester averaged 114 UCAS tariff points across all courses, according to the latest figures – ranking it =91st for entry standards. The university attracted more than 9,300 applications for entry in 2024 and around 2,300 new students were accepted onto courses, reflecting a continuing cooling of demand for places at Worcester over the past decade. Applications and enrolments were about 30% higher ten years ago.

A focus on work placements and employability translates into a top-50 place for the university in our analysis of the Graduate Outcomes survey, which found that 78.36% of Worcester graduates had found highly skilled work or returned to study within 15 months of finishing their degree.

Worcester's comprehensive programme of student welfare initiatives includes prompt access to counsellors and other mental health practitioners. Accommodation is guaranteed for first-years who firmly accept an offer and apply by the June deadline. Rooms are allocated on a first-come, first-served basis.

Worcester is up 11 places to 60th in our social inclusion index of England and Wales. Nearly a quarter of students (24.2%) register a disability, and its non-selective state school intake is in the top 20. But Worcester is less ethnically diverse than many other institutions, with 15.4% of students from black and ethnic minority backgrounds (90th).

Academic Achievement scholarships worth £1,000 are awarded to eligible undergraduates in their second and third year of a degree course.

Henwick Grove Worcester WR2 6AJ
admissions@worc.ac.uk
worcester.ac.uk
worcsu.com

Overall ranking 98
(last year 99)

Accommodation
University provided places 1,010
Self-catered £131–£228 per week

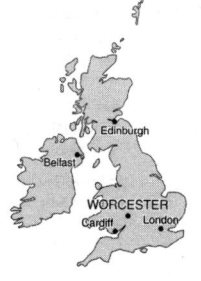

Student numbers
Undergraduates 6,055
Applications per place 4.1:1
Overall offer rate 78.0%

Fees
UK fees £9,535
International fees £16,700
Medicine £47,900

worcester.ac.uk/study/open-days
https://www.worcester.ac.uk/study/fees-and-finance

Wrexham University

A modern university guided by its civic role of driving regional – and global – economic and social change, Wrexham University has been investing £80 million into an ambitious campus overhaul, which includes the recently opened Health and Education Innovation Quarter and Cyber Innovations Academy.

A university since 2008, Wrexham has a small population of about 2,500 undergraduates. In the latest Research Excellence Framework (REF 2021), social work and social policy produced some of Wrexham's best results, with some world-leading research. However, the university fell to =124th in our research quality index in the face of improved performance across the sector compared with the previous national assessment, in 2014.

Down seven places in our main academic league table this year, Wrexham is ranked in the bottom ten. Discontent on campus is behind the dip in form, as reflected by a much weaker performance in the latest National Student Survey (NSS). Based on feedback from students, Wrexham has plunged 57 places to rank =61st for satisfaction with teaching quality, and it has lost even more ground for students' feedback on the wider undergraduate experience, placing 114th in our NSS analysis, a 96-place decline. Wrexham is also held back in our league table by a poor continuation rate, with 80.6% of students projected to carry on from the first to second year (126th).

Most degree courses require 120 UCAS tariff points; foundation programmes set the bar lower, at 48. Wrexham doesn't use the standard contextual admissions model. Instead, applications are considered in the round before a fair and achievable offer is made.

Graduate prospects are among Wrexham's strongest suits, with 74.7% of leavers in high-skilled jobs or further study 15 months after finishing their degree, according to the Graduate Outcomes survey. It ranks 73rd in our table.

Glyn's is the Students' Union bar on campus. Those looking for a change of scene can head over the border to Chester. The Plas Coch Campus has a modern sports centre with two floodlit artificial pitches, a performance laboratory and indoor facilities. Counselling and mental health support is available for free, and care-leavers are given extra support.

Demand for the 321 residential rooms is greater than supply, so not everyone who applies gets a place. Priority goes to full-time first-years, those who live the furthest from campus and students with social or physical needs.

After a long-term residence in our top spot for social inclusion in England and Wales, Wrexham is down two places to sit 3rd. Its overall rank is boosted by strong performances in most of our contributing measures, including the proportion of students who are the first in their family to go to university (59.6%, ranking 16th). All but 2.2% of the intake come from non-selective state schools (8th) and 7% of the intake fall into the white, working-class male category (one of the most under-represented groups, =15th).

Support includes ten £1,000 cash awards for students who are the first in their family to go to university, and £1,000 or 50% rent reduction for care leavers or estranged students.

Mold Road Wrexham LL11 2AW
enquiries@wrexham.ac.uk
wrexham.ac.uk
wrexhamglyndwrsu.org.uk

Overall ranking 122
(last year 115)

Accommodation
University provided places 321
Self-catered £125–£1785 per week

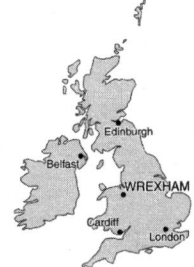

Student numbers
Undergraduates 2,525
Applications per place 4.9:1
Overall offer rate 59.8%

Fees
UK fees £9,535
International fees £11,750

wrexham.ac.uk/visit/undergraduate-events
wrexham.ac.uk/fees-and-funding

University of York

The University of York, a member of the Russell Group, the York Maastricht Partnership, and the Association of Commonwealth Universities, has dropped to 20th, three places down on last year. It does take a top ten spot for research quality (9th), following superb results in the latest Research Excellence Framework (REF 2021), when 93% of its work was rated world-leading or internationally excellent. Results were best in language and linguistics; education; philosophy; and sociology.

The university's reconfiguration of academic disciplines in 2022 created three schools for research and teaching: Business and Society; Arts and Creative Technologies; and Physics, Engineering and Technology. York's ambition to be a university for public good is evident in its research themes and its strength in teaching is recognised with a gold rating overall in the Teaching Excellence Framework (TEF 2023). Assessors rated York gold for the student experience and silver for student outcomes.

Feedback in the National Student Survey (NSS) hints at discontentment with the teaching on campus, however. In our latest NSS analysis, York has fallen outside the top 100 (=105th) for satisfaction with teaching quality. It has slipped outside the upper half of UK universities for evaluations of the wider undergraduate experience (=87th, down 23 places on last year).

From 2026, York will offer degrees in biodiversity, ecology and conservation; and medical engineering.

York requires A*AA to BBC at A-level. Contextual offers reduce the requirements by up to two grades.

Students enter the York Strengths programme from the first year of their degree and learn early on to consider the skills they need. All disciplines offer placement years in industry. Our analysis of the Graduate Outcomes survey shows such initiatives are paying off: more than four in five (82.7%) graduates were in highly skilled jobs or further study 15 months after leaving – a top 25 result for York.

Colleges named after the LGBTQ+ rights champions Anne Lister and David Kato are among the latest additions at Campus East, where Langwith, Goodricke and Constantine colleges opened in 2022. There are more than 5,000 cycle parking spaces on campus, to help cut the 30-minute walking time to the city centre, as well as a free bus service.

More than 2,000 York students are signed up to the university's sports system, which offers 65 clubs and the opportunity to take part regardless of ability or experience. For those with Olympic rowing potential, York has a British Rowing Start Centre and the university boathouse on the River Ouse is less than a mile and a half from campus. Talk Campus provides peer support in 26 languages online, and members of the Open Door Team of psychologists and student wellbeing officers are embedded in academic departments for mental health support.

First-years who apply by the end of July are guaranteed a room.

The university was the first Russell Group member to sign the Social Mobility Pledge and its programmes continue to target left-behind communities. York ranks 95th in our social inclusion index. The York Bursary of £1,000 per year is paid to students with a household income below £35,000, and care leavers, estranged students and refugees are eligible for further support.

Heslington York YO10 5DD
ug-admissions@york.ac.uk
york.ac.uk
yusu.org

Overall ranking 20
(last year =17)

Accommodation
University provided places 5,147
Catered £157–£252 per week
Self-catered £99–£218 per week

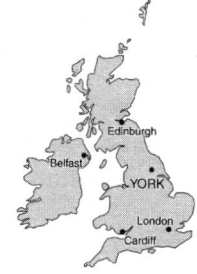

Student numbers
Undergraduates 14,705
Applications per place 5.9:1
Overall offer rate 79.3%

Fees
UK fees £9,535
International fees £25,800–£31,100
Medicine £47,000

york.ac.uk/study/undergraduate/visits/open-days
york.ac.uk/study/undergraduate/fees-funding

York St John University

Students at York St John University (YSJ) enjoy views of the medieval gothic masterpiece York Minster from their campus in the historic city. The original quad buildings create a handsome entrance and date from YSJ's founding as a teacher training college in 1841. They are still going strong as teaching spaces too, for subjects including law and dance, but are joined by an increasing estate of modern facilities.

The latest Research Excellence Framework (REF 2021) judged 58% of YSJ's submissions as world-leading or internationally excellent (115th). A research centre, the Institute for Health and Care Improvement, opened in 2023 to tackle issues such as health inequalities, an ageing population and pressure on the health service.

Underpinning a silver rating overall in the Teaching Excellence Framework (TEF 2023), YSJ earned gold for the student experience, and another silver for student outcomes. However, since the TEF assessment the university's superb record on student satisfaction has cooled. In our latest National Student Survey (NSS) analysis YSJ ranks =32nd for students' evaluation of teaching quality (down ten places) and it has plunged 52 places for their feedback on the wider undergraduate experience, to =94th.

As YSJ has diversified from training teachers into a much broader course offering it has spent £100 million in recent years to stay in step with its academic focus. The first students of new degrees in midwifery and diagnostic radiography began courses this term, their path paved with the addition of an MRI scanner and x-ray technology to campus, as well as operating department and midwifery suites.

From 2025 students can take degrees in midwifery, diagnostic radiography and user experience design. Two courses closing in 2025 are software engineering and games design.

Full degree courses require 128–104 UCAS tariff points, with foundation years needing 48 points. A contextual offer scheme applies to all courses except professional programmes, usually undercutting advertised tariffs by two A-level grades. In 2024, 10.9% of students arrived via clearing.

YSJ's graduate and work placement fair attracts employers that can offer graduate schemes and year-in-industry opportunities. But with our analysis of the Graduate Outcomes survey showing 69.1% of leavers in high-skilled jobs or postgraduate study 15 months on, YSJ is outside the top 100 (106th).

Appointments to spend time with the YSJ therapy dog, Blue, are among the university's wellbeing initiatives. Trained counsellors and advisers on mental health and welfare also tailor their services to the needs of students.

First-years who apply by the deadline are guaranteed a place in halls, which cost between £125 and £215 a week. None of the accommodation is catered.

Our outgoing University of the Year for Social Inclusion, YSJ shot up 31 places year-on-year to rank 16th in our previous edition. Featuring in the top 30 overall this year, YSJ succeeds in recruiting a relatively high proportion of students from one of the most under-represented groups – white working-class males – (7.4%, =13th) and more than a quarter of the intake has a registered disability (28.9%, 10th).

YSJ's package of support includes £800 per year scholarships for students from ethnic minorities with a household income below £42,000, care leavers and estranged students, and those entering with contextual offers.

Lord Mayor's Walk York YO31 7EX
admissions@yorksj.ac.uk
yorksj.ac.uk
ysjsu.com

Overall ranking 112
(last year 93)

Accommodation
University provided places 2,179
Self-catered £125–£215 per week

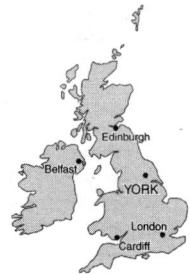

Student numbers
Undergraduates 6,460
Applications per place 4.8:1
Overall offer rate 85.0%

Fees
UK fees £9,535
International fees £12,100–£14,900

yorksj.ac.uk/study/undergraduate/meet-us/open-days
yorksj.ac.uk/international/funding-scholarships-and-paying-tuition-fees

Specialist and Private Institutions

This listing gives contact details for selected higher education institutions not listed elsewhere within the book. They range from small specialist colleges to private universities offering a wide range of courses. Some have degree-awarding powers of their own, while some are affiliated with other universities. Those marked * are members of GuildHE (**www.guildhe.ac.uk**). Where given, fees are for a single year of undergraduate study, correct for the most recent year of entry publicised by the institution. You should check the fees for the year you wish to begin your studies before you apply.

1 Specialist colleges of the University of London

Courtauld Institute of Art
Somerset House Strand,
London WC2R 0RN
www.courtauld.ac.uk
Fees: £9,275 (Overseas £28,350)

London Business School
Regent's Park,
London NW1 4SA
www.london.edu
Postgraduate only, fees vary

London School of Hygiene and Tropical Medicine
Keppel Street,
London WC1E 7HT
www.lshtm.ac.uk
Postgraduate only, fees vary

Royal Academy of Music
Marylebone Road,
London NW1 5HT
www.ram.ac.uk
Fees: £9,535 (Overseas £29,050)

Royal Central School of Speech and Drama*
Eton Avenue,
London NW3 3HY
www.cssd.ac.uk
Fees: £9,535 (Overseas £26,460)

Royal Veterinary College
Royal College Street,
London NW1 0TU
www.rvc.ac.uk
Fees: £9,535 (Overseas £47,960)

University of London Institute in Paris
9-11 rue de Constantine,
75007 Paris, France
www.ulip.london.ac.uk
Fees vary by course and modules taken

2 Specialist colleges and private institutions

Arden University*
Campuses in London, Birmingham,
Manchester, Leeds & Berlin
www.arden.ac.uk
Fees: £9, 275 (different fees apply for online learning or study at the Berlin campus)

Black Mountains College
Ennig Offices, The Square, Talgarth,
Brecon LD3 0BW
www.blackmountainscollege.uk
Fees: £9,250 (Overseas contact college)

BPP University*
Study centres across England
and the Channel Islands
www.bpp.com
Fees vary by course and study mode

Bristol Old Vic Theatre School
1-2 Downside Road, Clifton,
Bristol BS8 2XF
www.oldvic.ac.uk
Postgraduate only, fees vary

University of the Built Environment*
Horizons, 60 Queen's Road,
Reading RG1 5BS
www.ube.ac.uk
Fees: £9,270 (Overseas contact university)

Central School of Ballet*
21–22 Hatfields, Paris Garden,
London SE1 8DJ
www.centralschoolofballet.co.uk
Fees: £9,275 (Overseas £23,614)

Cranfield University
Campuses in Cranfield (Milton Keynes)
and Shrivenham (Swindon)
www.cranfield.ac.uk
Postgraduate only, fees vary

Dyson Institute of Engineering and Technology*
Tetbury Hill, Malmesbury,
Wiltshire SN16 0RP
www.dysoninstitute.ac.uk
Paid degree courses – no fees

Escape Studios
6 Mitre Passage,
London SE10 0ER
www.escapestudios.ac.uk
Fees: £9,535 (Overseas £17,995)

Glasgow School of Art
167 Renfrew Street,
Glasgow G3 6RQ
www.gsa.ac.uk
Fees: Scotland £1,820; RUK £9,535
(Overseas £24,800)

Guildhall School of Music and Drama
Silk Street, Barbican,
London EC2Y 8DT
www.gsmd.ac.uk
Fees: £9,535
(Overseas £24,980–£26,490)

Hereford College of Arts*
Folly Lane,
Hereford HR1 1LT
www.hca.ac.uk
Fees: £9,275 (Overseas contact school)

ICMP (Institute of Contemporary Music Performance)*
Campuses in Kilburn, Queen's Park,
Liverpool and Leeds
www.icmp.ac.uk
Feees: £9,535 (Overseas £16,250)

Istituto Marangoni London*
30 Fashion Street,
London E1 6PX
www.istitutomarangoni.com
Fees: £13,100–£14,300
(Overseas £21,000–£22,400)

The University of Law*
Campuses in Birmingham,
Bristol, Leeds, London, Manchester
and Nottingham
www.law.ac.uk
Fees: £9,535 (Overseas and varying
course lengths contact university)

Leeds Conservatoire*
3 Quarry Hill,
Leeds LS2 7PD
www.leedsconservatoire.ac.uk
Fees: £9,535 (Overseas £20,300–£20,700)

Liverpool Institute for Performing Arts*
Mount Street,
Liverpool L1 9HF
www.lipa.ac.uk
Fees: £9,535 (Overseas contact university)

London Academy of Music and Dramatic Art*
155 Talgarth Road,
London W14 9DA
www.lamda.ac.uk
Fees: £9,275 (Overseas £25,363)

London Contemporary Dance School
17 Dukes Road,
London WC1H 9PY
www.theplace.org.uk
Fees: £9,535 (Overseas £22,950)

The London Interdisciplinary School
20–30 Whitechapel Road,
London E1 1EW
www.lis.ac.uk
Fees: £9,275 (Overseas £20,000)

London School of Science and Technology*
Campuses in London, Birmingham and Luton
www.lsst.ac
Fees: £9,535 (Overseas contact school)

MLA College*
The Merchant, St Andrew Street, Plymouth PL1 2AX
www.mla.ac.uk
Fees: £9,535 (Overseas contact college)

Moorlands College*
Sopley, Christchurch, Dorset BH23 7AT
www.moorlands.ac.uk
Fees: £9,535 (Overseas contact college)

National Centre for Circus Arts*
Coronet Street, London N1 6HD
www.nationalcircus.org.uk
Fees: £9,535 (Overseas £18,000)

National Institute of Teaching*
Campuses in Birmingham, Bristol, London, Blackburn, Redcar and Doncaster
www.niot.org.uk
Postgraduate only, fees vary

Northeastern University London*
Devon House, 58 St Katharine's Way, London E1W 1LP
www.nulondon.ac.uk
Fees: £9,535 (Overseas £23,857-£28,411)

Northern School of Art*
Campuses in Middlesbrough and Hartlepool
www.northernart.ac.uk
Fees: £9,535 (Overseas contact school)

Arts University Plymouth*
Tavistock Place, Plymouth PL4 8AT
01752 203434
Fees: £9,535 (Overseas £17,500)

Rambert School of Ballet and Contemporary Dance*
Clifton Lodge, St Margarets Drive, Twickenham TW1 1QN
www.rambertschool.org.uk
Fees: £9,535 (Overseas £22,425)

Ravensbourne University London*
6 Penrose Way, Greenwich Peninsula, London SE10 0EW
www.ravensbourne.ac.uk
Fees: £9,535 (Overseas £17,000)

Regent College London*
Carmine Court, 202 Imperial Drive, Harrow HA2 7HG
www.rcl.ac.uk
Fees: £9,535 (Overseas contact university)

Regent's University London
Inner Circle, Regent's Park, London NW1 4NS
www.regents.ac.uk
Fees: £24,500-£27,750

Rose Bruford College*
Lamorbey Park, Burnt Oak Lane, Sidcup, Kent DA15 9DF
www.bruford.ac.uk
Fees vary by course and nationality

Royal Academy of the Dramatic Arts
62-64 Gower Street, London WC1E 6ED
www.rada.ac.uk
Fees: £9,535 (Overseas £26,500)

Royal Birmingham Conservatoire
200 Jennens Road, Birmingham B4 7XR
www.bcu.ac.uk/conservatoire
Fees: £9,535 (Overseas £20,960)

Royal College of Art*
Kensington Gore, London SW7 2EU
www.rca.ac.uk
Postgraduate only, fees vary

Royal College of Music
Prince Consort Road,
London SW7 2BS
www.rcm.ac.uk
Fees: £9,535 (Overseas £31,300)

Royal Conservatoire of Scotland
100 Renfrew Street,
Glasgow G2 3DB
www.rcs.ac.uk
Fees: Scotland £1,820; RUK £9,535
(Overseas £27,968–£28,919)

Royal Northern College of Music
124 Oxford Road,
Manchester M13 9RD
www.rncm.ac.uk
Fees: £9,535 (Overseas £29,650–£31,450)

Royal Welsh College of Music and Drama
Castle Grounds, Cathays Park,
Cardiff CF10 3ER
www.rwcmd.ac.uk
Fees: £9,535 (Overseas £20,790–£29,500)

St Mary's University College Belfast*
191 Falls Road,
Belfast BT12 6FE
www.stmarys-belfast.ac.uk
Fees: NI & ROI £4,855; RUK £9,250
(Overseas £20,800)

Scotland's Rural College
Campuses at Aberdeen, Ayr, Cupar,
Dumfries, Oatridge, West Lothian and
Edinburgh
www.sruc.ac.uk
Fees vary by course and nationality

University Centre Sparsholt*
Westley Lane, Sparsholt,
Winchester SO21 2NF
www.sparsholt.ac.uk
Fees: £9,275 (Overseas £13,000)

Stranmillis University College
Stranmillis Road,
Belfast BT9 5DY
www.stran.ac.uk
Fees: NI & ROI £4,855; RUK £9,535
(Overseas £20,800)

Trinity Laban Conservatoire of Music and Dance
King Charles Court, Old Royal Naval College,
London SE10 9JF
www.trinitylaban.ac.uk
Fees: £9,535 (Overseas £17,670–£26,060)

University Academy 92*
UA92 Campus, Brian Statham Way,
Old Trafford,
Manchester M16 0PU
www.ua92.ac.uk
Fees: £9,535 (Overseas £16,665–£16,965);
higher fees apply for two-year courses

University College, Birmingham (UCB)*
Summer Row,
Birmingham B3 1JB
www.ucb.ac.uk
Fees: £9,250 (Overseas £16,000–£19,750);
higher fees apply for two-year courses

UCFB (University Campus of Football Business)*
Wembley Stadium,
London HA9 0WS
14th Floor, 111 Piccadilly,
Manchester M1 2HY
www.ucfb.ac.uk
Fees: £9,535 (Overseas £16,950)

Walbrook Institute*
25 Lovat Lane, London EC3R 8EB
www.onlinedegree.libf.ac.uk
Postgraduate only, fees vary

Index

Aberdeen, University of 306
Abertay University 307
Aberystwyth, University of 308
access courses 40
accommodation
  after first year 45, 108
  bills 113–14
  catering 107
  choosing 109–10
  contracts 110
  deposits 113
  halls of residence 105–7, 110
  insurance 73, 111
  inventories 113–14
  lodging 110
  multiple occupation 112
  parental purchase 110
  private landlords 110, 112
  purpose built student accommodation (PBSA) 103, 104
  rent rates 45, 102, 103, 108
  rental code of standards 112
  Renters' Rights Bill 103, 104–5
  safety 114
  security 111, 114
  self-catering 107
  shared living experience 102, 109, 112
  staying at home 43, 102, 108–9
  supply issues 103, 104
  tenancy agreements 112–13
  tenancy problems 106
  websites 114
accounting and finance 136–8
admission tests 37, 38, 279
Adult Dependants' Grant 75
aeronautical and manufacturing engineering 139–40
affordability 30
agriculture and forestry 140–1
AI, impact on job market 55–6
alcohol 116–17
American studies *see* cultural studies
anatomy and physiology 141–2
Anglia Ruskin University 309
animal science 143–4
anthropology 144–5
applications *see also* UCAS
  Apply registration 78–9
  choices 79–80
  Clearing 16, 77–8, 86–8
  Clearing Plus 86
  deadlines 79–80, 82–4
  deferred places 88–9
  education details 80
  international students 82, 129
  interviews 84
  offers 85
  personal details 79

personal statements 78, 80–2
post-qualifications admissions model (PQA) 77
references 82
results day 86
timeline 7–8, 79–80, 82–4
apprenticeships 40–1, 63–4, 78
archaeology and forensic science 145–7
architecture 147–9
Arden University 439
art and design 149–51
Arts University Bournemouth 310
Arts University Plymouth 441
Aston University 312
astronomy 241–3
award winners 15

Balliol College, University of Oxford 279
Bangor University 313
Bath Spa University 315
Bath, University of 35, 314
Bedfordshire, University of 316
bioengineering and biomedical engineering 152–3
biological sciences 153–6
biomedical science *see* anatomy and physiology
Birkbeck, University of London 14, 39, 317
Birmingham City University 319
Birmingham Newman University 12, 320
Birmingham, University of 318
Bishop Grosseteste University *see* Lincoln Bishop University
black awarding gap 94–5
Black Mountains College 47, 439
Bolton, University of *see* Greater Manchester
Bournemouth University 321
BPP University 46, 63, 439
Bradford, University of 322
Brasenose College, University of Oxford 279
Brighton, University of 323
Bristol Old Vic Theatre School 439
Bristol, University of 324
Brunel University London 325
Buckingham, University of 40, 46, 63, 326
Buckinghamshire New University 327
budgeting 71–3
building 156–7
bursaries 12, 63, 66, 73–4
business, management and marketing 157–61

Cambridge, University of
  about 328
  admission tests 37, 38, 279
  application process 79, 84, 271, 279
  colleges 276, 293–303
  diversity 93, 99, 273–6
  graduate prospects 273
  league tables 16, 133, 271
  offer rates 271–2, 277
  satisfaction surveys 272–3
  Tomkins Table 273
campus universities 44
cancel culture 120
Canterbury Christ Church University 329
Cardiff Metropolitan University 47, 331
Cardiff University 330
career prospects *see* graduate prospects
Cathedrals Group 45
Celtic studies *see* cultural studies
Central School of Ballet* 440
chemical engineering 161–2
chemistry 163–4
Chester, University of 332
Chichester, University of 333
Childcare Grant 75
choosing a degree
  alternatives to higher education 30–1, 88
  checklist 47
  colleges 45–7
  course types 39–41
  information sources 47–8
  "insuranc" choice 85
  Joint and Combined Honours 37
  location 43–4
  Open Days 44, 48
  priorities 31–2
  private universities 46–7
  subject choice 29, 30, 31, 32–3, 47, 50, 56–7
  university choice 31, 41–7
Christ Church College, University of Oxford 280
Christ's College, University of Cambridge 293
Churchill College, University of Cambridge 293
cinematics 182–5
City St George's, University of London 13, 334
city universities 43
civil engineering 165–7
Clare College, University of Cambridge 293–4
classics and ancient history 167–8
classifications 21

Clearing 16, 77-8
Combined Honours 37
communication and media studies 168-71
computer science 38, 50, 171-4
consent 118-19
conservatoires 78, 440, 442
contextual offers 42, 91
continuation rates 22, 91
Corpus Christi College, University of Oxford 280
Corpus Christi College, University of Cambridge 294
cost of living 12, 30, 60
costs *see also* loans; tuition fees
 Adult Dependants' Grant 75
 affordability 30
 budgeting 71-3
 Childcare Grant 75
 insurance 73
 overdrafts and credit cards 73
 Parents' Learning Allowance 75
 rent rates 45, 71
 study costs 73
counselling 264-7
Coursera 40
Courtauld Institute of Art 439
Coventry University 126, 335
Cranfield University 440
Creative Arts, University for the 336
creative writing 174-6
credit cards 73
criminology 176-9
cultural studies 14, 133, 179-81
Cumbria, University of 337

dance 182-5
Data Futures 14
De Montfort University 338
debt 30, 60, 61-2, 66
degree apprenticeships 40-1, 63-4, 78
dentistry 181-2
Derby, University of 339
design 149-51
diplomas 40
Directory of Grant-Making Trusts 74
disabilities
 Disabled Student Allowances 74
 Diversity Index 97
 information sources 48
Discover Uni 47-8
distance learning 39-40, 126
diversity 12, 90-101, 273-6
Downing College, University of Cambridge 294
drama, dance, cinematics and photography 182-5
dropout rates 91, 96
drugs 117-18
Dundee, University of 340
Durham University 38, 133, 341
Dyson Institute of Engineering and Technology 47, 440

East and South Asian studies *see* cultural studies
East Anglia, University of 342
East London, University of (UEL) 343
ecology *see* biological sciences
economics 38, 50, 185-8
Edge Hill University 344
Edinburgh Napier University 346
Edinburgh, University of 345
education (subject) 13, 188-91
edX 40
electrical and electronic engineering 191-3
Emmanuel College, University of Cambridge 294-5
employability 58
employment outcomes *see* graduate prospects
engineering 38, 50, 199-200
 see also aeronautical and manufacturing engineering; bioengineering and biomedical engineering; chemical engineering; civil engineering; electrical and electronic engineering; mechanical engineering
English 193-6
English language proficiency 128-9
entrepreneurship 56
entry standards
 admission tests 37, 38, 279
 contextual offers 42, 91
 league tables 21, 134-5
 offer rates 15, 41-2, 271-2, 275-7
 "soft subjects" 36
 subject choice 32
 tariff points 33-5, 134-5
 vocational qualifications 37
environmental sciences 200-3
Escape Studios 440
Essex, University of 347
ethnic minority admissions 94
evening courses 39
Exeter College, University of Oxford 281
Exeter, University of 348

facilities at university 45
Falmouth University 349
finance (subject) 136-8
first generation students 96
Fitzwilliam College, University of Cambridge 295
food banks 71
food science 196-7
forensic science 145-7
foundation courses 40, 274
foundation degrees 40, 63, 68
fraud 73
French 197-9

further education (FE) colleges 46, 63
Futurelearn 40

gap years 88-9
gender gap, graduate prospects 57
general engineering 199-200
geography and environmental sciences 200-3
geology 203-4
German 204-5
Girton College, University of Cambridge 295-6
Glasgow Caledonian University 133, 351
Glasgow School of Art 440
Glasgow, University of 133, 350
Gloucestershire, University of 352
Goldsmiths, University of London 353
Gonville & Caius College, University of Cambridge 296
Graduate Medical School Admissions Test (GAMSAT) 38
Graduate Outcomes (GO) survey 13, 21, 29-30, 52, 57
graduate prospects
 choosing a degree 12, 13, 50-1, 56-7, 132
 employability 58
 future employment trends 50, 55-6
 gender gap 57
 league tables 21, 52-5, 135
 salaries 12, 13, 50-2, 54-5, 56, 62
 self-employment 56
 training schemes 32
 underemployment 56
grants
 priority courses 11-12, 60-1, 66
 UCAS central database 12
Greater Manchester, University of 354
Greenwich, University of 13, 355
Guildhall School of Music and Drama 440
GuildHE 45, 439

halls of residence 105-7, 110
hardship funds 74
Harper Adams University 356
Harris Manchester College, University of Oxford 281
Hartpury University 14, 357
health sciences 264-7
Hereford College of Arts 440
Heriot-Watt University 358
Hertford College, University of Oxford 281-2
Hertfordshire, University of 359
High Fliers survey 58
Higher Education Statistics Agency (HESA) 19, 93

Higher National Diplomas 40, 68
Highlands and Islands, University of the 360
history 205-8
history of art, architecture and design 208-10
Homerton College, University of Cambridge 296
honours classes 21
hospitality, leisure, recreation and tourism 210-12
Huddersfield, University of 361
Hughes Hall, University of Cambridge 296-7
Hull, University of 362

Iberian languages 212-13
ICMP (Institute of Contemporary Music Performance) 440
Imperial College London 38, 363
information systems and management 213-14
Informed Choices 48
insurance 73, 111
'insurance' choice 15, 85
international students
　applications 82, 129
　benefits of coming to UK 124-5
　English language proficiency 128-9
　families 123, 130
　fees 11-12, 13, 63, 67, 124
　numbers 11, 123-4
　origins 124, 125
　satisfaction surveys 126
　subject choice 127-8
　support systems 130
　university choice 126-7
　visas 123, 129-30
　websites 131
internships 58
interviews 38
Istituto Marangoni London 440
Italian 215-16

Jesus College, University of Oxford 282
Jesus College, University of Cambridge 297
Joint Honours 37

Keble College, University of Oxford 282-3
Keele University 364
Kent, University of 13, 365
King's College London (KCL) 366
King's College, University of Cambridge 297
Kingston University 367

Lady Margaret Hall, University of Oxford 283
Lancashire, University of 368
Lancaster University 369

land and property management 216-17
landscape planning *see* town and country planning and landscape
law 32, 37, 38, 217-20
Law, University of 46, 440
league tables
　methodology 19-22
　overall tables 23-8
　subject by subject guide 132-5
　see also individual subjects
Leeds Arts University 371
Leeds Beckett University 372
Leeds Conservatoire 440
Leeds Trinity University 373
Leeds, University of 370
Leicester, University of 374
liberal arts 220-1
librarianship *see* information systems and management
Lincoln Bishop University 376
Lincoln College, University of Oxford 283
Lincoln, University of 16, 375
linguistics 221-2
Liverpool Hope University 378
Liverpool Institute for Performing Arts 440
Liverpool John Moores University 379
Liverpool, University of 377
loans *see also* maintenance loans
　application 67
　budgeting 71-3
　funding timetable 72
　interest rates 62, 66
　Plan 5 loan 62, 67
　repayment scheme 13, 30, 60-2, 66-7
　shortfall in cover of living costs 12, 61, 70-1, 103, 108
　websites 75-6
location 43-4
London
　Birkbeck, University of London 14, 39, 317
　Brunel University 325
　City St George's 13, 334
　Goldsmiths, University of London 353
　Imperial College London 38, 363
　Istituto Marangoni London 440
　King's College London (KCL) 366
　Kingston University 367
　London Academy of Music and Dramatic Art 440
　London Business School 14, 439
　London Contemporary Dance School 440
　London Interdisciplinary School 47, 440
　London Metropolitan University 380

　London School of Economics and Political Science (LSE) 16-17, 36, 38, 381
　London School of Hygiene and Tropical Medicine 439
　London School of Science and Technology 441
　London South Bank University (LSBU) 382
　National Centre for Circus Arts 441
　Northeastern University London 46, 441
　Queen Mary, University of London (QMUL) 400
　Rambert School of Ballet an Contemporary Dance 441
　Ravensbourne University London 441
　Regent College London 441
　Regent's University 46, 441
　Royal Academy of the Dramatic Arts 441
　Royal College of Art 441
　Royal Holloway, University of London 406
　St Mary's University, Twickenham 408
　SOAS University of London 412
　Trinity Laban Conservatoire of Music and Dance 442
　University College London (UCL) 38, 426
　University of East London (UEL) 343
　University of Greenwich 13, 355
　University of, Institute in Paris 439
　University of Law 46
　University of Roehampton 404
　University of the Arts (UAL) 311
　University of West London (UWL) 16, 430
　University of Westminster 432
　Walbrook Institute 442
Loughborough University 383
Lucy Cavendish College, University of Cambridge 297-8

Magdalen College, University of Oxford 284
Magdalene College, University of Cambridge 298
maintenance grants 11-12, 60-1, 66
maintenance loans *see also* loans
　amount 11, 12, 60, 65
　budgeting 71-3
　funding timetable 72
　payment 65
　shortfall in cover of living costs 61, 70-1, 103, 108
management 157-61
Manchester Business School 14

Manchester Metropolitan University 385
Manchester, University of 384
Mansfield College, University of Oxford 284
manufacturing engineering 139–40
marketing 157–61
Massive Open Online Courses (MOOCs) 39–40
Masters courses 41
materials technology 222–3
mathematics 38, 50, 224–6
mature students 97
mechanical engineering 226–8
media studies 168–71
medicine
 admission tests 37, 38
 further study 32
 league tables 228–30
medicine, subjects allied to 50, 264–7
mental health 120–1
mergers 13
Merton College, University of Oxford 284–5
Middle Eastern and African studies *see* cultural studies
Middlesex University 386
million+ group 45
MLA College 441
Moorlands College 441
Murray Edwards College, University of Cambridge 298–9
music 231–3

National Centre for Circus Arts 441
National Institute of Teaching 441
National Student Survey (NSS) 16, 19, 20, 31, 132, 133
natural sciences 233–4
New College, University of Oxford 285
New Model Institute for Technology and Engineering (NMITE) 47
Newcastle University 387
Newnham College, University of Cambridge 299
NHS students 66
non-selective state school admissions 93–4
Norrington Table 273
Northampton, University of 388
Northeastern University London 46, 441
Northern Ireland
 fees 70
 grants and loans 61, 70
Northern School of Art 441
Northumbria University 389
Norwich University of the Arts 390
Nottingham Trent University 392
Nottingham, University of 391
nursing 66, 234–7
nutrition 264–7

occupational therapy 264–7
offer rates, supply and demand 15, 41–2
Ofsted grades 133, 188
Open Days 44, 48
Open University, The 14, 39, 393
ophthalmology 264–7
Oriel College, University of Oxford 285–6
orthoptics 264–7
osteopathy 264–7
overdrafts 73
overseas campuses 126
Oxford Brookes University 395
Oxford, University of
 about 394
 admission tests 37, 38, 279
 application process 79, 84, 271, 279
 colleges 276, 279–92
 diversity 93–4, 99, 273–6
 graduate prospects 273
 league tables 16, 133, 271
 Norrington Table 273
 offer rates 271–2, 275–6
 satisfaction surveys 272–3

Parents' Learning Allowance 75
part-time courses 39, 64
part-time work 12, 61, 75
Pembroke College, University of Oxford 286
Pembroke College, University of Cambridge 299
People & Planet 14–15, 19, 22
personal statements 78, 80–2
Peterhouse College, University of Cambridge 299–300
pharmacology and pharmacy 237–9
philosophy 239–41
photography 182–5
physics and astronomy 241–3
physiotherapy 243–5
Plan 5 loan 62, 67
planning *see* town and country planning and landscape
Plymouth Marjon University 397
Plymouth, University of 396
podiatry 264–7
POLAR4 92, 95
politics 245–8
Portsmouth, University of 398
Portuguese 212–13
private universities 46–7, 63
production engineering
 see aeronautical and manufacturing engineering
professional bodies 32
professional qualifications 32
psychology 248–51
psychotherapy 264–7
purpose built student accommodation (PBSA) 103, 104

qualifications *see* entry standards
Queen Margaret University, Edinburgh (QMU) 399
Queen Mary, University of London (QMUL) 400
Queen's College, University of Oxford 286–7
Queens' College, University of Cambridge 300
Queen's University, Belfast 401

radiography 251–3
Rambert School of Ballet an Contemporary Dance 441
Ravensbourne University London 441
Reading, University of 402
Regent College London 441
Regent's University 46, 441
religious studies 267–8
rent rates 45, 71, 102, 103, 108
Research England 21, 134
Research Excellence Framework (REF) 20–1, 133–4
research quality 20–1, 133–4
ResearchPlus 45
results day 86
Robert Gordon University 403
Robinson College, University of Cambridge 300
Roehampton, University of 404
Rose Bruford College of Theatre and Performance 441
Royal Academy of Music 439
Royal Academy of the Dramatic Arts 441
Royal Agricultural University 405
Royal Birmingham Conservatoire 441
Royal Central School of Speech and Drama 439
Royal College of Art 441
Royal College of Music 442
Royal Conservatoire of Scotland 442
Royal Holloway, University of London 406
Royal Northern College of Music 442
Royal Veterinary College 439
Royal Welsh College of Music and Drama 442
Russell Group
 Informed Choices 32, 36
 reputation 45
 "soft subjects" 36
Russian and Eastern European languages 253–4

safety on campus 12–13, 115–22
St Andrews, University of 17, 133, 407
St Anne's College, University of Oxford 287

St Catherine's College, University of Oxford 287-8
St Catherine's College, University of Cambridge 301
St Edmund Hall, University of Oxford 288
St Edmund's College, University of Cambridge 302
St George's, University of London *see* City St George's
St Hilda's College, University of Oxford 288-9
St Hugh's College, University of Oxford 289
St John's College, University of Oxford 289-90
St John's College, University of Cambridge 302
St Mary's University College Belfast 442
St Mary's University, Twickenham 408
St Peter's College, University of Oxford 290
salary data *see* graduate prospects
Salford, University of 409
sandwich courses 32, 58, 68
scams 73
Scholarship Hub 74
scholarships 12, 63, 73-4
schools, non-selective state school admissions 93-4
Scotland
 choosing a degree 41, 42, 43
 fees 64, 69
 grants and loans 61, 69-70
Scotland's Rural College 442
Scottish Index of Multiple Deprivation (SIMD) 92, 95
self-employment 56
Selwyn College, University of Cambridge 300-1
sexual consent 118-19
Sheffield Hallam University 411
Sheffield, University of 410
short courses 40
Sidney Sussex College, University of Cambridge 301
SOAS University of London 412
Social Inclusion Index 12, 90-101, 274
social media 121-2
social policy 254-6
social work 256-8
socialising 115
sociology 258-61
"soft subjects" 36
Somerville College, University of Oxford 290-1
South Wales, University of (USW) 413
Southampton Solent University 415

Southampton, University of 414
Spanish 212-13
speech therapy 264-7
sports science 261-4
Staffordshire University 416
staying at home 43
Stirling, University of 417
Stranmillis University College 442
Strathclyde, University of 133, 418
student experience 19, 20, 133
student/staff ratio 14
students' union 45
study skills 121
subject choice 13, 29, 30, 31, 32-3, 47, 56-7
subjects allied to medicine 50, 264-7
Suffolk, University of 419
Sunderland, University of 420
Surrey, University of 421
Sussex, University of 422
sustainability 14-15, 19, 22
Sutton Trust 90, 91
Swansea University 423

tariff points 33-5, 134-5
Teaching Excellence Framework (TEF) 14, 15
teaching quality 14, 19, 20, 133
teaching (subject) *see* education
Teesside University 424
Test of Mathematics for University Admission (TMUA) 38
theology and religious studies 267-8
thestudentroom.com 31
Tomkins Table 273
tourism 210-12
town and country planning and landscape 268-9
Trinity College, University of Oxford 291
Trinity College, University of Cambridge 302-3
Trinity Hall, University of Cambridge 303
Trinity Laban Conservatoire of Music and Dance 442
tuition fees *see also* loans
 amounts 11, 12, 60, 64, 66-70, 305
 bursaries and scholarships 63, 66, 73-4
 funding timetable 72
 history 62-3
 international students 11-12, 13, 63, 67
 websites 75-6
 work placements 63
Turing Scheme 13, 41

UCAS
 Apply registration 78-9
 hub 78

 registration dates 7
 UCAS Extra 86
 website 47, 48
UK Labour Force Survey 50
UK Research and Innovation (UKRI) 21, 134
UK University Overseas Campuses Network 126
Ulster University 425
underemployment 56
University Academy 92 442
University Alliance 45
University Campus of Football Business (UCFB) 442
University Centre Sparsholt 442
university choice 31, 41-7
University Clinical Aptitude Test (UCAT) 38
University College, Birmingham (UCB) 442
University College, University of Oxford 291-2
University of the Built Environment 440

veterinary medicine 269-70
vocational qualifications 32, 37

Wadham College, University of Oxford 292
Walbrook Institute 442
Wales
 fees 70
 grants and loans 61, 70
Wales Trinity St David, University of 427
Warwick, University of 38, 133, 428
wellbeing 120-1
West of England, University of the 429
West of Scotland, University of the 431
Westminster, University of 432
white working-class males 95
Winchester, University of 433
Wolfson College, University of Cambridge 303
Wolverhampton, University of 434
Worcester College, University of Oxford 292
Worcester, University of 435
work experience 32, 40, 58-9, 63
working part-time while at university 12, 61, 75
Wrexham University 93, 436

York St John University 438
York, University of 437

z-scores 19-20, 93
zoology *see* biological sciences

INDEX **447**